Living World History

SECOND EDITION

T. WALTER WALLBANK
University of Southern California

ARNOLD SCHRIER
University of Cincinnati

CRITIC READER   *Daniel Powell, Nicholas Senn High School, Chicago*

CONSULTANTS   GEOGRAPHY, *Charles M. Davis, University of Michigan*

STUDY AIDS, *Francine Pickow Lerner, formerly Charles Evans Hughes High School, New York City*

BIBLIOGRAPHY, *Ruby Crowe, Social Studies Consultant, Fulton County School System, Atlanta, Georgia*

COMMUNICATIONS, *Gene Dekovic*

DESIGNER   *Thomas J. Gorman*

GENERAL EDITOR   *I. James Quillen, Stanford University*

The authors wish to thank Robert Warth of Hunter College for his assistance in the preparation of Chapters 8 and 28.

History links the present with the past, the East with the West. Above is another view of the majestic Greek statue pictured on the front cover of this book. Below, a Japanese map of the late 18th century depicts Japan in the center of the world.

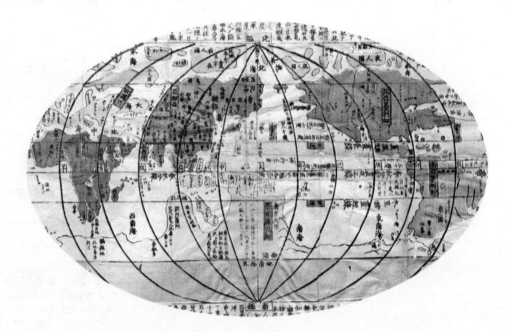

living
WORLD HISTORY

SECOND EDITION

Wallbank and Schrier

SCOTT, FORESMAN AND COMPANY

ATLANTA • DALLAS • PALO ALTO • FAIR LAWN, N.J.

table of contents

Photograph © Arnold Newman, courtesy *Holiday* Magazine, Curtis Publishing Company.

UNIT **11**

THE WORLD TODAY / 676

LIST OF MAPS

THE STRUCTURE OF *Living World History*

THE UNITS

The eleven units of *Living World History* correspond to well-defined historical periods. A full-page color photograph at the beginning of each unit symbolizes the basic themes of the unit. The unit introduction explains how the main ideas and events treated in the chapters within the unit relate to the historical period as a whole. The time lines in each unit show in parallel columns the chronological relationships of the significant events and famous personalities discussed in the chapters.

THE CHAPTERS

Shown in reduced size below are the first two pages of a typical chapter, Chapter 11, "Native Cultures in Africa and the Americas." These sample pages reveal how design and layout reinforce the structure of the chapter. The chapter elements are keyed as follows: A the chapter title, B the chapter numeral and the time span of the events treated in the chapter, C the explanatory caption for the thematic picture or pictures, D the beginning of the chapter introduction, E the conclusion of the introduction with its list of the main sections into which the chapter is divided, F the first main section heading, G the first subsection heading. Taken together, the chapter sections and subsection headings form a concise sentence outline, enabling the student to perceive the most important concepts, the supporting ideas, and the underlying details in the chapter. Chapter 11 is typical of many chapters, for it begins with a quotation from original source material which helps provide historical background.

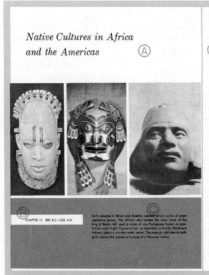

END-OF-CHAPTER MATERIAL

Also reproduced are the final pages of Chapter 11. The elements are keyed as follows: **A** section review questions, which appear at the end of each section in order to test the student's grasp of the main ideas of the section, **B** a chapter review, or summary, **C** the end-of-chapter review tests, which are designed to evaluate the student's command of important facts concerning time, place, people, and historical terms, **D** questions for critical thinking, which are intended to provoke further inquiry and mature thought.

THE MAP PROGRAM

The map program consists of a series of 98 maps drawn exclusively for this volume. Each map has been placed on the page where relevant text occurs. A great many of the maps illustrate one concept or a group of related concepts, such as "The Ice Age", p. 28. Other maps are more complex, such as "Roman Empire," p. 102.

GEOGRAPHY: A KEY TO HISTORY

Relationships between geography and history are described in a series of single-page essays. Each essay includes a schematic drawing pertinent to the topic discussed.

THE ILLUSTRATION PROGRAM

The majority of the pictures in *Living World History* are contemporary to the period depicted. The illustration program consists of picture groups, which are organized according to the following themes: daily life, significant events, great leaders, science and technology, and the arts. The picture groups which illustrate the daily life of ordinary people through the ages include, among others, "Daily Life in Egypt" (pp. 46-47), "Scenes of Greek Daily Life" (pp. 74-75), "Manor Life" (pp. 140-141), "Medieval Town Life" (pp. 160-161), and "Life in Japan" (pp. 244-245).

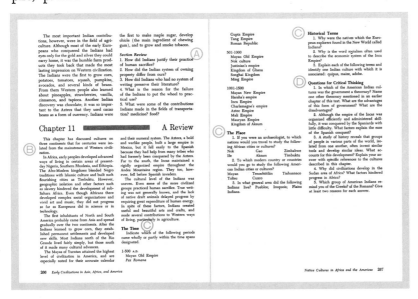

17

Concerning History:

An Introduction

The following statements deal with the subject of history—what it is, what the historian does, and why history is valuable. Opinions about these matters vary, and in no sense do the authors of *Living World History* agree with all of them. Indeed, it would be impossible to do so. Nevertheless, a sampling of opinions shows how history has been the object of speculation and controversy since men first began to record their actions and thoughts. Some of the quoted passages date from ancient times; others come from modern writers. All of them are worthy of study and analysis.

It is somewhat unfortunate that the word history should be used in several different senses. In its origin (Greek . . .) it meant learning by inquiry. The historian . . . was a searcher after knowledge, an investigator. But by a subtle transformation the term came to be applied to the record or narrative of what had been learned by investigation; and in this sense it passed over into the Latin historia and into modern speech. . . . Meantime another ambiguity . . . caused confusion in thought. The word history is used to denote not only the record of what has been learned by inquiry, but also the course of events themselves.

Allen Johnson, *The Historian and Historical Evidence*, 1926

History is the witness of the times, the light of truth, the life of memory, the teacher of life, the messenger of antiquity.

Marcus Tullius Cicero, 106-43 B.C., Roman statesman

History is . . . the record of what one age finds worthy of note in another.

Jakob Burckhardt, 1818-1897, Swiss historian

. . . history . . . is indeed little more than the register of the crimes, follies, and misfortunes of mankind.

Edward Gibbon, *Decline and Fall of the Roman Empire*, 1776-1788

History is made out of the failures and heroism of each insignificant moment.

Franz Kafka, 1883-1924, Czech novelist

The history of all hitherto existing society is the history of class struggles.

Karl Marx and Friedrich Engels, *The Communist Manifesto*, 1848

The history of the world is but the biography of great men.

Thomas Carlyle, *Heroes and Hero-Worship*, 1841

The subject of history is the life of peoples and of humanity.

Count Leo Tolstoy, War and Peace, 1865-1872

Human history is in essence a history of ideas.

H. G. Wells, Outline of History, 1920

The history of the world is the record of man in quest of his daily bread and butter.

Hendrik Van Loon, The Story of Mankind, 1921

THE ROLE OF THE HISTORIAN

History repeats itself, says the proverb, but that is precisely what it never really does. It is the historians (of a sort) who repeat themselves.

Clement F. Rogers, 1866-1949, English theologian

The whole past . . . consists of the infinite number of things which each person who ever lived has said, thought, and done. . . . Historians select a few of these thoughts, words, and deeds that seem to have general significance, and these become history as we ordinarily think of it. Because men's ideas of what is significant change from time to time and because new knowledge frequently becomes available[,] history is constantly being rewritten.

Bernard Norling, Towards a Better Understanding of History, 1960

Faithfulness to the truth of history involves far more than a research, however patient and scrupulous, into special facts. Such facts may be detailed with the most minute exactness, and yet the narrative, taken as a whole, may be unmeaning or untrue. The narrator must seek to imbue himself with the life and spirit of the time. He must study events in their bearings near and remote; in the character, habits, and manners of those who took part in them. He must himself be, as it were, a sharer or a spectator of the action he describes.

Francis Parkman, Pioneers of France in the New World, 1865

. . . historians ought to be precise, truthful, and quite unprejudiced, and neither interest nor fear, hatred nor affection, should cause them to swerve from the path of truth, whose mother is history. . . .

Miguel de Cervantes, Don Quixote, 1605-1615

The only completely unbiased historian is . . . the Recording Angel; and doubtless he has convictions which to Satan, as Mark Twain irreverently suggested, would seem prejudices.

Allan Nevins, The Gateway to History, 1938

THE USES OF HISTORY

To enable man to understand the society of the past and to increase his mastery over the society of the present is the dual function of history.

Edward H. Carr, What Is History?, 1962

Our custom of taking records and preserving them is the main barrier that separates us from the scatter-brained races of monkey. For it is this extension of memory that permits us to draw upon experience and which allows us to establish a common pool of wisdom. . . . Knowledge of things said and done . . . is a knowledge which not merely sees us through the trivial decisions of the moment, but also stands by in the far more important times of personal or public crisis.

Sherman Kent, Writing History, 1941

The study of history is said to enlarge and enlighten the mind. Why? Because . . . it gives it a power of judging of passing events, and of all events, and a conscious superiority over them, which before it did not possess.

John Henry Cardinal Newman, On the Scope and Nature of University Education, 1852

Those who cannot remember the past are condemned to repeat it.

George Santayana, 1863-1952, American philosopher

The Dawn of Civilization

All things must have a beginning, and so it was with the earth and the people who have lived on it for countless generations. Scientists who have studied the various rock layers, or *strata*, of the earth's outer crust believe that the earth is approximately four billion years old. In the strata of the earth are found the evidence of the origin of life forms, their changes, and development. *Fossils*, or hardened remains, which have been preserved in the strata, show that living things went through many changes during the passage of millions of years—from simple forms to more complex and advanced beings.

Manlike creatures first appeared on earth about a million years ago. These creatures differed in important respects from modern man, both physically and mentally. They had lower intelligence and smaller stature; they did not walk erect; and they had receding foreheads and massive jaws. It took almost a million years for these first man-types to evolve into man as known today.

The problem of survival was acute for early man. At first he was completely helpless before the forces of nature. He had no weapons or tools, no clothing, and his food supply was uncertain. Life was often short and violent. In order to survive, man had to learn how to master his environment. The story of this challenge is the theme of the first two chapters of *Living World History*.

Then, as now, man had certain basic needs: food, clothing, shelter, protection from enemies, forms of government to make group living possible, and religious beliefs to explain the mysteries of birth, death, and the hereafter. How people satisfy these wants—the various ways they produce food, build shelter, organize their families, create systems of government, worship their gods, and engage in many other forms of human activity—is called their *culture*. In this sense, culture has nothing to do with being "cultured"—that is, well-educated and refined. People possess a culture whether they are Indians in the rain forests of Brazil or apartment house dwellers in Paris.

Stone Age man learned to make simple stone tools and weapons, use fire, and fashion clothes. He also experimented with art forms, such as cave paintings, and began to have ideas about religion. Very slowly, after the passage of thousands of years, man developed new skills. He learned to work metals and to make pottery. He domesticated animals to assure a meat supply and planted seeds in the ground to produce crops. These developments, particularly those dealing with his food supply, gave man a significant degree of control over his environment. No longer did he have to wander about collecting berries and roots.

He ceased to be a nomad and could live in one place with many of his fellows. Thus the human community was born.

In studying Stone Age man, scholars refer to the *prehistoric* period, by which is meant the span of time before the invention of writing when there were no records and hence no history. About 4000 B.C. living conditions advanced so substantially in the river valleys of the Nile in Egypt and the Tigris-Euphrates in Asia Minor that *civilization* was achieved and the *historic* period began. The stage of development called civilization is reached when human culture becomes complex enough to include a system of writing, vocational specialization in a number of crafts, a

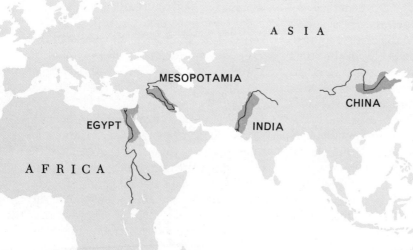

RIVER VALLEY CIVILIZATIONS

ASIA

MESOPOTAMIA

CHINA

EGYPT

INDIA

AFRICA

Prepared by
Rand McNally & Co., Chicago

single government affording protection and enforcing its own law, and cities. In short, it is a stage when men possess an extensive control over their environment.

The Egyptians built a remarkable civilization. The tomb painting of a religious ceremony reproduced at the beginning of this unit shows that more than 3000 years ago the people of Egypt had advanced ideas of religion and well-developed techniques of art. In addition, they had developed hieroglyphic writing and possessed the necessary engineering skills to build impressive structures.

In the river valley of the Tigris-Euphrates and in adjacent areas of the Near East, many different peoples took part in the advance of civilization: the Sumerians, Babylonians, Phoenicians, Hebrews, Hittites, and Persians. The Hebrew contributions were especially noteworthy: the idea of a single, all-powerful, and just God and the Old Testament, which described His works.

People today tend to overlook the immense debt owed to the men of the ancient world. They began the long struggle to conquer the forces of nature and to solve basic social and technical problems. In an important sense the first hatchet, the first written message, and the first seed planted in the ground to produce wheat were more significant in the story of human development than such awe-inspiring modern inventions as the atomic bomb, the electronic computer, and the space rocket.

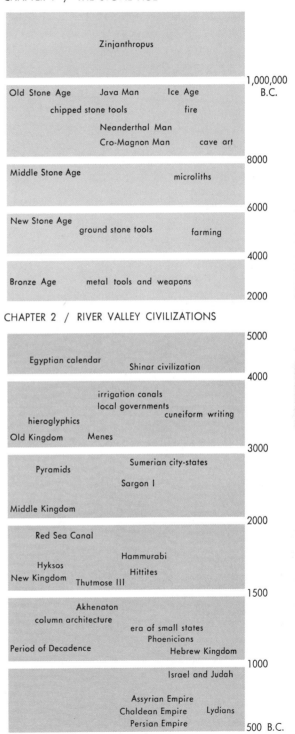

CHAPTER 1 / THE STONE AGE

Zinjanthropus

1,000,000 B.C.

Old Stone Age — Java Man — Ice Age
chipped stone tools — fire
Neanderthal Man
Cro-Magnon Man — cave art

8000

Middle Stone Age — microliths

6000

New Stone Age — ground stone tools — farming

4000

Bronze Age — metal tools and weapons

2000

CHAPTER 2 / RIVER VALLEY CIVILIZATIONS

5000

Egyptian calendar — Shinar civilization

4000

irrigation canals
local governments
hieroglyphics — cuneiform writing
Old Kingdom — Menes

3000

Pyramids — Sumerian city-states
Sargon I
Middle Kingdom

2000

Red Sea Canal
Hammurabi
Hyksos — Hittites
New Kingdom — Thutmose III

1500

Akhenaton
column architecture
era of small states
Phoenicians
Period of Decadence — Hebrew Kingdom

1000

Israel and Judah

Assyrian Empire
Chaldean Empire — Lydians
Persian Empire

500 B.C.

The Stone Age

Although prehistoric men had no system of writing, they left a record of their technical progress in tools and weapons. The simple hand ax at left dates from the Old Stone Age. More finely chiseled is a Neolithic flint dagger, center. The harpoon head and sickle blades at right, typical of the Bronze Age, show that men later discovered how to work metals and obtain food by fishing and farming.

One day in 1879 a five-year-old Spanish girl named María de Sautuola accompanied her father, Don Marcelino de Sautuola, as he explored the cave of Altamira on his estate in northern Spain. Suddenly Don Marcelino heard her cry out, "Toros! Toros!" (Bulls! Bulls!) He found her staring at the ceiling of the cavern where huge bison, painted in red and black, were drawn so skillfully that they seemed almost alive. Their eyes bulged in rage and terror; their flanks seemed to heave. Elsewhere in the cave Don Marcelino found pictures of horses, deer and wild boars. He was convinced that the pictures were made by primitive men.

Little María's discovery made the cave of Altamira famous, but scientists scoffed at Don Marcelino's theory. They claimed that the pictures could not have been painted by primitive men, for they were as well done as paintings by modern artists. Furthermore, they maintained that an artist who had visited Don Marcelino probably painted the pictures and that the Spanish nobleman was attempting a deception. Don Marcelino published an account of the discovery at his own expense, but few would believe his story.

In 1895 a French scholar, Emile Rivière, reported the discovery of prehistoric paintings and engravings on the walls of a cave in France. During the next two years, other cave paintings were discovered, and by 1900, scientists generally accepted cave art as the genuine work of primitive men. Don Marcelino had been right all along. The incredibly lifelike and colorful cave paintings at Altamira were at least 20 thousand years old.

Many of the discoveries relating to early men are the work of scientists called *anthropologists*, who study the origin, races, and customs of men, both ancient and modern. *Archaeologists*, the scientists who specialize in archaeology, a branch of anthropology, are concerned with excavating, classifying, and studying the remains of ancient cultures.

This chapter tells the story of ancient man in the following sections:

1. **Life began on the ancient earth.**

2. **Man developed basic skills in the Old Stone Age.**

3. **Man made great advances in the New Stone Age.**

4. **Important inventions appeared during the Bronze Age.**

1 Life began on the ancient earth

How old is the earth? How long has man lived on it? In the past few years scientists have found much new evidence for answering these two questions.

The earth was formed. Geologists—scientists who study the crust of the earth and its *strata*, or layers—believe that the earth is approximately 4½ billion years old. According to scientific theories, the earth began as a flaming mass of gas and vapor that gradually cooled enough to harden. Clouds appeared and for millions of years dropped rain onto the hot surface of the earth. The heat turned the rain to steam, which again became part of the overhanging clouds. As the earth cooled still more, the fallen water collected as deep oceans and shallow seas, which covered most of the earth.

It was in these oceans and seas that living things first appeared. And with them begins the story of life on earth.

Living things developed from simple to more complex forms. Scientists believe that the first living things—which existed about a billion years ago—were simple one-celled, water-dwelling plants and animals.

These tiny bits of living matter had no bony structure. As advanced life forms developed, they became more complex; that is, they were composed of more than one cell. Jellyfish, worms, snails, crabs, and then fish appeared in the water. The hardened remains of these life forms are called *fossils*.

All the earliest life forms lived in water. From them developed amphibians, which could live on land as well as in the water. Later, great reptiles such as dinosaurs appeared. And, after a long time, birds and higher animals developed. Each stage of animal development took millions of years.

Conditions were not easy for these early life forms. They had to struggle against other living things and against the strong forces of nature. Many plants and animals could not survive. Others did survive and became stronger as new generations changed to meet conditions on the earth. Some animals changed a great deal. For example, millions of years ago horses were only a foot high, with four-toed front feet and three-toed hind feet.

Skeletons gave clues to the appearance of early man. Although many theories about the origin of man exist, scientists believe that man came into being quite late in the long span of the development of life on earth—about 1¾ million years ago. Scientists have important clues to what the earliest men looked like. These clues are determined from the remains of ancient skeletons. Anthropologists can reconstruct the probable shape of an entire body from the bony parts which have been found.

In 1891 and 1892, Eugene Dubois, a Dutch surgeon and anthropologist, found the top of a skull, three teeth, and a left thighbone in a dry river bed on the island of Java. From these remains, anthropologists have reconstructed a type of early man which was called *Java Man*. He was shorter than the average man of today. His head hung forward on his chest, and his strong teeth and jaws stuck outward. His skull was small and very thick, and his forehead sloped back. Java Man, who probably lived about a million years ago, was considered until recently the oldest known man.

In 1959 Dr. L. S. B. Leakey, a noted British anthropologist, discovered in Olduvai Gorge in Tanganyika, Africa, a skull of a primitive man estimated to have lived 1¾ million years ago. According to the scientists who reconstructed this East Africa Man, or *Zinjanthropus*, he was low-browed and long-faced with large, deep jaws.

Parts of the skeletons of other early men have been found in Asia, Africa, and Europe. One of the oldest is the *Peking Man*, whose bones were found near Peking, China. Peking Man appeared on earth later than Java Man and is considered to have been more advanced, because he possessed a larger brain. Other and later finds include *Heidelberg Man*, first found near Heidelberg, Germany; *Neanderthal Man*, discovered in the Neanderthal, a valley near Düsseldorf, Germany; and *Cro-Magnon Man*, named for the cave in which his remains were found in France. The skeletons of these finds show the changes that occurred in man as thousands of years passed. The brain became larger and the teeth smaller. The back became straighter, allowing later man to stand more upright, with his head set farther back on his shoulders. His legs, too, became longer and straighter. The skeleton of the Cro-Magnon type of man was much like that of modern man.

Section Review

1. What information have geologists supplied about the age and formation of the earth?

2. According to scientists, through what

stages did living things develop from simple to more complex forms?

3. In what ways did the earliest man differ from modern man? What physical changes occurred in man from Zinjanthropus to the Cro-Magnon?

2 Man developed basic skills in the Old Stone Age

Generally, the time span from about one million years ago to about 3000 B.C. is called the Stone Age, because it was a period when man made most of his weapons and tools of stone. The Stone Age is divided into three periods, the earliest of which is called the Old Stone Age, or *Paleolithic* period. (The word *Paleolithic* is derived from two Greek words meaning "ancient stone.") The Old Stone Age lasted until about 8000 B.C.

Early man developed tools and skills. The earliest man probably did not know how to make or use tools or weapons. It is likely that he lived on insects, fish, and animals that he could catch with his bare hands. In addition, he gathered roots and wild plants for food. At this early stage, man's way of living was like that of the beasts.

The most important quality which makes man superior to other animals is his capacity to learn from experience and to devise ways of doing things—in short, his ability to think. Another important quality is his ability to exchange ideas with others —to talk. Such capacities have enabled man to rise far above the level of the wild beasts and to make steady advances in his way of living.

One of the first advances of man was the development of crude tools and weapons. He found ways of shaping rocks to the size and form that were helpful to him. He developed the fist hatchet, an early tool

Prehistoric Man was able to attain supremacy over his fellow creatures because of his erect posture, his complex brain, and his ability to grasp objects with his hands. He began to master his environment by learning to make fire, clothing, and shelter. Peking Man roamed the Far East about 360 thousand years ago. Above is a modern artist's drawing of Peking Man dragging a slain deer. Neanderthal Man lived 100 thousand years ago. The hunter shown below stalks a rhinoceros with a stone-tipped spear, an advance over the hand ax carried by Peking Man.

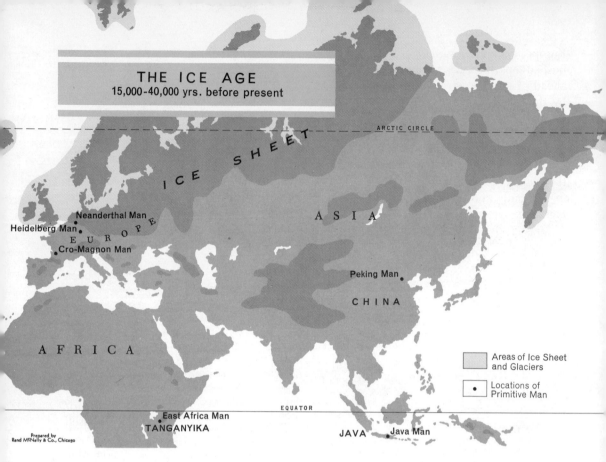

THE ICE AGE
15,000-40,000 yrs. before present

ARCTIC CIRCLE

I C E   S H E E T

A S I A

Neanderthal Man
Heidelberg Man
E U R O P E
Cro-Magnon Man

Peking Man

C H I N A

A F R I C A

Areas of Ice Sheet
and Glaciers

Locations of
Primitive Man

EQUATOR

East Africa Man
TANGANYIKA

JAVA   Java Man

Prepared by
Rand M?Nally & Co., Chicago

and weapon, by using one rock to chip another. He left one end thick so that it would fit snugly in his hand, and the other end he chipped to a point or edge that he could use for striking or cutting. With such weapons, man became a hunter of animals larger than those he could kill with his hands and teeth alone.

Man found uses for fire. Man knew of fire long before he learned to make it useful. He saw leaves, grass, or wood burning where lightning had struck. If the fire was small, perhaps he was not afraid of it. He may even have picked up a burning stick and waved it at an animal enemy. This would have taught him that here was another aid against his natural enemies. In a short time, as ages go (perhaps only a few thousand years!), he learned to keep a fire burning by adding wood or leaves.

He learned to cover his fire with ashes at night to keep coals glowing for rekindling new flames in the morning. But a longer time must have passed before man learned to start a fire.

Glaciers affected man's way of living. Fire became very important to man in the regions where his life was affected by glaciers. These giant masses of ice pushed down from the north during four different periods, which together made up what is called the Ice Age. In each period of the Ice Age, the glaciers formed in the north, gradually moved southward, and eventually retreated toward the North Pole. (The time span of the Ice Age coincides roughly with the time span of the Old Stone Age.)

As the glacial ice moved south, it covered much of northern and central

Europe, Siberia, and North America. It pushed tons of gravel, boulders, and stones ahead of it. In America, formations made by the glaciers may be seen as far south as the Ohio and the Missouri rivers. In the final period of the Ice Age, about 50 thousand years ago, the glaciers reached their farthest distance south. About 20 thousand years ago, this ice began melting in the south, and the remnant is still melting in the far north.

During the Ice Age, many men and animals died of exposure or starvation. Others moved to warmer areas. Still others adapted themselves to the cold. Some animals developed thick hides or coats of fur. Among these were the woolly mammoth and the woolly rhinoceros.

Man was also able to adapt himself to living in a cold world. He took refuge in caves and learned to wear animal skins for warmth. To make such clothing, he had to invent new tools—stone knives for skinning and bone tools for scraping the flesh and fat from the inner side of animal skins.

Neanderthal Man advanced beyond his ancestors. One type of Old Stone Age man who adjusted to cold was Neanderthal Man. He used fire, lived in caves wherever possible, and made his clothing of skins. From the tools and weapons he used, anthropologists have determined that Neanderthal Man learned to attach handles to chipped stones to make crude knives and spears. He also began to form religious beliefs. Remains of food and weapons found in the graves of his people indicate that he may have believed in some kind of afterlife.

Cro-Magnon Man developed art. Late in the Ice Age, about 30 thousand years ago, *Homo sapiens*, or the modern type of man, appeared. The chinless head, the receding skull, and the slouching posture of earlier types were replaced by features characteristic of modern man. The best known of these modern types was called Cro-Magnon Man.

Cro-Magnon Man invented better tools and weapons than did Neanderthal. He made spears with fine flint points and harpoons of reindeer horn and bone. To sew skins together, he developed bone needles. Cro-Magnon Man was also an artist. He carved figures of animals from horn and bone, molded statues in clay, and carved and painted the walls of caves. The Cro-Magnon hunter painted animals as magical symbols to bring him luck on the hunt. The first painters may also have been witch doctors or magicians.

Section Review

1. What kinds of tools and weapons did man develop in the Old Stone Age?
2. How did man probably learn about fire? How did fire change his way of living?
3. About when did the Ice Age begin? end? How did Neanderthal Man adapt himself to living in the Ice Age?
4. What advances did Cro-Magnon Man make over his ancestors?

3 **Man made great advances in the New Stone Age**

About 8000 B.C. another period in man's progress toward civilization began. This was the Middle Stone Age, or the *Mesolithic* period. Before the beginning of this age, the glacial ice retreated and the forests expanded to the north. A few important inventions appeared. One was the *microlith*, a small, pointed blade of stone used for knives, arrow points, and spearheads. The microlith was a crowning achievement in stone tools made by chipping because it was so light that hundreds of microliths could be made from a single pound of stone. Another notable Mesolithic advance was the first crude pottery.

Primitive Art

Peoples of primitive cultures the world over have revealed their creativity and vitality in various art forms. The wooden figure at right was carved by New Guinea tribesmen. Decorated with sea shells, it stands almost six feet tall. Below is a serpent-shaped mound nearly a quarter of a mile long, built by Indians in Ohio. The mound probably had religious significance. Above right on the facing page, his body painted with geometrical designs, is a hunter running through a herd of sheeplike animals. An early African painted the scene on a cave wall in the Sahara Desert about 3500 B.C. The animal below, possibly a bull, was drawn by a Cro-Magnon artist about 15,000 B.C. in the Lascaux Cave of southern France. Primitive art is not restricted to that created in remote times. For example, the New Guinea figure was carved in the 20th century.

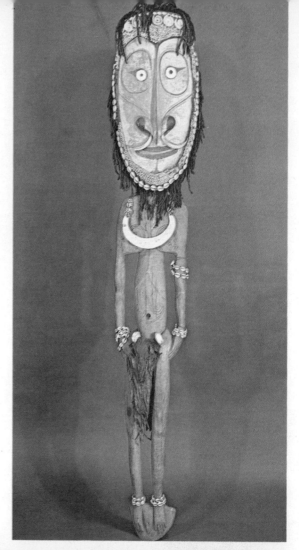

Made of sun-baked clay, pots were used to store food and water. The bow and arrow, invented either late in the Paleolithic period or in the Mesolithic period, served hunters and fighters until the firearm took its place in the 14th century A.D. Probably during Mesolithic times, wild dogs, such as jackals, attached themselves to human settlements. They became valuable to men in hunting and in guarding property. Since many Mesolithic peoples lived along the shores of rivers, lakes, and seas, fish was their main food. They invented the fishhook, numerous types of nets, and learned how to hollow out logs to make boats.

About 6000 B.C. the Middle Stone Age gradually gave way to the New Stone Age, or *Neolithic* period, which lasted until about 3000 B.C. New Stone Age peoples learned to sharpen stone tools and weapons by grinding them against gritty stones instead of by chipping or flaking them. This skill gave the period its name, but it is only one of many which distinguish New Stone Age peoples from their Old Stone Age ancestors.

Man began to farm. Of the important discoveries made in the New Stone Age, the most far-reaching were new ways of getting food. In addition to hunting and gathering, man learned to tame animals so that they would be near when he needed meat. Neolithic man learned to tame such animals as sheep, goats, pigs, and cattle. When herds and flocks of these domesticated, or tamed, animals ate most of the grass supply near a camping place, the herdsmen and their families moved on to fresh grazing lands. This way of life is called *pastoral,* or *nomadic,* and the people who wander from pasture to pasture are called *nomads.*

About this same time man made one of the greatest discoveries of all time when he found that seeds planted in the earth would grow into plants and furnish many seeds. Thus, man became a food grower—a farmer.

With this new knowledge of herding animals and raising plants, man could produce his food supply, and he no longer needed to depend on luck in hunting animals or in finding edible fruits, roots, and seeds. He and his family became safer from starvation.

New Stone Age man developed other skills. During the New Stone Age, man learned to spin and weave. Goats' hair could be woven directly into cloth. Later, man learned to spin the fleece from sheep and the fibers of flax to make thread and to weave threads into cloth. During this period, man probably learned to press and roll animal hairs together to make warm felt blankets.

Man kept on making important discoveries at an ever faster rate. The development of agriculture led to the invention of hoes and other stone tools for cultivating the soil and to the use of milling stones for grinding grain. He improved pottery-making by heating the clay in a fire, so that the pots were more substantial. In time, potters learned to make a wide variety of cups, bowls, and plates and to decorate them with paint.

Man learned to live in communities. During the Paleolithic and Mesolithic ages, men learned to help each other in hunting and fishing. Groups of families joined together for this purpose and formed a simple type of community. When men began to farm, they established permanent settlements. Farmers began to think of the land they farmed as belonging to themselves or to their own group, and not to other people. To protect their fields and animals, groups of farmers formed villages or small towns as strongholds against enemies.

Stone Age People Today

One way to learn about ancient arts and crafts is to observe the people of Stone Age cultures which still exist. Above left, members of the Watusi tribe in east Africa perform an intricate dance with gestures and movements which are parts of an age-old design. The Australian native at right above pursues an ancient craft, chipping crude stone knives. An Eskimo woman in a fur-trimmed parka, right, smooths a hide from which she will make warm clothing.

As people began to live together in larger groups, they had to make rules or laws regulating conduct and to create governments to enforce these laws. Scholars believe that in the earliest food-producing societies the government was controlled by a small group of arms-bearing men, each of whom had a voice in the government. In the more advanced food-producing societies, the government usually came under the control of wealthier members of the group. Often a chief became recognized as the ruler, and he made the decisions for the entire group.

Anthropologists believe that behavior among Stone Age men was regulated by custom. Different groups of Stone Age people formed their own rules for marriage, for the treatment and education of children, for the distribution of food, and for other relationships that existed among the members of the group. One who violated a custom was considered a wrongdoer.

Throughout much of the Stone Age, punishment for wrongdoing probably took the form of simple ridicule. A man who cheated or injured one of his fellows was subject to the scorn of all the members of his group. For people living in small bands in which everyone knew everyone else intimately, unpopularity was a severe form of punishment. Even within small groups, however, certain offenses, such as treason, were subject to formal punishment. The wrongdoer, if found guilty, could be executed or outlawed from the group. When men became farmers and when groups became larger, more and more offenses became subject to group punishment. Laws developed which specified the punishment to be given for each offense. The Code of Hammurabi, described in Chapter 2, represents an advanced stage in laws regulating group living. Such laws had their beginnings in the Stone Age.

Religion, too, became more elaborate as men learned to live in groups. Religion and magic were closely associated. People turned to medicine men to ward off droughts, famines, floods, and plagues. To gain favor with the spirits of nature, people of the New Stone Age developed religious ceremonies, particularly dances. These ceremonies often were carried out for the purpose of bringing good crops. In some groups the powers of nature were believed to be gods. To gain favor with the gods, men prayed to them and offered them gifts.

Section Review

1. What advances did man make in the Mesolithic period?
2. What improvements did New Stone Age man make in his tools and weapons? What new crafts did he develop?
3. Why was the herdsman safer from starvation than the hunter? Why was the discovery of how to grow plants from seed one of the greatest advances of all time?
4. How did farming change man's way of living?

4 **Important inventions appeared during the Bronze Age**

As long as man was dependent upon stone tools, he was limited in the kinds of work he could do. Stone tools and weapons broke easily. To make better tools, man needed a new, longer lasting material that could be molded more easily into different sizes and shapes.

Man learned to make tools and weapons of metal. Toward the end of the New Stone Age, men in the Near East found that they could use copper in an almost pure metallic state to make tools and weapons. At first, they hammered the copper to shape it. Later they learned that with heat they could melt the ore, pour the liquid metal into molds, and make tools and weapons of any desired size or shape.

Early metalworkers made another advance when they discovered that tin and copper melted together in the right amounts made a metal called bronze. Bronze was easier to shape, was harder, and gave a sharper cutting edge than copper alone. Because it was the chief metal for about 2000 years, the period in which it was used is called the Bronze Age. This era began about 3000 B.C.

Progress came in farming, transportation, and commerce. Along with metal tools came other inventions. One of these was the plow drawn by animals. At first the farmer had planted seeds in holes made with a crude digging stick. Then he had made a simple hoe which he pulled through the earth with a rope. The next step was to harness animals, such as the ox, to an improved hoe that became a plow. This invention enabled farmers to cultivate large fields instead of small plots. Another aid to farming was the development of better ways to control and use water for crops. In places where there was little rainfall, men learned to irrigate; that is, to bring water to their fields by digging ditches to lakes and streams. They also learned to build dikes to protect their fields from floods.

How to transport heavy loads was a problem for early man. Middle Stone Age man used a crude sled. Later, man harnessed an ox to this type of vehicle. Someone may have learned that a sled could be pulled more easily if poles or logs were put under it so that it moved forward as the logs rolled along the ground. It must have been much later that someone fastened pegs as axles to each end of the rolling logs. Some such series of experiments must have preceded the invention of the wheel, which is ranked as one of the greatest of human inventions.

Improvements in land transport were accompanied by improvements in water travel. An outstanding invention was the sailboat, which enabled men to move heavy goods safely on the seas. Sailors learned to chart the course of their voyages by taking advantage of prevailing winds, and learned the shortest sea routes from place to place.

Another important invention was the potter's wheel, which was a turntable on a vertical spindle. The potter threw a lump of wet clay onto the turntable, or wheel, and as he turned the wheel, he could guide the clay with his hand into the desired shape. The craftsman could shape pottery faster with the potter's wheel than without it.

All these new discoveries called for specialized services. No longer were all men hunters, herdsmen, or farmers. Some became metalsmiths, sailors, potters, or varieties of tradesmen. Trade, or commerce, began when people turned to one another for certain goods and services.

Different peoples passed through the prehistoric ages at different times. An important lesson of history is that people around the world did not advance from one stage of prehistoric development to the next at the same time. Some people remained hunters while others became herdsmen and farmers. Today, there are a few isolated areas in which men are still living in the Stone Age.

Not all peoples of the world passed through the prehistoric stages in the same order. For example, the Japanese skipped the Bronze Age and passed directly from the New Stone Age to an age of iron.

Section Review

1. In what respects was bronze superior to copper for making tools and weapons?
2. What achievements in farming, transportation, and pottery-making came about during the Bronze Age?

Chapter 1

A Review

According to geologists, the earth was formed about 4½ billion years ago from a flaming mass of gas and vapor. Seas and oceans were formed, and gradually early forms of life appeared in them. Millions of years later, land plants and animals appeared as living things developed from simple to more complex forms.

From skeletons of early men, anthropologists have learned about the changes that occurred in man from Zinjanthropus to the Neanderthal to the Cro-Magnon, the first modern type of man.

Man developed his first tools and skills during the Old Stone Age, which lasted from about one million years ago to about 8000 B.C. He learned to make stone tools and weapons by chipping one stone against another. He discovered uses for fire. Neanderthal Man learned to live in caves and to make clothing of skins, thereby adapting himself to living in the cold of the Ice Age. Cro-Magnon Man made advances in the tools and weapons of Neanderthal Man and carved and painted pictures on the walls of the caves he inhabited.

About 8000 B.C. the Middle Stone Age began, following the end of the Ice Age. Men of this period made microliths, tamed the dog, used the bow and arrow, made the first pottery from sun-baked clay, and hollowed out crude boats.

Many more improvements came in the New Stone Age, which began about 6000 B.C. Men learned to make sharper stone tools by grinding them, to spin and weave, and to fire clay to make pots. Men became food producers by domesticating animals and growing plants from seed. As men became farmers, they settled down to live in one place. They formed towns for protection against enemies, made laws and created governments, and developed more elaborate forms of religion than those of earlier men.

Bronze Age men learned to make metal tools and weapons, to improve farming with methods of water control and with plows drawn by harnessed animals, to transport goods in wheeled vehicles and sailboats, and to make pottery on a potter's wheel. Such improvements brought about specialization in work and the beginnings of trade.

The Time

1. During which stage of man's development—Paleolithic, Mesolithic, Neolithic, or Bronze Age—did the following achievements appear? (a) planting seeds for food crops; (b) using fire; (c) making microliths; (d) hunting with chipped stone weapons; (e) spinning and weaving; (f) forming villages and small towns; (g) specializing in metalwork, pottery-making, and other trades; (h) domesticating sheep, cattle, goats, and pigs; (i) making crude boats; (j) making clothing of animal skins.

2. About how many years elapsed from the appearance of Zinjanthropus to the appearance of Neanderthal Man? from the beginning of the Neolithic period to the beginning of the Bronze Age?

The Place

1. Although remains of early man are widely scattered, the following places are sites of important discoveries: Java; Peking; Heidelberg; the Neanderthal; Cro-Magnon Cave; Olduvai Gorge. What early man was found in each? In what modern country is each site located?

2. Name at least seven countries of modern Europe whose lands were entirely or partially covered by the glaciers during the greatest extent of the Ice Age.

Historical Terms

Use each of the following words or terms in a sentence which explains its meaning. Example: A *geologist* is a scientist who studies the crust of the earth.

strata	microlith
fossil	domesticated
anthropologist	pastoral
Ice Age	nomads
Homo sapiens	irrigate
potter's wheel	

Questions for Critical Thinking

1. In what ways was the specialization of labor an important development in the life of primitive man? Is labor in the world today becoming more specialized? Explain.

2. Name the inventions of primitive man which have made the greatest contribution to civilization today. Give a reason for each of your answers.

3. What sort of information can a scientific study of present-day primitive peoples reveal about prehistoric men?

4. Explain why different peoples have passed through prehistoric ages at different times.

5. Probably more inventions appear in one year today than appeared in 1000 years during the Stone Age. Why?

River Valley Civilizations

CHAPTER 2 4000 B.C.–500 B.C.

As man gained control of his environment, he was freed to pursue specialized occupations. Only then could he achieve the conditions necessary to civilization—a highly organized society, advanced skills in art and technology, and maintenance of written records. The Assyrian warriors, Babylonian priest, and Egyptian scribe above represent some of the varied professions which developed in the river valleys that were the first centers of civilization.

In December 1901 a team of French archaeologists at Susa, Iran, discovered three pieces of black stone upon which were found a long series of inscriptions. The archaeologists assembled the stones into one block nearly eight feet in height and sent it to the Louvre, a museum in Paris, where it still stands. The block of stone was one of the most important discoveries ever made about the ancient world, for it contained the law code of Hammurabi, a Babylonian monarch who had ruled the lower Mesopotamian valley over 3500 years ago. The code contained nearly 300 sections and covered in detail the everyday relations of the inhabitants of Hammurabi's empire. From the code, much can be learned about the way people lived in the ancient Near East.

Today, many of the provisions of the code seem extremely severe—even brutal. Disobedience to the head of the household was punished thus: "If a son has struck his father, his hands shall be cut off." Four sample laws dealing with theft show that in Babylonia human life was valued less than personal property.

If a man has stolen goods from a temple, or house, he shall be put to death; and he that has received the stolen property from him shall be put to death.

If a man has broken into a house he shall be killed before the breach [or place where the thief broke through] and buried there.

If a man has committed highway robbery and has been caught, that man shall be put to death.

If a fire has broken out in a man's house and one who has come to put it out has coveted the property of the householder and appropriated any of it, that man shall be cast into the selfsame fire.

Another feature which appears curious today is that penalties varied according to the social position of the injured: "If a man has knocked out the eyes of a patrician, his eye shall be knocked out," whereas if the same man knocked out the eye of a commoner, he was required to pay a fine only. Yet there are other provisions, more akin to modern concepts of justice, which bear out the claim made by Hammurabi in the prologue to the code that the law would "prevent the strong from oppressing the weak." Debt slavery was limited to four years, and corrupt business practices were penalized. Laws governing the fees of doctors and veterinarians allowed people of modest means to pay less for medical and surgical services than the highborn. And women were assured of certain rights which gave them a status not common in more primitive societies.

Hammurabi's code was not the first of its kind. He employed existing laws and revised another code which was already three centuries old. However, Hammurabi expanded the laws and changed some of them so that they would be all-inclusive. Most important, his law code served as the framework for other legal systems long after his death. As law is one of the basic means by which man establishes and maintains social order, the code represents a large step forward in man's journey toward an advanced stage of civilization. In the sections of this chapter which follow, the growth of civilization in the ancient Near East will be described.

1. **The Egyptians built the first empire.**

2. **Egyptian civilization advanced in many ways.**

3. **Nations developed in the Fertile Crescent.**

4. **Large empires were formed in western Asia.**

1 The Egyptians built the first empire

By 5000 B.C. New Stone Age people living along the Nile River in Egypt had learned to farm and to raise cattle. From this rather primitive culture developed one of the first civilizations in the world.

Egyptian civilization depended on the Nile. The civilization that developed in Egypt has been called "the gift of the Nile." This great river watered the land along its banks, and in floodtime it overflowed and deposited fertile soil on the fields. Because rain rarely falls in Egypt, water for drinking, bathing, and farming came almost entirely from the Nile.

The farmers of ancient Egypt lived in one-story, mud-brick huts in villages along the river banks. The fields were hard and dry except in spring when the river overflowed and flooded them with rich soil excellent for growing crops. During the other seasons, farmers dug irrigation ditches to divert water from the Nile into their fields.

The need to dig irrigation ditches, tend them, and construct dams for the benefit of all the farmers required group effort. Each group formed for these purposes had an administrator to direct the work and to make rules for the workmen to follow. In time the administrator assumed greater authority over the farmers. He directed the work of planting and harvesting crops, and he decided whether to store or distribute crop surpluses. These early cooperative efforts, accompanied by the rise of an administrative class, probably made up the earliest form of local government in Egypt.

Because the farmers needed to keep track of the passage of time in order to plan for planting and harvesting, they counted the days between Nile floods. To determine the seasons in which to carry out their farming duties, they studied the paths of the sun, moon, and stars. Their studies led to the development of a calendar which, it is believed, first came into use around 4000 B.C. The Egyptians noticed that on one day each year about floodtime a bright star—now known as the Dog Star, Sirius—appeared in the eastern sky before sunrise. By counting the days between appearances of this star, they determined that the length of a year is 365 days. By dividing the year into twelve months, each consisting of thirty days, they developed their calendar, with five days added at the end of the year. Because the year is actually about one quarter day longer than 365 days, the Egyptian calendar, though amazingly accurate for its time, eventually became erroneous.

The development of irrigation, the rise of local governments, and the invention of a calendar took place between 5000 and 3100 B.C. During this period the Egyptians also developed a system of writing and discovered how to make copper tools. They invented the plow, which greatly increased crop production, and much later, around 2000 B.C., they learned to make bronze by combining copper and tin.

The Old Kingdom began with the unification of Egypt (3100-2270 B.C.). At first Egypt consisted simply of a number of independent, separate villages. In time, local rulers won control over nearby villages, and then over larger areas. By 3100 B.C. two distinct kingdoms had developed. To the north lay Lower Egypt, which included the city of Memphis and the Nile delta, an area of land deposits at the mouth of the river. To the south lay Upper Egypt, which extended along the river valley southward from Memphis to Aswan.

About 3100 B.C. the ruler of Upper Egypt, King Menes, united Upper and Lower Egypt and established a single

Trade and travel along the Nile River in Egypt expanded greatly about 5000 years ago when the ancient Egyptians discovered how to take advantage of the Nile River currents and the prevailing summer winds. The river currents carried their boats downstream and, from mid-May to mid-October, the *Etesian winds* blew them upstream.

Etesian (meaning annual) is a name given to the summer winds which blow southward across the Mediterranean into Africa. In summer, the desert lands which extend from northwestern India across Egypt give off great amounts of heat into the air. The heated air expands, becomes lighter, and rises. This process, called convection, creates an area of low atmospheric pressure over the entire region. Lands to the north of this region have cooler and denser air masses, with resulting higher atmospheric pressure. After the low pressure zone has formed over the eastern Mediterranean region, and the high pressure zone to the north has built up, air from the high pressure area flows in to replace the warm air rising from the low pressure area. This flow of air forms the Etesian winds.

The Etesian winds appear about the middle of May and continue blowing until about the middle of October. During the day, the Etesian winds blow at speeds of from ten to thirty miles per hour, with occasional peak velocities of more than forty miles per hour. When the sun goes down, the desert lands and the air cool rapidly. The cool air becomes denser and the process of convection is reduced. Thus, the atmospheric pressure becomes higher and more nearly equal to the atmospheric pressure of regions to the north. As a result, the flow of air from the high pressure zone is reduced at night and the Etesian winds die out.

The southward-blowing summer winds and the northward-flowing Nile River currents enabled the ancient Egyptians to develop two-way trade along the Nile. From May to October, goods were shipped northward (downstream) in boats pushed by the currents, and return trips were made upstream by sailing with the wind.

As a result of this relatively quick and easy mode of transportation, Egyptian traders extended their activities along the Nile River. Under the stimulus of a thriving trade, many villages along the river became centers of commerce and government. This growth helped to promote the development of civilization in ancient Egypt.

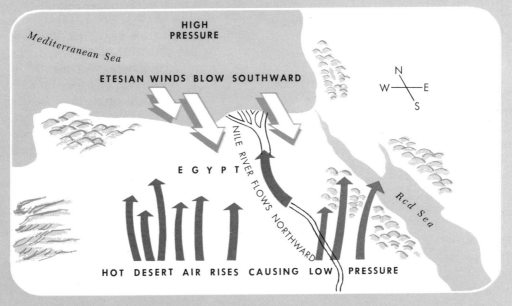

capital city, Memphis. The reign of King Menes marked the first time in history that a strong government ruled so large an area. He also founded the first Egyptian *dynasty*, that is, the first series of Egyptian rulers belonging to the same family. With the unification of Egypt, one of the great periods of Egyptian civilization began. This period is called the *Old Kingdom,* and it lasted for over 800 years.

During the period of the Old Kingdom, merchant ships sailed up and down the Nile, and expeditions left the Nile Valley to trade with peoples in other parts of Africa and the Mediterranean. Artists carved fine statues, and workmen wove soft linen cloth and made pottery with the use of a potter's wheel. Because Egyptians of the Old Kingdom did not know how to make bronze, they continued to use stone tools. However, they did make some implements from the copper that was mined in the Sinai Peninsula.

As generations passed, a ruling class of nobles and princes emerged. Perhaps because these nobles lived in large and luxurious houses, the Egyptian word *pharaoh,* which means "great house," also became the word for king.

The Pyramids were built during the Old Kingdom as tombs for the pharaohs. The largest, built at Giza for Pharaoh Cheops, is about 450 feet high and each of its four sides measures 756 feet across at the base. It is said that the building of this pyramid required thirty years and 100 thousand men. The larger stone blocks weigh several tons each. To quarry, transport, and raise these massive blocks into place with almost no machinery was a remarkable engineering feat. Almost as amazing is the fact that so early a government had the ability to organize and carry out so complex a task.

The Middle Kingdom arose (2060-1785 B.C.). Toward the end of the Old Kingdom, the power of the pharaohs declined.

Civil war brought the collapse of the Old Kingdom, and for more than two hundred years rival leaders fought among themselves for wealth and power. The struggle was won by princes from the city of Thebes, on the upper Nile, who succeeded in uniting the country for the period known as the *Middle Kingdom.* The princes from Thebes became the new pharaohs, and they made Egypt strong and prosperous. They encouraged art and literature and initiated new irrigation projects that greatly increased the crop area. Pharaohs of the Middle Kingdom built a canal which linked the commercial centers of the Nile Valley with the trade routes of the Red Sea. The strong dynasty that arose during the Middle Kingdom period was succeeded by a less capable one, which proved unable to maintain control of the country. The Middle Kingdom lapsed into civil war as rival leaders struggled for power.

About 1680 B.C., while weak from internal disorder, Egypt was conquered by the barbaric Hyksos from Asia. The Hyksos, who are sometimes called the "Shepherd Kings," ruled Egypt harshly for about 100 years. However, the Egyptians learned from them how to wage war with the horses and chariots which the Hyksos had introduced into Egypt. This knowledge proved useful to the Egyptians in the next period of their history.

Egypt freed itself during the New Kingdom and became an empire (1580-1085 B.C.). Thebes again provided leaders for Egypt. The Thebans, with the aid of the princes of the south, drove the Hyksos out, thus restoring Egyptian rule to Egypt. This victory marked the beginning of the *New Kingdom,* or Empire. During this period the pharaohs created an empire, which extended Egyptian rule far beyond the Nile River Valley up into western Asia.

The greatest pharaoh of the New Kingdom was Thutmose III, who ruled from

1501 to 1447 B.C. and who led Egyptian armies to victory over Syria, Phoenicia, and Palestine. During this time increased trade and booty from conquered countries enriched Egypt, and the capital, Thebes, became a city of statues, temples, and palaces.

By 1100 B.C., Egypt had again grown weak through quarrels among its leaders, rebellion among its conquered peoples, and costly battles with foreign enemies. From 1085 to 332 B.C., Egypt went through a period known as the *Period of Decadence,* during which the country was beset by civil war and a series of foreign invasions. Two countries that conquered Egypt were Assyria and Persia (discussed later in this chapter). Following these conquests, Egypt was ruled by Greeks, Romans, Arabs, Turks, and Britons. In fact, Egypt did not again become an independent nation until 1922.

EGYPTIAN EMPIRE
About 1450 B.C.

Mediterranean Sea

Thebes

Red Sea

Prepared by
Rand McNally & Co., Chicago

Section Review

1. What geographic factors encouraged the growth of civilization in Egypt?
2. What elements of Egyptian civilization developed before the Old Kingdom?
3. What were the outstanding achievements of the Old Kingdom? the Middle Kingdom? the New Kingdom, or Empire?

2 Egyptian civilization advanced in many ways

During the Old Kingdom, the Middle Kingdom, and the New Kingdom, Egypt developed a flourishing civilization. Many aspects of Egyptian life have played important roles in the development of Western civilization.

The power of the pharaohs was absolute. The pharaohs had absolute power over subjects—partly because most of these rulers governed justly, but primarily be-

cause the people believed the pharaohs were descended from a god and were gods themselves. (A government in which the ruler is presumed to possess both spiritual or divine power and civil authority is known as a *theocracy.*) In theory, the pharaoh owned all the land, commanded the army, controlled the irrigation system, and received the surpluses of crops produced on the royal estates. Since no one person could administer a huge kingdom, the pharaoh appointed officials to assist him. However, he was personally responsible for dispensing justice and for making all the important decisions regarding government affairs. Beginning with the Old Kingdom, the Egyptians created a complex but efficient administrative system that supported the absolute authority of the pharaoh.

Egyptian society was divided into three classes. The first class of people below the pharaoh was composed of the priests, the

Egyptian Religion was based on belief in life after death and the worship of many gods. Above is the pyramid built about 2600 B.C. to hold the body of Pharaoh Khafre. It was once connected by a covered passageway to the Great Sphinx, which has the body of a lion and the head of a man, possibly Khafre. The papyrus scroll below was buried with a female mummy. Osiris, lord of the afterlife, sits in judgment while his son, dog-headed Anubis, weighs the heart of the woman against the feather of truth.

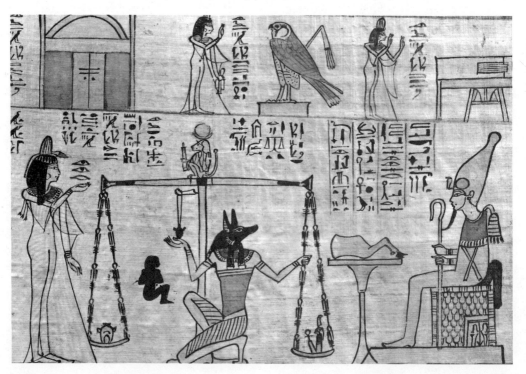

court nobility, and the landed nobility. The priests performed the religious ceremonies, especially those having to do with the burial of the dead. The court nobles advised the pharaoh and carried out his orders. The landed nobles managed their great estates, and some of them also served as generals in the royal army. From writings and pictures on tombs and temples, scholars have learned a great deal about life among the upper class. They lived in palatial homes, with luxurious furnishings and elaborate gardens. The women beautified their hair, wore rouge and lipstick, and painted their nails. It was not uncommon for both men and women to use perfume and wear jewelry.

Women of the upper class enjoyed a favored place in society largely because all landed property descended from mother to daughter, rather than from father to son as in most other ancient cultures. They could be merchants, eat and dance in public, and do most of the things men were allowed to do.

The middle class included the rich merchants and traders as well as the skilled artisans, who made furniture and jewelry, worked with leather and cloth, and directed the building of tombs and palaces. Professional people such as teachers, artists, doctors, and scribes were also considered middle class. Scribes, who wrote letters and documents for a living, held an important place in Egyptian life because few of their countrymen could read or write.

The lower class, to which the great mass of Egyptians belonged, was made up of slaves—usually war captives—and free laborers who worked on farms, irrigation systems, roads, and building projects. The free laborers, heavily burdened by taxes imposed on them by the pharaohs, had hardly any more political rights than the slaves. They lived poorly in small, mudbrick homes with few furnishings. From this class of free laborers, however, it was possible for bright and ambitious young Egyptians to rise to higher rank. Such persons might become merchants, priests, or even government officials. Sometimes loyal and able slaves were given their freedom. On a few occasions, a talented slave was known to rise to a position of authority in society.

Egyptian strength was built on farming and trading. The fertility of the Nile Valley and extensive irrigation systems enabled the Egyptians to reap large harvests. Because farmers produced more food than they needed for themselves, many of them became craftsmen or traders as well as farmers.

Egyptian traders relied mainly on ships to transport their goods. Trade reached its height during the New Kingdom, when Egypt controlled the trade routes of the Near East. Egyptian ships carried products such as wheat and linens across the Mediterranean to Europe and Asia, returning with lumber and metal weapons, which Egypt did not produce.

Religion in Egypt was concerned with life after death. Egyptians reasoned that just as plants decline in autumn and reappear in the spring, so also must man have life after death. Furthermore, they believed that the body in which the soul had lived in life must be preserved in death in order for the soul to live on. The process of preserving the body, called mummification, developed into a highly skilled art. Beliefs about the afterlife led the Egyptians to build large tombs in which to keep the bodies of their dead rulers.

Good conduct, as well as preservation of the body, was thought necessary for immortality, or life after death. In the *Book of the Dead,* the soul of a deceased man says to Osiris:

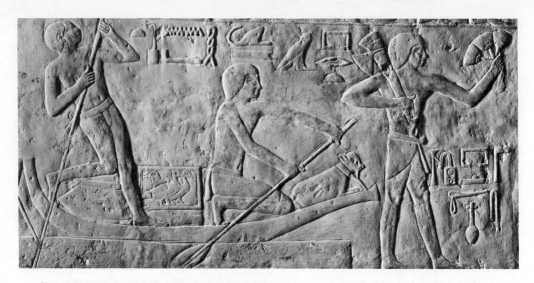

Daily Life in Egypt was portrayed on the walls of tombs in paintings and relief carvings. The Egyptians believed that figures came alive to serve the dead in the hereafter. In the relief at the top of this page, men transport cattle and fowl down the Nile to market. The man in the rear of the boat uses a pole to push the craft through the shallows while his companion steers with a paddle. Directly above, members of a female orchestra play a lyre, pipes, a lute, and a harp while a young girl dances. Workers harvest grain, top right, while an overseer counts the crop and kneeling scribes tally the figures. Depicted below are other common activities. In the upper panel, two men gather grapes and others crush them underfoot. The juice, pouring from a spigot, is stored in urns to ferment into wine. Below, bird catchers trap waterfowl in a net; the birds are then plucked and hung up to dry.

Here am I: I come to thee; I bring to thee
Right and have put a stop to wrong.
I am not a doer of wrong to men.
I am not one who slayeth his kindred.
I am not one who telleth lies instead of
truth.
I am not conscious of treason.
I am not a doer of mischief.

Polytheism, or the worship of many
gods, was characteristic of Egyptian religion during the Old Kingdom and the
Middle Kingdom. The most important
gods were Amon-Re, the sun god, and
Osiris, the god of the underworld and lord
of the afterlife. During the reign of Pharaoh
Akhenaton in the New Kingdom, who
ruled from 1375 to 1358 B.C., a new faith
was born. Akhenaton believed in one supreme god, rather than in many gods. The
supreme god, Akhenaton thought, was
Aton, the sun. Akhenaton forbade the worship of all gods but Aton, and withdrew
the government support previously given
to the priests of other gods.

However, the priests were numerous and
influential. They succeeded in terrifying
the already fearful people into believing
that if they obeyed Akhenaton they would
suffer the wrath of the gods. While Akhenaton lived, his orders were not openly dis-
obeyed, but after his death the priests persuaded Egyptians to return to the worship
of many gods. The concept of one god,
or *monotheism,* disappeared in Egypt for
a time, but it was born again later in the
Hebrew religion.

Hieroglyphic writing was developed.
Between 4000 and 3000 B.C. the Egyptians
developed a kind of picture writing known
as *hieroglyphics.* The first writings consisted of pictures of objects, such as a
house. Gradually, picture signs came into
use for ideas as well as objects. For example, a picture of an eye could mean
sight or *eye.* In time, the writers also used
picture signs to indicate sound. Although

these developments were the beginnings
of an alphabet, the Egyptians did not
create an alphabetical system of writing.

The first Egyptian books were written as
early as 4000 B.C. on a material made from
the *papyrus* plant, a kind of reed. Craftsmen sliced the pith of this plant into strips,
overlapped them, and pasted them together. Papyrus (the origin of the word
paper) was sold wherever Egyptian traders traveled. Egyptian books consisted of
long rolls of papyrus. (One such roll, now in
the British Museum, is 17 inches wide and
135 feet long.) Egyptian writings survived
the passage of centuries because they were
preserved in the dry climate of Egypt.

The early Egyptian writings were about
religion, such as the *Book of the Dead* already mentioned. During the Middle Kingdom, some adventure stories were written.
These works were probably the first story-
books ever published.

Mathematics and medicine advanced.
Because Nile floods washed away markers
for land boundaries, the Egyptians sur-
veyed the land frequently and used practical geometry in measuring the boundaries.
Their engineers also used mathematics to
work out the precise measurements necessary in the construction of their pyramids
and temples. Thus, the science of mathematics advanced in ancient Egypt.

Egyptian doctors were familiar with the
anatomy of the human body and the healing properties of certain herbs. They also
knew how to set broken bones and how to
cure wounds. However, their writings on
medicine, which describe different ill-
nesses and the treatments for them, show
that the Egyptians put much faith in the
healing properties of magic.

The Egyptians were skilled architects.
The Egyptians were good builders in stone,
and both sculptors and engineers delighted
in great size. The Great Pyramids and the

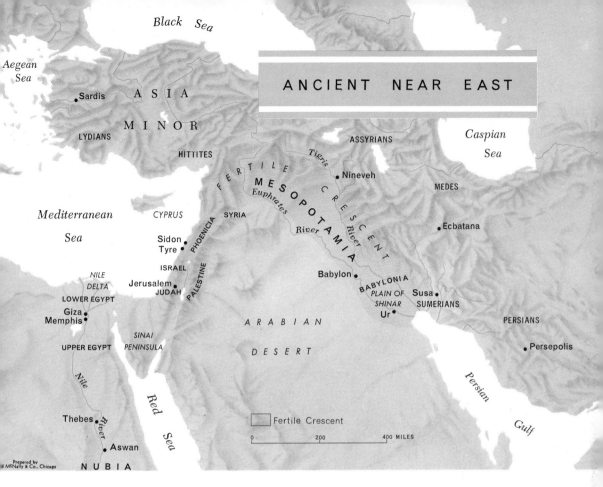

ANCIENT NEAR EAST

Fertile Crescent

0   200   400 MILES

Prepared by
d McNally & Co., Chicago

Sphinx are examples of the Egyptian fondness for huge structures.

Religion inspired the building of Egyptian tombs and temples. The most famous temple was that of the god Amon, at Karnak, which occupies part of the site of ancient Thebes. Part of this great temple still stands. Its hall is 400 feet long, 175 feet wide—larger than a football field—and 80 feet high. The roof was supported by rows of giant columns. The Egyptians were the first to support roofs with columns rather than with walls.

Section Review

1. Why was the pharaoh able to maintain absolute authority over his people?
2. Into what classes was Egyptian society divided?

3. By what means did Egyptians hope to achieve immortality?
4. What are hieroglyphics? What kinds of early Egyptian books were written on papyrus?
5. What achievements did the Egyptians make in mathematics? medicine? architecture?

3 **Nations developed
in the Fertile Crescent**

About the same time that a civilization was growing in Egypt, another civilization was emerging in western Asia, in the valley of the Tigris and Euphrates rivers known as Mesopotamia, or "land between the rivers." Mesopotamia was located in

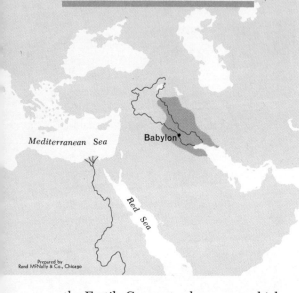

HAMMURABI'S EMPIRE
About 1760 B.C.

Mediterranean Sea

Babylon

Red Sea

Prepared by
Rand McNally & Co., Chicago

HITTITE EMPIRE
About 1300 B.C.

Mediterranean Sea

Red Sea

Prepared by
Rand McNally & Co., Chicago

the Fertile Crescent, a large area which extends in an arc from the southeastern end of the Mediterranean Sea to the Persian Gulf. It included all or parts of what are now Lebanon, Israel, Jordan, Syria, Turkey, and Iraq. Civilized living emerged in a small area of lower Mesopotamia in what is now Iraq. The area extended about 500 miles northwest from the Persian Gulf. The Bible calls this area the plain of Shinar. Some authorities believe that the earliest civilization in the world began here.

The Sumerians built a civilization. Civilization on the plain of Shinar first began to develop about 4000 B.C. At that time a tribe known as the Sumerians moved down from the hill country of the northeast into the fertile area bounded by the Tigris and Euphrates rivers. Like the Egyptians, the Sumerians dug canals to control the spring floods and to irrigate the land.

Unlike the Egyptians, who became a unified nation under the Old Kingdom, the Sumerians created a number of *city-states,*

each consisting of a city and dependent outlying territories. The city-states enjoyed their most prosperous period from 2900 to 2400 B.C. During this period, Sumerian farmers raised barley, oats, and dates. Some city dwellers were skilled craftsmen, and their products were traded as far away as India and Egypt.

Each city-state was a theocracy in which the local god, believed to be the real ruler of the city-state, was represented by an earthly ruler who served as high priest and city governor. This ruler officiated at religious ceremonies and performed administrative duties, such as supervising the irrigation system. Like the Egyptian pharaoh, he was an all-powerful ruler with absolute authority over his people. Although the Sumerian ruler governed his city-state in the name of the local god, unlike the Egyptian pharaoh, he was not considered divine himself.

The Sumerians made several important contributions to the civilization of the Near East. One was a form of writing.

The Sumerians manufactured no paper but used a stylus to make impressions on soft clay bricks or tablets, which were then baked to give them permanent form. The Sumerians' type of writing is called *cuneiform*, meaning "wedge-shaped," because of the marks made by their stylus. The writing had various combinations of the wedge-shaped impressions. Each sign stood for a syllable. The cuneiform writing of the Sumerians was later adopted by other peoples of the Near East, such as the Hittites, Babylonians, and Persians.

The plain of Shinar lacked stones for building, but clay was abundant, and the Sumerians used it to build their houses and temples. Although their buildings have largely vanished under the weathering of centuries, their invention of the arch continues to be important to architecture. The Sumerians probably made the earliest use of the wheel, although it may have been invented earlier, and they taught its use to the Egyptians.

Besides worshiping their own local god, the Sumerian people of each city-state worshiped other gods introduced into the plain of Shinar by invading peoples. The Sumerian religion gave rise to notable literary works, the most important of which is the epic poem *Gilgamesh*. In one of its sections, a fascinating account of a flood tells a story similar to the story of Noah in the Bible, inspired perhaps by the ever present possibility of river floods.

Hammurabi wrote a code of laws. Unlike Egypt, Mesopotamia had no natural barriers against invasion. Furthermore, the individual city-states were easy prey to outside foes. However, in spite of invasion, the Sumerian civilization persisted because the conquerors adopted Sumerian customs.

About 2500 B.C. the city-states were united by Sargon I, an invader from the north. Later, about 1760 B.C., Hammurabi, who came from what is now Syria, brought all of lower Mesopotamia under one rule. His capital was the city of Babylon, and all lower Mesopotamia became known as Babylonia.

Hammurabi's most important contribution to civilization was his written code of law. It comprised one of the earliest sets of laws in written form. Although his code contained many harsh and unjust laws, through it the state became responsible for their enforcement. State enforcement of laws was a great advance over the system of family vengeance practiced in more primitive societies, whereby the evil deeds of one wrongdoer were avenged by the family of the one who had been wronged.

After Hammurabi's death, his kingdom collapsed as wild mountain tribes invaded it from the east and north. The Hittites, one of these invading tribes, became powerful in the Fertile Crescent.

The Hittites conquered an empire with iron weapons. The Hittites occupied an area to the northwest of Babylonia, in what is now Turkey. For so early a time in history, their laws were just and humane, and their architecture was notable. Their most important gift to civilization, however, was the knowledge of how to work iron. In refining iron ore and using it to make tools and weapons, they marked the beginning of the Age of Iron, which succeeded the Bronze Age at about 1100 B.C.

Armed with their iron weapons, which were harder and stronger than those made of bronze, the Hittites drove southward into Syria, in the western part of the Fertile Crescent. Shortly after 1600 B.C. they conquered Babylonia and became rulers of the area once governed by Hammurabi.

These conquests aroused the fears of the Egyptian pharaohs, who sent armies north to challenge them. The ensuing long struggle between the two forces weakened both the Hittite and Egyptian empires.

Small Nations flourished in the Fertile Crescent before their inhabitants were subjugated by the Assyrians. The people of Sumer, shown in a procession on the inlaid stone panel at left, were among the first to use chariots. The spinner being fanned by a slave, center left, is from a relief found in Susa, a city which dates back to 1200 B.C. In the fresco below, from a synagogue in the ancient city of Dura-Europos, Philistines capture the Ark of Jehovah (a sacred box) from the Hebrews. The Hittite relief at right, carved about the 10th century B.C., shows lion hunters in a chariot.

By 1200 B.C. the Hittite kingdom was beginning to collapse, and Egypt had also lost much of its power. Since this situation left western Asia without a master, small states were able to develop and maintain their freedom. This era of small states lasted from about 1200 to 750 B.C.

The Phoenicians developed an alphabet. One of these small countries was ruled by the Phoenicians, who had been desert nomads. They moved westward into an area of the Fertile Crescent bordering the eastern Mediterranean. There they became sea traders and built the great trading cities of Tyre and Sidon. Their ships sailed to Greece, Italy, North Africa, Spain, south along the west coast of Africa, and possibly even to faraway Britain. The Phoenicians set up many distant trading colonies, the greatest of which was Carthage, in North Africa.

To keep account of their trading operations, the Phoenicians developed a more advanced system of writing than that devised by the Egyptians or Sumerians. They used letters or signs that represented sounds to make an alphabet, and this alphabet became their most important contribution to civilization. The word alphabet comes from their first two letters—

aleph and *beth*. The Phoenician alphabet consisted of twenty-two consonant symbols, and later, when the Greeks adopted it, they introduced vowel signs. From this combination of consonant and vowel signs came the alphabet used today by peoples of the West.

The Hebrews developed the belief in one god. Another small country was that of the Hebrews, or Jews. Much of the history of this people is told in the Old Testament of the Bible. It tells how the Hebrews, under their leader Abraham, came from the eastern part of the plain of Shinar. They sought a "promised land" in which to settle, and after years of wandering came to Canaan, or Palestine. The Book of Exodus in the Bible tells how some of the Hebrew tribes were enslaved by the Egyptians. After a long captivity, a great Hebrew leader named Moses led his people back to Palestine. Jewish scriptures relate how Moses gave the Jews the Ten Commandments which the Hebrew god, Jehovah, had revealed to him on Mount Sinai.

According to the Old Testament, the Hebrews had to fight the Canaanites and later the Philistines for possession of Palestine. Around 1025 B.C. Saul became their first king. He was followed on the throne by

Mediterranean   Sea

PHOENICIA

HEBREW KINGDOM
(under David and Solomon)

Red Sea

Prepared by
Rand McNally & Co., Chicago

brews were easy prey to invaders. In 722 B.C. the Assyrians conquered Israel. In 586 B.C. Judah fell to Nebuchadnezzar, a Chaldean king, who captured Jerusalem and carried off the inhabitants into exile. Later, the Persians defeated the Chaldeans and permitted the Hebrews to return to Jerusalem and to restore their temple.

Persian rule was followed by that of the Greeks and later, by the Romans. In 66 A.D. the Jews staged a revolt against Roman rule, but the Romans destroyed Jerusalem and drove many of the Jews from Palestine, from whence they scattered to many different parts of the world. In spite of this *Diaspora,* or "scattering," the Jews clung to their religion and customs and dreamed of someday returning to the "promised land." This dream was not realized until the 20th century, when the Jews were permitted to reëstablish a Jewish state in Palestine, which is now the nation of Israel.

The religion which the Hebrews developed is called Judaism. With its monotheism, or belief in one god, and teachings of the Old Testament, Judaism formed the base of two other great religions of the world—Christianity and Islam. From an early worship of many gods, the Hebrews developed the idea of one god for their own tribe. This idea, in time, developed into the idea of one loving Father who ruled over the whole universe. Building upon the Ten Commandments, prophets developed some of the noblest rules of human behavior, as shown in the following passage from the Holy Scriptures (Micah 6:8).

It hath been told thee, O man, what is good, And what the Lord doth require of thee: Only to do justly, and to love mercy, and to walk humbly with thy God.

About 66 A.D., the year the Jews revolted against Rome, a Jewish sect known as the

David who, as a boy, had slain the Philistine giant, Goliath, with a stone hurled from a sling. David, as the "singer of Psalms," is given the credit for having composed many of the sacred hymns which make up the Book of Psalms of the Old Testament. After defeating the Philistines, David established a promising kingdom with Jerusalem as its capital.

The Hebrew kingdom reached its height under David's son, Solomon, who reigned from about 977 to 937 B.C. In Jerusalem he built a great temple to God and sent his ships to trade in distant countries. His expenditures imposed such a high tax on the people that the Hebrew tribes in the north grew discontented with Solomon's reign. After his death they set up an independent kingdom, thereby dividing the land of the Hebrews into two parts: the Kingdom of Israel in the north and the Kingdom of Judah in the south. Thus weakened, the He-

Essenes hid many of their manuscript scrolls in caves near the Dead Sea. The scrolls, wrapped in linen and placed in jars, remained hidden for nineteen centuries. In 1947, the first of the Dead Sea Scrolls, as they are known, were found by shepherds. Since then, thousands of manuscript fragments have been unearthed. The scrolls, ranked among the most important discoveries of all times, furnish Biblical texts in Hebrew centuries older than the earliest text previously known. Included among the scrolls are two manuscripts from the Book of Isaiah, commentaries on Genesis, and portions of more than 100 scrolls of Old Testament books. Scholars have dated the earliest manuscripts to about 200 B.C. Others were written in the 1st century A.D.

Section Review

1. In what ways did Sumerian civilization compare with that of Egypt? In what ways did it differ?
2. How did the enforcement of laws under Hammurabi differ from the system previously in use?
3. What conditions in the Fertile Crescent enabled small states to enjoy a brief period of independence from 1200 to 750 B.C.?
4. What led the Phoenicians to develop an improved system of writing?
5. What contributions did the Hebrews make to religious thought?

4 Large empires were formed in western Asia

The era of small states ended with the rise of new empires in the Fertile Crescent. The first of these was the empire of the Assyrians, which lasted from about 750 to 605 B.C.

The Assyrians were mighty warriors. The original homeland of the Assyrians was a highland region north of the upper

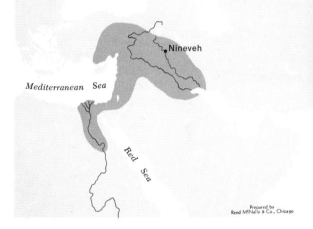

ASSYRIAN EMPIRE
About 700 B.C.

Nineveh

Mediterranean Sea

Red Sea

Prepared by
Rand McNally & Co., Chicago

Tigris River. Shortly before 1000 B.C. they began a series of attacks on their neighbors. Babylonia fell to them in 729 B.C. and Israel was conquered in 722 B.C. By 700 B.C. the Assyrians had created the largest empire the world had seen up to that time. It included the Fertile Crescent, the area surrounding it, and Egypt.

The Assyrians created their empire by developing an advanced system of political administration and by building a well-trained army equipped with iron weapons. Assyrian rulers, such as Ashurbanipal, governed a large area through governors placed in different parts of the realm. Communication between the ruler and the governors was maintained by a system of highways throughout the empire.

The Assyrian army was the most efficient of its day, using a bow with vicious iron-tipped arrows as its principal weapon. After Assyrian bowmen had weakened the enemy, heavy cavalry and chariots

Mediterranean Sea

Babylon

Red Sea

Prepared by
Rand McNally & Co., Chicago

A new Babylonian empire arose. With the fall of Nineveh, Babylonia again became powerful for the first time since Hammurabi. The victorious Chaldeans, guided by their strong King Nebuchadnezzar, created the Chaldean Empire by conquering the Fertile Crescent, including the Kingdom of Judah. Nebuchadnezzar rebuilt Babylon. Its marvels included the hanging gardens built on rooftops and considered by the ancient Greeks to be one of the Seven Wonders of the World.

The Chaldeans, extending the work of earlier peoples, made an intensive study of the stars, as well as the sun, the moon, and the planets. Without any telescopes or accurate time-recording instruments, the Chaldeans used mathematics to work out detailed tables of the movements of these bodies. In so doing, they made notable contributions to the science of astronomy. Like others who followed them, the Chaldeans named days of the week for the heavenly bodies. Later peoples named Saturday for Saturn, Sunday for the sun, and Monday for the moon.

The Chaldeans mistakenly believed that their study of the stars enabled them to foretell the future. From this belief arose astrology, a pseudo-science that still has some followers.

Nebuchadnezzar had a long reign, from 605 to 561 B.C., and with his death the Chaldean Empire began to decay. It was eventually succeeded by the great Persian Empire.

The Lydians invented coins for use in trade. Situated in Asia Minor in what is now eastern Turkey, the country of Lydia arose out of the ruins of the Hittite Empire. The Lydian capital, Sardis, was located near important trade routes and became a rich commercial center. Gold, found in Lydian streams, became a unit of exchange. Coins, issued in various sizes, were found to be much easier to carry around

smashed the ranks of the foes, driving them from the field. Few conquerors in history have been so cruel and heartless in war. They terrorized conquered peoples and forced them to bow to their will, frequently burning them alive or cutting off their heads.

Except for their developments in political administration and military science, their contributions to civilization were few, and their empire lasted little more than a hundred years. However, their fine library of clay tablets in their capital, Nineveh, helped preserve much of the knowledge of the Near East. Their art was noteworthy, particularly the sculptures of vigorous wild beasts, which decorated the walls of the royal palace.

In 612 B.C. Nineveh was captured by the Chaldeans from Babylonia and the Medes from Persia. Everywhere in the Near East the people rejoiced when their cruel Assyrian masters were overthrown. By 605 B.C. the Assyrian Empire had ceased to exist.

than weighted bars or rings of metal that formerly had been used for money.

Successful trade and gold resources brought great wealth to Lydia and to its most famous king, Croesus. A reminder of this prosperity is the phrase, "rich as Croesus." In 546 B.C. Croesus was defeated by the Persians, and his lands were absorbed into the Persian Empire.

The Persians built a vast empire. The Assyrian Empire had included two groups of related peoples, the Medes and the Persians. After helping defeat the Assyrians, the Median kings established a prosperous kingdom and ruled over their Persian kinsmen from their capital at Ecbatana.

While the Chaldean Empire was crumbling, the Persians, under Cyrus the Great, rebelled against the Medes and took over their lands, capturing Ecbatana in 525 B.C. Cyrus then conquered the Lydian kingdom and the Chaldean Empire. At the time of his death, the Persians ruled east to the borders of India, west to the Aegean Sea, and south to Egypt. Cyrus' successors conquered Egypt in 525 B.C. and even won land in southeastern Europe. The Persian Empire, established when Cyrus conquered Ecbatana, lasted until its conquest by Alexander the Great of Macedonia in 331 B.C.

The Persian government, like that of the Assyrian and Chaldean empires, was a *despotism*, or rule of a monarch having unlimited power. Unlike the cruel Assyrians, however, the Persian kings sought to give everyone in their empire equal rights and responsibilities. They respected the gods of conquered peoples and allowed them to use their own languages and to keep their own customs.

By 500 B.C. the Persian Empire, under Darius I, had reached its greatest size. Its government was modeled after that of Assyria, although it was much more efficient. Four capitals—Susa, Ecbatana, Babylon,

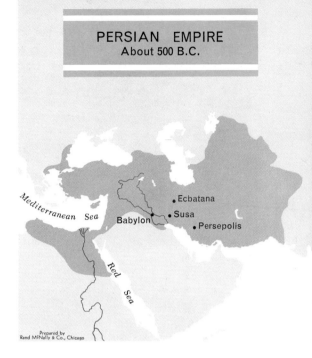

PERSIAN EMPIRE
About 500 B.C.

Prepared by
Rand McNally & Co., Chicago

and Persepolis—were established in various parts of the empire; and the total empire was divided into districts, or *satrapies*, each governed by a representative of the king, called a *satrap*. To keep himself informed on how well the satraps governed, Darius employed inspectors, called "The Eyes and Ears of the King," who traveled from district to district, reporting their findings personally to their ruler.

To improve communications throughout the vast empire, the Persian kings maintained a network of fine roads. Along these highways galloped the couriers of the king, changing horses every fourteen miles, much like the American pony express riders of the 1860's. Relays of these horsemen could cover 1500 miles in a little more than a week; ordinary travelers took three months to travel the same distance.

The Persian kings concerned themselves with the prosperity of the whole empire, partly because they wanted all districts to be able to pay taxes. The tax burden, how-

Great Empires in the Near East

Between 1000 and 700 B.C., the Egyptians and various peoples of the Fertile Crescent were conquered by the warlike Assyrians. A relief carving of a siege, above, shows Assyrian warriors storming a city. At left, soldiers with spears scale the walls. Bowmen at right take aim behind a four-wheeled war carriage. At the top are captives whom the Assyrians have impaled on stakes.

Assyrian dominance was followed by the establishment of the Chaldean Empire, which in turn fell to the Persians. In the relief at left, Darius, one of the great Persian kings, receives an emissary. Xerxes, his son and successor, stands behind the throne. The relief was found in one of the Persian capital cities, Persepolis, the ruins of which are shown below. The great columns once supported the wooden roof of a huge audience hall where kings held court. A magnificent double staircase, embellished with sculptured decorations, led to the hall, which was built during the reigns of Darius and Xerxes.

ever, was not oppressive. Trade throughout the empire was aided by the uniform monetary system of gold and silver coins, which the Persians had adopted from the Lydians.

The fair treatment of other peoples by the Persian kings resulted in part from the Persian religion, Zoroastrianism, founded by the teacher Zoroaster in the 7th century B.C. This religion demanded that its followers choose between Ahura Mazda, the god of good, and Ahriman, the god of evil. In time, the Zoroastrians believed, the world would come to an end with Ahura Mazda winning over Ahriman. At that time there would be a last judgment, and the righteous would go to heaven and the wicked to hell. In describing one of his victories, Darius I showed how he was influenced by the Persian religion:

... Ahura Mazda bore me aid ... because I was not an enemy, I was not a deceiver, I was not a wrong-doer, neither I nor my family; according to justice and rectitude I ruled . . . .

Although many of the Persian kings ruled with justice, they did not give their people a share in the government. The next chapter will tell how the Greeks set up the first democracy, a government in which the people had a voice.

Section Review
1. How did the Assyrians succeed in building so large an empire?
2. What contributions did the Chaldeans make to astronomy?
3. What policies of the Persians help explain the success of their government?

Chapter 2   A Review

In the river valleys of the Nile and the Tigris and Euphrates, man moved from the Stone Age into civilization. His advance into civilized living was marked by the development of writing, the use of metals, improved transportation, effective government, and the growth of towns and cities.

Egyptian civilization began in the Nile Valley, where the need for controlling the waters of the Nile helped bring about local governments. In 3100 B.C., King Menes unified Upper and Lower Egypt and set up the first strong central government over a large area. The great periods of ancient Egypt were the Old Kingdom, the Middle Kingdom, and the New Kingdom, or Empire. During these periods, the Egyptian religion and worship of the all-powerful pharaoh developed. Also during these periods the Egyptians established a prosperous trade along the Nile and the eastern Mediterranean Sea, and improved their system of writing. The Old Kingdom was famous for the Great Pyramids, the Middle Kingdom for the canal that connected the Nile with the Red Sea, and the New Kingdom, or Empire, for ex-

tending Egyptian control over other peoples. Outstanding Egyptian contributions to Near Eastern civilization included methods of precise mathematical measurements and columnar architecture.

In Mesopotamia, the Sumerians built a city-state civilization, developed cuneiform writing, and invented the arch. Their civilization lived on in spite of frequent invasions. Conquerors included Hammurabi, who wrote a code of laws and made the state responsible for enforcing them, and the Hittites, who introduced the Age of Iron. A struggle between the Hittites and Egyptians weakened both empires and permitted small states to enjoy a brief period of independence. The Phoenicians became successful traders and developed an alphabet. The Hebrews made an important contribution to civilization with the religion of Judaism, which stressed the existence of one all-powerful, fatherly God who demanded right conduct from men.

The era of small states was followed by a period of large empires. The Assyrians built an extensive empire by means of an efficient system of administration and communication, an excellent army, and terror tactics. The Chaldean Empire, which arose out of the defeat of the Assyrians, was developed by King Nebuchadnezzar. The Chaldeans were noted for their achievements in astronomy. They, along with the Egyptians, were eventually conquered by the Persians, who built one of the greatest empires the world had yet seen. Its government was modeled after that of the Assyrians, but the Persians, influenced by the principles of the Zoroastrian religion, ruled their people with consideration and justice.

The Time
Indicate the period in which the events described in the following statements occurred.

(a) 4000-3001 B.C.   (d) 1500-1001 B.C.
(b) 3000-2001 B.C.   (e) 1000-501 B.C.
(c) 2000-1501 B.C.

1. Hammurabi ruled in Babylon.
2. The Egyptian New Kingdom began.
3. The era of small states began.
4. Hyksos conquered Egypt.
5. Nebuchadnezzar ruled the Chaldean Empire.
6. The prosperous period of Sumerian city-states began.
7. The Egyptian Middle Kingdom ended.
8. The Assyrians conquered Babylonia and Israel.
9. The Egyptian Old Kingdom began.
10. The Persians conquered the Medes, the Lydians, the Chaldeans, and the Egyptians.
11. The Hittite Empire began to decline.
12. Solomon ruled the Hebrew kingdom.
13. Nineveh fell to the Chaldeans and to the Medes.

The Place
1. Name one empire for which each of the following cities served as the capital. On what river was each located: Thebes, Babylon, Nineveh?
2. What was northern Egypt (including the Nile delta and Memphis) called?
3. Which of the following modern countries are completely outside of the Fertile Crescent: Lebanon, Jordan, Egypt, Israel, Saudi Arabia, Turkey, Iraq, Iran?

4. Which geographical area is the largest: the plain of Shinar, Fertile Crescent, Mesopotamia?
5. What ancient empires at their greatest extent included parts or all of the following areas: Egypt, Palestine, Phoenicia, Syria?
6. Locate the following ancient cities and tell what each was noted for: Tyre, Sidon, Ecbatana, Persepolis, Susa.
7. Locate each of the following cities and name one kingdom of which it was once a capital: Memphis, Sardis, Jerusalem.

The People
1. With what religion was each of these names associated: Amon-Re, Ahura Mazda, Aton, Jehovah, Osiris?
2. Give one reason why each of the following persons was famous.

Moses	Zoroaster
Darius I	Ashurbanipal
David	Menes
Hammurabi	Nebuchadnezzar
Thutmose III	Sargon I
Akhenaton	Cyrus the Great
Solomon	Croesus
Cheops	Saul

Historical Terms
1. Define each of the following terms and tell how it applied to ancient Egyptian life.

dynasty	papyrus
pharaoh	court nobility
pyramid	immortality
theocracy	polytheism
mummification	

2. In what ways are hieroglyphic and cuneiform writing different?
3. Define the term despotism as it applied to the governments of the ancient empires.
4. Explain these terms and tell with what peoples each term was associated.

Shepherd Kings	"promised land"
city-states	astrology
monotheism	satrap
prophet	satrapies
empire	Exodus
Gilgamesh	Book of the Dead
Ten Commandments	Judaism
Psalms	
"The Eyes and Ears of the King"	

Questions for Critical Thinking

1. How did the influence of Zoroastrianism contribute to the generally humane rule of the Persian kings?

2. Of what significance is the discovery of the Dead Sea Scrolls to an understanding of the Hebrew religion?

3. What lessons in administration could later empire builders learn from the Persians?

4. Why did codes of law, such as that of Hammurabi, become important as men lived together in increasingly larger groups?

5. What do the excerpts from the Code of Hammurabi tell about Babylonian civilization?

6. In contrast to Egypt, which for centuries was under the rule of one dynasty, Mesopotamia was subject to frequent invasions and changes of rulers. Why?

The Classical World

Much of Western civilization can be traced to a common source—the world of ancient Greece and Rome. From this world came principles of law and government, fundamental concepts in science and mathematics, standards of art and architecture, and the root words of many living languages. Indeed, so much of Greco-Roman civilization serves as a standard that it is referred to as *classical*.

The first act in the drama of Greco-Roman history was the rise of civilization on the islands and shores of the Aegean Sea in the eastern Mediterranean. The island of Crete, in particular, grew wealthy through trade with advanced civilizations in Egypt and Asia Minor. Another important Aegean center was Mycenae in southern Greece. From about 1500 to 1200 B.C., Aegean civilization flourished. Then it was overrun by invaders from the north.

The newcomers belonged to a group of light-skinned peoples, the *Indo-Europeans,* whose original home was probably in central Asia. (In ancient times one branch of this large group moved westward into Greece, Italy, and western Europe. Others, such as the Hittites and Persians, emigrated to Asia Minor. Still others, referred to as the Aryans, pushed southeastward into India.) As the Indo-European tribes moved into the Greek peninsula, they mixed with the Aegeans and borrowed elements of their culture. From this intermingling of peoples came the Greeks, or *Hellenes.* The high point of Greek civilization was reached in the *Hellenic* period, which lasted from about 750 to 338 B.C.

The Greeks established city-states on the rugged peninsula of Greece. Two were especially important: Athens and Sparta. The government of Sparta was harsh, and its people had to conform to rigid military discipline. In Athens political and personal freedom was encouraged, and a workable democratic government was formed. Although the Athenians admired military prowess, the pursuit of beauty and truth was considered more important. In the 5th century, after taking the lead in repulsing a Persian invasion of Greece, Athens enjoyed a Golden Age. Important discoveries were made in science, mathematics, and medicine. Literature of enduring beauty and masterpieces of sculpture and architecture were created. Brilliant thinkers, such as Socrates, Plato, and Aristotle, inspired men to undertake the quest for truth and wisdom.

By the end of the 5th century, war and strife among the Greek city-states threatened the existence of Hellenic civilization. But it was not destroyed by the conquest of Philip of Macedonia in 338 B.C., which ended the Hellenic period. Philip admired Greek culture and so did Alexander, his son and successor. In the belief that it was his destiny to rule the world, Alexander invaded the huge Persian empire and conquered it. Within a few years, he had won an empire stretching from Greece through Asia Minor to the borders of India. After his death in 323 B.C., his empire split into three kingdoms that together make up what is called the *Hellenistic world.*

While Hellenic civilization was flourishing, dramatic events were taking place on the Italian peninsula. There, on the banks of the Tiber River, a Latin people of Indo-European origin built the city of Rome and established a republic. At the end of the 6th century B.C., the vigorous and aggressive Romans began a long program of conquest. First, they conquered the neighboring tribes and the prosperous Greek colonists on the Italian peninsula. Then they challenged the powerful state of Carthage and defeated it. By 100 B.C. all the lands around the Mediterranean Sea were theirs.

Roman conquests brought on serious problems, and the leaders of the republic proved unable to meet the needs of the state. Following a century of unrest and civil war, Augustus ended the republic and became the first emperor in 27 B.C. Augustus and the emperors who followed him extended Roman territory and established a *Pax Romana,* or "Roman Peace," throughout the imperial realm. The ruins of a Roman temple in Asia Minor, pictured at the beginning of this unit, suggest the grandeur of the empire.

The Romans displayed a genius for governing with justice the many different peoples in their empire. One of their greatest contributions to civilization was their comprehensive, flexible, and enduring system of law. The Romans were also great builders. They constructed magnificent public buildings, massive engineering projects, and durable roads. Although they were not creative in the arts, philosophy, or science, they admired Greek cultural achievements and preserved them for future generations.

THE CLASSICAL WORLD

Roman Empire
117 A.D.

Alexander's Empire
323 B.C.

BRITAIN

GAUL

SPAIN

Rome

Athens

Carthage

Alexandria

Babylon

PERSIA

INDIA

EGYPT

Prepared by
Rand McNally & Co., Chicago

Indo-Europeans invaded Greece

Minoan civilization

Indo-Europeans invaded Italy

1500

Mycenaean civilization
Troy

Dorian invasions

Latins in lower Tiber Valley

1000

rise of city-states

Hellenic period
Olympic games

Greek colonization

Solon
Pisistratus
Cleisthenes

Etruscans moved into Italy

Rome founded
Rome under Etruscan rule

Roman Republic

500

battle of Marathon   battle of Salamis

Golden Age of Pericles
Greek drama

Herodotus

Socrates
Peloponnesian War

Thucydides

creation of tribunes

Laws of the Twelve Tables

400

Plato
Aristotle

Hellenistic Age   Macedonian conquest   Alexander

Gauls burned Rome

300

Euclid

Stoics and Epicureans

Archimedes

Hortensian Law

Punic Wars   Roman conquest of Great Greece

Hannibal
battle of Zama

200

Aristarchus

Carthage destroyed   conquest of Greece

Gracchus brothers

100

Marius vs. Sulla   Golden Age of Latin literature

Julius Caesar dictator
Aeneid

Pax Romana   Augustus   battle of Actium

B.C.

A.D.

first school of medicine in Rome

Parallel Lives

100

"good emperors"   Roman Empire at greatest extent

Ptolemy
Galen

200

Diocletian

300

Constantine   capital moved to Byzantium

Greek Civilization

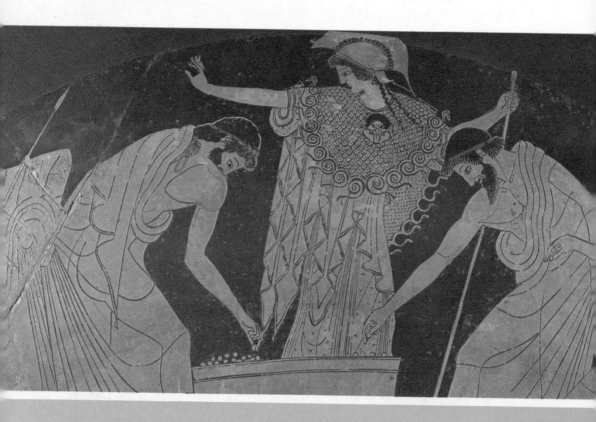

CHAPTER 3   1600 B.C.–31 B.C.

The Greeks were the first people in the world to establish a workable democratic government. They believed that every freeborn man should participate in the political affairs of his community, and they were fiercely proud of the right to vote which they enjoyed as citizens. Depicted in a vase painting of the 5th century B.C. are Greek warriors casting ballots. Watching over them is Athena, the patron goddess of Athens, the most enlightened city in ancient Greece.

Our constitution is called a democracy because power is in the hands not of a minority but of the whole people. When it is a question of settling private disputes, everyone is equal before the law; when it is a question of putting one person before another in positions of public responsibility, what counts is not membership of a particular class, but the actual ability which the man possesses. No one, so long as he has it in him to be of service to the state, is kept in political obscurity because of poverty. And, just as our political life is free and open, so is our day-to-day life in our relations with each other. . . . We are free and tolerant in our private lives; but in public affairs we keep to the law. This is because it commands our deep respect.

The speaker was Pericles, the famous general and statesman of Athens. The occasion was a memorial service for the Athenian soldiers who had fallen in battle against their rivals, the Spartans, in 431 B.C. Pericles' speech was effective propaganda. In it, he discussed why the Athenians were superior to the Spartans. Of more importance, his praise for his native city highlighted the nature and scope of the contributions which the Greeks of antiquity made to Western civilization.

First of all, the concepts of government by the people and of the equality of citizens before the law, mentioned in the passage quoted, are basic to the later development of Western democracy. Second, Pericles' description of public service as an honorable role for the citizen is an expression of a democratic ideal long admired in Western culture. Third, the freedom and individualism stressed by Pericles are values cherished by free peoples everywhere. Later on in his speech, Pericles speaks of the poise acquired from an awareness of beauty:

Our love of what is beautiful does not lead to extravagance; our love of the things of the mind does not make us soft.

He also touches upon the necessity for maintaining a balance of action and thought:

. . . we do not think that there is an incompatibility between words and deeds; the worst thing is to rush into action before the consequences have been properly debated.

These qualities of the best in Athenian society make up what is often described as the Greek view of life.

Western civilization owes even more to the Greeks. The classic forms of architecture and sculpture, history and philosophy, drama and poetry derive from Greek originals. Modern science had as a starting point the study of Greek treatises in physics, mathematics, biology, and medicine. It has been said that if anyone pursues what he feels is an original thought, he will meet a Greek along the pathway. How was it that these talented people were able to leave such magnificent gifts to civilization? Historians cannot agree; perhaps the only agreement possible is that no one factor can fully explain the achievements of Greek civilization. There are many aspects to consider: the origin of the Greeks, the relative isolation of their individual city-states, the freedom and individualism fostered by their society, the rivalries among themselves, and their conflicts with outsiders. This chapter discusses these aspects in the following sections:

1. **Aegean civilization centered on sea trade.**

2. **The Greeks established the basic principles of democracy.**

3. **The Greeks were threatened by Persia and by city-state rivalries.**

4. **The Macedonians united Greece and spread Hellenic culture.**

5. **Greek civilization formed the basis for Western culture.**

1 Aegean civilization centered on sea trade

To the men of early civilizations, the sea meant mystery and danger. In their sailboats and other small craft, they ventured upon it with caution, staying close to the shoreline by day and taking refuge in harbors at night. Little by little the sea grew in importance as a highway for trade. The Phoenicians were among the early traders who dared to navigate the open waters. Others who met the challenge of the deep were the people who lived on the islands of the Aegean Sea and along its shores.

Crete developed a flourishing culture. It is believed that Crete was first settled in the late Neolithic period by peoples from southwest Asia. In about 3100 B.C., Egyptians also immigrated to Crete. Between 1600 and 1400 B.C. Crete became a power in the ancient world, serving as a stepping stone on the trade routes between Europe and Africa and between Africa and Asia. The civilization which developed on Crete is called *Minoan* for King Minos. According to mythology, he was a semi-legendary figure who ruled Crete.

Ancient Greek legends include a number of references to Minoan civilization. One of the best-known stories concerns the Minotaur, a monster with the head of a bull and the body of a man, which was made an object of worship and kept beneath the royal palace in a labyrinth, an intricate and bewildering series of passageways. Every year the Minotaur was offered a tribute of seven youths and seven girls from Athens. Finally, it was slain by the Greek hero, Theseus, who escaped from the labyrinth by following a thread given him as a guideline by Minos' daughter.

Until the end of the 19th century, little definite knowledge of Minoan civilization existed. But in 1894 Sir Arthur Evans, an English archaeologist, began excavations on Crete. He found inscribed clay tablets and jewelry, which revealed that the Minoans had developed a system of writing. Copper and bronze tools and weapons indicated the advanced stage of Minoan technological development. An important find was the ruins of the royal palace at Knossos, the capital city. It was an amazing building, six acres in area and like a giant labyrinth with its many living quarters, corridors, tunnels, storerooms, and an ingenious underground plumbing system.

Crete achieved an abundance of wealth based on its overseas trade and metalworking industries. Prominent among Minoan manufactured goods were decorated clay vases, bronze weapons, and locks and keys, which were traded for gold, silver, and grain. Although Egyptian influences are prominent in much of Minoan art, the island people originated their own highly individualistic forms of architecture, painting, and sculpture. Their artistic works reflect the image of a pleasure-loving society whose members delighted in athletics and the world of nature. Depicted in many of the wall paintings is the hazardous sport of "bull dancing." The object of this sport was to meet the bull head-on, grasp his horns firmly, and somersault over his back to safety. Women as well as men participated in these events.

About 1900 B.C. a wave of invaders from the area around the Caspian Sea penetrated the Greek peninsula. Speaking an early form of Greek, these newcomers are known as Mycenaeans to distinguish them from the Greeks of a later day. At their fortified centers, especially at Mycenae and Tiryns, they began to engage in manufacturing and trade, successfully imitating the Minoans. About 1500 B.C. the Mycenaeans captured Knossos, and during the following century they attacked and destroyed other Cretan cities until they were driven from the island in 1400 B.C. While Minoan

Aegean Civilization

The Minoans, whose peaceful civilization thrived on the island of Crete 1000 years before the Age of Pericles, were nature worshipers. Their chief goddess was Mother Earth, the source of all life. Their favorite symbol was the double ax, displayed on a pillar in the sarcophagus painting above, which depicts a procession of Minoans honoring a dead king. The priestess at left pours a libation (liquid offering to the dead) into a large bowl. The other figures carry sacrificial offerings and a lyre. As in Egyptian art, people are shown in profile, the men painted red and the women pale yellow. Mycenaean soldiers, like those in the vase painting at right, attacked the Minoan cities. Their elaborate armor includes leather body armor, leg plates, and double-horned helmets. Each carries a spear, the principal offensive weapon, and a large, cumbersome shield, so heavy that a fallen soldier could be trapped beneath it.

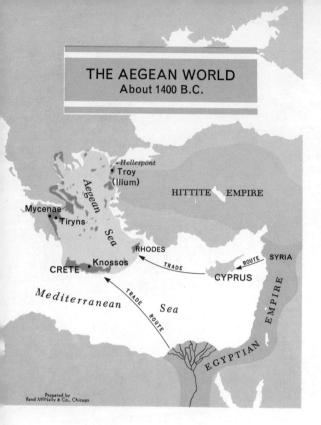

THE AEGEAN WORLD
About 1400 B.C.

←Hellespont
Troy
(Ilium)

HITTITE   EMPIRE

Aegean

Mycenae
Tiryns

Sea

RHODES

Knossos   TRADE   ROUTE   SYRIA

CRETE   CYPRUS

Mediterranean   Sea

TRADE

ROUTE

EGYPTIAN   EMPIRE

Prepared by
Rand McNally & Co., Chicago

trade and city life revived somewhat, commercial leadership in the Aegean had by this time passed to Mycenae, and Crete fell into decline.

Mycenae and Troy became centers of Aegean civilization. From 1400 to 1200 B.C., the dominant power in the Aegean was Mycenae. During this period, a feeling of fellowship developed among the Aegean peoples. A common language was a contributing factor. Also important was religion. At this time there developed the idea of a single, all-powerful deity, Zeus, who ruled over a family of gods and goddesses.

Aegean civilization also flourished in Asia Minor. Located strategically on the Hellespont, a narrow strait now known as the Dardanelles, was the city of Troy. It controlled the trade between the Mediterranean and the Black Sea.

After about 1300 B.C., Mycenaean trade began to decline for reasons still not fully

understood, and trade contacts with Egypt and the east coast of the Mediterranean were severed. This period of crisis is revealed in the *Iliad* and the *Odyssey,* the epic poems attributed to the blind poet Homer. The first poem tells of the siege of Troy. Probably the most familiar part of the poem is the story of how Troy was taken. The Mycenaean invaders built a huge wooden statue of a horse outside the city gates and then departed. The Trojans were impressed with the statue, and moved it into their city only to discover— too late—that the statue was filled with enemy soldiers. The *Odyssey* describes the wanderings of Odysseus (Ulysses) after Troy had been destroyed.

Section Review

1. How did civilization rise on Crete? What were the chief characteristics of Minoan culture?
2. Describe the elements which contributed to cultural unity on the Greek mainland during the Mycenaean period. In what respects was Troy strategically located for trade?

2   **The Greeks established the basic principles of democracy**

Throughout its existence, the Aegean civilization had been threatened by invaders. About 1100 B.C. warlike peoples later known as the Dorians began moving into the Greek peninsula from the north. The Mycenaeans were driven from their cities, and many of the survivors fled eastward into Attica and settled in Athens. Others took refuge on the islands of the Aegean and on a strip of seacoast in Asia Minor known as Ionia. Still others fell victim to the conquerors, but in time a peaceful mingling began to take place. From the mixture of various groups emerged the Greeks. During this period of transition

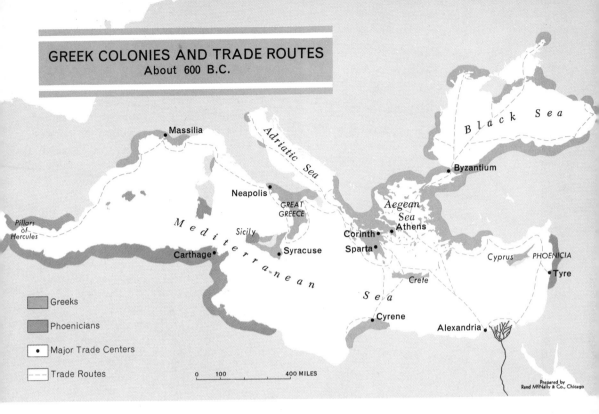

GREEK COLONIES AND TRADE ROUTES
About 600 B.C.

Massilia

Adriatic Sea

Black Sea

Byzantium

Neapolis

GREAT GREECE

Aegean Sea

M e d i t e r r a n e a n

Sicily

Corinth

Athens

Pillars of Hercules

Carthage

Syracuse

Sparta

Cyprus

PHOENICIA

Crete

Tyre

S e a

Cyrene

Alexandria

Greeks

Phoenicians

• Major Trade Centers

--- Trade Routes

0   100   400 MILES

Prepared by
Rand McNally & Co., Chicago

—from the first Dorian invasions to about the middle of the 8th century B.C.—the basis for Greek civilization was laid.

Little is known about this transitional period. Trade came to a standstill and the people lived in isolated agricultural communities. Gradually, Athens and other communities established contacts for mutual protection and for the observance of common religious festivals. From these contacts developed the famous Olympic games, beginning in the 8th century B.C. and held every four years in honor of Zeus. Little by little, the cultural unity was re-established which had existed when Mycenaean power was at its height.

The Greeks called themselves *Hellenes* after Hellas, an area in northwest Greece. The great period of Greek civilization which followed the era of transition is called the *Hellenic period,* which lasted from about 750 to 338 B.C.

Independent city-states were formed on the Greek peninsula. Early Greek society was simple. The people grouped into clans, ruled by a king or tribal chief. Each clan established a settlement, known as the *polis,* where the people might be safe from attack. The countryside around the polis was used for farming and grazing. The geographic isolation of the settlements among the mountains, valleys, and rocky coastline of Greece encouraged the growth of small, independent city-states. The members of the city-state were proud of their home city and only those born within the city-state could achieve full citizenship. The city-states were jealous of their independence and did not usually coöperate except when foreign invasion threatened.

One of the greatest contributions of the city-states to civilization was democratic government, which evolved gradually. The first step was usually the formation by the

The geography of Greece and the Aegean Sea favored the development of sea power by the ancient Greeks. The rugged mountains of the Greek peninsula and the scarcity of good roads and bridges made overland travel slow and difficult. Sea routes were easier to use. Ships could bypass the mountains and take shelter in the numerous fine harbors along the deeply indented coast. Timber for shipbuilding was available nearby in the wooded hills of the peninsula. As a result, the Greeks began to establish port cities along the coast, which afforded access to inland settlements.

The winds influenced the growth of navigation along the coasts of Greece. Breezes blew from land out to sea during the night and early morning, and blew toward land during the afternoon and evening. Greek sailors learned to put to sea early in the morning and to rely upon the landward breezes to return them to shore in the afternoon or evening.

Islands favored the development of travel across the Aegean Sea. The Aegean, studded with approximately 2000 islands, provided landmarks for sailors. Ships were seldom out of sight of land and were never more than fifty miles distant.

Sea trade was essential to the welfare of the Greeks. Their farmlands were not fertile enough to grow crops sufficient to feed all the people. The area around Athens, for example, produced enough grain for only about a quarter of the population, and it was necessary to obtain food from other regions. Beginning about 750 B.C. Greek traders and colonists built trading centers along the coasts of the Black Sea and in Asia Minor. From these centers food was shipped to Greece. By about 500 B.C. Greek maritime routes reached North Africa, Spain, and the Black Sea.

The development of naval power became necessary for the protection of the Greek city-states and their colonies. In the spring of 480 B.C., a huge Persian army and navy threatened to conquer all Greece. After losing a battle at Thermopylae, the Greeks decided to defend their homeland by sea. At the Battle of Salamis, in the fall of the same year, a fleet of Greek warships decisively defeated a great Persian fleet. After this victory, Greek naval power grew rapidly. Greek ships opened every port in the Mediterranean to Greek trade. As a result, the influence of Greek civilization spread throughout the Mediterranean.

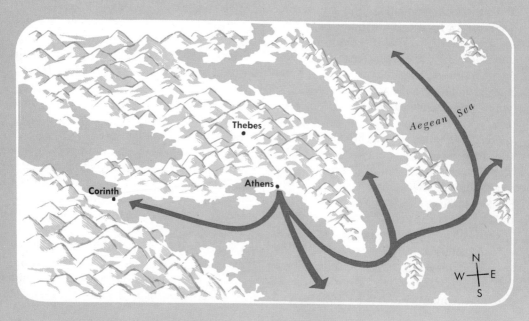

nobility of an *oligarchy*, or government by the few, which replaced the monarchy. As the power of the nobility increased, the common people at first benefited from the shift in political power. The first written legal codes were the work of the nobles; no longer was justice a matter of whim or guesswork. Penalties for lawbreakers were established by law rather than by a judge, and the laws were available for all to see.

Greek traders set up colonies and trade routes. By the middle of the 8th century B.C., the Greek world was controlled by nobles, who had become corrupted by power. They had increased their wealth through their control of the farmland, and had forced the small farmers to mortgage their plots of ground or to sell themselves into slavery. Many farmers abandoned the land in favor of small-scale manufacturing. Poor soils and scarcity of good land also contributed to the decline of agriculture.

Textile manufacturing, the making of pottery, and the fashioning of bronze weapons and implements developed rapidly. It was not long before Greek industry required additional markets for its goods and new sources of food supplies for the workers. An increase in population placed even greater demands on the available food supplies. Migration gave the people an opportunity to achieve wealth or attain increased political freedom; and the Greeks embarked upon a program of colonization.

Each new colony was bound by social and religious ties to the parent city-state, and thus the isolation of the original city-states decreased somewhat. Colonies were established in the north Aegean and the Black Sea areas, and in Egypt, Sicily, Italy, and southern France.

The power of the nobility was challenged by tyrants. The colonization system did not relieve the discontent in Greece, however. A number of trends combined to bring about the decline of the nobility. The first was the growth of the *hoplites,* a heavily armed infantry of citizens. The power of the *hoplites* increased until they were a match for the cavalry of the nobles, and they demanded improved living conditions for the common people. Second, the development of a system of coinage in Lydia quickly spread to Greece and a new basis of wealth was created which did not depend on land ownership. An important new social group appeared on the scene: a business class of merchants, shipowners, weavers, potters, and blacksmiths. They were discontented with the rule of the nobility and wanted a voice in government.

From about 650 to 500 B.C. a number of revolutions occurred in Greece. Many city-states came under the rule of *tyrants,* or leaders who had seized power unlawfully. To the Greeks, tyranny meant simply one-man rule. A tyrant was not necessarily a cruel or oppressive ruler; often he was a member of the nobility who had become democratic in outlook and to whom the people turned for leadership. In reality, the rise of the tyrants was a step in the direction of government by the people.

The first democracy grew in Athens. On the dusty coastal plain of Attica lay the city of Athens. The city hugged the slopes of a hill known as the Acropolis, where the Athenians built their forts and temples. As a seaport, Athens was exposed to a variety of commercial and cultural influences, which brought wealth and a diversity of ideas to the city.

From the 8th to the 6th centuries B.C., political control in Athens was concentrated in a council of nobles, with the most important public office held by the *archon,* or chief magistrate, elected annually from the nobility. By the end of this period, Athens was suffering from food-supply problems and from political unrest among the many poverty-stricken small farmers.

Scenes of Greek Daily Life decorated the graceful urns and vases made by skillful potters. In the vase painting at top left, two men wash in a public bathhouse, while water pours from animal-head spouts on the rear wall. Below, a Greek woman honors a dead youth by placing slender oil vessels at his tomb during a religious festival. Above left, the king of Cyrene, a Greek colony in North Africa, watches the weighing and loading of spices on shipboard. At dinner parties, men reclined on couches, like those above right, and amused themselves by singing, dancing, and playing instruments. The bearded man drinks from a shallow bowl called a cylix. His companion plays a tune on double pipes. In the painting below, a youth dons his armor, perhaps for the first time, with the assistance of his parents. Next to it, on a relief carving, masked actors perform a scene from a play on an elaborate stage.

Solon, who was elected archon in 594 B.C., came to the aid of the farmers. He canceled debts which they owed the nobles and forbade the practice of a farmer offering his services as security for a loan.

Solon created the Council of 400, which comprised 100 representatives from each of the four main tribes of Athens. The Council prepared the agenda for the meeting of the assembly, which was allowed by law to discuss only those matters brought before it. Trade was encouraged and the full rights of citizenship were offered to non-Athenian craftsmen if they moved their families to Athens. This step was important because citizenship had previously been granted only through birth. Solon did not create democracy, but his period of rule opened a new chapter in the history of Athens.

The shepherds were dissatisfied with their lot because they owned no land. They found a leader in the tyrant Pisistratus, a distant relative of Solon. Pisistratus seized the Acropolis in 560 B.C. and ruled for over thirty years. He redistributed the land and property of the nobles among the poor and landless and stimulated trade. The next important tyrant in Athenian history was Cleisthenes, who came to power in 508 B.C. Under Cleisthenes, the system of ostracism was introduced. This system allowed the citizens to banish any officials they judged to be dangerous to the Athenian state.

Other measures introduced by Cleisthenes strengthened the growth of democracy. To reduce the influence of the four Athenian tribes, he split their members into ten new tribes and set up a new system of political districts, or wards. He also increased the membership of the Council to 500. The new Council was composed of fifty members chosen annually by lot from each of the ten tribes. These changes were significant, for they enabled more people to participate in politics and allowed a greater variety of local interests to be represented in the governing bodies.

With the adoption of the reforms of Solon, Pisistratus, and Cleisthenes—the famous trio of tyrants who were champions of the people—Athens had taken large steps toward becoming a democracy. Other city-states followed the lead of Athens. By the end of the 6th century B.C., democratic governments were being set up in most city-states.

Sparta became a warrior state. An important exception to the trend toward popular government was the city-state of Sparta. When the ancestors of the Spartans, the Dorians, entered the Peloponnesus, they subdued the natives, who were classified as *helots.* Permitted to remain on the land as farmers, the helots supplied food for the conquerors. In the 8th century B.C., the Spartans invaded neighboring Messenia and subdued it. As a result, Sparta possessed adequate land and was not attracted by colonization and trade. Of greatest importance in the shaping of the Spartan system of government was the constant threat of rebellion by the Messenians and the helots.

In about 600 B.C., the Spartans set up a constitution, which was dedicated to ensuring the military strength of the state. An assembly of citizens was created, but it had little power. Control of the state was held by a small group of citizens, the Council of Elders, who presented measures to the assembly and appointed magistrates.

Sparta was organized as a military camp. To maintain high health standards, all weak or deformed children were killed. Only the strong and healthy were allowed to live. At seven years of age, boys were removed from their homes and sent to military camps, where they received strict training in gymnastics and military exercises. Each year they were flogged to test their powers of physical endurance. At twenty years of age, the young men became field soldiers and were permitted to marry, although they continued to live in the barracks. Ten years later men were admitted to the assembly and were given various government posts. The women of Sparta received equally severe training until marriage in order to be considered fit mothers.

The helots were regarded as state property and were little better than slaves. They were denied citizenship and were governed harshly. To spy on them and to prevent revolt, the Spartans created a secret police force. Once a year war was declared on the helots, so that potential rebels could be wiped out without breaking the law against murder.

The highly trained Spartan army was used against their neighbors with some success. But it was diplomacy, backed by threat of force, which enabled Sparta to extend its influence. In the 6th century B.C. the Peloponnesian League, a military alliance with nearby states, was formed.

Section Review
1. What geographic conditions led to the rise of independent Greek city-states?
2. How did trade expand Greek influence?
3. Describe the trends which contributed to the breakdown of the nobility's monopoly of power and the development of democratic government.
4. What factors account for the chief differences between the political development of Athens and Sparta?

3 **The Greeks were threatened by Persia and by city-state rivalries**

Inevitably the Greeks came into contact with other peoples as they expanded their colonial possessions and their power. The Persian Empire was the most dangerous foe. Hostilities between the Persians and the Greeks began when Cyrus of Persia attacked and defeated Croesus, the king of Lydia, in 546 B.C. Cyrus then continued his campaign until he had conquered most of the Ionian Greeks in Asia Minor.

The next Persian monarch to threaten the Greeks was Darius I, who began to rule in 522 B.C. One of his most important acts—the reorganization of the empire into administrative districts—aroused anger in the Ionian Greeks. Although included in one of these districts, they felt they had been given an insignificant status in the empire. In 499 B.C. the Ionian Greeks attacked the Persians. Although Athens sent ships to aid the Ionians, the Greeks were defeated decisively at the naval battle of Miletus in 494 B.C. The city of Miletus was burned by the Persians, an act of revenge which inflamed the Athenians. They began the construction of a navy to protect their own city. For his part, Darius was determined to seize the Greek mainland and punish the Athenians for the aid given their kinsmen in Asia Minor.

The Greeks were victorious at Marathon and Salamis. In 492 B.C. Darius tried to crush Thrace, an area north of Greece, and to subdue Athens at the same time. While attempting to navigate around Mount Athos, the Persian fleet was almost completely destroyed by a storm. Two years later, a Persian army and navy moved westward across the Aegean Sea to the Bay of Marathon, about twenty-five miles from Athens. The Greeks were prepared for this move; Athens and Sparta had agreed to an alliance to meet the Persian threat. However, when a runner was sent from Athens to Sparta requesting aid, the superstitious Spartans refused to march until the next full moon. Although aid from Sparta was withheld, the Athenians—outnumbered two to one—achieved an astounding victory. The Greek historian, Herodotus, described the battle of Marathon thus:

So when the battle was set in array, and the victims showed themselves favorable, instantly the Athenians . . . charged the barbarians at a run. Now the distance between the two armies was a little short of a mile. The Persians, therefore, when they saw the Greeks coming on at speed, made ready to receive them, although it seemed to them that the Athenians were bereft of their senses, and bent upon their own destruction; for they saw a mere handful of men coming on at a run without either horsemen or archers . . . the Athenians in close array fell upon them, and fought in a manner worthy of being recorded. . . .

The Persian fleet then set sail in a bid to capture Athens, but was repulsed. The fleet then withdrew to Asia Minor. The success of the battle of Marathon in 490 B.C. inspired the Greeks with confidence and touched off rebellions in other sections of the Persian Empire.

During the winter of 481-480 B.C., Xerxes, the son of Darius, prepared to attack Greece while Athens and the Peloponnesian League shouldered the burden of defense. After the Persians defeated the Spartan army at Thermopylae in 480 B.C., Xerxes captured Athens and burned the Acropolis. The Athenians placed their faith in "wooden walls"—the fleet—and assembled their ships at Salamis. The ensuing naval battle in the narrow straits of Salamis proved a disaster for the Persians. Xerxes returned to Asia Minor, and in 479 B.C. the surviving remnants of the Persian army on the Greek mainland were routed in the battle of Plataea. The Greeks became unchallenged in the Aegean, and Persia gave up its attempts to conquer them.

One of the most important results of the Hellenic victory was that the budding city-states of Greece had a chance to develop their democratic systems of government. Thus, the despotism of the East was not allowed to penetrate Europe and undermine the growth of freedom.

Athens became the leading city in Greece. After the defeat of the Persians, Athens took the lead in holding many of the city-states together in a loose federation called the Delian League. The power and wealth of Athens was based on a thriving trade, naval supremacy, and prestige. Under the leadership of Pericles, Athens reached the zenith of its democracy. The period of his rule, from 460 to 429 B.C., is called the Golden Age of Pericles. During this time, the Parthenon was built, and the arts and literature flourished.

Political power was vested in the popular assembly, in the Council of 500, and in a popular court. The real power of government lay in the popular assembly, of which all citizens over eighteen years of age were members. The assembly drafted laws, decided important issues, and elected an executive board of ten generals. The generals were subject to the will of the assembly, which could reëlect them, exile them, or sentence them to death. Pericles was president of the board of generals.

The Council of 500, which prepared legislation for the assembly, was divided into committees dealing with civic matters such as public buildings and street maintenance. Everyone serving the state was paid for his services, which meant that even poor men were able to serve. The juries of the popular court were also paid. The popular court was made up of as many as 2001 jurors, too many for even wealthy persons to bribe. To prevent corruption, judges and juries were chosen by lot.

Based on the principle that all citizens were equal, Athenian democracy made it possible for nearly every citizen to hold one or more public offices during his lifetime. This mass participation of citizens in political life is known as *pure* or *direct democracy* in contrast to the modern system of *representative democracy,* in which the citizens elect representatives to act for them in the government.

ILLYRIS
THRACE
Byzantium
MACEDONIA
Bosporus
Samothrace
△ Mount
Athos
Hellespont
PERSIAN
EMPIRE
Mount △
Olympus

Ionian

Sea

Aegean

Lesbos

LYDIA

THERMOPYLAE ✗
Delphi ●
Ithaca
LEUCTRA ✗ ● Thebes
Gulf of ✗ ● PLATAEA MARATHON
Corinth ✗
Corinth ● ✗ ● Athens
SALAMIS ATTICA
Olympia ●

Sea

IONIA

Ephesus

Samos

Miletus

Sparta ●
LACONIA

Halicarnassus

Cos

✗ | Battles

0 25 50 100 MILES

Rhodes

ANCIENT GREECE
about 480 B.C.

Crete

Prepared by
Rand M⁹Nally & Co., Chicago

Not all the inhabitants of Athens were granted citizenship. Women, foreigners, and slaves were excluded, and these groups far outnumbered the citizens. Therefore, limits to the principle of equality did exist.

A liberal education was stressed. Education in Athens was a primary factor in sustaining a healthy democratic government. The aim of Athenian education was to help students develop fine physiques and an appreciation for the arts, acquire the ability to think for themselves, and become good citizens.

Athenian boys started school at six years of age and continued until they were sixteen or older. Most of them learned to play the flute or lyre. At fourteen they entered a gymnasium, where they were trained in running, wrestling, boxing, and other athletic skills. Their academic subjects included geometry, astronomy, natural history, geography, and public speaking.

Because women in Athens did not take part in cultural or political affairs, the training of girls was more limited in scope. They did not attend school, but nevertheless they were taught in their homes to read, write, and play a musical instrument.

City-state rivalries undermined Greek power. The democracy practiced by the Athenians in their native city differed markedly from the policies pursued elsewhere. Athens forced the other members of the Delian League to pay tribute to the Athenian treasury. Farmers in other city-states were often forced off their land by Athenian settlers, and Athenian traders reserved the best commercial advantages for themselves. By placing its own interests first, Athens prevented the Delian League from becoming a true Greek union of states. Instead, the league was converted into an Athenian maritime empire.

During the final years of Pericles' leadership, other city-states tried to bring about the downfall of Athens. In addition to growing pressure from without, corruption crept into the government of Athens. Pericles' successors were inferior to him in intellect and morals. They used the ruling bodies for their private gain, and citizen juries frequently fined innocent men so that they could have regular employment in the courts at good wages.

The resentment of the other city-states erupted in open warfare; and in 431 B.C., with Sparta at their head, they allied themselves against Athens in the Peloponnesian War. After a long and costly struggle, Sparta defeated Athens in 404 B.C. Intermittent wars among the city-states, however, resulted in the collapse of Spartan leadership at the battle of Leuctra in 371 B.C. The disastrous Peloponnesian War left the Greeks weakened and divided. Meanwhile, to the north, a new power was gaining strength.

Section Review

1. Why were the battles of Marathon and Salamis important?
2. In what respects was the Athenian government democratic? undemocratic?
3. How did the training of the Athenian boy differ from that of the Spartan boy?
4. What caused the decline of Athens?

4 **The Macedonians united Greece and spread Hellenic culture**

North of Greece lay Macedonia, inhabited by an Indo-European people of the same racial stock as the Greeks. They were hardy mountain folk and Philip, their king, was a military strategist of the first rank.

After he came to power in 359 B.C., he organized a standing army of professional soldiers who were drilled in cavalry and infantry tactics and kept in trim through a rigorous program of athletics. Philip was also a ruthless master of intrigue, willing to use bribery, falsehood, or any other treacherous means to achieve his ends. He was determined to unite the Greeks under his rule, and little by little he encroached on Greek territory and incorporated outlying areas into his domain. Yet Philip desired the friendship of the Greeks and at first avoided the use of force. As a youth he had been a hostage in Thebes and had learned to respect Greek culture.

Philip's conquest of the Greeks ended the Hellenic period. Early in 338 B.C., an alliance was arranged between Athens and Thebes, the two most powerful cities at that time. Although the stated objective of this union was to maintain a balance of power among the city-states, the real reason was the fear of Macedonia. In the summer of 338 B.C. the Greeks attacked Philip, but the Macedonian king with his son, Alexander, almost annihilated the Athenian army. This clash marked the end of the power of the city-states, and all of the Greek peninsula except for Sparta quickly passed under Philip's control.

Within the year in which Philip's victories took place, delegates from all the major city-states of Greece (except Sparta) were summoned by Philip at Corinth, where the so-called Hellenic League was formed. The individual city-states were given a large degree of self-government, but control of internal security and external defense remained in Philip's hands. In 336 B.C., after preparing to invade Persia, Philip was murdered.

Fortunately, Philip was one of the few kings of ancient times who had prepared his successor for the task of ruling. His son, Alexander, was given the finest education

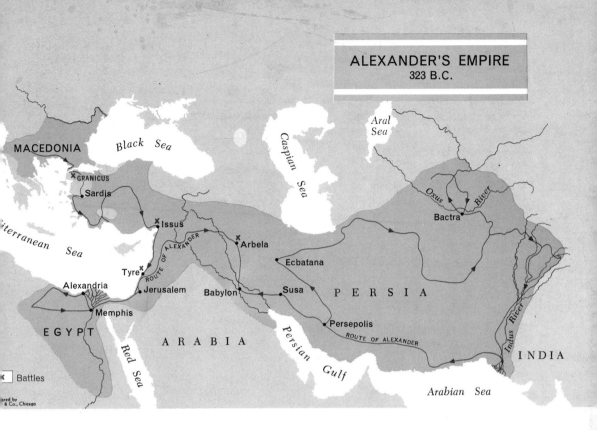

MACEDONIA

Black Sea

Caspian Sea

Aral Sea

GRANICUS

Sardis

iterranean Sea

Issus

ROUTE OF ALEXANDER

Arbela

Oxus River

Bactra

Tyre

Ecbatana

Alexandria

Jerusalem

Babylon

Susa

P E R S I A

Indus River

Memphis

E G Y P T

A R A B I A

Persepolis

ROUTE OF ALEXANDER

I N D I A

Persian Gulf

Red Sea

Arabian Sea

Battles

ared by
& Co., Chicago

---

available, including a period of tutoring by the famous Greek philosopher, Aristotle. While Alexander was still in his early teens, Philip shared state secrets with him, and at sixteen years of age Alexander took command of an elite guard. On his accession to the throne at the age of twenty, he proved himself a strong leader and mercilessly crushed a revolt by Thebes.

Alexander conquered the Persian Empire. The youthful Alexander resolved to carry out his father's plan to conquer Persia. He was a fervent admirer of Hellenic civilization and desired not only to preserve it but also to spread it abroad. His own ambition burned within him; he was convinced it was his destiny to rule the world. In 334 B.C., more than 30 thousand infantry and 5000 cavalry were assembled for the march to the east. It was a journey from which Alexander would never return.

In 334 B.C., Alexander won a great triumph at the battle of Granicus, which touched off a revolt of the Greeks in Asia Minor against their Persian overlords. The year following, Alexander's forces met the armies of the Persian monarch Darius III at Issus and, though outnumbered three to one, defeated them roundly. Darius fled ingloriously from the field of battle and Alexander's desire to defeat him once and for all increased. After a seven-month siege of Tyre and a successful expedition to Egypt, in which he founded the city of Alexandria, he swung north to face Darius again. In 331, Arbela fell to the young conqueror but Darius again eluded him. It was clear, however, that the Persian monarch could no longer rally his forces against the Greeks, and he was later murdered by one of his own men. Alexander marched on to Babylon and then Persepolis, where he took his seat on the royal throne of Persia.

Thus ended the Persian threat to the Mediterranean world, which had existed since the time of Darius I.

Alexander moved eastward through Persia to India, but at last his weary soldiers forced him to turn back. In 323 B.C., while planning the conquest of the western Mediterranean, he died in Babylon, a victim of fever. Although his many military successes were in some measure due to the disorganized state of the Persian Empire, Alexander in his own right was a skillful general and a gallant leader of men.

Outstanding as his military exploits appeared to the men of his own time and to later generations, of greater significance was Alexander's concept of "one world." He envisioned a blend of Greek and Persian culture with the Greek language and Greek law as strong unifying bonds. Marriages between his soldiers and native women were encouraged; Alexander himself married two Persian princesses. In the lands he conquered, a uniform coinage was adopted and the Persian system of *satrapies,* or administrative districts, was kept intact or modified only slightly. Over seventy new cities were founded and their governing bodies were staffed by Persians as well as Greeks and Macedonians. In short, Alexander believed firmly in the creation of a cohesive world government in which all men were brothers.

Commerce and culture spread during the Hellenistic Age. With the death of Alexander, the empire was left with no heirs to govern it. As a result, it was divided into three sections, each ruled by one of Alexander's generals. Antigonus ruled the kingdom of Macedonia, which had partial control over Greece; Egypt was ruled by Ptolemy; and Syria and Persia, by Seleucus. Dynasties were established in these kingdoms, and the three-part division made up what was called the *Hellenistic world.* The period of these kingdoms, called the *Hel-*

lenistic Age, lasted from Alexander's death until the Battle of Actium in 31 B.C., discussed in the next chapter.

The Hellenistic Age was a time of great economic growth and of cultural exchange between East and West. The network of cities founded by Alexander created new markets for a variety of goods and acted as focal points for the spread of Greek culture. The greatest city of all was Alexandria in Egypt, with a population of over a half million people. The city had wide, beautiful streets and a great library of 750 thousand books. A lighthouse nearly 400 feet in height was judged one of the Seven Wonders of the Ancient World.

Section Review

1. Why was Philip able to conquer the Greek city-states?
2. What was unusual about Alexander's early training in leadership? Name the areas included in his empire. How was his empire divided after his death?
3. What were the chief results of Alexander's conquests?

5 **Greek civilization formed the basis for Western culture**

The Hellenic and Hellenistic phases of Greek civilization differed in one basic respect: the first was a period in which cultural development was confined to the Greek peninsula, whereas the Hellenistic Age was a time in which almost the whole of the known world served as a setting for the spread of Greek culture.

Athenian philosophers searched for truth. The three greatest Greek philosophers were Socrates, Plato, and Aristotle. Socrates, who lived in the 5th century B.C., was known to his fellow Athenians as "the gadfly" because his persistent questioning of all ideas and actions stung his listeners into thinking. In fact, the so-called Socratic method consisted of asking questions and then carefully analyzing the answers in an attempt to arrive at truth. Socrates might begin a session by posing the question, "What is the beautiful and what the ugly?" Each response would be questioned and further questions would be posed until agreement had been reached by the participants about the precise definitions of the terms being discussed. Socrates' advice to everyone was to "know thyself."

Some Athenians believed that Socrates was an immoral influence on his students because he encouraged young men to question practices of all kinds. His questioning the acts of Athenian leaders led them to place Socrates on trial, charging that he was corrupting the youth of the city. He was sentenced to death and required to drink hemlock, a poison. Socrates accepted the verdict calmly; though his friends urged him to escape, he refused because he insisted that men must obey the laws of the state.

The most notable of Socrates' pupils was Plato, who lived from 430 to 347 B.C. He established the Academy in Athens, a famous school which existed for almost nine centuries. His most famous work, *The Republic*, describes an imaginary land in which each man does the work for which he is best fitted. Plato believed that there should be three classes of people: the workers to produce the necessities of life, the soldiers to guard the state, and the philosophers to rule in the interests of all. Private property was to be abolished and education was designed for the benefit of the rulers. Though Plato's ideas of communal life and a rigid class system seem harsh and akin to Spartan ideas, *The Republic* is an important work because it represents man's first attempt to devise a planned society.

Plato's most famous student was the 4th-century philosopher, Aristotle. He was a brilliant thinker whose interests ranged widely. He wrote treatises in biology, astronomy, physics, ethics, and politics. His most important work consisted of studies in logic. It was Aristotle who devised the *syllogism*, which consists of three propositions. If the major and minor premises are valid and related logically, the third proposition, or conclusion, inevitably follows. For example, (1) all Greeks are human; (2) Aristotle is a Greek; (3) therefore, Aristotle is human.

Like most Athenians, Aristotle believed that a person could be happy if he were moderate in most things. It is desirable, he felt, for all men to strike a balance between rash action and inactivity; to live between two extremes by following the Doctrine of the Mean. The best way to meet danger, for example, is through courageous action, which is the mean between foolhardiness and cowardice. In his *Politics*, Aristotle discussed the good and bad features of different kinds of governments: monarchy, aristocracy, democracy. Unlike Plato, he did not describe an imaginary state nor did he find a single system ideal. *Politics* serves to point out a significant difference between the two philosophers. Where Plato often appears to deal only with abstract ideas, Aristotle seems more down-to-earth, viewing men and things in a realistic fashion.

Two important schools of Greek philosophy arose in the Hellenistic Age: Epicureanism and Stoicism. The first was developed by Epicurus of Samos, who maintained that a temperate life was best for reducing pain and increasing pleasure. Some of his followers misunderstood his emphasis upon pleasure, thinking he meant that one should live only to eat, drink, and be merry. Thus Epicureanism is often misinterpreted in spite of its founder's emphasis upon mental activity as a way of gaining inner peace. Zeno of Cyprus developed the system of Stoicism.

Greek Art

The harmony of Greek architecture is perhaps best represented by the Parthenon, a temple which still majestically dominates the Acropolis, a rocky plateau in Athens, below. Dedicated to Athena, goddess of wisdom, the Parthenon has the appearance of perfect symmetry, achieved partly through such techniques as placing the middle columns farther apart than those at the ends. This effect and the graceful simplicity of the columns are shown in detail at right. The Parthenon and the carved marble maiden on the facing page were once brightly painted, as was most early Greek sculpture and architecture.

Unlike Egyptian art styles, which remained much the same for centuries, Greek art changed, becoming steadily more graceful and lifelike. The maiden, which dates from about 530 B.C., was found in the ruins of the Acropolis. She once held an offering to the gods in an outstretched hand. The realistic kneeling archer (partially restored) was carved around 480 B.C., and probably included a bronze bow and arrow. A youthful jockey molded in bronze typifies the animation achieved by Hellenistic sculptors.

Zeno taught that true happiness, or inner peace, can be achieved by man when he finds his proper place in nature. His followers were called *Stoics,* because they usually met on a *stoa,* or porch. Believing all nature to be good, the Stoics maintained that man must accept poverty, disease, or even death as the will of God. This philosophy led them to develop an indifference toward all kinds of experience, good or bad. Today the word *stoic* describes a person who does not show his feelings or emotions.

The Greeks achieved eminence in science. More important scientific discoveries and a greater degree of technological advance distinguished the Hellenistic period from the Hellenic. During the earlier period, however, Aristotle left his mark on the development of the natural sciences, and other Greeks made notable advances also. Pythagoras, a philosopher from the island of Samos, developed the geometric principle which bears his name, the Pythagorean theorem. Hippocrates, a Greek from Asia Minor, founded a medical school where diagnosis and treatment were based upon observation and healing practices rather than on magical formulas. "Every disease has a natural cause," he claimed. His work helped strip away superstitions and belief in magic which had hampered the study of disease. Physicians today swear an oath based on the original oath Hippocrates drew up for the ethical conduct of doctors.

During the Hellenistic Age, Archimedes of Syracuse calculated the way to measure the circumference of a circle. He also discovered the principle of specific gravity by noticing that the water in his bathtub overflowed when he lowered himself into it. From this experience he formulated what is known as Archimedes' principle: "A body immersed in a liquid is buoyed up by a force equal to the weight of the liquid displaced." Euclid, an Alexandrian, is often called "the father of geometry." His textbook *The Elements* still provides the basis for the study of plane geometry. Another Alexandrian scientist, Aristarchus, discovered that the earth rotated and revolved around the sun. Eratosthenes made a fairly accurate estimate of the circumference of the earth and drew the first rough system of longitudes and latitudes on a map of the world. More than 1700 years before Columbus, Hellenistic scientists had learned that the earth was round.

Scientists of the Hellenistic Age invented many machines that involved the use of levers, cranks, and geared wheels. Hero of Alexandria made a steam engine but used it as a toy. Other inventions included cogwheels, siphons, and derricks.

Herodotus and Thucydides were famous historians. So far as is known, the first man to apply the word *history* to a narrative of past events was Herodotus, a 5th-century Greek born in Halicarnassus, a city in Asia Minor. Driven into exile as a young man, he set out on his travels to Greece, Egypt, and the lands of the Persian Empire to gather information for his masterpiece, *History of the Persian Wars.* This work traced the rise of the Persian Empire under Cyrus and Darius I and came to a climax with the description of Xerxes' campaign against the Greeks. It is filled with anecdotes, legends, and many entertaining bits of odd information which are not always reliable as historical evidence. When relating events that he could not verify, however, Herodotus admitted it, allowing his reader to decide whether they were fact or fiction. Yet the *History,* for all its rambling style, is a unified account, for which its author has been dubbed "the father of history." Basic to Herodotus' beliefs was the idea that the gods punish those with excessive pride; to his mind, the Persians were guilty of great pride and were destroyed by the gods.

Like Herodotus, Thucydides lived in the 5th century and was an exile from his native city of Athens. While in exile, he wrote *History of the Peloponnesian War*, his only work. But there the resemblance to Herodotus ends. In his history, Thucydides included only material he considered relevant to the narrative. He weighed evidence carefully and admitted no facts to his history unless they had been meticulously checked. As he stated:

Of the events of the war I have not ventured to speak from any information, nor according to any notion of my own; I have described nothing but what I either saw myself or learned from others of whom I made the most careful and particular inquiry.

He did not believe that human events could be explained by fate or by the acts of the gods, and he searched for the human causes of the Greek wars. Thucydides himself had been an Athenian general before his exile. But no bias in Athens' favor mars his work, which has become a model for latter-day historians.

The Greeks invented drama. Greek tragic drama was an outgrowth of religious rites held at the festivals honoring the god of wine, Dionysus. A chorus of men chanted hymns in praise of the god and accompanied the songs with stately dances. In the 6th century B.C. changes were made in the performances which led to the development of the drama form. Individual actors were separated from the chorus and given roles to enact, and dialogue was introduced. Of greatest significance was the use of new themes based on heroic legends not related to worship of Dionysus.

The form and matter of Greek tragedy owed much to its association with religious practices. Poetic language was considered the proper mode of expression; the chorus remained a basic part of the play, commenting on the action as it unfolded; and both masculine and feminine roles were played by men. Most important, tragedy dealt with serious matters—man's destiny and the problems of good and evil.

Athens dominated the development of this art form and the most famous tragic dramatists were a trio of Athenian poets who lived in the 5th century: Aeschylus, Sophocles, and Euripides. Located on the slopes of the Acropolis was the open-air theater of Dionysus. It was semi-circular in plan and seated some 14 thousand spectators. Various devices were used to make a play understandable to the large audiences. The actors wore thick-soled sandals to increase their height and carried painted masks depicting grief, horror, and the other strong emotions portrayed. Speaking tubes were used to amplify the actors' voices.

Comedy also originated in the festivals of Dionysus. The greatest comic author was Aristophanes, who lived in the 5th century. No libel laws protected Athenians, and important citizens were often held up to ridicule in his plays.

Greek architecture and sculpture were widely imitated. Most Greeks, including those who were wealthy, lived in modest clay-brick homes; but they created beautiful temples of marble for their gods. Of those built during the Age of Pericles, the finest was the Parthenon, judged one of the most beautifully proportioned structures of all time. Many modern buildings employ architectural features created by the ancient Greeks.

Stiffness and formality characterized the bronze and marble figures of early Greek sculptors; but later workers, including the famous Phidias of the 5th century, used their materials to display the natural lines of the human body. A century after the Age of Pericles, Praxiteles carved figures that equaled or surpassed those of Phidias in grace and poise.

1. What were the chief contributions of the great philosophers, Socrates, Plato, and Aristotle? How did the Stoics differ from the Epicureans?

2. Name the scientific achievements of the Hellenic and Hellenistic ages.
3. How did the historical work of Thucydides differ from that of Herodotus?
4. Describe the development of drama.

Chapter 3 ▬▬▬▬▬ A Review

The prosperous Aegean civilization that flourished on Crete and, later, at Mycenae and Troy, was based on sea trade. In time, this civilization succumbed to the invasions of a warlike people, the Dorians, who settled in the Peloponnesus and drove the Mycenaeans into Attica and Ionia. Gradually, the invaders and the original inhabitants intermarried and from this mixture came the Greeks.

Although the Greeks had common customs and a common language, they did not unite as one nation but formed independent city-states. The two most important city-states were Athens, which developed a democratic government, and Sparta, which remained a rigid, militaristic state. Athens and many other city-states established colonies and trade routes throughout the Mediterranean region.

During the Hellenic period, the Greeks successfully defended themselves against the invasions of the Persians, and Athens became the most powerful city-state of Greece. It headed the Delian League, acquired great wealth through trade, and reached the height of its democracy in the Golden Age of Pericles. But jealousy and fear of Athens led to wars among the city-states, which weakened them and left them prey to Philip, the ambitious king of neighboring Macedonia. His conquest of Greece ended the Hellenic period. Philip was succeeded by his son Alexander, who was his equal in ambition and who surpassed his father in military and political achievements. Using Greek and Macedonian forces, Alexander conquered an empire and spread Greek culture through the conquered lands. His death was followed by the division of his empire and a new period in history, the Hellenistic Age.

The Greeks of the Hellenic period left great gifts to civilization: magnificent examples of sculpture, architecture, drama, and poetry, and outstanding contributions to philosophy and science. This period of history is studded with great names: Socrates, Plato, Aristotle, Herodotus, Thucydides, and many others. The Greeks' experiment with democratic government has for centuries inspired democratic movements the world over. In the Hellenistic Age, new centers of Greek culture arose in the Near East, especially in Alexandria. The chief contributions of this period were in science and technology, mathematics, and the philosophy of the Stoics and Epicureans.

The Time

Indicate the period in which each event in the following statements occurred.

(a) 2000-1501 B.C. (d) 500-401 B.C.
(b) 1500-1001 B.C. (e) 400-301 B.C.
(c) 1000-501 B.C.

1. The Greeks defeated the Persians in the battle of Marathon.
2. Sparta defeated Athens in the Peloponnesian War.
3. Crete emerged as a power in the ancient world.
4. Solon became archon of Athens.
5. Alexander the Great defeated Darius III in the battle of Arbela.
6. Athens flourished during the Golden Age of Pericles.
7. Philip of Macedonia conquered the Greek city-states.
8. The Dorians began their invasion of the Greek peninsula.
9. The Greeks defeated Xerxes in the battle of Salamis.
10. Mycenae became the dominant power in the Aegean world.
11. Cleisthenes came to power as tyrant of Athens.
12. Alexander's empire was divided among his generals.

Which of these events or developments occurred during the Hellenic period? during the Hellenistic Age? What was the time span of each period?

The Place

1. Locate each of the following cities that were centers of Aegean civilization: Knossos, Mycenae, Tiryns, Troy.

2. Name four modern countries and three islands in which Greek colonies were located. Locate the following Greek city-states that began as colonies: Massilia, Neapolis, Syracuse, Cyrene, Byzantium.

3. Locate each of the following Greek city-states which were on the Greek mainland: Athens, Sparta, Thebes, Corinth. Name one city-state located in Attica; one located on the Peloponnesus.

4. Name the contestants, tell the outcome and locate the site of each of the following battles: Miletus, Marathon, Salamis, Granicus, Issus, Arbela.

5. Name at least six modern countries, or parts of countries, which are in the area comprised by Alexander's empire.

6. Into what three sections was Alexander's empire divided after his death? In which part of the Hellenistic world was the city of Alexandria located?

The People

1. Give one significant fact about each of the following Greek statesmen: Solon, Pisistratus, Cleisthenes, Pericles.

2. What was one belief maintained by each of the following philosophers: Socrates, Plato, Aristotle, Epicurus, Zeno?

3. With what military victory or defeat is each of the following rulers associated: Darius I, Xerxes, Alexander, Darius III, Philip?

4. Name one contribution in science or mathematics made by each of the following Greeks: Hero, Pythagoras, Archimedes, Hippocrates, Aristarchus, Euclid, Eratosthenes.

5. Name two famous Greek historians and tell for what work each is best known.

6. What Greeks were famous tragic dramatists? Name a Greek writer of comedy.

7. Name two famous Greek sculptors.

Historical Terms

1. Give one significant fact about each of the following groups of people.

Dorians	Minoans	helots
Mycenaeans	Macedonians	hoplites
Spartans	Messenians	Trojans
Athenians	Ionians	

2. Explain each of the following terms as it applied to the political development of Greece.

tyrant	Council of 400
archon	Athenian Assembly
oligarchy	Council of 500
ostracism	pure democracy

3. What was the Peloponnesian League? the Delian League? the Hellenic League?

4. Explain the following terms that were significant in Greek life: theater of Dionysus, Olympic games, polis, Acropolis.

5. Name the author and describe briefly the theme of each of the following Greek books.

History of the Persian Wars	*Iliad*
The Republic	*Odyssey*
The Elements	*Politics*
History of the Peloponnesian War	

6. Explain by example the terms *syllogism* and *Doctrine of the Mean,* as devised by Aristotle.

7. What features of the Parthenon made it an outstanding work of architecture?

Questions for Critical Thinking

1. Why did the Greeks fail to unite permanently and thereby ward off the Macedonian conquest?

2. What characteristics distinguish the Hellenistic Age from the Hellenic period?

3. Some historians believe that Marathon and Arbela were among the most decisive battles in history. Explain why.

4. In what respects was Athenian democracy similar to that in the United States today? In what respects was it different?

5. Which philosophy do you think would have more appeal in the United States today, the Epicurean or Stoic? Why?

6. Do you think there is a connection between the growth of political democracy in Athens and the development of original thought and creativity in the arts? Why?

The Roman Empire

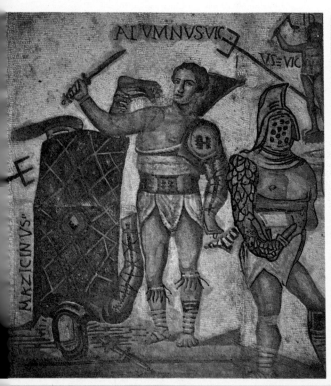

The Roman character combined a primitive enjoyment of cruelty with a highly developed proficiency in the art of government. In a 4th-century mosaic, left, the victorious gladiator Alumnus brandishes his sword over his fallen opponent. In stark contrast is the calm dignity of the emperor Trajan, right, one of the rulers who maintained order and stability throughout the vast Roman Empire.

To Edward Gibbon, the 18th-century English historian and author of *Decline and Fall of the Roman Empire*, "the period in the history of the world, during which the condition of the human race was most happy and prosperous" was the 2nd century A.D. It was during this century that the Roman Empire reached its greatest extent and was, according to Gibbon, "governed by absolute power, under the guidance of virtue and wisdom." A Roman subject of the 2nd century, Aelius Aristides, had this to say about the era in which he lived:

> . . . The whole world keeps holiday; the age-long curse of war has been put aside; mankind turns to enjoy happiness. Strife has been quieted, leaving only the competition of cities, each eager to be the most beautiful and the most fair. Every city is full of gymnastic schools, fountains and porticos, temples, shops, and schools of learning. The whole earth is decked with beauty like a garden.

There were those who would disagree with Gibbon and Aristides. To some, imperial rule was a mixed blessing at best; to others, it was oppressive and tyrannical. The famous modern-day historian, Arnold J. Toynbee, has interpreted the 2nd century A.D. as a time of stalemate when the world "lay more or less passive under the pall" of Roman power. Writing in the 2nd century, the Roman historian Tacitus stated: "They [the Romans] make desolation, which they call peace."

A set of conflicting opinions offers a good point from which to begin an examination of Roman history. In truth, military conquest made Rome a world state; the boundaries of the empire expanded as the Roman legions scored victory after victory. Yet force alone was not enough to maintain a unified state. Skillful diplomacy and effective government, a flexible system of law, a widespread network of roads and commercial towns—all these factors helped bring together a great number of peoples of varying customs and races. For over two centuries, from 27 B.C. to 235 A.D., the Romans maintained the *Pax Romana*, or "Roman Peace," throughout their far-flung domain.

The story of how Rome grew from a small city-state in central Italy to a vast empire is told in this chapter as follows:

1. **The Roman Republic arose in Italy.**

2. **The republic became a world state.**

3. **The empire endured for five centuries.**

4. **The Romans preserved Greek culture.**

1 The Roman Republic arose in Italy

Between 2000 and 1000 B.C., about the time that the Greek-speaking tribes were moving into their future homeland, another branch of Indo-Europeans filtered south through the Alps into the Italian peninsula. Most important were a group of tribes, the Latins, who settled along the west coast of central Italy in the lower valley of the Tiber River. About midpoint in the 8th century B.C., they built a small settlement on the Palatine, one of the seven hills in the area near a ford across the Tiber. From this modest beginning, the city of Rome emerged.

Early Rome was ruled by the Etruscans. In the 7th century B.C., the Latin tribes were conquered by their powerful neighbors to the north, the Etruscans. Little is known about these people although it is thought that they came originally from Asia Minor. The Etruscans drained the marshes around Rome, encouraged trade, and taught the Romans to use arches in their buildings.

During the period of Etruscan rule, many important features of Roman government developed. A king of Etruscan descent ruled the state and was elected to his office by the Latin tribal chieftains. He served as high priest as well as chief magistrate, and the symbol of his authority was the *fasces,* an ax enclosed in a bundle of rods. To advise him, the king chose a body of men of high rank known as the *Senate.* These high-ranking freemen were usually large landowners and were known as *patricians,* or fathers of the state. As such they formed the nobility of Rome. The non-nobles—small farmers and tradesmen—were known as *plebeians.*

The Roman Republic was established. In 509 B.C. the patricians engineered a successful revolt against their harsh Etruscan king, Tarquin the Proud. They then set up a *republic,* a state in which the citizens elected representatives to manage the government. Like the early oligarchies in Greece, power in the early Roman Republic was not in the hands of the people but was held tightly by the men at the top of the social scale.

The new republic was governed by two consuls and the Senate. In order to check the power of the consuls, a one-year limit was placed upon their term of office. If war or another emergency threatened the state, a dictator could be substituted for the consuls, but his term of office was limited to six months. The Senate, composed of 300 members appointed for life by the consuls, proposed the laws and nominated the consuls for office. Only patricians could become consuls or serve in the Senate.

The plebeians had their own assembly, which passed resolutions binding upon their class. At first, however, it was not important in the workings of Roman government.

Rome expanded within the Italian peninsula. Soon after the overthrow of the Etruscan monarch, Rome and the nearby Latin tribes formed the Latin League, an alliance against other Italic peoples on the peninsula. The Romans' motives for expansion were simple: to protect their emerging state from unfriendly neighbors and to secure more land for farming, since agriculture was the basis for the Roman economy. By the beginning of the 4th century B.C., Rome and the League controlled central Italy.

Two setbacks to Roman expansion occurred. The first was the invasion in 390 B.C. of the Gauls, insolent, fair-haired warriors who burned Rome to the ground. Although they withdrew after the payment of a tribute, the damage to Roman prestige was serious. The second setback took place in 340 B.C. when the members of the Latin League, jealous of Rome, revolted. Two years later, Rome defeated them, dissolved the League, and forced each tribe to sign a separate treaty of alliance. This policy of "divide and rule" was to aid Rome later in its career of conquest. The Romans then turned north and conquered the Etruscans, who had been weakened by repeated attacks of the Gauls. A defensive line on the Arno River was set up to check future attacks from the north.

The only serious rivals to Roman rule remaining on the Italian peninsula were the Greeks in southern Italy. They had settled there and in Sicily during the 8th century B.C. So successful were their trading cities that this area of Greek colonization was known as Great Greece.

The Greeks became alarmed at the growing power of Rome. To aid them, they called upon Pyrrhus, a kinsman of Alexander the Great and an ambitious military leader from northern Greece. In 280 B.C., with an army of 25 thousand men and twenty elephants, he defeated the Romans in battle but was astounded when their Italic allies refused to join forces with him against Rome. When his offer of peace was rejected by the Senate, he launched a second successful attack. But his losses were so great that he exclaimed, "Another such victory and we are lost." To this day, a costly victory is known as a Pyrrhic victory.

After Pyrrhus had returned to Greece, the Romans quickly conquered the Greek holdings on the Italian peninsula. By 270 B.C., less than 250 years after the founding of the republic, Rome was master of all central and southern Italy.

The early Romans had admirable qualities. Most of the early Romans were farmers, who lived simply, worked hard, and fought well. The Roman family was a close-knit group, held together by affection, the necessities of a frugal life, and the strict authority of the parents. Although the father was the absolute ruler of the family, the mother played an important role in family activities—she was not kept in seclusion as were the women of ancient Greece. Roman parents instilled in their children the virtues of loyalty, courage, and self-control. By performing civic and religious duties conscientiously, they strengthened the laws and customs of the republic.

The stern virtues fostered by Roman family life were a source of strength to the early republic. When increasing power and wealth began to undermine Roman family life, later generations viewed with dismay the passing of the old order. "Rome stands built upon the ancient ways of life and upon her men," wrote a poet of the 3rd century B.C., as if to warn the people of his day that Roman traditions were decaying.

Military strength and wise rule consolidated Roman gains. A large part of the success of the Roman conquests was due to the well-trained army of citizen-soldiers. The basic military unit was the legion, an infantry force of 6000 men at full strength. To achieve maximum flexibility and speed, the legions were broken up into companies of 120 men. As Rome expanded and the need for soldiers increased, the conquered tribes were forced to supply troops for the Roman army, but the captives were usually treated fairly and their loyalty was assured.

The most important factor in the consolidation of Roman power on the Italian peninsula was the Roman talent for organization. To some of the conquered, the full privileges of Roman citizenship were granted—the right to vote and to hold political office in Rome. To others were given less important rights, such as the right to hold property in Rome.

To the people it conquered, Rome granted a large measure of independence. They were free to manage their own affairs, set up their own assemblies, and elect their own magistrates while Rome controlled the administration of justice and handled city-to-city affairs. A tribute to Roman leadership was that the conquered peoples quarreled with Rome not to become free of Roman rule but to gain greater privileges within the republic.

The plebeians strove for equal rights within Rome. Soon after the founding of the republic, the struggle for plebeian rights began. As Roman power and territory increased and as the need for its loyal and well-trained citizen armies grew, the plebeians were able to gain a greater voice in the affairs of government.

An important step in the struggle for plebeian rights was the creation in 494 B.C. of two plebeian officials called *tribunes,* whose duty it was to protect the members of their class from injustice. Anyone who tried to harm a tribune could be killed, even a consul. In time, the number of tribunes was increased to ten. Allowed to witness Senate discussions, the tribunes could indicate their displeasure at any time by crying out, "*Veto,*" that is, "I forbid." Though at first the veto did not prevent the Senate from passing laws, it

The Powerful Roman Army helped the republic achieve a dominant position in the western world. The relief carving above shows infantry and cavalry in a parade. Standardbearers, such as the two at center, helped direct troop movements in battle. Troops and supplies were moved quickly over the well-paved Roman roads. Also important were Roman galleys, one of which is shown below. Oarsmen, who were usually slaves or prisoners of war, were stationed in the hold of the vessel.

worked as a check against unpopular legislation.

Another step in plebeian progress took place about 450 B.C. when the plebeians won the right to have laws put in writing, thus preventing judges from deciding similar cases differently. These written laws were called the Laws of the Twelve Tables, because they were carved on twelve bronze tablets hung in the Forum, an open-air meeting place. One of the laws prohibited marriage between plebeians and patricians, but in less than a decade this barrier fell and intermarriage became legal.

Little by little the plebeians made more gains. The veto power of the tribunes became effective and, in the 4th century, plebeians became eligible to hold one of the consulships. By the end of that century, plebeians were admitted to political offices formerly reserved only for patricians and were even allowed to become members of the Senate. In 287 B.C., the Hortensian Law made the resolutions of the plebeians binding on all citizens. Henceforth, the plebeian assembly was a popular assembly for the entire state. The old distinction between patrician and plebeian was wiped away, but the struggle for political power and social equality did not come to an end. In the centuries ahead, differences in wealth and status were fated to play an important role in the story of the internal affairs of Rome.

Section Review

1. Describe the government of the early Roman Republic.
2. What were the chief events in the Roman conquest of the Italian peninsula?
3. How did Roman family life contribute to the strength of the state?
4. What factors were important in the consolidation of Roman power on the Italian peninsula?
5. Trace the steps by which the plebeians gained power within the republic.

ROMAN REPUBLIC
About 264 B.C.

SPAIN
Sagento
Corsica
Sardinia
Rome
Cannae
Sicily
Carthage
Syracuse

Carthaginian Empire

Prepared by
Rand McNally & Co., Chicago

2 The republic became a world state

With Great Greece defeated and the heel and toe of Italy under its sway, Rome faced a powerful new rival, Carthage. Founded in 814 B.C. by Phoenician traders, Carthage had grown rich from the sea trade in the western Mediterranean. Its domain included territory in North Africa and Spain and important trading centers on the islands of Sardinia, Corsica, and Sicily. The strong Carthaginian navy blocked Roman expansion in the Mediterranean region.

Between 264 and 146 B.C. Carthage and Rome fought three wars, known as the *Punic Wars*. (The word *Punici* is Latin for Phoenicians, the ancestors of the Carthaginians.)

The Punic Wars strained the resources of Rome. Sicily was the prize in the First Punic War. The contest was clearly unequal, with the odds favoring Carthage, rich in gold, manpower, and ships. The Romans were not a seafaring people, but they realized that Carthage could be defeated only if its navy were smashed. With

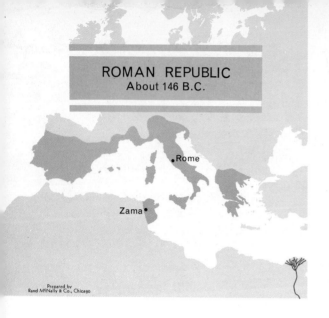

ROMAN REPUBLIC
About 146 B.C.

Rome

Zama

Prepared by
Rand McNally & Co., Chicago

amazing determination, the Romans built up a navy, training their soldiers as oarsmen on shore while building the ships. Several fleets were built before the Romans were able to hand the Carthaginians a decisive naval defeat off the coast of Sicily in 241 B.C.

Sicily became the first Roman province and was required to pay an annual tribute in grain to Rome. Three years after the end of the war, Sardinia was conquered; later, Corsica; and in 227 B.C. both were made into a single province. No longer was Roman power restricted to Italy, and the Roman navy was supreme in the western Mediterranean. Although the First Punic War had exhausted Rome and Carthage, both prepared for another struggle.

The Second Punic War has been called a "conflict between the nation Rome and the man Hannibal," for in Hannibal, Carthage possessed a military genius the equal of Alexander the Great. Hannibal began the war in 219 B.C. by attacking the city of Sagento in Spain, an ally of Rome. With cavalry, war elephants, and about 40 thousand infantrymen, Hannibal then crossed through southern Gaul and up over the Alps into Italy. The strenuous journey cost

him about half of his men, much of his equipment, and all but one elephant. With the Gauls of northern Italy as allies, Hannibal began to march down the peninsula.

To meet the emergency, the Romans made Fabius Maximus dictator. He was a cautious leader who refused to risk an all-out battle but contented himself with guerrilla tactics. Although this so-called Fabian policy of watchful waiting frustrated Hannibal, it was unpopular with many Romans. They staked success on a face-to-face battle with Hannibal at Cannae in southern Italy. There, in 216 B.C., the Carthaginian general encircled the Romans and wiped out a force at least a third larger than his own. But Hannibal dared not lay siege to Rome without reserves of manpower and supplies, which were cut off by Roman armies in Spain and in Sicily.

Finally, the Romans decided to open up another front. Under the leadership of Scipio the Elder, Roman forces invaded North Africa and forced Hannibal to rush to the defense of Carthage. At Zama in 202 B.C., Hannibal was defeated and fled to the East to save his life. The peace terms dictated by the Romans were harsh. Carthage gave up its navy, surrendered Spain, lost its freedom in foreign affairs, and paid annual tribute to Rome. Yet the Romans still feared a rebirth of Carthaginian power.

The fear that Carthage would recover was well founded. In 150 B.C., the Carthaginians attacked a Roman ally, and the Romans replied with an invasion of North Africa one year later. Carthage was besieged and, cut off from food supplies, most of the inhabitants starved to death. When the Romans entered Carthage, they sold the survivors into slavery, burned the city to the ground, and destroyed the fertility of the soil by throwing salt into the plowed land outside the city. Thus, in 146 B.C. the Third Punic War ended, and the former Carthaginian possessions in North Africa became the Roman province of Africa.

Roman armies were victorious in the East. Shortly after the end of the Second Punic War, the Roman legions turned eastward. After a series of wars, they defeated the Macedonians, and in 146 B.C. Macedonia became a Roman province. In the same year the Romans burned Corinth and made the other Greek city-states subject to Rome.

When the king of Pergamum in Asia Minor willed his realm to Rome in 133 B.C., the Romans began to take over lands in the Near East. Egypt and other countries allied themselves to Rome and later became Roman territories. By 100 B.C. all land bordering the Mediterranean was under Roman control, and the Romans called the great inland sea, *Mare Nostrum* (Our Sea).

The expansion of Roman territory led to changes within the republic. During the Punic Wars and the conquest of Mediterranean lands, changes were taking place in the republic that were destined to make the years from the midpoint of the 2nd century B.C. to the battle of Actium in 31 B.C. stormy and filled with civil strife.

As Rome became increasingly involved in foreign affairs, the best trained group in the state—the Senate—increased its power and prestige by conducting state negotiations. Although the ratification of treaties and declarations of war were still referred to the popular assembly, this body acted merely to rubber stamp the decisions of the senators, and the tribunes became yes-men of the Senate. The concentration of political power was accompanied by increased corruption in government, particularly in the provinces. Officials sent by the Senate to the provinces often took advantage of their jobs to amass riches.

Opportunities for graft grew as lucrative contracts for army supplies and for tax collection in the provinces were awarded by the Senate to individual men.

The effect of the wars of conquest on farming in the Italian peninsula was harmful. Southern Italy had been devastated by the ravages of Hannibal's army, and its farmers drifted to Rome in search of jobs. There, they found other Italian farmers unable to compete with large landowners employing slave labor captured in the wars. No large-scale industry existed in Rome to provide employment, and an idle and discontented mob was created which was capable of great mischief to the state.

As war booty poured into Rome, the opportunities to become rich increased, separating the interests of the rich from those of the poor. The new wealth also modified the Roman attitudes toward the state. The traditions of public duty and self-discipline began to give way to greed and luxurious living.

Civil war weakened the republic. Tiberius and Gaius Gracchus, two members of one of the leading families in Rome, viewed the widening gap between the rich and the poor as a menace to the stability of the republic. In 133 B.C., when Tiberius was elected a tribune, he proposed an agrarian reform law by which the land gained in Roman conquests— known as public land—would be divided to provide farms for the underprivileged. He also wished to limit the amount of existing land which an individual could hold, a proposal designed to strip the rich of valuable land already in their possession. To stop Tiberius and intimidate other reformers, a group of wealthy men had him murdered along with 300 of his followers, claiming that they were public enemies.

In 123 B.C., a decade after the murder of Tiberius, his young brother Gaius courageously stepped forth and was elected a tribune. He managed to pass a land reform bill and to win the support of the new rich to some of his legislative schemes. But again the entrenched men of wealth were alarmed. Gaius' supporters were attacked and slain, and Gaius himself committed suicide. The ability of the Romans to achieve reform gradually through peaceful compromise appeared to be a lost art.

The deaths of Tiberius and Gaius brought into sharp focus the rivalry of two bitterly opposed political groups: the supporters of the Senate and the enemies of senatorial rule. The latter group, known as the *populares,* included the new rich. Both groups used the Roman city mob for their own purposes, putting political power before principle to gain their ends. Into this dangerous situation came two military heroes, Marius and Sulla, both of whom wanted a command in the Near East.

Marius was supported by the *populares* and Sulla by the senatorial group. Sulla was chosen as a military commander in 88 B.C.; no sooner had he left Rome when civil war broke out. The *populares* cut off the grain supply to the city and forced their rivals to surrender, slaying hundreds of them. Marius was elected consul in 86 B.C. but died soon thereafter, and the consulships were held by *populares* until the triumphant return of Sulla four years later. He became dictator of the state by force, with the power to remodel the government.

In order to restore the power and prestige of the Senate, Sulla doubled the size of that body to 600 men and limited the veto power of the tribunes. Legislation introduced into the popular assembly was required to meet the previous approval of the senators. Sulla's changes wiped out many of the gains made by the plebeians in their long struggle for equality. In 79 B.C., convinced that his work was done, Sulla retired. He had restored order to the state, but his changes were not to last.

Julius Caesar became dictator of Rome. The conflict of Marius and Sulla had been complicated by a new factor which colored the political rivalry of the *populares* and the Senate. As consul, Marius had abandoned the traditional Roman method of recruiting a citizen army and had formed an army of volunteers drawn from the landless class. With the expectation of sharing in war booty and willing to serve for long periods, these professional soldiers owed their allegiance to their leader, not to the state. It was easy to see that a popular commander could use military force to gain political ends. Such a man was Marius' nephew, Julius Caesar, a brilliant general and a skillful politician as well.

After a successful military career in Spain, he threw in his lot with Pompey, another military hero, and Crassus, one of the wealthiest men in Rome. Their support made it possible for Caesar to become consul. In 60 B.C. the three men formed a union to rule the state jointly, called the First Triumvirate.

Soon thereafter Caesar became governor of Gaul, and from 58 to 51 B.C., in the so-called Gallic Wars, he extended Roman borders to include most of modern France and Belgium. He also led his legions across the English Channel to invade Britain. These accomplishments made Caesar so popular with the Roman masses that the Senate feared his growing power and ordered him to return to Rome without his army. Caesar knew that obedience meant imprisonment or possible death; Crassus was dead, and Pompey, jealous of Caesar, had conspired with the Senate to ruin him.

On January 10, 49 B.C., in defiance of the Senate, Caesar brought his army across the Rubicon River into Italy, knowing that the move would bring on civil war. (Ever since, the phrase "crossing the Rubicon" has meant making a decision from which there can be no turning back.) Fearful of the legions who were friendly to Caesar,

Roman Life was varied and busy. At top, two farmers crush olives in a stone press to make oil for cooking and lamp fuel. Government employees, like the tax collectors at left above, helped rule efficiently. In bustling cities, passers-by might be entertained by street musicians; those at right play a flute, cymbals, and a tambourine.

Pompey and most of the senators fled to Greece. Caesar pursued and defeated them. Upon his return to Rome, he became dictator and was elected to that office annually until 44 B.C., when he was made dictator for life.

During his five years of rule, Caesar's moderate reforms were put into effect without antagonizing many elements in the state. He weakened the power of the Senate, but at the same time increased its membership to 900. Roman citizenship was extended to persons living outside Italy. In the provinces, taxes were adjusted and the administration improved.

The Senate feared that Caesar meant to make himself king and establish a dynasty, thus ending the republic. A group of men including Marcus Brutus, one of the dictator's best friends, joined in a plot to murder Caesar. On March 15, 44 B.C., the "Ides of March," the plotters surrounded Caesar on the floor of the Senate and stabbed him to death.

Augustus became the first Roman emperor. Before his death, Julius Caesar had made his grandnephew and adopted son, Octavian, his heir. In 43 B.C. Octavian, with Mark Antony and Marcus Lepidus, formed the Second Triumvirate in order to restore order to Rome and punish the murderers. They attacked Brutus and his fellow conspirators, defeating them in the battle of Philippi in 42 B.C.

For ten years thereafter, Octavian and Antony, the two chief members of the Triumvirate, shared absolute power in the republic. Octavian ruled Rome and the West; Antony, Egypt and the East. The ambitions of each man brought them into conflict, however. While Octavian was shrewdly increasing his power in Rome, Antony had fallen in love with Cleopatra, the glamorous queen of Egypt. When word reached Rome that he had given Roman territory to Cleopatra and was plotting to seize the whole empire, Octavian persuaded the Romans to declare war on Egypt.

In 31 B.C. at Actium on the western coast of Greece, the fleet of Octavian clashed with the ships assembled by Antony and his queen. When Cleopatra fled the battle, Antony deserted his men and followed her to Egypt. The following year, when Octavian landed in Egypt, both Antony and Cleopatra committed suicide after failing to rally support against him. Soon thereafter, the ancient land of Egypt became a Roman province.

Upon his return to Rome, Octavian proclaimed that he would restore the republic. He was careful to observe the forms of republican government but held supreme power in his own hands, largely through his control of the army. As supreme leader of the army, he was called *imperator* from which the word "emperor" is derived. In 27 B.C. the Senate conferred upon Octavian the honorary title of Augustus, meaning "The Majestic." From then on, he was known by that name. After a century of civil war, Rome at last had been united under one ruler. The reign of Augustus ushered in the Roman Empire.

Section Review

1. How did the Romans meet the threat of the Carthaginian navy in the First Punic War? What factors prevented Hannibal from defeating Rome in the Second Punic War? Name the lands won by Rome in the Punic Wars.

2. What were some of the important changes that took place within the republic as it became a world state?

3. What events during the period from 133 to 79 B.C. weakened the Roman Republic?

4. List the chief events that led to Julius Caesar's rise to power. What reforms were put into effect during his rule?

5. How did Octavian become the supreme ruler of Rome?

3 The empire endured for five centuries

Augustus had fallen heir to a mighty world state. The empire extended in the east to the Euphrates River and west to the Atlantic Ocean, north to the Rhine and Danube rivers and south across the Mediterranean to North Africa and the sands of the Sahara. In the 2nd century A.D., during the reign of Hadrian, one of Augustus' most capable successors, the empire included 100 million people of different races, faiths, and customs.

Generally speaking, the first two and one half centuries of the empire were peaceful and prosperous. This period, from 27 B.C. to 235 A.D., is known as the *Pax Romana,* or "Roman Peace." Within the empire, trade flourished as conditions favorable to it became widespread. Bandits and pirates were hunted down, and roads and sea lanes were cleared for commerce. Ostia, at the mouth of the Tiber, served as a seaport for the city of Rome. Egypt, North Africa, and Sicily furnished grain for the entire empire, while timber and various farm products came from Gaul and central Europe. Spain supplied gold, silver, and lead; Britain, tin; Cyprus, copper; the Balkans, iron ore and gold.

Outside the empire, Rome carried on a thriving trade with distant lands, such as India and China. Silks, spices, perfumes, precious stones, and other luxuries from the Far East were in great demand. As many as 120 ships made annual voyages from the Red Sea to east Africa and India, and Roman trading posts were set up in southern India. During the 1st and 2nd centuries A.D. the empire carried on extensive trade with China (Chapter 10). Large quantities of silk were transported by caravan from northwestern China through Turkestan to western Asia. There, traders bought the silk and transported it by overland routes to Europe.

Augustus was the architect of the Pax Romana. Augustus proved to be a wise ruler, determined to restore order and encourage economic development. In greatest need of reform were the provinces which had suffered from misgovernment and heavy taxation under the republic. Augustus tackled the problem by dividing the provinces into two groups: the frontier provinces were placed under his direct control while the older, more stable provinces came under the rule of the Senate. For each of the frontier provinces, Augustus replaced the provincial governors with two carefully groomed civil servants, one dealing with military and civil matters, the other, with finances. One man served as a check on the other, thus helping to eliminate graft. Following a census and survey of the imperial resources, tax rates were adjusted. A program of public works was begun; and roads, bridges, and aqueducts were constructed.

Augustus had no desire to extend the outer limits of the empire, except along the northern frontier. To shorten the Roman defense line from the Black Sea to the North Sea, he believed that the territory lying between the Rhine and the Elbe should be acquired. This area was conquered, but in 9 A.D. the native Germans rose in revolt, defeating the legions decisively in the battle of Teutoburg Forest. After this setback, the northern frontier was maintained at the Rhine-Danube line.

Augustus was not successful in his attempts to restore the old ideas of Roman simplicity and home life. Laws were passed to encourage child bearing and to limit luxurious living—but with little lasting effect. Greater success awarded his efforts to reinstate religious rituals which lent dignity to the affairs of state. In time, worship of the emperor began and, as the years went by, the personal allegiance paid the emperor served as a bond for all peoples within the empire.

WALL OF ANTONINUS
WALL OF HADRIAN

BRITAIN
London
English Channel
TEUTOBURG FOREST
Rhine River

ROMAN EMPIRE
About 117 A.D.

GAUL
Lyon
Po River
Massilia
Danube
River
DACIA
CAUCASUS MTS.
Caspian

SPAIN
Corsica
Tiber R.
Rome
Black Sea
THRACE
Byzantium
Cordova
Ostia
Sardinia
MACEDONIA X PHILIPPI
Pergamum

ATLAS MTS.
M e d i t e r r a n e a n
Sicily
Carthage
Syracuse
Sparta
ACTIUM X
Athens
Corinth
Ephesus
Antioch
Babylon

Crete
S e a
Cyrene
Cyprus
Tyre
Damascus
Alexandria
Jerusalem
Petra
Memphis
ARABIA
EGYPT

Thebes
Red Sea

Prepared by
Rand McNally & Co., C

Roman Empire in 14 A.D.

Provinces added after 14 A.D.

Frontier Provinces

X   Battles

0   250   500   MILES

Both bad and good rulers followed Augustus. When Augustus died in 14 A.D., the Senate voted the title of imperator to his stepson, Tiberius. It was during his reign, which lasted until 37 A.D., that Jesus Christ was crucified in Palestine (Chapter 5). From the time of Tiberius to the end of the empire in 476 A.D., Rome was ruled by a wide variety of emperors, some good and some bad. Nero, judged the most wicked and worthless ruler ever to mount the throne, murdered his wife and his mother, and was accused of setting fire to Rome in 64 A.D., a great nine-day catastrophe which destroyed half the city.

In spite of incompetent rulers, the empire remained intact. Efficient administrators at many levels of responsibility ensured justice and order while commercial pros-perity contributed to political stability. Only when economic decline and social unrest set in did the lack of good leadership at the top become fatal to the health of the empire.

During the 2nd century A.D. the empire benefited from the rule of a group of good emperors. Trajan, who ruled from 98 to 117, was an ambitious military leader; before his death, the empire reached its greatest extent. His successor, Hadrian, ruled from 117 to 138. He made it his policy to strengthen the imperial frontiers. Traveling throughout the empire, he supervised the construction of numerous public works. One of the most famous projects was Hadrian's Wall in England. (A second wall, further northward, was built by Hadrian's successor, Antoninus Pius.) Marcus Aurelius, who ruled from 161 to 180, won both the respect and admiration of his people. His volume of essays, entitled *Meditations,* remains one of the best expressions of the Stoic philosophy (Chapter 3). It is one of the ironies of history that this scholarly, bookish man was forced to spend most of his years of rule as a soldier, defending the frontiers of the empire, which were under attack in the north and east.

Economic decline and political instability weakened the empire. By the end of the 2nd century A.D., attacks on the imperial frontiers became more and more frequent. To meet these threats, the empire doubled the size of its army. The increased drain on the supply of men and resources brought on an economic crisis which was made more severe by other factors. Poverty and unemployment were on the rise and trade started to decline. In an attempt to save valuable metals, the emperors reduced the gold and silver content of the money in circulation—a practice which created an inflationary rise in prices and further hardship.

Trade was hampered by civil disorder which, in turn, was caused by political instability. Meetings of the Senate and the popular assembly had become mere formalities; these two groups were no longer effective in governing the state. Political power was concentrated in the figure of the emperor, who was often at the mercy of the army. Peaceful succession to the imperial throne was rare; the death of an emperor signaled a free-for-all struggle. Of the twenty-nine emperors who ruled between 180 and 284 A.D., only four died a natural death. The others were murdered by army officers or by rival claimants to the throne. The soldiers had the real power to select the new emperor. As a result, emperors often followed the cynical advice of Emperor Septimus Severus, who is said to have told his sons, "Make the soldiers rich and don't trouble about the rest." The le-

gions were kept at full strength by the recruitment of barbarians and the forced enlistment of war captives. Few of these new legionaries cared for the empire so long as they received their pay.

Two emperors tried despotism to save Rome. After a century of decline and civil disorder, two emperors succeeded in halting the disintegration of the empire. The first was Diocletian, who reigned from 284 to 305 A.D. He believed that the empire had become too large for a single emperor to govern, and so he divided it, appointing a co-emperor to rule in the West while he ruled the eastern half. A sub-emperor, or heir, was appointed for each emperor to assure an orderly succession to the throne and to weaken the influence of the army on the imperial election.

To strengthen the empire, Diocletian set up a full-fledged *despotism,* or government by a ruler with unlimited power. Rigid rules for the economy were established. Merchants were told what prices they could charge for their goods, and secret police brutally punished those who defied the system. To bring in increased revenue, taxes were raised to new heights. Diocletian seemed to have forgotten the wisdom of an old saying, "a good shepherd shears his sheep but does not flay them."

In 305 Diocletian and his co-emperor retired according to plan. But war broke out between the contestants for the throne. A few years later, Constantine, one of the contestants, forged ahead and in 324 became sole ruler, reuniting the empire. He continued the despotic rule begun by Diocletian and instituted new, harsh laws to control the imperial economy. Aware that the western provinces were weakening and that the strength of the empire rested on its eastern provinces, Constantine removed the capital of the empire from Rome to Byzantium, which he renamed Constantinople after himself.

The measures of Diocletian and Constantine halted civil war and economic decline for a time. Yet, as a cure-all, despotism proved worse than the ills from which the empire suffered. State regulation of business killed individual initiative. The secret police choked off reform. Trade came to a standstill in many places, and the amount of wealth available for taxation decreased. After the death of Constantine in 337, rival contenders for the throne butchered one another with ruthless cruelty. The last ruler of a united Roman Empire was Theodosius I. Upon his death in 395, the empire was divided between his two sons: one to rule in the West and the other in the East. The next chapter will tell the story of the final breakup of the empire—how the decay within was accompanied and hastened by attacks from without.

Section Review

1. How did Augustus tackle the problem of improving the government and economy of the provinces?
2. How was the Roman Empire held together during the *Pax Romana*?
3. What conditions brought a decay within the empire after 180 A.D.?
4. What steps did Diocletian and Constantine take to strengthen the empire? With what results?

4 **The Romans preserved Greek culture**

The roots of Western civilization can be traced to the blend of Greek and Roman culture, known as *classical culture,* which flourished during the *Pax Romana.* The Romans admired Hellenic culture and borrowed extensively from the Greeks. In this process of assimilation, certain elements of culture were modified. For example, Roman sculpture became more lifelike than the Greek; Roman architecture, more elaborate. In addition, the Romans themselves made many contributions of their own which, added to the Greek heritage, helped to form a truly Greco-Roman culture. Perhaps the greatest single achievement of the Romans was the creation of a body of laws suitable for governing a world state.

Roman law welded the peoples of the empire together. In modern-day Italy, France, Spain, and Latin America, law codes based on Roman legal principles are still in use. The English common law, which forms the basis for the interpretation of legal principles in Great Britain, the Commonwealth, and the United States, was influenced greatly by Roman law. In fact, along with the Latin language, the system of law devised by the Romans is probably their most lasting gift to civilization.

The evolution of Roman law was a gradual process. The early Roman laws—represented by the Laws of the Twelve Tables—were relatively simple. As Roman power expanded, it became necessary to develop a system of law to cover not only Roman citizens but also those under Roman rule without citizenship rights. Special magistrates were appointed to conduct trials involving these two groups, and the bulk of Roman law arose from the accumulated decisions of the magistrates. Of course, the statutes enacted by the assembly were still important as a source of law, but the interpretations of the magistrates gave the law a chance to develop greater flexibility in meeting changing circumstances.

As the republic grew, the body of law grew also, incorporating local customs and traditions from the conquered lands within the framework of the Roman system. The Romans were tolerant of the existence of judicial and legal systems in the territories they conquered, and they borrowed certain aspects of these systems. Gradually, Roman law became international, particularly the laws dealing with commerce. A great stimulus to the development of Ro-

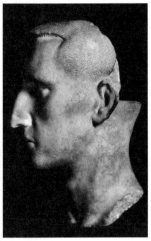

Roman Sculpture, although strongly influenced by Greek models, was noteworthy for its realism. Where the Greeks had idealized their subjects, creating types rather than individuals, the Romans tried to capture the essential personality of each subject. Four Roman rulers are shown above. At left, Julius Caesar's ambition is reflected in his strong, confident face. His kinsman, the youthful Augustus, appears quietly determined. Intellect and sensitivity are evident in the features of Hadrian, who instituted many humane laws. Diocletian is portrayed as an aging man, his mouth firmly set. A stern administrator, he halted the decline of the empire in the 3rd century.

man law was the organization of professional law schools under Augustus.

During the period of the empire, the magistrates exercised greater power than before as they drafted imperial edicts, which themselves became the chief source of legislation. In the 6th century A.D., Justinian, emperor of the Byzantine Empire (Chapter 8), ordered the huge mass of Roman law codified, an invaluable aid in its preservation.

The Romans were great engineers and architects. A network of roads knit together the Roman realm. Their primary purpose was the rapid movement of armies and military supplies, but they were free to the public for travel and commerce. Built of several layers of stone, the Roman roads were superior to any highways constructed in Europe until the 19th century. Roman engineering skill was employed throughout the empire in the construction of numerous aqueducts, dams, bridges, and drainage systems.

From the Etruscans, the Romans learned how to build vaults. Little by little, they improved vault forms so that large interior spaces could be enclosed. To roof these areas, domes were often used. Solidity and permanence were stressed by Roman architects, who used concrete and cement as basic materials. Exteriors were faced with marble or stucco and decorated with sculpture. The Romans preferred ornate display to the stark simplicity which was typical of Greek architecture.

The pride of the Romans in their state was displayed in the magnificence of their architecture, just as their practical nature was exhibited in the uses to which they put their engineering skill. The public baths were multilevel structures, which included steam rooms, pools, gyms, and libraries.

The Roman World

The remains of massive public buildings re-
call the magnitude of Roman power and
the breadth of the Roman world. That so
many of these structures still stand testifies
to the genius of Roman builders and the
strength of their materials. The extensive
theater, at left, once served Leptis Magna,
a city near Tripoli in North Africa. The Pont
du Gard aqueduct, below left, was built
in France in 19 B.C. and remains intact.
Stately columns lead to a triumphal arch
on a street at Timgad in Algeria, below
center. A tribute to Roman skill is the temple
at Petra, Jordan, right, which was carved—
not built—out of rose-colored stone. For an
occasional escape from hot and dusty cities,
the Romans maintained palatial country vil-
las. The seaside view, below, was painted
on a wall in Pompeii, a resort town in
Italy that was buried by volcanic ash.

The Roman baths served as popular meeting places for social and business purposes; by the 4th century A.D. the city of Rome boasted 1000 public baths. The huge Colosseum at Rome seated 50 thousand persons and was the scene of bloody gladiatorial combats and even mock naval battles. At the Circus Maximus, a vast stadium in Rome with a capacity of 150 thousand, thrilling chariot races were held.

The Romans are justly famous for city planning. Provincial cities and towns were usually built around a central forum, which was close to the crossing of two main roads. The principal civic buildings and the market place were centrally located in the forum area, and building codes were enforced to keep architectural styles uniform. The logical planning in the provinces presented a strong contrast to the capital city of the empire. With its narrow, winding streets, poor drainage system, and overcrowding, Rome could boast no systematic scheme. In the 2nd century A.D. the city had a population of over a million persons, jammed into nine square miles. Augustus claimed, with some justice, that he had found the city of brick and had left it of marble, but the splendid public buildings erected or repaired under his direction were often flanked by dark and flimsy tenement houses. Throughout the lifetime of the empire, Rome remained a sprawling, bustling metropolis, a city of magnificence and squalor.

The Romans used Greek models for literature. Throughout the history of Rome, Greek literature remained the most important influence on Latin literary works. An educated Roman was expected to know Greek as well as his native tongue. Wealthy persons often owned Greek slaves, who served as tutors for the children of the household. With Greek models to imitate, the Romans developed a literature of the first rank. Generally speaking, Latin literature is less imaginative than Greek and sometimes overly serious. While it was the Greek genius to speculate brilliantly about destiny and the universe, the Romans had a gift for describing less high-flown ideas, using literature to point out important ethical concepts.

The wealth and leisure resulting from Roman conquests stimulated the production of literature by providing a growing audience for it. From about 100 B.C. to 14 A.D., during the years which spanned the last century of the republic through the reign of Augustus, Latin literature was at its best. This period has been called the Golden Age of Latin literature. Foremost among writers of the Golden Age was the master statesman and polished orator, Cicero. His speeches, letters, and essays revealed his wide-ranging intellectual interests and nobility of character. The respect he commanded as spokesman for the Senate aroused the jealousy of Mark Antony, who had him put to death in 43 B.C. Another victim of political intrigue, Julius Caesar, was an important figure in the development of Latin literature. His military history, *Commentaries on the Gallic Wars*, is noted for its precise descriptive passages and vigorous style.

The greatest poet of the Golden Age was Vergil, known as the "Homer of Rome" because the *Iliad* and the *Odyssey* served as models for his epic, the *Aeneid*. The chief character in Vergil's work was Aeneas, a legendary Trojan hero who overcame numerous obstacles before founding the city of Rome. The most outstanding aspect of the *Aeneid* is Vergil's patriotic fervor; the glories of Rome were praised in stirring lines of poetry. Another writer with patriotic motives was Livy, whose history of Rome was entitled *From the Founding of the City*. By picturing the past greatness of Rome in glowing terms, he hoped to convince his readers to return to the simple ways of their ancestors.

Latin literature after the Golden Age was, for the most part, inferior in quality except for two authors: one Roman and one Greek. The Roman historian Tacitus is best known for *Germania*, his study of the German tribes who lived north of the imperial frontiers in central Europe. Like Livy, Tacitus urged the return to traditional Roman values by contrasting the strength and simplicity of the Germans with the weakness and immorality of his upper-class contemporaries in Rome. A second writer was the Greek biographer Plutarch, whose masterpiece was *Parallel Lives*. Arranged in groups of two were forty-six biographies in which a Greek statesman, orator, or warrior was paired with a Roman whose career and talents were similar. Plutarch did not flatter the Greeks at the expense of the Romans; his accounts were well balanced and his judgments of character sound. It was his special genius to have an eye for entertaining details; his descriptions of people and events are so colorful that *Parallel Lives* proved an invaluable source for latter-day writers. Shakespeare, for one, drew heavily on Plutarch's biographies when writing *Julius Caesar* and *Antony and Cleopatra*.

Long after the Roman Empire had crumbled, Latin continued in use as the written language for educated persons throughout western Europe. It became the official language of the Roman Catholic Church. The monks in the Church copied the works of classical authors, thereby preserving for modern times the literary heritage of Greece and Rome. Even today Latin serves as a universal language in many fields of knowledge. Over the centuries after the fall of Rome, spoken Latin changed gradually, forming the basis for the Romance languages—French, Italian, Spanish, Portuguese, and Rumanian (Chapter 7). The English language includes hundreds of words which can be traced to their Latin origins.

Greeks in the empire made important scientific discoveries. During the period of Roman rule, most of the noted men of science were Greeks, and Alexandria in Egypt, with its famous museum and library, was the center for research and experimentation. A famous Greek scholar was the astronomer Ptolemy. Between 127 and 151 A.D. he compiled in one book all that was then known about astronomy, and for 1500 years Ptolemy's views were generally accepted by educated men. Unlike Aristarchus before him, he believed that the sun revolved around the earth. Also a map maker, Ptolemy was the first to make a map showing the earth as round.

The Greek physician Galen, who lived in the 2nd century A.D., also studied in Alexandria. Next to Hippocrates, he was the most famous doctor of ancient times. He discovered that arteries contain blood—up to that time people had thought they were filled with air.

The Romans themselves made few contributions to scientific knowledge. However, they were skillful in applying Greek findings in medicine and public health. The Romans built the first hospitals, some of which gave free medical care to the poor. About 14 A.D. the first school of medicine was established in Rome, and it was there that Celsus, a Roman-born physician, wrote and taught. One of his books describes surgical procedures for removing tonsils and cataracts as well as the steps involved in elementary plastic surgery.

Section Review

1. How did Roman law become internationalized?
2. In what ways was the Roman talent for building exhibited?
3. Give examples that show why the period from 100 B.C. to 14 A.D. is called the Golden Age of Latin literature.
4. In what ways did the Latin language live on after the Roman Empire ended?

Chapter 4 ██████████ A Review

Conquered by the Etruscans in the 7th century B.C., the Romans overthrew their Etruscan monarch in 509 B.C. and set up a republic, which lasted until 31 B.C. After a long struggle for equal rights with the high-born patricians, the plebeians gained a measure of control over the government.

From 509 until about 100 B.C., the Roman state expanded. By 270 B.C. the Italian peninsula was conquered; by 146 B.C. Carthage was defeated in the Punic Wars. Campaigns in the Near East resulted in control over lands bordering the Mediterranean by 100 B.C.

Although conquest brought wealth to Rome, it also created serious problems for the republic. Civil wars broke out. The tribunes, Tiberius and Gaius Gracchus, were unsuccessful in their attempts to reform the state. Other leaders in conflict were Marius vs. Sulla, Caesar vs. Pompey, Octavian vs. Antony. After the Battle of Actium in 31 B.C., Octavian (later known as Augustus) became ruler of Rome. He was a strong ruler whose reign marked the beginning of the Roman Empire. The first 250 years of the empire were peaceful and prosperous, and the *Pax Romana* was extended from Britain to the Euphrates, from the Rhine to North Africa.

By the 3rd century A.D. the Roman Empire began to show signs of decay. Poverty increased, business activity declined, and the authority of the central government was weakened. Diocletian and Constantine resorted to despotism to strengthen the government, but the civil wars which followed their reigns indicated that despotic methods had failed to bring about a return of the *Pax Romana*.

The Romans developed a legal system which was effective in holding together the many different peoples and customs of the empire. Engineers and architects built excellent roads, bridges, and aqueducts, and massive public buildings. Literature flourished, particularly during the last century of the republic and the reign of Augustus. The Romans admired Hellenic culture and blended it with their own achievements to form a truly Greco-Roman world culture.

The Time

1. Some of the events named below are correctly placed under the period during which they occurred, and others are not. Rearrange the list so that all events appear in their proper time span.

800-401 B.C.
   The Second Triumvirate was formed.
   The Latins were conquered by the Etruscans.
   The Hortensian Law was put into effect.

400-201 B.C.
   Rome was founded.
   Caesar became dictator of Rome.
   The First Triumvirate was formed.

200-1 B.C.
   Constantine moved the Roman capital to Byzantium.
   The first Roman Republic was established.
   The good emperors—Trajan, Hadrian, and Marcus Aurelius—ruled Rome.

1-200 A.D.
   The Gracchus brothers attempted reform.
   Tribunes were created to protect the plebeians.
   Octavian defeated Antony in the battle of Actium.

201-400 A.D.
   Diocletian set up a despotism.
   The Romans destroyed Carthage.
   Scipio the Elder defeated Hannibal at Zama.

2. Give the time span of each of the following periods in Roman history: *Pax Romana; Golden Age of Latin literature; Punic Wars.*

The Place

1. Locate the following battle sites. Who were the contestants in each battle? Who was the victor in each battle?

Zama   Actium
Philippi   Cannae
Teutoburg Forest

2. How did the location of Carthage contribute to its wealth and power?

3. Locate the Roman territories listed below. Which ones had been part of Great Greece? of the Carthaginian Empire about 264 B.C.?

Egypt	Macedonia	Gaul
Sicily	southern Italy	North Africa
Pergamum	Sardinia	Spain

4. In what part of the Roman Empire were each of the following defensive lines or boundaries: Hadrian's Wall, Rhine-Danube line, Euphrates River?

The People

1. How did each of the following men attempt to restore order to Rome?

Tiberius Gracchus	Sulla
Gaius Gracchus	Julius Caesar
Diocletian	Constantine

2. Who were the members of the First Triumvirate? of the Second Triumvirate? What two dictators emerged from these groups?

3. Who was the chief opponent of each of the following: Marius, Pompey, Cleopatra?

4. What was one important literary or scientific contribution made by each of the following men?

Julius Caesar	Tacitus	Livy
Vergil	Cicero	Plutarch
Celsus	Galen	Ptolemy
Marcus Aurelius		

5. What role did each of the following men play in the Punic Wars: Scipio the Elder; Fabius Maximus; Hannibal?

6. What person and event inspired the term "Pyrrhic victory"?

Historical Terms

1. Describe each of these groups and name one political event with which it is associated: patricians; populares; plebeians. Who were the legionaries and how did they exercise political influence in the empire?

2. What would a Roman expect to see if he visited the Colosseum? the Forum? the Circus Maximus?

3. Identify each of the following terms, which are important to an understanding of Roman government.

First Triumvirate	Senate
tribunes	veto
dictator	consul
sub-emperor	co-emperor
Hortensian Law	imperator
Laws of the Twelve Tables	despotism

4. Who were the Etruscans? the Latins? the Gauls? the Punici?

5. Trace the expanding influence of Roman civilization by defining the following: Latin League, Mare Nostrum, Pax Romana, classical culture, Romance languages.

Questions for Critical Thinking

1. How did territorial expansion and increased trade under the republic contribute both to the wealth of Rome and to a decline in the basic strength of the Roman people?

2. To what extent do you think Julius Caesar was responsible for the collapse of the Roman Republic?

3. How did the flexibility of Roman law make it possible for the Romans to govern a world state?

4. In the development of Greco-Roman culture, what was the major contribution of the Romans? Explain your answer, using specific examples.

5. How did the decline of trade contribute to the weakening of the Roman Empire?

6. How did changes in the kinds of men recruited for Roman armies and the increasing need for more soldiers contribute to the political and economic decay of Rome?

7. What evidence can you cite to support the views of Gibbon and Aristides toward the Pax Romana? the views of Arnold J. Toynbee and Tacitus?

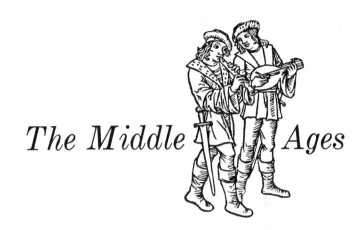

The Middle Ages

The Roman Empire had fallen into decline by the 4th century A.D. Near the end of the following century, it was divided into two parts. The eastern part—later known as the Byzantine Empire—survived for another thousand years. But the western Roman Empire was invaded by fierce, barbaric German tribes from the north. The following description, although somewhat exaggerated, is an account of this troubled time by a man who lived through the last dark days of the empire—Saint Jerome, a famous scholar and leader in the early Christian Church:

> My soul shrinks from reciting the ruins of our times. For twenty years and more, the blood of Rome has been poured out daily. . . . Bishops have been seized, elders and other officials slain, churches overthrown, horses stabled at the altars of Christ, the mortal relics of the martyrs dug up. Everywhere are lamentations, everywhere groanings, and on every hand the image of death. The Roman world is tumbling in ruins. . . .

Men like Saint Jerome believed that civilization could not survive the onslaught of the barbarians. Yet history shows that even after the most tragic setbacks, man has been able to recover and to create new ways of life—sometimes more advanced than those which preceded.

With the fall of the Roman Empire in the 5th century, the ancient period of European history ended. The next thousand years are called the Middle Ages—a middle period bridging ancient and modern history (the latter dating from about 1500). In the Middle Ages, some of the features of classical civilization were blended with various aspects of Germanic culture to form a new pattern of life called *medieval.*

During much of the Middle Ages, the Christian Church wielded the most important influence upon the lives of the people. This fact explains why the Middle Ages is often called the Age of Faith. As Imperial Rome declined, the Church took over many of its duties. Its servants, the

B.C.
A.D.

200

Jesus Christ Paul the Apostle

persecutions of Christians
Edict of Milan Council of Nicaea battle of Adrianople
Christianity made Roman state religion

400

battle of Châlons City of God "fall" of Rome
St. Benedict Clovis Theodoric
Gregory the Great

600

Venerable Bede
St. Boniface battle of Tours
coronation of Charlemagne

800

Treaty of Verdun
Viking invasions
feudalism and manorial system
Cluniac order founded
Peace of God

1000

Gregory VII vs. Henry IV College of Cardinals
Council of Clermont
First Crusade
Third Crusade Innocent III

1200

Fourth Crusade St. Francis St. Dominic
Inquisition
fall of Acre

1400

priests, helped enforce law and order, preserve learning, and teach children. They converted many of the Germans to Christianity and thus increased the power of the Church.

In the course of the early Middle Ages, the only form of government was a system of local authority or personal rule known as feudalism. Power in this system was held by the nobility, who were quarrelsome and warlike in the absence of an overall central authority. To alleviate the hardships of warfare, the Church encouraged a code of behavior known as chivalry. Knights were expected to protect the weak and the innocent and to be good Christians. Shown at the beginning of this unit is a kneeling knight from a stained glass window of a 15th-century church in Norfolk, England. The figure of the knight in prayer expresses the loyalty of the medieval warrior to Christian ideals.

A revival of trade and town life in the later Middle Ages was accompanied by progress in literature, the arts, and education. One of the great "inventions" of the Middle Ages was the university; another, in architecture, was the Gothic cathedral. In the towns and cities, a new social class rose to prominence—the middle class, or *bourgeoisie*. The members of this group were ambitious for wealth, social position,

Chapter 7 / The Growth of Medieval Towns	Chapter 8 / The Byzantine, Moslem, and Russian Empires	
		200 A.D.
	Constantinople made Roman capital Roman Empire split	
		400
	Justinian　Hagia Sophia Mohammed	
		600
	Heraclius　Hegira Moslem invasion of Spain Leo III　battle of Tours	
Carolingian Renaissance	Harun-al-Rashid	800
	Cyrillic alphabet	
epic poetry	Kievan Russia　Al-Razi	
advances in agriculture revival of towns and trade	conversion of Russians to Christianity Basil II	
		1000
mariner's compass Romanesque architecture Abélard Champagne fairs　Moslem learning entered Europe universities	Yaroslav the Wise　Seljuk Turks Greek Orthodox/Roman Catholic split battle of Manzikert　Omar Khayyam Averroës	
		1200
Gothic architecture St. Thomas Aquinas Hanseatic League　Roger Bacon Dante Black Death Chaucer	Latin Empire　Genghis Khan Tartar conquest of Russia Ottoman Turks Grand Duchy of Moscow battle of Kulikovo Tamerlane	
		1400
Everyman	fall of Constantinople	

and political power. As they became richer and better educated, they began to challenge the authority of the nobility.

When Rome fell in the West, classical civilization lived on and flourished in the Byzantine Empire. This empire was in peril most of the thousand years of its existence, but it protected western Europe from invasion by restless tribes from the Near East. Furthermore, the Byzantines preserved from harm the rich heritage of Greek and Roman learning. In the 7th century a new power arose, based on the faith of Islam— the Moslem Empire. The nomadic Arabs who embraced Islam extended their control over the Fertile Crescent, across North Africa, and into southern Spain. Because the Arabs were enterprising traders, they became important in the spread of culture, for they borrowed and preserved knowledge and customs from the people they conquered.

On the edges of the Russian plain, a Slavic state emerged in the Middle Ages. It too profited from culture borrowing, especially from Constantinople, the capital of the Byzantine Empire. In the 11th century, in the area which is now southwest Russia, the state of Kiev flourished. Kievan Russia was the forerunner of the Russian nation which would eventually expand over thousands of miles.

The Rise of Christianity and the Fall of Rome

CHAPTER 5   1 A.D.–800 A.D.

Barbarian invasions in the 5th century ended Roman political power, but not the influence of Christianity, which had swept the Mediterranean world. The cross that Jesus carried to his death inspired the Frankish king, Charlemagne, to conquer much of western Europe in the name of the Church. When Pope Leo III crowned Charlemagne "Emperor of the Romans" in 800 A.D., the act heralded the formation of a new empire based on a unified Christian Europe.

Six feet four inches tall, with massive shoulders and "great-chested like a steed," the king of the Franks was a giant among men. To the inhabitants of 8th-century Europe, he was the conqueror of a realm which in extent rivaled the Roman Empire in its greatest days. To Christian and pagan alike, he was a steadfast defender of the faith, who carried the word of God into the wilds of the Continent. It is interesting to note that he is the one ruler in history whose name in its French form has been blended with the epithet, "The Great." Thus he became known as Charlemagne; that is, Charles the Great.

The facts of history testify to the greatness of Charlemagne as a king, to his contributions to government and law, and to learning and the arts. Even the many legendary tales of which he is the hero yield a certain kind of truth to the student of history. Here was an extraordinary king, the legends say, who was capable of superhuman and incredible deeds. Most important, however, the perspective of time reveals Charlemagne as a key figure in the troubled era of the early Middle Ages. As king of the Franks, and later as head of a large empire, he served as the symbol of Europe united under a single emperor. And second, as a Christian warrior-king of German blood who admired the culture of the Roman Empire, he symbolized the forces which would reshape Europe.

In this chapter, the origins of a new Europe are traced in a discussion of the following:

1. **Christianity became a strong religion in the Roman world.**

2. **German tribes invaded the Roman Empire.**

3. **The Church became the bulwark of civilization.**

4. **An alliance of popes and Franks aided Western civilization.**

1 Christianity became a strong religion in the Roman world

By the middle of the 4th century, the once powerful and prosperous Roman Empire showed unmistakable signs of decay. The government was riddled by corruption, barbarian tribes threatened the imperial frontiers, excessive taxes burdened the citizens, and city mobs clamored for bread as food production continued to decline. In the face of these problems, many Romans turned to their old gods—Mars, Jupiter, and Minerva—while other Romans became absorbed in the teachings of Greek philosophy, chiefly Stoicism, which taught men to accept their fate with quiet courage. Still others turned to Oriental religions. The cult of the Egyptian goddess Isis, the Great Mother cult imported from the Near East, and the worship of the Persian god Mithras were among the most popular.

Of greater significance in the history of Western civilization was the rise of a new faith that had been founded in Palestine in the 1st century A.D. This faith—Christianity—was the religion based on the teachings of Jesus Christ.

Christianity began with the gospel of Jesus. Jesus was born in the city of Bethlehem near Jerusalem and spent His early years in the village of Nazareth, where He learned the trade of a carpenter. At the age of thirty, He abandoned this occupation and began to travel throughout Palestine, preaching a gospel of love for one's fellow man and condemning violence and selfishness. Accompanied by a devoted band of twelve disciples, Jesus attracted crowds of people wherever He appeared.

For centuries the Hebrew Prophets had taught that God would one day create a new Israel under a divinely appointed leader, a Messiah. In the New Testament (Luke 4:18), Jesus is quoted as saying:

The spirit of the Lord is upon me, because he hath anointed me to preach the gospel to the poor; he hath sent me to heal the brokenhearted, to preach deliverance to the captives, and recovering of sight to the blind, to set at liberty them that are bruised.

Many Jews believed, as Jesus Himself did, that He was the long-awaited Messiah, or Christ. They urged Him to help them win their freedom from Rome by force, but Jesus was not concerned with leading a Jewish rebellion. He sought to liberate men morally and spiritually. In anger and disappointment, many Jews turned against Him. He was condemned and turned over to Roman officials for execution, and the Roman governor, Pontius Pilate, ordered Him crucified.

The New Testament relates how Jesus reappeared to His disciples following the crucifixion and confirmed His teachings of eternal life. A few followers set about to spread the news of the Resurrection, dedicating their lives as missionaries of the new faith. They referred to themselves as "brethren" who were of "the way." Later, believers in "the way" were called Christians and their faith Christianity.

Paul spread the teachings of Jesus. The most important missionary was Paul, a well-educated Jew from the Hellenistic city of Tarsus in Asia Minor. As a young man, Paul believed that Christian teachings were in conflict with those of Judaism, and he took part in the persecutions of Christians. According to the Acts of the Apostles (9:1-5), Paul was on his way to arrest any men or women whom he found to be followers of "the way," when a vision of Christ appeared to him. After this experience, Paul became a dedicated convert to Christianity. Immediately he set out to bring Jesus' teachings to as many people as possible—to Jews and Gentiles alike. From about 37 A.D. until his death

in the year 67, he journeyed to many cities around the eastern Mediterranean, spreading the Christian gospel. His great contribution helped Christianity grow from a small Jewish sect in Palestine to a world religion.

Christianity triumphed over persecution. Officials of the Roman government tolerated the many existing religions in the empire so long as the people accepted government authority. The Christians, however, refused to comply with many of the Roman laws—particularly that of emperor worship. Consequently, Christians were regarded as enemies of the state.

Nero blamed the Christians for the burning of Rome in 64 A.D. and punished them severely. Other emperors, seeking excuses for unfavorable conditions during their reigns, used the Christians as scapegoats. They crucified them, threw them to wild beasts and to mad dogs in arenas, or had them burned alive.

The first widespread persecution was carried on from 249 to 251 A.D. by the emperor Decius. The last general anti-Christian drive was ordered by Dioclétian in 303. While the persecutions were at their height, Christians lived a hunted existence. But oppression failed to wipe out the religion. In fact, the courage with which Christians met death inspired Tertullian, a Roman writer of the 2nd century, to say that "the blood of the martyrs became the seed of the Church."

In 311 A.D. Christianity was made a legal religion in the East, and about two years later Emperor Constantine in the West, by the Edict of Milan, legalized Christianity throughout the empire. In 395 the emperor Theodosius made Christianity the official religion.

Christianity was strengthened by a common creed. Because Jesus left no written messages, disputes about Christian beliefs

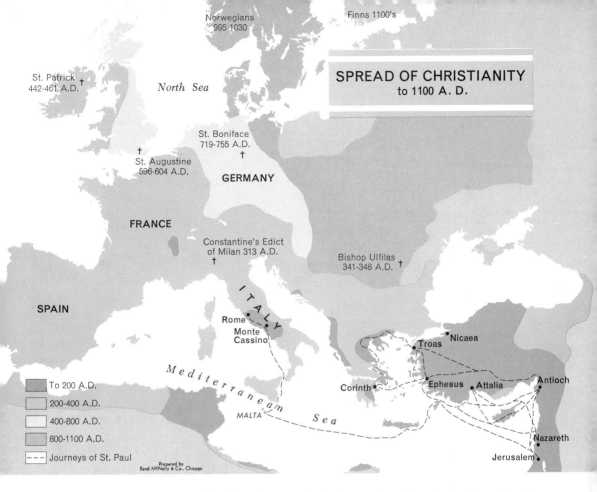

Norwegians
995-1030

Finns 1100's

North Sea

SPREAD OF CHRISTIANITY
to 1100 A. D.

St. Patrick †
442-461 A.D.

St. Boniface
719-755 A.D.
†

†
St. Augustine
596-604 A.D.

GERMANY

FRANCE

Constantine's Edict
of Milan 313 A.D.
†

Bishop Ulfilas †
341-348 A.D.

SPAIN

I T A L Y

Rome
Monte
Cassino

Nicaea

Troas

M e d i t e r r a n e a n

Corinth

Ephesus   Attalia

Antioch

S e a

MALTA

To 200 A.D.

200-400 A.D.

400-800 A.D.

800-1100 A.D.

Journeys of St. Paul

Nazareth

Jerusalem

Prepared by
Rand M?Nally & Co., Chicago

arose among his followers. To resolve this conflict, the emperor Constantine convened the Council of Nicaea in 325. This body formulated a creed supporting the doctrine that God and Christ were of the same substance. All members present agreed to the doctrine except a priest named Arius and his few followers, who maintained that God and Christ were of different substances. He and his followers were therefore banished from the Church as heretics (persons who hold a belief different from the accepted view). As the years passed, the Nicenes and the Arians vied for leadership in the Church, but finally, the Nicenes were victorious.

In addition to the Nicene Creed, there had developed an official book of sacred writings. To the holy writings of the Jews,

which the early Christians adopted and called the Old Testament, were added religious writings compiled after the death of Jesus. Twenty-seven of these compilations, or books, were selected to make the New Testament. In his travels from place to place, Paul the Apostle had kept in touch with Christians through letters of encouragement and advice. These letters, or epistles, constitute some of the most important books of the New Testament.

The official doctrines, or theology, of the Christian Church were systematized by a group of men known as the Church Fathers. St. Jerome, one of the most famous, lived from about 340 to 420 A.D. He made a Latin translation of the Bible, called the Vulgate, which is still used as the official version in the Roman Catholic Church.

Early Christian Art portrayed important scenes from the life of Christ and His followers. Painted in the 3rd century, the portrait of the Virgin and Child on the opposite page appears on the wall of one of the Roman catacombs, a series of underground tombs. At left is an ivory carving depicting Christ performing a miracle; He summons Lazarus, a devoted follower, from a tomb where he had lain dead for four days. The Byzantine enamel above shows the Transfiguration of Christ. The disciples Peter, James, and John kneel in astonishment as Christ, who is surrounded by a heavenly light, converses with Moses and Elijah, who represent the Old Testament Law and Prophets. The Bible tells how a voice from a cloud said, "This is my beloved Son: hear Him," convincing the disciples that Jesus was the Son of God. In the scene at left, two early Christian martyrs are brought before a Roman official. The courage of men like these, who were willing to die for their faith, helped win converts to Christianity.

In 426 another of the Church Fathers, St. Augustine of Hippo in Africa, finished *The City of God*. This book provided much of the foundation of Christian theology.

The Church established a well-knit organization. At first, Christians had no formal organization. Believers met in small groups, often in homes. In time, as Christianity won more followers, an organization evolved. Roman governmental forms served as models for the units of the Christian Church.

Presbyters, to be known later as priests, were ordained to conduct the business and services of churches in villages. Several of these units were placed under the direction of a bishop, who had charge of a diocese, or district. A number of dioceses made up a province under the authority of an archbishop, and a patriarchate was comprised of a group of provinces. The title of patriarch was given to the bishop of a large city, such as Rome, Constantinople, or Alexandria. Gradually the Bishop of Rome assumed leadership as pope, a word from the Greek meaning father.

The development of Church leadership in Rome resulted partly from the prestige held by the Eternal City as the great political capital of the empire. In addition, the decline of the western part of the empire gave the Roman bishops the opportunity to assume governmental leadership as it slipped from the hands of the puppet emperors. Finally, the popes claimed supremacy because of the Petrine Theory, a doctrine that the Roman church had been founded by Peter, leader of Jesus' Apostles. By the year 600, Rome was acknowledged as the capital of the Church and the pope as the head of the Church.

Section Review

1. How did Christianity begin?
2. What did Paul the Apostle contribute to the rise of Christianity?

3. Trace the steps by which Christianity triumphed over persecution.
4. In what respects did the Nicene Creed and the compilations of religious writings contribute to the unity and systematization of the Church?
5. What factors led to leadership by Rome in the organization of the Church?

2 **German tribes invaded the Roman Empire**

While the Church was growing stronger, the once mighty government of the Caesars was crumbling. Added to its many internal difficulties was a final crushing blow—invasion by Germanic tribes.

German tribes exerted pressure on the Roman frontier. In the 4th century A.D. most Germanic peoples in Europe were living east of the Rhine and north of the Danube. To the east, north of the Black Sea, were the East Goths (Ostrogoths) and the West Goths (Visigoths). To the west of these tribes and extending over a large area east of the Rhine were the Vandals, Lombards, Alemanni, Burgundians, and Franks. In and near present-day Denmark lived the Jutes, Angles, and Saxons.

These groups were seminomadic, herding their flocks and tilling the soil. Large and vigorous, the people prized strength and courage in battle. They worshiped many gods, including Tiw, the god of war; Wotan, the chief of the gods; Thor, the god of thunder; and Freya, the goddess of fertility. (The names of these deities are preserved in the English words Tuesday, Wednesday, Thursday, and Friday.)

The German tribal assemblies were made up of voting freemen, and their laws were based on long-established customs of the tribe. These political practices were to have a strong influence in medieval England, where they laid a foundation

Barbarian Tribes posed a constant threat to the later Roman Empire. To guard the border areas, the number of legions was increased, causing a steady drain on the treasury. As funds diminished, Rome lacked the money to maintain its soldiers, who foraged the countryside. Above, Roman troops sack a German village.

for the rise of parliamentary government and English common law. The Roman historian Tacitus, in his famous treatise *Germania*, gave a graphic account of how the Germans lived and wistfully compared these robust people with the weak, pleasure-loving Roman aristocracy.

For hundreds of years the Germans had exerted pressure on the frontiers of the empire. In 105 B.C. German warriors inflicted a terrible defeat on a Roman army, but four years later, a capable Roman leader, Marius, became a national hero when he outmaneuvered the Germans and defeated them. Again, in Julius Caesar's

time, German invaders tried to conquer part of Gaul but were defeated. During the reign of Augustus, the Romans launched a drive against the restless German tribes between the Rhine and the Elbe rivers, but in 9 A.D. the Roman legions suffered a crushing defeat in the Battle of Teutoburg Forest. Three legions were completely wiped out. From then on the Romans were content to hold the frontier on the Rhine-Danube line, and quiet continued for a long period. Again, in the reign of Marcus Aurelius, from 161 to 180 A.D., and for 120 years afterward, the Romans had difficulty holding the Germans at the frontier. But after 300 A.D. peace was maintained for some seventy-five years.

During tranquil interludes, the Roman and Germanic peoples had many opportunities for peaceful association. Some Germans were permitted to enter the Roman Empire to settle on vacant lands. Others, captured in war, became slaves on Roman estates, and still others accepted service in the legions. If intermingling had been allowed to continue, the Germans might have been gradually assimilated into the empire. However, pressure from the German tribes suddenly turned the gradual infiltration into a rushing invasion.

German tribes forced their way into all parts of the western Roman Empire. In Asia, during the 4th century, restless nomads called Huns were on the march from the east. Mounted on swift horses, they attacked with lightning ferocity all tribes in their path. Crossing the Volga River, they conquered the Ostrogoths in eastern Europe. Fearing that the Huns would attack them also, the Visigoths implored Roman authorities for sanctuary in the empire. The Roman officials agreed, promising them lands for settlement provided they came unarmed.

Neither side lived up to the agreement, however, and the Visigoths, without land and facing starvation, began to sack Roman settlements. When the Roman emperor Valens led a great army against the Visigoths, to the astonishment of Romans and Germans alike, the imperial force was scattered and the emperor slain. This battle on the field of Adrianople in 378 A.D. is considered one of the decisive battles in world history because it rendered the Roman Empire defenseless. German tribes outside the frontiers began to round up their cattle, mobilize their fighting men, and move toward the Roman borders.

Marching southwestward under their leader Alaric, the Visigoths reached Rome in 410 A.D. and looted the city. By that time other German tribes—the Franks, Vandals, and Burgundians—were moving into the empire. And about 450 A.D., Germans from northwest Europe—the Angles, Saxons, and Jutes—sailed to Britain, where they killed or enslaved the Britons whom they encountered and forced others to retreat into Wales and Scotland.

To add to the tumult, the Huns, led by Attila, had also invaded the empire and were threatening to enslave or destroy both Romans and Germans. So, forgetting their own differences for a while, the Romans and Germans united against a common enemy. They fought together in Gaul and defeated Attila, the "Scourge of God," at the Battle of Châlons in 451. Shortly afterward Attila died in Italy and his savage cavalry drifted apart.

The western empire collapsed. Meanwhile, the power of the emperors in Rome had fallen to a point where they had become merely puppets of the legionaries, many of whom were of German birth. In the year 476 Odoacer, a commander of the Roman armies, deposed the last of the Roman emperors and became the first German ruler of Rome. This date—476—is often cited as the date for the "fall" of Rome. In a strict sense, there was no "fall." The decline of Roman imperial power was a gradual and complex process marked by weakling emperors, corrupt bureaucrats, and the gradual admission of German soldiers into the legions.

Since the early decades of the 4th century, emperors at Rome had sensed the growing weakness of the empire in the West. In the year 330 A.D. Emperor Constantine had moved his capital to the city of Byzantium, in the eastern part of the empire, changing its name to Constantinople. By the end of that century, the Roman Empire had become permanently divided, with one emperor ruling in the

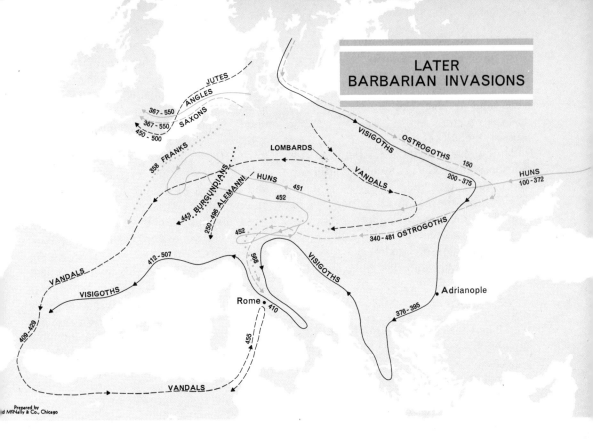

JUTES

ANGLES

367 - 550

367 - 550 SAXONS

450 - 500

FRANKS

358

LOMBARDS

VISIGOTHS

OSTROGOTHS

150

HUNS
100 - 372

BURGUNDIANS

ALEMANNI

HUNS

451

VANDALS

200 - 375

443

250 - 496

452

340 - 481 OSTROGOTHS

412 - 507

452

568

VANDALS

VISIGOTHS

VISIGOTHS

Adrianople

Rome

410

376 - 395

409 - 429

455

VANDALS

West and another in the East. Although separated, the two sections of the empire continued to be thought of as one.

But the western part of the empire was breaking up. By the year 476, when Odoacer ascended the throne, German kingdoms had been established in England by Anglo-Saxon invaders; the Visigoths had moved into Spain; the Vandals had built up a kingdom in North Africa; and, by 486, the Franks had gained control of Gaul. The Italian peninsula was to become the scene of conflict and strife, and near the end of the 5th century, it was to fall under the rule of the Ostrogoths.

The Ostrogoths had become free from the Huns after the death of Attila in 453, and they had built a settlement within the Roman Empire south and west of the Danube. In 471 they elected Theodoric their king, and soon afterward he led a march toward the eastern part of the empire. To prevent the Ostrogoths from encroaching on his lands, the emperor in the East encouraged Theodoric to invade Italy instead and to overthrow Odoacer who had ruled there since 476. Theodoric did so, and by 493 he was not only king of the Goths but of Italy also, with his capital established at Ravenna. His rule brought prosperity and peace to Italy, but at his death in 526, civil strife began again. In the middle of the 6th century a strong emperor at Constantinople, Justinian, won back Italy for a few years (Chapter 8). Then the Lombards, another German tribe, conquered it in 568 and established themselves there for 200 years.

The eastern part of the empire did not succumb to internal decay and barbarian invasions as the western part had. With its capital at Constantinople, it endured, carrying on the imperial tradition for a thousand years. It preserved much of Greco-Roman culture and served as a buffer for western Europe against invasions from the Near East.

Section Review

1. How did the relationship between the Romans and the Germans change after the 2nd century B.C.?
2. How did the battle at Adrianople in 378 affect the Roman Empire?
3. With what event was the "fall" of the Roman Empire associated?
4. To what extent did the "fall" affect the eastern part of the empire?

3 The Church became the bulwark of civilization

Three important forces helped shape a new pattern of civilization in western Europe. The first was the old Roman culture; the second was the vigor of the yet uncivilized Germanic tribes. The survival of the first and the civilizing of the second owed much to the third force that emerged during the decline of Rome. This third force was the Christian Church.

Although services of the Roman government were dropped little by little, and populations of cities declined during the German invasions, most persons saw little change in their daily lives. About two thirds of the land changed ownership, but usually only the wealthy landowners were affected. In a few regions the Germans outnumbered the old inhabitants, but the invaders soon adopted the customs of the Romans, and the blending of peoples that had been going on before the invasions continued. The invaders made use of some of the old Roman political forms and adopted Latin as the official language.

Many of the invaders had been Christianized by missionaries. They respected the Church and were impressed and awed by the solemnity of the Christian service.

The Church provided protection and order. During the invasions when security under Roman law was almost nonexistent, the Church assumed the task of protecting the helpless and punishing criminals. Persons fleeing for their lives could find refuge, called the right of sanctuary, in any church building.

As the power of the Roman emperors diminished, popes and their assistants took over governmental powers. Church courts were established and the right to collect taxes was authorized. The governmental power of the Church was especially evident from 590 to 604 when Gregory the Great was pope. He supervised the police, directed the generals of the army, coined money, and kept aqueducts in repair.

Missionaries spread Christianity. As early as the 3rd century, the teachings of the Christian Church had been carried beyond the frontiers of the Roman Empire by fearless missionaries. One of the most important was Ulfilas, an Arian Christian, who preached among the Gothic peoples. He invented a Gothic alphabet which he used in translating the Bible. Another famous missionary, St. Patrick, was born in Britain about 389. He journeyed to Ireland to convert the Celtic peoples to the faith and founded many monasteries which became famous as centers of learning. In 596 Pope Gregory sent a Roman monk, Augustine, as missionary to England; Augustine later became the first Archbishop of Canterbury.

In the early part of the 8th century, a young Benedictine priest named Winfrid was authorized to preach in Germany. He later changed his name to Boniface and became famous as the Apostle of Germany, where he founded churches and monasteries until his death in 755.

Monks helped preserve culture. During the era of Roman persecutions, a few Christians withdrew to the wilderness, giving up worldly interests and living in solitude. Others lived in groups, dedicating themselves to the service of God. Christian monasteries were first established in Egypt, springing up later in the eastern part of the Roman Empire. About the middle of the 4th century, monasteries began to appear also in the West.

About the year 520, St. Benedict established a monastery in Italy at Monte Cassino and drew up a set of rules that ensured a simple and useful life for monks. His rules required obedience and poverty, frequent daily services, and at least six hours of useful labor each day, mostly in outdoor work. The rules of the Benedictine order were widely adopted by other monasteries in western Europe.

In German lands beyond the old frontiers, where life was rough and semi-barbaric, the monks not only spread the teachings of Christianity but also became the agents of progress and civilization. Often in wild and forested lands, the monks cleared the forests, drained the swamps, and introduced new crops. The few schools that existed in Europe during the early Middle Ages were conducted by monks. The monasteries also served as hostels for travelers and as hospitals.

At a time when libraries were neglected, with their precious manuscripts destroyed or lost, copies of the Scriptures and occasionally of the classics were made by the monks and preserved in the monasteries. Nearly all the important monasteries had a scriptorium where monks copied manuscripts by hand which they illustrated, or illuminated, with decorative designs, borders, and initials done in gold and brilliant colors. The monks also kept historical accounts, called *Chronicles*. One, *The Ecclesiastical History of the English Nation*, written by the Venerable Bede, is the best account available of nearly two centuries of English history.

Section Review
1. What aspects of Roman culture did the barbarian invaders adopt?
2. In what ways did the Church provide order during the period of the invasions?
3. Describe the accomplishments of some of the missionaries.
4. How was learning preserved by the monastic groups?

4 An alliance of popes and Franks aided Western civilization

In the latter part of the 5th century, the Franks, a German tribe, began to build a nation in the north and east of Gaul. It was destined to become the greatest empire of early medieval times.

Clovis enlarged the Frankish realm and extended the power of the Church. Clovis began his remarkable career as the ruler of only one of the several petty kingdoms established by the Franks. By 486 A.D., he had subdued the last remnant of Roman authority in Gaul. He then turned against the other Frankish kings, put them out of the way, and crushed their forces. In 507 the Visigothic kingdom in southern Gaul was conquered and the Visigoths forced to flee to their kinsmen in Spain.

Clovis was converted to Christianity when he gained a victory in battle after an appeal to the Christian God. As a result, not only Clovis but all his warriors were baptized in the Christian faith.

As head of the Merovingian line of Franks, Clovis became one of the most powerful rulers in western Europe. He was the first important German king to become a Roman Catholic. All other Germanic rulers and their subjects—except those in England—were Arian Christians.

VERITATIS VERBA
in allegatione deficiunt sepe etia no
replicant ne tacendo ueti uide
...

The Work of the Early Church

The Church maintained inns and hospitals and encouraged private charity. Through lonely and dangerous lands, missionary priests traveled to preach the gospel and convert barbarian peoples to Christianity. Monastic communities provided the peace and order often lacking in the early medieval world. In some monasteries, there was a division of labor much like that in the world outside. In others, all the monks were required to perform some of the necessary menial tasks. At left, a painting by Stefano Sassetta depicts St. Anthony of Padua, a famous Franciscan preacher, distributing his wealth to the poor. Above is a bronze door from a Polish cathedral, showing a priest saying Mass. The relief commemorates the work of St. Adalbert, a missionary of the 10th century, who spent his life among the people of Poland and northern Germany. Above right is a monk harvesting grain; his curved body forms part of the letter "Q" in the word "Qui" from a medieval manuscript. At right, working on such a manuscript, is Pope Gregory the Great. One of the strongest Popes, he was first a Benedictine monk, and was the author of several important works on the Church.

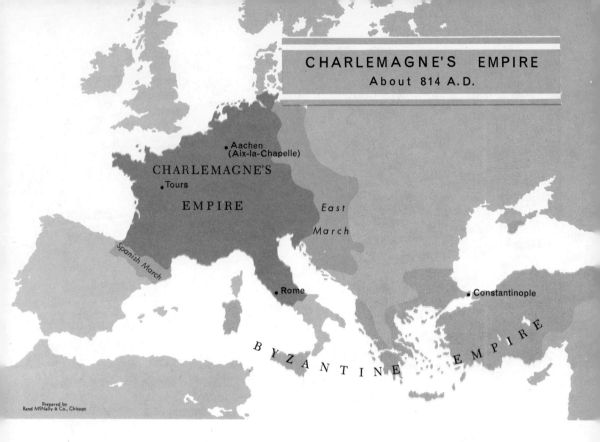

Aachen
(Aix-la-Chapelle)

CHARLEMAGNE'S

Tours

EMPIRE

East
March

Spanish March

Rome

Constantinople

BYZANTINE EMPIRE

Prepared by
Rand McNally & Co., Chicago

Thus they were regarded as heretics by the pope. This difference of doctrine gave Clovis an excuse to attack his Arian neighbors. He declared, "I cannot endure that those Arians should possess any part of Gaul. With God's aid we will go against them and conquer their lands." He defeated the Arians, extending his realm and the authority of the pope at the same time.

Clovis died in 511, and his kingdom was divided among his four sons. They extended Frankish authority into German lands north and east of the Rhine, but their four kingdoms were poorly governed. The Merovingian kings became immoral, weak drunkards who were dubbed the Do-Nothing Kings.

The Carolingian family won control of the Franks. Since the Frankish kings neglected their duties, the office of Mayor of the Palace assumed political impor-

tance. One mayor, Pepin, gained control of all Frankish lands and became in effect the sole ruler. He also coöperated with the Christian Church and supported papal missionaries. In 714 his son Charles inherited the office of mayor. Charles' most notable triumph was a military success won at the Battle of Tours in 732. Pitted against a host of Moslem invaders from Spain, he won a victory which saved northern Europe for Christianity; henceforth he was known as Charles Martel, or Charles the Hammer.

When Charles Martel's son, Pepin the Short, became Mayor of the Palace, he appealed to the pope to decide whether he or a Do-Nothing King should be considered the legal ruler of the Franks. The pope approved Pepin, and thus began the Carolingian line of kings.

In return for the pope's support, Pepin led an army into Italy against the Lombards, who menaced the papacy. In 756, after forcing them to surrender some of their lands, Pepin turned over to the pope a portion of the former Lombard territory. This Donation of Pepin came to be known as the Papal States.

Charlemagne built an empire and spread Christianity. In 768 Pepin's son Charles became the Frankish ruler and in time one of the greatest of all European monarchs. He was known as Charlemagne, or Charles the Great. At the request of the pope, Charlemagne brought his army into Italy, where he defeated the Lombards decisively, and in 774 he took the title King of the Lombards. Among his greatest military successes were the conquests of the heathen Saxons in the north and the Avars in the central Danube area. Eventually, he governed an empire stretching from the Danube to the Atlantic Ocean, from Rome to the Baltic and North seas. Accompanying his armies were priests of the Church. While the armies provided conquests for Charlemagne, the priests made converts for the Church.

Charlemagne appointed counts to preside over the counties, or districts, into which he divided his empire, and maintained law and order through agents called *missi dominici,* or "messengers of the lord." The *missi,* traveling in pairs, visited every county annually, held court, checked on the local courts, and reported their findings to Charlemagne. On the borders, he established defensive buffer districts called marks, or marches.

Charlemagne modeled his capital at Aix-la-Chapelle on Roman cities and imported statuary and marble from Italy to enhance its beauty. Aix-la-Chapelle was also famous for the revival of learning, often referred to as the Carolingian Renaissance. Charlemagne proved a benefactor to scholarship, urging priests to study and improve their education, sponsoring a refinement of the system of handwriting then in use, and generously supporting the monastic and cathedral schools. There boys were taught the Christian doctrine, arithmetic, grammar, and singing. The rebirth of learning during Charlemagne's rule helped preserve Roman culture and ensured the continuance of civilization in western Europe.

The coronation of Charlemagne symbolized the coöperation of Church and state. In the year 800 Charlemagne traveled to Rome. While he was attending service on Christmas Day, the pope placed a crown on the monarch's head and declared, "To Charles Augustus crowned of God, great and pacific Emperor of the Romans, long life and victory." Whether the pope planned this action with Charlemagne's knowledge is unknown. Of greater importance, the ceremony demonstrated that the idea of the Roman Empire still survived as a vital tradition in Europe and that there existed a strong desire to reëstablish the political unity of imperial Rome.

The coronation also illustrated another great theme of medieval history: the struggle between the Church and the state. Charlemagne was crowned not only by, but presumably with, the consent of the pope. He was emperor by the grace of God, with the Church on his side. But it was not all a positive gain for the ruler. The coronation signified that the Church could claim superiority over rulers. From that time on, both popes and kings claimed supreme authority.

Section Review
1. To what extent did Clovis lay a foundation for future Frankish power?
2. What contribution did Charlemagne make to the preservation of civilization?
3. What was the significance of the coronation of Charlemagne in Rome?

The Christian religion which began with the teachings of Jesus Christ became a strong force in shaping Western civilization. Although its founder was crucified and His followers harshly persecuted, the small group of "believers" gathered strength through the work of missionaries, especially that of Paul the Apostle. The development of a common creed and a Church organization, modeled after the government of Rome, further strengthened the movement. Eventually Christianity became the official religion of the Roman Empire.

German invasions which had begun as early as the 2nd century B.C., increased in the 4th century A.D. At that time Huns from Asia forced the German tribes to seek refuge in the empire. Once inside, they increased their power and landholdings at the expense of the Romans. Soon thereafter other German tribes advanced on Roman lands. In time they overthrew the puppet Roman emperors.

Although the western part of the Roman Empire crumbled, the Church at Rome, having become the head of all Christian churches, assumed leadership in governmental as well as in religious affairs. Its missionaries carried the Christian religion and Roman culture to the barbarian tribes while, in the monasteries, culture was preserved and education fostered.

In Gaul, about the year 500, the Frankish king Clovis grew powerful and extended Frankish territory through conquest. He allied his kingdom with the Church in Rome and established the Merovingian line of kings. The Do-Nothing Kings who succeeded Clovis allowed the Carolingian family to gain control.

The greatest member of this royal house was Charlemagne, who expanded the Frankish Empire still farther. His reign was noteworthy for good government, for the encouragement of education, and for the extension of the power of the Christian Church. When the pope crowned him emperor in 800, a precedent was established that would affect the relation of popes and monarchs for many centuries.

The Time

Arrange the sentences below so that events or periods given appear in their correct time sequence.

(a) The Roman Empire was rendered defenseless when the imperial army was defeated by the Visigoths, a barbarian Germanic tribe, at Adrianople.

(b) Clovis ended the last remnants of Roman authority in Gaul and extended the authority of the Church.

(c) Theodosius made Christianity the official religion of the Roman Empire.

(d) St. Boniface, one of many missionaries sent out to convert the barbarian tribes, became the Apostle of Germany.

(e) The Apostle Paul spread the gospel of Jesus to many cities throughout the Roman world.

(f) The coöperation of Church and state was symbolized when the pope crowned Charlemagne emperor of the Romans.

(g) The Council of Nicaea helped unify Church doctrine.

(h) Odoacer deposed the last of the Roman emperors.

(i) St. Benedict established a monastery and drew up a set of rules for monks.

(j) Constantine made Christianity a legal religion throughout the Roman Empire.

(k) Pope Gregory the Great, exemplifying the growing power of the Church in Rome, acted as both political and spiritual leader.

The Place

1. In what general areas did each of the following tribes establish kingdoms?

Visigoths	Lombards	Angles
Franks	Ostrogoths	Saxons
Vandals		

2. Locate the site, name the contestants, and tell the outcome of each of the following battles: Teutoburg Forest, Châlons, Adrianople, Tours.

3. What lands were included in both Charlemagne's empire and in the Roman Empire in 117 A.D.? Which areas were a part of

Charlemagne's empire only? of the Roman Empire only?

4. Locate the following places and tell what importance each one had in Church history: Nicaea, Milan, Nazareth.

5. Of what empires were Aix-la-Chapelle and Constantinople the capital cities? Under what name and in what country would each of these cities be found today?

The People

1. To what peoples did each of these missionaries carry the Christian religion?

Ulfilas   St. Augustine (of Canterbury)
St. Patrick   St. Boniface

2. Name the measures each of the following emperors took to hinder or to foster the spread of Christianity in the Roman Empire.

Diocletian   Theodosius   Nero
Constantine   Decius

3. What contribution did each of the following men make to the establishment and ultimate success of the Christian Church?

Paul the Apostle   Gregory the Great
St. Jerome   St. Benedict
St. Augustine (of Hippo)

4. For what achievements did each of the following men become heroes to their own people: Attila, Alaric, Theodoric? Of which tribal group was each a leader? Which leader was called the "Scourge of God," and why?

5. Name one achievement of each of the following kings or mayors of the palace in enlarging the Frankish kingdom or in extending the power of the Church.

Clovis   Pepin the Short   Charlemagne
Pepin   Charles Martel

6. How did Tacitus and the Venerable Bede contribute to the knowledge of history?

Historical Terms

1. Explain the meaning of each of these terms as applied to the beliefs and practices of the early Christians: Messiah, "the way," "brethren," missionaries.

2. Define each of the following terms as applied to the structure and organization of the medieval Church.

province   bishop
archbishop   pope
presbyters   diocese
patriarch   monastery

3. How did each of these writings contribute to the theology of the Christian Church?

Old Testament   *The City of God*
New Testament   Nicene Creed

4. How did the Petrine Theory strengthen the authority of the popes?

5. Why were Arians branded heretics?

6. Explain each of the following terms as applied to the Frankish kings and their kingdoms.

Donation of Pepin   Merovingians
marks or marches   *missi dominici*
Do-Nothing Kings   counties
Carolingians   Carolingian Renaissance

7. What was meant by the term "right of sanctuary"?

Questions for Critical Thinking

1. Why is it incorrect to say that the "fall" of Rome in 476 was a sharp break with the past?

2. What role did the Christian Church play in the building of the Frankish Empire?

3. How did the Christian Church strive to fill the political vacuum left by the disappearance of Roman authority?

4. Why did the early Christians encounter strong hostility from the Roman authorities? How was this hostility eventually overcome?

5. In what way did the coronation of Charlemagne mark a high point in the unity of Church and state but at the same time establish a point of conflict between kings and popes?

Feudalism and the Age of Faith

CHAPTER 6   800–1300

European life during the Middle Ages centered around two great institutions—feudalism and the Christian Church. The close relationship of the two is symbolized by the sculpture at left, where a priest offers the Eucharist to a knight. The most dramatic expression of this alliance was the crusades, a series of religious wars against the Moslems. The departure of Godfrey of Bouillon, right, for the Holy Land in 1096 marked the beginning of the First Crusade.

"In the name of God, St. Michael, and St. George, I dub thee knight. Be valiant." To a young Englishman of medieval times, these words, accompanied by the tap of a sword blade on his neck or shoulder, signified that he had become a knight and was expected to act in a manner becoming his newly acquired rank. John of Salisbury, a 12th-century English scholar, described the knight's code of behavior as follows:

What is the function of orderly knighthood? To protect the Church, to fight against treachery, to reverence the priesthood, to fend off injustice from the poor, to make peace in your own province, to shed your blood for your brethren, and if needs must, to lay down your life.

Knighthood reached its greatest importance in western Europe during the Middle Ages, when law was in the hands of the nobility. They held land, known as *feuds*, or *fiefs*, and governed the inhabitants through a system called feudalism. To protect his fiefs or add to them by seizing land from others, a noble needed a force of knights. Indeed, the usual occupation of the nobility was fighting; to keep in trim for warfare knights took part in tournaments that tested their skill.

Apart from the nobles and their knights, most medieval people had little interest in warfare. Peasants tilled the soil and hoped to stay free from trouble, although they were unable to prevent the hunting and fighting of the knights, which often destroyed crops and meadows. The Church used its influence to lessen bloodshed, but clergymen often found themselves involved in feudal rivalries, for the Church itself was a great landowner. The Church also encouraged Christians to fight on its behalf in the crusades.

Feudalism had taken shape in Europe by the 9th century and lasted until late in the 13th century. This period is described in the four sections of this chapter.

1. **Feudalism arose in western Europe.**

2. **The manor was the center of economic life.**

3. **Chivalry set standards for conduct.**

4. **The Church unified Europe.**

1 Feudalism arose in western Europe

To the people of his time, the empire of Charlemagne seemed powerful and destined to endure. The peace once enjoyed under the Roman Empire appeared to have been restored. However, after the death of Charlemagne, it was soon apparent that much of the success of the empire had depended upon this vigorous ruler. Little by little the power of the Carolingians was undermined. Weak successors were forced to grant special privileges, called immunities, to strong lords, allowing them freedom from any interference by royal officials. By the middle of the 9th century, kings ordered freemen to place themselves under the protection of a strong lord, a sure sign that the king was no longer able to guarantee law and order. The tendency toward strong local government, which had begun during the decline of Rome, once more came to the forefront. Some kind of authority was needed to replace the imperial power.

Division weakened the Carolingian Empire. Louis the Pious, Charlemagne's son, who became emperor in 814, was more interested in religion than in government, and he neglected his kingly duties. Three years after his death in 840, his sons signed the Treaty of Verdun, which divided the Carolingian Empire into three parts. Charles the Bald received West Frankland, west of the Rhine, which later be-

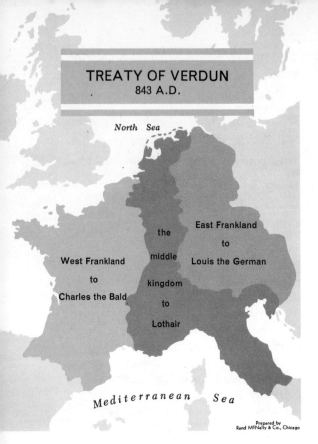

TREATY OF VERDUN
843 A.D.

North Sea

West Frankland

to

Charles the Bald

the

middle

kingdom

to

Lothair

East Frankland

to

Louis the German

Mediterranean Sea

Prepared by
Rand McNally & Co., Chicago

Vikings, Slavs, and Moslems attacked the empire. During Charlemagne's reign and continuing long after the Treaty of Verdun, the empire was invaded by bands of Scandinavian warriors, known as Vikings, Northmen, or Norsemen. More destructive than the German tribes that had invaded Rome four centuries earlier, they threatened all of Western civilization.

Venturing forth from their inlets, or fiords, in long boats, they journeyed to Russia, to England, to the shores of western Europe, and even into the Mediterranean area. There they landed on the beaches or on the shores of navigable rivers, set towns afire, seized all movable wealth, and sacked the churches. No wonder that the people prayed, "From the fury of the Northmen, O Lord, deliver us."

Some of the Vikings settled on the coast of West Frankland and, led by Rollo, they made an agreement in 911 with the ruler of West Frankland to remain there. Henceforth, they were known as Normans and the area became Normandy. They adopted Christianity and developed a well-governed and civilized state.

About the time of the Viking invasions, restless Slavic tribes from the northeast attacked Europe, particularly East Frankland. At the end of the 9th century, another group, the nomadic Magyars from Asia, laid waste an area in eastern Europe several thousand miles in extent. However, by the late 10th century the force of their attacks had waned, and, like the Normans, they became civilized and Christianized. They formed settlements and created a new state known as Hungary.

Meanwhile, the Moslems had pushed into southern Italy and along the coast of what is now southern France. They pillaged towns and sold their captives in the slave markets of North Africa. With bases on most of the strategic islands in the Mediterranean, their war vessels drove Christian commerce from the inland sea.

came France, while Louis the German received lands east of the Rhine, called East Frankland, the beginning of modern Germany. To Lothair was granted a narrow strip of land between these kingdoms, running from the middle of Italy to the North Sea. From his time to the present its ownership and government have been disputed, providing cause for many wars between Germany and France.

Although the empire was divided, the divisions were still thought of as parts of one great empire, with Lothair, the eldest, as emperor. However, neither the emperor nor his brothers held any real authority. The central imperial administration was breaking down, and government and economic life were controlled by hundreds of local counts, dukes, and other nobles. Furthermore, the empire was under attack by a new wave of invaders. They came from the north and from the east.

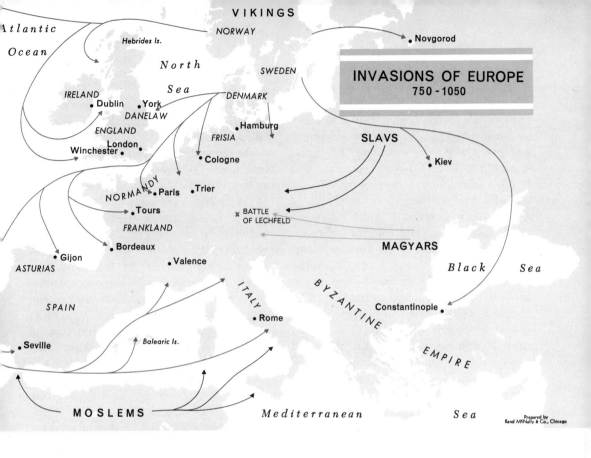

Atlantic
Ocean

NORWAY

• Novgorod

Hebrides Is.

North

Sea

SWEDEN

INVASIONS OF EUROPE
750 - 1050

IRELAND
• Dublin   • York
DANELAW

DENMARK

• Hamburg

FRISIA

SLAVS

ENGLAND

• Kiev

Winchester   London
•

• Cologne

NORMANDY   • Paris   • Trier
• Tours

BATTLE
OF LECHFELD

FRANKLAND

• Bordeaux

MAGYARS

• Gijon
ASTURIAS

• Valence

Black   Sea

SPAIN

ITALY

BYZANTINE

Constantinople
•

• Seville

Balearic Is.

• Rome

EMPIRE

MOSLEMS

Mediterranean   Sea

Prepared by
Rand McNally & Co., Chicago

During these invasions the kings in the lands of the old Carolingian Empire offered little protection to their people. In fact, no central government worthy of the name existed. The descendants of Charlemagne were dying out. In 911 the last Carolingian king in East Frankland died; seventy-six years later death claimed the last in West Frankland.

Feudalism, a new system of government, emerged. With the disappearance of a central government, landowning nobles had become virtually independent of kings or princes. As the power of the nobility increased, the system of government which is known as feudalism came into being.

Basic to feudalism were the arrangements for holding land and the relationships that existed among various elements of society. During the decline of Rome, when cities lacked law enforcement, small landholders sought protection from large landowners. They turned their property over to the stronger neighbor in return for protection and also surrendered legal ownership of it. In turn, they received the right to stay on their land and to farm it. This arrangement was called *precarium*, a Latin word meaning "something asked for and received by entreaty."

The personal services of feudalism known as vassalage derived from an early German tribal custom, called *comitatus*, in which a chief divided with his companions the spoils of war in return for pledges of loyalty and military service. From this custom arose the practice of *beneficium*, by which certain rights or certain lands were granted in return for specific services. Carolingian rulers who preceded

Charlemagne had parceled out land to warriors and thus had enlisted them in the royal armies as fighting men, or knights. When the *beneficium* became hereditary, the land, or *benefice,* was known as a fief or feud. While the system of landholding and personal service was more or less the same throughout Europe, feudalism differed in details from country to country and also from century to century.

A noble who received a fief became a vassal in a solemn and colorful ceremony called homage. The word *homage* stems from the Latin word *homo,* meaning "man," and in the ceremony the vassal promised fealty, that is, he promised to be the lord's faithful man. In a symbolic act called *investiture,* the lord then turned over the administration and use of the fief —but not the ownership—to the vassal.

By specifying certain duties and rights, the feudal contract—usually oral—provided a form of government for a relatively small political unit. It called upon the lord to protect the vassal, to defend the honor of the vassal's family, and to guarantee him justice in his court. If the vassal died without heirs or broke any of the provisions of the feudal contract, the lord could take back the fief.

The most important of the vassal's duties was military service. For each fief awarded him, he had to provide the services of a specified number of knights and horses for the lord, usually for a term of forty days a year. Because an important noble had many vassals, this part of the contract provided him with the armed forces necessary to defend his holdings and those of his vassals from attack. The vassal was also obliged to pay taxes to the lord and to provide ransom if the lord were captured by enemies.

Most vassals *subinfeudated* their fiefs. That is, each vassal kept enough land from his fief to provide food, fuel, and clothing for the maintenance of his own family and his servants. The rest of the land was then parceled out to other nobles, who in turn became vassals to him. This process of subinfeudation, or parceling out the land, divided Europe into thousands of local governments.

As the system of feudalism grew in extent, it also became complicated and clumsy. For example, a lord might be the vassal of several different lords, and so he would have to swear homage and fealty to different men. In case two of his lords went to war against each other, he would be obligated to fight for one of them and thus fail in his contract with the other. Sometimes a king with many vassals of his own might also become a vassal of another king, as was the case with King John of England, who held lands in France and was a vassal of the French king, Philip.

The Church entered into feudal contracts. Tracts of land given to the Church as gifts often carried with them feudal obligations. Consequently, a Church official holding a fief was at the same time the servant of the pope and a vassal of a lord. Frequently he had to decide to whom he owed first allegiance.

When a vassal not of the clergy died without heirs, administration of the fief reverted to its owner. Feudal lands held by the Church, however, were not fiefs of any one person. Therefore, when a Church official died, the feudal contract was not altered, for the Church still held the land. In this way, the extent of Church lands increased. Eventually, the Church owned about a third of the landed property in western Europe.

Medieval society consisted of fixed classes: nobility, clergy, and peasantry. The nobility consisted of the kings, their vassals, and lesser lords. Their status was inherited, and in an age of physical violence, it was not surprising that society accorded honor to the man with the sword. Because feudal law asserted that a noble could be judged only by his social equals or superiors, no member of the peasantry could bring a case against him.

Generally speaking, clergymen were the only group educated in a subject other than warfare. Bishops and high-ranking clergy lived on a par with rich lords, whereas the parish priests usually lived only slightly better than the peasants.

On the bottom rung of the social scale were the peasants, who were dependent on the nobility for their livelihood. With the exception of a small group who were free, nearly all of them were serfs who had inherited their social status. A peasant could not hope to attain the rank of a noble, but he could become a clergyman. With sufficient ability he could even become a bishop or pope.

Feudalism preserved order in a lawless era. Although based on contracts and promises, the system of feudalism could not guarantee political stability. Yet crude as it was, feudalism served to preserve order in a time of violence when no better government was available. And even though kings wielded little power, the feudal system kept alive the idea of kingship, enabling later kings to restore centralized government.

Section Review

1. What conditions weakened the Carolingian Empire after Charlemagne's death?
2. How did feudalism come to take the place of centralized government in western Europe?
3. How did subinfeudation complicate feudal relationships?
4. How did the Church obtain lands under the feudal system? How did it keep control of these lands?
5. In what respects was class division rigid during the time of feudalism?

2 The manor was the center of economic life

During the Middle Ages the economic counterpart of feudalism was the manorial system. By defining the duties and privileges of lords and vassals, feudalism secured a degree of political and social order in Europe. The manorial system, in similar fashion, governed the methods of agriculture, the lives of the peasants, and their relationships with one another and with the lord of the manor. Like the system of feudalism, the manorial system differed from one area to another and from one century to another.

Some manors can be traced back to Roman farms in the last days of the empire. Others can be traced to the time of the early Germanic invasions when freemen surrendered their independence and became semislaves of stronger neighbors. The manorial system of medieval times developed in a period when towns in Europe had diminished in size and number and when trade among them had almost disappeared. Throughout a great part of western Europe, life centered increasingly on the self-contained estates of the nobles.

The manorial system depended on farming. The fief of a large landowner might support several hundred manors, varying in size from 350 to 5000 acres each, while a small fief might support only one. The manor or manors that the lord used for himself were called his *domain*, and each manor became the center of the social and economic life of the persons who lived on it. Just as the peasants were dependent on the lord for protection and provisions, so also was the lord's power and wealth dependent on the peasants who worked his estates.

A manor house was the focal point of a manor; in many cases it was a large fortified structure, even a castle. The land on which it stood was the lord's *demesne.*

Manor Life

Self-sufficiency was the keynote of the manor, whose inhabitants produced almost everything they needed. Hunts, like the one above, were a source of both food and pleasure for the lord. Some of the peasants worked directly for the lord as servants or in specialized occupations such as beekeeping, left. However, most peasants tilled the lord's plots of ground, as well as their own. Above right, one peasant harrows while another keeps a sling handy to protect newly planted seeds from hungry birds. A reeve supervises the harvesting of wheat in the scene at middle right. Three men work with scythes.

At right is a map of a typical manor. Fields to the west, north, and east are divided into strips for the peasants. The lord has reserved the best land for his demesne, A. The manor house, B, occupies a dominant position. Nearby are stables, C; barns, D; and a bakehouse, E. Peasants' huts cluster in a small community, F. On the church lands, J, are a chapel, G, and the rectory, H. A windmill, K, stands near the river, L, which forms a boundary around the manor.

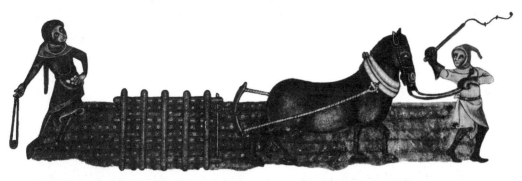

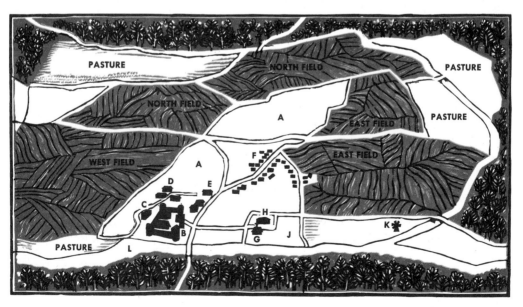

Also located on the demesne were such buildings as the lord's barns, stables, mill, bakehouse, and cookhouse. Near the demesne were the church, the priest's house, and the village where peasants' huts lined a narrow street. The lord allotted meadows and woodlands as he pleased, but made a pasture available to everyone in common.

The entire population of the manor shared in the division of farm land. The lord usually took the best portion and granted the remainder to the peasants. It was divided into long strips, usually separated only by sod ridges. Where work animals were scarce, the peasants pooled their oxen and plows and worked all the fields together. A system of three-field or two-field planting kept the farm land from being overworked. In the former system, two of three fields were planted each year, and in the latter, only half the land was used at one time; the remainder was allowed to lie fallow, or uncultivated.

Although the lord might reside on one of his manors, the day-to-day administration of each manor was in the hands of certain officials, known in England as the steward, the bailiff, and the reeve. The steward was the highest ranking official; he served as legal adviser to the lord and presided over the manorial court. He inspected the manor and, if the lord had more than one manor, he traveled from one to the other to check on their condition. The bailiff supervised the work of the peasants, the cultivation of the land, the financial accounts, and the collection of rents, dues, and fines. A reeve, or foreman, assisted the bailiff in the supervision of the farm work. A large manor might need many reeves to oversee such matters as the production and storage of hay, the care of bees and herds, and the harvesting of crops. It was the reeve who presented to the lord the villagers' complaints against the officials of the manor.

The lord's officials also saw to it that certain services were performed by the inhabitants of the manor. For example, the serfs were required to work two to three days a week on the demesne of their master and more during seedtime and harvest. In addition to this labor, the lord imposed special taxes on the peasants during the year, and by far the largest part of the flour, bread, and wine made by serfs in the demesne mill, oven, or press had to be given to the lord.

Freemen and serfs belonged to the peasantry. The peasantry comprised about 95 per cent of the population of the early Middle Ages in Europe. Although they were indispensable to the manorial system, they had no role in the feudal system. In theory, they were offered protection by the lord's knights and justice at the lord's court. In practice, the peasants were often at the mercy of their masters.

The smallest group in medieval society was made up of the freemen, who paid rent for their lands. They could hire someone to do their work if they were financially able to do so, or they could leave the manor if they located a new tenant satisfactory to the lord.

Serfs, who made up the largest percentage of the peasantry, could not leave the manor of their own free will. They were bound to the land, and the nobles considered them as property, scarcely above the cattle. Serfdom had its origin in the declining days of the Roman Empire, when men gave up their lands and independence for protection.

Medieval literature is filled with references to peasant ugliness, stupidity, and filthiness. Lacking opportunities for schooling and to a great extent unaware of its benefits, the serfs lived according to beliefs in magic, witches, and ogres. Only from time to time was their existence enlivened by folk dances on the village green, by church festivals, and by rough athletic contests.

The medieval manor was self-contained.
The manor was almost self-sufficient economically. Most of what was needed to feed, clothe, or shelter the people who lived on a manor was grown or made there. Sheep and flax furnished wool and linen for cloth; goats and cattle provided skins for leather; the woodland was a source of fuel. Peasants baked the bread, brewed the beer, pressed grapes for wine, and ground the grain. The food lacked variety and, too often for the serfs, was scanty in quantity. Grain was the important crop, and bread was the staff of life. Hay and grain for livestock were scarce in summer and so poor in winter that cattle often died from starvation or became too weak to walk to pasture in the spring. Most of them, therefore, were slaughtered in the fall, and only at that time was beef available for the serfs. Pork was somewhat more plentiful, for pigs found ample forage as they roamed the woods, living on shoots and acorns. The people's diet was sometimes supplemented by fowl and in season by fresh fruits and vegetables. Because the supply of milk was limited and peasants used most of it for making cheese, the chief beverages were cider, beer, and wine. Pure water was rarely available.

Manors were often surrounded by wild countryside, and while the lord traveled occasionally to distant places, many serfs never left the vicinity of the manor. Few changes disturbed their way of living, and time seemed to stand still.

Living conditions in the castle were primitive. The lord's manor house or castle was built primarily for defense against enemies. To provide a safe refuge during a siege, the great tower, or keep, was strongly fortified. The various buildings surrounding the keep were enclosed by a high wall often several feet thick. During a battle, defenders could take positions on ramparts near the top of the wall and pour burning oil or drop heavy stones on the enemy below. A moat, or ditch, outside the wall prohibited all entry to the castle until the drawbridge was lowered across the water from the massive gate. Unwelcome visitors were barred at the gate by an iron grating called a *portcullis.*

By modern standards the castle lacked many comforts. The rooms were dark, cold, and musty. In winter, hearth fires warmed only small areas, and the large rooms were often full of smoke, for chimneys did not come into use until the 14th century. When dining in the great hall, the nobles sat at boards placed on trestles, throwing scraps over their shoulders to the dogs. Rushes, spread over the floor to lessen the cold, became filthy and evil smelling from the refuse that collected in them. Not until late in the medieval period were carpets used as floor coverings.

The cumbersome beds of the nobility were usually built on platforms under canopies and enclosed with heavy curtains for privacy and for protection from drafts. Falcons, hounds, and even farm animals shared space with the family in the sleeping areas.

During the evenings jesters and clowns entertained the lords. Travelers were generally welcome, for they brought news and gossip from places outside the bounds of the manor. Welcome also were the traveling musicians, who journeyed from one castle to another, bringing their poems and music of heroic deeds, love, and great adventures.

Section Review

1. In what respects did the origins of the manorial system resemble those of feudalism?

2. Show how the medieval manor was a self-supporting unit.

3. Contrast the life of the serfs with that of the lords.

Chivalry and Knighthood developed from a simple relationship between lord and vassal into an elaborate way of life. In early medieval times, the training of knights emphasized only hunting and fighting. Knighthood was conferred with a single tap of the sword by another knight. In later times, training for knighthood became more formal and included intensive education in manners. Part of this training was spent in service as squire to a knight. Above right, a squire assists in dressing his knight in heavy armor. Knighthood also could be won through bravery on the battlefield; in the scene above left, a valiant lad kneels as he is dubbed "knight of the sword." When there were no real battles to fight, knights kept in trim by jousting in tournaments, following the strict rules laid down by the code of chivalry. On the facing page, knights display their skill and strength while noble ladies cheer their favorites. Chivalry also prescribed rules for gentlemanly conduct toward women. In the painting at left, a 15th-century artist has pictured knights gallantly escorting their ladies at a medieval garden party.

3 Chivalry set standards for conduct

Because the defense of his fiefs was crucial to his welfare, the lord needed armored knights for protection from his enemies. On the other hand, the knight needed weapons, armor, horses, personal attendants or squires, and a number of grooms or servants which the lord could supply. Armed and mounted for battle, the knight was a costly instrument of war, formidable in his day. Although fighting was his normal occupation, a knight preferred to capture his foe and collect the ransom for his return rather than kill him. When no wars were in progress, make-believe fighting and hunting were favorite pastimes; hunting replenished the meat supply and practice at fighting kept warriors in trim.

The manners of knighthood and the qualifications that the ideal knight supposedly possessed became known as chivalry. The term came from the French word *chevalier*, meaning "horseman"; in fact, during the Middle Ages, armed and mounted warriors, or knights, were referred to as the chivalry. As time passed, the courage, loyalty, and honor expected of the knighthood invested the word chivalry with meanings such as courtesy, gallantry, and honor.

Few knights lived up to the code of chivalry completely, and many disregarded it when convenient. Nevertheless, it served as an inspiration to the people

Medieval Castles were designed primarily for defense. A protective moat surrounds the thick walls of a 14th-century English stronghold, above left. The diagram below shows the principal parts of a typical castle. Ideally, the lord's keep could be defended even if the rest of the structure were captured. Only in the late Middle Ages did castle dwellers enjoy such refinements as windows and table linen, above.

of the Middle Ages. Even today many of the ideals of gentlemanly conduct derive from the chivalric code of medieval days.

A boy's schooling trained him for knighthood. The son of a noble began his training when, at seven years of age, his father placed him with another noble family. There he served as a page, waiting on the ladies and learning the rudiments of court etiquette. At fourteen or fifteen, he became a squire. He then waited on his lord and lady at table and studied music and poetry, but spent most of his time learning the craft of warfare. He practiced with arms, and was taught how to manage a charger, a knight's most important horse. By the time the squire was ready to become a knight, he had been instructed in the code of chivalry.

On the day before the knighting ceremony, the squire began his preparations with a solemn ritual bath. During the night he stood guard before the church altar on which his sword rested, and in the morning a priest or bishop blessed his weapon. The lord then dubbed him a "knight of the bath." A squire might also win knighthood after a battle in which he had fought gallantly; he would then become a "knight of the sword."

Jousting and tournaments were favorite sports. Jousting was a sport in which young men on horseback played at fighting, and a tournament was a free-for-all in which mounted knights charged one another in exhibition matches. Tournaments involved formal ceremonies in which banners, decorated shields, and plumed helmets added to the color of the spectacle. In the novel *Ivanhoe*, the 19th-century English writer Sir Walter Scott described a tournament:

> It was a goodly, and at the same time an anxious, sight to behold so many gallant champions, mounted bravely and armed richly, stand ready prepared for an encounter so formidable, seated on their war-saddles like so many pillars of iron, . . . As yet the knights held their long lances upright, their bright points glancing to the sun, and the streamers with which they were decorated fluttering over the plumage of the helmets. Thus they remained while the marshals of the field surveyed their ranks. . . . The marshals then withdrew from the lists, and William de Wyvil, with a voice of thunder, pronounced the signal words, *"Laissez aller!"* ["Go ahead!"] The trumpets sounded as he spoke; the spears of the champions were at once lowered and placed in the rests; the spurs were dashed into the flanks of the horses; and the two foremost ranks of either party rushed upon each other in full gallop, and met in the middle of the lists with a shock the sound of which was heard at a mile's distance.

Section Review

1. How was a noble's son trained for knighthood?
2. What standards of conduct were emphasized in the chivalric code?
3. Of what practical benefit were the games enjoyed by the nobility during the Middle Ages?

4 **The Church unified Europe**

In contrast to feudalism, which was a loosely organized and makeshift system of government, the Church boasted a strong, tightly knit organization which served as the chief unifying force in Europe throughout the Middle Ages. So thoroughly did the Church hold sway in the West that Europe was referred to as Christendom. Many of the functions of civil government were performed by the Church. Furthermore, the orders of the Church crossed political boundaries and extended into every aspect of daily life. Most Europeans swore loyalty to it, for to be outside its rule and its promise of salvation was unthinkable.

The Church had also grown immensely wealthy, its income exceeding that of all the important lay rulers put together. It was the constant recipient of large gifts of land in addition to the tithe, or tenth part of his income, that each member was required to pay to the Church.

Medieval people looked to the Church for salvation. The Church had developed a body of beliefs which everyone who became a Christian accepted. Most important were the seven sacraments: baptism, confirmation, penance, the Holy Eucharist, matrimony, holy orders, and extreme unction. The Church ruled that in partaking of baptism, a person was to become a Christian and to receive a Christian name in a christening ceremony; when the sacrament of confirmation was administered to him, he was received into the Church; by penance, a penitent wrongdoer was absolved of sins. In the celebration of the Holy Eucharist, the priest consecrated bread and wine in commemoration of the Last Supper; and marriage was recognized when it was blessed and regulated by the sacrament of matrimony. The sacrament called holy orders was conferred upon men who entered the priesthood. The sacrament of extreme unction was administered by the priest to the dying. People accepted the rule that partaking of the sacraments was essential to salvation and that the sacraments could be administered only by the clergy.

The village priest was likely to be of humble birth and with little education, but he was father confessor, social worker, policeman, and recreation director to his parishioners. The bishop was often (though not necessarily) of high social origin and had to maintain an elaborate household. As a rule he came into close personal contact only with the nobility.

During the Middle Ages the Church tried to ease the severity of warfare. By its Peace of God, inaugurated in 990, the Church cursed and banned from the sacraments all knights who pillaged sacred places or who refused to spare noncombatants. Also, in the 10th century, the Church in its Truce of God limited fighting to certain days of the week and prohibited it during certain religious seasons.

The Church enforced its rules. The Church maintained courts to help protect the weak and to punish evildoers. It also brought to trial clergymen and other persons guilty of religious offenses, judging them according to canon law, or the law of the Church. Canon law was compiled from the Scriptures, the writings of the Church Fathers, rules made by Church councils, and decrees of the popes. In time the Church issued its official body of canon law which guided Church courts.

Heresy was the most horrible of all crimes in medieval eyes. It was considered to be a crime not against society but against God, for it denied the teachings of the Church. The courts established to search for and punish heretics were designated by the name Inquisition.

The chief weapons used by the Church against offenders were excommunication, the interdict, and the deposition of rulers. Excommunication denied the services of the Church, including the sacraments, to the guilty one and forbade him association with Church members. If a heretic refused to renounce his heresy, he was turned over to civil authorities who usually burned him at the stake.

Interdict has been called a church lockout, for it was directed against the inhabitants of an entire area. To discipline a rebellious noble, all churches in his domain would be closed and most sacraments suspended. A prince thus singled out for punishment usually could not endure the pressure of his subjects to yield to the Church.

The third weapon of the Church—its right to depose rulers—was used to release subjects of a disobedient ruler from their vows of loyalty to him.

The Church became increasingly independent of lay rulers. After the fall of Rome, affairs of the Church and of new rulers, such as Clovis, had become closely intertwined. During the 8th and 9th centuries the Franks aided the popes, and churchmen took part in the coronation of kings. When officials of the Church entered into feudal contracts, they were obliged to serve both their lords and the pope or to choose between them. During the 10th century, the papacy itself depended upon a German king for protection against feudal abuses, unruly Italian nobles, and Roman mobs. This arrangement led German kings to interfere in Church affairs—even in the election of popes—in order to serve their own purposes. When a bishop or abbot assumed office, his spiritual authority was bestowed by a Church official, but his feudal authority was given by a king or noble. In Germany the king came to control the investiture of both spiritual and feudal powers.

The 11th century witnessed a great religious revival, which began at the monastic order of Cluny, founded in Burgundy in 910. Owing allegiance only to the pope, the Cluniac order spoke out against royal interference. It objected to the practice of clerics bequeathing property to their heirs rather than to the Church. It also instituted a reform program to remove all lay and feudal control over the pope, to forbid simony (buying and selling positions in the Church), and to stop interference by lay lords in the choice and investiture of bishops. In 1059 the College of Cardinals was created in Rome. Its function was to elect a successor to the pope who would be the choice of the Church, not of a king or Roman mob.

An enthusiastic supporter of reform was Pope Gregory VII, who reigned from 1073 to 1085. During his reign, the so-called investiture struggle came to a head in German lands. Gregory threatened to excommunicate any layman who tried to invest an official of the Church, or any cleric who submitted to it. Henry IV, emperor of the Holy Roman Empire, was determined that the Church should not interfere with the selection of the bishops who became his vassals. Branding some of Henry's acts illegal, Gregory excommunicated the king. When Henry defied the pope, a revolt among his barons forced him to make peace with Gregory. In 1077 he appeared at Canossa, a castle in the Apennines, dressed as a penitent, and stood barefoot in the snow three days before Gregory received him back into the Church.

In the 12th and 13th centuries the papacy and the ruling family of Germany clashed on numerous occasions. In these contests the Church was usually the winner, and its power increased under Pope Innocent III, who became the supreme overlord of Europe during his reign from 1198 to 1216. Claiming that his authority was above that of any other ruler and that the word of the Church was final, he forced King John of England to cede England to the papacy and then receive it back as a fief. He placed France under an interdict, and made vassals of the rulers of Denmark, Portugal, Poland, Hungary, and Aragon.

Religious orders were founded to strengthen the Church. During the 12th and 13th centuries, significant changes were taking place in European life. Cities and commerce were reviving, and schools and universities were being built. In response to these changes, two religious orders were inaugurated, both with the approval of Innocent III. The two orders were the Franciscan, founded by St. Francis of Assisi, and the Dominican, founded by St. Dominic. Unlike the monastic orders that renounced society, the Franciscans and Dominicans worked directly among the people. To spread the gospel and to fight heresy, their members preached in the towns and the surrounding countryside. Prominent as philosophers and theologians, the Dominicans became teachers at the universities of Paris, Bologna, and Oxford. Later, the Franciscans also became famous as educators, particularly in English universities. Both groups made a profound impact on an age that had grown critical of worldliness in the Church.

The Church urged crusaders to save the Holy Land for Christians. For hundreds of years Christians had visited the Holy Land to worship at places associated with the life of Jesus, particularly the Holy Sepulcher, where the body of Jesus was believed to have lain before the Resurrection. In the 11th century, Seljuk Turks—followers of Islam, the religion of the Moslems—swept into Palestine. By 1089 they had captured Jerusalem and were threatening Constantinople, the capital of the Byzantine Empire. This great city had long served as a bulwark against threats to western Christendom, for it was the seat of the eastern Christian Church and a strong outpost of Christian civilization. After the Byzantine emperor appealed to the pope for help, Pope Urban II called a council in 1095 to meet in Clermont, where he urged the thousands of knights present to "take up the Cross" and become crusaders, a word that means "marked with the cross." As a reward for driving the Moslems out of the Holy Land, the pope promised the crusaders forgiveness of their sins, a choice of fiefs in the land to be conquered, and freedom from their creditors. His stirring appeal generated tremendous enthusiasm. As the pope closed his speech, the audience roared, "God wills it!" Many knights were moved to become crusaders because of religious idealism; others enlisted for adventure, to escape debts or the long arm of the law, or to gain wealth.

The crusades began in 1096 and continued until nearly the end of the 13th century. Although the series of military operations involved are referred to as separate crusades, all of them were part of one continuous conflict against the Moslems. The First Crusade, led by princes and feudal barons from France, included 3000 knights and four times that many infantry. In 1099 the crusaders captured Jerusalem and created the Latin Kingdom of Jerusalem with Godfrey of Bouillon as ruler and defender of the Holy Sepulcher. The kingdom—a narrow strip of territory little more than fifty miles wide along the Mediterranean Sea—was divided into four great fiefs, sometimes referred to as the Crusader States. These principalities were then further subdivided into many smaller fiefs.

Within fifty years' time, the Turkish seizure of strategic cities in the Near East brought about another crusade. The Second Crusade was led by Conrad III of Germany and Louis VII of France in 1147, but it failed to accomplish anything of importance.

The recapture of Jerusalem in 1187 by the Moslem leader, Saladin, stimulated the Third Crusade, led by Frederick Barbarossa of Germany, Philip Augustus of France, and Richard the Lion-Hearted of England. Misfortune dogged this enterprise. On the way to Jerusalem, Frederick was drowned. Richard and Philip were in constant disagreement, and Philip returned home after Acre was captured in 1191. Richard fought with gallantry and courage, and in 1192 he secured the right for Christians to visit Jerusalem without fear of

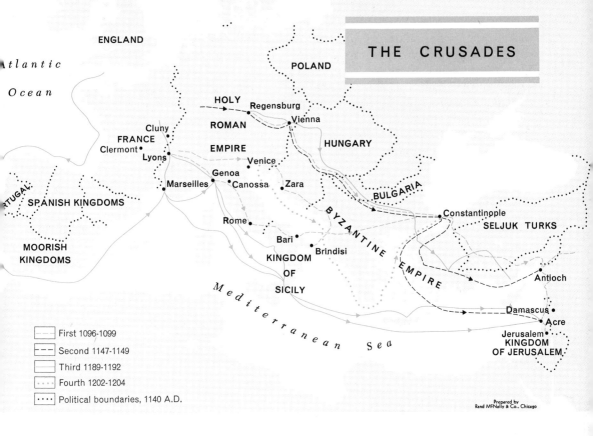

First 1096-1099
Second 1147-1149
Third 1189-1192
Fourth 1202-1204
Political boundaries, 1140 A.D.

Prepared by
Rand McNally & Co., Chicago

harm. For this slight gain, the Third Crusade paid dearly in human lives. More than
300 thousand men perished.

In 1202 a Fourth Crusade began, but
instead of fighting the Turks, the crusaders
captured and sacked Constantinople,
where they set up their own government,
the Latin Empire. When they were ejected
from their ill-gotten lands in 1261, the
Byzantine Empire was restored, but it
never wholly recovered from the blow
dealt it by the Fourth Crusade.

In the 13th century, other crusades and
various minor expeditions were under-
taken, including the tragic Children's Crusade, which began in 1212. In the belief
that the Turks could be routed without
fighting, the children enlisted under the
sign of the Cross. Most of them had no
idea of the perils of their undertaking and,

though many turned back before leaving
Europe, others were sold into slavery by
heartless Christian merchants at Marseilles.

After the Fourth Crusade, the survival
of the Crusader States was perilous. Even
though the roads and passes were well
guarded, Moslem pressure proved too great
for the knights to withstand. The year 1291
saw the fall of Acre, the last Christian
stronghold in the Near East, an event that
marked the end of the crusades.

Although the Holy Land was lost to
Christendom, the crusades cannot be written off as a series of military campaigns
that ultimately failed. In truth, they had a
wide and lasting effect upon European life.
Contact with the Near East ended the isolation of Europeans and exposed them to
a civilization in many ways superior to their
own.

New foods and fabrics were brought back from Moslem lands and the knowledge of the peoples and geography of the Near East enriched European culture. By depleting the ranks of the nobles, the crusades weakened feudalism and thereby contributed indirectly to the rise of royal power in western Europe. The crusades also reduced obstacles to widespread commerce and assisted indirectly in the growth of great ports and the rise of cities.

Section Review

1. In what respects was the Church the outstanding organization of the Middle Ages?

2. How did lay and Church government become intertwined? How did the question of supreme authority affect Church and lay rulers during the Middle Ages?

3. What was the primary purpose of the crusades? What gains were made?

4. How did the crusades benefit Europe?

Chapter 6   A Review

After the death of Charlemagne, the division of his realm and the invasions by Vikings, Slavs, and Moslems weakened the Carolingian Empire. Unable to maintain order, kings parceled out landholdings to nobles who promised loyalty and military service in return. The arrangements, or feudal contracts, between lords and vassals developed into a form of government called feudalism. It maintained a degree of law and order in a time of violence.

The manorial system formed the economic pattern of medieval times. As a rule, the manor was a self-sufficient unit, upon which the serfs worked indoors and outdoors for their lord in exchange for protection against robbers and invaders. Although peasant freemen enjoyed a measure of independence, serfs belonged to the land along with the livestock.

Social groupings were fixed in medieval times, the nobility being the privileged class. The armed knight, a member of the nobility, was trained for knighthood and chivalric conduct from early childhood.

The Church was the one unifying influence in western Europe during medieval times. The people looked to it for spiritual salvation, and its laws extended even to secular affairs. Through its own system of courts, the Church strengthened its position and used effective methods to enforce its laws. There were many clashes between kings and the papacy, but the Church usually won these contests for supremacy. The Church was a prime force in the lengthy conflict with the Moslems. Although few long-term territorial gains resulted from the crusades of the 11th, 12th, and 13th centuries, this series of military campaigns helped break down the isolation of medieval times.

The Time

Some of the events named below are correctly placed under the period during which they occurred, and others are not. Rearrange the list so that all events appear in their proper time span.

801-1000

The Treaty of Verdun divided the Carolingian Empire.

The Vikings began to invade Europe.

The Church inaugurated the Peace of God.

An investiture struggle took place between Gregory VII and Henry IV.

1001-1100

The College of Cardinals was created.

The last of the Carolingian rulers of East Frankland died.

The Seljuk Turks captured Jerusalem.

The First Crusade began.

1101-1200

Innocent III began his reign as pope.

The Cluniac order was founded.

The last of the Carolingian rulers of West Frankland died.

Saladin recaptured Jerusalem.

1201-1300

The Third Crusade began.

Urban II called the Council of Clermont.

Crusaders on the Fourth Crusade established the Latin Empire.

The period of the crusades ended with the fall of Acre to the Turks.

The Place

1. What nations or parts of nations of Europe today occupy the area that was included in the kingdom of Louis the German? of Charles the Bald? of Lothair?

2. Show on a map the Carolingian lands that were attacked by the following invaders: Vikings, Moslems, Magyars, Slavs. In what area did the Magyars settle? the Vikings who became Normans?

3. Which crusades followed primarily overland routes? sea routes? Why was Constantinople of strategic importance to the crusaders?

4. Locate the following places and name one event associated with each: Canossa, Cluny, Acre, Clermont, Jerusalem.

The People

1. How did each of the following persons raise the prestige of the medieval Church?

Gregory VII   Innocent III
St. Dominic   St. Francis of Assisi
Urban II

2. Identify each of the following men by naming the country or people over which he ruled and the crusade with which he is associated.

Godfrey of Bouillon   Saladin
Frederick Barbarossa   Philip Augustus
Richard the Lion-Hearted

Historical Terms

1. Show how each of the following practices was a forerunner of feudalism: *precarium, comitatus, beneficium.*

2. Explain each of the following terms as applied to the feudal system.

subinfeudation   feudal law   homage
feudal contract   benefice   fief
investiture   vassalage

3. Define each of the following terms as applied to the medieval manorial system.

manor   fallow   reeve
domain   steward   serfs
demesne   bailiff   freemen

4. What parts of the medieval castle were these: keep, moat, portcullis?

5. Explain each of the terms below as applied to knighthood.

knight of the bath   page   squire
knight of the sword   chivalry   jousting
tournament

6. What were the seven sacraments of the medieval Church?

7. Define each of the following terms as applied to the beliefs and practices of the medieval Church.

Peace of God   Inquisition
Truce of God   heresy
College of Cardinals   interdict
excommunication   simony
canon law   tithe
deposition of rulers

8. Explain each of the terms below as applied to the period of the crusades.

Seljuk Turks   Islam
Council of Clermont   crusader
Holy Sepulcher   Latin Empire
Latin Kingdom of Jerusalem

Questions for Critical Thinking

1. What aspects of the feudal and manorial systems seemed to stifle progress?

2. Why did the crusades have the effect of weakening the feudal system?

3. How did the development of chivalry among feudal nobles contribute to medieval society?

4. How did the involvement of the Church in the feudal system create conflicts between Church authorities and state rulers?

5. What conditions in 9th-century Europe made it difficult for the successors of Charlemagne to maintain a strong government?

6. In what ways did the Church act as a counterbalance to the warfare and lack of political unity within the feudal states of western Europe?

The Growth of Medieval Towns

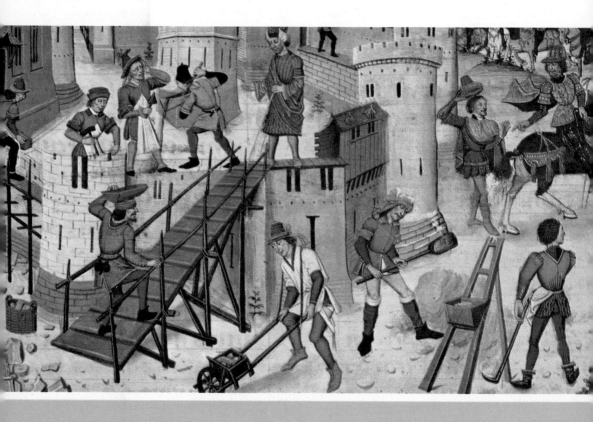

During the later Middle Ages, the town replaced the manor as the center of economic, social, and cultural life. Surrounded by thick walls, like the one being built above, towns afforded protection to merchants and provided a lively atmosphere for the exchange of ideas. Artists and scholars, no longer forced to take shelter in monasteries, benefited from the contacts which urban living offered.

He wore a forked beard and a beaver hat
From Flanders. High up in the saddle he sat,
In figured cloth, his boots clasped handsomely,
Delivering his opinions pompously,
Always on how his gains might be increased.
At all costs he desired the sea policed
From Middleburg in Holland to Orwell.
He knew the exchange rates, and the time to sell
French currency, and there was never yet
A man who could have told he was in debt
So grave he seemed and hid so well his feelings
With all his shrewd engagements and close dealings.
You'll find no better man at any turn;
But what his name was I could never learn.

This well-dressed, self-assured figure was a merchant and one of the characters that Geoffrey Chaucer, an English poet of the 14th century, included in his masterpiece, *The Canterbury Tales*. Whether or not Chaucer was describing a real person is unimportant except to literary scholars. To the student of history, the importance of the anonymous merchant is that in action and speech he is typical of a new group in medieval society—the middle class.

In 11th-century Europe, when trade began to expand beyond the local markets of the manor and town life revived, the middle class grew in strength and numbers. Often referred to by the French term, the *bourgeoisie*, this group was made up of carpenters, weavers, and other craftsmen as well as merchants. The wealth that the bourgeoisie accumulated enabled the most successful of them to live in mansions as good or better than those of princes. The positions of authority they attained ultimately made them rivals of feudal lords.

In some respects the medieval bourgeoisie may be compared to the shrewd merchants of ancient Egypt and Babylonia. They were as enterprising as the traders and craftsmen of Greece who supported tyrants in order to break the power of the landed aristocracy. And they came to wield authority in municipal governments, as did merchants in the days of the Roman Empire. But the comparison is incomplete. The middle class men of the medieval period differed in the ways used to obtain political power. They pooled their resources to purchase their freedom from feudal restrictions and to set up towns. Within the towns, they organized their own forms of government. Often, a group of towns banded together in a trade association. In short, the bourgeoisie worked together to achieve a common goal. Chapter 7 tells how:

1. **Town life revived in the later Middle Ages.**

2. **Education and learning advanced.**

3. **Literature and the arts expressed the spirit of medieval times.**

1 Town life revived in the later Middle Ages

From about 500 A.D. to the beginning of the 10th century, the economic life of western Europe was almost entirely agricultural. After the fall of Rome, cities within the empire slipped into varying degrees of decay. With the exception of the city-states of Venice, Florence, Genoa, and others in Italy, most of the former cities served chiefly to provide markets for local church administrations. The manors included a small group of peasant huts, but these villages, under the control of the feudal lord, were not towns. During the 10th and 11th centuries, as a result of a variety of factors, new towns and cities began to appear on the European landscape.

Hanseatic League
Trade Area

Prepared by
Rand McNally & Co., Chi

The resurgence of trade began in Italy.
After the collapse of the Roman Empire,
the trade between Europe and the East
was reduced to a trickle. Even trade between various regions of Europe itself was
reduced sharply. Because feudal estates in
Europe provided most of what was needed
for the lord and his household, there was
no impetus for a revival of trade. Furthermore, travel between distant points was
hindered by lack of roads and by highway
robbers, while pirates and unskilled crews
made travel by sea hazardous and uncertain. In addition, Moslems had won control of the Mediterranean during the 7th
century, and they monopolized most of the
commerce on the sea for 400 years.

The international trade that did exist
was chiefly in the hands of the Venetians.

This community of over a hundred islands
had become a republic in the 7th century,
with a *doge*, or duke, as leader. Through a
monopoly of the salt-fish trade, the inhabitants grew prosperous; and in the 9th century they formed the city of Venice. As
their wealth increased, so did their power,
and by the 11th century Venice controlled
the Adriatic Sea. In another hundred years,
Italian ships were calling at most Mediterranean ports.

After the Fourth Crusade, which ended
in 1204, the volume of trade between Venice and the Near East became greater than
any that had existed up to that time. The
goods flowing in from the East could not
be consumed entirely by the Italians, and
merchants began to transport their wares
by armed caravans over the Alpine passes

into northern Europe, where they found eager buyers at the feudal castles.

The first great trading system moved from east to west. Exports from India and China were brought to ports on the Persian Gulf and the Red Sea. From there they were taken by caravan to Alexandria in Egypt or to the seaports of Acre and Joppa, where ships picked them up and carried them to northern Italy. Another trading system tied regions of western Europe to the northern and eastern parts of the Continent. English wool, Flemish cloth, and the Oriental luxuries were traded for raw materials of the Baltic region, such as tar, fur, hides, and timber. Established by the Vikings in the 9th century was a third trade route, which followed along Russian rivers to the Black Sea and Constantinople.

Later, in the 13th and 14th centuries, other regional and international trade lanes developed on land and sea. Large fleets of galleys from Venice, Genoa, and other Italian towns defied pirates and rode out heavy storms to bring goods to England and to northern Europe. The revival of international trade was important in the growth of towns, and in turn the towns stimulated trade.

Trade fairs became an important feature of the European economy. It was common for serfs on the manors to barter home-manufactured products and surplus farm produce in the local market, held weekly in the open squares before castles or churches. As the volume of nonlocal trade began to increase, feudal lords set up fairs. These fairs not only became meeting places for merchants from all over Europe, but also brought an income to the lords through rents for space, taxes, and fines. Fairs differed from the local market, for they were great annual events. The custom of the yearly fair probably originated in the province of Champagne in northeastern France, and was well established in the

12th century. Troyes, a town in Champagne, held one of the largest fairs.

Regular laws of the region were set aside during the weeks of the fair and in their place was substituted a code called the "law merchant," or commercial law. Disputes were settled in special courts, which in France were called *pied poudre,* or "dusty foot" courts, because the shoes of the jurists and of the people in the courts were often dusty from the fairgrounds. In England, the term became pie-powder courts.

The fair provided a clearing house for both goods and ideas, as men from all over Europe exchanged information about arts and crafts, agriculture, and transportation. Leipzig and Frankfort, Venice and Genoa, Ypres and Lille also were scenes of famous fairs.

The use of money replaced the practice of barter. The trade fair played an important role in the development of a money economy. Barter had been a common practice during the early Middle Ages. For the most part, Church officials, kings, and lords hoarded precious metals; to them, the possession of gold and silver symbolized power. Although they could mint their own coins, there was little money in general use.

At the medieval fairs, money changers set up booths, where they not only converted coins of one kind to another, but also guarded sums which people deposited with them for safekeeping. Sometimes they lent money to those who attended the fair, charging interest. *Usury,* the practice of making a profit by lending money, was forbidden by the Church; and usurers who charged prohibitive fees were severely punished. In time laws were established to allow a just rate of interest, and the Church accepted the system.

As coins became a common feature of business life, simple forms of banking and credit appeared—first among the Lombards and Florentines in Italy. The important process of transferring funds was invented. By this means a man could deposit money in a bank and, with the receipt given him, he could collect an equal amount of money at a branch office of the bank in another city. The use of money helped break down the isolation of the feudal period.

Town sites were determined by several factors. Rivers were natural highways for transporting articles of trade, and many communities grew along important streams. Other towns were established where two streams joined or where there was a ford, bridge, or dam, such as *Ox-ford* in England, *Pont-oise* (bridge over the Oise) in France, or *Amster-dam* (dam on the Amstel) in the Netherlands.

Many towns began near the walls of a fortification, such as a castle. An example was the town begun in the 10th century around the castle of Count Baldwin Iron-Arm. The record reads:

> After this castle was built, certain traders began to flock to the place in front of the gate to the bridge of the castle, that is, merchants, tavernkeepers, then other outsiders drifted in for the sake of the food and shelter of those who might have business transactions with the count, who often came there. Houses and inns were erected for their accommodation, since there was not room for them within the chateau. These habitations increased so rapidly that soon a large ville [town] came into being which is called Brugghe [Bruges] by the people from the word for bridge.

Townsmen, like lords, built walls around the town for protection. As population increased, the houses and other buildings inside the walls grew more numerous and were crowded together. The rich and influential had the choice places inside the walls. The outer community was known as a *faubourg*, a French word meaning "outside the burg." ("Burg" originally meant a fortification and in time came to mean the town or city itself.) In Latin, the area was called *suburbium*, that is, "close to the urb, or city," or "a suburb." In time a suburb was often enclosed by a new wall, and the old one torn down. This process continued over and over again, and many medieval cities show marks of how their boundaries expanded.

Towns became increasingly independent of feudal control. All towns did not begin at the same time, of course. Nor did they advance at the same pace, become self-sufficient when others did, or win freedom in the same way. Many of the new towns had been established on the lands of feudal lords and were subject to their control and taxation. The townspeople resented the lords' demands, for they were not bound to a manor as were serfs.

Freedom was won by a few cities as early as the 11th century. Cologne in Germany, for example, won independence from a feudal bishop after a rebellion in 1075. In 1176 Lombard cities in Italy won freedom when they fought against Frederick I of Germany and defeated him at Legnano. However, rebellion was not the usual form of gaining independence. For the most part, freedom was won gradually. Often townspeople united to obtain grants and finally to win a charter that guaranteed independence.

Monarchs granted many charters to towns. The taxes a town paid to a king increased his wealth and therefore his power over the nobles. Increase of royal power ultimately strengthened central government and was a strong factor in the breakdown of feudalism.

When a town charter was won, it often benefited only the inner circle of merchants and craftsmen who made the local laws and who had led the movement for freedom. However, in German towns, serfs who escaped from the manors could establish themselves as freemen if they lived in a chartered town for a year plus one day. This custom encouraged many serfs to run away to cities for, as the saying went among them, "City air makes free."

Merchants and craftsmen organized guilds. Usually, the privileged citizens of a town were members of a guild. At a time when central government was inadequate, merchants had set up organizations to regulate business dealings within a city. The merchant guilds ruled that none but members might sell merchandise within certain areas, and in this way they enjoyed a monopoly of the trade in their localities. Their courts settled disputes and judged and sentenced dishonest members. For example, the court decided that John Penrose, a vintner, or wine merchant, should

> drink a draught of the same wine which he sold to the common people; and the remainder of such wine shall then be poured on the head of the same John; and that he shall forswear the calling of a vintner in the city of London forever. . . .

The guilds assisted needy members, built homes for the poor, and conducted banquets and other events in the guildhall.

Craftsmen had their own guilds, as did the merchants. Each craft had its own organization, with the goldsmiths in one, the arrow makers in another, the shoemakers in another, and so on. Anyone not a member of a specific guild was forbidden to engage in the craft of that guild. The system created such a degree of specialization that members of one guild might be able to make only one kind of hat.

To become a member, a worker began when a youth to serve three to twelve years as an apprentice to a master craftsman. He lived in the master's house, and although he received no wages, his food and clothing were supplied. When his schooling was completed, the youth became a journeyman (from the French *journee*, meaning "day's work") and was eligible to receive wages. Usually at the age of twenty-three, a journeyman could seek admission to a master guild. He might be required to present a sample of his work, and if this sample, or *master piece*, won approval, he might then have to set up a shop, a costly undertaking. As rules for admission to master guilds grew more strict, journeymen organized associations of their own.

Towns and guilds made treaties and alliances with other towns and guilds, extending privileges to their merchants and ensuring mutual defense against pirates and rival cities. One of these trade organizations, known as the Hanseatic League, was a loose federation founded on alliances. By the late 14th century, it included coastal and river towns in Germany, Scandinavia, England, and Russia. Its monopoly of the Baltic and North seas trade made it one of the greatest trade associations in northern Europe during medieval times.

A new class of people arose in western Europe. With the rise of towns and the expansion of trade and industry, a powerful class of people had developed in Europe. Unlike the nobility, their interest was in business rather than war, and they were referred to as men of the burg, that is, *burghers*, or the *bourgeoisie*. At the top of the scale were the prosperous merchants and bankers. Their sons attended the universities and became eminent professional men, even advisers to kings. Feudal lords looked down their noses on the middle class as mere upstarts, but the bourgeoisie continued to prosper. They became patrons of the arts and established a kind of nobility of their own. In turn, they were contemptuous of those beneath them on the social scale, such as the skilled workers.

Medieval Town Life

Medieval towns were bustling centers of commercial activity. From stores which opened directly onto the streets, merchants enticed strolling shoppers. In the picture at right, tailors cut and stitch clothes in a shop festooned with finished garments. A barber, beneath a display of bowls used in his trade, shaves a customer. On sale at a grocery are tarts and sugar from a large loaf. Both merchants and craftsmen, like the cloth dyers below left, formed guilds to protect and maintain high standards in commerce and industry. Perhaps the craftsmen below with various tools—spades, hammers, and saws—are discussing important issues of their different guilds.

As a result of greater commercial activity, money replaced the barter system. With the increased use of money came thieves known as cutpurses, the medieval counterparts of pickpockets. The one at left is caught by a law officer while slashing the purse strings of a passer-by. New economic conditions also provided for more leisure time. Amusements for townspeople ranged from comic puppet shows, above left, to crude bearbaiting, below right on the opposite page. In the latter, enjoyed by all classes, dogs were set upon a chained bear.

Thus, class distinctions were developing along lines of wealth rather than birth.

The bourgeoisie were the city landholders, and while they hired former serfs, they withheld from them the right to own land in the cities, to hold political office, or to vote. Thus they consolidated their power.

Other factors aided the development of towns. The recovery of trade was of prime importance to the growth of towns, but other strong forces also contributed to this movement.

Changes in agriculture had a marked effect on town growth. Improved farm methods and technology increased food production, bettered living standards, and contributed to an increase in population. At the same time, technological progress reduced the number of persons needed to do the work on the manors. For example, the use of water power to drive mills, invented before the time of Christ, came into common use in Europe about the time of the crusades. Three inventions, perfected in Europe during the 10th century, helped transportation and farming: (1) the tandem harness made possible the use of horses in teams; (2) the horse collar shifted weight from the horse's neck to its shoulders and permitted it to pull heavy loads without being choked; (3) horseshoes improved traction and protected the horse's hoofs.

At the beginning of the 11th century more land became available for cultivation when forests were cleared, swamps drained, and land reclaimed from the sea. The lords who developed many of these wilderness lands needed laborers to dig ditches, build dikes, cut timber, and uproot tree stumps. To enlist workers, the lords promised serfs freedom from feudal obligations and the right to rent land at fixed fees. The serf with a little money in his pocket could now bargain with the lord and decide for himself whether to remain on the manor or move to the town.

As towns gained independence and grew in political stability, city living became increasingly desirable and serfs continued to leave the manors. This exodus of the Middle Ages, extending over hundreds of years, constituted one of the great social, political, and economic revolutions of history.

Town life had attractions and limitations. In their early stages, towns were so rural in character that to leave the country and live in a city did not deprive one of fresh air which was part of country living. Even in the country, houses were built close together for protection and warmth. In the cities, rows of houses served as a protective wall, while the gardens they surrounded provided space for recreation and food. The home of a burgher might house his shop, workrooms, and the family's living quarters.

In crowded cities, opportunities to acquire wealth, personal freedom, and improved status outweighed discomforts and dangers, which increased when populations within city walls grew dense. The narrow streets barely allowed two horsemen to pass, but their crooked routes protected pedestrians and riders from cold winter winds. The streets also were likely to be dark, but the overhanging top stories of the houses helped guard against the hot sun and the rain.

As cities grew larger, public health and safety laws began to appear. Fireproof roofing was required of builders in Lübeck after 1276, and in 1388, England forbade people to throw waste into ditches and rivers.

Very few persons could boast of running water in their homes, but water from wells, springs, and rivers was piped to central fountains, and public and private bathhouses were in wide use from the

1300's on. Paris began to pave its streets in 1185, and all the streets of Florence were paved by 1339.

In 1348 and 1349 a pestilence called the Black Death ravaged Europe, spreading by way of the trade routes and appearing at its worst in the cities. More people died during this plague than in any other epidemic, and some medieval records say that cities lost almost 50 per cent of their population. Even so, by the middle of the 15th century, 150 cities in Germany had populations up to 35 thousand. London had 40 thousand and Brussels 35 thousand, while Paris had grown to 300 thousand.

Section Review

1. What effect did the resurgence of trade between Europe and the East have on the growth of towns?
2. What was the function of the medieval fairs? How did they encourage the use of money?
3. How were some town sites determined?
4. Describe the circumstances which enabled towns to win independence. What purposes did the guilds serve?
5. What changes in social relationships accompanied the rise of towns?
6. What factors other than trade accounted for the development of towns?
7. What were some of the appeals and dangers of town life?

2 **Education and learning advanced**

Following the fall of Rome, the Church took over the few schools that existed in western Europe in order to prepare young men for holy orders. Because many of the nobility disdained the "unmanly" skills of reading and writing, young nobles trained chiefly for warfare. The isolation and disorder of the times also worked against the spread of learning. As a result, formal education (except for the clergy) had almost disappeared in Europe by 600 A.D.

Charlemagne was a notable patron of learning. To preserve the purity of its teachings, the Church attempted to destroy paganism and pagan literature. By so doing, many of the classical works of the Greeks and Romans from the pre-Christian era were destroyed. Even though some monasteries maintained a study of Latin and Greek, a general decline in classical learning began, affecting such branches of study as science, linguistics, literature, and philosophy. By the 7th century, medieval culture reached its lowest point, and very little advance was made until the time of Charlemagne.

However, monks in Ireland had pursued a study of the classics and had carried their learning into parts of England, Scotland, and Germany. In the 8th century, Charlemagne brought scholars, such as Alcuin of England, to his court. They were put to work to improve the literacy of the Frankish clergy and to prevent careless alterations in classical and Biblical manuscripts. Charlemagne also encouraged the development of architecture and the advancement of art.

Historical and biographical writing revived under royal patronage. Paul the Deacon, an Italian monk, wrote the *History of the Lombards*, and Charlemagne's secretary, Einhard, wrote a biography of the great emperor. These authors, like many of the scholars who came to Charlemagne's court, wrote in Latin. The emperor also wished to develop a literature in the native tongue of his people, and he directed the collecting of old German songs and began the compilation of a German grammar.

The rebirth of learning that Charlemagne inspired in the 8th century has been called the Carolingian Renaissance, or revival. Many schools that sprang up during this revival of learning died out after Charlemagne's death, but students of his scholars became teachers, and a few of the monastic schools later became the bases for universities. Most of the oldest Latin manuscripts that exist today were made in Charlemagne's centers of learning.

The Moslems in Spain achieved a high level of cultural development. After the Moslem Arabs gained control of the Mediterranean, they invaded Spain in 711 and conquered it seven years later.

Moslem culture had been enriched by contacts with Hindus in India, with Near Eastern peoples, and with Greeks. When the Arabs came to Spain, they were already in possession of a rich body of learning and practical knowledge. To Spain they brought new foods, such as rice and sugar, and introduced water-driven mills and advanced methods of agriculture. Their manufacture of wine and olive oil became successful industries; their linens, silks, leather goods, weapons, glass, and tapestries were unmatched elsewhere in Europe. Cordova, the capital of Moslem Spain, had a population of more than a million. Upper-class homes had balconies, marble fountains, and marble baths with running hot and cold water.

Learning thrived in this atmosphere of prosperity. Education was available to all who could afford it, and most men of the upper classes could read and write. Cordova became the intellectual center of the western world.

A group of Christians in northern Spain had survived the Moslem invasions of the 8th century. Gathering strength through the ensuing years, they began a reconquest, or *Reconquista,* of Spain in the 11th century. After they gained control of most of Spain, many European scholars came there to study, and Averroës, a famous Arab philosopher who lived from 1126 to 1198, became a teacher of Christian students. Many classical works became available to Euro-

peans through his translations of Greek writings, especially those of Aristotle, and they had a profound influence in Europe.

Universities were established throughout Europe. During the 1100's, the rise of cities and of a wealthy middle class, monastic reforms, and contact with other cultures acted as stimulants to the growth of learning in Europe. The Church, which had grown steadily in wealth, power, and size, needed trained lawyers for its courts and for drawing up documents. Kings and princes also needed men trained in civic matters. To meet these demands, teachers and students formed organizations comparable to craft guilds with their masters and apprentices. These guilds of learners were called *universities,* and early ones were poorly organized with no definite courses of study, no permanent buildings, and few rules. In time they were granted charters by kings and by popes, which gave them legal status. Certain rights were also granted to students, such as freedom from military service and from the jurisdiction of town officials. One famous university was established at Bologna (about 1158) and another at Paris (about 1200).

Bologna gained a reputation for the study of law, and its students were often professional men and government officials. The student guilds controlled the administration of the university, hired teachers, and made the rules for the school. At Paris, the university had grown from a cathedral school. It was attended by young boys, and its government was headed by a chancellor, with rules made by teachers and other adult authorities. Both systems influenced the organization of other universities.

The faculties or departments into which the universities were divided included arts, theology, medicine, and law. A student was awarded a bachelor's degree after about three years and a master's degree after a total of eight years. The master's degree permitted him to teach and, with four to eight years further study, he won a doctor's degree. Because the governments and the Church employed so many people, theology and law were valuable vocational subjects. The study of law was so popular by the 13th century that many schools were devoted almost entirely to that field.

Classrooms were cold in winter, and students wore heavy gowns and hoods and sat on floors covered with straw for warmth. They attended one or two classes every day, each class several hours long. Lectures began at dawn, with breakfast in the late morning as the only break until four or five o'clock in the afternoon. Once darkness fell, studies were discontinued, for candles were expensive. Youths sometimes spent their evenings drinking, gambling, or fighting. Their conflicts with townspeople over students' rights led to quarrels, referred to as town-and-gown riots.

Scholars argued over basic truths. During the Middle Ages, scholars were deeply concerned over conflicts between faith and reason. Early teachers of logic were often criticized by the Church. After the writings of Aristotle became more widely circulated among Europeans, his philosophy and the teachings of the Church became the two great influences on medieval thinking. Some scholars argued that Aristotle's teachings were contrary to those of the Church. Others attempted to apply the logic of Aristotle to Church teachings. They believed that the Christian religion could be better understood in the light of Aristotle. The term *Scholasticism* came to be associated with the latter group.

Pierre Abélard was a Scholastic of the 12th century. His lectures drew so many students to the cathedral schools of Paris that the beginning of the university there is often credited to him. In his work, *Yes and No*, he presented opposing opinions concerning faith and reason. The most fa-

MEDIEVAL UNIVERSITIES

Uppsala

St. Andrews

Copenhagen

Cambridge
Oxford
Cologne
Erfurt
Cracow
Prague
Paris
Heidelberg
Vienna
Basel
Budapest
Pecs
Turin
Pavia
Padua
Ferrara
Montpellier
Bologna
Siena
Valladolid
Toulouse
Pisa
Perugia
Coimbra
Salamanca
Rome
Naples
Palma
Salerno
Seville
Catania

● Organized like University of Paris
● Organized like University of Bologna

Prepared by
Rand McNally & Co., Chicago

mous of the Scholastics was St. Thomas Aquinas, who lived from about 1225 to 1274. He joined the Dominican order as a youth and became a brilliant lecturer and writer. Some of the great Christian hymns of the Middle Ages were composed by him. During his lifetime the controversy between faith and reason reached its height. St. Thomas disagreed with the extremists on either side, and through his writings and teachings he attempted to resolve the conflict. According to St. Thomas, man's reason and his faith are both gifts of God, and certain truths can be understood by man's powers of reasoning; other truths, basic to Christianity, can be perceived only by faith. So convincing were his arguments that his work, the *Summa Theologica*

FINNISH

MEDIEVAL LANGUAGE GROUPS

CELTIC

GERMANIC

SLAVIC

HUNGARIAN

ROMANCE

ROMANCE

BASQUE

TURKISH

HELLENIC

(The Highest Theology) is still an authority for Roman Catholic teaching.

Scientific knowledge made some progress in the later Middle Ages. The Greek and Arab works that flowed into Europe, particularly after the beginning of the 12th century, made up a rich legacy of scientific knowledge. Arabic numerals and the zero symbol made possible the decimal system of computation. Algebra from the Arabs, trigonometry from the Moslems, and Euclid's *Geometry* increased the scope and accuracy of mathematics.

Roger Bacon, an English monk of the 13th century, criticized the methods of the Scholastics and recommended that learning be based upon observation and experience. As a result, he was attacked by many learned men of his day and toward the end of his life, he was imprisoned for fifteen years and his works were condemned. In one of his famous statements, he said:

> There are four principal stumbling blocks to comprehending truth, which hinder wellnigh every scholar: the example of frail and unworthy authority, long-established customs, the sense of the ignorant crowd, and the hiding of one's ignorance under the show of wisdom.

It was Roger Bacon who prophesied the coming of power-driven ships, cars, and flying machines.

In the 12th century the mariner's compass was invented, followed by the invention of a rudder for a ship in about 1300. The 14th century also saw the introduction of the blast furnace and progress in ironworking. Greek and Arab treatises on biology were popular among medieval doctors, whose techniques were improved through this knowledge.

Section Review

Section Review
1. What contributions did Charlemagne make to the preservation of learning?
2. To what degree did the level of culture in Moslem Spain differ from that in northern parts of Europe during the 9th and 10th centuries?
3. What helped stimulate the rise of universities in medieval Europe? What were the basic differences between the two most famous medieval universities?
4. How did the wide circulation of the teachings of Aristotle influence medieval thinking?
5. Name some of the advances made in science during the Middle Ages.

---

3 **Literature and the arts expressed the spirit of medieval times**

The isolation that had settled over the whole of Europe during feudal times began to break down under the influences of city life, international trade, and contact with other cultures. The revival of interest in education stimulated expression in literature and in the arts. The Church remained the dominant influence, and literature, music, and architecture for the most part were characterized by religious themes.

Popular languages replaced Latin. The educated people of the Middle Ages used the Latin language as a means of communication. Virtually all literature—including documents and treatises of the Church, the government, and the schools—was in Latin. The common people heard classical Latin spoken in their churches, but the majority of Europeans could neither speak nor understand it. They used the speech that was native to their locality.

As in all languages, modifications of Latin went on constantly. Changes appeared gradually in the meanings of words, the structure of sentences, and the accents of speech. The greater the distance between groups, the greater the difference in their speech, or native tongues. The native tongues, or vernaculars, formed the basis of the languages used today in various countries. French, Italian, Spanish, and Portuguese vernaculars became the foundation of the Romance languages. The Latin original and its variations can be seen clearly in the English words *mountain, lunar,* and *chant.*

LATIN	ITALIAN	FRENCH	SPANISH
mons	montagna	montagne	montaña
luna	luna	lune	luna
cantare	cantare	chanter	cantar

Hundreds of English words derive from Latin, though the major influence upon English was Germanic. Germanic vernaculars became the foundation of the Dutch and Scandinavian tongues as well as of the modern German language, and Germanic and Latin vernaculars influenced each other. Several hundred Germanic words crept into the Romance languages from the time of the earliest barbarian invasions, while contact with the Arab and Near East countries brought in words from the Greek, Persian, and Arabic languages as well.

Medieval literature took many forms. Latin was the vehicle for poetry, as shown in the great hymns of the Middle Ages, and also for less serious works, such as the saucy Goliardic poetry composed by university students. This poetry, named perhaps after a legendary writer, Archbishop Golias, described the joys of wine, love, and song in a gay, irreverent, and sometimes shocking manner. Wandering students sang Goliardic verses in exchange for food and shelter.

Medieval Art, usually inspired by the Church, took many forms. The gilt book cover above bound a medieval manuscript of the Gospels; precious jewels and enamel inlays surround the central figure of Christ. Members of the holy family are dressed in contemporary style in the 15th-century Flemish wood carving on the facing page. This type of sculpture often decorated the altars of Gothic cathedrals, like the one at Amiens, below. Typical Gothic features include the round rose window, pointed arches, and triple doors. The tapestry at right above depicts chivalrous courtship in an idyllic forest. Not merely decorative, tapestries also served to shield castle rooms from chill drafts. Below right is a book illustration of a moral fable in which a flying fish, representing people with good intentions but few accomplishments, races unsuccessfully with a ship that symbolizes the perseverance of those who work hard.

The earliest form of vernacular literature was the epic, which described the adventures of great heroes. *Beowulf,* written in the Anglo-Saxon vernacular in the 8th century, is an example of an early epic. Others, composed in Scandinavia, date from about 900 to 1250 A.D. *The Song of the Nibelungs* appeared in German in the 13th century. In French, epics called *chansons de geste* told chiefly of the great deeds of Charlemagne and his knights. *The Song of Roland* dates from the 11th century and describes the heroic death of a Christian knight fighting against the Moslems in Spain. The Christian-Moslem struggle is also recounted in the Spanish epic, *El Cid.*

The troubadours of southern France composed a type of poetry in the vernacular, which was sung to the accompaniment of a lute. They praised the beauties of nature, the loveliness of fair ladies, and the supremacy of love. The word *minstrel* has its origin in the Latin term for minister, or servant, and minstrels served as entertainers, traveling from one castle or manor to another. In Germany, their counterparts were known as *minnesingers,* from the German words *minne* (love) and *singen* (to sing). Minnesingers were often members of the lower nobility who posed as wandering musicians in order to sing messages to high-born ladies.

After the 12th century, literary expression in the localized languages gained momentum, and Latin could not compete successfully against it. With the rise of the city and the influence of the bourgeoisie, another type of vernacular literature developed. Merchants and artisans of the 12th and 13th centuries liked the comical, scandalous, and cynical short stories called *fabliaux.* Popular with them also were animal stories, such as *Reynard the Fox,* and the many ballads telling how Robin Hood stole from the rich to give to the poor. *The Vision of Piers Plowman,* a poem of the 14th century, expresses the attitude of the people toward corrupt government, abuses by the clergy, and oppression of the lower classes.

Chaucer and Dante were two great medieval poets. Geoffrey Chaucer was born about 1340 in London, the son of a wine merchant. After serving as a page in the castle of a prince, he held many official government positions and carried out diplomatic missions in Italy. Although writing was never his primary occupation, Chaucer is one of the great figures in medieval literature. His best known work is *The Canterbury Tales,* which tells the story of thirty pilgrims on their way to Canterbury cathedral. It offers a vivid picture of the England of his time. The Midland dialect Chaucer used was the base from which the future English language developed.

Dante Alighieri was an Italian poet, philosopher, and student of politics, who was born in Florence in 1265. While in exile for his political beliefs, he wrote the *Comedy,* a poem which later admirers entitled the *Divine Comedy.* This work reflects the religious spirit of the Middle Ages, narrating a story of Dante's mythical journey through Hell, Purgatory, and Paradise. His writings both in Latin and in the Italian vernacular became an inspiration for many poets who succeeded him. The Tuscan dialect which he used became the basis of modern Italian.

The arts served the needs of the Church. Many of the tunes of minstrels and minnesingers dated from ancient times. They continued to be popular in the medieval period, but the music composed in the Middle Ages was produced chiefly for the Church. Church services were sung, or chanted, in a simple melody, or plain-song. Its notes were written above the words to be sung. In the 11th century, a music staff of four lines was developed, and improvements in the staff and in the notation system led to the interweaving of several melodies, called *polyphony*. Musicians of the Middle Ages used various types of organs, violins, dulcimers, and lutes, but these instruments were crude.

Few persons of the Middle Ages knew how to read or write, and few could understand the Latin speech used in church services. To make the services meaningful to the congregation, dramatizations of Bible stories and religious teachings were performed in the churches. They began as choral singing of sacred stories and later developed into simple dramas dealing with Biblical themes. The plays were performed inside the church proper, under the supervision of the clergy. Later on, plays in vernacular languages were performed, but many of them retained their religious character. They were called morality plays and were not performed in the churches, but in market places, at fairs, and in guildhalls. *Everyman,* a play written in the 15th century, is a morality play, telling how the chief character, Everyman, rebuffs the temptations of life through the aid of his religious belief.

Artists and sculptors of the Middle Ages were encouraged to use their talents in depicting religious subjects, and the Church hired the best artists of the day to decorate churches and cathedrals. On outside walls and façades of the buildings, sculptures illustrated the life of Christ and of the Virgin Mary and described events in the lives of saints and stories from the Bible. The stories that were depicted on the outside of the building were often continued on the interior walls and columns and also in the pictures in the stained-glass windows. Although the use of stained glass in windows dated from ancient times, it became a fine art during the medieval period. By adding minerals to molten glass, craftsmen achieved brilliant hues. Glaziers, working from artists' sketches, fitted small pieces of glass into various designs.

During the religious revival in the 11th century, many churches were built throughout Europe. Most were of the Romanesque style of architecture, that is, a style influenced by the building of ancient Rome. Romanesque architecture varied in different localities, but the churches of that style usually had walls of stone and roofs of wood. The wood often caught fire, and many churches lay in ruins as a result. To make them fireproof, builders designed roofs of stone and made them barrel-shaped, that is, rounded, or vaulted. These vaulted roofs were too heavy for the walls that supported them. They thrust out the sides of the buildings, many times falling on hundreds of worshipers. For years architects sought the answer. They made walls thicker, added extra rooms to support the sides of the main building, and devised various types of arches to support the vaulted roof.

Architects were faced also with the problems of providing more space for the worshipers and more light for the interiors of churches. Their efforts resulted in a massive church building, comprised of a large nave and many separate units, such as arcades, aisles, chapels, and galleries, each unit lending support to the others. Thick interior piers occupied a great amount of the space; small windows pierced the thick walls, but let in little light.

By the middle of the 12th century, architects were making use of the pointed arch for roofs, a feature that originated in Persia. The pointed arch permitted more freedom and control in planning than builders had had with the barrel-shaped vault. The weight of the roof was shifted to piers and braces, called buttresses. With the use of flying buttresses on the exterior of the buildings, churches could be built to great heights. This new style, originating in France, was called Gothic. Throughout the 13th century, towns competed in erecting Gothic cathedrals to exceed the height of any in neighboring communities. The tallest one, at Beauvais, France, rose to 154 feet.

Walls, no longer necessary to support the roof, could be thinner. As stained glass became more available, wall space gave way to window space, and in some churches, such as Sainte Chapelle in Paris, the sides of the building serve chiefly as framework for the beautiful jewel-like windows. Interior pillars in the Gothic churches were less massive than in the Romanesque, and architects achieved to some extent the light, space, and safety that had been objectives of builders for hundreds of years.

Section Review

1. What is a vernacular? How did vernaculars develop among European peoples in the Middle Ages?
2. What different forms did medieval literature take? Give examples.
3. How did two famous poets of the Middle Ages influence the development of language?
4. What advances were made in music during medieval times? How did medieval drama develop? How did artists, sculptors, and artisans serve the Church?
5. What were some of the problems and the objectives of medieval church builders? How were these objectives achieved?

Chapter 7 ████████████ A Review

After the fall of Rome, cities declined and trade was reduced to a mere trickle. During the 10th and 11th centuries, however, a resurgence of trade began between Italian city-states and the East, and many of the goods imported into Italy flowed into regions farther north. As trade routes developed throughout Europe, a money economy replaced the barter economy of the early Middle Ages. Trading centers were established. They prospered, grew into towns, and were chartered as independent city governments. Their wealth increased royal treasuries, thus giving kings power over the nobles and helping break down feudalism.

Merchants and craftsmen organized guilds to protect their interests, and towns and guilds formed trading associations, such as the Hanseatic League. Townsmen became prosperous and developed a new class of people, known as the bourgeoisie, who were influential in city governments. Wealth rather than birth distinguished them.

Among many factors contributing to the growth of towns, an important one was the migration of serfs to the cities.

The rise of towns and trade stimulated education and the arts. Universities were established in Europe from the 1100's on, and

Averroës, Abélard, St. Thomas Aquinas, and Roger Bacon were among the great scholars of the later Middle Ages.

Native tongues, or vernaculars, became the languages of storytellers and poets. One of the earliest forms of medieval literature in the vernacular was the epic, and two famous poets of the Middle Ages, Geoffrey Chaucer and Dante, influenced the formation of the future English and Italian languages through their writings.

Musicians, dramatists, artists, sculptors, and architects used their talents to serve the Church. The making of stained-glass windows became a fine art during the Middle Ages, and building techniques advanced, as seen in the building of Romanesque and Gothic churches.

The Time

Give the century in which each of the following events or developments occurred.

1. The city of Venice was formed.
2. A revival of learning took place under Charlemagne.
3. Cologne won its independence.
4. The mariner's compass was invented.
5. The vernacular poem *The Vision of Piers Plowman* was written.

6. The *Reconquista* began.

7. Fairs were well established in the province of Champagne.

8. The University of Bologna was founded.

9. The Black Death spread throughout Europe.

10. The Moslems conquered Spain.

11. The tandem harness, horse collar, and horseshoes came into use.

The Place

1. Locate each of the following cities and tell which were (a) in the Mediterranean trade area; (b) in the Hanseatic League trade area; and (c) sites of famous medieval fairs.

Acre	Venice	Troyes
Leipzig	Lübeck	Bruges

2. In what respect was each of these cities a medieval center of learning: Paris, Bologna, Cordova? Locate each.

3. Name one or more countries of today in which the following language groups developed.

Romance	Germanic	Slavic

The People

1. What contributions did each of the following make to the revival of learning that took place under Charlemagne: Einhard, Alcuin, Paul the Deacon?

2. Name one achievement of each of the Scholastics Abélard and Aquinas.

3. What did Roger Bacon contribute to the development of scientific knowledge during the later Middle Ages?

4. How did Averroës contribute to the revival of learning in western Europe?

5. For what famous works are Dante and Chaucer known? Explain the contribution each man made to (1) the development of vernacular languages and to (2) the understanding of medieval life.

Historical Terms

1. Define each of these terms as it applied to the expansion of European trade.

law merchant	usury
pied poudre courts	Hanseatic League

2. Burg and urb are the roots of the words *faubourg* and *suburbium*. Tell the meaning of these four words. What do they reveal about the growth of towns in the Middle Ages?

3. Who was the *doge?* With what city is he associated?

4. Define each of the following terms as it applied to merchants and craftsmen of the Middle Ages.

merchant guilds	apprentice
craft guilds	master craftsman
journeyman	masterpiece

5. Describe the special place in medieval society held by the burghers, or bourgeoisie.

6. What was the Black Death?

7. Explain the term Scholasticism.

8. Describe the various types of medieval literature embodied in these terms: Goliardic poetry; *chansons de geste; fabliaux.* Which were composed in the vernacular? Which were epics?

9. Who were the troubadours, minstrels, and minnesingers?

10. Identify each of the following works of medieval literature.

The Song of Roland	*Beowulf*
Reynard the Fox	*Everyman*
Song of the Nibelungs	*El Cid*
The Vision of Piers Plowman	

11. Why was polyphony an innovation in music?

12. In what respects did Gothic architecture differ from Romanesque architecture? Why was the invention of the flying buttress an architectural achievement?

Questions for Critical Thinking

1. How did the rise of towns in medieval Europe stimulate education and the arts?

2. How did town life contribute to the growth of a class called the bourgeoisie?

3. Why do you think Roger Bacon was unsuccessful in convincing learned men of his day to adopt his views?

4. What features did early French, Spanish, and Germanic literature have in common?

5. Did the intellectual stirrings of medieval Europe indicate a trend away from the teachings of the Church or merely a changing attitude toward these teachings? Use examples to support your answer.

6. How did the rise of towns weaken feudalism?

The Byzantine, Moslem, and Russian Empires

For centuries the Byzantine Empire served as a buffer for Europe against Moslem invasions. Byzantine rulers like Justinian and his wife, Theodora, left, sought to preserve the traditions of the Roman Empire, although Rome itself had fallen to barbarians. For their part, the Moslems created a dynamic new culture based on the religion of Islam. Caravans like the one at right carried the word of the prophet Mohammed to peoples from Spain to the Far East.

"The universal verdict of history is that the [Byzantine Empire] constitutes, without a single exception, the most thoroughly base and despicable form that civilization has yet assumed. . . ." So wrote the famous 19th-century British historian, W. E. H. Lecky. His disapproval of Byzantine civilization reflected the strict moral standards of England during the reign of Queen Victoria. The word *Byzantine* had long been used to suggest moral corruption and political intrigue. Present-day historians can agree with Lecky that there was much that was evil in the Byzantine Empire. However, no civilization can endure a thousand years, as did the Byzantine, without elements of greatness. In the last few decades, historians have shown increased respect for the splendid cultural heritage the Byzantines left the Western world.

The Moslem Empire was far larger than the Byzantine, though its civilization was relatively short-lived. Moslem scientists and philosophers were among the most illustrious of medieval times. Islam, one of the world's great religions, is an enduring monument to the faded glory of this once proud empire.

The early Russians did not build a state comparable to that of the Byzantines or the Moslems. Under the leadership of the city of Kiev, the Russian city-states enjoyed a modest commercial and agricultural prosperity until domestic conflict and foreign invasion disrupted a promising beginning. The principality of Moscow then revived the Russians and forged a new nation.

This chapter traces the fortunes of three civilizations from their origins, showing their relationship to each other and to the medieval West. The chapter is divided into five parts:

1. **The eastern empire survived the fall of Rome.**

2. **The Byzantines made notable contributions in many fields.**

3. **The Moslem Empire arose from the religion of Islam.**

4. **The Moslems created an advanced civilization.**

5. **A Slavic state began on the Russian plain.**

1 The eastern empire survived the fall of Rome

In the southeastern corner of Europe, on a strategic peninsula between the Black Sea and the approaches to the Aegean Sea, lies the Turkish city of Istanbul. On its site a Greek colony called Byzantium was established in the 7th century B.C. In 196 A.D., it fell under Roman control.

Constantine, emperor of Rome from 306 to 337 A.D., ordered a new city built there, and in 330 it became the second capital of the Roman Empire. Known as Constantinople, or the city of Constantine, it eventually emerged as a thriving metropolis and the center of a new civilization, sometimes labeled late Roman but usually called *Byzantine* after the original Greek settlement.

The Byzantine Empire was the continuation of the Roman Empire. After the death of Emperor Theodosius in 395, two emperors ruled the Roman Empire—one in the east and one in the west. While Germanic chieftains carved out kingdoms in Italy, Spain, and North Africa, Constantinople, as the center of Roman rule in the eastern provinces, stood firm. The city was protected on three sides by water and, on the fourth side, massive walls offered a virtually impregnable barrier to would-be conquerors.

Justinian restored Roman greatness. During the 6th century the power and grandeur of Rome was briefly revived by the Emperor Justinian, who ruled from 527 to 565. In a brilliant campaign, the Vandal

Battle of Châlons
✕ 451

FRANKS

LOMBARDS

SLAVS

BULGARS

Milan

Ravenna

VISIGOTHS

BALKANS

Rome

Dyrrachium

Constantinople

PERSIANS

ASIA MINOR

SYRIA

Cordova

Cartagena

Smyrna

Antioch

Ceuta

SICILY

Athens

Syracuse

Carthage

Damascus

Jerusalem

Tripoli

Alexandria

Memphis

Prepared by
Rand McNally & Co., Chicago

kingdom in North Africa was destroyed, and a foothold was gained in southeast Spain, the farthest west that Byzantine rule ever penetrated. Another military expedition was launched against the Ostrogoths in Italy, and after many years of desperate fighting Byzantine authority was established. But in the process of restoring imperial control, Italy was devastated. The fields lay untilled, cities fell into ruin, and famine and disease stalked the stricken land. Justinian's triumphs were a hollow mockery to the population he had "rescued" from barbarian domination. Late in the 6th century the Lombards, a Germanic tribe, established their own kingdom in Italy.

Justinian's most enduring contribution to Western civilization was his preservation of the Roman law in a systematic form. He organized a commission of lawyers to revise and codify the law of the great Roman jurists. This *Code* was supplemented by the *Digest* and the *Institutes*, two works which expressed the philosophy of law as understood in Justinian's time. Roman law, which otherwise might have been lost, was therefore preserved for hundreds of years and passed on to posterity.

Another of Justinian's memorable achievements was the magnificent church of Hagia Sophia (meaning "Holy Wisdom") in Constantinople. A triumph of Byzantine architecture, it was built at a tremendous cost by the labor of thousands of workers and artisans. The emperor also lavished funds on roads, aqueducts, public buildings, and other civic projects. He helped to make the capital city one of the wonders of the Middle Ages, far larger and more beautiful than any metropolis in western Europe.

For all the splendor and pomp of his rule, at his death Justinian left a realm dangerously weakened by his extravagant ambitions. The treasury was exhausted, and the outposts of the overextended empire in the West were difficult to defend. In mustering his resources to reclaim the lost territories of Rome, Justinian had neglected the eastern provinces which were periodically attacked by Persians, Slavs, Bulgars, and others.

The eastern empire became Byzantine. In the years after Justinian's death, the painfully acquired western empire was eaten away by further barbarian conquests. Only Sicily, portions of Italy, and several Mediterranean islands remained. Syria, Palestine, and Egypt, added to the "core" territory of Asia Minor and the southern Balkans, constituted the eastern empire. The concept of a united Roman Empire was never entirely discarded, but by the 8th century the eastern empire developed a civilization more Hellenic and Oriental than Roman.

In medieval Europe, Greek was an unknown language except to a few learned monks. But to the Byzantine population, largely Greek but including Slavs, Syrians, Jews, and others, it was the national tongue. Latin was reserved for state documents and official functions until the 7th century when it was discarded for even these formal occasions. The Greek classics formed the basis of Byzantine literature.

The Oriental tradition of the Byzantine Empire came from the ancient empires of Persia and Mesopotamia. Eastern customs were reflected in the elaborate etiquette at the royal court and the lavish ceremonies associated with the semi-divine status of the emperor. Noneastern influences were also important. Roman influence was obvious in the law and in the political tradition of imperial authority. The empire was also Christian, but the Byzantine church evolved in a pattern different from that of western Europe.

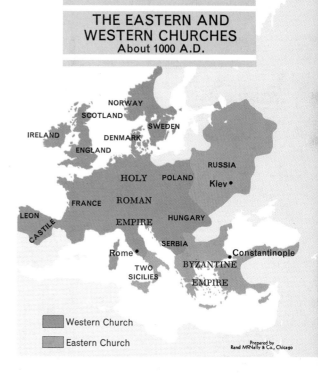

THE EASTERN AND WESTERN CHURCHES
About 1000 A.D.

Western Church

Eastern Church

Prepared by
Rand M?Nally & Co., Chicago

The Eastern Church split off from Rome. In the West the power of the Christian church increased as the secular authority declined. In the East the relationship between church and state was reversed. The emperor was supreme in church affairs, although, in practice, he customarily observed the wishes of the patriarch, the highest church official, just as he left the details of civil administration to his chief advisers.

Increasingly poor feelings strained the relationship between the eastern and western churches. As early as 381 A.D., the church in Constantinople rejected the theory that the bishops of Rome were entitled to rule over the universal church. As the papacy in Rome increased in power, frequent clashes with the patriarch in Constantinople resulted. Controversies over dogma and ritual added to the bitterness of the quarrel. A complete break came in

1054 when Pope Leo IX and Patriarch Michael Cerularius excommunicated each other. Even then the break might not have become permanent had not the Fourth Crusade occurred, in which the crusaders plundered Constantinople. After that time, the Eastern (Orthodox) Church and the Roman Catholic Church went their separate ways.

The Byzantines withstood many invaders. Periods of imperial instability and economic decline alternated with periods of political strength and commercial prosperity. There were few great emperors to exert effective leadership, and the safety of the empire was often threatened by external enemies. Yet, for ten centuries, like an island fortress in a raging sea, the Byzantine capital withstood numerous attempts to breach its inner defenses. The outer ramparts were repeatedly attacked and sometimes taken. In the 7th century, the emperor Heraclius, a great general in his own right, ended the Persian threat and recovered Syria, Palestine, and Egypt. But a new menace soon replaced the old—the Moslem Arabs. By the end of the 7th century, the Moslems had conquered North Africa, the eastern Mediterranean lands, and parts of Asia Minor. The Balkans also came under attack by the Bulgars, a nomadic people similar to the Huns, who subjugated the Slavic population and settled in what is now Bulgaria.

Under Leo III, who ruled from 717 to 741, the Byzantine Empire regained its strength. He increased imperial authority by weakening the power of the provincial governors. This administrative reform is credited with prolonging the life of the empire. A Moslem army was repulsed at the very gates of Constantinople (717-718), and the Byzantine navy drove off the invader's fleet. A vital element in Byzantine naval success over the years was the use of "Greek fire," an inflammable liquid containing lime, sulfur, and other chemicals which set fire to the enemy ships.

Another outstanding ruler, Basil II, who ruled from 976 to 1025, revived the power and prosperity of the empire after a long period of decline. He became known as the "Bulgar Slayer" because of his ruthless conquest of the Bulgars. On one occasion thousands of Bulgars were blinded and only a handful left with a single eye each to guide the rest home. The Bulgarian king is said to have died of shock when this sightless multitude returned. But once the fighting was over, Basil acted in statesmanlike fashion, giving the Bulgars self-rule in the empire.

As so often happened after the reign of a strong emperor, the empire lapsed into another era of decay following the death of Basil. New commercial rivals, notably the city-state of Venice, offered serious competition to Byzantine trade in the eastern Mediterranean. And a foe more powerful than the Persians or the Bulgars appeared from Central Asia—the Seljuk Turks. After the Turks routed a Byzantine army at Manzikert in 1071, the whole of Asia Minor was overrun by these hardy invaders.

Constantinople suffered a crushing blow in 1204 when the Fourth Crusade was diverted from a campaign against the Moslem Turks to an invasion of the city itself. Christian crusaders looted the great city in an orgy of destruction. Priceless art treasures were pillaged, and a vast quantity of rich booty was carried away.

A French noble of the Fourth Crusade described the downfall of the city:

> . . . the great churches and the rich palaces melting and falling in, and the great streets filled with merchandise burning in the flames. . . . The booty gained was so great that none could tell you the end of it: gold and silver, and vessels and precious stones . . . and cloth of silk . . . and ermine, and every choicest thing found upon the earth . . . never, since the world was created, had so much booty been won in any city.

Turks overwhelmed the Byzantine Empire. Disastrously weakened by the ravages of the crusaders, the Byzantine Empire never fully recovered from the Fourth Crusade. Rival claimants to the throne provoked disunity and even civil war, while religious disputes further disrupted domestic peace. Peasant unrest and rebellion resulted from the heavy tax burden exacted by the landowners, and economic decay set in, caused largely by the Mediterranean conquests and commercial rivalry of Venice and Genoa. The disintegration of the once mighty empire was also accompanied by financial ruin. Even the imperial court suffered acute distress. At the marriage of Emperor John V in 1347, "the wedding feast was served in vessels of earthenware and pewter, and not one item of gold or silver appeared on the table." Yet the final collapse might have been delayed indefinitely had the Ottoman Turks not come upon the scene.

The Ottomans, former subjects of the Seljuk rulers, by-passed Constantinople and crossed the straits into Europe in 1354. The Balkans were subdued in a long and bloody struggle, and by 1446 only the Byzantine capital remained of the once mighty empire. In 1453 the end came. Barely 8000 defenders—many of them foreign-born troops serving only for their pay—were left to fight the besieging Turkish army of 160 thousand men. After eight heroic weeks the valiant band was overwhelmed. Emperor Constantine XI perished with his men, fighting to the last. As the Turks stormed the walls of the city, the emperor rushed to meet them, crying out as he was cut down, "God forbid that I should live an Emperor without an Empire! As my city falls, I will fall with it."

Section Review

1. How did Justinian seek to preserve Roman greatness?
2. In what ways was Byzantine civilization influenced by Roman, Hellenic, and Oriental traditions?
3. Why did the Byzantine church break with the papacy at Rome?
4. During what periods was the Byzantine Empire strong? What enemies attacked the Byzantine Empire?
5. What circumstances led to the final collapse of the empire in 1453?

2 **The Byzantines made notable contributions in many fields**

Although Byzantine civilization lacked the originality of classical Greece and Rome, it was superior to the civilization which existed in medieval Europe. The armies of the empire held back the nomadic hordes which would have flooded the West and swept away the promising beginnings of medieval culture. Not until the 14th century were Byzantine standards of art and scholarship achieved by the peoples of western Europe.

The Byzantine Empire was also the champion of Christendom against Islam. Arab expansion was checked between the 8th and 11th centuries, and the Turkish assault upon Europe, which began in the 14th century, was weakened by the tenacious resistance of the faltering empire. The amazing strength and endurance of Byzantine civilization was due to several factors: a centralized government and a well-trained bureaucracy; an efficient and well-led army and navy; the vitality and leadership of the Orthodox Church; and a high level of prosperity sustained by a vigorous economy.

Businessmen kept industry and trade alive. With its flourishing commercial life the Byzantine Empire was able to survive the perils of domestic conflict and the steady assaults of foreign aggressors. Situated at the crossroads of Europe and Asia,

Constantinople was the greatest center of trade in the early medieval world. At a time when the commerce of western Europe had slowed to a trickle, the Byzantine capital was thronged with merchants from many lands. A stable currency based on gold greatly enhanced the empire's economic advantage. Because money was scarce in the West, the gold *bezant* became a recognized medium of international exchange.

The Black Sea furnished access to the major waterways of southern Russia—the Dnieper and Don rivers. Over these routes flowed a steady stream of goods. Wines, silks, fruits, glassware, and various luxury products were exchanged for Russian furs, fish, and honey. By merchant caravans across the desolate wastes of Central Asia came spices, perfumes, precious stones, and other rare and costly goods from the Far East. Merchant vessels plied the Aegean and Mediterranean seas, carrying both Byzantine manufactured goods and foreign merchandise to western ports. The revival of trade in Europe beginning in the 12th century was due partly to the stimulus of Byzantine commerce.

The government acted as a stern watchdog over all aspects of economic activity. Industry was rigidly controlled: wages, prices, and working conditions were set; the quality of products was checked; and exports were subject to strict regulation. Articles made by skilled artisans and craftsmen—jeweled ornaments, magnificent tapestries, carved ivory, and exquisite leather work—were the pride of Constantinople. In quantity of output, textiles were the chief industrial product. About 550 A.D. silkworms were smuggled out of China, and thereafter splendid fabrics and garments were made in Constantinople from the raw silk. The silk industry became a profitable state monopoly.

The lower classes failed to share the general prosperity. Yet their standard of living, meager as it was, would probably have been envied by people in the West. The economy was relatively stable, and the lot of the peasants, many of whom were reduced to serfdom, was at least improved by governmental supervision of the great estates.

Rulers maintained a centralized government. Unlike western Europe, with its feudal system, the Byzantine state was centralized. In theory, imperial authority was despotic—it was above the law. But custom and tradition limited the arbitrary use of power, and the weaker emperors were often overshadowed by strong ministers or ambitious patriarchs. An army of civil servants was responsible for the actual workings of government. Despite the common abuses of corruption and bribery, the administrative officials were generally conscientious and efficient.

As in Imperial Rome, a grave defect marred Byzantine political life: the lack of legal succession to the throne. Any upstart, with courage and luck, could aspire to supreme power. Many did so, and the story of the rise and fall of Byzantine emperors is a record of intrigue and violence. Of the 107 emperors who ruled between 395 and 1453, only 40 died a natural death in office.

The excitable city population of Constantinople added to the normal hazards of government. Arguments about religion frequently led to bloodshed, and the chariot races held in the Hippodrome often aroused the spectators to a frenzy. Spontaneous popular uprisings were apt to break out at any time. The most famous of these outbursts was the terrible Nika Revolt in 532 during the reign of Justinian. Named for the rallying cry of the rebels (*Nika* means "victory"), the revolt lasted for a week. Before it was over, some 30 thousand corpses were said to have littered the streets of the city.

The Empress Theodora's bravery inspired her husband to remain in the city

The Byzantine Empire was a world of opulence compared with feudal Europe. In Constantinople stood the magnificent church of Hagia Sophia, above. This structure represents a great architectural achievement of the Byzantines—the construction of a circular dome on top of a rectangular building. Hagia Sophia (Greek for "Holy Wisdom") was converted into a mosque by Moslem conquerors, who added four slender minarets. Chariot races, reminiscent of those held in Rome, took place at the Hippodrome in Constantinople. At right, an emperor with scepter and orb enjoys a day's games. The whole Byzantine Empire was protected by a mighty navy and its "Greek fire," an inflammable liquid sprayed at enemies, as shown below.

The Byzantine, Moslem and Russian Empires   181

and crush the rebellion. According to the historian Procopius, she said to Justinian:

> If . . . it is your wish to save yourself, O Emperor, there is no difficulty. For we have much money, and there is the sea, here the boats . . . as for myself, I approve a certain ancient saying that royalty is a good burial-shroud.

Byzantine civilization spread throughout eastern Europe. The Slavic peoples of Russia and the Balkans were the most deeply influenced by the Byzantine Empire. Missionaries carried the Christian gospel to these pagan tribes in the 9th century. Today the Orthodox faith is predominant in Russia, Yugoslavia, Greece, and Bulgaria. The Cyrillic alphabet, used in the Russian, Serbian, and Bulgarian languages, is derived from the modified Greek letters of Byzantium.

The autocratic tradition of czarist Russia owes much to Byzantine example. The term *czar* given to the Russian rulers comes from the word *caesar,* the Roman title taken over by the Byzantine emperors. Russian architecture, the calendar in use during czarist times, and much of the literature of early Russia, especially the lives of saints, is Byzantine in origin.

Scholars preserved classical learning. Byzantium was heir to the intellectual treasures of ancient Greece. Although the empire produced no Plato or Aristotle, the works of both were studied with profound respect. The most eminent scholar, Michael Psellus, served on the faculty of the university in Constantinople during the 11th century. He wrote widely on many subjects, yet his writings display little originality, for he shared with other men of learning a preference for commentaries on the ancient classics rather than creative scholarship. Only in the field of history and theology did the empire produce works of real excel-lence. Anna Commena, daughter of the 11th-century Emperor Alexius, produced a notable work on the life and times of her father, and Nicephorus Gregoras wrote movingly of the declining empire in the 14th century. Probably the best-known historian, however, is Procopius, whose notorious *Secret History* is a biased but fascinating account of Justinian's reign.

The public and private libraries of the empire were rich in the masterpieces of Greek philosophy and literature. Manuscripts of priceless value were lost in the plunder of Constantinople by the crusaders in 1204 and by the Turks in 1453. Nevertheless, the classics that did survive made a significant contribution to the cultural revival in western Europe in the 14th and 15th centuries (Chapter 13).

Architects and artists created domes, mosaics, and paintings. The vitality of the empire in art and architecture is in direct contrast to the imitativeness of its scholarship. Greek, Roman, and Persian influences can be seen in the architectural splendors of the capital, but in the glorious church of Hagia Sophia, Byzantine genius in the arts came to full flower. It was a church, wrote Procopius, "the like of which has never been seen since Adam, nor ever will be." Rectangular in shape and surmounted by a huge dome suspended 179 feet above the floor, the structure was both an artistic and engineering triumph.

Among the decorative arts, the finest achievement was the use of mosaics—small bits of colored glass or stone formed into vivid patterns. Mosaics were usually placed on the walls and ceilings of churches. Most of the designs depicted scenes of religious significance. Wall paintings and icons (painted images of sacred figures) added further richness to church interiors.

The nonreligious art which glorified the imperial palaces was likewise conceived on a dazzling scale. Polished marble, inlaid bronze, rich fabrics, gold and silver dishes, and jeweled ornaments were all representative of the Byzantine genius for artistic craftsmanship.

Section Review

1. What characteristics of Byzantine civilization enabled it to endure so long?
2. Why did Constantinople enjoy great prosperity?
3. What were the strengths and weaknesses of the Byzantine government?
4. How did the Byzantine Empire influence the Slavs?
5. What were some of the achievements of Byzantine civilization in scholarship and the arts?

3 The Moslem Empire arose from the religion of Islam

In the 7th century, a new faith and a new empire burst forth from obscure and humble origins in the Arabian peninsula. A land of scanty rainfall and trackless wastes, much of it shifting desert sand, Arabia was an unlikely setting for the development of one of the great religions of the world.

Near the Red Sea coast were prosperous trading cities, but the interior of Arabia was sparsely inhabited by primitive nomads. These desert peoples had no organized government and lived a precarious existence. They depended on their flocks for food, and their meager possessions were sometimes supplemented by raids on passing caravans. Their religion was simple nature worship, although Christianity and Judaism had made some impression upon the better-educated townspeople. The most important Arab shrine was the Kaaba (cube), a temple in the city of Mecca which contained a sacred black stone along with images of several hundred tribal deities.

Mohammed started a new religion. About the year 570 the future prophet of Islam was born in Mecca. He was given the common Arabic name of Mohammed. Little is known of his early life, except that he was left an orphan as a child and reared by relatives. As a young man he entered the service of a wealthy widow engaged in the caravan trade. He later married his employer, raised a family, and lived a quiet and simple life despite the economic security and social prestige gained by his marriage.

Mohammed claimed to receive divine revelations, and finally became convinced that he was the appointed prophet of the one true God, Allah. At first he made few converts beyond his immediate family. As his doctrines became more widely known, he aroused opposition from the wealthy merchants who dominated Mecca, for they feared mass conversion to a new religion and possible loss of income from pilgrimages to the Kaaba. But the common people remained indifferent to the new prophet.

In 622 Mohammed decided that a more promising field for missionary work lay to the north in Medina. He and his followers left secretly in a migration known as the *Hegira* (flight), an event that marks the beginning of the Moslem calendar. He soon established himself as the city's political and religious leader. Winning converts from the surrounding tribes, he launched a holy war against his enemies. In 630 Mohammed returned to Mecca in triumph. The Kaaba was purged of its idols and preserved as sacred to the Moslem faith. At the time of the prophet's death two years later, Islam had spread to most of Arabia.

Islam was a simple, inspiring faith. The term *Mohammedanism*, widely used in the West to describe the religion founded by Mohammed, is inaccurate. *Islam* ("submission to the will of Allah") is the correct

Mohammed founded Islam, a religion which now has over 400 million believers. His early life is shrouded in legend. One such story is illustrated above: a Christian monk bows before the young Mohammed, in whom he recognizes the signs of a prophet. An angel anoints the head of the youth. Mohammed did not begin to preach until he was about 40, after divine revelations had convinced him of his mission. Below, he addresses the faithful in a mosque during his last visit to Mecca.

word, and the "true believer" is a *Moslem.* The basic principles of Islam are found in the *Koran,* the holy book of the Moslems. It contains the teachings of Mohammed, which to the devout are the inspired words of Allah spoken through his prophet. The authorized version of the Koran was prepared soon after the death of Mohammed by his followers.

The essence of Islam is contained in a single statement, "There is but one God, Allah, and Mohammed is His Prophet." One may become a Moslem simply by accepting and repeating this simple creed. Islam is a religion derived from many sources, and the influence of Christianity and Judaism on Islam is great. Many figures in both the Old and New Testament, including Moses and Jesus, are accepted as prophets, but Mohammed is considered the last and the most important.

Four obligations are required of all Moslems: prayer five times daily, almsgiving, fasting from sunrise to sunset during the sacred month of Ramadan (the ninth month of the Moslem year), and a pilgrimage to Mecca at least once a lifetime. The ethical teachings of the Koran forbid the worship of idols, gambling, drinking, and the eating of pork. Polygamy, or multiple marriage, is permitted, though the number of wives is limited to four. The doctrine of immortality is stressed, and the painful reality of hell in contrast to the joyful paradise of heaven is described in terms appropriate to a desert people. The faithful will be rewarded with the eternal joys of heaven:

In gardens of delight . . .
Upon inwrought couches,
Reclining thereon face to face.
Youths ever young shall go unto them
    round about
With goblets and ewers and a cup of
    flowing wine—
Their heads shall not ache with it, neither
    shall they be confused;

And fruits of their choice,
And flesh of birds to their desire;
And damsels with bright eyes like hidden
    pearls.—
A reward for what they have wrought . . . .
Amid thornless [date]-trees,
And bananas laden with fruit,
And shade outspread,
And water flowing,
And fruit abundant,
Never failing nor forbidden.

But the condemned

shall be cast into scorching fire to be broiled. They shall be given to drink of a boiling fountain. They shall have no food but of dry thorns and thistles, which shall not fatten, neither shall they satisfy hunger. . . . They who believe not shall have garments of fire fitted unto them. Boiling water shall be poured on their heads . . . and they shall be beaten with maces of iron.

Equality of all Moslems in the sight of Allah is a leading feature of the religion. Although class and racial distinctions were therefore minimized, such Arabic customs as slavery and the inferior status of women were accepted. Islam has no organized priesthood, nor have churches or church services developed that are comparable to Christian services or centers of worship. However, temples, or *mosques,* exist for prayers, and *mullahs,* or learned teachers, are available to explain religious doctrine.

The Islamic community became a *theocracy,* a system of government in which the religious leader also assumes political control. Mohammed's successors were known as caliphs, and they accepted the prophet's command to spread the faith by the sword. Islam was a fighting religion which soon spread beyond the borders of Arabia.

The Arabs conquered a huge empire. Religious fervor was only one of several reasons for Arabic expansion. The pressure of overpopulation, together with poor eco-

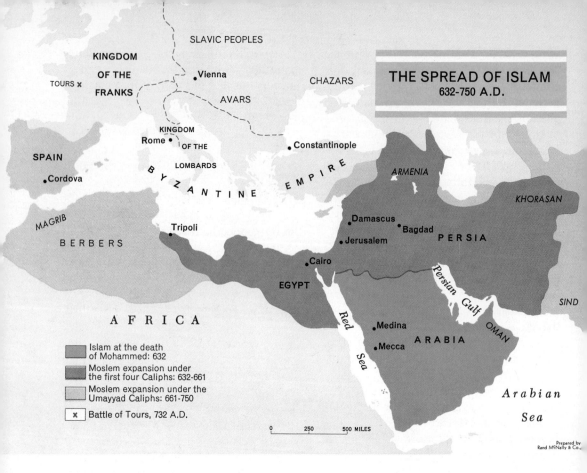

KINGDOM
OF THE
FRANKS

TOURS x

• Vienna

CHAZARS

AVARS

THE SPREAD OF ISLAM
632-750 A.D.

KINGDOM
Rome • OF THE
LOMBARDS

• Constantinople

B Y Z A N T I N E   E M P I R E

SPAIN

• Cordova

ARMENIA

KHORASAN

MAGRIB

BERBERS

• Tripoli

• Damascus
• Bagdad
• Jerusalem

PERSIA

• Cairo

EGYPT

SIND

A F R I C A

Red Sea

• Medina
• Mecca

ARABIA

Persian Gulf

OMAN

Arabian
Sea

Islam at the death
of Mohammed: 632

Moslem expansion under
the first four Caliphs: 632-661

Moslem expansion under the
Umayyad Caliphs: 661-750

x   Battle of Tours, 732 A.D.

0   250   500 MILES

Prepared by
Rand McNally & Co.

nomic conditions brought on by severe drought early in the 7th century, caused a crisis in Arabia. An outlet for the increasing population was found in the north, where the Byzantine and Persian empires had become exhausted by prolonged warfare. In 636 Arab armies invaded Syria, and by mid-century Egypt, Palestine, Iraq, and most of Persia had fallen to the hosts of Islam. In 661, under the Umayyad rulers, the Moslem capital was moved from Medina to Damascus.

Further Arab conquests were temporarily halted by civil war, and in the latter part of the 7th century, they were resumed at a slower pace. The Arabs advanced across North Africa, subdued the Berber tribes, and converted the native population to Islam. The conquered peoples were generally treated with leniency and seldom converted to Islam by force. But unbelievers were obliged to pay special taxes.

In 711 the Moslems ventured across the Strait of Gibraltar into Spain. Under Tarik, their able Berber commander, the Moslem forces crushed the Visigothic kingdom and pressed on across the Pyrenees Mountains into France. They were defeated near Tours in 732 by the Frankish leader Charles Martel and thereafter retreated into Spain. Meanwhile, other Moslem armies were harrassing the Byzantine defenses and pushing into Central Asia. Within a century of Mohammed's death, a great Moslem empire stretched from Spain in the west to the frontiers of India in the east.

The Moslem Empire fell into decline.
The decline of the empire conquered by the Arab followers of Islam was almost as

swift as its rise. Political unity in so huge an area was difficult to achieve under any circumstances, and the Arabs lacked experience in the art of government and administration.

In 762 the capital was transferred from Damascus to a newly built city on the banks of the Tigris River in Iraq. Named Bagdad, it rivaled Constantinople in its wealth and beauty. Here the Abbasside dynasty ruled. The most famous of its caliphs was the 8th-century ruler Harun al-Rashid, whose legendary deeds are recorded in the tales of the *Arabian Nights*. But even the powerful Abbassides failed to hold together the disintegrating Moslem Empire. Religious and political strife was nearly continuous after the 8th century. Independent caliphates were established in Spain and in North Africa, and in the 11th century the appearance of the Seljuk Turks altered the nature of Islamic rule.

The Turks assumed leadership of the Moslem world. About the year 1000, Turkish nomads from Central Asia migrated into Abbasside territory. A great chieftain, Seljuk, gave his name to these tribes, which became known as Seljuk Turks. Bagdad was taken in 1055, Asia Minor was wrested from Byzantine rule, and before the end of the century the Seljuk Empire dominated the world of Islam from the Mediterranean to the borders of China. Moslem by adoption, the Seljuks were an illiterate people similar to the Arabs of the 7th century. They were capable of appreciating the high state of Abbasside civilization, however, and under their patronage Bagdad regained some of its lost glory as the center of Moslem culture in the East.

The resurgence of Moslem power, particularly in the holy places of Palestine sacred to the Christian faith, led to the First Crusade in 1096. Largely because the Seljuk forces were split by rivalries and thereby weakened, the crusaders were success-

ful. They established the Crusader States along the shores of the eastern Mediterranean. But during the 12th century the great Seljuk soldier and statesman, Saladin, founded a new dynasty in Egypt, brought most of North Africa and the eastern Mediterranean lands under his rule, and inflicted heavy losses on the Christians in the Third Crusade.

In the 13th century the Mongols swept into the Middle East. These fierce invaders captured Bagdad in 1258, and the Seljuk domain was soon splintered. Better warriors than statesmen, the Mongols never founded a permanent Moslem state. The vigorous Ottoman Turks, named for their leader Osman, who lived from 1259 to 1326, fell heir to the disrupted rule of the Seljuks. Converted to Islam early in the 14th century, they built up an empire comparable to that of the Arabs. They extinguished the remnants of Byzantine power, conquered the Balkans, and twice drove to the gates of Vienna (1529 and 1683) before the armies of Christendom hurled them back.

Section Review

1. How did the Arabs live at the time Mohammed began to preach his new religion?
2. Trace the events that led to Mohammed's triumph in Mecca in 630 A.D.
3. Describe briefly some of the characteristics of Islam.
4. What pressures drove the Arabs to their conquests? What lands did they rule?
5. Why did the Arab empire decline so quickly? Who gained control of it?

4 **The Moslems created an advanced civilization**

Islamic culture had a vitality unmatched in the relatively backward society of Europe during the Middle Ages. Like the civilization of the Byzantine Empire, it was lacking in creative genius.

Moslem Achievements in art and science often were the result of a combination of the best elements from cultures that came under Islamic domination. Thus, architectural styles throughout the Moslem world vary. The sunny patio of the Alhambra palace in Spain, above, is typical of Moorish architecture, characterized by the horseshoe arch and intricate geometrical decoration. In the Royal Mosque in Isfahan, Iran, far left, pointed arches are used as decorative motifs. A dome based on a Byzantine model is embellished with bright Persian tile. Decorative tile also is used extensively in the bath shown above left. Enjoying a high standard of living, wealthy Moslems could bathe each morning. (Medieval Europeans seldom bathed at all.) The Moslems also borrowed from Greek and Roman writings, which they translated into Arabic. A druggist, lower left, makes cough medicine from a Greek formula.

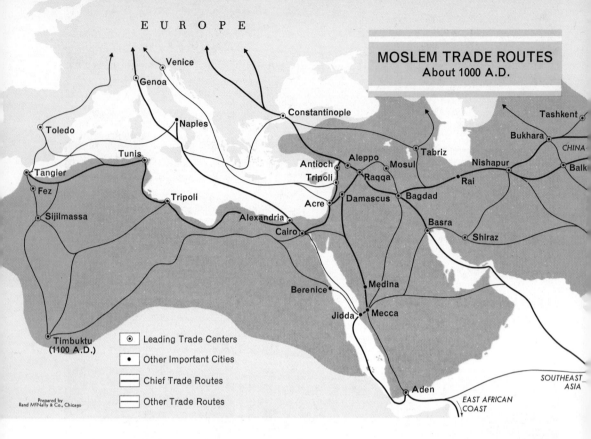

EUROPE

MOSLEM TRADE ROUTES
About 1000 A.D.

Leading Trade Centers

Other Important Cities

Chief Trade Routes

Other Trade Routes

Prepared by
Rand McNally & Co., Chicago

For three centuries, however—beginning in about the middle of the 8th century—Moslem civilization preserved the best elements of the Greco-Roman and Persian cultures and made significant contributions of its own. The Arabs themselves were hardly more than rude conquerors—or at best men of business and public affairs. Yet their religion and their language furnished a solid foundation upon which the varied peoples of the Moslem world built a remarkable civilization.

The Moslems improved agriculture and industry. The caliphs promoted vast irrigation projects, extended the canals of ancient Mesopotamia, and encouraged such scientific farming methods as crop rotation and the use of fertilizer. The arid regions of the Middle East and North Africa blossomed as never before.

The diversity and richness of the produce was unequaled in Christian Europe until modern times. Wheat and other grains were grown in the valley of the Nile; cotton, flax, and sugar cane were cultivated in North Africa; olives, fruits, and fine wines were produced in Spain; and stock breeding flourished in Asia Minor, Persia, and Syria. New varieties of sheep furnished raw material for fine woolens; the Arabian horse, renowned for its speed and endurance, was brought to its full development; and the camel, the "ship of the desert," became the chief means of land transportation.

The great estates were worked by tenant farmers and serfs. Though slavery was fairly common, most slaves were personal or household servants and were not used for plantation labor. Small landholdings predominated, and even if the peasants seldom prospered, they were better off as a class than the serfs of western Europe.

Moslem industry centered around the great cities of the empire, most of which specialized in the manufacture of certain products. Bagdad was noted for its glassware, jewelry, silks, and luxury goods; Damascus for its tempered steel and "damask," or embossed linen; Cordova for its leather products; and Toledo for its fine steel and swords. Papermaking was introduced from China, and some of the secrets of Byzantine metalworking in gold, silver, and bronze were learned by Moslem craftsmen. Guilds of craftsmen controlled most of the goods that were made.

Moslem trade spread culture. Commerce was even more thriving than industry and agriculture. Such business terms as *bazaar, tariff, traffic, check,* and *caravan* are of Arabic origin. The Moslems invented a variety of business practices—the use of receipts, checks, bills of lading, and letters of credit. They also formed trade associations and developed joint-stock companies similar in nature to those which appeared in Europe during the Age of Discovery (Chapter 15). Daring explorers opened up new overland routes to the Far East; and sea voyages to India and China by way of the Persian Gulf, the Red Sea, and the Indian Ocean were commonplace centuries before Western navigators discovered the Atlantic route. It is believed that Europeans acquired knowledge of the compass and the astrolabe (the predecessor of the sextant) from Moslem sailors.

Moslem merchants were more enterprising than their Byzantine competitors, for they did not wait for their customers to seek out their merchandise. They linked the trade of three continents, and the spread of Islam to East Africa, India, parts of China, and the East Indies was due largely to the entering wedge of commerce. Christians, Jews, and others were encour-

aged to settle in Moslem lands for business purposes. Despite far-flung commercial interests, the bulk of Moslem trade was carried on within the empire. Next to religion and language, trade was the unifying tie of the Moslem world.

Science developed in Moslem lands. In medicine, mathematics, astronomy, chemistry, and physics, Moslem achievements were particularly noteworthy. Well-equipped hospitals, usually associated with medical schools, were located in the principal cities. At a time when superstition still hampered the practice of medicine in western countries, Moslem physicians were diagnosing diseases, prescribing cures, and performing advanced surgery. Probably the greatest of all medieval physicians was the 9th-century figure, Al-Razi, known in the West as Rhazes. He was the author of scores of scientific works, including a comprehensive medical encyclopedia and a pioneering handbook on smallpox and measles. A 10th-century physician, Avicenna, compiled a huge *Canon of Medicine* which was considered the standard guide in European medical circles until the late 17th century.

The science of astronomy was hindered by the practice of astrology, but the Copernican theory (discussed in Chapter 17) was foreshadowed in the writings of several scholars. Omar Khayyám, also celebrated as a poet, devised a calendar so accurate that it contained an error of only one day in 3770 years compared to an error of one day in 3330 years in the Gregorian calendar, now used in the Western world. Chemistry developed from alchemy, the pseudo-science that sought to transmute the baser metals into gold. Experiments by the alchemists led to the discovery of alum, borax, nitric and sulfuric acid, carbonate of soda, cream of tartar, and other substances. Physicists founded the science of optics. Alhazen, who lived from 965 to 1039, challenged the mistaken Greek view on the refraction of light by his theory that vision is due to the impact of light rays on the eye.

Arabic numerals were apparently adopted from India and transmitted to the West, although the indispensable zero is often credited by some scholars to Moslem mathematicians. Important advances were made in algebra, analytical geometry, and plane and spherical trigonometry.

Literature, scholarship, and the arts flourished. Poetry was highly esteemed among Moslems. The riches of this literary form are unfortunately lost in translation, and the fame of Omar Khayyám's *Rubáiyát* derives from the 19th-century English translations by Edward FitzGerald.

> The Moving Finger writes;
>   and, having writ,
> Moves on; nor all thy
>   Piety nor Wit
> Shall lure it back to
>   cancel half a Line,
> Nor all thy Tears wash
>   out a Word of it.

The same gift for colorful imagery is found in Islamic prose, parts of the Koran, and even in philosophical essays. The renowned tales of the *Arabian Nights* were collected from Persian sources and perfected in 14th-century Egypt.

Moslem scholars, like the Greek scholars in the Byzantine Empire, revered the works of the ancient Greek philosophers. A century before Saint Thomas Aquinas attempted to reconcile the teachings of Aristotle with those of Christianity, the most distinguished Moslem philosopher, Averroës of Cordova, sought to harmonize Aristotelian principles and the faith of Islam. Excellent histories and biographies were written. The 14th-century writer, ibn-Khaldun, sometimes regarded as the first modern historian, produced a lengthy history of the Arab states, emphasizing Spain

and North Africa. His contemporary, the adventurous ibn-Batuta, traveled thousands of miles from Spain to Ceylon and China and left a fascinating account of his journeys, which was rediscovered when the French occupied Algeria in the 19th century.

Because the followers of Islam believed that the representation of human and animal figures was a form of idol worship, Moslem artists concentrated on intricate geometrical designs. In decorative handicrafts—rug weaving, pottery making, and jeweled metalwork—the exquisite quality of the workmanship equaled that of Constantinople's best artisans. Architecture drew heavily upon that of Byzantium and Persia, but in time a distinctive Moslem style developed. The typical Byzantine domes used in mosques were supplemented by minarets, slender towers from which the faithful were called to prayer. The arcade and the horseshoe arch are other graceful features of Moslem architecture.

1. What unifying ties bound the Moslem world?
2. What contributions did the Moslems make to agriculture and industry?
3. Give examples to show how Moslem trade spread culture.
4. What were some Moslem achievements in science, literature, scholarship, and the arts?

5 **A Slavic state began on the Russian plain**

The original homeland of the Slavs is unknown, but it is thought that they were one of many peoples who migrated from Asia long before the Christian era. Three distinct groups eventually emerged: the southern or Balkan Slavs; the western Slavs, including the Czechs and the Poles; and the eastern Slavs, who later became known as Russians. By the beginning of the 8th century, the eastern Slavs were settled in communities between the Baltic and Black seas. In the more isolated areas they lived by agriculture, hunting, and fishing. In the growing towns, however, a bustling commercial life offered additional opportunities. Lacking a central government, the Slavs were organized in city-states in which the ruling class was composed of wealthy merchants.

Viking invaders ruled the first Russian state. Viking raids along the coasts and inland waterways of Europe in the 9th century (Chapter 6) extended into the Slavic settlements. According to tradition, in 862 a Viking chieftain named Rurik became the ruler of Novgorod, an important city in the northern part of what is now European Russia. In 882 his successor, Oleg, captured Kiev. Later on, he conquered Smolensk and formed the first Russian state. Vastly outnumbered by the Slavs, the Vikings soon lost their racial identity. The name *Russia,* which came into use much later, presumably derives from *Rus*, a term once employed by foreigners to describe both the Slavs and their Viking rulers.

For three centuries Kiev was the capital of a loose confederation of city-states, and the Dnieper River served as the major trading route with the Byzantine Empire. Special commercial rights were granted the Russians to prevent an attack on Constantinople in 907. Merchants from the important Russian cities were allowed access to Byzantine markets without paying customs duties, and boats for the return voyage were equipped at the emperor's expense.

Russia adopted some of Byzantine culture. The early Russians practiced a variety of pagan customs. By the middle of the 10th century many merchants, impressed by the wonders of Constantinople, were baptized into the Christian faith. In 957 Olga, the reigning princess of Kiev, was converted by Byzantine missionaries. Her grandson, Vladimir, followed her example in 988, and Russia's official acceptance of the Orthodox Church came some two years later when the pagan idols in Kiev were destroyed and the whole population was baptized in the waters of the Dnieper. Couriers were dispatched to the other cities to carry out a similar program. Both Olga and Vladimir were later canonized, although their piety seems to have been rather superficial. For several centuries Christian rites vied with the heathen customs of the common people.

The Russian church, as in Byzantium, was wholly subordinate to civil authority. The adaptation of the Greek alphabet to the Slavic tongue stimulated the growth of a native literature. But it had the unfortunate additional effect of cutting off much of the cultural heritage of Christendom, for priests and monks, the only educated class, were usually ignorant of Latin and seldom more than semiliterate in Greek. Russia's cultural isolation from the mainstream of European thought has been in part due to this unusual feature of its development.

Yaroslav was the Charlemagne of Russia. Kievan Russia reached the summit of its power during the reign of Yaroslav the Wise, from 1019 to 1054. His prestige among European rulers was demonstrated by his sister's marriage to the king of Poland and the marriage of three of his daughters to the kings of France, Hungary, and Norway. Kiev became the religious and cultural center of Russia as well as the political capital. A patron of scholars and artists, Yaroslav founded schools and libraries, and with the help of Byzantine architects the impressive cathedral of Hagia Sophia was built in honor of the original one in Constantinople. A bishop

Russian Civilization was disrupted in the 13th century when Tartars from central Asia overran the Kievan states. During the two centuries of Tartar domination, Moscow emerged as the center of Russian culture. The Muscovites preserved a distinctive architectural style that had developed in Kiev—the onion-shaped dome, as shown on the Cathedral of St. Basil in Moscow, left (now a museum). Below, a Moscow prince receives ambassadors. The Russian horsemen above left are dressed in Tartar style. European visitors to Moscow were rare, especially during the long, harsh winters when sledges and skis were the chief means of transportation, as shown above right.

EARLY RUSSIA
About 1000 A. D.

Gulf of Finland
ESTONIANS   Lake Peipus   Novgorod
Pskov
LITHUANIANS
Rostov
Baltic Sea
W. Dvina River   Kazan
Murom
Smolensk
PRUSSIA
Oder River
Vistula River
Bug River
K I E V A N   R U S
Kulikovo
POLAND   Turov
Vladimir
Cracow   Kiev
Dnieper River
Don River
Volga River
Ural River
Danube River
CARPATHIAN MTS.
Dniester River
HUNGARY
P E C H E N E G S
CHAZARS
Caspian Sea
B Y Z A N T I N E
SERBIANS   WALLACHIA
BULGARS   Black   Sea
CAUCASUS MTS.
Constantinople (Istanbul)
E M P I R E

Kievan Rus
Paying tribute to Kievan Rus
Often controlled by the Pechenegs
Major Trade Routes
Other Trade Routes

0   100   200   300 MILES

Prepared by
Rand McNally & Co., Chicago

was sent by the Byzantine patriarch to preside over church affairs.

Yaroslav extended his domain by defeating the Lithuanians and annexing portions of their territory, now part of eastern Poland. He also checked the Finns and overcame the Estonians in order to give the Russians a firmer hold over the southern shores of the Gulf of Finland. The Pechenegs, one of many formidable nomadic raiders from Asia, were decisively beaten in 1036 and never again menaced Kiev or blocked the river road to Constantinople.

Like the empire of Charlemagne, the famous leader of the Franks with whom Yaroslav has been compared, the Kievan state never regained its preëminence after the death of its great ruler. Russian unity was shattered by civil war among his heirs.

It was regained only temporarily during the brief reign, from 1113 to 1125, of Vladimir Monomakh, the prince of Chernigov called to the throne by the desperate townspeople of Kiev.

Russia survived attacks from east and west. Periodic waves of Asiatic barbarians had swept into Europe from the time of the Huns, who in the 5th century helped to destroy the Roman Empire. However severely they suffered from these fierce invaders, the Russian people always managed to hold them off and retain their independence. But in the 13th century a more powerful conqueror, the Tartars, appeared on the Russian steppes. Under Genghis Khan these Mongol horsemen overran North China, Central Asia, Persia, and southern

Russia. After the great khan's death in 1227, his grandson Batu captured and pillaged Kiev in 1240 and brought the other Russian states under his control.

The Tartars were fierce warriors who showed their enemies no mercy. Using original sources, a well-known scholar of Russian history, Bernard Pares, described them as follows:

> . . . they despised other races and believed they were destined to carry out their master's command to conquer the world. [Genghis] Khan had organized them in multiples of ten; and if some of a "ten" were taken prisoners, the rest on their return were put to death. Hand-to-hand fighting they avoided where possible. . . . They liked to envelop an enemy by sheer numbers or to retreat before him, drawing him under a cross fire of their archery. "In this sort of warfare," writes Marco Polo [the famous 13th-century traveler], "the adversary imagines he has gained a victory, when he has in fact lost the battle." They could live for a month . . . on mare's milk, of which they made a kind of porridge; they could stay on horseback for two days on end, and sleep while their horses grazed. Each man took about eighteen horses with him and rode them in turns; if without other food, they would draw blood from their veins. In battle they executed their cavalry manœuvres like one man with extraordinary rapidity. Besieging an important town, they began by building a wooden wall all around it, which blocked all outlet and gave cover to their men. They gave no quarter, quoting a saying of [Genghis] Khan that "regret is the fruit of pity."

Tartar headquarters were maintained at Sarai on the lower Volga. For more than two centuries the Russians remained under the sway of the Golden Horde, as these Mongols were called (see map of Mongol Empire, Chapter 10). Russians were allowed self-government in exchange for the payment of tribute and the acknowledgment of Tartar supremacy.

Russia's national hero during the early years of the Tartar yoke was Prince Alexander of Novgorod. Known as Alexander Nevsky because of his rout of a Swedish army on the Neva river in 1240, he also repelled other aggressors from the west. His most notable victory was achieved two years later at the expense of the Teutonic Knights, a German order of crusaders, in the "battle of the ice" at Lake Peipus. Nevsky never dared challenge the Golden Horde, however. His rule in Vladimir as leader of the Russian nation from 1252 to 1263 rested upon the formal consent of the Tartar khan, with whom he negotiated to protect his people from further invasions. When he died, the bishop announced the news in the cathedral of Vladimir with these words: "My dear children, know that the sun of Russia has set."

Daniel, Alexander Nevsky's youngest son, inherited the principality of Moscow. Hardly more than a few villages dominated by the Kremlin, a walled fortress protecting the inner city, Moscow gradually expanded during the next century. Favored by strong rulers and a strategic location, it became the new center of the Russian church when the bishop moved there in 1328.

The princes of Moscow were obedient and reliable servants of the Tartars. In return they were given a dominant position over the other Russian rulers. After the Horde had begun to disintegrate in the latter part of the 14th century, Russian forces under Muscovite leadership crushed a huge Tartar army at Kulikovo in 1380. The victory was short-lived, for Tartar power was revived under Timur the Lame (Tamerlane). Moscow was sacked in revenge, and regular tribute was again exacted from the Russian princes. Not until 1480 was the Tartar threat ended forever. Moscow was then free to "gather in the Russian land," and when the process was completed, a mighty new state joined the other great powers of Europe.

1. What peoples were the traditional founders of the Russian state?
2. How did Christianity come to Russia? Why was Russia culturally isolated from the rest of Christendom?
3. Why is Yaroslav the Wise compared to Charlemagne?

4. Who were the Tartars and what role did they play in Russian history? What characteristics of these people enabled them to conquer a huge empire?
5. What aggressors from the west did the Russians succeed in turning back?
6. How did the princes of Moscow gain a dominant position in Russia?

Chapter 8   A Review

During the early Middle Ages three civilizations developed on the fringes of Europe: the Byzantine, the Moslem, and the Russian. The first inherited its territory and much of its political tradition from the Roman Empire, and it conferred upon the Russians the Orthodox religion and other aspects of its culture. The Moslem Empire encompassed many nationalities under the common tie of the Islamic faith and the Arabic language. The Ottoman Turks finally absorbed both Moslem civilization and the remnants of Byzantine territory.

Constantinople, the strategically placed Byzantine capital, nurtured a prosperous society and the best of Greco-Roman culture. Autocratic emperors but an unstable imperial succession; Christianity but a faith alien to the Roman Catholicism of the West; a Latin heritage but a Greek-speaking people—these were some of the contrasting features of a brilliant civilization which survived the fall of the western Roman provinces by a thousand years. Looted by Christian crusaders in 1204, the last Byzantine citadel—Constantinople—was captured in 1453.

Inspired by Mohammed, the prophet of Islam, restless Arabs conquered Byzantine and Persian territory in the 7th century and went on to found a huge empire in the Middle East, North Africa, and Spain. They were unable to hold these sprawling lands under one government for long. But such Moslem cities as Bagdad, Damascus, and Cordova equaled the wealth and splendor of Constantinople. Throughout the Moslem world, scholars, scientists, and artists made outstanding contributions in their fields. Both Moslem and Byzantine civilization easily surpassed the barbarism of early medieval Europe and helped preserve classical learning.

The eastern Slavs and their Viking rulers created what has proved to be the most enduring of the three states—Russia. The precarious unity maintained by the Kievan princes lasted about three hundred years. Then rival principalities contested Kiev's position, and in the 13th century the Tartar yoke was fastened upon the Russian people. Not until two centuries had passed were the dukes of Moscow able to win independence for Russia.

The Time

Indicate the correct period for each event.
(a) 301-600   (c) 901-1200
(b) 601-900   (d) 1201-1500

1. Seljuk Turks captured Bagdad.
2. Arab armies invaded Spain.
3. Oleg captured Kiev.
4. Mohammed made his *Hegira.*
5. Harun al-Rashid ruled the Moslem Empire.
6. Constantinople became the capital of the Roman Empire.
7. Ottoman Turks captured Constantinople.
8. Tartars captured Kiev.
9. Justinian ruled the Byzantine Empire.
10. Bagdad became the capital of the Moslem Empire.
11. Constantinople was looted in the Fourth Crusade.
12. Yaroslav the Wise ruled Kiev.
13. The Eastern Church broke completely with the Roman Catholic Church.
14. Moslems were defeated near Tours by the Franks.

The Place

1. Locate the site and name the contestants and victors in the "battle of the ice." In the battle of Kulikovo. What was the outcome of the battle of Manzikert?

2. Name the empire or state of which each of the following cities was the capital: Bagdad, Constantinople, Kiev. On what water body was each capital located?

3. Name one event in Moslem history with which each of the following cities is associated: Mecca, Medina, Tours. Locate each city.

4. Why was the Dnieper River a major trading route between Kievan Russia and the Byzantine Empire?

5. Name one product for which each of these Moslem cities was famous: Bagdad, Damascus, Cordova, Toledo. In which modern country is each of these cities located?

The People

1. What steps did each of these Byzantine rulers take to strengthen the Byzantine Empire: Justinian, Heraclius, Leo III, Basil II? For what act of bravery is Empress Theodora remembered?

2. With what Moslem group and Moslem conquest is Tarik associated? Saladin?

3. Name one achievement of each of the following Moslem scientists: Al-Razi, Omar Khayyám, Avicenna, Alhazen.

4. For what literary works were ibn-Khaldun and ibn-Batuta noted?

5. What contributions to Byzantine history were made by Anna Commena, Nicephoras Gregoras, and Procopius?

6. In what respects was the work of Michael Psellus typical of Byzantine scholarship?

7. Who was the most famous caliph of the Abbasside dynasty?

8. Give one achievement or event associated with each of the following leaders who influenced Russian history.

Vladimir Monomakh Rurik Olga
Alexander Nevsky Oleg Vladimir

9. Give two reasons why Yaroslav the Wise is called "Russia's Charlemagne."

10. What areas came under the sway of Genghis Khan? What actions did Batu and Tamerlane take to keep Russia subject to Tartar control?

Historical Terms

1. What were the following Byzantine contributions to art: mosaics, icons?

2. Why were the following achievements of Justinian noteworthy: *Code, Digest* and the *Institutes*, Hagia Sophia?

3. Define or identify each of the following terms as it applies to the religion founded by Mohammed.

Islam	Koran	mosque
Moslem	Ramadan	mullah
Hegira	polygamy	caliph
minaret	theocracy	

4. Give one event in Byzantine, Moslem, or Russian history associated with each of the following peoples.

Seljuk Turks	Berbers	Tartars
Ottoman Turks	Mongols	Bulgars
Teutonic Knights	Vikings	Pechenegs
Lithuanians		

5. What three groups of Slavs emerged in eastern Europe?

6. What was the Kremlin of Moscow at the time of Daniel Nevsky?

7. Identify the following Moslem books: *Rubáiyát, Arabian Nights, Canon of Medicine.*

8. How did "Greek fire" contribute to the success of the Byzantine navy?

Questions for Critical Thinking

1. To what extent did Justinian succeed in restoring Roman greatness? In what respects did he fail?

2. How does Islam differ from Christianity?

3. What factors contributed to the rapid spread of Islam? How did the methods used in spreading Islam compare with those used in spreading Christianity?

4. Do you agree with historian W. E. H. Lecky in his critical judgment of Byzantine civilization?

5. How did the Moslems and Byzantines contribute to the advance of Western civilization?

6. In what ways and for what reasons did the development of early Russia, from the 9th to the 14th century, differ from that of western Europe?

7. In what respects was Western civilization of about 1000 A.D. inferior to that of the Byzantines? of the Moslems?

Early Civilizations in Asia, Africa, and America

Most Westerners still imagine that ancient history is largely concerned with the Mediterranean countries, and medieval and modern history is dominated by the quarrelsome little continent of Europe.

This criticism of Western narrow-mindedness was made by India's famous political leader Jawaharlal Nehru. For too long, the study of non-Western areas has been neglected in schools and by textbooks of history. Why? Because, after 1600, much of the non-Western world fell under the colonial rule of the Western powers. The people of Asia and Africa were overwhelmed by the power and energy of the West, and for a time their past days of glory and greatness were obscured. In Europe, the peoples of the non-Western world were considered backward or, at best, strange. Their history was not examined seriously or systematically; in fact, it is not surprising that the history of these peoples was considered far less important than European history.

In the 20th century, the non-Western peoples have come alive. They have adopted the nationalistic creeds, the democratic ideals, and the modern science of the West, and they have demanded freedom from imperial rule. After World War II, colony after colony achieved independence. Former subject peoples, determined to be heard, eagerly entered into the drama of world history.

The emergence of the Afro-Asians is one of the most significant happenings of the 20th century. This condition of awakened vigor was well described at the first Asian Conference held in New Delhi, India, in 1947. Representatives of twenty-eight countries attended. In the opening address, Nehru declared:

> We stand at the end of an era and on the threshold of a new period of history. . . . we can look back on our long past and look forward to the future that is taking shape before our eyes. Asia . . . has suddenly become important again in world affairs. . . .

Asia . . . has played a mighty rôle in the evolution of humanity. It was here that civilization began and man started on his unending adventure of life. . . .

This dynamic Asia from which great streams of culture flowed in all directions, gradually became static and unchanging. Other peoples and other continents came to the fore and with their new dynamism spread out and took possession of great parts of the world. . . .

A change is coming over the scene now and Asia is finding herself. We live in a tremendous age of transition and already the next stage takes shape when Asia takes her rightful place with the other continents.

More than half of the world's population demands attention. In order to understand their problems, one must learn about the history, the culture, and the achievements of the non-Western peoples.

The Indus Valley in India and the Hwang Ho Valley in China, like the river valleys in Egypt and the Fertile Crescent, were cradles of civilization. In both India and China, the essentials of civilization had been developed by about 2000 B.C. In the Indus Valley, great cities such as Mohenjo-Daro flourished. With the invasion in 1500 B.C. of the Indo-Aryans, who were related to the Greeks and Romans, India entered a new era. Two features of the Indian way of life, which developed gradually at this time, were the caste system and the religion of Hinduism. These important cultural elements have come down to the present relatively unaltered. During the long span of Indian history, much of its culture was exported by Indian immigrants, traders, and colonists to other Asian areas, especially Southeast Asia. In Hindu history two empires were outstanding: the Maurya and the Gupta. After about 650 A.D. Hindu power declined, and India was overun by Moslem invaders from central Asia. From about 1000 to 1500, they set up a number of Moslem kingdoms in the land. In the

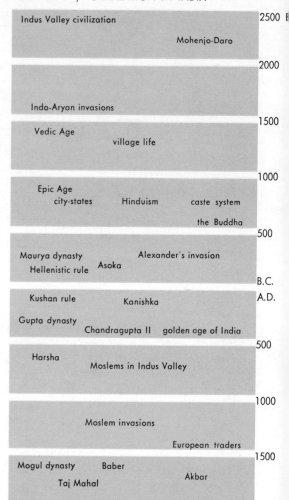

16th century a new group of Moslems came to India and established a remarkable state, the Mogul Empire.

China is comparable to India in its long history and contributions to world civilization. China's series of imperial dynasties, including the Chou, Han, Tang, and Manchu, covered an immense time span—from 1027 B.C. to 1912 A.D. From the Chinese came silk, the compass, the first adding machine, and printing. Chinese art stands in a class by itself. The picture at the beginning of this unit, "Spring Festival on the

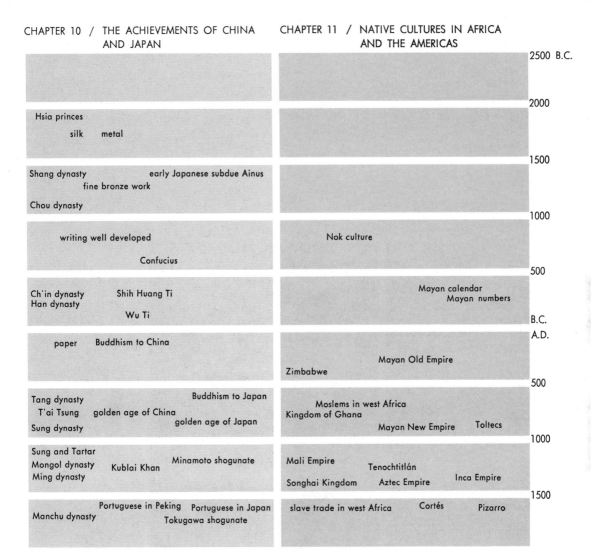

River," was painted on silk hundreds of years ago. It illustrates the formal manners of the people, the sophistication of their culture, and the delicacy of their art. Chinese culture played a prominent part in the development of Japan. There were important differences between the two peoples, however, so that Japanese culture is not just an off-shoot of the Chinese.

Other non-European areas that were almost unknown to white men until late in the 15th century were Africa south of the Sahara Desert and the two American continents. The vast area in Africa south of the Sahara lay static and largely undisturbed until early modern times, although advanced cultures grew up in what is now Southern Rhodesia and in the empires of Ghana and Mali. North America was populated by Indian tribes whose ways of life were relatively simple. But to the south, the Mayas in Yucatan, the Aztecs in Mexico, and the Incas in Peru built remarkable civilization. The Mayas were the most advanced, for they were creative in both art and science.

Civilization in India

CHAPTER 9   2200 B.C.–1700 A.D.

Civilization in India—as in Mesopotamia and Egypt—grew up along a river. An artist of the Indus Valley carved the head at left, found at Mohenjo-Daro. Over the centuries, the development of the Hindu religion provided stability. The Hindu god Siva, center, was worshiped throughout the land. Mogul invasions beginning in the 11th century introduced a new element, Islam, into Indian life. Strong rulers such as Akbar, right, consolidated Mogul power.

In the 4th century B.C., when ways of life in northern Europe were primitive, the Mauryan Empire flourished in northeastern India. About 302 B.C., Megasthenes, a Greek envoy from western Asia, came to the Mauryan court. Luckily for historians, he spent much of his spare time writing an account of the products, customs, and government of this first great Indian empire.

Megasthenes lived in Pataliputra, the capital, a walled city covering some eighteen square miles and surrounded by a deep moat. The city walls were of wood with 64 gates and 572 towers placed at regular intervals. Streets were laid out in orderly fashion, and in the heart of the city was located the palace of the king, Chandragupta Maurya. The palace was a beautifully carved wooden structure. Its pillars were plated with gold and silver and ornamented with intricate designs.

Chandragupta was a stern ruler and a master of intrigue. For the most part he lived in seclusion in his palace, but on special holidays, he toured the capital city. Megasthenes described one such occasion in which the monarch, seated on the back of an elephant, led a colorful procession.

Then came a great host of attendants in holiday dress, with golden vessels, such as huge basins and goblets six feet broad, tables, chairs of state, drinking and washing vessels, all of Indian copper, and many of them set with jewels, such as emeralds, beryls and Indian garnets. Others bore robes embroidered in gold thread and led wild beasts, such as buffaloes, leopards and tame lions, and rare birds in cages.

The prosperity and wealth of the empire impressed Megasthenes favorably. All land belonged to the state, and a tax on farm products was the chief source of government income. Irrigation and crop rotation were practiced, and Megasthenes claimed that famine was almost unknown in the land. Commerce and handcraft industries thrived. Textiles, cutlery, and agricultural implements were made for export. Displayed for sale in the bazaars of Pataliputra, Taxila, and other cities of the empire were products from southern India, China, Mesopotamia, and Asia Minor.

The organization of the Mauryan Empire was remarkable for its time. It was one of the first large, well protected, and efficiently administered states in history. The empire was divided into three provinces, each of which was governed by a viceroy who had his own staff of civil servants. City administration was progressive. In Pataliputra, for example, government committees guarded the rights of craftsmen, registered all births and deaths, regulated the quality of merchandise traded, and collected taxes. The Mauryan army included 600 thousand infantrymen, 30 thousand cavalrymen, and 9 thousand war elephants—the "armored tanks" of the ancient East. Excellent roads, marked by milestones, connected the many villages and towns. One road extended for 1200 miles, from Taxila to the capital city.

After the fall of the Mauryas in the 2nd century B.C., other great empires arose on the Indian subcontinent. Each made noteworthy contributions to science, mathematics, literature, and art. In this chapter, the rich panorama of Indian history to about 1700 A.D. is described in the following sections:

1. **The earliest civilization of India began in the Indus Valley.**

2. **Many features of Indian life evolved in early times.**

3. **Strong rulers established Indian empires.**

4. **India enjoyed a golden age during the Gupta Empire.**

5. **Moslems controlled India for centuries.**

BACTRIA

INDO-ARYAN INVASIONS

HINDU KUSH MTS.

KHYBER PASS · Peshawar
GANDHARA · Taxila

HIMALAYA

DESERT

River

· Harappa

BOLAN PASS

DESERT

Indus

Mohenjo-Daro ·

DESERT

SIND

MOUNTAINS

Jumna

Gogra River

Ganges River

Ganges River

Brahmaputra River

BENGAL

BURMA

River

Narbada

Arabian

Godavari

Bay

Sea

DECCAN

River

of Bengal

Kistna

River

0 ———— 300 MILES

TAMIL LAND

CEYLON

Prepared by
Rand McNally & Co., Chicago

The earliest civilization of India began in the Indus Valley

Chapter 2 pointed out that the four earliest civilizations grew up in river valleys, and discussed the two that arose along the Nile and along the Tigris and Euphrates rivers. The third of the four civilizations lay in the valley of the Indus River in what is now West Pakistan. The Indus Valley is a fertile plain located in the shadow of the Hindu Kush mountain range.

Evidence uncovered since 1922 shows that a civilization flourished in the Indus Valley between 2500 and 1500 B.C. Archaeologists have found the remains of sixty villages and towns in an area about 950 miles long. Their inhabitants lived mainly by farming. They also carried on wide commerce, and were skilled at weaving cotton and making pottery, jewelry, and utensils of copper, silver, and lead.

An ancient city had modern features. Archaeologists have learned much about the Indus Valley people by studying the remains of a city at the site now called *Mohenjo-Daro*. It had industrial and business areas and wide, straight streets. Along the streets stood flat-roofed brick houses with wells and bathrooms. The city sewage system was so well planned that it had no equal in the modern world until the middle of the 19th century. At Mohenjo-Daro the people made toy birds and animals; they made small statues of people and arm bands carved with figures of tigers, elephants, and crocodiles. Scholars believe that some of their gods influenced later Indian religion.

Disaster created "the place of the dead." About 1500 B.C. a disaster struck Mohenjo-Daro, and possibly the entire Indus Valley civilization. Skeletons were found in groups, as though these long-dead people had huddled together for comfort in the face of an overwhelming catastrophe. But what happened is still a mystery. Later the area was given the name Mohenjo-Daro, which means "the place of the dead."

Even before the decline of the Indus Valley culture, another group of people had apparently created a strong, well-organized society in India, especially in the south. These were the *Dravidians*, who were short and dark-skinned. They built large cities and castles, and traded with Babylonia. The Dravidians may have been descended from the people of Mohenjo-Daro. No one can be sure, however, because the history of India is not completely known. It is known that the people of prehistoric India were dark-skinned, because they were so described by invaders from the west, who are discussed in the next section.

Section Review
1. Where was the first civilization of India? When did it flourish?
2. Of what importance to modern historians is Mohenjo-Daro? What modern features did it have?
3. Who were the Dravidians?

2 **Many features of Indian life evolved in early times**

The life of the average Indian villager today is governed by ancient traditions. They regulate how he makes his living, how he worships, and even how he dresses and eats. Most of these customs date back to the period of Indian history discussed in this section.

Indo-Aryans invaded from the northwest. About 1500 B.C. tribes of invaders began pouring through the mountain passes into northwestern India. These were the Indo-Aryans, part of the large group of Indo-European peoples described in Chapters 3 and 4. Like their relatives who were invading Persia, Greece, and Italy at about that same time, the Indo-Aryans were fair-skinned and tall, with long heads and regular features. They were hearty eaters and drinkers, fought hard, and had a simple, seminomadic existence. They lived mainly by herding cattle and by farming small plots of ground.

The wealthiest men among them were those who had the most cattle. (The Indo-Aryan word for war meant "a desire for more cows.") The wealthiest man in a tribe was probably also the ruler, or *rajah*. The Indo-Aryans considered the Dravidians coarse, ugly, and inferior. Actually, the Dravidians were the more civilized. Although they defeated the Dravidians, the Indo-Aryans adopted many Dravidian customs and ideas, including certain features of their religion.

Indian Art, like that of medieval Europe, was usually inspired by religion. The carving above right is an example of the Gandharan style. While the Buddha's gracefully draped robes and wavy hairstyle show the influence of Greek and Roman sculpture, his serene pose is typically Indian. The Gupta artist who made the relief carving below depicted dancing girls performing in a temple. In contrast to the calm Buddha, an animated Hindu warrior god, dating from about 750 A.D., fiercely waves his many arms, above left.

Village life took shape in the Vedic Age. The first Indo-Aryan civilization lasted around 600 years, from about 1500 to 900 B.C. This period is called the *Vedic Age,* a term which comes from the word *Vedas* (meaning "knowledge"), the name of the Indo-Aryans' first literature. Information about the Indo-Aryan invaders came from the *Vedas,* which were collections of writings on religion, philosophy, and magic.

The Indo-Aryans killed some Dravidians, drove others southward, and made slaves of those who remained. During this period many Indo-Aryans became farmers and settled down in villages.

Indian village life assumed much the same pattern it has today. There was a village leader called the *headman,* sometimes inheriting the post, sometimes elected to it. The village men worked as farmers or craftsmen, or both. Their houses had mud walls, clay floors, and thatched roofs. A villager's chief garment was a wraparound skirt, the end of which he threw over his shoulder.

City-states developed during the Epic Age. The Indo-Aryans had been gradually pushing eastward to the valley of the Ganges River and south toward the Narbada River. Settlement reached these rivers about 900 B.C., the beginning of the *Epic Age* (so called because our knowledge of it comes from epics composed during the period).

By the beginning of the Epic Age, the Indo-Aryans had created many kingdoms around city-states much like those of early Greece. These kingdoms were almost always at war, and the stories of war heroes gave rise to many epics.

These well-built city-states were surrounded by moats and walls. In the center stood the palace of the rajah, or king, who had much greater power than the village headman. The rajah maintained an army and consulted a royal council made up of relatives and other nobles. In theory, at least, the rajah owned all the land. A middle class emerged in the cities, partly as a result of trade.

Because cattle were prized as a symbol of wealth, as such they represented a unit of standard value—a sort of money. A man often bought his bride with cows. Copper coins came into use later, and toward the end of the Epic Age traders used letters of credit, which would indicate that the people had some form of banking.

Indo-Aryans set up the basis of the caste system. Beginning at the time of their first invasions, some Indo-Aryans had married Dravidians. The invaders probably soon began to feel that if the fair Indo-Aryans continued to marry Dravidians, they would be almost as dark as the Dravidians in a few generations. To prevent this, the Indo-Aryans developed a system of rigid social groups. Dravidians were forbidden to marry Indo-Aryans or even to associate closely with them.

For some time the system remained a simple division between the dark Dravidians and the lighter Indo-Aryans. Gradually, however, four distinct groups appeared among the Indo-Aryans: (1) the *Brahmans* or priests; (2) the *Kshatriyas,* or warriors; (3) the *Vaisyas,* or traders and landholding farmers; and (4) the *Sudras,* or serfs. In addition, there was a fifth group, the *pariahs,* also called *untouchables* because other Indians believed that the touch of one of them, or even his shadow, would contaminate them. For a long time, the Kshatriyas, or warriors, ranked first. But as warfare declined and religion became more important, the priestly Brahmans became most important.

The Epic Age ended about 500 B.C., and afterward the people of India developed a more rigid and complex division of society, the *caste system,* which they fitted into the original structure. The hundreds of castes were based on purity of race, politics, position in society, kind of work, wealth, and religion. The members of each caste had to follow caste rules governing marriage, occupations, religious rites, and social habits such as eating and drinking. People had to marry within their own caste and remain in the caste into which they were born. No amount of success or achievement could enable a person to move from a lower to a higher caste.

Indians created enduring literature. The invading Indo-Aryans brought a language related to those of the Greeks and Romans. During a thousand years in India, this tongue developed into a language known as *Sanskrit.* By the 4th century B.C., Sanskrit had three forms—the religious Sanskrit of the Brahmans, the Sanskrit of the poets, and the Sanskrit of the arts and politics.

Early Sanskrit literature includes the *Vedas,* and the most important in these collections of writings is the *Rig-Veda,* meaning "Hymns of Knowledge." It has 1028 hymns of praise to various gods. The Brahmans passed these hymns down by word of mouth from generation to generation. It has been said that some Brahmans could recite as many as 100,000 verses. Scholars wrote many commentaries on the *Vedas,* called the *Upanishads,* which speculate about the beginning of the world and of man.

The Epic Age produced two great epic poems, the *Mahabharata* and the *Ramayana,* both describing the adventures of Indo-Aryan heroes. Like the *Iliad* of the Greeks, the *Mahabharata* tells of a great war, and is probably the work of many poets. The *Ramayana,* like the Greek *Odyssey,* tells of a hero's wanderings and of the patient wait of his faithful wife. The *Mahabharata* glorifies war and adventure; the *Ramayana* shows the growth of knightly ideals among the Indians.

Hinduism stressed rebirth. The Indian religion of Hinduism developed from the early Indo-Aryans' sacrifice of animals to a number of gods. The greatest god was Indra, who—like the Greek Zeus and the Roman Jupiter—threw thunderbolts, ate bulls by the hundred, and drank lakes of wine. But the *Rig-Veda* tell hymns about something more vital than the gods—a moral law that rules both gods and men. In short, Hinduism progressed to a belief that the universe and everything in it was God. This principle was termed *Brahma.* It was personified in many gods, the most important being Brahma (the creator), Siva (the destroyer), and Vishnu (the preserver).

Hinduism developed elaborate ceremonials and rituals. It stressed a deep respect for all living things, and the cow became holy as a symbol of the sacredness of life. One of the basic aspects of later Hinduism was its emphasis on escape, which Hindus desired because they believed the world to be evil and unimportant. Every Hindu wished to escape from the physical world into a world of the spirit. He believed he could be truly happy and at peace when his soul was taken by the "world-soul" and was made a part of it.

Hinduism taught that the soul escapes through a process of rebirth connected with the caste system. A man lives and dies many times. Each time he dies he is *reincarnated,* or born again in a new body. This process is called the *transmigration of the soul.* Each existence gives a man a chance to improve himself by living according to Hindu ethics. As he improves, he is born into a higher caste. If the Hindu's soul improves in each life, he is finally born into the highest caste—the Brahman. And if he continues to improve as a Brahman, his soul is absorbed by the world-soul and does not return to earth. If a Hindu should not improve—that is, if he should break the religious law—his soul is reincarnated in a person of a lower caste or even in an animal.

It is because Hindus believed the world and all physical things in it were evil that some of their holy men have starved themselves, lived as hermits, and actually inflicted pain on their own bodies. By this privation and self-torture, the Hindu holy men have shown their disapproval of the physical world.

Because of his beliefs, the Hindu has not feared death, believing that the soul merely changes its form. A death is only one incident in perhaps a thousand or more lives and deaths as the spirit makes its long journey to reach the world-soul.

Buddhism originated in India. Some thinkers grew dissatisfied with the elaborate rites of Hinduism and its enforcement of the caste system. One of these was Gautama Siddhartha, who was born about 563 B.C., and who died in 483 B.C.

Gautama was the son of a king whose domain lay close to the Himalayas. When Gautama was twenty-nine, he left his wife and child and his easy life to search for an answer to the question, "Why do men suffer pain and sorrow?" He lived with holy men, fasted, and inflicted tortures upon himself. Then one day as he sat meditating under a sacred tree, he felt that the truth had come to him. Thereafter, he was known as the Buddha, a name meaning "The Enlightened One." He taught and preached for the rest of his life, and formulated these beliefs, the Four Noble Truths:

1) Human life—as manifested in birth, old age, sickness, and death—is full of pain and sorrow.
2) Pain is caused by man's craving for life, passion, and pleasures.
3) Pain can be stopped by putting an end to craving.
4) The way to stop craving, and thus to end pain, is to travel the *Eightfold Path,* along which one must practice right belief, right intention, right speech, right action, right livelihood, right effort, right thinking, and right meditation.

The Buddha believed that if one followed these rules, his soul would finally be freed of the bondage of rebirth and would enter *nirvana.* Nirvana, according to the Buddha, cannot be defined, but it is the final result of the end of all earthly desires when the soul finds perfect peace.

As a reformer of the Hinduism of his time, the Buddha preached against the rites and dogmas of the Brahmans, and broke with their rules of caste by treating all men alike. He also attacked the extremes of self-punishment practiced by some Hindus, and taught the Middle Way, or moderation in all things.

During the Buddha's lifetime, his teachings spread over all central and northern India. He founded several orders of monks, who built monasteries that became centers of learning. In spite of his ban against the worship of deities, the Buddha's followers made a god of him after his death. They established a religion called Buddhism based on his teachings.

Section Review
1. Why is the early Indo-Aryan period called the Vedic Age?
2. How did the caste system develop? How did it relate to Hindu beliefs about death?
3. What developments in Indian culture took place in the Vedic Age? the Epic Age?
4. What Hindu beliefs and practices did the Buddha attack?

3 **Strong rulers established Indian empires**

Shortly after the end of the Epic Age, India was threatened by a new invasion from the northwest. Alexander the Great had defeated Persia in 328 B.C. Two years later, hoping to conquer still more territory,

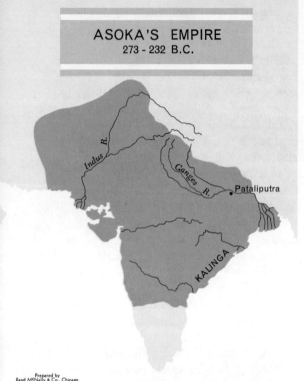

ASOKA'S EMPIRE
273 - 232 B.C.

he crossed the Indus River into India. He defeated an Indian army and pushed on toward the east. However, his soldiers refused to go farther, and he had to turn back.

The Maurya dynasty brought unity and peace. Alexander is said to have met and influenced a young Indian named Chandragupta Maurya. In 321 B.C., Chandragupta seized an Indian kingdom and established himself in its capital, Pataliputra. His power grew, and in the years following he conquered all of northern India. He was the first ruler of the Maurya dynasty.

In 273 B.C., Chandragupta's grandson, Asoka, became emperor. He led a military campaign which enlarged the Mauryan Empire to include all but the southern tip of India. But the cruelty of the campaign horrified him, and he never fought again.

Sickened at the bloodshed and the loss of thousands of lives, Asoka determined to give his people peace rather than war. At about this time he was converted to Buddhism, an event that may well have helped turn him away from warfare. Asoka commanded his people to be kind, truthful, and liberal. He had rules of conduct carved on pillars, some of which still stand. He enshrined relics of Buddhist saints in domed monuments called *stupas,* and had Buddha's life pictured in sculptures. Yet Asoka also allowed other religions in his empire.

Asoka sent Buddhist missionaries north to the lands of the Himalayas, to the southern tip of India, and to Ceylon, Burma, Syria, Egypt, Cyrene (in North Africa), and Macedonia. As a result, Buddhism became the religion of a large part of the world. It could be said that Asoka was to Buddhism what the Apostle Paul was later to be to Christianity.

Asoka, one of the outstanding rulers in history, gave India unity and peace. But soon after his death in 232 B.C. his empire began to fall apart. The last Mauryan emperor was assassinated in 184 B.C., and a series of invasions brought northern India under foreign rule.

Hellenistic kings came from the West. In the eastern part of Alexander's empire, bordering northern India, was the Greek kingdom of Bactria. It had achieved independence in the mid-3rd century B.C. Demetrius, a Bactrian ruler, conquered part of northern India in 183 B.C. The enlarged state of Bactria formed an area in which Hellenistic and Hindu culture mingled. The most important result of this intermingling was the rise of a famous school of art in the area of Gandhara, which blended eastern and western traditions. Hellenistic rule ended about 130 B.C., and most of the Hellenistic influences diminished.

Kushan rulers helped spread Buddhism. During the Hellenistic period in northern India, strong nomadic tribes were sweep-

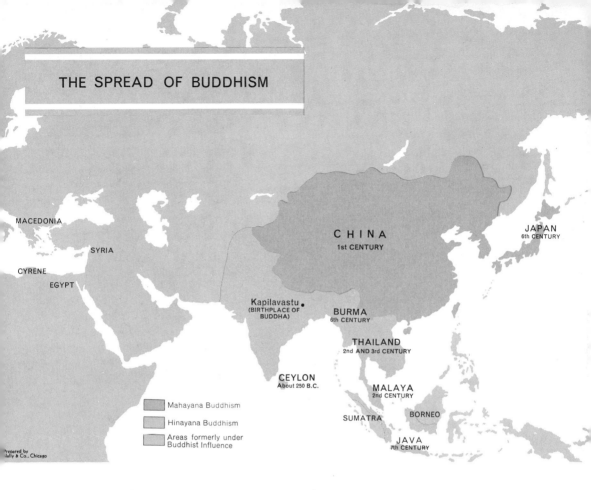

MACEDONIA

SYRIA

CYRENE

EGYPT

CHINA
1st CENTURY

JAPAN
6th CENTURY

Kapilavastu
(BIRTHPLACE OF
BUDDHA)

BURMA
6th CENTURY

THAILAND
2nd AND 3rd CENTURY

CEYLON
About 250 B.C.

MALAYA
2nd CENTURY

SUMATRA

BORNEO

JAVA
7th CENTURY

Mahayana Buddhism

Hinayana Buddhism

Areas formerly under
Buddhist Influence

Prepared by
Jally & Co., Chicago

ing south and east from central Asia. By the 1st century A.D., one tribe, the Kushans, had conquered much of northwestern India. Their rule lasted until about 200 A.D.

The most powerful Kushan king, Kanishka, became ruler about 78 A.D. He ruled over a large area of Asia, including what is now Afghanistan and northwestern India. He pushed his boundaries south, perhaps as far as the Narbada River. He built fine buildings in his capital, Peshawar, and encouraged the study of medicine.

Kanishka was a patron of Buddhism, and called a council of 500 monks, who developed the *Mahayana* school of Buddhism. Believers in this school supplemented the original Buddhist traditions, which they called *Hinayana* Buddhism. One development was belief in a great number of minor deities, called *Bodhisattvas*, who aided men in their achievement of nirvana. Mahayana Buddhism spread through much of northern Asia, becoming the Buddhism of China, Mongolia, Tibet, and Japan. Hinayana Buddhism prevailed in Burma, Thailand, and Malaya, and also on the island of Ceylon.

Southern India traded with Rome. During the Kushan period, India carried on a flourishing trade with the Greco-Roman world, and the Kushan emperors were on friendly terms with the Romans. There was a large exchange of goods between the two countries, most of it passing through the ports of southern India.

The people of the south, the *Tamils*, were descendants of the Dravidians who

THE GUPTA EMPIRE
320-480 A.D.

R.
Indus
Ganges
Ajodhya
Pataliputra
R.
Narbada R.
• Ajanta

Prepared by
Rand McNally & Co., Chicago

had been driven from the north by Indo-Aryan conquests. They had established several independent and usually quarrelsome kingdoms. The prosperous Tamils were remarkable builders, and constructed great irrigation works and temples. Roman coins found in southern India show that there was extensive trade between the Roman Empire and India. In fact, some of the first Indian coins were copied from Roman coins. Roman ships brought precious metals, wine, pottery, glass, and silverware to south India. There the Romans bought coral, spices, silk, precious stones, and rice to sell in Europe.

Section Review

1. Why was Asoka's first military campaign also his last? How did he encourage Buddhism?
2. How did the Hellenistic invaders influence Indian civilization?
3. What new form of Buddhism grew up under Kanishka? Where is it practiced today?
4. What evidence shows that Indians traded with the Roman Empire?

4 **India enjoyed a golden age during the Gupta Empire**

After the fall of the Kushans, northern India broke up into many small states. A period of cultural decline lasting about 100 years came to an end in the 4th century, when a new line of kings, the Guptas, came to power. The Guptas arose in the same area as the Mauryas. Their reign is called the golden age of Hindu culture.

The first Gupta king became ruler of the Ganges Valley about 320 A.D. The Gupta Empire reached its height in the period between 380 and 413, during the reign of Chandragupta II (not related to the Chandragupta Maurya discussed earlier). The Guptas reigned until about 535 A.D.

The people prospered. The Gupta emperors ruled strongly but fairly. Their income came from port duties, the royal lands and mines, and a tax on farm produce. Trade and manufacturing flourished. A Chinese Buddhist on a pilgrimage to India wrote:

> . . . The people are many and happy. They do not have to register their households with the police. There is no death penalty. Religious sects have houses of charity where rooms, couches, beds, food, and drink are supplied to travelers. . . .

Buddhism, however, was no longer one of the chief religious sects, and in time was to disappear almost entirely from the land of its founder. Buddhism had been losing its Indian followers partly because of its tolerance of foreign invaders such as the Greeks and Kushans. People began to feel

During the 1st century A.D., a sea captain named Hippalus observed certain regularities in the winds in the Indian Ocean. His observations led to the discovery of the *monsoons*, winds that blow steadily in certain directions at different seasons of the year.

By utilizing winds of the southwest summer monsoon, ships were able to sail directly across the Indian Ocean to India from the Red Sea, the Persian Gulf, Arabia, and East Africa. Use of this direct route, instead of the old route along the coasts of Arabia, Persia, and India, cut the Africa-to-India sailing time from twelve months to two. Return voyages were made from India after the northeasterly winter monsoon set in during October. As a result, sea trade to India increased and an all-water trade route to China developed.

The action of the monsoons can be explained simply. In summer, air masses over India are warmed, become lighter, and rise, creating low atmospheric pressure in the area.

Meanwhile, over the Indian Ocean the air is cooler and denser, and the atmospheric pressure is high. Air flows naturally from areas of high pressure toward areas of low pressure, and thus winds sweep across the Indian Ocean into India. The April-to-October summer monsoon brings storms and heavy rains.

Autumn brings cooler weather and cooler, denser air over India and most of Asia, producing high atmospheric pressure. Air over the Indian Ocean, however, remains warmer because water tends to lose or gain heat more slowly than land—and the water thus warms the air at this season. The warm air rises, creating a low pressure area in the Indian Ocean. As a result, when the "high" over India builds up and the "low" over the Indian Ocean develops, the winter northeast monsoon begins. Winds sweep from India out across the Indian Ocean and the Arabian Sea from October to March. By December the winds bring dry, clear weather which is ideal for sailing.

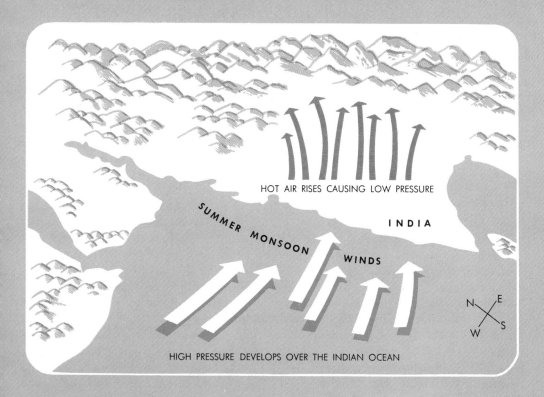

HOT AIR RISES CAUSING LOW PRESSURE

INDIA

SUMMER MONSOON WINDS

HIGH PRESSURE DEVELOPS OVER THE INDIAN OCEAN

that Hinduism was a more truly Indian religion. Support of the Brahmans by Gupta rulers also aided Hinduism.

Learning and art flourished. Scholarship and science throve under the Guptas. The astronomer and mathematician Aryabhata discussed in verse the value of pi (π), and the rotation and spherical shape of the earth. Other Indian astronomers calculated the diameter of the moon and wrote on gravitation.

The contributions of Indian mathematicians to world civilization were among the greatest of any people. They developed the number symbols which served as the basis for our own numerals. (Because these symbols were adopted and carried westward by Arab traders, they were called *Arabic numerals* by people in the West.) Gupta scholars also worked out the decimal system and were probably also the first—aside from the Maya Indians of Yucatan—to make use of the zero.

Indians found new uses for chemistry in manufacturing, and their steel was the best in the world. They were the first to make cotton, calico, cashmere, and chintz. Gupta doctors were far more skilled than the European doctors of the period. In the universities established during this time, physicians learned to sterilize wounds and perform surgery. They were especially skilled in treating snake bites.

Gupta literature is famous for its fairy tales and fables. The most famous storybook of the time is the *Panchatantra*, a collection of eighty-seven stories written between 300 and 500 A.D. Other Indian writings included the world-famous story of Sinbad, which finally found its way into *The Arabian Nights.* Some Indian fables were later translated into European languages, and were used by such authors as Chaucer, the Grimms, and Kipling in their tales. Much good poetry and drama also belongs to the Gupta period.

During the time of the Gupta Empire, Indian painters and sculptors freed themselves from Hellenistic influences to create a basically Indian art. Artists, inspired chiefly by Hinduism, produced dignified and restrained work. The Ajanta cave paintings, which date from this period, are well known for their beauty.

Indian culture influenced other peoples. From about the 2nd to the 10th centuries, Indian emigrants, traders, and conquering armies carried their way of life to all of southeast Asia. The influences had a gradual effect, but eventually reached as far away as Madagascar and Formosa.

Indian influence was strongest in such places as Ceylon, Burma, and central Thailand, where the cultures became almost entirely Indian. In more distant areas such as Java, Cambodia, and southern Indo-China, Indian culture was not so strong, and blended with local customs.

Indian art, however, made a strong impression on all of southeast Asia. It influenced a Buddhist dynasty of central Java, which built the world's largest Buddhist shrine at Borobudur in the 8th or 9th century. About the same time, Hindus in Cambodia began one of the greatest religious buildings in the world, the temple of Angkor Wat. This building, finished in the 12th century, also owed much to Indian architecture.

Centuries of disunity followed Gupta decline. Gupta power began to decline after Chandragupta II died in 413 A.D. The Huns invaded northwestern India near the end of the 5th century, while their kinsmen under Attila were invading Europe. By the middle of the 6th century, the Gupta Empire had been brought to ruin.

Small states continued to make war on one another until early in the 7th century. A ruler named Harsha brought order when he made himself master of most of the area of the Gupta Empire between 606 and 612. Harsha was a patron of the arts, a poet, and a good military leader and administrator. But he was a despot, though a kindly one. When he died in 647, he left no one trained to take his place, and all of northern India again plunged into discord.

The strife that followed Harsha's death brought more than a political decline. In Jawaharlal Nehru's history of India, he writes that there was a

> . . . decline all along the line—intellectual, philosophical, political, in techniques and methods of war, in knowledge of and contacts with the outside world. . . .

The Hindus had become overconfident and self-satisfied with what they had and what they were, an attitude that not only halted progress but also weakened the country. Because of this weakness, the Indians were unable to defend themselves against a new wave of invaders.

Section Review

1. Why did Buddhism lose most of its followers in India?
2. What contributions did Gupta scholars make in science, technology, and mathematics?
3. In what areas of southeast Asia was Indian influence strongest? Where did it have less effect?
4. What weakened India after the Gupta and Harsha regimes?

5 **Moslems controlled India for centuries**

Arab Moslems had established a province in the southern Indus Valley as early as the year 711, but Indian rulers had prevented them from expanding. Then, 300 years later, another Moslem force came to India.

Invaders came from the north. During the 11th and 12th centuries, warlike Moslem invaders came from the mountainous country of Afghanistan through the passes into northwest India. Some were Afghans and some were Turks, but all of them believed in the religion of Islam, the faith of the Prophet Mohammed. They believed their faith should be spread by the sword, and they looked down on the Indians because of their different religion.

At first these Moslems came as robbers to loot the gold and jewels of the Indian cities. But when it became apparent to them how weak and rich India was, they began to set themselves up as kings and princes. Between the years 1000 and 1500, they established many sultanates, or Moslem kingdoms. The sultanate centering around the great city of Delhi was one of the most powerful. By 1318, the Moslems had conquered all of India except the extreme southern part. Firuz Shah Tughluk, an enlightened Moslem ruler, abolished tortures for crime and built towns, colleges, irrigation projects, and mosques. He died in 1388, and ten years later Timur the Lame, or Tamerlane, another Moslem, marched into India. Tamerlane had already conquered central Asia and, defeating all armies sent against him, looted Delhi and killed perhaps 100 thousand prisoners in cold blood—Moslems and infidels alike. Afterward, he departed westward, leaving the few survivors in Delhi to perish of famine and plague.

The Moguls united most of India. About 1500 came new Moslem invaders led by Baber, whose name meant "Tiger." He was a Turk, descended from Tamerlane, and was also related to Genghis Khan, the great Mongol leader. The Indians thought of Baber as a Mongol, and applied their word for Mongol, *Mogul,* to his dynasty.

The Moguls quickly set about strengthening their power in northern India. In

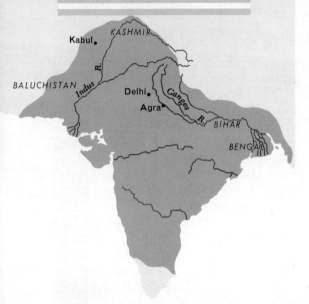

THE MOGUL EMPIRE
About 1690

Kabul

KASHMIR

BALUCHISTAN

Indus R.

Delhi

Ganges R.

Agra

BIHAR

BENGAL

mate knowledge not only of military and political matters, but of many of the mechanical arts. He took delight in watching the casting of pieces of artillery, and in his own palace kept workmen constantly employed in the manufacture of guns and arms of various descriptions. In short, he was well informed on a great variety of subjects . . . He always entertained at his court a dozen or so [learned men] . . . To their discussions . . . he was a willing listener, believing that by this means he could overcome the disadvantage of his illiteracy.

Akbar believed that religious tolerance was essential for the stability of his empire. Therefore, he declared freedom of religion for all his subjects. It was also his personal belief that truth could not be restricted to one religion. In 1582 he created a religion of his own, which included ideas from several different religions. Known as *Din Ilahi* (meaning "divine faith"), it did not gain followers outside the royal court and died out after his death.

Akbar improved the administration of justice and restricted the use of physical torture and the death penalty to the most serious crimes. An orderly man, he was conscientious in the performance of his duties toward the people. As reported by the priest previously quoted:

1556, the Mogul ruler Akbar, grandson of Baber, began to conquer other territories from his capital at Agra, near Delhi. By 1576, he had extended his rule eastward by conquering Bihar and Bengal. Ten years later, Kabul and Kashmir in the north were annexed. In 1595, when Baluchistan became a part of his empire, Akbar was the undisputed ruler of northern India.

Akbar was the greatest of all Mogul rulers. Akbar could neither read nor write, but he had an agile mind and a great desire to learn. In order to increase his knowledge, he surrounded himself with philosophers, artists, architects, priests, and poets from many countries. One of his visitors, a Roman Catholic priest, described him in this fashion:

Akbar . . . was a man of sound judgment, prudent . . . kind, affable, and generous . . . He was interested in, and curious to learn about many things, and possessed an inti-

That any person might be able to speak to him on business of importance, Akbar appeared twice daily in public, to give audience to all classes of his subjects. . . Eight experienced officers, whose judgment he could trust, were in constant attendance on him. Amongst these he apportioned the days of the week, so that each had his special day for introducing those who desired an audience. . . When giving audience, the King is also attended by a number of secretaries, whose duty it is to record in writing every word he speaks.

Akbar ruled for forty-nine years. At his

The Moguls brought to India a rich Moslem style of art and architecture. The miniature painting, which reflects Persian influence, depicts an audience in the court of a Mogul ruler. Akbar allowed all his subjects to appear before him with petitions. The white marble tomb, inlaid with semiprecious stones, was built in Agra for one of Akbar's officials.

death in 1605, northern India was a unified state. Later Mogul kings pushed their control southward. At its peak, about 1700, the Mogul Empire was the largest in the history of India up to that time. After 1707 it disintegrated, but the Mogul dynasty continued in weakened form until 1857.

The Moguls were great builders. Akbar and his successors had many magnificent buildings constructed in the empire, including Moslem mosques, palaces, forts, and tombs. One of their palaces at Delhi is the largest in the world. On one of its walls can still be seen this inscription: "If anywhere on the earth there is Paradise, it is here, it is here, it is here."

The most famous Mogul building, and one of the most beautiful in the world, is the Taj Mahal, at Agra. It was modeled after a tomb that Akbar designed for his mother and father. The emperor Shah Jehan built the Taj Mahal in the year 1632 for his favorite wife. A total of 22 thousand workmen labored on it for more than twenty years. Built of white marble, it is inlaid with precious stones. Shah Jehan and his wife are buried there side by side.

Section Review
1. Why did Moslem invaders decide to settle in India?
2. For what were Mogul rulers noted?
3. Why is Akbar considered one of the outstanding rulers of history?

Chapter 9 A Review

The first civilization of India developed in the Indus River Valley somewhat later than the river valley civilizations of Egypt and Mesopotamia.

A mysterious disaster destroyed this early culture, but a new one grew up under the Indo-Aryans, who had invaded India from the northwest. During the Vedic and Epic ages, some of India's greatest literature was composed. This period also witnessed the development of such distinctively Indian institutions as the village community, the caste system, and the Hindu religion. Another Eastern religion, Buddhism, was also established in India at this time. Its founder, Gautama Buddha, wanted to reform Hinduism. Instead, his followers made a religion of his teachings and a god of him after his death.

Shortly after an invasion by Alexander the Great, northern India was united under the Maurya dynasty. This dynasty produced an important ruler, Asoka, who brought peace and fostered the spread of Buddhism. The decline of the Mauryas in the 100's B.C. was followed by other invasions. Rule by Hellenistic Greeks from Bactria had little lasting effect on India, but the Kushans, who controlled northern areas for about 200 years,

had a strong influence, especially on the growth of Buddhism. The Kushan period was one of lively trade with the West, most of it moving through Tamil ports in southern India.

A new line of emperors, the Guptas, ruled during India's Golden Age. They favored Hinduism, and Buddhism almost disappeared from the land of its birth. India under the Guptas made many contributions to the world, including the numerals now used in the West, the decimal system, and advances in astronomy and medicine. Writers and artists also made noteworthy contributions to the civilization of India.

With the decline of the Guptas, starting in the 5th century, India was thrown into discord. During a brief period in the 7th century, Harsha provided strong rule. Then in the 11th century, Moslem invaders began establishing small kingdoms in India. In the 1500's, a fresh wave of Moslems, the Moguls, swept into India. Their greatest ruler, Akbar, united northern India and was noted for his great love of learning. The Mogul rulers became famous for the construction of beautiful mosques and palaces, including the Taj Mahal at Agra.

The Time

Indicate the period in which the events described in the following statements occurred.

(a) 3000-1001 B.C.   (d) 1-500 A.D.
(b) 1000-501 B.C.   (e) 501-1000 A.D.
(c) 500-1 B.C.   (f) 1001-1500 A.D.
       (g) 1501-1700 A.D.

1. Alexander the Great crossed the Indus River into India.
2. Indo-Aryan invaders began their conquest of northern India.
3. Mahayana Buddhism was spread by the Kushan kings.
4. A flourishing civilization arose in the Indus Valley.
5. A city-state civilization developed during the Epic Age.
6. The Moslems established sultanates in India.
7. Gautama Buddha died.
8. The Vedic Age began.
9. Asoka sent out missionaries to spread the message of Buddhism.
10. The Moguls created a great Indian empire.
11. Disaster struck Mohenjo-Daro.
12. The Mauryan Empire flourished in India.
13. Harsha brought India a short period of peace and order.
14. Gandharan art rose during the rule of the Hellenistic kings.
15. The golden age of the Guptas stimulated learning and the arts.

The Place

1. Locate each of the following places and give one reason why each place was significant in Indian history: Mohenjo-Daro, Pataliputra, Peshawar, Delhi, Bactria.
2. Name and locate the city or country to which one would go to visit the following shrines or works of art: Ajanta cave paintings, the Taj Mahal, the largest Buddhist shrine in the world, the temple of Angkor Wat.

The People

1. Identify each of the following persons (1) by indicating the kingdom or empire he governed and (2) by citing one of his achievements: Chandragupta Maurya, Asoka, Demetrius, Kanishka, Harsha.
2. Name one accomplishment of the following Moslem leaders: Firuz Shah Tughluk, Tamerlane, Baber, Akbar, Shah Jehan.

Historical Terms

1. Identify each of these Hindu castes: Brahmans, Kshatriyas, Vaisyas, Sudras.
2. Hinduism is the religion of most of the people of India today. Explain the meaning of these terms which are associated with Hindu philosophy.

transmigration of the soul   Brahma
reincarnation   "world-soul"

3. Explain the meaning of the following Buddhist terms and concepts.

Four Noble Truths   nirvana
Eightfold Path   Middle Way
Mahayana Buddhism   stupas
Hinayana Buddhism   the Buddha
Bodhisattvas

4. Identify these Indian writings.
Mahabharata   *Upanishads*
Panchatantra   *Ramayana*
Rig-Veda

5. Define each of the following terms as it applied to early Indian life: rajah, headman, Sanskrit.
6. Give one significant fact about each of the following Indian peoples: Indo-Aryans, Dravidians, Tamils, Moguls. With which group are the sultanates and Taj Mahal associated?

Questions for Critical Thinking

1. Contrast the rule of the Guptas and the Moguls. Which period is more deserving of the title "golden age of Indian culture"? Why?
2. To what extent was Indian civilization, up to about 1600 A.D., influenced by foreign peoples?
3. Which teachings of the Buddha resemble those of Christianity? Which differ?
4. What conditions account for the golden age of the Guptas? How did these conditions compare with those which brought about the golden age of Pericles? Explain.

The Achievements of China and Japan

CHAPTER 10 2000 B.C.–1644 A.D.

For centuries, the Chinese held scholarship in great respect. (The emaciated man with a scroll is a scholar sitting at his work table, his writing instruments nearby.) The Japanese, who borrowed many elements of Chinese civilization, did not share this reverence for learned men. They admired the military valor of their samurai, or warrior, class; shown above is a band of warriors.

One of the most interesting aspects of world history is *culture diffusion,* the process by which inventions, beliefs, and customs have been transmitted from one group of people to another. Traders, courtiers, missionaries, and warriors have acted as agents in the process. Sometimes warfare stimulates culture diffusion, but long periods of peaceful intermingling have also resulted in profitable exchanges.

Throughout its history, China has been a rich source of inventions for people from other lands. Silk, printing, paper, the compass, tea, and porcelain originated in China, and their introduction in the West had far-reaching effects. It is not surprising, however, that the greatest impact of the whole of Chinese culture took place in the areas close to China itself—that is, in Japan, Korea, southeast Asia, and to a lesser degree, in central Asia.

In the 3rd and 4th centuries A.D., the Chinese established a strong province in southern Manchuria and northern Korea. This area, well known to Japanese raiders and traders alike, served as a link for the exchange of ideas and goods between the Chinese mainland and the islands of the Japanese archipelago. In addition, Chinese immigrants introduced their arts, crafts, and system of writing to the islands. Buddhism, which originated in India and later had taken a strong hold in China, also spread to Japan, and Buddhist temples were built there, particularly after the 8th century A.D. Chinese law codes played an important role in the evolution of Japanese government while Chinese sculpture, painting, and literature exerted a powerful influence on the Japanese people. Until the 19th century heralded the arrival of the Industrial Revolution, Japan looked to China for cultural leadership.

Yet Japanese culture should not be viewed as merely an outgrowth of Chinese civilization. An intriguing element in the process of culture diffusion is the manner and degree to which ideas and techniques passing from one group to another are modified according to the needs and traditions of the borrowers. Such was the case with Japan. The Chinese civil service system, which was set up to provide a pool of officials from all classes, was borrowed by the Japanese, who restricted the eligible candidates to members of the aristocracy, thereby radically altering a testing system based on merit. The complicated Chinese writing symbols were adopted by the Japanese, who used them to represent syllables of their own language, not ideas, as the Chinese did. And, little by little, Chinese art forms were modified so that in time unique Japanese styles appeared.

In this chapter, the rise and development of China and Japan are discussed in the following sections.

1. **The first civilization in China arose in the Hwang Ho Valley.**

2. **The Chou dynasty ruled longest in China.**

3. **Two dynasties united China.**

4. **The Tang dynasty gave China a golden age.**

5. **Invasions failed to destroy Chinese civilization.**

6. **Mings and Manchus maintained Chinese culture.**

7. **Japan developed its own traditions.**

1   **The first civilization in China arose in the Hwang Ho Valley**

Man's story in China began many thousands of years ago. As discussed in Chapter 1, remains of an early form of man, Peking Man, were discovered in China. This discovery indicates that Stone Age men lived in the area as long as 500,000 years ago. During the centuries that followed, their descendants laid the foundations of civilization in China. The earliest civilization there, as in the three other "cradlelands" of Egypt, Mesopotamia, and India, arose in the valley of a great river.

China's cradle of civilization lay to the northeast, in the valley of the Hwang Ho, or Yellow River. As in the other three cradle areas, the river brought new fertile soil with every flood. In addition, strong winds from the west blew in a fine-grained soil called *loess*, which further enriched the land.

Hsia princes ruled in legendary times. Knowledge of early China comes from legends, which say that for a long period— from about 2000 to 1500 B.C.—the land was ruled by the Hsia princes. Yü, the first prince of Hsia, is described as being brave and strong, somewhat like the Greek Zeus. He is said to have fought a mighty river to save his people from floods. According to an early Chinese saying, the people claimed that, "But for Yü we should all have been fishes."

Such legends are unreliable, but it is true that people of a New Stone Age culture settled in the Hwang Ho Valley. They farmed, raised cattle, and made fine pottery. Walls of pounded earth surrounded their villages of mud houses. The people had a simple form of government, and were divided into upper and lower classes. These early Chinese learned to mix tin and copper to make bronze, and to cast the melted bronze into useful and pleasing shapes. They also invented a form of picture writing, and found out how to make fine cloth from the unraveled cocoons of silkworms.

Shang kings were religious leaders. The recorded history of China begins about 1500 B.C. with the rise of the Shangs, whose capital was located north of the lower part

THE RULE OF CHOU
1027—256 B.C.

Prepared by
Rand McNally & Co., Ch

of the Hwang Ho, near the present city of Anyang. The Shang kings controlled only a small area around their capital, while strong nobles ruled the more distant parts of the kingdom. However, the nobles recognized the Shang king as the head of the armies and as the high priest, or religious leader. They believed he governed by command of heaven. As high priest, he paid homage to his ancestors and made animal sacrifices to gods to bring about good harvests.

Much of the knowledge of Shang history comes from excavations of sites near Anyang. One important source of information is the writings on pieces of animal bones and tortoise shells, which were used to foretell the future. Priests wrote questions on the bones and shells. They heated the bones and interpreted the cracks that resulted as answers from gods or ancestors. The inscriptions show that Chinese writing was well advanced at this time. Shang writing, like that of the early Egyptians, used pictures, and had a total of about 2000 symbols. Writings were inscribed on tablets of wood or bamboo.

The people of the Shang kingdom are best known for their fine bronze work. The pieces found are balanced and beautifully decorated. Shang sites have also yielded pieces of carved ivory and jade, marble sculptures, dagger-axes, and chariot fittings. These discoveries indicate that the Shang period was highly civilized. The people, however, were conquered by a less civilized group that invaded the country from the northwest.

Section Review

1. Where did the earliest civilization of China arise? What geographical conditions helped the people there?
2. What were three important achievements of the Chinese Stone Age culture in the Hwang Ho Valley?
3. Who ruled China in the earliest historical period? What were their main duties?
4. What Shang period remains indicate the level of civilization at that time?

2 **The Chou dynasty ruled longest in China**

The Shang period, like many other eras in Chinese history, ended with a successful invasion by a less civilized people. The leader of this less civilized group was known as *Chou.* The dynasty named after him began in 1027 B.C., and ruled for almost eight centuries, until 256 B.C.

During the first phase of the Chou period, lasting about 250 years, the kingdom consisted of over a thousand feudal states, each under the control of a noble. The nobles were loyal to the king and furnished him with soldiers to keep order and to extend the boundaries of the kingdom. Toward the end of the period, however, the nobility used the soldiers to extend the boundaries of their own states at the expense of other nobles. In 771 B.C., some of the nobles joined forces, marched on the Chou capital, Honan (Loyang), and killed the king.

A new Chou king was allowed to take the throne, but he had little power. He became hardly more than a high priest who performed state religious rituals and tried to ease tensions among the nobles. During this period, the Chinese moved into and settled the richly fertile river valley of the Yangtze. The stronger nobles gained control over the land of the weaker nobles, and, as a result, the number of feudal states decreased, but those that survived increased in power.

During the last two centuries of the Chou period, sometimes called *The Era of Contending States,* the strong nobles warred constantly with one another. They invented catapults to break down the mud walls of enemy towns, and for the first time used companies of mounted archers to make sudden attacks.

The Chou period made lasting achievements. The eight centuries of Chou rule were perhaps the most important in Chinese history. This era is often called the *classical* period because the great literary classics were collected at that time.

The Chou period saw changes in the economic life of China. Many people gave up farming and became merchants or craftsmen. Towns grew in size and number. Craftsmen who practiced the same trade organized guilds to help each other and improve the quality of work. Trade grew during the Chou dynasty, although most of it took place within the Chou kingdom itself. The goods traded included jade ornaments, bronze mirrors and vessels, iron tools, silks, furs, and furniture.

Three Great Religions—Confucianism, Taoism, and Buddhism—helped shape Chinese history. The philosophy of Confucius was preserved by his pupils. He is pictured above by a Tang artist. Lao-tse himself, according to legend, wrote the Taoist "Book of the Way" while visiting at the home of an official, below. Buddhist pagodas dotted the Chinese countryside after missionaries brought the faith from India. The miniature porcelain pagoda above probably was used as a family shrine.

The Chou era was also important for the government of China. The Chinese, like the Egyptians, believed that their ruler was divine and, beginning with the Chou period, they called their king the *Son of Heaven.* Unlike the Egyptians, however, the Chinese limited the power of their kings. When the Chous seized the throne, they declared that they had been justified in doing so because the Shangs had not ruled well, and thus had not had the support of the gods. According to this theory, the *Mandate of Heaven,* all rulers were expected to govern justly and to look after the well-being of their subjects. If a king neglected this duty, he would no longer enjoy the support and favor of the gods, and could be dethroned by his people. This belief provided a justification for revolution.

The king was assisted by a chief minister and six department heads who were chosen because of their intelligence rather than their birth. The department heads consisted of: the Director of the Multitude (agriculture), the Director of the Vast Labors (public works), the Director of the Horses (war), the Director of Rites (religious affairs), the Director of the Royal Household (finance), and the Director of Criminals (justice).

Confucius was a great Chinese teacher. During the Chou period, great thinkers and teachers drew up rules of conduct for the Chinese people. Among other things, they regulated what should be worn for special occasions, the serving and eating of food, the way in which people talked to one another, and the conduct of a son toward his father. This code of politeness changed little until recent times, and still has an influence on Chinese life.

One of the greatest Chinese teachers, Kung-fu-tse, is better known today by the Latinized form of his name, Confucius. He is the most honored and revered man in all Chinese history.

Confucius was born in 551 B.C., only a few years after the Buddha. He began to teach when he was twenty-two. According to one tradition, he won such fame that when he was fifty-two, the prince of his state asked him to become governor of a province. He gave the people good government, but a jealous neighboring governor forced him to resign. After trying unsuccessfully to persuade other princes to adopt his plans of government, he returned to teaching.

Confucius did not think of himself as an inventor of new ideas; he called himself a transmitter, not a maker. He is believed to have preserved the literature of China for later times. Fearing that it would be lost during the troubled era in which he lived, he gathered earlier writings to prepare what are called the "Five Classics."

Unlike the Buddha, Confucius did not seek to escape from the world, but wanted instead to find a way for man to be happy on earth. He taught that human nature was good, not bad. If men would think and act properly, he believed, most evils would disappear. His teachings held that men should develop the virtues of kindliness, tolerance, and respect for older people and ancestors. In government he believed the ruler was like the father in a family: he directed the government, but was responsible for the welfare of his people. Confucius also stressed the importance of education, good manners, and tradition.

The teachings of Confucius provided an admirable system of practical ethics for the people of China, and had a great influence on them. His followers thought so highly of him that they combined his teachings with their religious ideas about ancestor worship to develop a religion called *Confucianism,* which continues today.

Great as Confucius was, he may not have been altogether good for China. He loved tradition and the past, and stimulated in the Chinese a strong dislike for change. Their extremely conservative attitudes were to have serious consequences in later years.

Taoism grew out of Lao-tse's teachings. Chou China produced another great teacher, Lao-tse. Very little is known about him as a person, but his teachings, organized into a religion known as *Taoism*, have had a great influence on China. This religion holds that the best way to live is not by complicated rules or artificial restraints, but according to nature. The word *Tao* means "way," and Taoists believed that those who followed this way, as taught by Lao-tse, would learn the meaning of the universe. The religion held that men should be kind, free from pride, humble, and thrifty, and should return an injury with a great kindness. Unlike Confucius, who stressed the importance of good government, Lao-tse believed that the less people are governed, the better off they are.

Over the centuries, simple Taoism has been buried under a great deal of superstition and magic. But early Taoists, because of the stress on nature, made important contributions to Chinese science.

Art and literature flourished. Chou artists made many beautiful pieces of cast bronze, as well as wooden sculptures, lacquer ware, and pottery. They also did especially fine carvings in jade. Once, when Confucius was asked why the Chinese prized jade so highly, he replied:

> . . . It is because, ever since the olden days, wise men have seen in jade all the different virtues. It is soft, smooth and shining, like kindness; it is hard, fine and strong, like intelligence; its edges seem sharp but do not cut, like justice . . . the stains in it, which are not hidden and which add to its beauty, are like truthfulness. . . .

The Chinese language is not an easy one, although Chinese words have only one syllable. A single word may have several meanings. For example, *fu* can mean "rich," "store up," or "not." The speaker gives the meaning by the tone of his voice. As a result, spoken Chinese varies in tone, and has a "sing-song" quality.

Long before the Chous rose to power in 1027 B.C., the Chinese people developed a system of writing. By the end of the Chou period, writing was so well developed that it has come down to the present with few changes.

Chinese writing, like Egyptian, developed from picture writing. The Egyptians went on to develop symbols for consonant and vowel sounds combined—though they did not use them much—but the Chinese continued to use a symbol for each word or concept. There are about 40,000 Chinese picture symbols. Only a few scholars learn all of them.

The classical literature of China dates to Chou times. Among the most famous works are the "Five Classics," which were com-

THE RULE OF CH'IN
221—206 B.C.

piled by Confucius. Of these, the *Book of History* and the *Book of Poetry* are the best known. A poem from the *Book of Poetry* tells the thoughts of a young girl whose lover has neglected her:

You student, with the collar blue,
Long pines my heart with anxious pain.
Although I do not go to you,
Why from all word do you refrain?
O you, with girdle strings of blue,
My thoughts to you for ever roam!
Although I do not go to you,
Yet why to me should you not come?

Section Review

1. What were the lasting achievements of the Chou period? Why is this era sometimes called the classical period?
2. How did Confucius serve as a transmitter of ideas?
3. In what way did the teachings of Confucius have a good influence on the Chinese? In what way did they prove to be a bad influence?
4. How did Taoism differ from the teachings of Confucius?
5. Why is Chinese a difficult language to write?

3 Two dynasties united China

The centuries immediately preceding and following the birth of Christ witnessed much expansion and exchange among the civilized peoples of the world. Alexander's conquests established a brilliant Hellenistic culture, but it gave way before the vigorous Romans. In the East, India prospered under the Mauryas, the Bactrian kings, and the Kushans. Merchants traveled back and forth between East and West, exchanging goods and ideas.

China, too, took part in the expansion and cultural interchange that characterized this period. Two dynasties, the Ch'in and the Han, provided strong government that

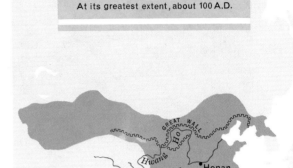

THE HAN EMPIRE
At its greatest extent, about 100 A.D.

fostered outside contacts with peoples from other lands.

A Ch'in emperor centralized the government. In the closing years of the Chou dynasty, the king of Ch'in, one of the warring feudal states, became China's strongest ruler. The Chou dynasty fell in 256 B.C., and after a power struggle among several states, the Ch'in ruler seized control of China in 221 B.C. and established a new dynasty. It is from the name of this dynasty that China got its name.

Although Ch'in control lasted only until 207 B.C., it was absolute and the ruler had complete authority over all the people. Only a very able, strong man could bring about such a state of affairs. This man was called *Shih Huang Ti* ("First Emperor").

Shih Huang Ti extended China's boundaries southward, and united the country by making Ch'in laws the laws of the whole nation, setting up uniform systems of weights and measures, and building a net-

The Great Wall of China winds along the tops of mountain ridges. From tall towers located at regular intervals, sentries commanded a wide view of the countryside. When a guard saw enemies approaching, he signaled by smoke during the day or by rocket flare at night. The wall, located in the northern part of the country, served as protection against Hun tribes attracted by the warm climate and rich soil of China.

work of tree-lined roads. Most important, he strengthened the central government by destroying the power of the nobles. He then organized China into thirty-six military provinces, each governed by an appointed official. This basic form of government, with modifications, lasted more than 2000 years, until 1912 A.D.

To bolster his rule, Shih Huang Ti tried to erase from the minds of the Chinese the ideas of Confucius. Because Confucian literature fostered tradition and described the old Chou system as virtuous and just, the First Emperor ordered all of it burned. Many books survived, however, and were later collected and saved.

To protect the northern and western border areas from invasion by the barbaric Huns, Shih Huang Ti added to and joined together several protective walls to make the Great Wall of China. This great fortification extended 1500 miles, from the northwestern limit of China eastward to the Yellow Sea. The wall, built of stone, brick, and earth, was in most places twenty-five feet high and fifteen feet thick. A roadway ran along the top. Because of the hardships they endured, the men forced to build it died by the thousands, and, according to an old Chinese saying, "every stone cost a human life."

The Han dynasty extended the boundaries of China. Civil war broke out in China shortly after the death of the First Emperor in 210 B.C. After eight years of disorder, a new dynasty gained control. It took the name *Han* because its first ruler, a general, had once led an army on the Han River. The Han dynasty was one of the most illustrious in Chinese history; Chinese still call themselves "sons of Han." In four centuries from 202 B.C. to 220 A.D., China grew as large and prosperous as the Roman Empire of the same period.

The greatest Han ruler was Wu Ti, who lived between 140 and 87 B.C. He drove the Huns back from the Great Wall, took part of Korea, and extended the empire southward to Indo-China and westward to central Asia. Before the Romans established the *Pax Romana*, or Roman Peace, around the Mediterranean, Wu Ti brought a Chinese Peace to central and eastern Asia. Later Han emperors pushed their boundaries to the borders of India and Persia.

During the Han period, the Chinese made several cultural advances. They invented the first shoulder collar for draft animals, which made it possible for animals to pull heavier loads than before. (Europeans did not know about this device for another 1400 years.) By the end of the 1st century A.D., the Chinese had invented paper. They also compiled the world's first dictionary and wrote the first scholarly history of China.

China met other civilizations. The expansion of China during the Han period brought the nation into contact with other peoples. Trade with the West prospered especially along the so-called "Silk Road." This route ran from China through central Asia, crossing deserts and mountains, to the borders of the Middle East. Along this highway, probably in Chinese Turkestan, merchants from the West met Chinese trade caravans bringing luxury wares, especially silks, spices, and furs, which were highly prized. The traders swapped ideas as well as goods, and exchanged much information. People of the Roman Empire learned about such fruits as peaches, apricots, and rhubarb from the Chinese. Roman influence led the Chinese to adopt a more lifelike approach to art and design, and

possibly new musical ideas and advanced knowledge of chemistry; from central Asian peoples the Chinese learned about grapes and alfalfa.

Chinese contact with India led to an important result—the introduction of Mahayana Buddhism into China. A Chinese mission went to the Kushan Empire and brought back the religion about 67 A.D., and it spread rapidly.

Section Review

1. What dynasty gave China its name? What were some of the accomplishments of the period?
2. Why did Shih Huang Ti attack Confucian literature?
3. What did Wu Ti accomplish for China? What cultural advances were made during the Han period?
4. What did the Romans learn from the Chinese? What did China learn from other peoples?

4 **The Tang dynasty gave China a golden age**

The glory of the Hans faded in the 3rd century A.D. War lords seized parts of the empire, and the last of the Hans was deposed in 220 A.D. China broke up into little warring kingdoms, and barbarians broke through the Great Wall. Science, art, invention, and trade stood still or declined. China, like Europe during the same era, underwent a period of darkness and confusion, but China recovered faster. Its recovery began in 623, when a new group of rulers, the Tangs, came into power.

The Tangs provided good rule for almost 300 years. This extremely productive period was a golden age for China because the country was prosperous and free from invasion, and its people made advances in education, literature, and the arts. New canals were built, foreign trade increased,

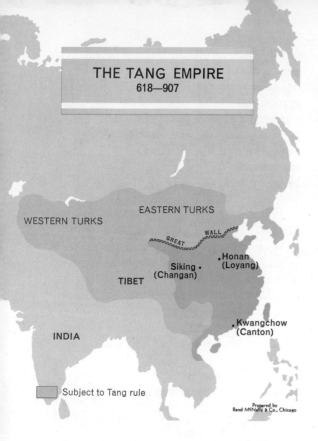

THE TANG EMPIRE
618—907

WESTERN TURKS

EASTERN TURKS

GREAT WALL

TIBET

Siking
(Changan)

Honan
(Loyang)

INDIA

Kwangchow
(Canton)

Subject to Tang rule

Prepared by
Rand McNally & Co., Chicago

and once said: "By using a mirror of brass you may see to adjust your cap; by using antiquity as a mirror you may learn to foresee the rise and fall of empires."

T'ai Tsung refused to make harsher laws to discourage crime because, he explained, "If I diminish expenses, lighten the taxes, and employ only honest officials . . . this will do more to abolish robbery than the employment of the severest punishments." This emperor knew that he owed it to his people to govern wisely. One day, when in a boat with his son, he said: "The water bears up the boat, but it can also overturn it. So with the people—they uphold the prince but they can also overthrow him!"

Education strengthened Chinese government. The Chinese were among the first to develop a civil service, in which government positions are filled by public examination. The system, which began during the Han dynasty, was greatly strengthened under the Tangs.

Education played an important role. Good students were sent from local schools to the colleges of their provinces, and the best students then went to the imperial university in the capital, where several thousand of them studied for the civil service. This educational system provided China with intelligent and well-trained officials. It also carried Chinese influence abroad, because other countries of Asia sent their young men to China to be educated.

Thousands of officials of the Chinese government belonged to the civil service system. They were selected after taking written tests, given every three years. Each candidate sat in a separate room, where he had three days to answer the examination questions. So important was the examination that the strain on the candidates was extreme, and some went mad or even died of exhaustion. The final examination included essays on current events and Confucian classics, an original poem and

and the population grew to 50 million. Some scholars believe that at its height the Tang Empire was the strongest, most enlightened, most progressive, and best governed in the world.

A great emperor governed wisely. An exceptional Tang ruler, T'ai Tsung, became emperor in 627, when he was only twenty-one. He pushed back the invading barbarians and extended the frontiers of China. Later, his son extended the empire farther until it included all of Korea and stretched westward to Afghanistan—about the same distance as that from New York to San Francisco.

After several military campaigns, T'ai Tsung concentrated on the peaceful development of China. He strengthened government administration, curbed the growth of large estates, and tried to equalize the tax burden. He valued the study of history, prose composition, and special tests in law and mathematics.

Many poets wrote during the Tang period. A common saying about the Tang era held that "Whoever was a man was a poet." One of the greatest and certainly one of the most carefree of the Tang poets was Li Po. He wandered around with a group of companions who called themselves "The Six Idlers of the Bamboo Streams" and later with another group, "The Eight Immortals of the Wine Cup." He found time, however, to write some of the best poetry of China. One of his poems entitled "The Moon over the Mountain Pass" reads:

> The bright moon soars over the Mountain of Heaven,
> Gliding over an ocean of clouds.
> A shrill wind screaming ten thousand li away,
> And a sound of whistling from Yu-men pass.
> The imperial army marches down White Mound Road.
> The Tartars search the bays of the Blue Sea.
> The warriors look back to their distant homes:
> Never yet has one been seen to return.
> Tonight, on the high towers she is waiting.
> There is only sorrow and unending grieving.

Another great poet was Tu Fu, whose love of nature is expressed in the following lines from his poem, "The Rain at Night."

> The good rain knows when to fall,
> Coming in this spring to help the seeds,
> Choosing to fall by night with a friendly wind,
> Silently moistening the whole earth.
> Over this silent wilderness the clouds are dark.
> The only light shines from a river boat.
> Tomorrow morning everything will be red and wet,
> And all Chengtu will be covered with blossoming flowers.

The Chinese invented printing. Literature flourished under the Tangs, not only because the people were prosperous and the government stable, but also because of the invention of printing. They had used ink as early as 1200 B.C., an excellent type which they made from lampblack and which is known in English as India ink or China ink. During the Han dynasty the Chinese invented paper.

Early Chinese printing, as developed under the Tangs, is called *block printing*. The printer carved raised characters on a block of wood, wet the surface of the characters with ink, and pressed sheets of paper against them. Printers in the 11th century went on to invent movable type of baked clay. The characters of the movable type could be rearranged to form different words and thus be used over and over again. The Chinese alphabet has about 40 thousand characters. Because of the difficulty of producing so many pieces of type, most Chinese printers continued to use block printing.

Most early Chinese books were not books in our sense of the word, but printed rolls of paper. Gradually, however, the Chinese developed books with pages and covers. They also invented paper money and printed playing cards.

Section Review

1. After the decline of the Hans, how did China resemble Europe during the same period?
2. How did the Tang ruler T'ai Tsung strengthen China?
3. How did the Chinese educational system spread Chinese influence to other countries? In what way was the Chinese system of government administration unusual? What other achievements made the Tang period a golden age?
4. Why did Chinese printers prefer the system of block printing even after they had invented movable type?

Chinese Arts and Crafts

Throughout the long history of China, its people have produced works of great beauty and charm. During the prehistoric Bronze Age, a Shang craftsman made the intricately detailed metal sculpture on the opposite page. This owl-like figure is actually a vessel for holding liquids and probably was used in the elaborate funeral ceremonies characteristic of the time. The pottery figurines at right below reflect the elegant, refined court life of the Tang dynasty. Two dancers and three musicians entertain a princess. The ceramic group at left—two men with a cart and bullock—was also made during the Tang era, a time when commerce thrived under stable and efficient government. A portion of an exquisite Sung scroll painting, above, depicts women preparing silk, a major trade item between East and West. At far right above, a farmer and water buffalo plow a rice field. This jade carving from the Manchu period is a fine example of the Chinese craftsman's skill.

Invasions failed to destroy Chinese civilization

Signs of decay in China could be seen as early as 751. In that year, Arabs intent on spreading Islam defeated the Chinese in central Asia and took the province of Turkestan. Other defeats and political corruption further injured the Tangs, and their dynasty came to an end in 906.

China was divided under the Sungs. Five weak dynasties followed the Tangs. It was not until 960 that a strong new dynasty, called the *Sung*, came to power. Even then, fierce barbarians beyond the Great Wall were a constant danger.

For 400 years after the fall of the last Tang, the history of China is largely the story of barbarian attacks. These savage tribes had been a threat to China and to other countries from earliest times. Among the fast-riding barbarians were the Huns, Mongols, Turks, and Tartars (or Tatars). The nomadic Tartars were a mixture of Turks, who conquered the Byzantine Empire, and the Mongols, who overcame the Russians. (Chapter 8.) They had often invaded China. Usually the Chinese had quickly closed the gap in the Great Wall and driven off the tribesmen or bribed them to return to their highlands.

During the reign of the Sungs, barbarian invasions grew more and more violent. Soon after the dynasty was established, the Tartars began to fight their way into northern China. The Sung emperors, rather than fight, tried to appease the Tartars with bribes of money and silks. This appeasement encouraged the Tartars to ask for more. Then the Sungs tried to bribe one group of Tartars to destroy another. Although this trick worked at first, the victors grew strong and turned against China. They captured the Chinese emperor and set up a Tartar empire in northern China, with its capital at Peking.

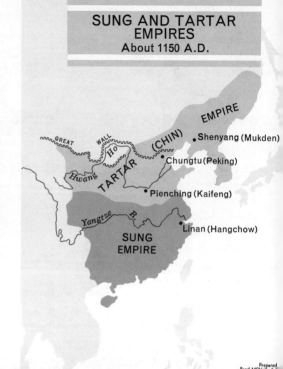

SUNG AND TARTAR EMPIRES
About 1150 A.D.

Prepared
Rand McNally & C.

The Sung dynasty was not destroyed, however. The son of the captured emperor established a new capital at Hangchow in southern China. China then, in 1127, consisted of two empires—the Tartar in the north and the Sung in the south.

The Sung Chinese produced many inventions. Although the Sung dynasty ruled during a time of constant danger and frequent strife, scholars made several contributions to Chinese civilization. Learned men wrote on botany, chemistry, and geography. They also produced many historical writings; one such history covered events from the 5th century B.C. to the 10th century A.D. The first full study of *historiography*, the art of writing history, also appeared. The techniques of map making also improved.

Important progress was made in science and technology. The Sung Chinese developed inoculation for smallpox and learned how to make gunpowder; at first they used the new explosive only in religious ceremonies, but later they made bombs and hand grenades with it. The Sung introduced the first adding machine, the *abacus,* a device which is still used by many people in the Orient.

Sung artists and craftsmen created masterpieces. While the Tang period had been an age of great poets, the Sung era was one of great artists. Chinese painting reached a degree of perfection never again achieved. In fact, many experts believe that the distinctive style of the best Chinese painting of this period has never been equaled by any other people.

Chinese painting is not photographic. Painters try to show the spirit of what they picture. Many Chinese paintings consist of long rolls. When a person wants to enjoy such a painting, he unrolls and "reads" it.

Many stories are told about Sung artists. One artist could draw a perfectly straight line 1000 feet long. Another could draw a detailed map of China in a one-inch square. Landscape paintings were especially popular during the Sung dynasty. One artist is said to have painted an enormous landscape so realistic that he stepped into the mouth of a cave in the picture and disappeared forever.

Another art in which the Sung Chinese surpassed all other peoples was the making of porcelain. This type of pottery was made with a special white clay, which was mixed with powdered rock and sand, moistened, and made into a smooth paste. The potter shaped this mixture and fired it in a kiln. The Chinese discovered unusual glazes and used them to beautify porcelain surfaces in soft rich colors. One piece of green-glazed porcelain was described as "like curling disks of the thinnest ice, filled with green clouds."

Many factories made porcelain plates, cups, bowls, candlesticks, and other objects. Later, when Europeans came to China, they set up shops that copied Chinese porcelain models. They exported their porcelain to Europe as *chinaware,* a word still used to describe porcelain.

The Mongols conquered China. About the year 1200, Mongols struck at the Tartar emperors of northern China. The Mongol cavalry was invincible. Under their chief, Genghis Khan, the Mongols invaded Russia and swept east as well as west, conquering and often destroying everything in their path. For twenty years, Genghis Khan terrified and conquered the peoples from southern Russia to Korea. His armies killed more than 5 million persons.

After Genghis Khan's death in 1227, the Mongols extended their conquests. Kublai Khan, the grandson of Genghis, became the emperor in 1260. He conquered the Sungs in southern China in 1279, ending that dynasty and bringing both north and south China under his rule, which lasted until 1294. At the height of their power, the Mongols controlled China, Russia, Persia, and central Asia. In theory, Kublai Khan was the only Mongol ruler, but actually the Mongol conquests were divided into four empires: that of the Great Khan; the Empire of Jagatai; the Ilkhan Empire; and the Golden Horde, or Kipchak Empire.

The Mongols showed great ability in governing the countries they conquered. Kublai Khan built roads, filled granaries with wheat for use in times of famine, and gave state assistance to orphans and the sick. He also rebuilt the capital at Peking.

Marco Polo visited the Mongol court. A famous book, *The Travels of Marco Polo,* gives a great amount of information about Kublai Khan's empire. Marco Polo, a Venetian, traveled with his father and uncle in 1271 to the court of Kublai Khan.

THE MONGOL EMPIRE
About 1290

SIBERIA

RUS

GOLDEN HORDE
(KIPCHAK EMPIRE)

Black Sea

•Sarai

•Karakorum

JAPA

Mediterranean Sea

Caspian Sea

Tabriz •

EMPIRE OF JAGATAI

•Samarkand

ILKHAN EMPIRE

KOREA

EMPIRE
Khanbalik •
(Peking)

OF THE

GREAT KHAN

PACIFI

OCE

ARABIA

AFRICA

INDIA

INDO-
CHINA

INDIAN   OCEAN

Prepared by
Rand McNally & Co., Chicago

The journey through central Asia and across the terrible Gobi Desert took four years. Marco Polo became a favorite at the court of the Mongol emperor, and he stayed in China for seventeen years, serving much of that time as an official of the government.

Marco Polo returned to Venice in 1295, where he had trouble convincing his countrymen of the truth of what he had seen. They thought his stories exaggerated the population and wealth of China, and they called him "Marco Millions." Other Europeans—missionaries and merchants—followed his route to distant China and brought back the same reports, however.

Under the Mongol rulers, life in China went on much as before, and the influence of the Sung period remained strong. Kublai Khan encouraged his people to adopt Chinese ways and in time, the Mongols absorbed much of the Chinese way of life. Because this process of assimilation has happened again and again with foreigners, there is a saying that "China is a sea that salts all rivers that flow into it."

Section Review

1. How did the Sungs try to keep the Tartars out of China? What happened when their methods failed?

2. What practical inventions came out of the Sung period?

3. What were the chief characteristics of Chinese painting during the Sung period?

4. How did Mongol rule benefit China?

6 Mings and Manchus maintained Chinese culture

The Mongol kings governed China for nearly 100 years. In time, however, their rule weakened, and the people began to revolt against their foreign masters. The Chinese had continued to regard the Mongols as intruders, in spite of all the Mongol efforts to adapt themselves to Chinese life. One leader of the discontented Chinese, Hung Wu, gathered an army that captured Peking in 1368 and drove out the Mongol rulers. China returned to the rule of a Chinese dynasty, which was called the *Ming*, or "Brilliant," dynasty.

Ming China prospered. The Ming rulers tried to restore and strengthen all things Chinese. They had waste fields made fit for farming, and additional mulberry trees planted to provide food for silkworms. As trade with distant countries increased, shipbuilding and navigation improved. Chinese ships sailed to the Philippines and other islands of the Far East, to India, and even to Africa.

The Ming emperors rebuilt the capital of Peking into one of the finest cities in the world. With many palaces, temples, and walls, it was really four cities in one, each surrounded by a wall. In the center of the main city was the *Forbidden City*, in which only members of the royal family could live. Outside the Forbidden City was the Temple of Heaven, where the emperor prayed to the Supreme God for all of his people.

Although many of the Ming emperors were not very good rulers, the Chinese made some cultural advances during this period. For example, the use of three-color glazes made porcelain more beautiful than ever before.

Ming rulers limited contact with the West. After the downfall of the Mongols, Chinese contact with Europe stopped. It

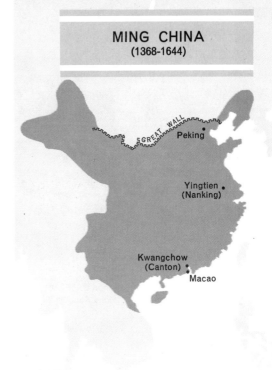

MING CHINA
(1368-1644)

GREAT WALL · Peking

Yingtien (Nanking)

Kwangchow (Canton) · Macao

Prepared by Rand McNally & Co., Chicago

was renewed, however, during the European age of exploration and discovery that began late in the 15th century.

The Portuguese, eager for trade with the East, first sent representatives to Peking in 1520. This early contact did not work out well. The Portuguese plundered, kidnaped, and murdered, much to the horror of the Chinese, who called these Westerners the "ocean devils." As a result, the government banned foreigners from China. However, it did allow the Portuguese to establish themselves at Macao, in southern China. Christian missionaries also came to the Far East, but they, like the merchants, did not always respect the wishes of the Chinese government. Thus, foreigners continued to be unwelcome in China.

China tried not only to exclude foreigners, but also to keep its own people from leaving the country. Although Ming emperors of the 15th century had encouraged

MANCHU CHINA
1644 - 1912

Area temporarily held
or tributary

MANCHURIA

MONGOLIA

SINKIANG

Peking•   KOREA

TIBET   Nanking•

NEPAL

CHINA

TAIWAN
(FORMOSA)
BURMA   •Canton
          Macao••Hong Kong

INDO-
CHINA

Prepared by
Rand McNally & Co., Chicago

quered Korea in 1627. Discontent grew within China, and bands of robbers roamed the countryside. One powerful robber chieftain seized much territory and, in 1644, threatened the capital at Peking. The Chinese asked the Manchus to help them put down this chieftain. The Manchus did so, but then took Peking for themselves and made their own prince the emperor of China. The new Manchu dynasty ruled from the capital at Peking until 1912.

The Manchu Empire was vast in extent. It included Mongolia, Manchuria, Korea, Indo-China, Tibet, and eastern Turkestan, as well as China proper. The Manchus kept the Chinese system of government that had been set up by the Ch'ins. They divided the important political jobs evenly between Chinese and Manchu nobles, but Chinese held most of the lesser governmental offices. The Manchus did try to keep their own customs and language, and forbade intermarriage with the Chinese. They made the Chinese wear *queues*, or pigtails, as a sign that they were inferior to their Manchu masters.

During 150 years of this rule, China enjoyed prosperity and well-being. The Manchu emperors built roads and canals, tried to stop famines, and helped farmers clear new land. Population increased rapidly. Like their Ming predecessors, however, the Manchus maintained an isolation policy which kept ideas developed in other lands from reaching China. The Manchus also failed to solve the problem of increasing pressure on China from the expanding nations of the West. This pressure and its consequences is discussed in Chapter 24.

Section Review

1. What were some of the achievements of the Ming rulers? Why did they want to reverse their former policy of encouraging trade with other nations? What effects did isolation have on China?

trade with other nations, those of the 16th century believed in a policy of isolation, and forbade almost all contact with the outside world. In 1619, the Ming emperor wrote to the czar of Russia: "By my custom, O Czar, I neither leave my own kingdom nor allow my ambassadors or merchants to do so." This isolation came to have serious consequences. It prevented China from exchanging ideas and thus learning from other peoples.

The Manchus overran China. Isolation, together with government corruption and high taxes, weakened the Ming Empire. Several peasant uprisings occurred in the early 1600's.

Meanwhile, a Tartar tribe of Manchuria, the Manchus, started to expand their territory. They began breaking through the Great Wall and raiding the borders of Ming China, and they con-

2. Who were the Manchus? How did they establish themselves in China?

3. How did the Manchus differ from the Mongols in their attitude toward assimilation with the Chinese? What policies of earlier dynasties did they continue?

7 Japan developed its own traditions

The Japanese, like all other peoples, have been influenced by the geography of their land—its size, climate, resources, and natural features. Japan consists of many islands, the largest of which are Honshu, Kyushu, Shikoku, and Hokkaido. The total area of Japan is approximately the size of California. The islands closest to the mainland of Asia are less than 150 miles from the Korean peninsula. In climate, Japan is fortunate. It has plentiful rainfall, and ocean currents from the south prevent severe winters in most areas.

The land is rather poor, however, and only about 17 per cent of it is suitable for farming. Overcrowding has always been a problem. Every inch of available land must be farmed in order to feed everyone. Japan also lacks such natural resources as iron, coal, and oil. Because of these disadvantages, plus the nearness of Japan to the Asian mainland, the Japanese have always been interested in the continent. From early times they looked longingly toward it as a source of raw materials and a place to settle their surplus population.

The early Japanese lived simply. According to Japanese tradition, the islands were first settled by the gods. Legends say that a grandson of the Sun Goddess was chosen to rule over the islands, and that one of his descendants became the first Japanese emperor. For this reason, the Japanese worshiped the emperor as one who descended from the gods.

Legend aside, the ancestors of the Japanese came to the islands shortly after 1500 B.C. Perhaps they came from Korea, perhaps from the East Indies. They found living on the islands a people called the Ainus. The Japanese were more advanced than the Ainus and had little trouble conquering them, driving them to the island of Hokkaido, where their descendants still live today.

From earliest times the Japanese seem to have been a warlike people. Perhaps their wars with the Ainus made them this way. At any rate, the soldier's profession was always much more honored in Japan than in nearby China.

Gradually, in the centuries that followed their invasion, the Japanese developed a government and nation. Yet most of the land was still covered with forests. The people had no money system, and no written form of their language. Their lives centered mainly on farming and fighting.

Chinese culture changed Japan. China was the most important foreign influence on the culture of early Japan, beginning especially with the fall of the Han dynasty and the troubled times that followed. Chinese and Korean refugees came to Japan and taught their arts and crafts. The Japanese also borrowed the Chinese system of writing. In 552 A.D., a Chinese Buddhist monk brought his religion to Japan and soon won many converts.

In the days of the mighty Tang Empire, a constant stream of merchants, artists, scholars, and craftsmen came from China to Japan. The Japanese eagerly read Chinese literature, and learned about Chinese philosophy, history, and poetry. They adopted the Chinese calendar, system of weights and measures, and style of dress. They even built Nara, their first capital, in imitation of the capital city of the Tangs.

The Japanese also adopted Chinese methods of government. Their emperor had greater power than the emperor in China, however. Unlike the Chinese, who believed that the people could overthrow a bad ruler, the Japanese thought that their divine emperor should never be removed, no matter what he did.

Japan enjoyed two prosperous periods. The period from the 8th to the 12th century A.D. is often called the golden age of Japan. The country was rich and prosperous. Kyoto, the capital from 794 to 1868, had become one of the largest cities in the world by 1200. But gradually the power of the emperors declined, and a form of feudalism grew up, not unlike that in Europe in the Middle Ages. Great noble families began to seize power. Finally, in 1192, one such noble, of the Minamoto family, became very strong. He placed himself at the head of the government, with the title of *shogun,* or military governor. The emperor was still greatly respected, but the shogun held the real power.

Government by shoguns lasted for more than 600 years. For a time noble families fought with each other trying to win the *shogunate*—that is, the office or right to rule as shogun. Finally, the Tokugawa family seized the office, which they held from 1603 to 1868. Under their rule, Japan became more prosperous than ever before. Education, art, and literature thrived.

Soldiers were highly respected. The Japanese developed several social classes. At the top were the shogun and the feudal lords, who were called *daimios.* Another important class consisted of the warriors, or *samurai.* Below them were officials and priests, merchants, and artisans. More than three fourths of the people, however, were farmers. The average family worked on a small farm of about two acres, which enabled them to earn only a very poor living.

The samurai occupied an important position in Japanese society especially after

JAPAN

the establishment of the shogunate, with its emphasis on the military. In some ways they resembled the knights of Europe. Their ideals were closely connected with the religion called *Shinto,* which glorified the emperor and the nation. The samurai followed a stern code called *Bushido,* which advocated a simple life. This code taught a samurai to bear pain without flinching and, above all, to be always loyal to the emperor and to his lord. In the event of defeat or dishonor, the samurai was expected to commit suicide by plunging a knife into his abdomen—a method called *seppuku,* or *hara-kiri.*

The Japanese excelled in many arts. In art, the Japanese began by copying the Chinese, but in time achieved a fine and distinctive style of their own.

Japanese painting followed strict rules. For example, the painter had to use a conventional series of symbols to indicate a tree. Yet Japanese artists showed great skill and imagination, and managed to achieve remarkable variety while following these rules exactly. They often painted landscapes and battle scenes; humorous pictures of people and animals were also popular.

In literature, the Japanese have shown a great interest in poetry. Writing poems has even been organized as a sport, with as many as 1500 poets competing. Most Japanese poems are very short; the object is to concentrate a great amount of meaning in a few lines.

It is said that a master poet of Japan was once asked by some peasants to compose a poem to the full moon. He began:

'Twas the new moon—

The peasants laughed, "The poet is crazy, for this is a full moon." Then the last two lines followed:

Since then I have waited
And lo! Tonight!

The peasants then understood the poet's skill. He had praised the full moon with beautiful simplicity just by implying what a miracle it seemed to him.

Japanese architects, like the Chinese, used mostly wood in their buildings. Some of the oldest examples of wood architecture in the world are to be found in Japan. The temples were very similar to those of China, but had more carving and ornamentation. In contrast, Japanese homes have usually been simple, one-story buildings. Even the rich had very little furniture, using a few pads for beds and chairs, and small lacquer trays as tables. Straw matting covered the floor, and sliding screens, usually of paper, divided one room from another.

The refinement and formal simplicity of Japanese painting, poetry, and domestic architecture have been carried over into other aspects of Japanese life. Even the simplest gardens followed strict aesthetic standards. The Japanese developed flower arrangement into an art. In the past, trained "flower masters" taught the subject, and no Japanese girl was considered educated until she had learned to arrange flowers with taste and beauty. Even the serving of tea came to be the object of much ceremony, with each gesture part of an elaborate ritual.

Japan adopted a policy of isolation. The seas separating the islands from the mainland of Asia served as protective barriers against invasion. Kublai Khan, the Mongol emperor of China at the time of Marco Polo's visit, did try to conquer Japan. In 1281 he sent 900 ships and 25,000 Mongol soldiers to the islands. But the Japanese resisted fiercely, and were helped by a storm which sank the ships and drowned the soldiers. The Japanese called this storm *Kamikaze,* or "Divine Wind." Several other early attempts to invade Japan from the mainland also failed.

In 1592 the situation was reversed. Since Japan was growing stronger, and Ming China seemed to be weaker, the Japanese endeavored to invade China. They sought help from Korea, but the Koreans refused and fought instead on the side of China. While Chinese and Korean armies engaged the Japanese on land, the Korean navy destroyed the Japanese fleet. Finally, the Japanese returned to their island home in defeat.

Europeans came to the Japanese islands in the 16th century. The Portuguese were first on the scene, as they had been in China. Their ships sailed in 1542 into Japanese harbors, where the Portuguese sailors gazed at the neat houses and the great snowy mountain, Fujiyama. Before long the Portuguese were trading with the Japanese. A famous priest, Francis Xavier, introduced the Christian religion. Others

Life in Japan intrigued the first European visitors, who found many sights and customs unlike their own. A harsh and demanding military code played an important role in Japanese society. This aspect is reflected in a fiercely grimacing wooden head, below left. At the same time, the Japanese were a pleasure-loving people of cultivated tastes. In a teahouse, below, a young couple plays a game while other guests watch. Outside, a display of fireworks entertains the townspeople. On the opposite page, actors perform a drama to the music of a drum and stringed instrument. Plays sometimes lasted all day, and peddlers wandered among the audience selling rice cakes and tea. For their part, the Japanese had a sharp eye for the unusual appearance of their visitors. In a 16th-century painting of Portuguese traders arriving in Japan, above, the artist ridicules the newcomers' trousers, a style of dress strange to the Japanese.

carried on his work, and by 1581 there were 150 thousand Japanese Christians.

The Portuguese were followed to Japan by the Spaniards, Dutch, and English. At first the shoguns were friendly to European missionaries and traders, but in the early 17th century they decided that the foreigners were in Japan to gain political power, and thus were a danger to the Japanese government. Their suspicions were increased by the foreigners themselves: the Portuguese Jesuits intrigued against the Spanish Franciscans, and both groups plotted against the Protestant Dutch. In 1614 the shogun issued an edict ordering all foreign priests to leave, churches to be burned, and Japanese converts to renounce Christianity. A few years later another edict made it a capital offense for a Japanese to become a Christian.

The shogun then forbade all foreigners to come to Japan and prohibited the Japanese from leaving. Only the Dutch were allowed to maintain a trading post on an island off the port of Nagasaki. During the next two centuries, Japan had little contact with the outside world.

Section Review

1. How has the geography of Japan affected its relations with the mainland of Asia?

2. What were some of the things the Japanese learned from China?

3. How did the Japanese attitude toward their emperor differ from that of the Chinese?

4. What principles did the code of Bushido impose on the samurai?

5. In which arts did the Japanese excel?

6. Who were the first Europeans to come to Japan? Why did the shoguns later forbid contact with foreigners and outlaw Christianity?

Chapter 10 ▬▬▬▬▬▬▬ A Review

The first Chinese civilization began in the Hwang Ho, or Yellow River valley. Then came the legendary Hsia rulers and the first truly historical era, that of the Shangs. The Chou dynasty which followed ruled longer than any other, from 1027 to 256 B.C. During this classical period, the Chinese developed a governmental system, social customs, and literary and artistic traditions that were to last throughout the nation's history. The Chou period was also important because of its two great teachers, Confucius and Lao-tse.

The Ch'in dynasty of the 3rd century B.C., although not a long one, united China and set up a form of government that was to endure until 1912 A.D. Its greatest ruler, Shih Huang Ti, built the Great Wall as a barrier against barbarian attacks.

The Hans governed until the 3rd century A.D. They had won control of eastern and central Asia, and over this great area established a Chinese Peace. Contact with the world beyond the borders of China led to increased trade with the West and to the introduction of Buddhism from India. The greatness of the Han period remained unequaled until the golden age of the Tang dynasty, between the 7th and 10th centuries. Education and a civil service system were improved, great poetry was written, and printing was developed.

In spite of barbarian invasions and the loss of half of China to the Tartars, the Sung period saw great advances in technology and art. Then new invaders, the Mongols, succeeded in conquering China. According to the account of the famous traveler, Marco Polo, they accepted Chinese life, and in time they were absorbed by it.

A native Chinese dynasty returned to power when the Mings took over in the 14th century. Under them and the Manchus who followed, China enjoyed peace and stability. Both dynasties maintained the high level of Chinese culture, but the people tended to preserve old ways instead of progressing to new ones.

China had a strong influence on nearby Japan, although the Japanese gradually created their own distinctive way of life. Actual political power changed hands several times, but an unbroken line of emperors continued to hold the respect of the people. The loyalty toward superiors received its most characteristic Japanese expression in the code of Bushido, adopted by the warrior class. Along with their admiration for military ideals, however, the Japanese developed a refined and graceful way of life.

From the 1600's on, both China and Japan tried to limit European contacts by shutting their doors on the outside world and isolating themselves. This policy had important consequences in later years.

The Time

Indicate the period in which the events described in the following statements occurred.

(a) 2000-1501 B.C. (e) 1-500 A.D.
(b) 1500-1001 B.C. (f) 501-1000 A.D.
(c) 1000-501 B.C.   (g) 1001-1500 A.D.
(d) 500-1 B.C.   (h) 1501-1900 A.D.

1. The Japanese shoguns began a policy of isolation by outlawing Christianity and foreign trade.

2. Marco Polo visited Mongol China.

3. The Han dynasty took over control of China.

4. Recorded history of China began with the establishment of the Shang kings as rulers.

5. In an announcement to the czar of Russia, the Ming emperor declared the isolation of his country.

6. Confucius began his teaching in China.

7. The ancestors of the Japanese migrated from Korea or the East Indies to the Japanese islands.

8. The Tang rulers ushered in the golden age of China.

9. The golden age of Japan began.

10. Kublai Khan made an unsuccessful attempt to invade Japan.

11. The Tokugawa family won the Japanese shogunate.

12. The Chou, or classical, period of China began.

13. The Ch'in dynasty centralized Chinese government.

14. China was divided between the Sungs and Tartars.

15. The prosperous rule of the Mings began with the capture of Peking.

16. The Hsia princes ushered in the legendary period of China.

17. The Japanese made an unsuccessful attempt to invade China.

The Place

1. If you were flying in Japan from Kyushu Island to Hokkaido Island, in what direction would you be going? What other island or islands would you cross?

2. Which of these dynasties controlled the largest area of China: Chou, Ch'in, Han, Ming, Manchu?

3. Of which four empires was Peking the capital?

4. With what empire is the city of Hangchow associated?

5. On what island was the Japanese capital located from 794 to 1868?

6. The Great Wall of China was constructed to keep out invading Huns. From which direction was the invasion anticipated?

7. With which river of China was the early Chinese civilization associated? On the map "Asia," locate this river.

The People

1. What special contributions to Chinese civilization were made by Confucius? Laotse? Li Po? Tu Fu?

2. Identify each of the following rulers with a Chinese dynasty and cite at least one of his achievements: Shih Huang Ti; Wu Ti; T'ai Tsung; Kublai Khan; Hung Wu.

3. What made Francis Xavier's name well known in Japanese history?

4. Why were the Minamoto and Tokugawa families important in Japanese history?

Historical Terms

1. In an exhibit of ancient Chinese skills and inventions, with what period in Chinese history would each of the following items be identified: India ink; an abacus; a green-glazed porcelain vase; an example of block printing?

2. These terms are important to an understanding of Chinese civilization. Give their meanings: historiography; the classical period; queues; "ocean devils"; Mandate of Heaven; loess; Five Classics.

3. These terms are important to an understanding of Japanese civilization. Give their meanings.

shogunate	Shinto
daimios	Bushido
samurai	hara-kiri

4. Define culture diffusion by citing examples from the history of China or Japan.

Questions for Critical Thinking

1. For centuries, control of Korea has been a point of conflict between China and Japan. What is the reason?

2. Did Shih Huang Ti's policy of stamping out Confucianism indicate a strength or weakness in his rule?

3. Generally speaking, what do these periods of history have in common: Athens under Pericles; Rome under Augustus; India under the Guptas; China under the Tangs?

4. In what ways did the samurai class of Japan resemble the feudal knights of medieval Europe.

5. What is the meaning of the saying, "China is a sea that salts all the rivers that flow into it"?

6. To what extent was Japanese culture merely an extension of Chinese culture?

7. Was the Ming policy of isolating China from foreign influences a wise one? Explain.

8. How did the thinkers and teachers of the Chou period influence the Chinese in establishing codes of conduct?

Native Cultures in Africa and the Americas

Early peoples in Africa and America created artistic works of great expressive power. The African who carved the ivory head of the king of Benin, left, used a crown of tiny Portuguese traders to symbolize royal might. Figures of fish, so important to Pacific Northwest Indians, adorn a wooden mask, center. The vase at right depicts with grim realism the impassive features of a Peruvian Indian.

I spoke to Montezuma one day, and told him that Your Highness was in need of gold . . . and I besought him to send some of his people, and I would also send some Spaniards, to the provinces . . . ordering them to go to the lords of those provinces and cities, and tell them that I had commanded each one of them to contribute a certain measure of gold . . . Thus it was done, and all those lords . . . gave . . . gold, and silver, and the featherwork, and the [precious] stones, and the many other things of value which I assigned and allotted to Your Sacred Majesty, amounting to the sum of one hundred thousand *ducats,* and more. These, besides their value, are such, and so marvellous, that for the sake of their novelty and strangeness they have no price, nor is it probable that all the princes ever heard of in the world, possess such treasures . . .

This enthusiastic report to Charles V, the king of Spain, was written in October 1520 by Hernando Cortés, the daring adventurer who was the first European to describe the riches of the Aztec Empire in Mexico. In the land of Montezuma, the Aztec chieftain, Cortés and his band of followers found wealth beyond their wildest dreams.

The search for gold and other valuables was a driving force in the penetration of the African continent. In 1472 a Portuguese explorer named Ruy de Sequiera entered the busy streets of the west African city of Benin, in what is now Nigeria. He was amazed to see the city thronged with merchants and artisans, and to find beautiful articles of ivory, bronze, and iron being made and traded. As further explorations by Europeans revealed the abundance of valuable products in Africa, trading posts were established along both the west and east coasts of the continent.

Of course, the narrative of European discovery does not "begin" the history of Africa and the Americas. The advanced cultures which the Europeans found there were the result of centuries of growth and development. The following chapter describes how civilization came about in ancient Africa and the Americas.

1. **Several cultures flourished in early Africa.**

2. **American Indian culture evolved over many centuries.**

3. **The Mayas achieved the highest Indian civilization in America.**

4. **The Aztecs conquered much of Mexico.**

5. **The Incas controlled a vast empire in South America.**

6. **Indians had distinctive customs.**

1 **Several cultures flourished in early Africa**

One of the cradles of civilization lay in Africa, along the Nile Valley in Egypt. Egyptian culture flourished from about 3100 to 100 B.C. After its decline, the northern coast came under the influence of various Mediterranean peoples, including the Phoenicians, Greeks, and Romans. It was conquered by the Arabs during the 7th and 8th centuries. Later, Arabs also founded towns along the east coast of Africa.

The vast interior south of the Sahara Desert, however, remained unexplored and mysterious until the 1800's. Since about 1850, historians and archaeologists have been reconstructing the early history of Africa. This process has been difficult, because most African peoples left no written records. Many old traditions were preserved only by passing them on orally.

Some advanced peoples built cities. Archaeologists have found evidence of a few important African cultures. One of these, in Nigeria, is known as the *Nok* culture, and existed from 800 B.C. to 200 A.D.

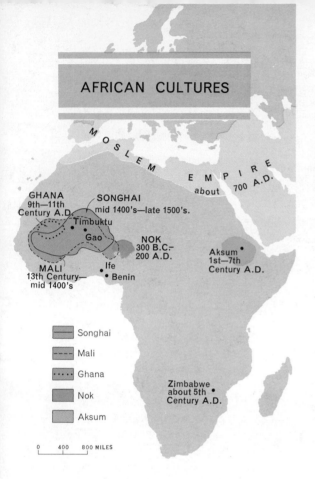

AFRICAN CULTURES

MOSLEM EMPIRE about 700 A.D.

GHANA
9th—11th
Century A.D.

SONGHAI
mid 1400's—late 1500's.

Timbuktu

Gao

NOK
300 B.C.–
200 A.D.

Aksum
1st—7th
Century A.D.

MALI
13th Century—
mid 1400's

Ife

Benin

▨ Songhai

▨ Mali

▨ Ghana

▨ Nok

▨ Aksum

Zimbabwe
about 5th
Century A.D.

0   400   800 MILES

The people developed a beautiful form of glazed, sculptured clayware. Although generally in the Neolithic stage of development, they did work tin and iron.

Far to the south, in what is now Southern Rhodesia, a flourishing civilization grew up around a large city known as Zimbabwe. Its ruins revealed a large temple of granite bricks with walls fifteen feet thick. On a nearby hill stood a massive fort, similar to the upper fortified part of a Greek city. Little is known about the people who built Zimbabwe. Authorities believe that the city became a trading center in the 5th century A.D.

Another promising African civilization flourished in Ethiopia between the 1st and the 7th centuries A.D. This kingdom of Aksum was the legendary home of the Queen of Sheba, the Ethiopian queen who

visited King Solomon. The people of Aksum were converted to Christianity in the 4th century.

Afro-Moslem kingdoms flourished in the Sudan. The most important early cultures of Africa appeared in the geographical region called the *Sudan,* (not to be confused with the African country of that name). The Sudan is a long, narrow belt of land stretching from the Atlantic to the valley of the Nile. It is bounded on the north by the arid sands of the Sahara and on the south by the tropical jungle forest fronting on the seacoast.

Beginning in the 8th century, Moslem merchants began to cross the Sahara in trade caravans in order to obtain gold in west Africa. Moving southward from North Africa, these traders set up important kingdoms. Their African Negro subjects borrowed much of the Moslem culture, such as methods of warfare, the Islamic religion, and the Arabic language. The Negroes gradually absorbed their conquerors through intermarriage and became the rulers themselves.

Between the 9th and 11th centuries, an early Negro kingdom, Ghana, controlled a large area of the western Sudan. Its people farmed, raised cattle, and traded elephants and gold for salt, wheat, and cloth.

Ghana was destroyed in the 13th century by the people of Mali, whose empire at one time stretched 1500 miles from the Atlantic to Lake Chad. One of their cities, Timbuktu, was a large and busy trade center. Merchants thronged its streets. Some came with caravans that included as many as 12 thousand camels. Craftsmen produced well-made wares of iron, tin, and leather.

Mali domination in the Sudan lasted until the middle 1400's. Then another kingdom, Songhai, in turn rose to power. Its capital was at Gao, but Timbuktu remained an important city. It became known as a

Early African Peoples established a variety of cultures. An artisan of the Nok civilization carved the terra cotta head of a woman, below right, in a realistic style. The people who worshiped in the temple at Zimbabwe, below left, seem to have disappeared mysteriously, leaving no traces except the ruins of their great city. Above, a bronze plaque depicts a king of the Benin people, who ruled southern Nigeria during the 16th century. He is flanked by two guards.

The heart of the African continent is a large region of equatorial (tropical) rain forest. This region, central Africa, extends along both sides of the equator from the Atlantic Ocean to eastern Africa. Almost until the 20th century this region was virtually cut off from communication with outside areas and did not share the cultural and technological progress of other regions in Africa which maintained contact with the world. As a result, central Africa remained stagnant for centuries, with weak, tribal forms of government, almost no industry or agriculture, and a population of less than two persons per square mile.

The stagnant condition of central Africa was chiefly the result of geographic barriers, an unfavorable climate, and disease. Barriers included the African coast, unnavigable rivers, the tropical rain forest, and deserts.

The African coast was a formidable barrier to penetration of central Africa by Europeans. It has few deep-water harbors—fewer than any other large continent—and approaches to the coast are endangered by pounding surfs and long sand bars. Transportation inland from the coast is made difficult by dense forests and by the steep slope of the interior plateau, which averages about 2000 feet above sea level. Rivers leading inland are blocked in many places by rapids, waterfalls, and sand bars. Even the great Congo River, 3000 miles long, is navigable by ocean vessels for only 95 miles.

The dense tropical rain forest formed another barrier. Larger than western Europe, its very size made communication and travel within the area difficult. In addition, many roads in the region were overgrown by vegeta-

tion or were washed out during the course of the rainy season.

On the north, central Africa is bordered by grasslands and by the huge Sahara. This desert is about equal in size to the United States, and forms the greatest single barrier between central Africa and North Africa. It has in effect created *two Africas*—North Africa and sub-Saharan Africa.

On the south, central Africa is bordered also by grasslands and desert. Vast tracts of rolling grassland, plateaus, and the great Kalahari Desert separate central Africa from southern Africa.

One of the most effective obstacles to European communication with central Africa was the prevalence of disease. The hot, wet climate sapped the strength of Europeans and reduced their resistance to disease. Central Africa became known as the "white man's grave" because so many died there. The tropical vegetation was a breeding ground for insects carrying the germs of malaria, yellow fever, and other diseases. The relationship between vegetation and disease was discovered in 1900.

The pattern of stagnation in central Africa has been changed gradually during the past half century by modern technology and science. The use of DDT sprays, antibiotics, and vaccines has reduced the disease rate. Geographic barriers also have been largely overcome. Beginning in 1898 railroads were built, and all-weather motor roads were constructed during the 1930's. Air service, telephones, and radio networks have aided the development of industry and speeded the emergence of central Africa from its long period of isolation.

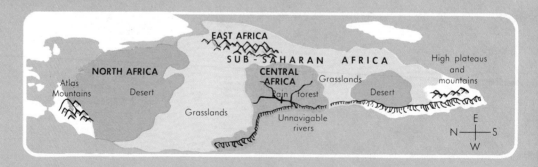

religious and intellectual center, with a famous mosque and a fine university. Songhai flourished until the late 1500's, when it was conquered by the Moors.

Most Africans lived simply. Outside the areas of advanced cultures, the great majority of African people lived a primitive tribal existence, with few of the tools and skills needed for civilization. They had no system of writing or counting, and no knowledge of the wheel or the sail. This backwardness resulted, not from any inherent inferiority, but from various external factors such as isolation and slavery.

For many hundreds of years, Africa below the Sahara was geographically isolated. To the north stretched the desert, a barrier which merchant caravans crossed only with difficulty. The coasts were forbidding. They had few natural harbors, and dangerous falls and cataracts blocked the rivers into the interior. In the inland areas, wild animals and the prevalence of disease made life difficult.

Slavery was another bar to progress. Long before the coming of Europeans, Arabs in east Africa traded in slaves, disrupting the life of the Africans and carrying away their best men. In the 16th century, Europeans introduced the slave trade into west Africa.

When the isolation of Africa ended in modern times, the rest of the world learned that, even during the long period of isolation, Africa had made progress toward civilized ways. Although science and technology had remained crude, society had grown extremely complicated. Africans had worked out varied codes of conduct, methods of education for the young, systems of law, and complex ideas about religion. They also created vigorous traditions in the arts. Their sculpture was outstanding; that of the city of Ife in Nigeria has become famous. African art influenced Western painting and sculpture in the 20th century, particularly the school known as *primitivism*. Music and dancing also played a large part in the life of primitive Africans. Strong and rhythmic African music, brought to America by Negro slaves, greatly affected the development of jazz and many Latin-American musical forms.

Section Review

1. Why is it difficult to reconstruct early African history? What have archaeologists discovered about early native cultures in Nigeria and Southern Rhodesia?
2. How did Moslems contribute to African culture?
3. In what ways did geographic features affect the people of Africa? How did slavery hinder progress?
4. What progress did the Africans make toward civilization during their long isolation?

2 **American Indian culture evolved over many centuries**

While the peoples of Europe, Asia, and Africa were working out distinctive patterns of living, the first inhabitants of North and South America were also developing their own ways of life. Most of their cultures were destroyed so completely that little remains, except a number of impressive ruins. Yet it should not be forgotten that in the New World, as well as in the Old, man made the long climb from primitive toward civilized ways of living.

When Columbus reached the shores of America in the 15th century, he called the people he met *Indians,* because he thought he had landed in India. The name survives in spite of its inaccuracy.

The first American Indians probably came from Asia. It is believed that man first appeared in the Western Hemisphere between 12 and 15 thousand years ago.

North American Indians achieved various levels of civilization. Among the most advanced were the Indians of the Southwest, whom the Spanish called Pueblo, their word for village. The Pueblo Indians often built their "apartment houses" on sheer ledges for protection against enemies. The structure below, called the Cliff Palace, stands on the ledge of a deep canyon at Mesa Verde National Park in southern Colorado. At least 400 Indians once lived in this eight-story village. The Songish Indians of the Pacific Northwest, who were great hunters and fishermen, carved the mother and child at left. The baby's head has been bound at the sides to make it longer, an effect which these Indians admired. Plains Indians of Wyoming painted the elk hide at right with scenes of a buffalo hunt. Dancers around the tepees were probably performing a good luck ritual. The shell below, etched with a fierce-looking Indian, is believed to be a religious object of prehistoric Indians from Oklahoma. It was unearthed in a mound which served as the base of a temple where these Indians worshiped.

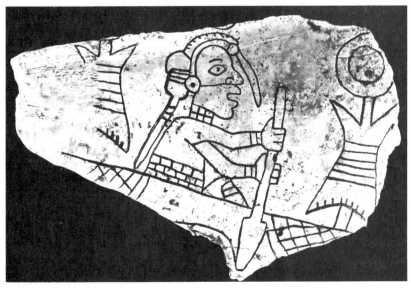

The first Americans probably came from regions of Asia across the Bering Strait between Siberia and Alaska; a land bridge may have connected the two continents at that time. Most of the newcomers probably resembled the people of China and Mongolia.

At that time, the peoples of the world were still living in the Old Stone Age. Scholars are fairly sure that the first American immigrants had fire, stone tools, skin clothing, and the domesticated dog. Most of them lived as hunters or gatherers. In the long years before the coming of the Europeans, descendants of these people pushed southward and eastward until they had settled in most areas of North and South America.

The American Indians were isolated from the civilizations of the Old World. Some anthropologists believe, however, that daring seafarers may have crossed the Pacific or Atlantic oceans to America centuries before the Vikings or Columbus. Other authorities believe that the Indians developed their cultures independently. They maintain that similar inventions in the Eastern and Western hemispheres indicate merely that peoples often hit upon similar devices or ideas when they encounter similar problems.

Farming changed Indian life. Several hundred years before the Christian era, some Indians learned to grow *maize,* or corn. They may have first domesticated the wild plant as early as 4000 B.C. Scholars are not yet sure whether corn originated in Mexico, Central America, or South America. They do know that it spread over much of the New World, and became as important there as wheat was in the Old World.

As happened in the Eastern Hemisphere, farming enabled men in America to settle in communities, to develop New Stone Age skills such as weaving and pottery making, and to set up a division of labor. These skills spread slowly throughout the Americas, although some people made faster progress than others.

Many Indians made little progress. When the first Europeans arrived in the Americas, they found several groups of Indians, each with a special way of life. In both North and South America there were many tribes that had not yet developed a true civilization; they built no cities and had no writing.

One such group included the Indians of the northeast woodlands of North America, who lived by hunting and farming. The Five Nations of the Iroquois are known for their well-organized form of government. In the northwest, along the Pacific Coast, various tribes lived comfortably without either farming or domesticating any animals other than dogs. They enjoyed a rich supply of food—fish, game, and wild fruits—and they became famous for their wood carvings.

The famous Plains Indians, such as the Sioux and Cheyennes, have been called the best fighters in the world. Before the 1600's, most of them made a meager living as farmers, but after the Spanish brought horses to America, these Indians became buffalo hunters.

Some groups created higher cultures. One of the few advanced cultures north of the Rio Grande was that of the Pueblo tribes in what is now the southwestern United States. Pueblo Indians lived mostly by farming. They used *adobe,* or sun-dried brick, to build several-storied houses that have been called the first American apartment buildings. Some people believe they had one of the oldest republican governments in history, because the people chose their own chiefs.

Indians in Mexico and in Central and South America built more advanced civilizations than their neighbors to the north. They began their development at about the time the Hans of China and the Romans were building their empires thousands of miles away. The Mayas in Yucatan, the Aztecs of Mexico, and the Incas in Peru had civilizations that in some respects rivaled those of ancient Egypt and Mesopotamia. These cultures of the south advanced further than those of the north probably because they had learned earlier how to raise corn. As a result, they had lived in one place for longer periods than the northern Indians and had had more time to develop the skills associated with civilization.

Section Review

1. From what lands did the Indians probably come? What skills did they bring with them? How did farming change their way of life?
2. What distinguished the Iroquois? the Plains Indians? the Pueblo Indians?
3. What was the main reason why the Indians south of the Rio Grande were able to develop a high culture sooner than those in the north?

3 **The Mayas achieved the highest Indian civilization in America**

Beginning about 500 B.C., the Mayan Indians developed a high culture in the peninsula of Yucatan (present-day British Honduras and parts of Mexico and Guatemala). By the beginning of the Christian era, they had invented writing, a system of numbers, and a calendar. These achievements made them the most advanced of the Indians in America.

Most Mayas were corn farmers, who lived in thatched huts located on the outskirts of cities. These cities were religious centers, and did not have a large permanent population.

Mayan culture had two main periods. By 300 A.D., in Honduras, northern Guatemala, and nearby areas of Mexico, the Mayas had established a distinctive civilization. Its early phase, which lasted until the 9th century, is called the *Classic* period, or *Old Empire.* During this time the Mayas perfected their arts, science, and learning, and built several cities. During the 800's, however, the people began to abandon these centers. They may have left because their poor farming methods had exhausted the soil of the minerals necessary for good crop production.

After the Old Empire crumbled, large numbers of Mayas drifted northward and built new cities in the northern tip of the Yucatan Peninsula. Around them grew up city-states somewhat similar to those of ancient Greece. Their governments were theocratic, being dominated by priests. This later Mayan phase, called the *Mexican* period or *New Empire,* flourished from about 980 to 1200. It is characterized by Mexican influences, particularly the worship of a god in the form of a feathered serpent. These Mexican culture traits probably originated with a northern tribe called the Toltecs.

The Mayas excelled in many fields. In the field of the arts, Mayan architecture and sculpture were outstanding. The commonest type of building resembled a pyramid but had a flat top. The whole structure was faced with stone and surmounted by a temple. Carved stone figures of the many gods served as decorations. These were so well made that some people consider Mayan sculpture superior to that of the ancient Egyptians.

The Mayas were the only American Indians to develop a true system of writing. No one has learned to read it, although scholars can pick out the symbols that stood for gods, stars, and dates. The Mayas produced paper from bark or the tough fibers of the maguey cactus, and used it to make folding books. Spanish conquerors destroyed all but three of these, however, and most examples of Mayan writing that now exist are those carved on stone.

Perhaps the greatest accomplishment of New World science was the Mayan calendar, developed sometime between 400 and 200 B.C. Mayan astronomers discovered that the year was slightly less than 365¼ days long. Not until the 16th century A.D. did Europeans have a calendar nearly so accurate. In fact, the Mayan calendar was only slightly less accurate than the Gregorian calendar used today.

The Mayas were also skilled in mathematics, and worked out a system of numbers. At least 300 years before the birth of Christ, they had invented the idea of zero, which mathematicians of Gupta India were to develop independently several hundred years later.

The Mayan zero looked like this: 👁 The Mayan numbers up to nineteen were made by adding ones and fives. For example:

The Mayan number system was based on the number 20 instead of 10, which the decimal system uses. That is, zero at the end of a number meant 20 times the number before it, instead of 10 times.

Section Review
1. What were the achievements which made the Mayas the most advanced Indians in America?
2. What characterized the civilization of the Mayan Old Empire? the New Empire?
3. What important invention did Mayan mathematicians make?

4 The Aztecs conquered much of Mexico

North of the Mayas lived other, more warlike tribes. They exchanged ideas with the Mayas, and gradually extended their power and influence through military conquest. The early Toltecs laid a foundation upon which the Aztecs later built a large empire.

The Toltecs preceded the Aztecs. At the time of the Maya Old Empire, the Toltec Indians began to develop a culture of their own in central Mexico, near present-day Mexico City. They had come from the north about the 1st century A.D. By 700, the Toltecs were carving interesting statues from stone and building great pyramids. Their way of life influenced the Mayas of Yucatan, especially between 900 and 1200, when the Toltecs were at the height of their development. Some scholars believe that the Toltecs migrated to the land of the Mayas and ruled various Mayan cities.

The Aztecs built a great city. In the 13th century, a savage Indian people swept into Mexico from the northwest. They were the Aztecs, who may have come from what is now New Mexico or Arizona. They defeated the already weakened Toltecs. Aztec culture reached its height during the 15th and early 16th centuries. The Aztecs themselves were not inventive, but they learned from the Mayas and the Toltecs. Although they did not develop a true system of writing, they did use a simple form of picture writing. They had a calendar, which, like that of the Mayas, was very accurate. They maintained hospitals with doctors and surgeons who were at least as good as those of Europe at that time.

According to legend, the Aztecs decided to locate their capital where they saw a heaven-sent eagle, with a snake in its beak, sitting on a cactus growing from a rock in

NORTH PACIFIC
COAST TRIBES
1800's—1800's A.D.

PLAINS

INDIANS

1500's—1800's A.D.

IROQUOIS
1000's—1600's A.D.

AMERICAN
INDIAN CULTURES

PUEBLOS
about 500—1690 A.D.

TOLTECS
about 700—1200 A.D.

•Chichen Itza
MAYAS
about 500 B.C.—1200 A.D.

•Tenochtitlán

AZTECS
1200's—1520 A.D.

TROPIC OF CANCER

ATLANTIC

OCEAN

EQUATOR

PACIFIC

OCEAN

INCAS
1000's—1532 A.D.

•Cuzco

•Tiahuanaco

TROPIC OF CAPRICORN

0   250   500   1,000 MILES

45°

30°

15°

0°

30°

45°

45°

30°

105°   90°   75°   60°

ed by
Co. Chicago

a lake. (This scene is pictured on the flag of Mexico.) Actually, the tribe decided in 1325 to build its city, Tenochtitlán, on the islands in Lake Texcoco because there were too many enemies on the mainland. Mexico City now stands on the site of Tenochtitlán and the vanished lake.

Tenochtitlán prospered, and had a population of 300 thousand by the early 15th century. The setting of this city was magnificent. Because it lay out in the water, on islands and land reclaimed from the shallow lake, it has been called a New World Venice. Canals interlaced the islands, and a visitor could enter the city either by canoe or by walking over one of the long stone causeways which connected the city to the mainland.

Striking features of Tenochtitlán were the great temples and pyramids which stood in the city square. Near the temples were schools that prepared boys to be warriors or priests, for the Aztecs were both warlike and religious.

The Aztec Empire fell to the Spanish. Authorities are not sure what kind of government the Aztecs had. Some believe the emperor had absolute power. Others hold that the Aztecs had a form of democracy.

By the early 1400's, people of Tenochtitlán were ruling the other Aztec tribes. In 1500, the city was the center of an empire that included at least 5 million persons. To the Aztecs, making an empire meant merely adding to the number of conquered peoples from whom they could gather tribute. They did not try to integrate these conquered peoples into Aztec society.

Spanish troops landed in Mexico in 1519, and were led by Hernando Cortés, an adventurer of great ability who wanted gold. When he and his followers reached Tenochtitlán, they were amazed at the wealth and brilliance of the city. The Aztecs, awed by these strange white men on horseback, thought they might be messengers from a god. They offered gifts of gold, and Montezuma, the emperor, received Cortés with great courtesy. The Spanish leader seized Montezuma, however, and held him in prison; he was later killed in an uprising.

Cortés went on to subdue the Aztec Empire completely. He and his small group of adventurers were able to do this with comparative ease because they had the help of many Indian tribes who had been conquered by the Aztecs. These tribes welcomed the opportunity to turn on their cruel Aztec masters.

Section Review

1. What Indian cultures were influenced by the Toltecs?
2. What were the outstanding achievements of the Aztecs?
3. What helped the Spanish conquer the Aztec Empire so easily?

5 **The Incas controlled a vast empire in South America**

Far to the south of the Mayas and Aztecs, various groups of Indians in the Andes Mountains and Pacific Coast regions of South America began to develop high cultures in the first few centuries of the Christian era. Their descendants were to be united in the greatest of the American Indian empires.

The Tiahuanaco culture developed in the Andes Mountains. High in the Andes, near the shores of Lake Titicaca, lies a jumbled mass of gigantic stones—the ruins of Tiahuanaco. Like Mohenjo-Daro in India, the name of this site means "the place of the dead."

Little is known about the people who lived in Tiahuanaco, but apparently they were excellent builders. Some of the stone slabs they worked with weighed 200 tons. Without using mortar, they fitted these blocks together tightly; in fact, it is impossible to slip a knife blade between them.

Archaeologists do not know what caused the end of the Tiahuanaco culture. The people had conquered tribes both along the coast and in the mountains of what is now Peru. Their culture and that of the Mayan Old Empire declined at about the same time. After 900 A.D. the Indians of this region made little progress for several centuries.

The Incas unified an extensive empire. A few centuries after the decline of Tiahuanaco, a people of the Peruvian mountains began to develop a distinctive way of life. The ruler of these people was known as the *Inca*, and the term has since been applied to the entire group.

Around the 11th century, the Incas settled in a valley of the Andes. They conquered the Indians there and set up a capital at Cuzco. The Incas soon expanded their rule to neighboring mountain valleys, and by 1400—like the Aztecs far to the north—they were conquering distant regions. By the 16th century, the Incas were ruling an empire greater from north to south than the distance between New York and San Francisco.

The cultural foundations of the Inca Empire had been laid by the earlier Peruvian cultures, especially that of Tiahuanaco. For example, the Incas, too, were great builders; some of their forts and temples have withstood centuries of damaging earthquakes. Although the Incas had no system of writing, they devised a clever way to keep records on knotted strings called *quipus.* Of various kinds and colors, the knots recorded crop production and other data needed by the Inca government.

The Incas were great empire-builders. Unlike the Aztecs, they absorbed those they conquered into their own culture. They brought the sons of conquered chiefs to Cuzco and educated them in the Inca schools. In addition, they sent colonies of loyal subjects to live in conquered areas, where they showed the new subjects the Inca way of life.

The Incas maintained highly organized systems of government, communications, and transportation in order to unite their vast empire. One great Inca road ran from one end of the empire to the other along the Pacific Coast. Another climbed along the crest of the Andes Mountains. Many sections of the roads were paved, and suspension bridges hung over gorges and rivers. These bridges were marvels of engineering for the age in which they were built. From stone towers swung cables of rope as much as a foot thick. Wooden planks laid across the cables made a bridge about 8 feet wide that might stretch as far as 400 feet. Over these roads and bridges, relays of swift Indian runners rushed messages from one part of the country to another.

Inca life was carefully regulated. At the head of the Inca government was the emperor, or Inca, who ruled as a hereditary absolute monarch. Since he claimed to be a descendant of the sun god, the government was actually a theocracy.

The Inca government owned and controlled all means of making and distributing goods. Land belonged to the state, not to those who lived on it. There was little private manufacture or trade because the government handled the exchange of goods. For example, officials would collect wool from a village of llama herdsmen, send it to another village for weaving, to another for dyeing, and then distribute the cloth where it was needed. The officials fed the inhabitants of the herdsmen's village with grain supplied from villages whose people worked only at farming.

Latin American Indians reached a higher level of civilization than the tribes north of Mexico. The Maya Indians, famous for their architectural achievements, constructed elaborate temples on high mounds of earth. The Mayan temple above right (its tower has been reconstructed) stands on a mound thirty feet high in Palenque, a city of the Old Empire. Among Mayan ruins, archaeologists have found stone pillars, like the one at far right above. The pillars, most of them about nine feet tall, were carved with figures of gods and with hieroglyphics relating to the passage of time. In Peru, the Incas built a great civilization. Both of the decorated jugs at right were made by people absorbed into their empire. One is painted with battling warriors who clutch maces and shields. The other is shaped in the form of a seated god.

The Aztecs of Mexico, contemporaries of the Incas, enjoyed an advanced culture, but the religion that dominated their lives was cruel and bloodthirsty. They believed that failure to satisfy their many gods would eventually bring about the end of the world. A blood sacrifice was considered the highest form of offering to the demanding gods. In the gruesome ceremony shown in the scene above, a priest cuts out the heart of a prisoner. Because the Aztecs needed hundreds of victims each year, they waged continuous warfare with other Indian tribes in Mexico.

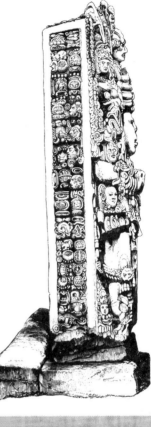

Some authorities have regarded the Inca system as an early form of socialism because the state, rather than private individuals, owned all of the means of production.

The population of the Inca Empire was about 10 million persons. (Even later, in 1600, England had less than half that many.) The vast extent of the empire required a great deal of organization and regulation. All persons were classified according to their age and ability to work. Most men had to serve in the army and to spend a certain amount of time working on government projects. Quipu records in Cuzco kept officials aware of the man power available everywhere in the empire.

The government even regulated the private life of the individual. If a young person were unmarried by a certain age, he had to choose a mate or take one selected by lot.

The Inca Empire fell to Spain. When the Spaniards, led by Francisco Pizarro, reached Peru in 1532, the Incas' gold aroused their greed. After inviting the emperor, Atahualpa, to visit him, Pizarro captured him and killed 2000 of his followers. Atahualpa offered as his ransom one roomful of gold and two of silver. Pizarro accepted and seized this fabulous treasure, and then treacherously executed the emperor. So much power had been concentrated in the hands of the emperor that his death made effective resistance almost impossible. Even though small groups of Incas continued to fight for some years, the empire as a whole collapsed quickly.

Section Review

1. What is known about the Tiahuanaco culture?
2. How did the Incas' treatment of conquered peoples differ from that of the Aztecs? What means did they use to keep their empire united?

3. Why has the Inca Empire been called socialistic? Give an example of how the state controlled the lives of the people.
4. Why did Inca resistance crumble after the death of the emperor?

6 Indians had distinctive customs

Out of the thousands of different customs practiced by the many groups of American Indians, some are of special interest. Indian religious beliefs, for example, reveal a great deal about the people who held them. Achievements in various fields indicate their cultural levels, and help explain the nature and extent of the Indian contributions to Western civilization.

Religious practices often were cruel. Religion was an important influence in the lives of most Indians, and among the Mayas, Aztecs, and Incas, the priests exercised great power. Many American Indians worshiped the sun, and several tribes had other gods that might represent something in daily life, such as agriculture or an aspect of nature. Religious ceremonies took place constantly.

To the Spanish, the most shocking feature of Indian religion was human sacrifice. This custom had grown out of the belief that man must give something of great value to the gods in order to receive favors in return. As nothing was more valuable than human life itself, sacrifice took on a noble and holy quality. Although the Incas and the Old Empire Mayas practiced it only on rare occasions, the Aztecs offered thousands of human sacrifices every year. For the dedication of the great pyramid temple at Tenochtitlán, 20 thousand Aztec captives were killed.

Religious practices among some Indians indicated progress beyond the beliefs in human sacrifice and nature gods. The people of Tiahuanaco, for example, apparently worshiped a creator god who ruled other gods. During the last years of the Inca Empire, people had begun to revive this belief, and seemed to be tending toward faith in one single god. Some of their hymns to this god show great beauty and feeling.

Indians stressed group living. Indian life among most groups centered around the tribe or the clan and not around the individual. Often, the tribe owned all the land and no one person could keep any for himself.

Among Indians who farmed for a living, the land was often given out to the people on a supposedly equal basis; it could be redistributed at any time. For example, the land of an Aztec farmer might, and probably would, pass to his son. Neither he nor his son, however, had the right of private ownership, and could not prevent the village council from giving the land to someone else.

Indian achievements varied. In the field of writing and literature, only the Mayas created a genuine system of writing, although the Aztecs had a kind of picture writing, and Incas used quipus for record keeping. (Both Mayas and Aztecs made paper and books.) Yet all American Indians had a literature. It was passed on by word of mouth from generation to generation, and finally written down when the white men came. Most of the literature took the form of poetry, and often expressed religious ideas or tribal traditions. Indians also liked to tell myths and legends about animals and war.

In arts and crafts, Indians produced distinctive basketry, weaving, embroidery, metal work, painting, sculpture, and architecture. Sculpture decorated temples and palaces, and low-relief carvings adorned walls, illustrating some historical event or religious ceremony. Although Indians never invented the potter's wheel, they made fine pottery, especially in the southwestern United States and in Peru. These same groups also did excellent weaving. Indians did not know how to work iron, but several of the Latin-American tribes excelled in metal work with gold, silver, and copper.

One serious obstacle to progress in such fields as science and technology was the lack of draft animals. There were no horses or cattle in America before the coming of the white man, and so man power had to be used for many laborious and time-consuming tasks. Probably because of lack of draft animals, the Indians never learned to use the wheel. They did know about this important principle, for ancient Indian toys with wheels have been found, but they did not put it to practical use.

Some Indian contributions enriched Western culture. Indian influences are seen in several aspects of American life. Indian names occur throughout the Western Hemisphere. They have been given to nations, provinces, states, towns, cities, rivers, and lakes throughout Canada, the United States, and Latin America. For example, the Canadian province Saskatchewan, and Winnipeg in the province of Manitoba, have Indian names. Alaska, Mississippi, Illinois, and Wyoming are among states in the United States that have Indian names. Others appear in Latin-American countries such as Mexico, Nicaragua, and Peru. Indians invented the snowshoe, toboggan, and canoe. In medicine, they first used quinine, cocaine, cascara, ipecac, and the bulb syringe. Indians first discovered the properties of rubber, developed adobe for building, and invented the game of lacrosse. Their ingenuity also provided such varied contributions as cochineal dye, henequen fiber for rope, and moccasins.

The most important Indian contributions, however, were in the field of agriculture. Although most of the early Europeans who conquered the Indians had eyes only for the gold and silver they could carry home, it was the humble farm products they took back that made the most lasting impression on Western civilization. The Indians were the first to grow corn, potatoes, tomatoes, squash, pumpkins, avocados, and several kinds of beans. From them Western people also learned about pineapples, strawberries, vanilla, cinnamon, and tapioca. Another Indian discovery was chocolate; it was so important to the Aztecs that they used cacao beans as a form of currency. Indians were the first to make maple sugar, develop chicle (the main ingredient of chewing gum), and to grow and smoke tobacco.

Section Review

1. How did Indians justify their practice of human sacrifice?
2. How did the Indian system of owning property differ from ours?
3. How did Indians who had no system of writing preserve their literature?
4. What is the reason for the failure of the Indians to put the wheel to practical use?
5. What were some of the contributions Indians made in the fields of transportation? medicine? food?

Chapter 11 A Review

This chapter has discussed cultures on three continents that for centuries were isolated from the mainstream of Western civilization.

In Africa, early peoples developed advanced ways of living in certain areas of present-day Nigeria, Southern Rhodesia, and Ethiopia. The Afro-Moslem kingdoms blended Negro traditions with Islamic culture and built such flourishing cities as Timbuktu. However, geographic isolation and other factors such as slavery hindered the development of sub-Sahara Africa. Even though Africans there developed complex social organizations and vivid art and music, they did not progress so far as Europeans did in science or in technology.

The first inhabitants of North and South America probably came from Asia and spread gradually over the two continents. After the Indians learned to grow corn, they established permanent settlements and developed new skills. Most Indians north of the Rio Grande lived fairly simply, but those south of it made many cultural advances.

The Mayas of Yucatan attained the highest level of civilization in America, and are especially noted for their accurate calendar and their numeral system. The Aztecs, a bold and warlike people, built a large empire in Mexico, but it fell easily to the Spanish because they had help from many tribes who had formerly been conquered by the Aztecs. Far to the south, the Incas maintained a rigidly organized empire throughout the Andes Mountains region. They too, however, fell before Spanish invaders.

The cultural level of the Indians was uneven. Even some of the more civilized groups practiced human sacrifice. True writing was not generally known, and the lack of native draft animals delayed progress by requiring great expenditure of human energy. In spite of these factors, Indians created useful and beautiful arts and crafts, and made several contributions to Western ways of living, particularly in agriculture.

The Time

Indicate which of the following periods came wholly or partly within the time spans designated.

1-500 A.D.
Mayan Old Empire
Pax Romana

Gupta Empire
Tang Empire
Roman Republic

501-1000
Mayan Old Empire
Nok culture
Justinian's empire
Kingdom of Ghana
Songhai Kingdom
Ming Empire

1001-1500
Mayan New Empire
Harsha's empire
Inca Empire
Charlemagne's empire
Aztec Empire
Mali Empire
Mauryan Empire
Kingdom of Aksum

The Place

1. If you were an archaeologist, to which nations would you travel to study the following African cities or cultures?

| Nok | Gao | Zimbabwe |
| Ife | Aksum | Timbuktu |

2. To which modern country or countries would you go to study the following American Indian cities or cultures?

| Mayan | Tenochtitlán | Tiahuanaco |
| Toltec | Cuzco | |

3. In what general area did the following Indians live? Pueblos; Iroquois; Plains Indians.

Historical Terms

1. Why were the natives which the European explorers found in the New World called Indians?

2. Why is the word socialism often used to describe the economic system of the Inca Empire?

3. Explain each of the following terms and identify one Indian culture with which it is associated: quipus, maize, adobe.

Questions for Critical Thinking

1. In which of the American Indian cultures was the government a theocracy? Name one other theocracy mentioned in an earlier chapter of this text. What are the advantages of this form of government? What are the disadvantages?

2. Although the empire of the Incas was organized efficiently and administered skillfully, it was conquered by the Spaniards with little difficulty. What factors explain the ease of the Spanish conquest?

3. A study of history reveals that groups of people in various parts of the world, isolated from one another, often invent similar tools and develop similar ideas. What accounts for this development? Explain your answer with specific references to the cultures described in this chapter.

4. Why did civilizations develop in the Sudan area of Africa? What factors hindered progress in Africa?

5. Which group of American Indians remind you of the Greeks? of the Romans? Give at least two reasons for each answer.

Medieval Europe in Transition

In Europe during the Middle Ages, men lived according to a fairly well-defined pattern. This underlying unity was expressed through membership in a universal church and acceptance without question of the same ideas. Life was static or, at best, slow moving. Class divisions were rigid in an agricultural society dominated by a feudal nobility. Aside from a few cities, most activity centered on the manors, which were usually isolated and self-sufficient. Medieval Europe was a narrow world whose people had little knowledge of, or contacts with, other lands and peoples.

Dynamic forces began to alter the medieval pattern beginning about the 12th century. In a transitional period extending roughly to about 1600, a new Europe was in the making. Important changes in government, in learning and the arts, in religion, and in economics helped prepare the way for the birth of the so-called modern period.

The most remarkable and important political development was the rise of nations.

Medieval feudal lords were replaced by powerful kings, who gradually perfected new and more efficient forms of government. A national army protected a nation and helped increase its size. The royal court of law created uniform standards of justice throughout the realm. The picture on the opposite page illustrates the grandeur and power of a monarch in his royal court. It shows Charles VII of France in 1458 condemning one of his dukes for treason. The figures in white cowls are judges.

The new national courts symbolized the victory of the king over the noble and of the nation over the feudal fief. Royal justice made a great impression on the people, as seen in an extract from a biography of Louis IX (Saint Louis) of France written during his lifetime:

> . . . The king governed his land rightly and loyally, and according to God. . . . Many a time it happened that in summer he would go and sit down in the wood at Vincennes,

CHAPTER 12 / THE DEVELOPMENT OF NATIONS	CHAPTER 13 / THE RENAISSANCE	
Alfred the Great		
		900
Otto the Great Capetian dynasty Battle of Lechfeld		
		1000
Norman conquest Reconquista		
		1100
Henry II Portugal independent Frederick Barbarossa		
		1200
Magna Charta Louis IX Las Navas de Tolosa Model Parliament		
		1300
Hundred Years' War Battle of Crécy	Petrarch Giotto Black Death Boccaccio	
		1400
Battle of Agincourt Joan of Arc fall of Constantinople Wars of the Roses Ivan the Great Ferdinand and Isabella Tudor dynasty	Donatello Van Eyck Gutenberg Bible Lorenzo de' Medici Leonardo da Vinci	
		1500
Ivan the Terrible Russians capture Kazan	Raphael Erasmus Michelangelo The Prince Utopia The Courtier Titian	
		1600
	Shakespeare Don Quixote Rubens Rembrandt	
		1700

with his back to an oak, and make us take our seats around him. And all those who had complaints to make came to him without hindrance from ushers or other folk. Then he asked them with his own lips: "Is there any one here who has a cause [complaint]?" Those who had a cause stood up[,] when he would say to them; "Silence all, and you shall be dispatched [judged] one after another." Then he would call Monseigneur de Fontaines or Monseigneur Geoffrey de Villette and would say to one of them: "Dispose of this case for me." When he saw anything to amend in the words of those

who spake for others, he would correct it with his own lips.

The Renaissance, which first appeared in Italy early in the 14th century, constituted a great revival of learning and the arts. This movement emphasized individual freedom, beckoning men to think and act for themselves in order to enjoy life on earth. A similar spirit of individual inquiry produced the Reformation, which split the universal church and created divided religious loyalties. During the transitional

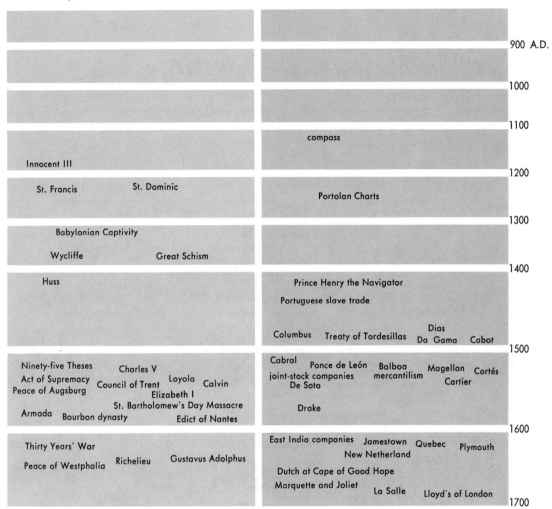

900 A.D.

1000

1100

compass

1200

Innocent III

St. Francis   St. Dominic

Portolan Charts

1300

Babylonian Captivity

Wycliffe   Great Schism

1400

Huss

Prince Henry the Navigator

Portuguese slave trade

Dias

Columbus   Treaty of Tordesillas   Da Gama   Cabot

1500

Ninety-five Theses   Charles V

Act of Supremacy   Loyola

Council of Trent   Calvin

Peace of Augsburg   Elizabeth I

St. Bartholomew's Day Massacre

Armada   Bourbon dynasty   Edict of Nantes

Cabral   Ponce de León   Balboa   Magellan   Cortés

joint-stock companies   mercantilism   Cartier

De Soto

Drake

1600

Thirty Years' War

Peace of Westphalia   Richelieu   Gustavus Adolphus

East India companies   Jamestown   Quebec   Plymouth

New Netherland

Dutch at Cape of Good Hope

Marquette and Joliet   La Salle   Lloyd's of London

1700

period in European history, the increased emphasis on the individual was seen in other ways. Seeking riches and adventure, bold men crossed uncharted oceans to discover new worlds. Overseas expansion stimulated trade, increased wealth, and introduced to Europe a host of products previously scarce or unknown. The quickening of town life and the growth of commerce increased the influence and wealth of middle class men, who were vigorous supporters of the system of economic individualism known as capitalism. The bar-

ter system of the Middle Ages gave way to one of money, banks, and stock exchanges as Europe rapidly became the economic center of the world.

The Development of Nations

CHAPTER 12   871 A.D.–1552 A.D.

During the later Middle Ages, feudalism was on the wane as trade and towns revived and strong monarchs undermined the authority of feudal lords. By improving the administration of justice, encouraging commercial life, and rallying the people around them, aggressive kings created nations. Above, Church leaders officiate at a coronation as nobles promise their allegiance to the new monarch.

The afternoon of August 26, 1346, was chilly and cloudy. Heavy showers pelted down as a large army of French knights urged their horses across a muddy field near the village of Crécy, France. On a hill before them stood a small English army—foot soldiers, dismounted knights, and stout archers armed with longbows.

The showers ended, and the French knights charged toward the outnumbered English. Suddenly, the English archers bent their longbows and sent flights of arrows whistling toward their attackers. As one who was there said, "It was like snow." The deadly arrows pierced the heavy armor of the charging knights, leaving many dead and wounded. Again and again the French charged in vain. By midnight, more than a thousand French knights lay dead on the field of Crécy. The English lost only about fifty men.

This battle, one of many between the English and the French, in the Hundred Years' War (1337-1453), disclosed many signs for the future. The defeat of the French knights by the English bowmen forecast the end of chivalry and the dominance of mounted knights, who had been the backbone of feudalism. The longbow had made knights' armor almost useless. The English also used primitive forms of cannon at Crécy—the first use of gunpowder in a field battle.

Also important was the fact that the victors were beginning to think of themselves as Englishmen and not merely as the inhabitants of a certain village or the followers of a certain noble. In other words, they were developing loyalty to their country rather than to an individual. With their love of country, their common language, customs, and traditions, and their growing central authority, the English were becoming a nation.

This chapter describes how feudalism faded in western Europe, as kings grew more powerful and as new weapons destroyed the supremacy of the medieval knights. It tells how kings, aided by the rising middle class, began to replace the local governments of feudalism with strong central authority. Thus a few nations, united and protected by new centralized governments and by the loyalty and support of the people, took the place of hundreds of separate fiefs. Finally, the chapter shows how the development of nations varied from country to country, moving rapidly in some and slowly in others.

The account of the development of nations is found in the following sections:

1. **Feudalism grew outmoded.**

2. **England became a unified nation.**

3. **The French monarchy created a national state.**

4. **Nation making occurred elsewhere.**

1 **Feudalism grew outmoded**

During most of the Middle Ages in Europe, strong national governments did not exist. France, for example, had at least 10 thousand separate parcels of land that were more or less countries unto themselves. There were kings, to be sure; theoretically, they owned all the land, but they had little actual power. In theory they ruled supreme over their nobles, who owed them loyalty. But the nobles often did just about as they pleased.

Feudalism provided government in an age of disorder, and the brawling nobles did furnish some protection for the people. But this protection was limited, and some feudal lords were more dangerous than the bandits they were supposed to be fighting.

The expansion of trade required improvements in government. Times changed. By the year 1100, cities had begun to grow fairly rapidly. Trade expanded and the

EUROPE
About 1000

■ Holy Roman Empire

SCOTLAND

North
Sea

IRELAND

WALES ENGLAND

NORWAY

SWEDEN

Baltic

Sea

DENMARK

POMERANIA

KINGDOM OF GERMANY

KINGDOM OF
FRANCE

KINGDOM
OF
ITALY

M O S L E M S

Mediterranean

KINGDOM
OF
SICILY

Sea

FINNISH
TRIBES

LITHUANIA

PRUSSIA

R U Ś

POLAND

HUNGARY

NOMADIC

WALLACHIA

BYZANTINE EM

Prepared
Rand M&Nally & C

population increased. As was learned in
Chapter 7, a new class of merchants and
tradesmen, the *bourgeoisie*, developed in
the cities. They disliked the lack of law
and order which interfered with business and threatened their property. The
middle class was also dissatisfied with
feudal obligations and conflicting legal
systems. Each noble had his own court,
and the Church also maintained a complete system of courts. The latter tried not
only churchmen, but also students, crusaders, and servants of churchmen. Many

persons tried to secure the right to a
Church trial, called *benefit of clergy*, because Church courts usually gave lighter
penalties than did other courts.

Increasing trade and commerce also
called for safer, more efficient transport.
Under feudalism, a noble could decide for
himself whether the highway passing
through his fief should be kept in good repair. He could and often did charge out-
rageous tolls for the use of a road or river
that he controlled. To make matters worse,
there was no effective police force. The

rocky, muddy roads were full of bandits who preyed on defenseless travelers.

The situation seemed to demand a change. The feudal system could not supply what was needed because it was made up of many small political units, ruled by rival nobles. Government had to be taken over by larger units.

Strong kings extended their power. Almost all nations that established central national governments during this period followed a similar pattern. It was the kings who increased their power at the expense of the Church (as discussed in Chapter 14) and the nobility. Kings collected taxes from the rising merchant class in exchange for protecting their property. This new source of wealth helped them become more independent of their nobles. Military support was the most important service a vassal gave to his lord. Each vassal had to equip a certain number of knights for military service. In this way kings assembled their armies—when they could. However, when they began to collect taxes from the growing merchant class, they could afford to hire *mercenaries,* or professional soldiers and officers. Husky peasants could become good soldiers of the king.

At the same time, mounted and armored knights were losing their supremacy to other kinds of fighting men. For many years ordinary soldiers, on foot and without armor, had been helpless in front of the knights' huge war horses and battle-axes. But three new developments in the late Middle Ages destroyed the knights' fighting mastery. One of these was the pike, which was developed by sturdy Swiss peasants in their fight for freedom against German knights. The pike was a long spear, usually about eighteen feet in length. Solid ranks of Swiss pikemen, fighting shoulder to shoulder, held off the charges of the knights, and the Swiss were soon in demand all over Europe as mercenaries. A second development was the increasing use of the English longbow. An archer using this weapon could shoot, with deadly accuracy, as many as twenty arrows a minute at a distance of 200 yards. The sharp, steel-tipped arrows could pierce many kinds of armor.

Most important was gunpowder, which had been invented by the Chinese, but was probably "reinvented" in Europe. Cannons, the first European weapons to use gunpowder, could batter down the walls of medieval castles, formerly the nobles' strongholds. Later, firearms made it possible for any private soldier to cripple the ablest knight long before he got close enough to fight with his battle-ax.

As kings became more powerful, they centralized governments. They employed civil servants, who specialized in finance, military affairs, or the law, to advise them in the task of ruling. They granted townsmen freedom from many feudal obligations, lightened the tolls paid by merchants, and extended their protection to make traveling safer. They also worked to bring all the people under one group of royal courts, which attempted to administer uniform justice.

In short, the kings were building new political units called *nations.* A nation is usually characterized by: (1) a strong central government powerful enough to defend itself from enemies without and capable of enforcing its own law within; (2) a population set off from other neighboring groups by language, religion, traditions, and a distinctive way of life; and (3) a feeling among the people of loyalty and pride in the group—a feeling known as *nationalism* or *patriotism.*

Section Review

1. What class of people particularly favored a strong king? Why?
2. Why was commerce difficult in feudal times?

New Methods of Warfare

The development of new weapons marked a change in waging war. Fighting became more "scientific," and tactical maneuvers involving common soldiers replaced the hand-to-hand combat of knights. A dangerous new weapon, the pike, was equally effective in the hands of both mounted knights and foot soldiers, as shown at right. A line of pikemen could serve as a bristling defense for cannoneers while they were reloading. The 14th-century drawing at far left below is the earliest known representation of a cannon. A soldier triggers the mechanism, which ejects a spear. Longbows, crossbows, and cannons are among the 15th-century weapons used by soldiers besieging a town from a movable tower, left. Aboard a galley of the same period, below, some of the soldiers take aim with crude muskets, while others are equipped with crossbows and pikes.

3. How did taxes from the merchants help kings gain independence from the nobles?
4. What developments changed medieval methods of making war?
5. In what ways did kings, as they became more powerful, improve governments?
6. What are the main characteristics of a nation?

2 England became a unified nation

Roman authority in Britain collapsed around 450 A.D., when Germanic tribes invaded the island. These Angles, Saxons, and Jutes murdered, enslaved, or drove out most of the native people. Then they set up several small kingdoms.

These petty kingdoms quarreled among themselves, and first one and then another gained supremacy. At the same time, they were all defending themselves against raiding Norsemen from Denmark. The kingdom of Wessex finally managed to make itself dominant and unite southern England. This success was largely the work of King Alfred the Great, one of the ablest rulers of England, who reigned from 871 to 899. A capable general, he reorganized the army for better defense against the Danes. But he was more interested in peace than in war. To restore law and order, he improved the system of local government and issued a set of laws. Alfred ruled with more authority than any Saxon king before him, and his admirable character won him the love of his people.

William of Normandy conquered England. The Wessex line of King Alfred continued to rule until 1016, when the Danes overran England and seized the throne from the English king, Ethelred the Unready. The first Danish king, Canute, ruled well, but his two sons, who succeeded him, were hated tyrants. After the second son died, the English invited Edward the Confessor, Ethelred's son, to become king.

King Edward the Confessor died childless in 1066. His cousin William, duke of Normandy, made a claim to the English throne, based on a distant relationship to the English royal family, but the council of the kingdom selected Harold, a powerful

Thomas à Becket was appointed archbishop of Canterbury by his friend King Henry II. The two men quarreled, as shown above, when the king tried to bring the clergy under royal law and Becket defiantly asserted Church authority. In a fit of anger, Henry denounced the archbishop, whereupon a group of knights journeyed to Canterbury and killed Becket in the cathedral. Public furor over the crime thwarted the ambitions of the king, even though he had not specifically ordered the murder.

English noble, as the ruler. In response, William raised an army by promising lands to his followers and by winning the pope's approval of his cause. In 1066 he crossed the English Channel and defeated King Harold in the Battle of Hastings. Harold was killed, and William became king.

William the Conqueror was too strong a king to let his nobles challenge his power. Although he brought the political feudal system from Normandy, he changed it so that it became a pillar of his strong government. He required all the nobles to swear direct allegiance to him and broke up the largest feudal holdings. By continuing the Anglo-Saxon militia system, whereby all men had to bear arms for the king, he lessened his reliance upon the military service of his great nobles. William also increased his sources of revenue. He ordered a census of all the taxable wealth in his kingdom. The results

were collected in the famous Domesday Book, which today furnishes an excellent description of 11th-century England.

England was not a unified nation in 1066, nor did William make it one. The Norman and Saxon strains did not merge for about 200 years, and it took a series of wars with France to kindle a spirit of patriotism. But William did lay a firm foundation for a strong monarchy.

Henry II improved the legal system. After the Norman kings, as William and his first three successors are called, England came under the rule of the Plantagenet family. Henry II, a great-grandson of William and founder of the line, ruled England from 1154 to 1189. The Plantagenets ruled until 1399. During that time, there began to develop three new institutions that have become the basis of many modern democracies—common law, the jury system, and representative government.

The reign of Henry II was one of the greatest in English history. This freckle-faced, redheaded king was determined to unite all of England under his rule. He wanted all the people to look to him and to their national government for justice and protection.

Henry II made his royal law the main law of the land. Because of its uniformity, it was fairer and more efficient than the many different kinds of law that existed at the time. Gradually it came to be known as the *common law*, because it applied to the whole country. It was based on custom and court decisions. Common law is used today in the United States (except for Louisiana) and in nations and colonies established by Great Britain.

Henry II extended an old custom of sending judges on regular tours all over the country. These traveling judges combined local legal customs with legal opinions from the king's court to develop the common law as the uniform law of the land. Going from place to place, they had the advantage of being strangers in each district and therefore not subject to bribes, threats, or the pressures of friendship. Each judge had a *circuit*, or route that he followed. This practice, which has remained an important part of the judicial system of England, served as the basis for the circuit courts of the United States.

The jury system also developed under Henry II. The first juries consisted simply of the people who came before the royal judge to accuse someone of committing a crime; they did not decide whether the person was guilty. An outgrowth of this early jury is the *grand jury* of today, whose purpose is to decide whether there is enough evidence against an accused person to hold him for trial. About a century after Henry's time, another kind of jury began to develop. It heard a trial and decided on the guilt of the accused. This kind is called a *petit* (little) *jury,* or *trial jury.*

Henry II had great ability and energy. A lesser man would have failed, for he faced great difficulties. The nobility—and even his own sons—resisted him. The Church fought him because it resented his interference with its own system of courts. Henry believed that Church courts were often too lax and that all his subjects should be brought under one system of justice. His stand led to a famous quarrel with the Church, in which Thomas à Becket, the archbishop of Canterbury, opposed Henry. The murder of Becket by some of Henry's knights outraged public opinion and hurt Henry's cause. His ambitions for equal justice for all Englishmen were not realized until after the Middle Ages.

Magna Charta assured some rights. When Henry died in 1189, his oldest son came to the throne. Richard the Lion-Hearted, as he was called, was a famous soldier but a poor king. He was more interested in deeds of bravery than in statesmanship. During the ten years of his reign he spent most of his time fighting in the Crusades or in western Europe, and made only two brief visits to England. During Richard's absence, his deceitful brother, John, plotted to overthrow him. Although John did not succeed, he became king when Richard died.

John ruled cruelly and arbitrarily. He quarreled with the king of France and with the pope, and ruthlessly stifled opposition at home. In 1215 his nobles rebelled at his unjust demands. They forced King John to agree to a document called *Magna Charta,* or the Great Charter, which was designed to limit his power and protect their feudal rights. The Magna Charta did not, at the time, guarantee representative government, taxation by consent of the people, or trial by jury. But these principles developed from the rights it did grant.

The Magna Charta forced the king to make this promise: "To no one shall we sell, deny, or delay right or justice." He also had to promise to stop seizing the property of his vassals and forcing large payments from them. The Magna Charta stated that the king could collect no money beyond that allowed by the old laws of feudalism "save by the common council of our kingdom." Later scholars interpreted this clause to mean that the king could not levy any taxes without the agreement of the people through their representatives. (The colonists in the American Revolution referred to this principle when they objected to "taxation without representation," because they had no representatives in the British government.)

Another clause of the Magna Charta declared:

> No free man shall be seized, or imprisoned . . . nor shall we pass sentence on him except by the legal judgment of his peers or by the law of the land.

This was later taken to mean a guarantee of trial by jury to all freemen. The number of freemen was quite limited at that time, since most Englishmen were still serfs. But as they became free, they also gained the rights that were promised to freemen in 1215.

Parliament took shape under Edward I. Edward I, one of the greatest Plantagenets, tried to bring the entire island under one rule. In 1284 he conquered Wales, made it part of England, and designated his oldest son as the prince of Wales. Edward wanted to take Scotland, but several expeditions failed to subdue its fiercely independent people.

This warfare was costly, and Edward needed extra funds. He collected money through special taxes, which were approved by representatives of the people in an institution called *Parliament*.

English kings had long had a group of advisers known as the Great Council, which included members of the higher clergy and the feudal nobility. In 1295, Edward called these great nobles and princes of the Church to meet with him. In addition he ordered the *sheriffs*, or local law enforcement officers, to hold elections in their *shires* (counties). Freemen chose two knights from each shire and two *burgesses*, or citizens, from each chartered town, called a *borough*.

This assembly came to be known as the Model Parliament because it contained the essential features of later parliaments.

At first, the knights met with the nobles, and the clergy and burgesses each met as separate groups. In time, the clergy withdrew entirely, and the knights sat with the burgesses. The nobles made up what became the House of Lords. The elected knights and townsmen made up what became the House of Commons. This group was a *representative* body, because each member represented other persons besides himself and voted in their interests.

At first, the House of Lords and the House of Commons probably met in the same room, although as separate groups. In time, it became more convenient for the House of Commons to have its own quarters, and so it met in Westminster Abbey. The monarch could call these two houses together and address them in joint sessions from the throne.

The early kings called Parliament mainly to get money, but Parliament began to have other ideas. Its members hit upon the idea of holding up a grant of money until the king righted wrongs they brought to his attention. This procedure was called *redress of grievances*. Parliament drew up formal statements of demands called *bills*. These became acts, or statutes, when the sovereign gave his assent. In this way, Parliament became a legislative, or lawmaking, body. The word *parliament* has thus

The English Channel is a 350-mile-long arm of the Atlantic Ocean which links the North Sea with the Atlantic and forms a water barrier between England and the continent of Europe. A better understanding of the English Channel as a geographic barrier may be gained by examining facts about the Channel itself.

The English Channel lies on the continental shelf, an underwater stretch of land, or plain, which gradually slopes westward from the European continent before dropping off suddenly to the deep sea bed of the Atlantic Ocean. The English Channel is relatively shallow, with an average depth of about 175 feet.

The Channel is narrow, as well as shallow. Its average width is 75 miles, but at its narrowest point—between Dover, England, and Calais, France—the Channel is only 21 miles wide.

The Atlantic Ocean and North Sea tides sweep into the Channel about every 12½ hours. The gravitational pull of the moon and the sun cause the surface of the ocean to rise one or two feet, on the average. The narrowness and shallowness of the Channel, however, heightens the effect of the tides. As a result, waters in the Channel rise from about 12 feet to more than 40 feet at high tide. The opposing influence of the North Sea and Atlantic tidal currents in the Channel causes many local variations in the time and height of the tides and often makes navigation difficult.

Waters of the Atlantic Ocean enter the English Channel from the southwest and flow northeast through the Channel. A portion of the stream turns northwest as it enters the Channel and flows in a gigantic counterclockwise movement between England and Ireland. This flow brings Atlantic water southward across the entrance to the Channel. The splitting and conflict of currents, together with the movement of the tides, tend to make the Channel waters choppy and rough.

The prevailing westerly winds add to the rough seas in the English Channel. Moist winds from the west blow across the Channel all year, except in March or April, when dry easterly winds prevail. The west winds bring storms and rain over the Channel, and high winds occur frequently from October to January. As a result, calm seas in the Channel are rare. The English Channel is noted for its roughness, bad weather, and fogs.

The combined effects of the tides, currents, and winds increased the effectiveness of the English Channel as a geographic barrier between England and the continent of Europe. No invader has successfully crossed the Channel and conquered England since William of Normandy in 1066. Today, however, modern weapons of attack cannot be stopped by the English Channel. It has lost much of its strategic value as a geographic barrier.

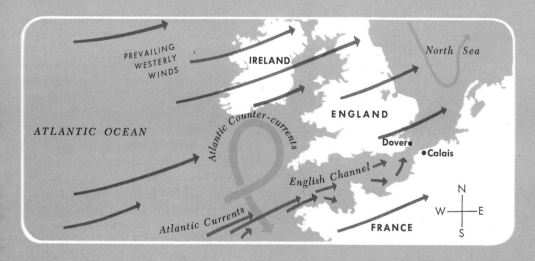

come to mean the highest lawmaking body of any country, and England has earned the title "Mother of parliaments."

The Wars of the Roses resulted in a new line of strong kings. After the reign of Richard II ended in 1399, a long series of foreign and civil wars weakened the land. The Hundred Years' War, which had begun in 1337 when Edward III invaded France, went badly for England in its later years. Scarcely had it ended when two branches of the English royal family, the House of York and the House of Lancaster, started a series of conflicts for the throne. This struggle, which began in 1455 and lasted for thirty years, destroyed many of the noble families of England. It was called the *Wars of the Roses* because the Yorkists used the white rose as an emblem and the Lancastrians, a red rose. Finally, in 1485, Henry Tudor defeated the Yorkist King Richard III at the battle of Bosworth Field. As Henry VII, he united both families and began the famous Tudor dynasty, which ruled England until 1603.

The reign of the Tudor family was a period of strong royal power. Parliament was comparatively weak. The nobles had been subdued. The king's judges enforced the common law, and an efficient group of civil servants helped govern the kingdom. England under the Tudors gained increasing leadership in European affairs and enjoyed a great flowering of culture. The reign of Elizabeth I, discussed in Chapter 14, was especially important.

By the end of the 15th century, the English nation had become firmly established. All the people lived under the common law, and a national government ruled in all parts of the realm. The once separate Norman and Saxon customs and languages had merged into something new—English nationality. The people felt united by a common pride in their monarch and their country.

Section Review

1. What steps did William the Conqueror take to strengthen the power of the English monarchy?
2. How did Henry II improve the legal system?
3. What was the Magna Charta? What principles of democracy are based on its provisions?
4. When did the Model Parliament meet? What groups of people did it include? How did the kings' need for money aid the development of Parliament as a lawmaking body?
5. Who was the first Tudor? For what was his dynasty noted?
6. In what respects had England become a firmly established nation by the end of the 15th century?

3 **The French monarchy created a national state**

France lagged far behind England in developing a national government. Here the collapse of central authority after Charlemagne's death was followed by the growth of a completely feudal government organized around strong local leaders. In the late 10th century, the name *France* referred merely to a small section around Paris. What was vaguely thought of as a kingdom consisted only of a collection of feudal states. As a result, the French kings had a harder task uniting their nation than did their royal neighbors across the English Channel.

In 987, the French nobles elected Hugh Capet as king. He had been count of Paris, ruling an area only about 100 miles wide and 200 miles long. Many of his feudal nobles were much more powerful than he, but the Capetian family extended its control by warfare and through alliances and treaties with powerful nobles. The family ruled until 1328.

Kings strengthened the government.
The first task of the Capetian kings was to force the nobles to accept their authority. Louis VI (Louis the Fat), who ruled from 1108 to 1137, was the first king to have much success with this problem. He acquired complete control over his royal domain, called the *Ile de France,* which served as a center from which royal law could be extended. His grandson, Philip II (Augustus), won Normandy, Anjou, and other English possessions in France from King John. Year by year, Capetian kings pushed out from their capital at Paris to enlarge their country. Each one left his successor a little more power than he had inherited.

As in England, the kings of France gave the people better government than the feudal barons had provided. Louis IX, who ruled from 1226 to 1270, is a good example of the true knightly king of the Middle Ages. He led his knights in the Crusades, and won fame for his bravery and dignity as a prisoner of the Moslems. Peace and justice seemed to him far more important than conquests, however, and the Church made him a saint after his death because of his nobility of character. Louis established a system of royal courts and declared private warfare and trial by combat illegal. He encouraged the people to appeal to his officials if the nobles oppressed them. In this way he convinced all classes of the French people that their government was important to their own well-being. The French, however, did not develop a strong parliament, or place much emphasis upon the rights of the people.

England threatened French independence. In addition to their problems at home, French kings faced a constant danger of trouble with England. England still owned some territory in France, and English rulers had to pay homage to the French kings because of these possessions. English

ENGLAND AND FRANCE
About 1337

English possessions in France

Battle during Hundred Years' War

WALES · Bosworth · London Hastings · CALAIS FLANDERS AGINCOURT CRÉCY NORMANDY · Rouen · Reims BRITTANY Paris · CHAMPAGNE ANJOU ORLÉANS × POITIERS POITOU BURGUNDY AQUITAINE Bordeaux · GASCONY LANGUEDOC

Prepared by
Rand McNally & Co., Chicago

rulers, considering themselves to be the equals of French kings, were unfaithful vassals.

From the middle of the 12th century to the middle of the 15th, the English and French were often at war. In 1328 the last Capetian king died without leaving any direct male heir. Edward III of England was related to the Capets through his mother, and claimed to be the king of France. The French refused to honor his claim, and Edward used this refusal as an excuse to invade France with an army in 1337. His invasion began a series of wars that became known as the Hundred Years' War. The fighting in all these wars took place in France, but better generalship and weapons often gave the English the advantage. In 1346 Edward's troops, with the help of their longbows, won a smashing victory at Crécy; the next year they captured Calais. Under a later king, Henry V, English longbowmen defeated a large French army at Agincourt in 1415, and reconquered Normandy.

Joan of Arc inspired patriotism. By 1425 it looked as if England would conquer and rule France. Then an amazing story unfolded. A simple country girl, Joan of Arc, "knowing neither A nor B," as she said, had visions and believed that she heard the voices of saints calling on her to rid France of the English soldiers. In 1429 she went to Charles, the uncrowned heir to the throne, and asked for an army. She promised that she would defeat the English and save the throne for the king of France. Charles and his court were skeptical, but, unable themselves to stop the steady advance of the English, they gave her the soldiers she asked for.

Clad in shining armor and mounted on a white horse, Joan appeared to the French soldiers as a heaven-sent leader. Filled with new hope, they fell on the English like a thunderbolt. For a short time Joan of Arc led her soldiers to victory after victory. Charles, with her at his side, was crowned king of France at Reims Cathedral. Then Joan fell into the hands of the English, was tried as a heretic, and was burned at the stake in 1431.

But Joan's work had been done. Frenchmen thrilled at the memory of the simple peasant girl, her love for her country, and her courage. Her loyalty helped develop a national spirit in France, a new feeling that France was united and that no foreigner should be allowed to rule it. From this time on, the English fought a losing battle. By the end of the war in 1453, they held only the city of Calais.

The French victory ended England's costly attempts to conquer France. Both nations could now concentrate upon their own problems. The war also did much to encourage patriotism on both sides. Lastly, because of new methods of warfare, the Hundred Years' War helped end the long supremacy of mounted knights.

Section Review
1. Why did French kings have a greater task in increasing their power than the English kings?
2. What steps did the Capetian kings take to enlarge their holdings and to improve the French government?
3. Why was England a threat to French independence?
4. What were three results of the Hundred Years' War?

4 **Nation making occurred elsewhere**

While England and France were being strengthened and unified, nations were beginning to develop in other areas of Europe.

Spain and Portugal became separate nations. A Germanic tribe, the Visigoths, had settled in Spain during the German invasions of the Roman Empire. Their kingdom lasted until early in the 8th century. Then, in 711, Moorish invaders crossed from Africa and conquered most of the Iberian Peninsula. A few Christians continued to hold out in the mountains of the north. Their communities were so small, however, that the Moors made only a half-hearted effort to subdue them.

As discussed in Chapter 7, the Moors built up a Moslem kingdom in Spain that reached a high level of culture. In 1031, however, it was split by internal quarrels, and broke up into more than twenty small states. Moslem disunity helped the Christians in the north, who were determined to carry out a crusade against the Moslems and regain Spain for Christendom. In this task they were aided by nobles from many parts of Europe. Alphonso I of Portugal

UNIFICATION OF SPAIN

Christian States
Moorish Influence

PYRENEES
NAVARRE
CASTILE
ARAGON
BARCELONA
LEON
LEON
LIPHATE OF CORDOVA

1000

PYRENEES
LEON
NAVARRE
ARAGON
PORTUGAL
CASTILE
CALIPHATE OF CORDOVA

1150

PYRENEES
NAVARRE
ARAGON
PORTUGAL
KINGDOM OF SPAIN
Las Navas
de Tolosa •
GRANADA
To Spain in 1492

1450

Prepared by
Rand McNally & Co., Chicago

defeated the Moors in his country in 1139, and declared Portugal an independent kingdom in 1143. The Christian kingdoms of northern Spain gradually drove back the Moslems. After a decisive victory at Las Navas de Tolosa in 1212, only Granada remained in Moslem hands.

In 1469 the two leading Christian countries of Aragon and Castile were joined when Ferdinand, the future king of Aragon, married Isabella, later queen of Castile. The *Reconquista* (reconquest), as it was called, finally succeeded in 1492 when Ferdinand and Isabella captured Granada. United Spain was at last ready to become a strong nation.

Other Europeans began building nations. Nation making in medieval and early modern times had its greatest success in western Europe, along the shores of the Atlantic Ocean. However, other national groups were forming elsewhere in Europe. In the north, the Swedes, Norwegians, and Danes were emerging as separate peoples. The Bohemians, a Slavic people, were united in the 11th century by one of their tribes known as the Czechs. The Poles

formed a strong group, and organized the Duchy of Poland. The Magyar tribes of Asia settled down in a fertile area along the Danube River and formed a kingdom of Hungary.

Two rulers strengthened Russia. The development of a Russian nation began with the story of two fierce but capable rulers, both named Ivan. The first of these men was Ivan III, sometimes called Ivan the Great; the second was his grandson, Ivan IV, usually known as Ivan the Terrible.

Ivan the Great, who ruled from 1462 to 1505, brought to completion the work of the grand dukes of Moscow. Slowly but surely he gained control over one small feudal state after another until he ruled most of the Russian people. In 1480 he stopped all tribute to the Tartars. They sent an army against Ivan, who amassed a great force of his own. After the two armies had faced each other across a small river for weeks, both decided to withdraw. Although there was no battle, this event brought to a close the two centuries of Tartar domination in Russia.

Strong Leaders were essential to the development of nations, providing inspiration both on the battlefield and in the halls of government. Frederic Barbarossa, above, a great German king, led the Third Crusade. Edward I, above right, curtailed feudalism in England and strengthened the monarchy. Before Joan of Arc was burned at the stake, right, she inspired French troops to victory over English invaders during the Hundred Years' War.

Having won out over the Tartars, Ivan III attacked the Polish-Lithuanian kingdom, which had taken over the western regions of Russia during the Tartar occupation. After two invasions, he won back several border areas.

Under Ivan the Terrible, who ruled from 1533 to 1584, the Russians pushed their way into the eastern *steppes,* or plains, defeated the nomad tribes, and brought vast lands under the sway of the Moscow grand duke. In 1552, Russian troops captured Kazan, one of the chief cities of the Tartars. Russian peasants began to till the soil in the land once ruled by Genghis Khan.

During the era of the two Ivans, these rulers made progress toward uniting Russia and establishing a strong central government. They took the title of *czar* from the Roman word *Caesar,* showing that they considered themselves heirs to the Eastern Roman Empire of the Byzantines. After this empire fell to the Turks in 1453, the czars of Russia claimed to be the new Roman emperors of the East. They kept the tradition of despotic rule inherited from the Byzantines and the Tartars.

Nation making failed in Germany and Italy. By 850 A.D. the people of East Frankland were calling themselves *Germans,* and were developing a language distinct from that spoken in West Frankland (France). The German kings set out to unite their country under a strong central government. All went well for a time. Hungarian and Slav raiders from the east were defeated, and many German nobles promised to obey and serve their kings.

Shortly after 900, Henry the Fowler, a Saxon noble, ascended the throne of East Frankland. He succeeded in forcing from his powerful nobles the loyalty they owed him. Yet each noble, as master in his own lands, continued to raise his own army and form alliances to increase his power.

Henry's son, Otto the Great, became one of the strongest kings of Germany. First, he defeated the Hungarians at the Battle of the Lechfeld in 955; then he began to expand eastward into the land of the Slavs. (This pressure against the Slavs has been a continuing feature of German history; perhaps 60 per cent of modern Germany originally belonged to the Slavs.)

After his victory over the Hungarians, Otto was considered the strongest king in Europe, and his country the most powerful. But instead of making himself supreme at home, Otto turned his attention toward Italy. This country had declined greatly from its glory in the days of the Roman Empire.

In the year 962, Otto the Great made a mistake that had far-reaching consequences. He invaded Italy, and had the pope crown him as a new Roman emperor. From this time on, German emperors thought of themselves as the rulers of a great European empire. They hoped to be like the Roman Caesars, ruling over what came to be called the Holy Roman Empire —which, the 18th-century French writer Voltaire said, "was neither holy, nor Roman, nor an empire."

The establishment of the Holy Roman Empire was a sad blunder. While the German emperors wasted their time, money, and armies fighting in Italy, the nobles at home regained their power. Instead of a united German nation, there was only a hodgepodge of free cities and tiny feudal states. The emperor had little power, but seven of his feudal vassals became so important that they claimed the right to elect the ruler, and were called *Electors.*

Some of Germany's greatest kings could not resist the temptation to possess an Italian empire. Frederick Barbarossa ("red-beard") was founder of the royal house of Hohenstaufen. His great ambition was to restore the glory of Charlemagne, to unite Germany and Italy in one strong empire under his rule. Crowned emperor at Rome in 1155, he spent much of his reign—which lasted until 1190—in wasteful fighting. The liberty-loving Italian cities, supported by the papacy, completely defeated his efforts.

The grand ambitions of the German emperors not only destroyed the hope for a unified nation at home but also had unfortunate effects on Italy. German emperors interfered there constantly. Instead of one nation, there were the Papal States, the kingdom of Naples and Sicily, and such city-states as Venice, Milan, Florence, and Genoa. Each of these independent city-states controlled the land around it and had its own army and ambassadors. Their jealousies and rivalries led to continual warfare and kept Italy from nationhood. Neither Italy nor Germany became united kingdoms until the 19th century.

Section Review

1. How did nation making in Spain differ from that in France and England?
2. How did Ivan III and Ivan IV enlarge Russia?
3. After a promising start, why did nation making fail in Germany?
4. What hindered nationhood in Italy?

Chapter 12   A Review

The development of modern European nations took place during the late Middle Ages. As the population increased, cities grew, and trade expanded, feudalism became inadequate as a form of government.

Kings strengthened their authority at the expense of feudal nobles. New methods of warfare further limited the supremacy of mounted knights. As kings built up their strength, they improved their national governments with better administration and legal systems.

Some kings had begun fairly early to establish efficient central governments. In England, Alfred the Great succeeded in uniting southern England against the Danes in the 9th century. Troubled times undid much of his work, however. It was not until the Norman Conquest of 1066 that England emerged again as a strong kingdom—under William the Conqueror, who made his central government supreme. Henry II fostered the development of the common law and trial by jury. The Magna Charta, signed by King John, guaranteed basic rights to freemen. And, under Edward I, Parliament began its slow but steady progress as a representative lawmaking body. Thus England made a start, not only as a nation, but as a democratic one. After a period of confusion during the Wars of the Roses, the Tudors came to power and ushered in a great era of English political and cultural expansion.

In France, the Capetian kings enlarged their holdings gradually by reducing the power of the nobles and by providing better government. The Hundred Years' War resulted from English claims to territory in France. Although England won several victories early in the war, the French regained lost ground under the inspiration of Joan of Arc. The war helped both nations by settling the question of English claims in France, by stimulating patriotism, and by helping end feudal methods of warfare.

In Spain and Portugal, the Christians fought for centuries to expel the Moors. Portugal succeeded in the 12th century. Then, more than 300 years later, Spain's two most important kingdoms were joined with the marriage of Isabella of Castile to Ferdinand of Aragon. In 1492 these monarchs led their people in the final expulsion of the Moors, and Spain took its place as a unified nation.

Several regions of northern Europe had had some success in nation making by 1500. Under Ivan III and Ivan IV, Russia freed itself from Tartar domination. Strong German kings, especially Otto the Great, made a promising start in uniting German states. However, they made a mistake by setting up the Holy Roman Empire. They tried unsuccessfully to control Italy, with the result that neither Germany nor Italy developed political unity.

The Time

Indicate in which of the four periods the following events occurred.

(a) 801-1000   (c) 1201-1400
(b) 1001-1200   (d) 1401-1600

1. The *Reconquista* was completed.
2. William of Normandy conquered England.
3. Otto the Great was crowned emperor by the pope.
4. Edward I convened the Model Parliament.
5. King John agreed to sign the Magna Charta.
6. Tartar rule of Russia ended.
7. The Byzantine Empire fell to the Turks.
8. The Hundred Years' War ended.
9. The Wars of the Roses ended.
10. Portugal became independent of Moorish control.

The Place

1. Tell why each of the following places is associated with the making of a modern nation.

Wessex   Castile   East Frankland
Granada   Aragon   *Ile de France*
Wales   Kazan   Normandy

2. What event occurred at each of these places?

the Lechfeld   Reims   Crécy
Bosworth Field   Agincourt   Hastings
Las Navas de Tolosa

The People

The following persons were outstanding men and women of their times. Name the country with which each person is associated, the century in which he lived, and the achievements for which he is noted.

Alfred the Great   Louis IX
William of Normandy   Joan of Arc
Edward I (Plantagenet)   Ivan the Great
Henry Tudor   Otto the Great
Henry II (Plantagenet)   Hugh Capet
Ferdinand and Isabella

Historical Terms

If newspapers had existed in the period covered by this chapter, the following headlines might have appeared. Write the meaning of the italicized word or phrase in each one.

1. *Bourgeoisie* Growing in European Cities
2. Accused Demands *Benefit of Clergy* in Murder Case
3. French King Reported Recruiting *Mercenaries*
4. *Borough* Election for *Burgesses* Held Yesterday in *Shire*
5. Parliament Delays Appropriations by Insisting on *Redress of Grievances*
6. *Czar* Reports Capture of Kazan
7. Successor to throne of *Holy Roman Empire* Sought by *Electors*
8. Swiss Peasants Use *Pikes* in Their Fight for Independence
9. Hundred Years' War Spurs *Nationalism* in France and England
10. *Domesday Book* Reveals Sources of English Wealth
11. London Thief Accused by *Grand Jury*
12. Ivan the Terrible Brings Eastern *Steppes* Under His Domain

Questions for Critical Thinking

1. In what ways were the steps taken by Henry II and Louis IX to strengthen their national governments similar?
2. What obstacles to unification did both the Spanish and Russians face? How were these obstacles overcome?
3. How did the development of strong central governments help business and trade during the late Middle Ages?
4. Using the reference map, "Europe," tell what geographical features helped or hindered the efforts of the German kings to control both Germany and Italy.
5. It has been said that whoever holds the purse strings of a nation controls that nation. How did control of the purse lead to growth of representative government in England?
6. Why is it incorrect to apply the term *nation* to the England of William the Conqueror's time?
7. How was the development of the French nation affected by the Hundred Years' War?

The Renaissance

Around 1300, a revival of learning and the arts began in Italy, later spreading to northern Europe. This new movement was termed the Renaissance. Two famous German artists of the period were Hans Holbein the Younger and Albrecht Dürer. At left is Holbein's portrait of Erasmus, the "scholar of Europe"; at right is a drawing by Dürer of an artist using a so-called perspective machine to achieve a greater degree of realism in the portrait he is painting.

Men and women of the Middle Ages perhaps gave more serious thought to life after death than to life on earth. They were taught by the Christian Church that worldly concerns were of little importance. Church authority, along with the regulated system of feudalism, gave the individual few chances to express independent ideas. He was expected to accept his position in society without question.

During the period from the 14th to the early 17th century, this approach to life changed gradually. Pleasures and problems of earthly life became important to people, who wanted to live their own lives and to form their own opinions. Confident of their own powers, they also became defiant of authority. During this period towns grew, trade expanded, and political units increased in size. Men's interests also widened; they became aware of their own individual traits and of the world around them.

Out of this increased awareness of life, this new spirit of curiosity and independence, came a revival of learning and an outburst of creative activity that produced some of the greatest art and literature the world has known. These changes—a rebirth of learning and a great creative flowering—are known as the *Renaissance* (a French word meaning "rebirth"). The term is also applied to the period during which the changes took place, a period of transition from medieval to modern times.

In the following sections, this chapter describes the Renaissance and the outstanding figures who were a part of it:

1. **The Renaissance began in Italy.**

2. **The Renaissance was based on humanism and a revival of learning.**

3. **Italians created masterpieces of Renaissance art.**

4. **The Renaissance spread to other countries.**

1 The Renaissance began in Italy

An important aspect of the Renaissance concerned the revival of classical learning. It was logical that this movement should start in Italy, a region where many traces of Greco-Roman civilization still remained. Italy had another advantage in being close to Constantinople, which had preserved the Greek language and much of Greek learning.

More important than old cultures was a new vigor, which Italy enjoyed partly because of wealth from increased trade and partly from political independence.

New wealth supported art and learning. Earlier chapters have described how trade was stimulated by the Crusades and how towns began to increase in size and importance in the 11th century. Northern Italy benefited especially from the increased trade, chiefly because of its strategic location. Most of the trade routes from the East, whether by sea across the Indian Ocean or overland through Asia and the Near East, converged on the eastern end of the Mediterranean Sea. Italian merchants purchased their goods there and transported them to the ports of northern Italy, from which they were carried across the Alps into northern Europe.

Northern Italy was divided into a number of city-states, similar in plan to those of ancient Greece. Each consisted of a city proper and a tract of surrounding land. The growth of trade brought great prosperity to these cities, the most important of which were Venice, Florence, Milan, and Genoa. Venice, the "Queen of the Adriatic," was built on 117 small islands, and drew its power and wealth from the sea. As early as 1500, Venetian merchants had a fleet of 3000 ships. Florence was famous for its textile industry, which employed 30 thousand persons.

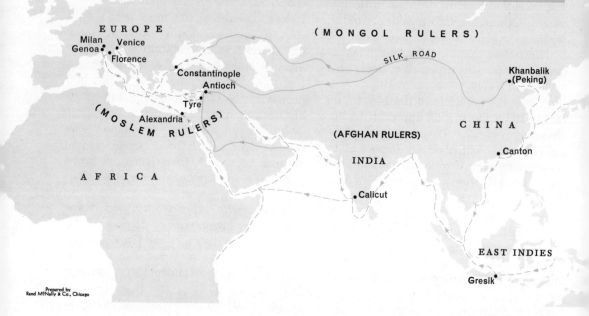

TRADE ROUTES FROM ASIA TO ITALY

EUROPE

Milan · Venice
Genoa · · Florence

(MONGOL RULERS)

SILK ROAD

Constantinople
Antioch

Khanbalik
· (Peking)

Tyre

(MOSLEM RULERS)

Alexandria

(AFGHAN RULERS)

CHINA

· Canton

INDIA

AFRICA

· Calicut

EAST INDIES

Gresik

Prepared by
Rand McNally & Co., Chicago

As Italian bankers and merchants grew rich from trade, their new wealth enabled them to enjoy leisure, to study, and to learn to appreciate the arts. They invited artists and philosophers to live and work in their palaces. Because of their patronage of the arts, it has been said that "the oil of commerce lighted the lamp of culture."

Italian rulers also took a leading part in encouraging artists and writers, for the glory not only of their own families but also of the cities they ruled. The Este family, which governed the city of Ferrara, supported such painters as Leonardo da Vinci, Raphael, and Titian. The Medici family of Florence were patrons of the artists Donatello and Michelangelo, among others. The popes, too, played an important role in supporting culture. Leo X, himself a Medici, made Rome a great center of art and learning.

Political conditions encouraged individualism. German kings during the Middle Ages wanted to unite Italy and Germany in the Holy Roman Empire. This ambition aroused strong opposition from the popes. In order to gain the support of the Italian cities, both sides—the German emperors and the popes—granted them special privileges, including the right to elect their own officials, to make their own laws, and to levy taxes. Most of the cities developed a republican form of government.

Because there was no effective central government in Italy, each city became a law unto itself. As trade grew, the merchant class became more powerful. Quarrels broke out between various groups of wealthy merchants; often noble families joined in the feuds. People longed for law and order, and in response to this need, a class of *despots,* or dictators, arose in the 14th century. These daring men seized power by force and guile, but most of them were interested in the people's welfare and gave their cities efficient government. Some despots, like the Medici family of Florence, had been bankers and merchants. Others, like the Sforzas of Milan, began as soldiers called *condottieri.*

The Italian despots came to power because of their strength, cleverness, and ability. If their heirs lacked these qualities, they soon lost influence. Birth hardly mattered; talent was the chief essential. Once on top, a ruler had to be constantly alert for plots to overthrow him. Life in 14th-century Italy was both exciting and dangerous. People were skilled in the use of the dagger, the poisoned drink, and the convenient "accident."

In such an atmosphere, the old medieval idea of the unimportance of the individual gave way to the notion that he was all-important. Old barriers to freedom of thought and action broke down. Men began to express their own ideas about life and art, to criticize long-held customs and beliefs, and to glory in their own strength.

Machiavelli justified the use of force and deception in politics. In the Middle Ages, treatises on government were rare and consisted for the most part of manuals describing the desirable traits a ruler should possess. These guidebooks were pious, well-intentioned, and dull. In 1532 was published a slim volume entitled *The Prince* by Niccolò Machiavelli. It too contained advice to a hypothetical ruler, but it differed radically from its predecessors. It was to become one of the most notorious works ever written.

Born in 1469, Machiavelli served his native city of Florence for many years as a diplomat and government official. While in retirement from public life, he wrote *The Prince*, intending it as a realistic set of rules by which a strong ruler could create a unified government for Italy and ward off invasions by other newly powerful European nation-states. Central to his thinking was the concept that society is subject to the passions and interests of men, not divine rule or moral law. In this respect, Machiavelli offered an example of Renaissance man's revolt from traditional ideas of authority.

Ever since its publication, which was five years after Machiavelli's death, *The Prince* has been the subject of heated debate and analysis. To some, Machiavelli was a shrewd observer of his fellow man and a clever judge of human motives and actions; to others, he appeared as an evil influence, callous to the demands of morality and religion. Machiavelli believed that the state should be all-powerful and that every political action must be measured against one standard only: success. In *The Prince*, he frankly proposed the use of any available means to achieve and maintain power. Lying, cheating, and murder were of no consequence if these methods were necessary for the ruler's purposes. The rights of citizens included only those granted them by the ruler for the benefit of the state; in truth, the people were viewed as mere putty in the hands of their ruler. In his emphasis upon the stability of the state at all costs, Machiavelli offered a blueprint for the development of the strong and cohesive nation-state.

Section Review

1. Why was the geographic location of Italy important in making it the home of the Renaissance?

2. Why was it said of Renaissance Italy that "the oil of commerce lighted the lamp of culture"?

3. How did the quarrels between the popes and the Holy Roman emperors affect the Italian city-states? What factors encouraged individualism there?

4. Why did Machiavelli write *The Prince?* What were the basic ideas of this work?

2 The Renaissance was based on humanism and a revival of learning

A movement called *humanism* was one of the first products of the spirit that characterized 14th-century Italy. Humanism is a way of looking at life that is marked by an interest in man and in the beauties and opportunities of existence here on earth. Humanists taught that man should live a full life and welcome new experiences. They believed that he should try to better his life in this world, rather than to expect improvement only in the hereafter.

The new humanistic movement was closely related to a revived interest in classical learning, because humanists felt that the writings of Greece and Rome best embodied their attitudes toward the world.

It was to this rebirth of learning that the word Renaissance originally referred.

Petrarch and Boccaccio were pioneer humanists. Humanism owed much to the work of an Italian writer named Francesco Petrarca, better known as Petrarch. This writer, born in 1304, resented his father's desire to have him become a lawyer and, for consolation, turned to reading Cicero and Vergil. According to one story, Petrarch's father once hurled the boy's books of these two writers into the fire. The youth set up such a wail, however, that his father snatched them from the fire.

Petrarch dedicated his life to a study of classical writers, and from his study developed a new approach to life. He found that the Romans had believed in the importance of this world, as indicated in their

The Renaissance Spirit stressed individualism and worldliness. Men and women wished to become well versed in the social graces and able to enjoy life fully. Left, a public game in 16th-century Florence typifies the elaborate kind of festival that people of the Renaissance enjoyed. Two teams play a ball game while spectators surround the field and crowd the windows of a nearby palace. Above left, fashionably dressed ladies in a garden listen to the music of a lute. No longer confined to the home, women played an important part in civic and cultural affairs. The two gentlemen at right, each armed with a rapier and dagger, square off for a fencing match, an activity that replaced jousting as one of the favorite sports of the wealthy class.

writings about love, the beauties of nature, and the pleasures and problems of everyday existence.

Petrarch and the later humanists tried to recover both the spirit and the actual writings of the ancient authors. They studied Greek and Latin and spent much money and time trying to find old manuscripts. They ransacked ruins, sent agents to Constantinople to buy what they could, and searched monasteries for the precious pieces of parchment. Greek manuscripts became more plentiful after 1453, when the Turkish seizure of Constantinople forced many Greek scholars to flee from the Byzantine Empire and take refuge in Italy.

As a writer, Petrarch tried to imitate the Latin works of Cicero and Vergil. However, it was the group of sonnets written in Italian and inspired by his love for a woman named Laura that made him one of the greatest lyric poets of all time. This love poetry of Petrarch indicates the great interest which humanism had in human emotions.

Another noted humanist was Giovanni Boccaccio, famous for both his poetry and prose. In 1348 the horrible plague known as the Black Death struck Florence, where Boccaccio was living. Thousands died from the dreaded disease. Boccaccio made this event the background for his famous work, the *Decameron*. This is a series of diverting tales, in Italian, told by three young men and seven young women who have fled to an isolated country house to escape the plague. Many of the stories mirrored the spirit of the times by ridiculing feudal customs.

Education broadened in aim and content. In medieval times education had served chiefly to train the priest for preaching and the scholar for debating with other scholars. During the Renaissance men came to believe that education should not be so limited, but should aim toward developing the individual as "the complete man." The ideal Renaissance gentleman was courteous in manners, witty in speech, and educated broadly enough to appreciate good literature, painting, and music. He was athletic, well formed in body, and proficient in sports. In the arts of war the complete man was a brave and capable soldier. A famous book outlining this all-round individual was *The Courtier*, by Baldassare Castiglione, himself a scholar, poet, and courtier.

In order to achieve the goal of Renaissance education, Italian schools tended to concentrate less on theology and more on literature, especially Latin and Greek. The classical writings were known as *literae humaniores* ("humane letters," or literature dealing with humanity), and it is from this term that the word humanism is derived. The humanists, who taught Greek and Latin language and literature, gained great respect. People came long distances to attend their lectures. Rich men and rulers employed them in their own households to teach their daughters as well as their sons.

Although humanists stressed the importance of man and his earthly life, most of them remained religious. Those who criticized the Church believed in reform, not revolt. Humanistic scholars performed a service by carefully translating Greek and Hebrew sources of the Bible.

Versatile men typified the Renaissance. The Renaissance attitude toward the individual gave men faith in their own powers. They were eager to search for new continents, explore the secrets of nature, question the authority of the established Church, and express their love of life in works of literature and art.

Seldom has the world seen so many amazingly versatile men as during the Renaissance. Many were able not only to do many different things, but also to do them extremely well. Leonardo da Vinci, as one example of this many-sided ability, was one of the greatest painters of all time. As an engineer and architect, he designed buildings, canals, and military devices. In addition, he studied geology, chemistry, and human anatomy.

Leonardo da Vinci left over 5000 pages of notes and drawings. The notebooks contained sketches, not only of human figures, but also of cannons, engines, flying machines, and hundreds of other devices, some of which were not to be developed until centuries later. Leonardo left many projects unfinished, but people marveled at his many skills and admired him almost as if he were superhuman.

Some of the people of the Renaissance went to extremes in overstressing the importance of the individual. They scorned the group, had no concern for laws or morality, and openly admired the successful scoundrel. Anything a man could get away with seemed to be all right to them. Benvenuto Cellini was an example of this type of person. A great artist in metalwork and sculpture as well as a good writer, he was also an unscrupulous liar, braggart, and murderer. In his autobiography, he wrote honestly of his adventures, many of which reveal his cool ruthlessness.

Section Review

1. How did humanism offer a change in outlook? Why did humanists study Greek and Roman classics?
2. What aspects of the Renaissance spirit are seen in Petrarch's life and works?
3. How did education change during the Renaissance?

4. In what way does the life of Leonardo da Vinci provide an example of Renaissance versatility?

3 Italians created masterpieces of Renaissance art

During the Middle Ages, religion had inspired the building of beautiful churches, although painting and sculpture had been restricted because they were considered mere parts of church architecture. Artists worked anonymously to illustrate the teachings of the Church, and concentrated on depicting human suffering and the joys of the hereafter.

Artistic expression changed with the growth of humanism and the Renaissance emphasis on the importance of man and life on this earth. Painting and sculpture became independent art forms. Individual artists expressed their own observations of life by depicting the grace of the human body and the beauties of nature.

Florence led the way. Changes in the art of painting became evident early in the 14th century. The forerunner of the new style was a Florentine, Giotto di Bondone, born about 1266. He was the first European artist to give figures a sense of movement, of being alive. Giotto decorated the walls of churches in Florence, Padua, and Assisi with *frescoes,* or paintings on wet plaster. Most of these illustrated scenes in the life of Christ.

In the years following Giotto's achievements, Florence became the art center of Europe. Perhaps only in ancient Athens has such a brilliant group of artists ever been assembled in one place. The Florentines learned to draw human figures accurately, and attempted to portray ideas and emotions by means of human posture and facial expressions. They used shading to achieve special effects and developed new colors. Perhaps most important, they solved the problem of perspective so that their paintings achieved a lifelike three-dimensional quality. One Florentine artist noted for this technique was Paolo Uccello. Although his works are often crowded with figures, his careful placement of them and his use of perspective create a pleasing sense of order.

Three artists were outstanding. Within less than a century, from the late 1400's to the middle 1500's, three of the most important figures in the history of art—Leonardo da Vinci, Michelangelo, and Raphael—created masterpieces that are known throughout the world.

Leonardo da Vinci, born in 1452, left fewer than twenty paintings, but their influence on Renaissance art was great.

RENAISSANCE ITALY
About 1490

MONTFERRAT
SAVOY
MILAN
SALUZZO
GENOA
MODENA
LUCCA
Pisa
FLORENCE
Venice
Padua
MANTUA
FERRARA
Bologna
Urbino
PAPAL
Assisi
SIENA
STATES
CORSICA
(To Genoa)
Rome
KINGDOM
Naples
OF
NAPLES
SARDINIA
AND
Palermo
SICILY

⊙ Capital city having same name as state

Prepared by
Rand McNally & Co., Chicago

Painting of the Italian Renaissance was more realistic than that of the Middle Ages. In Giotto's "Lamentation over the Dead Christ," left, the figures have a solidity and roundness not found in medieval painting. Uccello concentrated on discovering scientific principles of perspective. In his painting "The Hunt," above, the geometric arrangement of trees and careful placement of men and animals create a three-dimensional quality. Raphael was a master of realistic portrait painting. He captured a mood of deep contemplation in the portrait of his friend Count Tommaso Inghirami, an Italian poet, above right. In Tintoretto's "Jacob Wrestling with the Angel," below right, the subtle contrast of light and shadow heightens the vitality and dramatic interest of a popular Bible story.

Two of Leonardo's paintings, "Mona Lisa" and "Virgin of the Rocks," are noteworthy for the formal dignity of their composition and also for their detailed backgrounds. Leonardo's interest in experimentation led him to try new techniques of fresco painting on the "Last Supper"; they did not work well, and little of the original painting remains.

Michelangelo, like Leonardo a man with many talents, was a skilled sculptor, painter, and architect, and even a fair poet. He was born Michelangelo Buonarroti, near Florence in 1475. At thirteen he became an assistant to a painter and learned to make frescoes. For a number of years, Lorenzo de' Medici, ruler of Florence, helped him carry on his studies.

Michelangelo liked sculpture better than painting, and many of his painted figures have the massive solidity of statues. He was fond of saying, "It is only well with me when I have a chisel in my hand"; but people always wanted him to paint. Against his wishes, Pope Julius II persuaded Michelangelo to paint frescoes on the walls and ceiling of the Sistine Chapel in the Vatican. Lying on his back on a scaffold most of the time, Michelangelo painted the Bible story of Genesis from the Creation to the Flood, a gigantic task that took him four years. The design covers nearly 10 thousand square feet and includes over 300 figures, some of which are 10 feet high. These frescoes have been called "the greatest single masterpiece in the history of painting."

Michelangelo lived only for his art and had little interest in money or comfort. According to men who knew him, he took no pleasure in eating or drinking, and was satisfied with a little bread, a bit of cheese, a bed, and a workshop. He slept in his clothes to save time, and worked so hard that his sides became swollen, his face grew seamed with wrinkles, and his back became misshapen.

Raphael, whose full name was Raffaello Santi, was born in Urbino in 1483. He began to paint at an early age. Most of his paintings were of religious subjects, and he became especially noted for his tranquil, sweet-faced Madonnas. Critics consider him a master of space composition. Raphael was a great favorite of two popes. For Julius II he painted several frescoes in the Vatican, and Leo X appointed him chief architect of St. Peter's Church.

Venice rivaled Florence as an art center. By the 16th century, Venetian painters had created their own traditions. They became particularly known for their use of rich, glowing colors. Giovanni Bellini, born about 1430, came from a family of famous painters. He created a gentle, soft style, which influenced two famous pupils, Giorgione and Titian. The former painted many scenes from Greek and Roman mythology. Titian, born Tiziano Vecellio in 1477, was the greatest master of the Venetian school. Like many other Venetian painters, he was skilled in the use of color and gave his name to a particular shade of red-brown.

Titian's work typifies a change that occurred in art in the middle of the 16th century when painting became more worldly. Artists still painted scenes from the Bible, but they also began to depict scenes and people from the world around them. They did fewer frescoes and more easel paintings on canvas, especially portraits of rich and powerful patrons.

Another great Venetian artist, born in 1518, was Jacopo Robusti, known as Tintoretto. His bold use of light and space make his paintings of religious and mythological subjects extremely dramatic.

Sculpture and architecture flourished. An outstanding sculptor of the early 15th century was a Florentine, Donatello. He was the first sculptor of this period to show a knowledge of human anatomy. Perhaps his greatest claim to fame is his magnificent statue of a Venetian *condottiere*, Gattemelata. This statue was the first monumental figure on horseback since Roman times. In the face of the general, Donatello caught the spirit of the Italian despot—proud, powerful, and cruel. Another soldier on a horse, Colleoni, was the subject of a great bronze statue by a pupil of Donatello, Andrea del Verrocchio, who became the teacher of Leonardo.

In a class by himself was Michelangelo. Great as he was with brush and paint, he was even greater with chisel and stone. In his statue of the Biblical character David, the sculptor presented his idea of the ideal young hero, with a fine head, classic features, and supple body. Michelangelo also carved sculptures for the Medici chapel in Florence and for the tomb of Pope Julius.

Italian Renaissance architects based their work on Greek and Roman models, but adapted them to their own times to produce original work of great beauty. Types of buildings unknown to classical architects—churches and palaces—called for different treatments of the pillars and domes of Greek and Roman architecture. New combinations of classical elements included barrel-vaulted naves and domes crowned with cupolas. Several buildings were the work of more than one architect. One of the greatest Renaissance structures, the church of St. Peter in Rome, represented the efforts of ten different architects. It is the largest Christian church in the world and is especially noted for its huge dome, designed by Michelangelo.

Section Review

1. How did artistic expression change with the coming of the Renaissance?
2. What developments characterized Florentine painting after the time of Giotto?

3. For what artistic qualities were the following Italian Renaissance artists known: Giotto? Leonardo? Raphael? Titian? Uccello? Tintoretto?
4. What changes occurred in painting in the mid-16th century?
5. On what earlier styles was Renaissance architecture based? Why and how did it differ from them?

4 **The Renaissance spread to other countries**

From its home in Italy, the Renaissance spread to many parts of Europe. Scholars and artists from the north traveled southward to study with Italian masters and returned home with new attitudes and knowledge. The Renaissance also spread through books printed by means of a new invention—movable type.

Printing helped spread the Renaissance. During the Middle Ages, writing had been done on *parchment,* made from sheepskin or goatskin, and on *vellum,* made from calfskin. Parchment was expensive; one book might require the skins of twenty-five sheep. Vellum cost even more. Early in the 12th century, Europeans learned about paper from the Moors in Spain. The Moors knew about it through the Arabs, who in turn had learned its use from the Chinese. Even though paper was less expensive than parchment or vellum, books were still expensive because they were written by hand. When the Medici family in Florence wanted 200 books for their library, forty-five skilled copyists worked two years to make them. Under such conditions, it was not surprising that even large libraries had only a few hundred volumes. The average man never saw a book, much less owned one.

The technique of imprinting, or marking by pressure, is as old as man himself.

Italian Architecture and Sculpture

A renewed interest in classical traditions influenced Renaissance architecture. In the palace under construction above, Roman features include the columns, an extravagant use of statues, and a symmetrical design. The dome of Florence Cathedral, above right, was conceived by the Renaissance architect Filippo Brunelleschi after he had observed ancient Roman ruins. Next to it is Michelangelo's sketch for the dome of St. Peter's in Rome. He did not live to see his plan realized, but his successor carried it out. Both of these churches are the products of many architects.

An expressive work of sculpture located in Florence Cathedral is Michelangelo's "Pieta," left. The body of Christ sinks heavily into the arms of sorrowful mourners. Another famous sculptor, Verrocchio, depicted the forceful character of his patron, Lorenzo de' Medici, in the terra cotta bust at right.

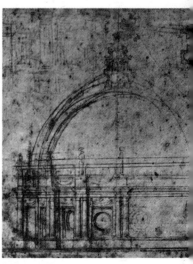

However, the application of printing to making copies of books or pictures was delayed in Europe until the late Middle Ages. The first printing in Europe, like that in China, was block printing. Europeans may have learned the art from the Far East; Marco Polo described the printed paper money he had seen in the court of Kublai Khan. In late medieval Europe, wooden blocks became quite common for printing playing cards and pictures of saints.

The Chinese invention of movable type may have affected the development of printing in Europe, though it is not known whether the influence was direct or indirect. Credit for the first use of movable type in Europe is usually given to a German, Johann Gutenberg. Probably the first European book printed with movable type was the famous Gutenberg Bible, completed about 1456. The process was introduced into Italy in 1464 and into France about four years later. The oldest example from England dates back to 1476. By the end of the 15th century, printing presses using movable type had been established in eighteen countries. European presses had printed 8 million books by the early 1500's.

The invention of movable type had important results. Books could be produced rapidly, in great quantities, and for a fraction of the cost required by the old system of hand copying. The new books were far more accurate, too. Formerly, producing two exact copies of the same book had been almost impossible, because copyists always made mistakes. More important, typographical printing made books available to a large number of persons.

Printing helped the spread of the Renaissance spirit. Italian books were sent all over Europe. The new movement in the rest of Europe, called the *Northern Renaissance,* took on a distinctive character as each country added some of its own native genius.

Northern humanists emphasized social and religious problems. In general, the humanists of northern Europe were more serious and scholarly than those of Italy. Italian humanists were interested in their personal fortunes and in expressing themselves. Northern humanists were concerned with social problems, particularly those involving religion and ethics.

Erasmus, a Dutch scholar born about 1466, is often considered the greatest of the humanists. Although he was born in the Netherlands, his interests were cosmopolitan, and he knew many languages and many countries.

Erasmus was a priest who spent much of his time studying Greek and Latin writings. He wrote many books, all in Latin. In 1511, he published his famous satire, *The Praise of Folly*, which lashed out at the vices and evils of the time. Erasmus attacked superstition, warlike princes, insincere priests, and scholars who wasted time with silly problems. Erasmus also produced a Latin translation of the New Testament from Greek sources, showing that there were many errors in the Bible used at the time.

All his life, Erasmus carried on a struggle against ignorance, stupidity, and vice. He kept up a vast correspondence with scholars throughout Europe, and so helped spread humanistic ideals. When he died in 1536, he left behind a foundation on which later thinkers could build.

In England, humanism was introduced by a group of English scholars who had gone to Italy to study medicine and Greek. On their return, these English humanists gathered at Oxford University and became known as the *Oxford Reformers*. As teachers, preachers, and authors, they sought to bring the new learning to England.

The Oxford Reformers had a great influence on a young Oxford student named Thomas More. So did Erasmus, whom he met at an early age and corresponded with for the rest of his life. Thomas More became a lawyer and served in many governmental posts under King Henry VIII. His most famous book, *Utopia*, indirectly criticized many contemporary evils by describing an ideal, imaginary community. His criticism was effective later on in bringing about legislation to help the poor.

Northern artists created distinctive styles. Even before the innovations of Italian Renaissance art reached northern Europe, painters in the Low Countries had begun to break away from medieval traditions. Among the first to do so was Jan van Eyck, born about 1370. He painted realistic landscapes and portraits, taking infinite pains to show trees, grass, and flowers as they appeared in nature. It is to Van Eyck that credit is due for the invention of oil paints.

The skill of Italian painters, particularly their use of perspective and mastery of anatomy, impressed the artists of northern Europe. One of the earliest to be influenced directly was a German, Albrecht Dürer, who first visited Italy about 1494. He was struck by the high social position of artists there, commenting "Here I am a lord, at home a parasite." Dürer's work blended medieval and Renaissance styles. He realized the possibilities for illustrating the new printed books, and he produced a great number of woodcuts and engravings for this purpose.

Another German artist was Hans Holbein the Younger, who excelled in portraiture. He was appointed court painter to King Henry VIII of England, where he became famous for his lifelike portraits of the royal family. He also painted excellent portraits of the great humanists Erasmus and Sir Thomas More.

The Flemish artist Pieter Brueghel the Elder devoted his life to painting country landscapes and robust scenes of peasant life. This type of art, concerned with everyday life, is called *genre* painting. It reached its height in the Netherlands in the 17th century with the work of Frans Hals and Jan Vermeer. Two of the greatest 17th-century painters were Peter Paul Rubens, a Flemish artist known for his large, dramatic canvases, and Rembrandt van Rijn, a Dutch painter whose sensitive portrayal of character has made his works acclaimed among the most outstanding of all time.

Renaissance literature culminated in Shakespeare and Cervantes. The English poet Chaucer, discussed in Chapter 7, is often considered a forerunner of English Renaissance literature. It was on the foundations laid by Chaucer and the Oxford Reformers that English writers of the late 16th and early 17th centuries created a literature unsurpassed in any nation. Queen Elizabeth I, like many rulers of the period, supported and inspired the work of writers. The *Elizabethan Age* boasted the poets Edmund Spenser and Sir Philip Sidney and such dramatists as Christopher Marlowe and Ben Jonson. But the greatest name in Elizabethan literature—and one of the greatest the world has ever known—was that of William Shakespeare.

The plays of Shakespeare, like the King James Bible, are part of the priceless literary heritage of the English-speaking people. The Renaissance spirit was reflected in the breadth of his interests and in his deep understanding of human personality, manifested in such different characters as Hamlet, Macbeth, Julius Caesar, Othello, and Falstaff. Out of the richness of his writing came not only the poetic imagery of *Romeo and Juliet* and *The Tempest,* but also hundreds of sayings that have become part of the English language.

In France and Spain there were outstanding humanists who criticized the evils of their day. One of the most important of these was a Spaniard, Miguel de Cervantes.

Northern Renaissance art was noted for vivid scenes of everyday life and penetrating character analysis. In the painting of John Arnolfini and his wife, above, Jan van Eyck rendered with loving detail the clothing and room of a wealthy Flemish couple. A rowdy country marriage feast is the subject of "Peasant Wedding" by Pieter Brueghel the Elder, left above. Below, left, is a sensitive portrait of his mother by Rembrandt. Next to it, glowing with rich color, is Rubens' painting of himself and his wife.

Cervantes, who lived from 1547 to 1616, was the author of *Don Quixote,* one of the world's greatest novels. By the latter part of the 16th century, when Cervantes wrote his novel, feudalism and knighthood were outmoded although the codes of chivalry still appealed to many persons. The hero of Cervantes' book, Don Quixote, was a poor but proud Spanish gentleman who loved to read knightly romances. At the age of fifty, he made himself a suit of armor and, taking his old horse for a charger, went to seek adventure. He was accompanied by his servant, Sancho Panza, as his squire.

Cervantes showed himself to be a Renaissance figure both by vividly portraying contemporary Spanish life and by ridiculing the ideals of knighthood and chivalry through the amusing adventures of Don Quixote. In spite of his absurd actions, the hero's bravery and goodness represented ideals which Cervantes respected, although he seems to have felt that they were impractical in the world as he knew it.

Section Review

1. What were some results of the invention of movable type?
2. How did northern European humanists differ from those of Italy? In what ways did Erasmus and More typify northern humanism?
3. For what were the following northern Renaissance artists known: Jan van Eyck? Albrecht Dürer? Pieter Brueghel the Elder? Rembrandt van Rijn?
4. How do Shakespeare and Cervantes reflect the Renaissance spirit?

Chapter 13 ▮▮▮▮▮▮▮▮▮▮ A Review

The Renaissance, a movement characterized by a revival of learning and a great outburst of artistic creativity, first began in Italy. The key location of the Italian city-states on the trade routes between East and West brought new wealth to Europe, which enabled merchants and rulers to help support artists and writers. Rivalries among and within the city-states stimulated a new spirit of individualism and free inquiry.

One of the most important elements of the Renaissance was humanism, closely linked to a rebirth of interest in the classic writings of Greece and Rome. Italian humanists such as Petrarch and Boccaccio inspired much of this interest, which was transmitted through a broadened and more varied education. Renaissance humanism rediscovered man as an individual. People admired not only the versatility of a man like Leonardo da Vinci but also the successful intrigue of a scoundrel like Benvenuto Cellini.

The greatest manifestation of the Renaissance spirit occurred in the field of art, especially painting. Famous Italian artists of the period include Giotto, Leonardo, Michelangelo, Raphael, and Titian.

The Renaissance spread from Italy to the rest of Europe through personal contact and, more importantly through books printed from movable type. The writings of Italian humanists influenced two of the greatest European scholars, Erasmus and Sir Thomas More, although these and other northern writers concentrated more on social problems than had their Italian predecessors. Northern painting also profited from the Italian example, and boasted such names as Dürer, Holbein, Brueghel, Rubens, and Rembrandt.

In England, the Renaissance blossomed in the Elizabethan Age with an amazing number of fine writers, the greatest of whom was Shakespeare. Cervantes of Spain created in Don Quixote one of the most memorable figures in fiction, and a symbol of the end of the medieval era.

The Time

Some of the events named below occurred during the time of the Renaissance in western

Europe (1300 to about 1650). Others did not. Rearrange the items on the list so that all events appear in their proper chronological order, and name those events that occurred during the Renaissance.

Capture of Constantinople by the
  Ottoman Turks
Norman conquest of England
Establishment of the Mogul dynasty in India
Hundred Years' War
Spanish conquest of the Aztecs and Incas
Establishment of the University of Bologna
Beginning of Tudor rule in England
Golden age of the Tangs
Reign of Yaroslav the Wise in Russia
Completion of the *Reconquista* by Ferdinand
  and Isabella

The People

1. What contributions did each of these men make to the Renaissance?

Petrarch	Cervantes
Shakespeare	Erasmus
Castiglione	Gutenberg
Lorenzo de' Medici	More
Boccaccio	Machiavelli

2. Arrange the following names of artists under the headings "Italian Renaissance" or "Northern Renaissance."

Leonardo da Vinci	Holbein
Dürer	Donatello
Jan van Eyck	Brueghel
Rubens	Rembrandt
Raphael	Giorgione
Giotto	Michelangelo
Titian	Bellini
Uccello	Tintoretto

From the preceding list pick two men and tell how the paintings of each are typical of the Renaissance style.

3. With what cities are the following families identified: (a) Sforzas; (b) Medicis; (c) Estes? Name two artists supported by the (1) Medici family and (2) Este family.

4. Who were the Oxford Reformers?

Historical Terms

1. Define the following terms as they applied to 14th-century Italian politics: despot; condottieri.

2. Why was Greek and Latin literature called *literae humaniores*? Explain how humanism was related to the revival of interest in classical writings.

3. What are frescoes? In what way did genre painting reflect the spirit of Renaissance times?

Questions for Critical Thinking

1. Why did the Renaissance begin in Italy almost two centuries before it spread to northern Europe?

2. In what ways would humanistic ideals conflict with traditional medieval religious beliefs and practices?

3. How did Renaissance art reflect the spirit of humanism? Cite two or more specific examples.

4. Some historians date the modern period of history from Renaissance times. In what ways did developments in the Renaissance represent a break with medieval times?

5. Why would Machiavelli's ideas about government appeal to despots of his time?

The Reformation

CHAPTER 14   1309–1648

Reforming the Church had become a burning issue as early as the 13th century, when the Dominican and Franciscan orders sought to revive the spirit of early Christianity. At right, the Franciscan friar St. Bernardino preaches to a group of townspeople. Criticism continued, however, culminating in the Reformation of the 16th century. The force and eloquence of Martin Luther, left, were vital factors in the break with Rome and the birth of Protestantism.

Out of love for the faith and the desire to bring it to light, the following propositions will be discussed at Wittenberg under the chairmanship of the Reverend Father Martin Luther, Master of Arts and Sacred Theology . . . those who are unable to be present and debate orally . . . may do so by letter.

With these words, an earnest, rough-hewn German priest, Martin Luther, prefaced a document which he posted on the main door of the Castle Church of Wittenberg at noon on October 31, 1517. It was a custom of the time for scholarly debates to be announced in this way, and Luther knew that a large crowd was expected in Wittenberg on the day following—November 1, All Saints' Day. His document, written in Latin and composed of ninety-five theses, or statements, was an attack on a practice of the Church which many people felt was being abused by unworthy churchmen—the sale of papal indulgences. Luther had the theses printed and sent to friends in other cities, who translated the document into German. His strong voice of protest against the "holy trade" was the opening salvo in a great movement which came to be known as the Reformation.

The Reformation of the 16th and 17th centuries included two basic phases: the Protestant Reformation and the Catholic Reformation, sometimes called the Counter Reformation. In both phases, strong leaders sought to bring Christian practices closer to the ideals of Christianity. Roman Catholics believed that reforms had to take place within the existing Church structure and that no changes in doctrine were permissible. Protestants believed that reforms could not be achieved without drastic changes. They withdrew their allegiance from the Church of Rome and set up their own churches. They rejected the authority of the pope and his right to interpret the Scriptures for all men of the Christian faith.

The events of the Reformation were closely linked with the political fortunes of aggressive and expanding nations. Religious quarrels often led to political and social strife. Unscrupulous kings and princes used religious differences to gain political ends.

This chapter tells how:

1. **The power of the medieval Church declined.**

2. **The Reformation divided Europe.**

3. **Religious differences aggravated political conflicts.**

1 **The power of the medieval Church declined**

The medieval period had been truly an Age of Faith, with the Church acting as a great unifying and civilizing influence. The Church reached the summit of its political power in the 12th and 13th centuries, and especially during the reign of Innocent III, from 1198 to 1216. As told in Chapter 6, this strong pope, who gave orders to kings and whom no one dared disobey, was considered the universal ruler of the Western world. After his time, however, the Church began to lose some of its power.

Abuses aroused opposition. In the later Middle Ages, weaknesses gradually arose within the Church. Some of the clergy led immoral lives, disregarding their religious vows and duties. Many had grown worldly; some popes, for example, became involved in Italian politics and in humanistic scholarship and art patronage. Furthermore, the increasing wealth of the Church encouraged corruption. Men bought positions in the Church—a practice known as simony—so they could enjoy ease and luxury.

Reformers attempted to return the Church to its ancient ideals of poverty and service. As early as the 13th century, two new orders of friars were established to help purify the Church. Both the Franciscans, founded by St. Francis of Assisi, and the Dominicans, founded by St. Dominic of Spain, became known as preachers and teachers among the people.

Nevertheless, abuses continued, and critics attacked the Church openly. In the 14th century, John Wycliffe, an Englishman, denounced Church rituals as formal and empty, and taught that salvation was an individual matter between man and God; he also translated the Bible from Latin into English so that common people could read it. Wycliffe's views influenced John Huss, a Bohemian, who criticized the wealth and worldliness of the Church. He was condemned as a heretic and burned at the stake in 1415. Huss became a martyr in the eyes of his countrymen, and his ideas did not die out.

The Renaissance spirit of free inquiry encouraged men to question established religion. Humanists particularly in northern Europe criticized Church teachings and practices. They claimed the Church had too much authority at the top and laid too much stress on ceremony. Erasmus lashed out at what he labeled religious hypocrisy and the worship of images. Like most humanist critics, he felt that the Church could reform itself from within.

New forces challenged Church supremacy. Movements outside the Church also tended to decrease its authority. One of these trends was nationalism. Kings extending their power in rising young nations did not want popes dictating to them. Nor did the people welcome the rules and commands of foreign churchmen. They also resented the fact that most of the money they gave the Church went to Rome. Some people began to think it

might be better to have a national church, controlled in their own country.

Several rulers, including Henry VI of the Holy Roman Empire and Edward I of England, defied the authority of the pope. Philip IV of France went further. In 1309 he forced the pope to leave Rome and live at Avignon in southern France. This Babylonian Captivity, named for the time when the ancient Hebrews were prisoners of the Babylonians, lasted for sixty-five years. Then in 1378 a controversy known as the Great Schism split the papacy. Italian cardinals elected an Italian pope, who ruled at Rome. French cardinals chose a Frenchman, who maintained a papal court at Avignon. Each pope claimed to be the only true head of the Church, and each enjoyed the support of several European rulers. Finally, a majority of cardinals met in 1409, deposed both popes, and elected a third. Because neither of the deposed popes would resign the office, the three became rivals. The controversy ended with the election of a new pope in 1417. By that time, however, the long conflict had greatly lowered the prestige of the papacy.

Another development that tended to challenge Church authority was the growth of business and commerce. The rising merchant class did not like the Church laws forbidding the lending of money at interest. In addition, many of them looked with envy upon the broad lands and rich treasure owned by the Church; they were ready to welcome any movement that could help them obtain this wealth.

Section Review
1. What were some weaknesses within the Church in the late Middle Ages?
2. On what grounds did the following men criticize the Church: John Wycliffe? John Huss? humanist thinkers?
3. How did the rise of nationalism threaten the Church?

4. Why did some businessmen resent and envy the Church?

2 The Reformation divided Europe

Conditions in Germany especially favored opposition to papal authority. Living far away from the headquarters of the papacy, many Germans were bitter about the large sums of money collected by the Church within their country and sent to Rome. The Church had difficulty imposing its authority over the hundreds of independent German states. As opposition grew, all that was needed to bring about a revolution against the Church was a leader.

Luther led the Protestant Reformation.
Martin Luther was born of German peasant parents in 1483. His father sent him to the University of Erfurt, hoping that he would be a lawyer. The young man became so absorbed in the question of gaining salvation, however, that he gave up his law studies and became a monk. In 1512 Luther took a position as professor of religion at the University of Wittenberg, where he soon made a name for himself as a brilliant lecturer. As he probed the problem of eternal salvation, Luther came to the conclusion that salvation was a matter between man and God, and did not necessarily require the sacraments and ceremonies of the Church, nor, for that matter, the intervention of priests. Later, he recognized only two sacraments, baptism and the Holy Eucharist, which he called the Lord's Supper. The Church taught that man gained salvation through faith and good works—the manifestation of faith by performing virtuous acts and participating in Church ritual. It was Luther's belief that man gained salvation through faith alone, a doctrine called justi-

fication by faith. Luther's views were to bring him into direct conflict with the Church authorities.

This conflict came to a head over the practice of granting indulgences. An indulgence was a kind of pardon, a remission of punishment due to sin. The Church granted indulgences on condition that the recipient confess his sins and truly repent. As a penance, the sinner usually said special prayers and gave a donation to some cause favored by the Church. Gradually the Church came to rely on the sale of indulgences when it was in need of money.

Pope Leo X announced a sale of indulgences during the years 1515-1517 in order to raise money for the completion of St. Peter's Church in Rome. In 1517 an agent for the Church named Johann Tetzel began to sell indulgences near Wittenberg. Tetzel was a vigorous salesman and did not always explain that an indulgence was of no value to the sinner if he did not really repent.

Luther objected to the sale of indulgences, maintaining that they were valueless to the sinner, whose sins could be forgiven only by faith in Christ's sacrifice. In October of 1517 Luther nailed to the door of the Wittenberg church a list of statements about the sale of indulgences. These Ninety-five Theses, as they were called, caused a great stir. Two years later in a public debate with a churchman named Johann Eck, Luther went further and questioned fundamental Church beliefs relating to the rights of the papacy.

Luther continued to attack the Church in sermons and writings, and in 1521 the pope excommunicated him. When he refused to change his views, Luther was branded a heretic and his life was endangered. The elector of Saxony and other German princes rallied to his protection, however, whereupon Luther plunged into a campaign to organize a new church.

Religious Leaders in the 16th century wielded great influence. Martin Luther's revolt from Church authority encouraged German serfs to rebel against feudal lords in the Peasants' War of 1524-1525. Luther, however, took the side of the nobles, who repressed the revolt with great severity. Defeated serfs, below right, swear allegiance to their victorious lords. John Calvin, below left, imposed strict rules in his Protestant theocracy at Geneva and employed spies to make sure they were obeyed. Yet this city became a haven for Protestants from other nations. St. Ignatius Loyola, left, founded the Society of Jesus as a "spiritual militia" to strengthen the Church. The Jesuits gained influence in royal courts and helped win many people back to Catholicism. Devoted to the cause of education, they established a number of fine schools and colleges.

IOHANNES · CALVINVS ·
ANNO · ÆTATIS ·53·
·B·

Luther's writings were reproduced on the new printing presses, and they received wide circulation. He translated the Bible from Latin into German, so that the people could read the Scriptures in their own language.

Luther's views on religion reflected the emphasis placed on the importance of the individual during the Renaissance. He taught that every person had a direct relationship with God, and was able to interpret the Bible for himself. In some ways, however, Luther disappointed the humanists. He lacked flexibility and tolerance and, once he had completely broken away from the pope and organized his own church, he felt that everyone else who broke with the Roman Catholic Church should accept his beliefs.

Luther's doctrines came to be called *Lutheranism,* and won many followers in Germany. The Holy Roman Emperor, Charles V, and some principalities remained Catholic, however, and disagreements between the two religious groups led to oppression of the Lutherans and to civil war. When Catholic leaders took action against the reformers, several Lutheran princes issued a protest; it was this incident that gave rise to the word Protestant. Finally, delegates met in 1555 to draw up the Peace of Augsburg, which decreed that each prince could decide for himself between Catholicism and Lutheranism, and that his subjects would be bound by his choice. The settlement also provided that Protestants could keep all Church property confiscated before 1552 but that bishops who had adopted Lutheranism after that date had to give up their church lands.

Luther's ideas spread to many parts of Europe. In particular, they affected Scandinavia, where Protestantism gained the support of the governments of Denmark (which included Norway at that time) and Sweden.

Calvinism became a driving force. Meanwhile another reformer, Huldreich Zwingli, had won a following in Switzerland. Many cantons, or districts, adopted his form of Protestantism. After a brief Catholic-Protestant war in which Zwingli lost his life, a truce allowed each canton to keep its own religion.

Geneva, an independent republic, had adopted Protestantism. When a French Protestant scholar, John Calvin, visited the city in 1536, the people asked him to stay and organize a church. He accepted the invitation.

Calvin, born in 1509, had had to flee from France because of his Protestant views. Although he had been inspired by Luther, he disagreed with him on various matters of doctrine. One of Calvin's important theories was that of predestination, which held that God predetermined human salvation or damnation, and that a man could do nothing to alter his fate. Man's purpose in life, according to Calvin, was not to work out his salvation but to honor God. Calvin outlined his ideas in a famous book, *The Institutes of the Christian Religion.*

Calvin set up a theocracy in Geneva, which controlled not only church affairs, but also politics, education, amusements, and family life. Taking the Bible as his supreme authority, this stern reformer established a rule in Geneva based upon the belief that man should live a serious, dignified, and moral life. He held that wearing jewelry and gaudy clothes, singing frivolous songs, dancing, and playing cards were sinful in the eyes of God.

The Calvinists at Geneva organized their church so that the members could take part in its management, a practice which helped unify the movement. They placed much emphasis on the education of their ministers and invited Protestant scholars to Geneva, where they set up a school to train preachers. Calvinism had a

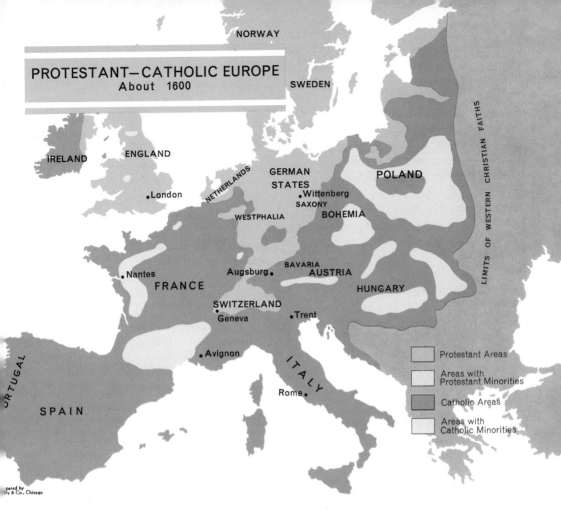

PROTESTANT–CATHOLIC EUROPE
About 1600

NORWAY

SWEDEN

IRELAND

ENGLAND

NETHERLANDS

•London

GERMAN
STATES

•Wittenberg

SAXONY

WESTPHALIA

BOHEMIA

POLAND

•Nantes

FRANCE

Augsburg•

BAVARIA

AUSTRIA

HUNGARY

SWITZERLAND

•Geneva

•Trent

•Avignon

ITALY

Rome•

PORTUGAL

SPAIN

LIMITS OF WESTERN CHRISTIAN FAITHS

Protestant Areas

Areas with
Protestant Minorities

Catholic Areas

Areas with
Catholic Minorities

prepared by
ly & Co., Chicago

special appeal for businessmen because it taught that a man's work was actually part of his religious life. Hard work, ambition, and thrift were considered Christian virtues, and prosperity was regarded as a sign of the elect, those people who were predestined to salvation.

People from other countries came to Geneva to listen to Calvin's sermons and returned home to set up new churches based on the Calvinist model. Calvinism became the heart of the Swiss Reformed Church. It was established in the Netherlands as the Dutch Reformed Church and by John Knox in Scotland as the Presbyterian Church. In France, Calvinists were known as *Huguenots.*

England broke with Rome. The influence of Protestantism was also felt in England, but most Englishmen remained loyal to the Church. King Henry VIII even wrote a pamphlet in 1521 attacking Luther, for which the pope rewarded him with the title "Defender of the Faith." Soon afterward, however, the king quarreled with the pope.

Henry VIII had married his brother's widow, the Spanish princess Catherine of Aragon. The royal couple had six children, but only one, Mary Tudor, survived. Henry was dissatisfied. He wanted a son to succeed him because he felt that the newly established Tudor dynasty needed a strong ruler. Besides, he had fallen in love with a court beauty named Anne Boleyn.

Henry asked the pope to dissolve his marriage to Catherine on the grounds that it had been contrary to Church law for him to marry his brother's widow, and that papal permission obtained at the time of the marriage was in error. The pope refused, in part because of threats from Catherine's nephew, the powerful Emperor Charles V of Spain. His action enraged the stubborn king, who was not accustomed to having his wishes denied. He appointed a new archbishop of Canterbury, who declared in 1533 that Catherine was not the king's lawful wife, leaving Henry free to marry Anne Boleyn. In 1534, through a law called the Act of Supremacy, the king had Parliament make him head of the Church in England. Henry VIII also abolished monasteries and seized a large amount of Church property.

As head of the Church, Henry made few changes in the Catholic religion. However, the Protestant ideas of Luther and Calvin gained ground among the people. During the six-year reign of Henry's son Edward VI, the Church in England adopted several Protestant reforms.

Henry's daughter Mary came to the throne in 1553. As a stanch Roman Catholic, she was determined to reverse the trend toward Protestantism. Her severe persecution of English Protestants discredited Roman Catholicism and led to the epithet by which she is commonly known, "Bloody Mary." Elizabeth I, who succeeded Mary in 1558, reinstated a moderate Protestantism. Parliament confirmed it in a series of documents establishing the *Anglican* Church. The more extreme forms of Protestantism did not die out in England, however, but remained strong in the Puritans and other Nonconformist sects, as dissenters from the Anglican Church were called.

Roman Catholics organized the Counter Reformation. Within a few years after Luther's revolt, Protestantism became firmly established throughout Scandinavia, England, and Scotland, and in most of Switzerland and Germany. There were also many Protestants in France, Poland, Hungary, and the Netherlands. The Roman Catholic Church undertook a program, known as the Catholic Reformation or the Counter Reformation, to institute reforms and win people back to the Church.

The establishment of several new religious orders helped strengthen the Church. The Capuchins, an offshoot of the Franciscans, preached and cared for the poor and sick. The Ursulines, an order of nuns, undertook the education of girls. The most famous was the Jesuit order, founded by a Spaniard, St. Ignatius Loyola, in 1534. Jesuits became known for their excellent schools, their influence in European royal courts, and their missionary work in Africa, America, and the Far East.

The Church had for centuries held councils to consider problems and to make reforms, and many persons had been urging such a meeting since Luther's revolt. In 1542 Pope Paul III called the Council of Trent (in Austria). Delegates, meeting from 1545 to 1563, reaffirmed without compromise all existing Roman Catholic doctrine. However, they did make several changes in Church discipline and administration. The Council ordered a reform of monastic life, made plans to establish seminaries for the education of priests, and denounced the appointment of immoral men to Church office.

Another aspect of the Counter Reformation involved strengthening and expanding the Inquisition. The papacy also began issuing the *Index*, a list of books which Church members were forbidden to read. The Church had formerly controlled the spread of what it considered heretical ideas by confiscating and burning unacceptable books, but this system became too difficult after the advent of printed books.

The Counter Reformation, especially the work of the Jesuits, was extremely successful. By the 17th century, the Roman Catholic Church had stopped the spread of Protestantism in France, won back Hungary and Poland, and maintained Catholicism in Bavaria, Austria, Ireland, and the southern Netherlands (now Belgium).

The effects of the Reformation were widespread. The Reformation affected Europe in many ways. It weakened the political power of the Roman Catholic Church and helped new nations become more independent. In some respects, the Reformation increased the power of kings; they profited from the limitation of papal authority and from the wealth they seized from the Church. But the Reformation also helped democracy and representative government. Protestantism, by limiting the authority of the clergy, increased the role of the people in church government, particularly among the followers of Calvin. This idea of self-government was carried over into political affairs.

Protestantism also strengthened the middle classes. Calvinism especially glorified the work of the businessman, dignified thrift, and justified profits. Many members of the middle class also benefited from the seizure of Church land and property.

The Reformation also served to encourage education. Since most Protestants believed that everyone should read the Bible, schools became necessary. At the same time, Roman Catholics also improved the education of their children. The Jesuit order in particular developed an excellent school system that attracted many Protestant youths.

The Reformation helped strengthen and improve religious practices throughout Europe. It reawakened an interest in religion, which had begun to decline in the late Middle Ages. Both Roman Catholics and Protestants were quick to point out each other's errors, and accordingly both groups worked to prevent abuses. More important, in the long run, the Reformation encouraged religious toleration and freedom. At first, Catholics and Protestants tried to convert each other forcibly, but by the end of the 17th century, many men began to realize that they could not compel others to accept religious ideas that were inconsistent with the individual's faith and belief.

Section Review

1. Why did conditions in Germany favor a revolt against the Church?
2. What views brought Luther into conflict with the Church? How did he reflect Renaissance ideas? In what way did he disappoint the humanists?
3. What were the chief characteristics of Calvinism? Where did it spread?
4. How did Protestantism become established in England?
5. What were the most important features of the Counter Reformation? How successful was this movement?
6. What were the chief effects of the Reformation?

3 **Religious differences aggravated political conflicts**

As the religious differences among European peoples became established along national lines, political conflicts among nations were intensified. As a result, from the middle of the 16th to the middle of the 17th centuries, Europe underwent a series of wars involving religion. In many cases, questions of faith served only as an excuse to wage war for political reasons.

Spanish power threatened Europe. The next chapter discusses how Spain gained a vast colonial empire in America and became the richest nation in Europe in the

Spanish Hapsburgs

Austrian Hapsburgs

Boundary of
Holy Roman Empire

SWEDEN

NORWAY

AND

DENMARK

RUSSI

IRELAND

ENGLAND

LITHUANIA

NETHERLANDS

HOLY
ROMAN
EMPIRE

LUXEMBURG

POLAND

BOHEMIA

BURGUNDY

FRANCE

AUSTRIA

HUNGARY

MILAN

VENICE

GENOA

FLORENCE

PAPAL
STATES

CORSICA
(To Genoa)

SPAIN

OTTOMAN EMPI

NAPLES

SARDINIA

SICILY

Prepa
Rand McNally

16th century. Spain also had great political power at that time. King Charles, who ruled the nation from 1516 to 1556, was the strongest ruler of Europe. He was a member of the Hapsburg family of Austria, which had been steadily gaining influence through wise marriages. Charles had inherited the Low Countries, southern Italy, and Austria. In 1519 he was elected Holy Roman Emperor Charles V. Since he was primarily king of Spain, these were the days of Spanish glory.

The immense power and many lands inherited by Charles V threatened the independence of other states and led to the development of a new concept in European politics—the *balance of power*—which was

a kind of equilibrium that resulted when no one nation had overwhelming superiority. Nations shifted alliances continually in order to preserve this equilibrium. When Francis I of France invaded Italy in 1515, other nations moved to prevent him from getting too strong. For example, Henry VIII of England allied England with the Hapsburgs. Then, when the latter defeated France, Henry transferred his support to the French in hopes of restoring the balance of power. Francis I in turn allied his nation with various German Protestant princes and with Sultan Suleiman, ruler of the Ottoman Empire. This later alliance—between a Catholic and a Turk, the foe of Christianity—showed how religious differences could be subordinated to political considerations.

Charles, in failing health and exhausted from his efforts to maintain his vast empire, abdicated in 1556. Austria went to his brother Ferdinand I, king of Bohemia and Hungary; two years later Ferdinand succeeded as emperor of the Holy Roman Empire. This branch of the family became known as the *Austrian Hapsburgs*. Charles' son, Philip II, inherited the rest of his father's realm. He and his successors were known as the *Spanish Hapsburgs*. Philip expanded his territories by annexing Portugal in 1580. But his Dutch Protestant subjects, who had rebelled against Spain in 1566, announced their independence in 1581.

England defeated Spain. Philip, wanting to strengthen his own rule and to defend Roman Catholicism, saw Protestant England as his chief foe. He had been married to Mary Tudor for four years, but her anti-Protestant campaign had met with little success, and he lost his influence in England when she died in 1558. Mary's successor, Queen Elizabeth I, was hostile to Spain. She helped the Dutch in their rebellion against Philip. She also condoned the piratical expeditions of English sea captains, including Sir Francis Drake, who seized many Spanish treasure ships as they returned with gold and silver from the New World.

In 1588, Philip launched an invasion against England, hoping to punish the nation and crush Protestantism. He sent the Spanish Armada, a fleet of over 130 ships, to attack England and to prepare the way for an army invasion. Every Englishman prepared to turn out and fight for his country and its liberty. The smaller but faster ships of the English navy were expertly sailed and led by such bold seamen as Drake, John Hawkins, and Martin Frobisher. The English won a great victory in the English Channel, and the defeated Armada sailed for Spain. A storm drove many of the ships ashore, and fewer than eighty returned to Spanish ports.

Elizabeth had gained two objectives. England remained free and Protestant. The nation had also established itself as a sea power—the beginning of its long mastery over the oceans of the world.

Civil war disrupted France. While the Spanish were fighting the Dutch and English, civil war broke out in France. Huguenots contended with Roman Catholics in a series of conflicts between 1562 and 1598 over the issue of which faction would control the throne. During most of this time, France was ruled by weak kings. A regent, Catherine de' Medici, exercised great power. Although at first she tried to steer a middle course between Protestants and Catholics, she finally went over to the Catholic side. Her hatred of Protestantism grew, culminating in the St. Bartholomew's Day Massacre of 1572, in which she planned to have all the Huguenots killed. Although at least 10,000 Huguenots were slain, Protestantism was not extinguished in France.

In 1589 the French king, Henry III, was assassinated. Henry of Navarre, leader of the Huguenot party, was heir to the throne, but the French Catholics and Philip II of Spain denied his right to be king. He had to fight for his throne—with the aid of Queen Elizabeth—and become a Catholic before he could be crowned as Henry IV in 1594, the first of the Bourbon dynasty.

Although Henry IV remained a Catholic, he did not forget the Huguenots. In 1598, he issued the Edict of Nantes, which protected the liberties of the Huguenot minority. It gave them freedom of religion in many cities. Thus France became the first large nation to permit more than one form of Christianity within its borders.

National Rivalries

Conflicts among nations increased after the Reformation, partly because the religious revolt ended the Church's role as a negotiator in international affairs. With few restraints on their power, European rulers used every means at their command in competing for supremacy. Henry VIII, left (as sketched by Holbein the Younger), was a skillful diplomat who shifted English support from one Continental ruler to another in order to maintain a balance of power. Charles V, king of Spain and Holy Roman emperor, employed military force to maintain the unity of his empire. The painting above right depicts Charles and his army near the Italian town of Orbetello.

During the reign of Charles' son Philip II, the Spanish tried unsuccessfully to invade England. Above, the English (at right) scatter the "Invincible Armada" by launching flaming boats at the cumbersome Spanish galleons. Both religious and political motives played an important part in the Thirty Years' War. At right, the Swedish monarch Gustavus Adolphus rides in triumph after capturing Munich in 1632, while kneeling officials offer him the keys to the city. Only a few months later, the king was killed in battle.

The Thirty Years' War weakened the Hapsburgs and strengthened France. The last phase of religious warfare was a savage struggle waged in Germany from 1618 to 1648, known as the Thirty Years' War. An important cause of the war was the failure of the Peace of Augsburg to settle all the religious problems of Germany. It had recognized only Lutheranism among the Protestant sects and had ignored Calvinism. Nor did it prevent struggles for Church property. Some of the clergy who became Lutheran after 1552 kept the lands they had held as Catholics. Protestant princes had continued to take over Church territory, a practice which Catholics felt the Peace had prohibited.

Political rivalry also played an important role. Many of the leaders involved in the war used it to satisfy their desires for land, money, and power. Ferdinand II, the Holy Roman Emperor, wanted to unite the principalities of his empire in order to strengthen his position in Europe.

Germany formed the main battleground for the Thirty Years' War, which broke out in Bohemia. At first, the fighting involved mainly the Protestant princes, organized in the Protestant Union, and their opponents, the Catholic princes and Holy Roman Emperor, who formed the Catholic League. Then other countries entered the fight.

First came Denmark, which entered the war on the side of the Protestants in 1625. The armies of the Catholic League, under Albrecht Wallenstein, defeated the Danes and drove them out of Germany. Then Sweden came to the aid of the Protestants in 1630. Although Swedish forces under King Gustavus Adolphus won several brilliant victories, the Swedish king was killed in battle in 1632.

When it seemed that the fighting had ended, France suddenly entered the war on the side of the Protestants. France was primarily a Roman Catholic country, and the power behind the French throne was Richelieu, a cardinal in the Church. Protestantism, however, worried France less than did the power of the Hapsburgs. France had been fighting the Spanish Hapsburgs in the Netherlands, Italy, and Spain, and had aided German Protestants secretly with money. Beginning in 1635 it sent troops to Germany under two able generals, Prince Louis de Condé and Henri de Turenne. After savage fighting, the French and their allies won a victory, and the war ended in 1648 with the Peace of Westphalia.

The Thirty Years' War had important results. It caused widespread destruction in Germany because the armies lived off the land instead of furnishing their own supplies. Numerous cities lay in ruins, and many people died of starvation. Historians have estimated that it took Germany a century to recover.

The Peace of Westphalia settled the question of the ownership of Church property by specifying that those who held the land in 1624, whether Protestant or Catholic, would retain ownership. The Peace also granted the same privileges to Calvinism as had been given Lutheranism in the Peace of Augsburg. Of greatest significance, Westphalia symbolized the victory of individual nations over more far-reaching organizations—such as the Church and the Holy Roman Empire —that attempted to transcend national boundaries.

The Thirty Years' War established France as the strongest nation in Europe. It was also an important step in the decline of the Hapsburgs. The Austrian branch was weakened by the rise of the individual German states, which won almost complete independence. During the war, the Spanish Hapsburgs lost Portugal, which became independent. They also were defeated by the French in a series of conflicts that lasted until 1659.

Queen Elizabeth I provided England with stable government for forty-five years. Though vain and flirtatious, she was an adroit diplomat. She refused all offers of marriage, partly to avoid involving England in European political struggles. One such offer came from King Philip of Spain, who had been her sister Mary's husband. When Elizabeth refused him, he tried to gain influence in England by supporting Mary Stuart, the Roman Catholic queen of Scotland, who was next in line for the English throne. Elizabeth imprisoned Mary for several years. Finally, at the urging of Parliament, Elizabeth ordered Mary beheaded for allegedly taking part in an assassination plot.

1. Why was Spain so powerful in the 16th century? What steps did European powers take to prevent Spain from upsetting the balance of power?
2. What was the importance of the English victory over the Spanish Armada in 1588?

3. What were the issues of the civil wars in 16th-century France? Why was the Edict of Nantes noteworthy?
4. What were some of the causes of the Thirty Years' War? Why did France enter the war?
5. What were the most important results of the Thirty Years' War?

Chapter 14 ▉▉▉▉▉▉▉▉▉▉ A Review

The Protestant Reformation that divided Europe in the 16th and 17th centuries and reduced the power of the Church had several causes. Corruption and worldliness weakened the Church from within and aroused criticism from many reformers. New trends from outside also reduced Church authority. As Europeans developed strong feelings of loyalty to their own nations, they began to resent papal control. Merchants wanted to be free of religious restrictions on trade.

The Reformation started in Germany when Martin Luther attacked the Church. It spread to Scandinavia and to Switzerland, where John Calvin established a new sect of Protestantism. Calvinism inspired the French Huguenots, the English Puritans, the Scotch Presbyterians, and other sects. England first broke with Rome after an essentially political quarrel between Henry VIII and the pope. Major differences in religious doctrines appeared only when the English Church became more Protestant under Henry's successors.

As Protestantism expanded, the Catholic Church organized the Counter Reformation to regain lost ground. New religious orders added vigor to help bring this about. The Council of Trent reaffirmed Roman Catholic beliefs and instituted reforms, while a strengthened Inquisition and the issuing of the Index enforced conformity.

The Protestant Reformation shattered religious unity and aided both royal power and the democratic spirit in the emerging nations of Europe. It also encouraged business and education. Although religious hatred was intensified for a time, the Reformation on the whole led to toleration.

Religious quarrels aggravated the political conflicts that plagued Europe from the mid-16th to the mid-17th centuries. Under the Hapsburgs Charles V and Philip II, Spain enjoyed its greatest glory. Jealous nations tried to check Spain, however, and keep a balance of power. The revolt of the Dutch Protestants lessened Spanish power in the Low Countries, and the English defeat of the Armada further diminished Spanish prestige and established England as a sea power.

Civil war between Protestants and Catholics weakened France for a time, but the Edict of Nantes granted a measure of religious liberty. Religious warfare culminated in the Thirty Years' War, which devastated Germany, humbled the Hapsburgs, and left France the most powerful nation in Europe.

The Time

Arrange the following events in their correct chronological order.
Anglican Church established
Defeat of the Spanish Armada
Thirty Years' War
Reign of Innocent III
Edict of Nantes
St. Bartholomew's Day Massacre
Ninety-five Theses
Babylonian Captivity
Council of Trent
Great Schism
Act of Supremacy

The Place

1. In 1600, which of the following countries or areas had Catholic majorities? Which had Protestant majorities?

Poland	Hungary	Switzerland
France	north German	England
Spain	states	Ireland
Italy	Portugal	Austria
Sweden	Bohemia	Netherlands

2. What areas from the empire of Charles V were included in the empire of his son, Philip II? What addition did Philip make to his domain in 1580? Which area did he lose in 1581?

3. What were the events important to the history of religion which occurred at each of the following places? Avignon; Geneva; Wittenberg; Trent.

The People

1. What two religious leaders founded orders of friars to help purify the medieval Church?

2. In what ways are the following men associated with the breakup of the medieval Church?

John Wycliffe	Henry VIII
Erasmus	Philip IV
Johann Tetzel	John Huss
Martin Luther	

3. How was each of these women involved in the Protestant-Catholic controversies of England? Catherine of Aragon; Anne Boleyn; Mary Tudor; Elizabeth I.

4. How did St. Ignatius Loyola and Pope Paul III contribute to the Catholic Counter Reformation?

5. Explain the role of each of the following persons in the religious-political struggles of the 16th and 17th centuries.

Sir Francis Drake	Ferdinand II
Gustavus Adolphus	Sultan Suleiman
Albrecht Wallenstein	Henry IV
Catherine de' Medici	Charles V
Cardinal Richelieu	Philip II

6. What contributions to the Protestant Reformation were made by John Calvin, John Knox, and Huldreich Zwingli?

Historical Terms

1. The Reformation period resulted in the division of the Christian world among several Christian groups, including Roman Catholics, Huguenots, Lutherans, and Calvinists. With which group was each of the following associated? *Institutes of the Christian Religion;* Edict of Nantes; Council of Trent; Ninety-five Theses. What was the Anglican Church?

2. Explain how the prestige of the medieval Church was lowered by the Great Schism; the Babylonian Captivity; simony.

3. Give the meaning of each of the following terms and tell whether it is associated with Catholic, Lutheran, or Calvinist doctrine: (a) predestination; (b) indulgences; (c) justification by faith.

4. How did the following groups contribute to the Catholic Counter Reformation? Jesuits; Ursulines; Capuchins.

5. What was the purpose of the *Index?*

6. Explain what was meant by maintaining the "balance of power."

7. In what ways did the Peace of Augsburg and the Peace of Westphalia strengthen Protestantism and foster the growth of independent states?

Questions for Critical Thinking

1. Of the various forces contributing to the decline of the medieval Church, which was the most powerful? Explain with specific examples.

2. In what ways did Calvinism seem to encourage the growth of a middle class?

3. Was the Thirty Years' War primarily a religious or a political struggle? Support your answer with pertinent examples.

4. What were the requirements for a true "balance of power" in 17th-century Europe? Was a balance of power achieved in the Peace of Westphalia? Explain.

5. The 16th century is often called the "Spanish Century." What were the factors which explain the maintenance of Spanish power? Why did the defeat of the Armada herald the end of Spanish glory?

The Age of Discovery

The energetic spirit that characterized Renaissance Europe led people to venture beyond familiar shores, cross uncharted oceans, and explore new lands. Adventurous men like Christopher Columbus, left, laid the foundations for great colonial empires. As Europeans took advantage of increased trade opportunities, the resulting economic changes created a Commercial Revolution. A moneylender and his wife, shown at right, typify the growing prosperity of Europe.

During Roman times, travel to far-off lands was not uncommon and trade prospered. Merchants exchanged goods with China and India, and many of them had a fairly clear understanding of the geography of North Africa, the Near East, and western India. However, the collapse of the Roman Empire, and later, the Moslem seizure of most Mediterranean trade routes, largely isolated Europe from the rest of the world. For centuries, few Europeans dared to travel. Roads were poor and infested with wolves and bandits, while sea travel was endangered by pirates. Most people stayed close to home; they knew and cared little about the rest of the world.

There were some exceptions. During the 10th century, Norsemen from Scandinavia voyaged far to the west across the Atlantic to North America, landing probably in the vicinity of Labrador, Nova Scotia, and New England. Few Europeans knew of their discoveries, however, and they were soon forgotten. The Crusades, beginning in the late 11th century, restored European contact with the East, although most of the resulting commerce was confined to the Mediterranean Sea. In the 13th century, Marco Polo journeyed to China, lived at the court of the Mongol emperor Kublai Khan, and returned to report the wonders he had seen. His book influenced Europe, but the Ming rulers who succeeded the Mongols discouraged contact with foreigners.

By the beginning of the 15th century Europe stood on the verge of a dynamic, exciting new era—the Age of Discovery. This chapter discusses how:

1. **Two chief factors stimulated exploration.**

2. **Explorers discovered new lands.**

3. **Overseas empires arose.**

4. **A Commercial Revolution resulted.**

1 Two chief factors stimulated exploration

Europeans of the late Middle Ages knew little about the world beyond their own continent and the lands around the Mediterranean. Not until the 15th century did they venture out into the unknown.

Europeans wanted to find new trade routes. The revival of trade in the late Middle Ages spurred the growth of commerce between Europe and the East, particularly India, China, and the East Indies. Chapter 13 discussed how this commerce especially benefited the Italian middlemen who traded between the eastern end of the Mediterranean Sea and the rest of Europe. All trade routes between Europe and the East made the use of both sea and land transportation necessary. Goods passed through many hands before reaching a destination, and each handler naturally wanted to make a profit. Italian merchants made the largest profit of all because they had a virtual monopoly on the Mediterranean portion of the trade. As a result, Europeans outside of Italy paid high prices for spices, silks, and other wares from the East.

The people of Europe were eager to buy imported goods, but not at the high prices charged by the Italians. Merchants realized that they could avoid the high prices if merchandise were transported by a single sea voyage instead of in several stages across both land and sea. In addition, merchants in nations along the Atlantic Ocean —England, Portugal, France, Spain, and the Low Countries—were interested in breaking the Italian monopoly and in trading directly with the East. Thus a combination of factors—a demand for more and cheaper imports and the desire of Atlantic nations to enter the Eastern trade—resulted in a search for all-water routes to the East.

Improvements made travel easier. Since about the 12th century, men had been improving their ships and learning to sail them more accurately and safely. For one thing, ships were increasing in size; builders had doubled their capacity in the years between 1200 and 1500.

Two new inventions aided mariners—the compass and the astrolabe. Before the use of the compass, sea captains had guided their ships by the stars and sun, but on cloudy days and nights, sailors had no way to find their bearings in the open sea or in unfamiliar waters. The compass may have originated in China or with the Arabs. European sailors began to use it in the 12th century, although at first it consisted only of a magnetized needle floating on a reed in water. The astrolabe is thought to have been developed by Greek scientists of the Alexandrian period, but it was not used widely by mariners of western Europe until the 15th century. A forerunner of the sextant, it was used to determine a ship's latitude. By checking the position of the stars against this instrument, sailors could determine to what extent their ship was north or south of its course.

Improved mathematics also helped in finding a ship's location at sea. For example, by using their ship and a distant object as points on a geometric figure, sailors measured their location and distance by means of the angles of the figure.

During the 13th century, sailors began to use *Portolan* Charts (from the Italian word *porto*, meaning "harbor"); these showed coasts, harbors, and ports with considerable accuracy.

Section Review

1. Explain why goods imported from the East cost so much in Europe.
2. What changes in trade routes did the Atlantic nations seek?
3. What improvements made sailing easier by the 15th century?

2 Explorers discovered new lands

A desire for new trade routes, together with improvements in transportation, stimulated a great period of exploration, which lasted roughly from 1450 to 1650. It is often called the Age of Discovery because of the new lands explorers found; these lands eventually became much more important than the trade routes originally sought.

Prince Henry aided the Portuguese. One of the first nations to set out beyond the Mediterranean Sea was Portugal. Its achievements owed much to a member of its royal family, Prince Henry the Navigator, who wished to promote Portuguese power and spread the Christian faith.

Born in 1394, Prince Henry was the third surviving son of the king of Portugal. He had fought against the Moors in Morocco, and his military fame earned him tempting offers, such as command of the armies of England. Prince Henry turned them all down, however, and devoted himself to the study of navigation and exploration. He did not travel himself, but used his wealth and position to promote the work of others.

Prince Henry opened a naval school and observatory at Sagres, on the coast of Portugal, and hired the best captains and map makers he could find. Beginning about 1415, he sent ships out year after year to sail south along the coast of Africa and to bring back reports of what they saw. They discovered the so-called Gold Coast of Africa (now part of Ghana), the Azores, the Cape Verde Islands, and the Madeiras. Their voyages were extremely profitable trading ventures.

In 1460 Prince Henry died, but he had given the Portuguese a good start in the field of exploration. Bartholomeu Dias sailed from Portugal in 1487 and the following year succeeded in reaching and rounding the southern tip of Africa, giving it the name Cape of Storms. His voyage proved that a sea passage south of Africa did exist. This news pleased the king of Portugal so much that he renamed the region the Cape of Good Hope.

Columbus found the New World. Spain had meanwhile joined the search for an all-water route to India. Christopher Columbus, a native of Genoa, Italy, was sure that he could reach the Orient by sailing west. Like many men of his time, he was certain that the world was round. He based his geographic information, however, on the maps and writings of the 2nd-century Greek scholar Ptolemy, who had exaggerated the size of the Europe-Asia land mass and had underestimated the circumference of the earth. Columbus believed, therefore, that a route westward to India would be shorter than one eastward around Africa.

Columbus won the support of the Spanish rulers, Ferdinand and Isabella, who provided him with three small ships. The fleet set sail in August 1492. In spite of threats of mutiny from his frightened crews, Columbus kept his ships pointed westward and finally sighted one of the Bahama Islands—probably the one now known as Watling Island—where he landed on October 12, 1492. Columbus went on to discover Cuba and the island of Hispaniola (the location of present-day Dominican Republic and Haiti), where he made a settlement.

Columbus returned triumphantly to Spain and later made three more trips across the Atlantic, discovering various other islands and once reaching the mainland of South America. Some historians maintain that as long as Columbus lived, he believed that he had found an outlying region of Asia rather than a New World. In their opinion, this is why he called the islands the Indies and the inhabitants Indians.

The pope divided new lands between Spain and Portugal. Three papal decrees in the 1450's gave Portugal a monopoly on African exploration and trade. In 1480 the pope granted Portugal all lands from Cape Bojador on the west African coast to the East Indies. In order to confirm their rights to newly discovered lands and prevent conflicts with Portugal, the Spanish sovereigns asked Pope Alexander VI to define the pagan areas of the world which they might claim. In 1493 he drew an imaginary north-south line, called the *papal line of demarcation,* through the Atlantic 100 leagues (about 250 miles) west of the Azores; all newly discovered lands west of the line were to go to Spain. Because of Portuguese protests, envoys from both nations met the following year and drew up the Treaty of Tordesillas, which moved the line 270 leagues farther west. Thus Portugal was later able to claim Brazil.

Da Gama sailed to India. While Spaniards were voyaging westward looking for India, the Portuguese continued their search for a southern route around Africa. In July 1497, Vasco da Gama set sail from Lisbon with four ships, reaching the Cape of Good Hope in November. The expedition rounded the Cape, sailed north along the east coast of Africa, and then set out boldly across the Arabian Sea. At last in May 1498, the ships reached the city of Calicut, India. Because of a hostile reception there, the expedition went on to a nearby city to buy spices and jewels.

Da Gama's return to Lisbon in September 1499 was greeted with wild enthusiasm, and the goods he brought back sold for sixty times the cost of the expedition. Though he had lost half his ships and nearly two thirds of his men, Da Gama had found the first all-water route to India and had finally broken the monopoly of the Italian city-states.

Ships and Aids to Navigation

The Age of Discovery was made possible not only by adventurous men, but also by improvements in ships and sailing. With T squares and globes close by, the geographer at left works in his study, possibly charting a course for an ocean voyage. In the foreground, a loadstone (magnetic rock) floats in a container of water; the loadstone was an early form of compass. Portolan Charts supplied 15th-century explorers with details of coastlines. The one at right, from a Portuguese atlas, shows the Caribbean area.

During the 15th century, shipbuilders improved sails and hulls so that ships could make long journeys in all kinds of weather. Below left, depicted on a bowl, is a Portuguese ship of the early 15th century with three masts and three sails. The small triangular sail in the stern helped steer the vessel. Ships of this type, which sailed the Mediterranean, were about 85 feet long. Below center is the *Victoria*, the only one of Magellan's five ships to return to Spain. By this time —the early 16th century—ships averaged 125 feet in length. Large merchant vessels helped maintain colonial empires. Those below right are Dutch "East Indiamen," which measured about 210 feet long. They are shown in Amsterdam Harbor in 1599, laden with precious cargo from the Orient.

The success of Christopher Columbus' first voyage to the New World was due chiefly to a combination of favorable winds and currents, some of which were familiar to him. As an experienced sailor, Columbus knew that ships venturing into the Atlantic had encountered winds blowing from the west (the *prevailing westerlies*) at about 35 to 40 degrees north latitude. Since much of Spain lies in this latitude, Columbus reasoned that his best course could not lie directly to the west against the prevailing winds. He had sailed to the Canary Islands before and knew that winds blowing toward the west prevailed in that latitude. Therefore, on August 2, 1492, he set sail from Palos, Spain, southwest toward the Canary Islands, at 28 degrees north latitude.

From the Canary Islands, Columbus sailed westward, in the belief that the Indies lay due west on the 28th parallel. Columbus' fleet of three ships was able to proceed steadily westward, aided by ocean currents. Two of these, the Canaries Current and the North Equatorial Current, flow westward across the Atlantic. Columbus was aided also by the favorable winds, the *northeast trade winds*, which are usually steady and accompanied by fair weather. For a short time, however, his course carried him into the *horse latitudes,* a zone of light variable winds, lying between the trade winds and the prevailing westerlies at about 35 degrees north latitude. The lack of favorable winds slowed the ships, but at about 55 degrees west longitude they again caught the northeast trade winds and made 142 miles per day for five days. After 33 days land was sighted, and on October 12, the ships anchored —probably near what is Watling Island.

On the return voyage, Columbus chose to take a direct course for Spain, northeast by east. He was unaware that this course, if followed, would have taken him past the British Isles into the Arctic. However, the Gulf Stream, which flows northeast across the Atlantic, and the prevailing westerlies swept his ships eastward at a rapid rate and enabled him to reach the port of Palos on March 15, 1493.

Columbus made three other voyages to America—in 1493, 1498, and 1502. From the knowledge gained by his pioneering voyages, other explorers were able to sail to America with less fear of the winds and currents.

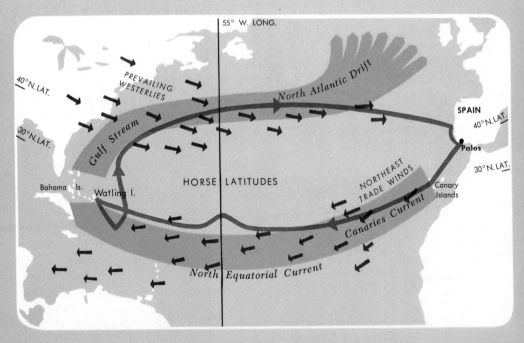

Other explorers made discoveries. The voyages of Dias, Columbus, and Da Gama excited the curiosity of many Europeans and inspired further explorations. One of the first men to realize that the newly discovered lands to the west were not part of Asia was Amerigo Vespucci, an Italian, who sailed first in the employ of the Medicis of Florence and later for Portugal. He maintained that he made four voyages to the New World between the years 1497 and 1503 and that he was the first European to set foot on the mainland. Most of his explorations were along the east coast of South America. Because of Vespucci's success in spreading the idea that a new continent had been found, a German geographer named the new lands America after him. Some historians dispute his claims, but the name endures.

In 1500, a Portuguese fleet under Pedro Cabral, sailing to India around Africa, swung so far westward in rounding Africa that the men sighted the easternmost region of South America. Before continuing his voyage to India, Cabral asserted the Portuguese claim to the new land, Brazil.

In 1510 a Spanish explorer, Vasco de Balboa, established the first Spanish settlement on the American mainland on the Isthmus of Panama. He explored nearby regions, and in 1513, was the first European to gaze out at what he called the South Sea. (Magellan later gave this greatest of oceans the name Pacific, from the Latin word meaning "peaceful.")

Magellan's expedition circled the world. Ferdinand Magellan was a Portuguese explorer who, like Columbus, believed it was possible to reach India by sailing west. Like Columbus, he gained support from the king of Spain.

In September 1519, Magellan set sail with five ships and 243 men. His Spanish officers did not like being commanded by a Portuguese captain, but Magellan gave his orders: "Follow the flagship and ask no questions."

The expedition reached the bay of Rio de Janeiro in December and explored the Rio de la Plata in January and February, 1520. The men wintered at San Julian, in what is now southern Argentina, during which time Magellan quelled a mutiny and one ship went out exploring and disappeared forever. During the fall, Magellan sailed around the southern tip of South America; another mutiny broke out, and he put several men ashore. The ships then edged their way through the narrow strait since called the Strait of Magellan. Ice formed on the sails and rigging, and one ship returned to Spain, but Magellan forced the rest of his frightened expedition onward.

Once in the Pacific, the small fleet sailed boldly westward. Food and water became scarce, and the men suffered acutely. Finally, in the spring of 1521, Magellan reached the Philippine Islands. After landing, he and several crewmen were killed in a battle with the natives. The survivors burned a ship because it was unseaworthy and continued to the East Indies; another vessel remained there (it was later wrecked), so that only one ship —the *Victoria,* with a rich cargo—crossed the Indian Ocean, rounded Africa, and dropped anchor at Seville in September 1522. After three years and twelve days, with only eighteen men left, the first ship to go around the world returned to prove that the earth was round and that the Americas constituted a New World.

Gold drew Spanish adventurers westward. During the 16th century, Spanish adventurers explored many parts of the Americas. In 1513 Juan Ponce de León, seeking a "Fountain of Youth," discovered and explored Florida for Spain. Chapter 11 told how Hernando Cortés and Francisco Pizarro fought American Indians.

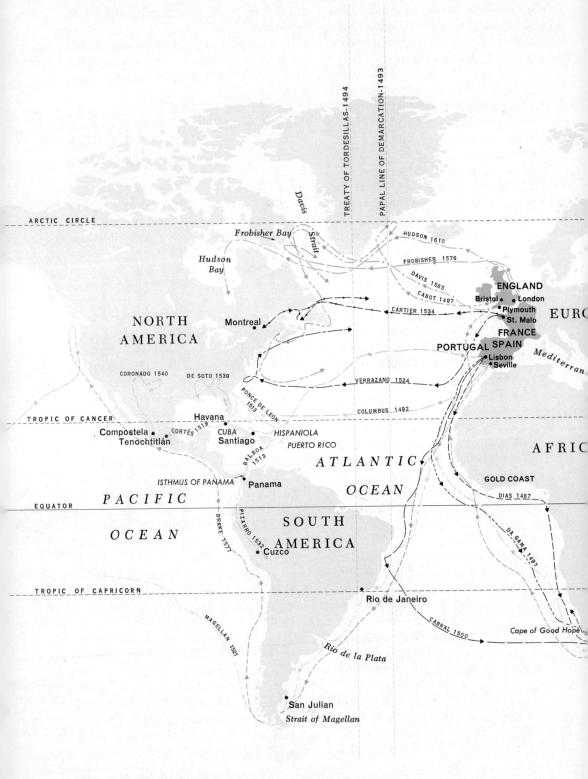

ARCTIC CIRCLE

Davis

TREATY OF TORDESILLAS·1494

PAPAL LINE OF DEMARCATION·1493

Frobisher Bay

Strait

HUDSON 1610

Hudson Bay

FROBISHER 1576

DAVIS 1585

CABOT 1497

ENGLAND

Bristol • • London

• Plymouth

• St. Malo

NORTH AMERICA

Montreal

CARTIER 1534

EUROP

FRANCE

PORTUGAL SPAIN

Mediterran

• Lisbon

• Seville

CORONADO 1540

DE SOTO 1539

VERRAZANO 1524

PONCE DE LEON 1513

TROPIC OF CANCER

Havana

COLUMBUS 1492

Compostela •

CORTÉS 1519

CUBA

AFRIC

Tenochtitlán

Santiago

HISPANIOLA

PUERTO RICO

ATLANTIC

BALBOA 1513

OCEAN

GOLD COAST

ISTHMUS OF PANAMA

• Panama

DIAS 1487

EQUATOR

PACIFIC

DRAKE 1577

PIZARRO 1532

SOUTH

OCEAN

AMERICA

DA GAMA 1497

• Cuzco

TROPIC OF CAPRICORN

Rio de Janeiro •

MAGELLAN 1521

CABRAL 1500

Cape of Good Hope

Rio de la Plata

• San Julian

Strait of Magellan

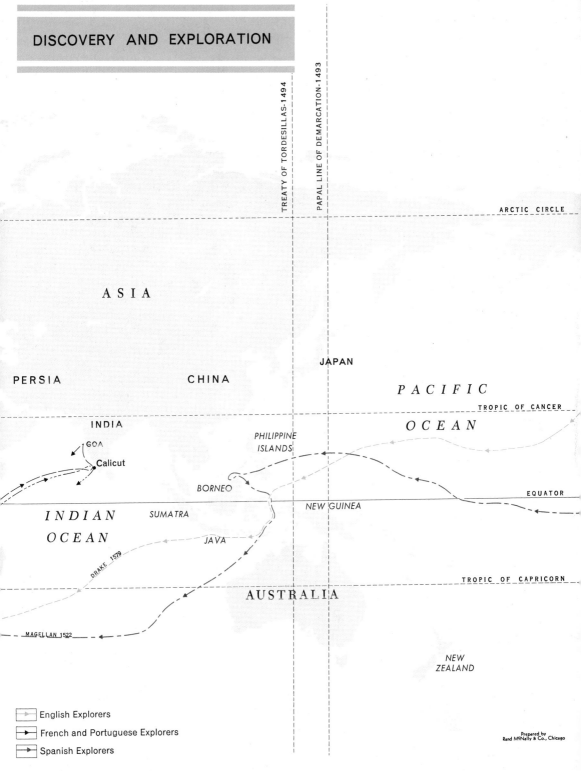

DISCOVERY AND EXPLORATION

TREATY OF TORDESILLAS-1494

PAPAL LINE OF DEMARCATION-1493

ARCTIC CIRCLE

ASIA

PERSIA

CHINA

JAPAN

PACIFIC

INDIA

TROPIC OF CANCER

OCEAN

GOA

Calicut

PHILIPPINE
ISLANDS

BORNEO

EQUATOR

INDIAN

SUMATRA

NEW GUINEA

OCEAN

JAVA

DRAKE 1579

TROPIC OF CAPRICORN

AUSTRALIA

MAGELLAN 1522

NEW
ZEALAND

English Explorers

French and Portuguese Explorers

Spanish Explorers

Prepared by
Rand McNally & Co., Chicago

The Age of Discovery 337

Cortés conquered the Aztecs of Mexico in 1521 and, ten years later, Pizarro invaded Peru and seized immense treasures of gold and silver. Between 1539 and 1542, Hernando de Soto explored the southeastern portion of the United States, and may have been the first white man to sight the Mississippi River. In 1540 Francisco de Coronado led an expedition into the area which is presently the southwestern United States. There he and his men discovered the Grand Canyon and marveled at the buffalo herds roaming the plains.

These Spanish explorers, called conquistadors (from the Spanish word for "conquerors"), were chiefly interested in gold; as they told the Indians, they "suffered from a fever that only gold could cure." Many of them were cruel and ruthless, but their courage enabled them to overcome great difficulties and their explorations added to Europeans' knowledge of the world. In addition, the Catholic missionaries who came in their wake did much to transmit European civilization and improve the lot of the Indians.

Many explorers looked for a Northwest Passage. Even though it soon became apparent that the New World was not Asia, most people were still more interested in getting to the East than in exploring the Americas. England, France, and the Netherlands wanted their share of the Eastern trade, and were not inclined to abide by the papal line of demarcation, which had divided all new claims between Spain and Portugal. The king of France remarked that he would observe the line of demarcation when he was shown "the will of Father Adam." Because of Spanish and Portuguese domination of the southern regions of the Americas, northern European nations tried for years to find a route to the East around or through North America. But they were unsuccessful in the search for what they called the Northwest Passage.

As early as 1497, John Cabot, an Italian mariner, was sent out by King Henry VII of England to "seek out, discover, and find whatsoever . . . countries . . . which before this time have been unknown to all Christians." He landed on the coast of Nova Scotia, Canada, and claimed the territory for the king. Cabot was the first European after the Norsemen to set foot on the mainland of North America. Most important, his discovery gave England a claim to the whole rich continent.

Giovanni da Verrazano, an Italian, was sent out by the French king in 1524; he failed to find the Northwest Passage, but did explore eastern North America from North Carolina to Newfoundland. Jacques Cartier, also sailing under the flag of France, in 1534 eventually made his way up the broad St. Lawrence River in hopes of reaching China. The vast territory of eastern North America to which he laid claim was given the name New France. This claim duplicated that of England.

Other Englishmen continued searching for a Northwest Passage. Martin Frobisher from 1576 to 1578 and John Davis from 1585 to 1587 tried and failed to find a way through the icy waters of arctic North America. One of the most famous English sea captains, Sir Francis Drake, combined exploration with freebooting, or piracy. In 1577 he sailed through the Strait of Magellan and up the west coast of the Americas as far as California, seizing gold and silver from Spanish ships on the way. He sailed northward, possibly as far as Vancouver Island, in an unsuccessful search for a western exit from the Northwest Passage, then headed back south. Fearing the Spaniards whom he had robbed, he directed his ships westward and journeyed home via the East Indies. He reached England in 1580, becoming the first Englishman to sail around the world. His voyage brought a profit of 4700 per cent and proved that the small English ships, contrary to the opinion of many, were more than adequate for long voyages.

Henry Hudson, an English navigator and explorer, made several voyages in an unsuccessful search for a Northwest Passage. In 1609, in the service of the Dutch, he discovered and sailed up the Hudson River. The following year, sailing for the English, he spent three months exploring the Hudson Bay area. A quarrel led to discontent among the crew, and they put Hudson and a few companions into a small boat and abandoned them. The mutinous crew made its way back to England, but Hudson was never heard of again.

Section Review

1. How did Prince Henry help Portugal in the field of exploration? Why was Dias' voyage significant?
2. How did reliance on Ptolemy's ideas about geography encourage Columbus to sail westward to reach the Orient? What areas in the New World did he discover?
3. Why and how did the pope divide the pagan world between Spain and Portugal?
4. What was important about the voyages of Da Gama? Cabral? Balboa? Magellan?
5. What discoveries did the conquistadors make in their search for gold?
6. Why did explorers for northern European nations look for a Northwest Passage? Describe the achievements of five men who failed to find it.

3 Overseas empires arose

After their first discoveries, the nations of Europe began to consolidate their positions in the areas they claimed. Whether they traded goods or developed natural resources or set up colonies, competition among them was keen. Rivalry was intense also because many claims were vague and the nature and extent of the territories was not well known.

Portugal established a far-flung empire. The Portuguese set up several bases in Africa in order to ensure their toe hold there and to provide fresh supplies for their ships trading with the East. On the west coast they founded the colony of Angola; on the east coast they established posts at Mozambique and on the island of Zanzibar. In India, the Portuguese built forts at Goa and Diu. Their posts at Malacca on the Malay Peninsula and in Java, Sumatra, and the Spice Islands (the Moluccas) helped them control the rich trade of the East Indies. They also began to deal with merchants in Japan and China, and were given trading rights in Macao, in southern China. Brazil was the only Portuguese territory in the Americas. Throughout these areas, missionaries, especially the Jesuits, served to extend Portuguese influence.

The Portuguese overseas empire was based on trade. Except in Brazil, the Portuguese did not settle abroad in large numbers; merchants sent out only enough men to protect their commerce by controlling native rulers. Portugal was too small a country to spare the people for colonization. Besides, most of the territory it controlled lay in hot, humid lands, with climates that most Europeans disliked. These disadvantages made it difficult for Portugal to hold on to its widespread possessions, especially when competition from other nations increased. In addition, the Portuguese had little religious tolerance; they introduced the Inquisition into India, arousing opposition among the natives.

Spain took over Portugal in 1580, restricting some of its commercial activity and turning over the administration of Portuguese possessions to Spanish officials. Although the Portuguese regained their independence in 1640, the British and Dutch meanwhile had succeeded in seizing much of the Portuguese empire, and during the latter 17th century its power overseas waned rapidly.

Colonial Empires

Europeans had many reasons for developing colonies in newly discovered areas of the world —reasons sometimes summarized as "glory, gold, and God." Kings sought to increase their prestige with other monarchs and to enrich their royal treasuries. Merchants were interested in establishing ports along new trade routes. Spreading Christianity and escaping from religious persecution were still other motives for colonization.

At left above is a 1584 view of the Potosí silver mine in the Spanish colony of Bolivia. Llamas carry heavy loads of ore down from the high mountain, Cerro Rico de Potosí, as Indians in the foreground pile the silver and prepare it for smelting. This area was one of the richest sources of silver the world has ever known.

When French Huguenots tried to establish a settlement in the North Carolina area in 1562, they became embroiled in a feud between native Indian tribes. In the scene below left, the muskets of the Frenchmen help one group of Indians defeat a stronger force. (The French settlement was later destroyed by the Spanish.)

Most expeditions sent out to explore new territories included missionaries, who preached Christianity among the natives. Above right, Portuguese priests in the Congo baptize a native before a church still under construction.

A scene at Peking in 1668, below right, depicts Dutch merchants seeking permission to trade in China. Seated in the center of the courtyard of the imperial palace, the Dutch bargain with one of the many court officials who had to be bribed before an audience with the emperor could be obtained. In the foreground are gifts to be distributed, including a globe. At right in the background, a satisfied official kneels as he receives his gift. At left are two men greeting each other with the traditional deep Chinese bow, called a kowtow.

Most Spanish possessions lay in the New World. Except for the Philippines, most Spanish overseas possessions were in the Western Hemisphere. From their first settlement on the island of Hispaniola in the West Indies, explorers and settlers moved out to other islands—Cuba, Puerto Rico, and Jamaica, among others—and to the mainland of South America. Within fifty years after the conquest of Mexico, a large Spanish colony flourished there, and others dotted South America. By 1575 the New World contained about 200 Spanish settlements, with a total of about 160 thousand Spanish inhabitants.

Because Spain was much stronger than Portugal, it could establish more colonies, better develop their natural resources, and transplant European ways of living more effectively. Spanish colonial policy had shortcomings, however. The central government exercised strict control over the colonies; for example, only Catholics were allowed to settle there. By awarding large tracts of land to royal favorites—thus re-creating the aristocratic system of the mother country—the system further stifled individual initiative. (Additional discussion of the Spanish colonial empire in America will be found in Chapter 23.)

England entered the game. Drake's voyage around the world encouraged English ambitions overseas; they were further stimulated by the defeat of the Spanish Armada in 1588, dramatic evidence of England's emergence as a strong naval power.

The first successful English settlement on the American mainland was founded in 1607 at Jamestown, Virginia. Plymouth, Massachusetts, was established in 1620, and other colonies followed shortly. England also claimed a large area around Hudson Bay in Canada, where it set up posts to aid its fur traders. In addition, the English settled on islands in the West Indies, and on the Bermudas; they seized Jamaica from Spain in 1655. By 1640 about 60 thousand Englishmen had emigrated to the New World.

English colonies in the New World became populous and strong, partly because England allowed religious minorities to settle there; these groups provided a large number of colonists, whose sturdy independence made them ideal settlers. In addition, many English colonies overseas were established by private companies, which allowed their settlers some degree of self-government.

England became interested in the East, too, particularly as the power of Portugal declined. Businessmen organized the English East India Company in 1600, and England later gained control of such prosperous trading posts as Bombay, Calcutta, and Madras.

France sent out traders and missionaries. Although Cartier had founded a colony in Canada in 1541, it did not survive. The first permanent French settlement was made at Quebec in 1608 by Samuel de Champlain. This fortified post high on a bluff overlooking the St. Lawrence River became the capital of the region called New France. Farther up the river the French built another fort at Montreal.

Fur was to France what gold was to Spain. Fur trappers, called *coureurs de bois,* a French phrase meaning "runners of the woods," were among the first white men to explore the Great Lakes region, and were followed by soldiers and missionaries. In 1673 Louis Joliet, a fur trader, and Father Jacques Marquette, a Jesuit missionary, discovered that the Mississippi flowed into the Gulf of Mexico, although they did not follow the river to its mouth. This feat was accomplished in 1682 by Robert de la Salle, who claimed for France the vast area watered by the Mississippi and its tributaries; he called it Louisiana in honor of King Louis XIV.

Several French trading posts and forts were scattered along the Great Lakes and down the Mississippi, including those at Detroit, St. Louis, and New Orleans. The French made few sizable settlements outside the St. Lawrence area, however; by 1660 Canada had no more than 2500 French settlers. Most Frenchmen did not want to migrate to the cold wilderness of Canada. The Huguenots, who might have been interested in going, could not, because France, like Spain, excluded non-Catholics from its colonies. As in the Spanish colonies, rigid government control and a feudal land system discouraged the independent farmer. For these reasons, French colonization in North America lagged behind the English.

French colonists emigrated in much greater numbers to French settlements in the Caribbean—Martinique, Guadeloupe, Tortuga, and Haiti. In Africa, France set up posts at the mouth of the Senegal River and on the island of Madagascar. French outposts in the East included one at Pondichéry, India, which was established in 1674.

The Netherlands set up many colonies.
The Netherlands, like Portugal, was a small country that built a large, prosperous empire. During its long struggle for freedom from Spain, from 1567 to 1648, the nation had developed a strong navy. In this same period, Portugal had come under Spanish control, so that its hold on the East Indian spice trade was weakened. The Dutch East India Company was founded in 1602, and by 1619 the Dutch had established themselves at Batavia on Java. They seized Malacca in 1641 and completed their conquest of the Spice Islands (the Moluccas) in 1667. They set up way stations on the African coast, where ships could take on fresh food and water; the most important was a settlement at the Cape of Good Hope founded in 1652.

In the New World, Dutch colonists settled Curaçao and other islands in the West Indies, and Dutch Guiana on the coast of South America. They bought the island of Manhattan from the Indians in 1626 and planted a colony, New Netherland, along the Hudson River. In 1664 the English seized this colony and renamed it New York.

Section Review
1. What was the basis of the Portuguese empire? Where were its posts and colonies established? Why did its empire overseas decline?
2. How did the overseas empire of Spain differ from that of Portugal? What were some shortcomings of the Spanish colonial system?
3. What led the English and the French to seek territories overseas? In what areas did they establish colonies and trading posts? Why did the English colonies attract more settlers than the colonies of France?
4. In what way did the relations between the Netherlands and Spain affect the Dutch overseas empire?

4 A Commercial Revolution resulted

The creation of European empires overseas, with the resultant increase in trade and in the supply of precious metals, led to far-reaching changes in the business life of Europe. These changes, called the *Commercial Revolution*, included the introduction of new business methods, especially banking and insurance; an increase in prices; the growth of modern capitalism; and the development of the economic system of mercantilism. Along with these changes in business went a rise in the standard of living and improvements in Europeans' everyday life.

GREENLAND
(TO DENMARK)

ARCTIC CIRCLE

ICELAND
(TO DENMARK)

*Hudson
Bay*

LABRADOR

NEWFOUNDLAND

London
Bristol

Amsterd
Antwerp

VANCOUVER
ISLAND

Quebec
Montreal

NOVA SCOTIA

Detroit
LOUISIANA
St. Louis
Jamestown

Boston
New York
Philadelphia
Williamsburg

Lisbon
Seville

OTTO

AZORES

MADEIRA
ISLANDS

New
Orleans

Charleston

Mobile

BERMUDAS

CANARY
ISLANDS

CALIFORNIA

MEXICO

FLORIDA

Gulf
of
Mexico

BAHAMAS

TROPIC OF CANCER

Mexico
City

CUBA

TORTUGA

HAITI

WEST INDIES

Belize

JAMAICA

PUERTO
RICO

GUADELOUPE

MARTINIQUE

CAPE VERDE
ISLANDS

St. Louis
GAMBIA

CURACAO

BARBADOS

SIERRA
LEONE

GUINEA

PANAMA DARIEN VENEZUELA GUIANA

GOLD COAST

EQUATOR

MARANHÃO

DUTCH
BRAZIL

PERU

ANGOLA

Lima

ST. HELENA

BRAZIL

TROPIC OF CAPRICORN

Rio de Janeiro

CHILE

Santiago

Cape Tov

Buenos Aires

San Julian

Strait of Magellan

ARCTIC CIRCLE

RUSSIAN EXPANSION ACROSS SIBERIA

MANCHU CHINA

JAPAN

IRE

PERSIA

sra

Ormuz

MOGUL

DESHIMA ISLET
(NAGASAKI HARBOR)

TAIWAN
(FORMOSA)

TROPIC OF CANCER

Diu

Bombay

Goa

Calicut

Cochin

INDIA

Calcutta

Madras

Pondichéry

CEYLON

Macao

SIAM

PHILIPPINE

ISLANDS

Aden

SOCOTRA

Malacca

BORNEO

EQUATOR

ZANZIBAR

SUMATRA

CELEBES

MOLUCCAS

NEW
GUINEA

Batavia

Barabudur

JAVA

TIMOR

Mozambique

MADAGASCAR

MALAY ARCHIPELAGO
(EAST INDIES)

AUSTRALIA

TROPIC OF CAPRICORN

NEW
ZEALAND

British

Dutch

French

Spanish

Portuguese

Trade routes and trade increased. The discovery of new trade routes ended the long trade monopoly enjoyed by the middlemen of the Mediterranean Sea. Proud and prosperous Genoa, Venice, and Florence declined as trade shifted to the north Atlantic ports of London, Amsterdam, Bristol, and Antwerp.

The volume of trade increased greatly. From Asia went larger shipments of spices, gems, paper, ivory, porcelain, and textiles, and new commodities, such as tea and coffee. The Americas supplied a flow of goods, many of which—including potatoes, tobacco, cocoa, and corn—were also new

to Europe. Other American exports included furs and codfish from Canada; lye, ship timbers, pitch, and turpentine from New England; and sugar, molasses, rum, and indigo from the West Indies. Africa contributed hardwoods, ivory, gold, and ostrich feathers.

The most profitable export from Africa, however, was Negro slaves. The Portuguese, the first Europeans to export slaves from Africa, transported the initial group to Portugal in 1441, but the trade expanded most rapidly after the discovery of America. The several nations that eventually took part seized and shipped altogether

Changes in Everyday Life resulted from the Age of Discovery. Goods that previously had been scarce and expensive—hardwoods, glass, fine textiles, and certain food products—now flowed into Europe from all areas of the world. The 17th-century drawings above represent three new imported beverages. At left is a seated Arab with coffee plant; at center stands a New World "savage" with his contribution, the cacao bean, from which chocolate is made; at right, beneath a smiling tea drinker, are Chinese farmers harvesting tea leaves. The interior of a Dutch home at left shows some of the refinements which Europeans could now afford. Bright curtains grace the glass windows, and a gilt-framed mirror reflects a woman seated on a chair playing a small piano-like instrument called a virginal. An oriental rug, left, lies beside a bed hung with rich fabrics, and chandeliers add further elegance to the home. A woman sweeps the tile floors, a far cry from the rush-covered stone of medieval castles.

about 20 million Africans to the Americas to work the mines and plantations. Negroes were chained in cramped, unsanitary quarters on the slave ships, and conditions were so bad that hundreds died on each voyage. It has been estimated that about one fourth of the total died before reaching the Americas.

Merchants adopted new business methods. As European merchants grew rich, they sought ways to safeguard, invest, and borrow money. Italians, who were the first European bankers, had begun handling papal revenues as early as the 1100's.

Banking did not become big business until the 16th century, however. Checks, bank notes, and bills of exchange all came into widespread use.

Increased commerce also led to the development of insurance. Merchants had to be prepared for loss through fire, shipwreck, and piracy. Since one of these disasters could ruin a man, merchants banded together and contributed to a common fund, out of which an owner could be compensated for losses. Marine, life, and fire insurance companies began to operate in the late 17th century. One of the most famous of these was Lloyd's of London, an association of men and companies specializing in ship insurance.

Another important innovation during the Commercial Revolution was the joint-stock company. Any person could acquire a part ownership in this type of company by buying one or more shares. The total shares, or stock, purchased by investors constituted the wealth the company needed for conducting business. An investor's earnings rose or fell depending on the success of the business and in proportion to the number of shares he owned. If the company made a profit, each shareholder received part of it, called a dividend. The Dutch East India Company and the English East India Company were joint-stock companies.

Along with the growth of joint-stock companies went the establishment of stock exchanges, where businessmen could buy and sell shares of stock. These exchanges acted as thermometers of business, because the rise and fall in the price of stocks showed whether business was good or bad.

Modern capitalism was born. The rapid expansion of commerce, the rise of banking and insurance, the establishment of joint-stock companies, and the introduction of the stock exchange—all these business changes signaled the beginning of modern capitalism. The word can be defined simply as the private control of the means of production for private profit. As known today, however, capitalism implies the accumulation and investment by private individuals of large amounts of capital, or wealth used to produce more wealth. During the Middle Ages people had dealt more in services, goods, and land than in money. The increased supply of precious metals, however, enabled Europeans to coin more money. The freer flow of coinage made it easier to save and reinvest money. Merchants and bankers could accumulate capital because they made huge

profits handling the expanded volume of trade. They could then reinvest surplus funds, often in joint-stock companies. The capitalism of the period is called mercantile capitalism because it was based on trade and commerce, particularly with territories overseas.

The rise in prices and expansion of business did much to enrich the bourgeoisie. (At that time, the term signified not all townsmen, but only the well-to-do middle class to which the capitalists belonged.) Thereupon, the bourgeoisie were to have an ever increasing effect on government policies. One of the earliest examples of this trend was the development of the economic policy of mercantilism.

Nations developed mercantilism. As discussed in Chapter 12, the central governments of many European nations were extending their political power during the late Middle Ages. With the growth of commerce and capitalism, the new national states wanted to establish their rule over the economic life of their people as well. In practice, mercantilism meant that government controlled the entire economy. The basic idea of the system was that a nation was prosperous and strong if it had a large amount of gold and silver and if it did not need to rely on other nations for important materials.

Because mercantilism stressed self-sufficiency, each nation tried to sell as much as it could to other nations and to buy as little as possible in order to maintain a favorable balance of trade. A mercantilist government aided export and shipping companies because such businesses brought money into the country. Such a government discouraged the importation of foreign goods and created many new industries to supply products previously purchased from other nations.

Colonies were important to the mercantile system. National governments regarded them as closed markets and kept foreign traders out so that merchants from the mother country could establish monopolies. Colonies were forbidden to produce anything the mother country sold. Colonies were also sources of supply for the home country, particularly for raw materials.

Mercantilists regarded business between nations as a kind of economic war. A business deal could not benefit both sides; one had to gain, the other lose. The system led to intense competition among nations, to struggles over colonies, and to war. Many of the conflicts in the period from 1650 to 1800 can be explained partly or wholly in terms of the mercantile policy.

Daily life in Europe changed. Except for the upper classes, standards of living were still low for most Europeans in 1500. Houses were small and uncomfortable. Windows usually had no glass, floors were covered with rushes that accumulated dirt, and most furniture was crude. Because clothing was expensive, most people wore out one outfit before they acquired a new one. Diet was monotonous, and table manners unrefined.

In the period between 1500 and 1750, habits of life in Europe changed more than they had in the preceding 1000 years. A rising standard of living enabled more people, especially the merchant class, to live comfortably.

New kinds of timber, such as mahogany from the West Indies, increased the supply of wood for houses and furniture; for instance, chairs began to replace stools in many homes. Window glass, carpets, and wallpaper came into use. Feather beds, pillows, and mirrors became more common. Textiles, particularly cotton and linen, became cheaper, and people began to wear underwear and to use handkerchiefs. The use of forks, napkins, and delicate china helped to refine table manners.

There was increased variety in food. Europeans learned to eat potatoes, oranges, lemons, strawberries, bananas, and peanuts. Sugar replaced honey as a sweetening agent. When a pineapple was given to King James I of England, he was "so ravisht with its charming deliciousness," that, according to a writer of the times, he said: "It was not fit to be tasted by a Subject, but only proper to Regale the Gusto of Princes accustomed to the highest delicacies."

New beverages included cocoa, from America; tea, brought from China by the Dutch in 1606; and coffee, introduced from Arabia in the 16th century. Part of the vogue for coffee and tea resulted from the medicinal qualities claimed for both drinks. It was said that coffee would prevent and cure the dropsy, gout, and scurvy. Inhaling the vapors of coffee was also supposed to stop headaches and coughs. The popularity of coffee led to the development of coffee houses, which became centers for literary and political discussions. Lloyd's of London began as a coffee house.

Tobacco smoking, an ancient custom of the American Indians, became popular. Even high-born ladies "would not scruple to take a pipe sometimes very sociably." Like coffee and tea, tobacco was said to possess miraculous healing powers for all sorts of ailments.

Section Review
1. What were two important results of the discovery of new trade routes?
2. How did increased commerce stimulate banking? the development of insurance? the growth of modern capitalism?
3. Why did mercantilism require strong governmental controls over business? Explain why colonies were important to the mercantile system.
4. Describe the changes in European life that took place between 1500 and 1750.

Chapter 15 ▃▃▃▃▃▃▃▃▃ A Review

The great era of European exploration and discovery began late in the 15th century, and, with the rise of overseas empires, resulted in a Commercial Revolution.

At the beginning of this period, Europeans were interested primarily in finding new trade routes to the East, hoping to break the Italian monopoly on East-West trade. Improvements in sailing helped their search, and with the encouragement of Prince Henry, Portuguese sea captains explored the coast of Africa in hopes of finding a southeastern route to India. Although Columbus failed to reach India by going westward, he made the vastly more important discovery of a New World. After Columbus' discovery, the pope established a line, defining lands which Spain and Portugal might claim. Shortly afterwards Da Gama succeeded in reaching India by the southern route around Africa. Meanwhile Vespucci, Cabral, and Balboa contributed to European knowledge of America.

In 1519 Magellan led an expedition that succeeded in accomplishing what Columbus had attempted—reaching the East by going west. The crew members surviving the voyage became the first men to go around the world. The New World became increasingly important as conquistadors fanned out from Spanish territories in search of gold, and English, French, and Dutch explorers looked for a Northwest Passage.

Following these explorations, the nations of Europe were quick to exploit their newly won territories and to establish overseas empires. Portugal, France, and the Netherlands were interested chiefly in trade, while Spain and England also established populous colonies, particularly in the New World. Most European nations tried to maintain a widespread system of outposts and colonies, and competition was keen.

The Age of Discovery led to a great increase in trade and in the supply of precious metals, which in turn brought about several changes known collectively as the Commercial Revolution. The changes included the development of banking, insurance, joint-stock companies, and stock exchanges; a rise in prices; and the growth of modern capitalism. Other developments were the increasing importance of the bourgeoisie, the flowering of mercantilism, and a higher standard of living for the people of Europe.

The Time

From these 50-year periods, choose the proper one for each of the events described in the sentences below.

(a) 1451-1500   (d) 1601-1650
(b) 1501-1550   (e) 1651-1700
(c) 1551-1600

1. The first permanent French colony in the New World was established.
2. Dias rounded the Cape of Good Hope.
3. Magellan discovered the Philippines on his voyage around the world.
4. The Treaty of Tordesillas was signed.
5. The English settlement at Jamestown was established.
6. Ponce de León discovered Florida.
7. Cabot landed on the mainland of North America.
8. The Dutch established a settlement at the Cape of Good Hope.
9. Cartier sailed up the St. Lawrence River and laid claim to New France.
10. The Dutch East India Company was founded.

The Place

1. In 1700, what European countries had colonies or trading posts in each of the following areas?

North America	East Indies
South America	West Indies
Africa	China
Japan	India

2. In which of the above areas was each of the following colonies or trading posts located?

Goa	Batavia	Philippines
Brazil	Calcutta	Mozambique
Peru	Jamaica	Pondichéry
Java	Virginia	Puerto Rico
Cuba	Haiti	Louisiana
Florida	New York	New Orleans

3. To which European country did each of these colonies and trading posts belong in 1700? What colony did the Netherlands lose before this date? To whom did the Portuguese lose their colonies in the East Indies?

4. Is there a "northwest passage" by sea from Europe to Asia?

5. What man-made shortcut of the 20th century would have eliminated many miles of Magellan's voyage?

6. If you had been a Portuguese in the late 15th century, would you have preferred the Treaty of Tordesillas to the papal line of demarcation of 1493? Explain.

The People

1. For each of the following explorers tell the flag under which he sailed and the area he explored.

Cabot	Marquette and Joliet
Cartier	Columbus
Coronado	Vespucci
Pizarro	La Salle
De Soto	Cabral
Da Gama	Cortés
Verrazano	Drake
Balboa	Ponce de León
Dias	Hudson

2. Which of these statements in the group (a) through (c) might have been made by Prince Henry the Navigator? by Magellan? by Champlain? (a) "Below us lies the mighty St. Lawrence River." (b) "My students sail forth, eager to challenge the unknown." (c) "Look how calm is this sea; I shall call it Pacific."

Historical Terms

1. What descriptive information would you provide for these items in a museum exhibit on navigational equipment of the Age of Discovery: (a) compass; (b) astrolabe; (c) Portolan Charts?

2. Who were the conquistadors?

3. What is meant by the term Commercial Revolution? What is the meaning of these terms used in connection with the Commercial Revolution?

joint-stock company	dividend
share of stock	stock exchange

4. Three business enterprises associated with the Commercial Revolution were the Dutch East India Company, the English East India Company, and Lloyd's of London. What were they?

5. Capitalism and mercantilism grew out of the Commercial Revolution. What do these terms mean? What is mercantile capitalism?

6. Explain what is meant by a favorable balance of trade and closed markets. How were these terms related to the economic policy of mercantilism?

Questions for Critical Thinking

1. In what ways does the Space Age resemble the Age of Discovery?

2. Why is the term "revolution" applied to the economic changes which occurred between 1500 and 1750?

3. In your opinion, which European country gained the most power during the Age of Discovery? Explain carefully.

4. Had there been no voyages of Columbus to set the course, which explorer do you think would have discovered the New World first? Give reasons for your answer.

5. If you were a merchant during the Age of Discovery, what might be your reaction to the mercantile system?

6. With the creation of overseas empires and the rise of capitalism, more and more of the policies of government came to be decided by the bourgeoisie. Why?

7. How did the economic policy of mercantilism tie in with the growth of nationalism in western Europe? Explain why mercantilism would lead to increased competition among nations.

Early Modern Times

The early modern period of history began about midway in the 17th century. For more than 150 years afterward, royal power in Europe steadily increased. The feudal nobility and the universal church had been humbled in the early stages of nation making, and the voices of the people were either unheard or unheeded. Therefore, with little to restrain them, the monarchs of Europe built up their power. *Absolutism,* a system of unchecked personal rule, became widespread.

One-man rule reached its height under Louis XIV of France. All over Europe, monarchs tried to imitate his style of living. On the opposite page is shown a magnificent staircase from the residence of the grand duke of Wurzburg in Bavaria. The halls and stairway are designed in the rich baroque style, with ceiling frescoes by Giovanni Battista Tiepolo, a famous Venetian artist. The palace of Wurzburg symbolizes the pride, power, and extravagant tastes of European rulers in early modern times.

Absolute rulers often felt compelled to extend their power beyond the boundaries of their nations. Since each state was considered a law unto itself, unhampered by moral scruples, monarchs operated in a kind of political jungle of power politics. Competition among nations involved the skillful use of diplomacy and war to gain national aims. The attempts of ambitious rulers to seize desirable territories, destroy the commerce of rival nations, and otherwise enhance their own prestige resulted in a period of unrest and violence. It was the wish of Louis XIV, who headed the most powerful country of his time, to make France dominant in Europe. Fearful of Louis' ambitions, other nations came together in alliances against him in order to maintain a balance of power. A long series of costly European and colonial conflicts resulted.

What made the early modern period different from preceding eras was not absolutism (whose roots lay deep in the past) but a new approach to life. Basic to this change was the growth of science. Building upon discoveries which had been made during the Renaissance by Copernicus and Galileo, the English mathematician Sir Isaac Newton defined the workings of gravitational forces. New branches of mathematics (analytic geometry and calculus) were devised, and instruments were invented to observe and measure the world of nature: the telescope, the barometer, the thermometer, the microscope. The study of chemistry was separated from the pseudo-science of alchemy and put on a scientific basis. Physicists investigated magnetism and electricity, and medical knowledge increased.

Underlying the developments in science was a firm belief that reason should be the guiding authority for human actions, a belief known as *rationalism*. So widespread was this conviction that the entire period from the publication of Newton's law of gravitation in 1667 to the outbreak of the French Revolution in 1789 is termed the Age of Reason. Rationalist thinkers turned searching eyes on philosophy, politics, religion, and the arts in a kind of intellectual revolution, known as the *Enlightenment*.

Many leaders of the Enlightenment were concerned with government. Voltaire was a sharp critic of the abuses of absolutism. Locke and Rousseau contributed new theories of society and government. Many people became convinced that absolutism must give way to more reasonable and democratic forms of rule. The English philosopher John Locke justified the use of force to remove despotic governments in these words:

> . . . Whenever the legislators endeavour to take away and destroy the property of the people, or to reduce them to slavery under arbitrary power, they put themselves into a state of war with the people who are thereupon absolved from any further obedience, and are left to the common refuge which God hath provided for all men

CHAPTER 16 / THE POWER STRUGGLES OF EUROPEAN KINGS

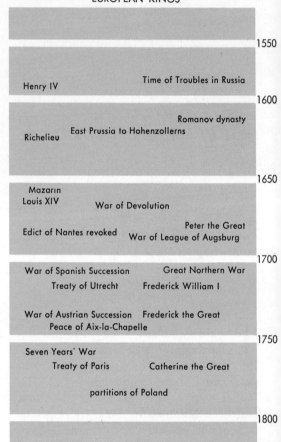

1550

Henry IV   Time of Troubles in Russia

1600

Romanov dynasty
East Prussia to Hohenzollerns
Richelieu

1650

Mazarin
Louis XIV   War of Devolution

Peter the Great
Edict of Nantes revoked   War of League of Augsburg

1700

War of Spanish Succession   Great Northern War
Treaty of Utrecht   Frederick William I

War of Austrian Succession   Frederick the Great
Peace of Aix-la-Chapelle

1750

Seven Years' War
Treaty of Paris   Catherine the Great

partitions of Poland

1800

against force and violence. Whensoever, therefore, the legislative shall transgress this fundamental rule of society, . . . by this breach of trust they forfeit the power the people had put into their hands. . . .

Three great political revolutions occurred in early modern times. In England, one king was beheaded and another exiled as a prelude to the Glorious Revolution of 1688, which established the supremacy of Parliament. In 1689 the famous Bill of Rights was enacted, marking the end of absolutism in England and guaranteeing the basic rights of the individual. The second revolution transformed thirteen British

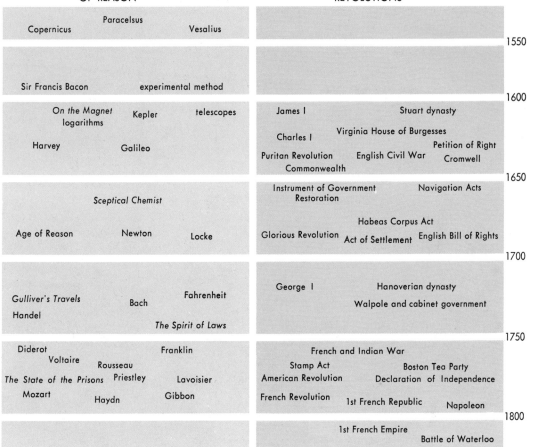

CHAPTER 17 / SCIENCE AND THE AGE OF REASON	CHAPTER 18 / THE AGE OF DEMOCRATIC REVOLUTIONS	
Copernicus Paracelsus Vesalius		
		1550
Sir Francis Bacon experimental method		
		1600
On the Magnet Kepler telescopes logarithms	James I Stuart dynasty	
Harvey Galileo	Charles I Virginia House of Burgesses	
	Puritan Revolution English Civil War Petition of Right Cromwell	
	Commonwealth	
		1650
Sceptical Chemist	Instrument of Government Navigation Acts Restoration	
Age of Reason Newton Locke	Habeas Corpus Act	
	Glorious Revolution Act of Settlement English Bill of Rights	
		1700
	George I Hanoverian dynasty	
Gulliver's Travels Fahrenheit Bach	Walpole and cabinet government	
Handel		
The Spirit of Laws		
		1750
Diderot Franklin	French and Indian War	
Voltaire Rousseau	Stamp Act Boston Tea Party	
The State of the Prisons Priestley Lavoisier	American Revolution Declaration of Independence	
Mozart Gibbon Haydn	French Revolution 1st French Republic Napoleon	
		1800
	1st French Empire Battle of Waterloo	

colonies into the independent federal republic of the United States.

A third great revolution broke out in France in 1789. The aim of this revolt was to sweep away unjust feudal customs and to liberalize the government. At first, relatively moderate reforms were achieved. Later the revolution took a violent turn and the monarchy was replaced by a republic. Radical changes were enacted and the king was executed. A Reign of Terror began which finally resulted in a reaction against radicalism and bloodshed. A vigorous leader, Napoleon, then rose to the forefront. Although he restored order and gave the people prosperity and military triumphs, democratic government was scrapped and Napoleon became a virtual dictator. Finally a coalition of European powers destroyed the empire he had created. Following the Battle of Waterloo, Napoleon was proclaimed the "enemy and disturber of the tranquillity of the world." Exiled to St. Helena in 1815, he was left with little but his dreams of past glory.

The Power Struggles
of European Kings

Non est potestas Super Terram quæ Comparetur ei Iob. 41. 24

On the title page of Thomas Hobbes' *Leviathan* appears a king towering over his land. His body is made up of his subjects and his hands hold the symbols of royal authority (the sword) and religious power (the bishop's staff). All-powerful monarchs controlled many European nations in the 17th and 18th centuries; conflicts among them made that period a time of constant, widespread warfare.

Political absolutism was not born during the 17th or 18th centuries, for its basic ideas can be traced back to the pharaohs of Egypt, Alexander the Great, and the Roman emperors. However, some of the typical forms of absolutism developed during early modern times, following the upheaval and turmoil of the late Middle Ages and wars of religion. Many men believed that strong government was necessary to bring order, efficient rule, and prosperity to the growing nation-states. In addition, the medieval idea that God ruled the state through His chosen agents lingered on to support political absolutism.

One of the important theories developed to convince men of the necessity for obeying the government was the doctrine of the divine right of kings. According to this doctrine, the king, by the grace of God, was absolute in his power, sacred in his person, endowed with extraordinary wisdom, and responsible to God alone. The Grand Monarch, Louis XIV of France wrote to his grandson Philip V of Spain:

> You must be master; never have a favourite nor a prime minister. Consult your council and listen to what they have to say, but decide for yourself. God, who has made you a king, will give you the necessary wisdom, so long as your intentions are good.

Other monarchs, such as Frederick William I and Frederick the Great of Prussia, and Peter the Great and Catherine the Great of Russia, adapted these ideas to meet their own needs and the changing times.

A second important theory of absolutism in government was developed by the Englishman Thomas Hobbes in his masterpiece *Leviathan*, published in 1651. He likened the state to a great leviathan, or sea monster, that forced men to do its will. Without the strong rule of the state, the life of mankind would be "solitary, poor, nasty, brutish, and short." Men would be constantly at war with their fellow men. Although Hobbes preferred a monarchical form of government, he conceded that a republic might supply the necessary authority to keep men at peace. In either case, the "great Leviathan" was formed by men surrendering their right of self-government to protect themselves at home and to defend themselves against foreign enemies.

Supported by these theories, the European kings waged internal power struggles and succeeded in crushing those opposed to absolute rule. Even though the central government affected all phases of town and city life, many men were willing to accept this strong monarchical rule because it promised a better life and seemed to be the answer to the religious, political, and economic difficulties of the age. Not only did the monarch seek to exert his will at home but he also sought to demonstrate his superiority and increase his prestige among his fellow rulers. This state of affairs resulted in a series of international wars among the absolute monarchs. These domestic and foreign power struggles are discussed in this chapter.

1. **Absolutism reached its height in France.**

2. **Powerful rulers helped Russia grow.**

3. **Prussia stressed militarism.**

4. **Power politics dominated Europe.**

1 **Absolutism reached its height in France**

King Henry IV of France, who ruled from 1589 to 1610, laid the foundations that enabled his country to become the first nation of Europe during the reigns of his son and grandson. Chapter 14 described how he established law and order by ending the civil war in France and issuing the Edict of Nantes. To foster prosperity, he promoted the manufacture of fine textiles and tapestries. These luxury industries furthered the aims of mercantilism by keeping in the country large sums of money that had formerly been paid for importing such articles. During Henry's reign, agriculture improved, roads and canals were built, and the French made their first permanent settlement in the New World, at Quebec.

In 1610 Henry was assassinated, leaving the throne to his eight-year-old son, Louis XIII. Louis' mother, Marie de' Medici, acted as regent, and her mismanagement plunged France into disorder again. Soon, however, she came under the influence of an able, ambitious churchman named Richelieu. Largely because of her patronage, he was made a cardinal in 1622 and chief minister two years later.

Richelieu and Mazarin ruled behind the scenes. When Louis XIII was old enough to reign as king, he proved to have little ability, and although he disliked Richelieu, he found him indispensable and allowed him virtually absolute rule over France. The cardinal, pale and delicate from an incurable disease, had a will of iron. He succeeded in his two aims: to strengthen the power of the king in France and to make France supreme in Europe. To accomplish the first goal, he took steps to destroy the political rights of the Huguenots and the power of the nobles. By attacking their chief town, La Rochelle, he forced the Huguenots to give up their privilege of maintaining fortified towns garrisoned by their own troops. He issued an edict for the destruction of all nobles' castles that were not necessary for national defense. Nobles lost their jurisdiction over local districts to new royal officials called *intendants,* who kept a watchful eye on the king's enemies.

Cardinal Richelieu achieved his second aim chiefly by weakening the power of the Hapsburgs. He plunged France into the Thirty Years' War, from which it emerged as the strongest nation in Europe.

Richelieu, harsh and relentless, showed little concern for the common people of France, who had to bear heavy tax loads, and they rejoiced at his death in 1642. Louis XIII died a year later, and his son became king—Louis XIV—at the age of four. Richelieu had trained Jules Mazarin, an Italian-born cardinal, to be his successor, and during Louis' childhood, Mazarin held the reins of rule in his capable hands. Strong nobles tried to gain control of the government, but after a civil war known as the *Fronde,* Mazarin in 1653 suppressed the challenge of the nobles to royal power. When Mazarin died in 1661, Louis XIV, then twenty-two years old, personally took over the direction of the government.

Louis XIV was one of the most powerful French kings. Louis XIV ruled France until 1715, and has been called the perfect example of an absolute ruler. He is supposed to have declared "*L'État, c'est moi*" ("I am the state"), a saying that accurately describes his attitude toward France. Louis believed in the divine right of kings and had a burning ambition to make his reign a glorious one. His courtiers called him *Le Roi Soleil* (the Sun King), and he was also known throughout Europe as the Grand Monarch. He ruled with unlimited power. Dignified and regal in his bearing, he fully enjoyed playing the part of God's agent on earth. People flattered the monarch outrageously, and a cook is said to have killed himself because fish for the king's dinner had not arrived on time.

Louis was intelligent and worked hard at being king. He kept a regular schedule and spent many hours a day in consultation and paper work. His capable economic adviser, Jean Colbert, made France

The Palace of Versailles was the center of European social life during the reigns of Louis XIV and Louis XV. It was the site of many elaborate festivals held to impress visiting nobility with the glory of France. The royal family lived in the buildings at center, nobles in the surrounding mansions. In the 17th-century view above, a stately procession heralds the arrival of King Louis XIV in a red coach.

a model of mercantilism by fostering overseas development and minutely regulating business practices and the quality of merchandise. To compete with the powerful Dutch and English East India companies, the French East India Company was founded in 1664. Louis XIV also increased the powers of the *intendants,* reorganized the army, and strengthened the navy.

Luxury surrounded the court at Versailles. Louis XIV wanted a splendid setting worthy of his exalted conception of

the monarchy. The Louvre in Paris, the traditional royal palace, did not suit him, mainly because he disliked the city itself; uprisings there in connection with the Fronde had humiliated and endangered the royal family, and Louis never forgot the unpleasant experience. He decided to build his palace at Versailles, a village about ten miles outside the French capital.

The palace required thirty-two years to complete, had rooms enough to house about 10,000 persons, and was lavishly decorated with mirrors, mosaics, priceless

carpets, and tapestries. The marshland surrounding the palace was transformed into a vast park.

Louis maintained his officials and many of his nobles at Versailles, where they lived on the generosity of their royal master and had nothing to do but serve and amuse him. They idled away their time at balls and parties, hunting, gambling, gossip, and intrigue. Louis thus strengthened his absolutism by making the nobles dependent on him and by keeping them under his watchful eye.

Life at Versailles was governed by a rigid etiquette, all revolving around the person of the king. Everything he did was accompanied by ceremony. When he rose in the morning, he was attended by 150 nobles, who considered it a privilege to hand him his clothing. When he dined, the food was carried into him in a formal procession, and courtiers stood while he ate. Other European kings tried to model their courts after that of Louis and even built palaces in imitation of Versailles.

Some domestic policies had unfortunate effects. Versailles was an example of the imprudence of some of Louis' policies. For one thing, it involved enormous expense. Its construction required the labor of 35 thousand men and may have cost as much

Powerful Figures dominated European politics in the 17th and 18th centuries. Richelieu, shown in a triple portrait at left, ruled France for Louis XIII. Skillful and unscrupulous, he did not hesitate to crush those who opposed the power of the king. Louis XIV, below center, in contrast to his father, kept royal authority in his own hands. The "Sun King" served as his own prime minister and forbade his advisers to sign any documents without his permission. The creation of a navy was part of the westernization program of Peter the Great of Russia, depicted below left against a background of ships. The new navy battled successfully against the Swedes and Turks. The Prussian King Frederick the Great, below right, a cynical and autocratic monarch in his youth, was an "enlightened" ruler in his old age. Influenced by contemporary philosophers, he instituted reforms aimed at relieving the burdens of the serfs.

as $100 million—the king himself destroyed the accounts so no one would know how much he had spent. Maintaining the large court was also a severe financial drain on France, and required approximately six out of every ten francs collected in taxes. In addition, by moving his court to Versailles, Louis isolated himself and his successors from contact with the French people, an isolation that had serious consequences for Louis' successors.

Louis' religious intolerance was as damaging to France as was Versailles. In 1685 he revoked the Edict of Nantes depriving Huguenots of their freedom of worship. As a consequence, thousands of these prosperous, industrious citizens fled to Prussia, England, and the English colonies in America. Louis' action weakened France economically by depriving the nation of some of its most progressive citizens.

In spite of these domestic policies Louis might have been one of the best kings in French history, but as he grew older he became interested in military conquest.

Louis' wars weakened France. Louis' great ambition—to increase his glory and that of his family—resulted in nearly fifty years of war. It was his desire for prestige, rather than concern for national security, that motivated his attempts to gain for

EUROPE IN 1721

SWEDEN
St. Petersburg
Stockholm
RUSSIA
Baltic
Sea
Copenhagen
PRUSSIA
GREAT BRITAIN
BRANDENBURG
(TO PRUSSIA)
POLAND
HANOVER
UNITED
NETHERLANDS
Amsterdam
Berlin
Warsaw
Kiev
London
Utrecht
SAXONY
Oudenarde
English Channel
AUSTRIAN
Aix-la-Chapelle
NETHERLANDS
HOLY ROMAN
Paris
Blenheim
Vienna
Versailles
LORRAINE
AUSTRIA
Buda
Augsburg
BAVARIA
EMPIRE
HUNGARY
La Rochelle
FRANCE
SWITZERLAND
Venice
MILAN
SAVOY
(TO AUSTRIA)
Genoa
VENICE
Avignon
GENOA
Adriatic Sea
(To The Pope)
TUSCANY
Constantinopl
PAPAL STATES
CORSICA
(TO GENOA)
Rome
OTTOMAN EM
Madrid
Naples
NAPLES
Lisbon
(TO AUSTRIA)
SPAIN
BALEARIC ISLANDS
MINORCA
SARDINIA
(TO GREAT BRITAIN)
(TO AUSTRIA)
Mediterranean
SICILY
Sea
MOREA
Gibraltar
(To Great Britain)

Prep.
Rand McNally

France its so-called "natural boundaries" —the Rhine, the Alps, and the Pyrenees. In trying to achieve this goal, he continued the Bourbon feud with the Hapsburgs, which had been initiated by Henry IV and continued by Richelieu in the Thirty Years' War. Because the other nations of Europe did not want France to upset the balance of power, they opposed Louis in four conflicts.

The first war, 1667-1668, is called the War of Devolution, or War of the Spanish Netherlands. It began when French armies invaded the Spanish Netherlands (now Belgium). The Dutch, fearing for their security, formed a coalition, or alliance, to stop the invasion, and forced Louis to halt

his attack. Angered by what he regarded as Dutch interference, Louis bought off their allies, England and Sweden, and attacked the Netherlands in 1672. After desperate resistance and great peril, the Dutch managed to secure other allies, including Austria and Spain, and in 1678 ended this second war by halting the advance of the French king. A third conflict, the War of the League of Augsburg, followed after Louis had seized border districts along the Rhine. His actions alarmed Europe, and several rulers—including the Holy Roman Emperor and the rulers of Spain, Sweden, and several German states —formed the League of Augsburg to curb him. This coalition became the Grand Alliance when England joined it in 1688. The war—which lasted from 1689 to 1697 —brought Louis a few border territories at the cost of heavy losses in men and money.

The last of Louis' wars was the most costly, however. It grew out of a conflict over who was to succeed to the throne of Spain, and was called the War of the Spanish Succession. Although Spain had declined since the 16th century, it still controlled a large part of Europe. Its territory included the Spanish Netherlands, the Kingdom of Naples and Sicily, the Duchy of Milan, and Sardinia—and also land in the New World. Charles II, the last Spanish Hapsburg, died in 1700 leaving no direct male heirs but willing his possessions to Louis XIV's grandson Philip. Louis XIV promoted the claims of Philip, but the other nations of Europe refused to acknowledge him as king of Spain. They did not like the idea of Bourbon kings in both Paris and Madrid, fearing that Louis would unite the two crowns and thus gain an empire stretching from the Netherlands to Sicily.

England, the Dutch Netherlands, Austria, and Prussia allied themselves against France to keep Louis' grandson from becoming king of Spain. The war began in 1702, and was fought in Europe and in North America (where it was called Queen Anne's War after the English monarch). The allies were fortunate in having a brilliant English general, John Churchill. This officer was an outstanding statesman, a natural and popular leader of men, and a master of battle strategy. Under his leadership the allies won a number of victories over the French, notably at Blenheim on the Danube in 1704 and at Oudenarde in the Spanish Netherlands in 1708. These successes dealt a blow to French prestige.

Peace was agreed upon by the Treaty of Utrecht in 1713. France was allowed to keep some of the conquests of Louis XIV, but it lost Newfoundland, Nova Scotia, and the Hudson Bay territory to England. Spain ceded Gibraltar to England; Austria received Naples, Milan, Sardinia, and the Spanish Netherlands, which then became the Austrian Netherlands. In addition, the treaty recognized two new royal families, that of Savoy in Italy and that of Hohenzollern in Germany. Louis' grandson was allowed to assume the Spanish throne as Philip V, but the crowns of Spain and France were never to be united. Thus the nations of Europe emerged from the war —and indeed from the entire fifty-year period of Louis' wars—having achieved a balance of power.

Louis' wars left France with an empty treasury and a large debt. As he grew older, Louis doubted the wisdom of his many military exploits. On his deathbed in 1715, he warned his heir: "Try to preserve peace with your neighbors. I have been too fond of war."

Section Review

1. What steps did Henry IV take to build France into a strong nation?
2. What were Richelieu's aims? How did he accomplish them?
3. In what respects was France an absolute monarchy under Louis XIV?
4. How did the court at Versailles enable Louis to strengthen his absolutism? How did it weaken France?
5. In the wars of Louis XIV and the peace treaties that followed, what steps were taken to preserve the balance of power?

2 Powerful rulers helped Russia grow

During the 15th and 16th centuries two famous Russian rulers—Ivan the Great and Ivan the Terrible—extended the power of Russia and centralized its government. A period of unrest known as the Time of Troubles followed the death of Ivan the Terrible in 1584. It ended in 1613 when a popular assembly elected Mikhail Romanov as czar. The Romanov dynasty was to remain in power until World War I.

Peter the Great tried to westernize Russia.

Mikhail's grandson, Peter I—usually called Peter the Great—came to the throne in 1682 (although he did not become sole ruler until 1696). One of the greatest figures in Russian history, Peter was tall, strong, and full of enthusiasm. He had a violent temper and could at times be extremely cruel. But he also possessed an excellent mind and a strong determination to work for Russian progress.

Peter was greatly impressed by European technology; he took a trip in disguise to Prussia, to the Netherlands, and to England, where he visited workshops and shipyards. When he returned to Russia, he took with him a large number of scholars, craftsmen, and engineers. He was determined to modernize Russia and to introduce European customs, by force if necessary. He tried to end the Asiatic practice of secluding women and encouraged the men to adopt European breeches instead of flowing oriental robes. He also decreed that men should cut off their long beards, and even carried a pair of scissors with him to snip off the beards of men he met in the street. However, Peter did more than attempt to change fashions. He founded scientific institutions, reformed the calendar and alphabet, and sent young men to western Europe to study. He created a small navy and modernized the army. A stanch mercantilist, he started new industries in order to make Russia more self-sufficient.

Peter the Great, like most other European rulers of the time, believed firmly in absolutism. He completely removed all traces of local self-government and authority. Under him the Russian Church became a tool of the central government and a strong supporter of Russian absolutism.

Peter extended Russian boundaries.

The goal of Peter the Great and later Russian rulers in foreign affairs was to obtain "windows on Europe"—that is, seaports on the Black Sea or Baltic Sea that would enable Russia to trade with western Europe by water. To gain these "windows," Peter had to wage war against the Turks in the Black Sea area and against the Swedes, who controlled much of the Baltic region.

In 1695 and 1696 Peter sent expeditions against the Turks at Azov on the Sea of Azov. The second expedition won this port for Russia, but Peter lost it to the Turks again in 1711.

In 1699 Peter allied Russia with Poland, Saxony, and Denmark against Sweden. Denmark and Saxony began the Great Northern War by attacking Swedish possessions in 1700. Charles XII of Sweden retaliated by invading Denmark and crushing Peter's army at Narva on the Gulf of Finland. Peter was confident of success, however, and in 1703 laid the foundations of St. Petersburg (now Leningrad), his new capital, on a region of the Baltic shore he had captured from Sweden. The war later turned in favor of the Russian forces, which in 1709 won a smashing victory at Poltava in southern Russia. From that time on, Sweden was increasingly hard pressed by enemies, which by then included several German states. When the war ended in 1721, Sweden had lost nearly all of its possessions along the Baltic, and Russia had not only secured its Baltic "window" but had also become the dominant power in northern Europe.

Catherine the Great continued Peter's policies.

Several weak rulers followed Peter the Great, who died in 1725. His grandson came to the throne as Peter III in 1762. He was mentally unfit to rule and antagonized many persons. His wife, a German princess, led a rebellion and seized the

GROWTH OF EUROPEAN RUSSIA

- Moscow in 1462
- Acquisitions to 1676
- Growth to 1725
- Growth to 1796

lf of Finland
Narva • St. Petersburg

• Moscow

SSIA

RIA

• Poltava

GARY

Azov
Sea of Azov
CRIMEA
Black Sea

Caspian Sea

OTTOMAN EMPIRE

Prepared by
Rand McNally & Co., Chicago

tion policy by improving schools and modernizing laws, she was rigid in her opposition to any reforms that threatened the absolutism of her rule. The condition of the peasantry actually became worse; Catherine extended serfdom to over a million peasants who had formerly been free.

Catherine, like Peter the Great, wanted to expand Russian territory, especially in the south, where the Ottoman Empire seemed unable to offer effective resistance. She goaded the Turks to war in 1768, and by 1774 had won back Azov and territories on the Crimean peninsula, as well as free access to the Black Sea and the right to protect Christians living within the Ottoman Empire. A few years later she seized the Crimea, bringing about a second war with the Turks in 1787. A treaty signed in 1792 confirmed Russian ownership of the Crimean and other Turkish lands north of the Black Sea. During the same period Russia took part in the division of Polish territory (see page 371). When Catherine died in 1796, Russia had not only won its Black Sea "window" to the West but had become one of the great powers of Europe.

throne for herself, taking the title Catherine II. (She later became known as Catherine the Great.) Her husband was murdered in prison, probably with Catherine's consent, but she announced gravely that he had died of colic.

By the time of Catherine's accession to the throne, the philosophical doctrines known as the Enlightenment had spread through the intellectual circles of Europe (Chapter 17). Several European rulers who tried to put into practice some of the new ideas about political liberty and religious toleration were called enlightened, or benevolent, despots. Catherine, gifted and well educated, corresponded with learned men in western Europe and considered herself an enlightened ruler. Although she continued Peter's westerniza-

Section Review
1. How did Peter the Great try to westernize Russia? How did he strengthen Russian absolutism?
2. What was Peter's goal in foreign policy? To what extent did he achieve it?
3. How did Catherine the Great continue Peter's policies?

3 Prussia stressed militarism

During the late Middle Ages a new state began to take shape in northeastern Europe. This nation, later called Prussia, owed its rise to the Hohenzollern family, originally from the south German state of Swabia. The family produced a long series of capable rulers who wanted land and

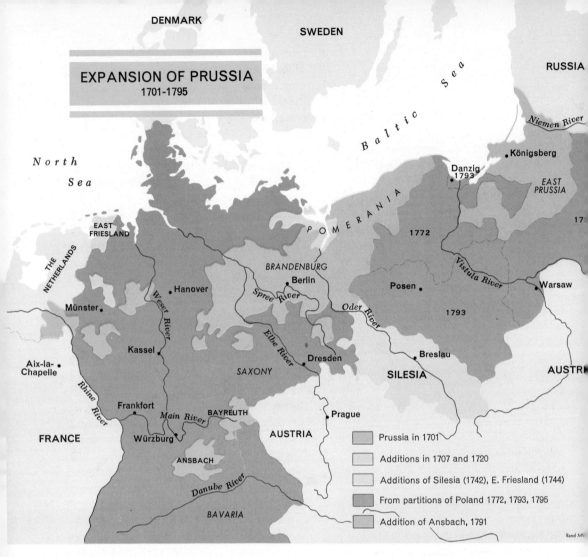

DENMARK

SWEDEN

RUSSIA

Baltic Sea

North Sea

Niemen River

Königsberg

Danzig
1793

EAST PRUSSIA

17

EAST FRIESLAND

P O M E R A N I A

1772

THE NETHERLANDS

BRANDENBURG

Berlin

Vistula River

Warsaw

•Hanover

Spree River

Posen

Münster•

Oder River

1793

Kassel

Elbe River

•Dresden

•Breslau

Aix-la-
Chapelle

SAXONY

SILESIA

AUSTR

Rhine River

Frankfort

Main River

BAYREUTH

Würzburg

ANSBACH

•Prague

AUSTRIA

FRANCE

Danube River

BAVARIA

Prussia in 1701

Additions in 1707 and 1720

Additions of Silesia (1742), E. Friesland (1744)

From partitions of Poland 1772, 1793, 1795

Addition of Ansbach, 1791

Rand M⁝

power and obtained both with the aid of sharp diplomacy.

In 1415 the Holy Roman Emperor gave the province of Brandenburg to the Hohenzollerns as a reward for military services. In the 17th century the family obtained lands along the Rhine and the valuable region of East Prussia. By astute strategy the elector of Brandenburg emerged from the Thirty Years' War as the most important Protestant ruler in the German states. His successor aided the Holy Roman Emperor in the War of the Spanish Succession in return for royal rank; in 1701 he was crowned King Frederick I of Prussia.

Frederick William built up the army. Frederick William I, the second king of Prussia, ruled from 1713 to 1740. He transformed his country into a militaristic state, tripling the size of the army and making it the most efficient fighting force in Europe. His hobby was recruiting men over six feet tall for his Potsdam Guard—"My dear blue children," he called them. Frederick William, however, never risked his army in battle.

In addition to building a strong army, Frederick William did much to improve the efficiency of the Prussian government by developing a class of well-trained, obedient public servants who had a strong sense of duty to their sovereign.

Frederick William was hard working and conscientious but a confirmed absolutist, considering himself the father of his people. He claimed that he alone knew what was good for them and once said, "Salvation belongs to the Lord, everything else is my business."

Frederick the Great increased Prussian strength. As a boy, Frederick William's son, Frederick, was not interested in a military life, preferring reading and music. After years of harsh discipline, however, he learned to be an excellent soldier and became a hard and cynical diplomat. Soon after he took the throne as Frederick II in 1740, he began a war with Austria. The forty-six years of his reign saw almost constant warfare, and by the end of this period, the army had reached a strength of 200 thousand men.

However, Frederick the Great, as he is usually called, had interests other than war. He enjoyed the study of history, poetry, and philosophy and never lost his love of music nor of playing the flute. He spoke and wrote French well and, like other benevolent despots, was interested in the humanitarian ideals of the Enlightenment. As an "enlightened" monarch, Frederick abolished torture in criminal cases, reformed the civil courts, and granted religious toleration to all people in Prussia.

He worked hard to improve the government and the living conditions of his people, believing that kings " . . . must be active, hard-working, upright, and honest, and concentrate all their strength upon filling their office worthily." Among other improvements, he promoted elementary education, and had canals extended and marshes drained. By fostering industries, especially the manufacture of woolen and linen textiles, he showed that he, too, was influenced by the policy of mercantilism.

Careful management left the treasury well filled at his death. Like his father, Frederick was a strict absolutist and ruled with little interference. Both monarchs helped strengthen a state which later became the center of the German nation.

Section Review
1. What were some of the chief steps in the growth of Prussia prior to 1700?
2. What steps did Frederick William take to make Prussia a strong state?
3. In what ways did Frederick the Great improve the economic and social conditions of Prussia?

4   **Power politics dominated Europe**

The 18th century, like the 17th, witnessed one war after another. France and England were bitter enemies during this period because each wanted colonial dominion in America and in the East. Spain usually sided with France because Spain was ruled by a branch of the Bourbon family. Russia and Prussia had no fixed friends or enemies, but were interested in expanding their territories.

The War of the Austrian Succession involved many countries. The Austrian emperor Charles VI had no sons, and he foresaw difficulties when his successor, his young daughter Maria Theresa, should come to the throne. At that time only a male ruler had the authority to reign over Hapsburg lands. In 1713 he secured the Pragmatic Sanction, a pledge of several rulers, including Frederick William of Prussia, that they would respect Austrian boundaries and acknowledge Maria Theresa as the sole heir of his dominions. When the emperor died in 1740, however, Frederick the Great, ignoring the Pragmatic Sanction, led his troops against Austria, claiming the rich province of Silesia.

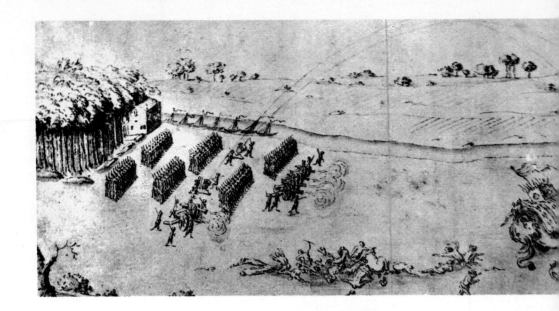

World-wide Warfare characterized rivalries among European nations in the 18th century. During the Great Northern War, the battle of Poltava, below, was waged on the plains of southeastern Russia. An exhausted Swedish army fighting far from home was defeated by superior Russian troops. Battles between France and England during the Seven Years' War were fought in Asia and in the New World. At Plassey field in India, above, the noise of British cannons caused frightened elephants to stampede the combined French and Indian forces. Quebec was besieged for two months by the British before the city's protective heights were captured from the French, as shown at right.

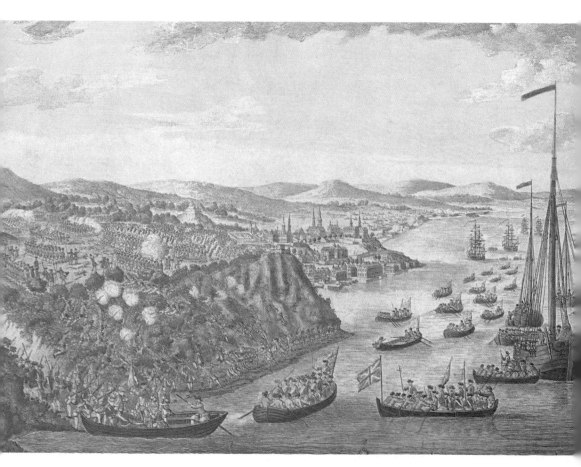

France, Spain, Saxony, and Bavaria joined in the scramble for Austrian territory. In this War of the Austrian Succession, England sided with Austria, not so much to help Maria Theresa as to oppose France.

Frederick defeated the Austrians in 1745, but the other combatants continued to fight, mainly over the question of colonial possessions. The war ended in 1748 with the Peace of Aix-la-Chapelle, which confirmed the transfer of Silesia to Prussia (first made in 1742). Colonial possessions seized during the war were returned to their original owners, but resentments smoldered and soon warfare began again.

The Seven Years' War strengthened England. In the years immediately following the War of the Austrian Succession, European powers switched sides so completely that the realignment has been called the Diplomatic Revolution. By 1756, France was allied with Russia, Sweden, and its long-time enemy, Austria; England had made an alliance with its recent foe, Prussia. A conflict that erupted between these new rival alliances was called the Seven Years' War, and it was fought both in Europe and in the overseas colonies. It broke out over the question of colonial rivalries in North America, where it was called the French and Indian War.

By 1733, England had established thirteen colonies along the Atlantic seaboard. The French were in possession of the St. Lawrence River Valley and had posts along the Great Lakes and the Ohio and Mississippi valleys. The English were fearful that the French would hem in the British colonies along the Atlantic coast. Another cause of conflict was the continued British harassment of Spanish trade in Latin America, annoying to the French because Spain had become a French ally.

The French and Indian War began in 1754 without a formal declaration of war when the French defeated a force of Virginia militia under George Washington near Fort Duquesne (now Pittsburgh). A year later the English under General Edward Braddock attacked Fort Duquesne; Braddock was killed and his English regulars were badly beaten. The next year England and France formally declared war on each other, and, anticipating an attack upon his lands by Austria and its allies, Frederick the Great attacked Austria.

Things went badly for England until 1757, when a great leader, William Pitt, became secretary of state and took over direction of strategy. Pitt provided his ally Frederick the Great with large sums of money to be used in fighting France. This plan kept the French occupied in Europe and left England free to attack them on the seas and in the colonies.

Pitt's strategy paid off. In India a remarkable leader, Robert Clive, defeated the French and their Indian allies in the Battle of Plassey, in 1757. In America colonial troops and English regulars drove the French from the Ohio Valley in 1759. Another English army under James Wolfe attacked Quebec and won the city after a sharp battle in which both Wolfe and the French commander, the Marquis de Montcalm, were mortally wounded. The rest of New France passed into the hands of the British when French forces surrendered Montreal in 1760. Meanwhile, Prussia, fighting the combined forces of Austria, Russia, and France, managed to stave off defeat, although not without severe losses.

The European phase of the conflict was settled by the Treaty of Hubertusburg in 1763; Frederick did not gain additional territory, although he had greatly increased Prussian prestige by his success in war against heavy odds. War overseas ended the same year with the Treaty of Paris. France ceded Canada and all lands east of the Mississippi, except New Orleans, to England. (New Orleans and French territory west of the Mississippi had gone

PARTITIONS OF POLAND

TO RUSSIA 1772

TO PRUSSIA 1793

TO PRUSSIA 1772

TO PRUSSIA 1795

TO PRUSSIA 1793

TO RUSSIA 1795

TO AUSTRIA 1795

TO RUSSIA 1793

TO AUSTRIA 1772

Prepared by
Rand McNally & Co., Chicago

to Spain in 1762.) In India no European rivals were left to obstruct English conquest. England emerged from the war as the leading nation of Europe and the greatest colonial power in the world.

Poland lost its identity as a nation. One of the outstanding examples of unprincipled statecraft during this period was the ruthless partition of Poland. Although Poland had enjoyed some influence and prosperity during the late Middle Ages, it had declined after the 16th century. At the beginning of the 18th century, it was still the third largest country in Europe, but it was growing steadily weaker. Its kings had little authority, while corrupt nobles, who still had great feudal power, were constantly quarreling among themselves. The backward peasants suffered grinding poverty. Lack of natural boundaries and an efficient army further hampered Poland.

The weakness of Poland greatly interested its neighbors, Russia, Prussia, and Austria. In 1772, Frederick the Great convinced Catherine of Russia and Maria Theresa of Austria that Polish territory could be easily seized. The three nations bribed members of the Polish parliament, which approved the first partition. Russia, Prussia, and Austria together took portions of Poland that totaled more than one fourth of the country.

In 1793 Russia and Prussia invaded Poland and forced it to repudiate a newly adopted constitution. They then seized more land in a second partition. The desperate Poles, determined to regain some of their lands, united in a national uprising behind a brave leader, Thaddeus Kosciusko, but it was too late. After an unequal struggle against the forces of Russia and Prussia, Kosciusko was taken prisoner and the insurrection collapsed. In 1795 Russia,

Prussia, and Austria divided what remained of Poland in a third partition, and it ceased to be an independent nation.

Section Review

1. What led to the War of the Austrian Succession? What did each of the major participants hope to gain from the war?

2. What were some of the causes of English-French friction in North America? What were the chief results of the Seven Years' War?

3. Explain some of the causes of Polish weakness in the 18th century. Show on a map how the country lost its identity as a nation between 1772 and 1795.

Chapter 16 ▬▬▬▬▬▬▬▬ A Review

The period of the 17th and 18th centuries in European politics was the heyday of royal absolutism in government and of the unprincipled use of military force in international relations. In France absolutism was fostered by Henry IV and two powerful churchmen, Richelieu and Mazarin. It received its fullest expression under Louis XIV, whose grandeur was symbolized by the magnificent palace of Versailles. Unfortunately, Louis' desire for military glory led to four costly wars.

In Russia, Peter the Great used his extensive power to modernize his country, strengthen the central government, and increase Russian territory. Probably his most lasting accomplishment was the establishment of his capital city of St. Petersburg on an arm of the Baltic. A successor, Catherine the Great, continued Peter's policies by adopting some Western ways and by seizing the Crimea and large areas of Poland.

Another absolutist state, Prussia, emerged as an important nation under such strong rulers as Frederick William I and Frederick the Great. An excellent military machine and efficient central government enabled this relatively small country to exert an influence out of proportion to its size and population.

During the latter part of this period, warfare involved an increasing number of nations and widespread areas of the globe. By the end of the Seven Years' War in 1763, Prussia had become one of the foremost nations of Europe, France had lost most of its overseas empire, and England had assumed first place both in Europe and as a colonial power. The unethical statecraft of the era culminated in the partitions of Poland, which completely erased this nation from the map of Europe.

The Time

1. Arrange the lettered sentences below so that events or periods appear in their correct time sequence.

The period of the 17th and 18th centuries in European politics was the heyday of royal absolutism in government and of the unprincipled use of military force in international relations. (a) Louis XIV of France involved the major countries of Europe in a number of wars designed to increase French power. (b) Cardinal Richelieu, as the chief minister of France, took steps to strengthen the monarchy and make France the leading power in Europe. (c) The rise of Prussia as a major power began when Brandenburg became a Hohenzollern possession. (d) Frederick the Great increased the prestige of his nation by gaining Silesia from Maria Theresa. (e) By the time of his death, Peter the Great had acquired new and substantial territories for Russia. (f) In Russia, the Time of Troubles ended with the founding of the powerful Romanov dynasty. (g) The long French-English struggle in India and North America ended with the Treaty of Paris. (h) Three nations—Prussia, Russia, and Austria—became partners in the destruction of Poland.

2. Name a treaty concluded on each of the following dates: 1713; 1748; 1763.

The Place

1. In what part of the world did France have its largest holdings in 1700? What overseas territories did it lose in 1713? in 1763? What country took possession of each of these French territories?

2. Why was St. Petersburg considered a Russian "window on Europe"?

3. Where were these battles fought and who were the victors and losers in each:

Blenheim	Narva	Poltava
Oudenarde	Azov	Plassey
Quebec		

4. Why would the Hohenzollern acquisition of East Prussia stimulate Prussian expansion from Brandenburg eastward?

5. From what countries did Prussia and Russia gain European territory during the 18th century?

6. For what reasons would Louis XIV regard the Rhine, the Alps, and the Pyrenees as the "natural boundaries" of France?

7. What European territories did Spain lose in 1713? To what countries? What overseas lands did Spain gain from France in 1762?

The People

1. What contribution to France did each of these figures make?

Henry IV	Louis XIV
Cardinal Richelieu	Jean Colbert
Cardinal Mazarin	

2. The men whose names are listed below were involved in the English-French rivalry of the 18th century. Explain the role of each.

Edward Braddock	James Wolfe
William Pitt	Marquis de Montcalm
Robert Clive	John Churchill

3. By the end of the 18th century, Prussia was a major power in Europe. What contributions did each of these rulers make to the development of the Prussian state: Frederick I; Frederick William I; Frederick the Great?

4. What Hapsburg queen is discussed in this chapter? Name one event with which she is associated.

5. "The Great" was a title held by both Catherine II and Peter I of Russia. What did each do to earn this title?

6. With what event in the European power struggles is Thaddeus Kosciusko associated?

Historical Terms

1. Why are the epithets "Grand Monarch" and *"Le Roi Soleil,"* appropriate to the absolutism of Louis XIV?

2. Each of these terms was related to the problem of maintaining the balance of power in 17th- and 18th-century Europe. Explain the meaning of each.

coalition	Pragmatic Sanction
Grand Alliance	Diplomatic Revolution

3. With what internal struggle in the France of Richelieu and Mazarin are the *intendants* and the *Fronde* associated?

4. What war was concluded by each of the following treaties: (a) Peace of Aix-la-Chapelle; (b) Treaty of Utrecht; (c) Treaties of Paris and Hubertusburg? By the terms of each treaty, what countries gained territory or prestige? at the expense of what other countries?

5. Explain each of these terms and tell with what European ruler or rulers it is identified: benevolent despot; regent; Potsdam Guard.

Questions for Critical Thinking

1. How do you think the partitions of Poland affected the balance of power in Europe?

2. In what respects were both Catherine the Great and Frederick the Great enlightened rulers? Who was more enlightened? Why?

3. The 17th century may be considered the "French Century." During the next century, however, France lost its position as the leading power in Europe. What reasons can you give for French decline?

4. It has been said that in power politics national interest always takes precedence over morality. To what extent do the events of 17th- and 18th-century Europe substantiate this statement?

5. What benefits to European society were provided by absolute monarchs? What were the disadvantages of living in an absolutist state?

Science and the Age of Reason

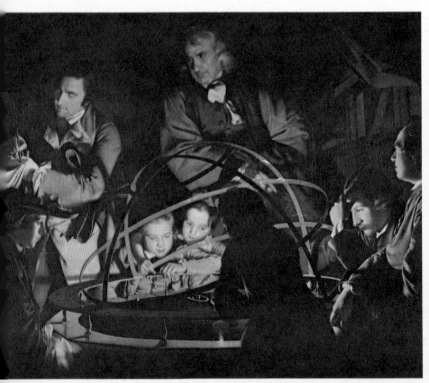

Beginning in the 16th century, discoveries in science led to a new era in Western thought. Devices such as the orrery, a mechanical model of the solar system, captured the imagination of many ordinary people, while men of learning applied scientific concepts to the study of human society. In the Age of Reason, Voltaire, a brilliant French sage, campaigned vigorously against superstition.

In a general sense, science has been defined as knowledge of the world that can be tested and proved by observation and experiment. In their search for truth, scientists meticulously record a host of facts in order to arrive at general laws about the universe.

Today, most persons speak casually of living in a scientific age and discuss eagerly the latest achievements of science. It is often assumed that scientific study can solve most economic and social problems. These attitudes, however, would not have been shared by the people of the Middle Ages. In fact, the scientific approach to life is a fairly recent development in Western thought.

Earlier chapters in this book told how the ancient Greeks studied the physical world and tried to develop rules about it. Because they based many of their theories merely on the appearance of things, rather than on experiment and accurate observations, some of their conclusions were incorrect. For example, they concluded that the earth is stationary because it does not appear to move.

The great thinkers of the Middle Ages like Thomas Aquinas devoted themselves primarily to harmonizing the classical theories—particularly those of Aristotle—with Christian teachings so that they carried the weight of Church authority. In the case of phenomena not included in this scheme of things, or where observations seemed to contradict the system, medieval scholars worked out ingenious explanations to keep the theories intact.

Beginning about the 16th century, several factors contributed to the growth of a new attitude, the scientific way of looking at the world. During the Renaissance and Reformation, traditional ideas were attacked and often discarded while new ideas took their place. Voyages of exploration and discovery added much to men's knowledge of the world. Of great importance also was the invention of the printing press, which made it possible to spread new ideas quickly and widely.

As early as the 15th century, Leonardo da Vinci had written: "Those sciences are vain and full of errors which are not born of experiment, the mother of certainty. . . ." This principle of experimentation was basic to the system of the 16th-century English philosopher Sir Francis Bacon, who urged all scientists to follow a fixed pattern in their search for truth. First, he said, the scientist should experiment or try things out. Next, he should carefully observe and record the results of his experiments. He should then be able to generalize from his experience and to state valid conclusions.

Bacon's stress on experimentation became an essential part of what is called the scientific method. This pattern of reasoning, the basis of all modern science, differed so much from past practice that it caused a revolution in the way men thought about the world.

This chapter tells how:

1. **Scientists developed new theories about the universe.**

2. **Several branches of science progressed.**

3. **Medical knowledge increased.**

4. **The Age of Reason saw the scientific method applied to many fields.**

1 Scientists developed new theories about the universe

The Greek astronomer Ptolemy, discussed in Chapter 4, believed that the earth stood still at the center of the universe, and that the sun, moon, stars, and planets moved around it. For more than a thousand years, most people accepted the Ptolemaic view of the universe, also called the *geocentric* (earth-centered) theory. It was approved by the Church, which held that since God had created the universe to serve man, man's home—the earth—must stand at the center. By the end of the Middle Ages, however, some thinkers were beginning to doubt Ptolemy's theory because of the growing number of phenomena it failed to explain.

Copernicus challenged an ancient belief. In the 16th century, a Polish churchman named Nikolaus Copernicus, who was greatly interested in mathematics and astronomy, developed his own theory about the motions of the sun and the planets. In his view, the sun, not the earth, is the center of the solar system; the earth and all the planets move around it. In addition, Copernicus argued, the earth rotates on its axis every twenty-four hours as it makes its yearly trip around the sun.

Copernicus set forth his *heliocentric* (sun-centered) theory in a book called *On the Revolutions of the Heavenly Bodies,* but he delayed publishing it for twenty years because he knew how disturbing his ideas would be to all those who accepted the Ptolemaic system as a proven fact. The book was finally published in 1543, only six weeks before Copernicus died.

As it turned out, the Copernican theory attracted very little attention at first. Hardly anyone believed it, and even astronomers found it difficult to accept. For one thing, it contradicted some astronomical observations. According to Copernicus, the stars should have been seen in different places at different times of the year, and this had not yet been observed. Copernicus also gave unsatisfactory explanations of some implications of his theory; for example, people could not understand why things did not fly off the earth if it were in motion. As these problems were resolved, the validity of the Copernican theory was reinforced; in consequence, it began to arouse greater interest and opposition.

Kepler strengthened the Copernican theory. The first professional astronomer to uphold Copernicus' views openly was a brilliant German scholar named Johann Kepler. During the early 17th century, he formulated three laws of planetary motion. Kepler's first law stated that a planet moves, not in a circle, but in an oval orbit called an ellipse, with the sun at one focus. In the second, he demonstrated that the speed of a planet increases when it comes closer to the sun. The third, or harmonic, law defined the mathematical relationship between the time required for a planet to go around the sun and its distance from the sun.

Kepler's formulas described the movements of the planets more exactly than Copernicus' writings had. They showed that the universe operates according to regular laws. One question that troubled Kepler, and one he could not answer, was why the planets remained fixed in their orbits and did not fly off into outer space.

Galileo made important discoveries. The heliocentric theory received further confirmation from a great Italian astronomer, Galileo, who has been called the father of modern experimentation. Born at Pisa, Italy, in 1564, Galileo entered the university there and at age twenty-six became professor of mathematics.

Some of Galileo's greatest contributions to science were made in the field of physics shortly after he began to teach. By rolling weights down an inclined plane set up in his laboratory, he disproved Aristotle's theory that bodies fall at speeds proportional to their weight and demonstrated that bodies of different weights fall at the same speed in the absence of air. (The story that he performed this experiment by dropping weights from the Leaning Tower of Pisa is probably only a legend.) Galileo also explained the principle of the lever and the motion of projectiles.

When he investigated the problem of sound, he was able to show that differences in tone resulted from differences in wave length—the shorter the wave length, the higher the tone.

Galileo eventually left Pisa and went to the University of Padua. There he heard about the invention of the telescope in the Netherlands and set about making his own. Eventually he built one that would enlarge the appearance of distant objects more than thirty times. Using his telescope, he discovered mountains on the moon, the stars of the Milky Way, the satellites of Jupiter, the rings of Saturn, and spots on the sun. As his knowledge of astronomy increased, Galileo became convinced that the ideas of Copernicus were correct. One reason was his discovery of the moons of Jupiter. The fact that these satellites moved around Jupiter showed that not all heavenly bodies revolved around the earth. Thus, Galileo reasoned, it was possible for at least some planets to move around the sun.

Galileo feared to say anything about his conclusions because of opposition to the heliocentric theory. In fact, in 1616, the Church had forbidden him to teach or defend the Copernican system. Not until 1632 did he publish his *Dialogue on the Two Great Systems of the World,* in which he implied that the Copernican theory was true. As he had feared, he was called before the Inquisition (a Church court) in 1633 and severely examined. Finally, his spirit broken, Galileo, almost seventy years old, agreed to retract what he had written and deny that the earth moves around the sun. According to a legend, after he publicly denied the movement of the earth, Galileo whispered to himself: "But it does move!"

Newton unified scientific knowledge. In 1642, the same year that Galileo died, a boy was born in England who was destined to become one of the greatest scientific geniuses the world has ever known. His name was Isaac Newton, and his work represented the climax of the movement that began with Copernicus.

Newton was a brilliant mathematician who taught at Cambridge University. While still in his twenties, he invented a system of mathematical calculation called calculus. He also studied light and was able to break up white light by means of a prism into the colors of the rainbow.

Newton's supreme achievement, however, was the formulation of the *law of universal gravitation,* which stated that every planet has a gravitational force whose strength depends on its mass and its position in the universe. Combined with the law of inertia (which holds that moving bodies continue to move in the same direction unless acted on by an outside force), this principle accounted for the motion and position of all bodies in the heavens, in particular for the regular movement of the earth around the sun. The law of gravitation explains why objects fall to the ground, what keeps planets in their orbits (the question that had baffled Kepler), and why bodies of water have tides. In short, the law is true not only on the earth, but anywhere in the solar system. It can be said that the law of gravitation summed up the previous century and a half of scientific discoveries by linking them in exact mathematical terms. The publication in 1687 of Newton's book outlining his theories, *Mathematical Principles of Natural Philosophy,* marks one of the great milestones in the development of science.

Section Review

1. Compare the geocentric and heliocentric theories. Which theory did the Church favor?

2. Why did the Copernican theory fail to attract much notice at first?

3. How did the work of Kepler and Galileo strengthen the Copernican theory? What were some of Galileo's other accomplishments?

4. Why was Newton's work important?

2 Several branches of science progressed

The 16th and 17th centuries saw great advances not only in astronomy, but also in chemistry and physics. Improved mathematics and new instruments helped make these advances possible.

Improved mathematics and new instruments benefited scientists. Modern mathematics began as early as the 13th century with the introduction of Arabic numerals into Europe. Other important steps were the perfection of the decimal system and the development of mathematical symbols, such as $+$, $\div$, $\times$, $=$, and $\overline{)}$.

In the 17th century, the invention of logarithms by a Scotsman named John Napier made it possible to perform multiplication and division by means of simple addition and subtraction. Moreover, finding square and cube roots became a matter of simple division. Because the time required to solve difficult mathematical problems was reduced drastically, it was said that Napier had doubled the lives of his fellow mathematicians. Other developments included analytic geometry, invented by a French mathematician and philosopher, René Descartes, and calculus, devised independently by Newton and a German philosopher, Gottfried Leibnitz.

By the 17th century, the work of science was becoming notable for its exactness and precision because new and more accurate instruments of measurement and observation had been devised. The first telescopes, made in the Netherlands about 1608, were refracting telescopes, with the image focused by a lens. This type of instrument was unwieldy because of its excessive length. In 1668 Newton invented an improved device, the reflecting telescope, with the image focused by a mirror.

Evangelista Torricelli, a disciple of Galileo, invented a mercury barometer in 1645 with which he measured atmospheric pressure. The barometer is employed in forecasting the weather. Somewhat later Gabriel Fahrenheit, a young German physicist, made the first mercury thermometer, which registered freezing at 32° and boiling at 212°. (Thermometers made previously had been able to measure temperatures only as high as 173° F. because they contained alcohol, which has a boiling point lower than that of mercury.) A Swedish astronomer, Anders Celsius, used another scale, reading 0° for freezing and 100° for boiling, when he invented the centigrade thermometer.

The first air pump capable of creating a vacuum was invented by the German physicist Otto von Guericke. In 1654, he demonstrated his apparatus. The air within two hollow metal hemispheres was withdrawn so that only the pressure of the atmosphere held them together; to pull the hemispheres apart, sixteen horses were needed, thus indicating the great strength of atmospheric pressure.

Galileo had pioneered in studying the pendulum, and his observations regarding its movements were employed later on in constructing clocks. In 1656, a Dutch astronomer, Christian Huygens, built the first successful pendulum clock, which enabled scientists to measure small intervals of time accurately.

Experimentation stimulated modern chemistry. Long a mixture of fact and magic, the study of chemistry was not put upon a scientific basis until the middle of the 17th century. Medieval alchemists believed, as did the Greeks, that all matter was made of four elements: earth, fire, water, and air. It was also thought that all things that burn contained a mysterious substance called *phlogiston* that made fire possible and was given off in burning.

The first man to practice the scientific method in chemistry was Robert Boyle, the son of an Irish nobleman. In his book *The Sceptical Chemist* (1661), he criticized alchemists and attacked the theory of the four elements. He proved that air could not be a basic element because it was a mixture of several gases. (A century later, an English scientist named Henry Cavendish proved that water could not be an element because it consisted of hydrogen and oxygen.) Boyle also defined an element as a substance that cannot be broken down into simpler parts by chemical means. He did not attempt to say how many elements there were; but within fifty years of his death, over thirty were recognized, and more were added to the list in later centuries.

Joseph Priestley, an English minister, produced several chemical substances, including ammonia and carbon monoxide. In 1774 he discovered what is known now as oxygen, calling it "dephlogisticated air." It remained for his contemporary, Antoine Lavoisier of France, to prove that a burning substance does not give off phlogiston but instead combines with "dephlogisticated air," which he termed oxygen.

Physicists studied magnetism and electricity. The first section of this chapter described some important discoveries of Galileo and Newton in the branch of physics concerning motion, sound, and light. Another branch of physics, the study of magnetism and electricity, owed much to William Gilbert, a physician to Queen Elizabeth of England. Gilbert's book *On the Magnet,* published in 1600,

explained the action of the compass needle by describing the earth itself as a large magnet. Gilbert also investigated static electricity. Ever since the time of the Greeks, thinkers had been perplexed by the power of amber, which, when rubbed, picked up bits of feathers or paper. Gilbert found that several other substances, including sulfur and glass, behave similarly. He coined the word *electric* (from the Greek word for amber, *elektron*) to apply to them.

Scientists next invented machines to produce the force that Gilbert had studied. One mechanism consisted of a globe of sulfur mounted on a revolving axis; when it was rubbed by a cloth, it produced sound and light. With this device, an electric current could be sent from one end of a thread to the other. Scientists also found a way to store electricity in the Leyden jar, one of the earliest forms of condensers.

The first important American scientist, Benjamin Franklin, believed that lightning was identical with the static electricity in the Leyden jar. In 1752 he tested his hypothesis by flying a kite with a wire tip during a thunderstorm. Electricity was conducted through the rain-soaked string to a key attached to it, thus proving Franklin's theory. This experiment led to Franklin's invention of the lightning rod to protect buildings.

Section Review

1. Of what benefit were the 17th-century discoveries in mathematics?
2. How was the work of scientists aided by the inventions of the following men: Napier; Torricelli; Fahrenheit; Celsius; Guericke; Huygens?
3. What theories delayed the scientific study of chemistry? What was proved by Boyle? Cavendish? Priestly? Lavoisier?
4. What did Gilbert and Franklin contribute to the study of electricity?

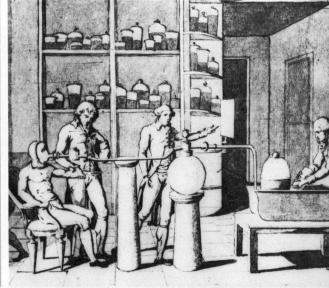

Scientific Discoveries

The first important advances in modern science were made in astronomy. Among the basic discoveries in this field were those describing how planetary movements followed systematic laws. Tycho Brahe, a Danish astronomer and teacher of Kepler, is shown above in his laboratory; he was one of the first scientists to plot the courses of celestial bodies accurately. Developments in other branches of science are shown on the opposite page. The force of air pressure was demonstrated dramatically when Otto von Guericke staged the experiment shown above. Using a pump which he invented, he removed the air from two hollow metal hemispheres after they had been sealed together. Observers were amazed that it took sixteen horses to pull the device apart. A drawing of Antoine Lavoisier's laboratory, below right, depicts him investigating the breathing process. Some discoveries captured popular interest not for their scientific importance, but simply as amusements. Below left, a scientist entertains onlookers by demonstrating the properties of electricity; a bystander amuses herself by drawing a spark from the lady's nose.

The study and practice of medicine in the Middle Ages, like other sciences, suffered from a heavy reliance on traditional ideas that were often erroneous. Physicians used "magical" potions and based their medical knowledge on the writings of authorities from ancient times, such as Galen.

Modern medicine is said to have begun with Philippus Aureolus Paracelsus, a Swiss doctor of the early 16th century, who applied chemistry to medicine. He attacked the alchemists, declaring that they should aim not to make gold but to prepare medicines. He discarded such remedies as powdered Egyptian mummy and crushed sow bugs, and instead urged experimentation with various chemical drugs to see which would be effective.

Vesalius founded the study of anatomy. Another important figure in the history of medicine was Andreas Vesalius, a native of Brussels. As a medical student at Louvain and Paris, he became disgusted with his professors; instead of examining the human body themselves, they merely read Galen. In order to perform his own dissections, Vesalius collected cadavers (sometimes robbing the gallows) and got into trouble for his illegal activity. Finally, he fled to Padua, which he helped make the most important medical center in Europe.

In 1543, the same year in which Copernicus published his revolutionary theory, Vesalius published a book entitled *On the Fabric of the Human Body*. It was the first accurate description of the anatomy of the human body. Vesalius was so bitterly attacked for his ideas by jealous colleagues that he abandoned university life while still in his thirties and became the personal physician to the Holy Roman Emperor, Charles V.

Harvey explained blood circulation. The research of William Harvey, an English physician, greatly furthered physiology, the study of the functioning of the human body. He observed his patients closely and experimented with fish, frogs, and birds in his attempts to determine how the heart worked and whether the blood moved in a continuous stream. In 1628 he wrote a book entitled *An Anatomical Exercise on the Motion of the Heart and Blood in Animals*. This slim volume of seventy-two pages explained for the first time the pumping action of the heart and how the blood circulates through the body and then returns to the heart.

Inventions aided diagnosis and treatment. Galileo is often credited with helping invent the microscope because he combined lenses to secure large magnification. The first microscope was built about 1590 by a Dutch eyeglass maker named Zacharias Janssen. In the 17th century another Dutchman, Anton van Leeuwenhoek, first saw bacteria. A careful observer, Leeuwenhoek made all his own microscopes and left a wealth of information describing the wonders he saw: red blood corpuscles, bacteria, yeast plants, and other tiny forms of life. However, he remained unaware of their significance in helping and harming man. Other aids to medical science included the clinical thermometer, which came into use in the late 1700's.

Section Review

1. What was Paracelsus' greatest contribution to modern medicine?
2. How did Vesalius' method of studying anatomy differ from that of his professors? What did he accomplish?
3. What did Harvey discover about the human body?
4. How was the study of medicine aided by Janssen? Leeuwenhoek?

4 The Age of Reason saw the scientific method applied to many fields

The inventions and discoveries of scientists indicated that the physical universe was a well-ordered machine, working according to laws of nature. Many thinkers reasoned that there must also be natural laws that would apply to men and society. All that was needed, they believed, was to discover these laws by the new scientific methods, just as astronomers had discovered the laws governing stars and planets.

Along with this devotion to science went faith in reason as the primary source of truth, and a firm belief in progress. The thinkers of the scientific era had great hopes for the future. Descartes declared:

If we use the proper methods, we shall be able to outstrip our ancestors. The Golden Age is not behind us. Not only is progress possible, but there are no limits that can be assigned to it in advance.

The period in which scientific reasoning influenced almost all intellectual life is called the Age of Reason. It lasted from about 1687 to about 1789, or from the publication of Newton's theory of gravitation to the French Revolution. It may be thought of as an age when many great thinkers examined laws, constitutions, kings, religions, and the arts to see whether they could be squared with natural law. The intellectual movement of the Age of Reason is called the Enlightenment.

The ideas of Locke and Montesquieu influenced government. Perhaps the most influential figure of the Age of Reason was John Locke, an English philosopher born in 1632. Like many men of his time, Locke believed that progress was certain if men would use their minds and follow reason. According to his theory of government, men possessed certain natural rights, chiefly to life, liberty, and property. When the people established a government, he argued, they had given it the power to protect these rights. This had been done by means of an agreement, which he called a social contract, between the people and the government. If a government did not protect their natural rights, Locke said, the people had a right to establish a new government.

Locke's social contract theory offered a powerful argument for the right of revolution against tyranny and the establishment of government by the people. Eagerly studied in Europe and America, his teachings played a large part in the American Revolution, and his ideas are to be found in the Declaration of Independence and in the United States Constitution.

Another famous thinker who applied reason to the study of government was a French nobleman and judge, the Baron de Montesquieu. In his most important work, *The Spirit of Laws,* which took him twenty years to produce, he described and analyzed many laws and constitutions from ancient times to his own age. This book, published in 1748, established Montesquieu as one of the founders of the scientific study of government, called political science. His description of a separation of powers among the three divisions of government—the executive, the legislative, and the judicial—strongly influenced the men who drafted the United States Constitution.

Voltaire attacked intolerance. An outstanding representative of the Age of Reason was François Arouet, who was born in Paris in 1694 and later gave himself the name Voltaire. A brilliant writer with a keen and sarcastic wit, Voltaire had no patience with fools or their folly.

Men of the Enlightenment responded to the spirit of the times in different ways. The English writer Swift, below left, satirized man's petty vices. In contrast, the French philosopher Rousseau, below right, praised the natural nobility of man. The Austrian composer Mozart, above, created music both graceful and profound.

His attacks on the stupidities of his time often got him into trouble. At one time he was held for eleven months in the Bastille prison in Paris because of his criticisms of nobles and high officials. Although he wrote over fifty plays and several books of history and criticism, Voltaire's best-known work is the brilliant satire *Candide* (1759), which ridicules the idea that this is "the best of all possible worlds."

Voltaire's most important influence lay in the field of religious toleration. He was himself a follower of a new religious movement, *deism*. The deists believed that God created the universe, set it up to operate by natural laws, and left it alone. Moreover, God did not interfere in the daily lives of men. Believing that it was useless to pray for help, the deists felt that religious rituals were unimportant. They criticized the quarrels and persecutions resulting from religious differences. Because Voltaire bitterly attacked the corruption he saw in organized religion, he was called an atheist. He saw the necessity of having religious beliefs, however, and once said, "If there were no God, it would be necessary to invent one."

As a skeptical rationalist, Voltaire hated fanaticism and intolerance above all else. In several cases of religious persecution, he intervened directly to secure justice. A famous saying attributed to him is: "I do not agree with a word you say, but I will defend to the death your right to say it."

Rousseau praised freedom. Although he held many of the advanced beliefs of his day, Jean Jacques Rousseau approached them through emotion rather than reason. He was born in 1712 in Switzerland of French parents; his mother died when he was an infant, and his father turned him over to the care of relatives. After being apprenticed to a lawyer and then to an engraver, Rousseau ran away and became a vagabond. For twenty years he led a hand-to-mouth life as servant, tutor, music teacher, and hack writer. Undisciplined and emotional, he was a slave to his feelings.

In 1750 Rousseau became famous overnight when an essay with which he had won a contest was published. This *Discourse on the Arts and Sciences* claimed that before man was civilized he had been pure and good; that mankind had been corrupted by laws, religion, education, and business, and could recover its lost purity and goodness only by getting "back to nature." This idea of the nobility of the simple life became especially popular in France. The queen had a peasant village built at Versailles, where she and her attendants played at being milkmaids.

One of Rousseau's most important books was *Social Contract* (1762). Like Locke, Rousseau believed in a social contract between people and their government. However, he did not justify revolution but instead argued that men are restrained by the General Will—that is, the concept of what is best for the state. Rousseau, who championed freedom and individual dignity, believed that democratic elections would reveal the General Will. However, his doctrine has also been used to justify dictatorship, on the grounds that one man of superior talents can interpret the General Will for all the people.

Diderot's encyclopedia helped spread the new ideas. Another giant of the Age of Reason was Denis Diderot of France, who conceived the idea of compiling the new knowledge and ideas of the Enlightenment in an encyclopedia. He wanted his encyclopedia to champion tolerance, denounce superstition, and criticize unjust practices of the time, as well as to give facts about all branches of learning.

The Arts in the Age of Reason mirrored a sophisticated society dominated by pleasure-loving aristocrats. At left, a sketch illustrates the carefully prescribed arm motions for a dance of the period. Antoine Watteau, a French artist famous for his elegant style, painted "The Music Party," above, a leisurely group gathered on a spacious porch. The columns are typical of baroque architecture. Artificial elegance became even more pronounced in rococo architecture and art. An example is the German porcelain group above right, where a boy presents a birthday bouquet to his mother as his sister and a maid look on. Below right, a caricature by the English artist Thomas Rowlandson depicts aristocratic idlers in a coffee house.

Many important writers, including Voltaire, Montesquieu, and Rousseau, submitted articles to Diderot. Thirty years in preparation, this encyclopedia ran to thirty-five large volumes. This huge work, published between 1751 and 1772, played a major role in circulating the new ideas of the Enlightenment. Thousands of sets were published in France, and many editions appeared in other parts of Europe.

Reformers wanted to improve human welfare. The Age of Reason stimulated concern for the welfare of all human beings because thinkers demanded reform of customs that they considered unreasonable. Religious liberty greatly increased, and notable improvements were made in public health and in the treatment of the sick and the insane.

Prison reform also received attention. Jails had always been dirty, unhealthful places, governed by cruel and inhuman laws. For example, in England—which was more advanced than most nations—some persons who had been acquitted of crimes were not discharged from prison until they had paid their "board bill" to their jailers who, receiving no regular salary, depended for their living upon fees collected from the inmates. Such conditions improved partly as the result of a reform movement led by John Howard, a county sheriff, who appeared before Parliament to urge improvement. In 1777 he published a book called *The State of the Prisons in England and Wales,* which stressed the need for better prison administration. Prisons, Howard argued, should not exist for punishment alone; rehabilitation or reform of the convicts should be considered a primary function.

Education also felt the breath of reform. The harsh methods of discipline common at that time were relaxed, and efforts were made to provide schools for the common people. One of the most important influences on education was Rousseau. He wrote that children should not be treated as miniature adults or burdened with the useless customs of high society, but should be encouraged to express themselves in their own way.

Elegant refinement characterized the arts. Reason ruled not only scientists and scholars but also writers, painters, and musicians. The creative artists of the 18th century prided themselves on their rationalism and self-control and tried to follow definite rules in their works. Many of them admired and imitated the classical arts of Greece and Rome—a movement known as neoclassicism.

The Age of Reason was notable for its satire. The most successful poet of the time was Alexander Pope of England, whose elegant verses exposed the follies and pretensions of contemporary society. One of the best-known prose works was *Gulliver's Travels,* written in 1726 by Jonathan Swift in the form of an adventure story. Although the tale has since become a great favorite with children, the deeper meanings of its bitter satire on the pettiness of man's quarrels, wars, and vices were intended for adults.

Other types of writing benefited from the emphasis during this period on reason and clarity. One of the first works in the novel form was Daniel Defoe's realistic adventure story, *Robinson Crusoe.* Many critics, however, consider the first novel to be Samuel Richardson's *Pamela,* the romantic adventures of a servant girl which today would be classified as "soap opera." Another famous early novel was Henry Fielding's *Tom Jones,* a fascinating picture of 18th-century England. A landmark in the writing of history was Edward Gibbon's masterful six-volume study, entitled *Decline and Fall of the Roman Empire.*

The French produced three great dramatic writers: Pierre Corneille and Jean Racine retold stories from classical mythology in their tragedies; the witty comedies of Molière exposed pretense and hypocrisy, particularly among physicians, lawyers, and the newly rich bourgeoisie.

The music of the 18th century, like the literature, was balanced, controlled, and refined. While England and France set the tone for literature in the Age of Reason, its greatest musicians came from Germany and Austria. Religious themes predominated in the work of two Germans, George Frederick Handel, composer of the *Messiah,* and his great contemporary, Johann Sebastian Bach. The Austrian musician, Franz Joseph Haydn, is noted for his chamber music and for the introduction of a new musical form, the symphony. His pupil, Wolfgang Amadeus Mozart, one of the most gifted composers in the history of music, wrote more than 600 musical compositions, including the famous operas *Don Giovanni* and *The Marriage of Figaro.*

In architecture, the grand and elaborate baroque style typified by Louis XIV's palace at Versailles was refined into the more delicate style called rococo. Beginning about 1750, there was a reaction against both these forms in favor of a simple, restrained neoclassicism; buildings influenced by this trend included St. Paul's Cathedral in London and Mount Vernon, George Washington's home.

Section Review

1. How did the important inventions and discoveries of scientists lead to the Age of Reason?
2. What was Locke's social contract theory? How did it tend to encourage revolution?
3. How did Voltaire reflect the Age of Reason in his religious beliefs and in his attacks on intolerance?
4. What were some of Rousseau's basic ideas in the fields of government and of education?
5. Why did the Age of Reason lead to humanitarian reforms? What were some of them?
6. Show, with examples, how works of literature and art expressed the ideals of the Age of Reason.

Chapter 17   A Review

A new era in Western thought began in the 16th century with the development of experimental science. One of its most important aspects was a changed view of the solar system. Some men of the Middle Ages had questioned the Ptolemaic theory that placed the earth at the center of the universe. Copernicus went further by proposing a new heliocentric theory. Though his system received little attention at first, the observations and writings of later scientists refined it and brought it into wider acceptance. Kepler's laws of planetary motion strengthened the heliocentric theory, and some of Galileo's many discoveries helped confirm the Copernican system, although the Church forced him to retract his views. The so-called Copernican revolution culminated in Newton, who unified the discoveries of his predecessors by developing the law of universal gravitation.

Scientists were aided both by new mathematical tools (logarithms and calculus) and instruments of measurement (clocks, barometers, and thermometers). Chemistry emerged from the superstitions of the alchemists with the work of Boyle, Priestley, and Lavoisier. Physics advanced markedly after the outstanding discoveries of Galileo, Newton, Gilbert, and Benjamin Franklin.

Medical science, too, made great strides forward through the work of Paracelsus, Vesalius, and Harvey. The invention of the microscope and the thermometer aided doctors in their diagnosis and treatment of disease.

Men were impressed with the fact that the universe seemed to run according to scientific principles that could be discovered by reason. During the Age of Reason, they tried to find similar principles that would apply to almost every field of knowledge. Locke and Montesquieu investigated government; Voltaire and Rousseau turned searching eyes on morality, religion, and education. Diderot helped popularize the new ideas in his encyclopedia. Humanitarians urged reforms in several fields. Reason ruled the arts, as seen in the satire of Pope, Swift, and Molière, the formal music of Haydn and Mozart, and the balanced restraint of neoclassic architecture.

The Time

Some of the following are correctly placed under the period during which they appeared, and others are not. Rearrange the list so that all appear in their proper time span.

1501-1600
first telescopes
On the Fabric of the Human Body
An Anatomical Exercise on the Motion of the Heart and Blood in Animals
On the Revolutions of the Heavenly Bodies
Don Giovanni

1601-1700
Diderot's encyclopedia
logarithms
Dialogue on the Two Great Systems of the World
The Spirit of Laws

1701-1800
The Sceptical Chemist
Candide
Mathematical Principles of Natural Philosophy
Gulliver's Travels
The State of the Prisons in England and Wales
Social Contract (Rousseau)

The People

1. How did each of these men challenge the traditions of their society?

Locke	Rousseau	Diderot
Vesalius	Swift	Montesquieu
Voltaire	Howard	Boyle
Pope	Molière	Bacon
Cavendish	Paracelsus	

2. Copernicus, Galileo, Kepler, and Newton all worked on a related set of problems in astronomy. Explain how each added something new to an understanding of the solar system.

3. What common interest was shared by Fahrenheit and Celsius? by William Gilbert and Benjamin Franklin? by Joseph Priestley and Antoine Lavoisier?

4. The study of higher mathematics depends on the use of logarithms, analytic geometry, and calculus. Who were the inventors of each of these mathematical advances?

5. In what field did each of these men make a major contribution?

Mozart	Gibbon	Fielding
Harvey	Bach	Defoe

Historical Terms

1. Sir Francis Bacon's belief in experimentation was the basis of modern *science* and the *scientific method*. Explain the meaning of these terms.

2. How does a view of the universe based on the *heliocentric* theory differ from one based on the *geocentric* theory?

3. Technology and scientific theory are often interdependent. For each of these inventions tell what scientist is responsible for it, the date it was invented, and why it was important: mercury barometer; microscope; pendulum clock.

4. The first true chemists asked themselves these basic questions: Of what is matter composed? What happens during the process of burning? The following terms were important in their research. Define each one: phlogiston; dephlogisticated air; oxygen; element.

5. Both Locke and Rousseau thought of government as a *social contract*. What did Locke mean by this? What did Rousseau mean by the General Will?

6. In what order did the artistic styles, *rococo, baroque,* and *neoclassicism,* appear in

Europe? What were the characteristics of each style?

7. How did the beliefs of the religious movement known as *deism* reflect the ideas of the Age of Reason?

8. What was meant by the Enlightenment?

Questions for Critical Thinking

1. Why is it said that Galileo rather than Copernicus is the father of modern experimentation?

2. Explain with pertinent examples why the 17th century might be called the "century of genius."

3. Upon what basis could Montesquieu be considered an honorary citizen of the United States?

4. The philosophy of the 18th century is often called the Enlightenment. In what ways were writers and philosophers "enlightened"?

5. During the 18th century, organized religion was under attack. How does an understanding of the Age of Reason help explain this situation?

6. Choose one person who, in your opinion, best exemplifies the ideas of the Age of Reason. Explain your choice.

7. Explain what is meant by this statement: "The law of gravitation summed up the previous century and a half of scientific discoveries by linking them in exact mathematical terms."

8. Was the 18th century an era of optimism or pessimism? Explain.

9. How successful were the 18th-century philosophers in applying scientific method to the study of society as a whole?

The Age of Democratic Revolutions

The liberal ideas of the Enlightenment stimulated revolutionary movements aimed at abolishing absolutist monarchies and extending the rights of ordinary citizens. In America, colonists broke away from England and signed a Declaration of Independence, left, carefully summarizing their grievances. In France, a long and bloody revolution erupted many times into mob violence. At right, an executioner displays the head of Louis XVI to the waiting crowd.

On the night of October 17, 1787, a young Englishman traveling in France returned to his quarters after having had dinner with a group of French friends. Throughout the meal the major topic of conversation had concerned the political conditions in France. What the young man heard deeply disturbed him. In his diary he recorded his impressions of the evening.

> One opinion pervaded the whole company, that they are on the eve of some great revolution in the government: that everything points to it . . . a great ferment amongst all ranks of men, who are eager for some change without knowing what to look to or to hope for: and a strong leaven of liberty, increasing every hour since the American revolution. . . .

The troubled young diarist was Arthur Young, who later became well known throughout Europe as an agricultural expert. For many months he traveled all over France, carefully noting conditions, recording his observations, and becoming more and more convinced that the nation was on the verge of a profound upheaval. Less than two years after that disturbing dinner party, the most important revolution of modern times erupted in France.

The French Revolution had been in the making for a long period of time. By the end of the 18th century, the people had lost faith in the existing system of government, feeling it to be unjust and unfair. Loyalty to the monarchy was undermined by a growing desire for change, an attitude that reforms were necessary and right.

A similar sense of dissatisfaction had existed among the American colonists scarcely twenty years before Young's visit to France, as it had among the English themselves a century earlier. The specific conditions differed in the case of each nation, but the general problem was the same: People were unhappy with the way they were being governed. The idea of the divine right of kings and royal absolutism gave way to the idea that kings must share their power with parliaments, the representatives of the people, because governments existed for the benefit of the people and not for a privileged few.

These democratic ideas grew so widespread that the late 17th and the 18th centuries became an age of democratic revolutions, as first Englishmen, and then Americans and Frenchmen, resorted to force to change their governmental systems. When the age came to a close, these revolutions had established more firmly than ever before the principles and practices of constitutional government, of representative institutions, and of democratic procedure.

This chapter tells how:

1. **The Puritan Revolution curbed absolutism in England.**

2. **England strengthened its democracy with a bloodless revolution.**

3. **The American Revolution gave birth to a new nation.**

4. **Growing dissatisfaction paved the way to revolution in France.**

5. **The French Revolution brought drastic changes.**

6. **Napoleon was a son of the revolution.**

1 **The Puritan Revolution curbed absolutism in England**

The 17th century was an age of absolutism in most of Europe. In England, however, conditions were different. The power of the English kings never became so great as that of their European contemporaries because of the importance of

Parliament. Even the Tudors, who had almost unlimited power, had to reckon with Parliament. Without its consent, a ruler could not make or repeal laws, or impose new taxes. Parliament's "power of the purse" was an effective tool for curbing an overly ambitious king.

The Tudors shrewdly avoided conflicts with Parliament, particularly over finances. Although they acted upon the principle of divine right, they refrained from discussing it. With strong support from the middle class, to whose interests they catered, the Tudors achieved a high degree of success and England enjoyed a long period of prosperity.

James I raised an important issue. Trouble began when Elizabeth I died in 1603 and James, king of Scotland, succeeded to the throne as the first of the Stuart kings. (He was the son of Mary, Queen of Scots, who had been imprisoned and finally beheaded on the charge of plotting against Elizabeth.) For the first time, England and Scotland had the same king, though each maintained its own separate government.

James I, born and raised in Scotland, did not understand the English very well. He was a learned man who lacked common sense; his contemporaries called him "the wisest fool in Christendom." To make matters worse, James had exaggerated notions about the powers of the king. He was a firm believer in the divine right of kings and even wrote a book about it. Particularly annoying to the English was his habit of lecturing Parliament on the subject of royal power. Not content with exercising the considerable authority he inherited from the Tudors, he insisted that any restriction whatever on his power was wrong.

Since the English had a long tradition of parliamentary checks on royal power, James' position was unwise, especially since he was in constant need of money.

Parliament became so irritated with him that it refused to grant him the revenues he needed. In effect, the monarch had raised an important constitutional question—whether the king or Parliament was supreme in England.

The problem was intensified by the profound changes which English society had undergone during the 16th century. Two classes had grown greatly in importance. One, the gentry, included landed gentlemen (also called squires) ranking just below the nobility. The other consisted of merchants and manufacturers. Both groups had considerable economic strength and, through their representatives in the House of Commons, were eager to increase their political power at the king's expense.

Another factor that complicated the situation was religion. The religious compromise worked out during the reign of Elizabeth proved satisfactory to many Englishmen but displeased several groups. One group included the Roman Catholics; another was the High Church party, composed of people who wished to reintroduce more Roman Catholic practices and ceremonies into the Anglican Church. At the other extreme were Calvinist Protestants, including many of the politically ambitious gentry and middle class, who felt that the English Church was too "popish." Most of them wanted it to reform, particularly by abandoning such rituals as kneeling and making the sign of the cross at baptism. Because these reformers insisted on "purifying" the English Church, they were generally referred to as Puritans. Another group of Calvinist Protestants, the Presbyterians, wanted a new type of national church without bishops; they were especially strong in Scotland. Still another group of Protestants favored completely independent congregations, and were known as Separatists.

When James became king, the Puritans presented him with a petition asking for reforms, which he refused to grant, warning them that if they did not conform to the practices of the Church of England, he would "harry them out of the land."

Charles I complicated the quarrel. When James died in 1625, his son Charles succeeded him on the throne as Charles I. Like his father, Charles I favored absolutism and opposed the Puritans. Parliament, with many Puritan members, was just as suspicious of Charles as it had been of his father. Hence, it continued the practice of voting the monarchy inadequate revenues, much to the irritation of the new king.

Charles tried to raise money by forcing his subjects to contribute funds to the government; rich men who would not pay were imprisoned and poor men were drafted into the army. In 1628 Charles particularly needed funds because of the naval expeditions he had sent to aid the French Huguenots of La Rochelle. Parliament took advantage of the situation to force the king to agree to the Petition of Right, which condemned arbitrary taxation and imprisonment. Friction continued, however, and Charles finally reached such a deadlock with Parliament that he decided to by-pass it altogether. In 1629 he dismissed it and ruled alone for the next eleven years.

Charles hoped that by providing the country with efficient personal government he could diminish the stature of Parliament, but he antagonized too many important groups. He made enemies of the Puritans by persecuting their leaders and supporting the High Church party; as a consequence, thousands of Puritans emigrated to America in the 1630's. In addition, Charles alarmed property owners with his attempts to raise money through forced loans. When he tried to impose the Anglican religion upon the Presbyterian Scotch, open rebellion broke out in 1638.

Desperately in need of funds to put down the Scottish rebellion, Charles finally recalled Parliament in 1640. Its members refused to vote any money, however, unless Charles made certain concessions. He refused and after only three weeks dismissed the assembly, known as the Short Parliament. He then called for new elections. The Parliament that reconvened later in 1640 remained in session for the next twenty years, and was appropriately called the Long Parliament.

The Long Parliament, with essentially the same membership as the Short Parliament, was no more accommodating than its predecessor. Before it would grant any money, it demanded important reforms:
1) Parliament must meet at least once every three years.
2) Royal courts, responsible only to the king, must be abolished.
3) The king must no longer levy taxes without the consent of Parliament.
Although Charles reluctantly agreed, he had no intention of keeping his word.

Cavaliers fought Roundheads in the Civil War. Led by the Puritan faction, Parliament made further demands. The king, at the head of a band of soldiers, invaded the House of Commons to arrest five of its leaders, but they had fled. Armed Londoners came to the defense of Parliament, and the king went northward to collect an army. About 120 Lords and 200 Commoners joined him, and he gathered an army from the north and west of the country. The followers of Charles were called Cavaliers; they included most of the nobles and large landholders, and they opposed extreme Protestantism.

About 30 Lords and 300 Commoners, including many Puritans, remained in Parliament to govern the country. They raised an army which drew its support from the south and east of England. The men of Parliament and supporters of the

ENGLISH CIVIL WAR
1642-1646

SCOTLAND

Royal Authority

Parliamentary Authority

x Battle

MARSTON MOOR x

•Preston

•Hull

•Nottingham

NASEBY x

Worcester•

EDGEHILL x

Oxford•

•London

•Bristol

NEWBURY x

•Plymouth

Prepared by
Rand McNally & Co., Chicago

Puritans were called Roundheads because they cut their hair short as a protest against the elaborate hair styles of the day.

Civil war began in 1642. Fighting took place on a small scale, and, though the Battle of Edgehill in October was indecisive, other early engagements favored the royalists. Then the Roundheads discovered within their midst an unknown country squire with extraordinary military and leadership qualities. He was Oliver Cromwell, a devout Puritan. Using severe discipline, he trained an army which defeated the Cavaliers at Marston Moor in 1644 and again in 1645 in the Battle of Naseby. A year later the king surrendered and the war ended.

For the next two years king and Parliament tried unsuccessfully to come to terms. Cromwell strongly distrusted the king, but Parliament was reluctant to deal harshly with him. Finally Cromwell took matters into his own hands and, with the support of the army, excluded nearly 100 members from Parliament. The remaining members convicted Charles of treason and had him beheaded in 1649.

A Commonwealth replaced the monarchy. After the death of Charles I, Parliament declared England to be "a Commonwealth and Free State . . . without any king or House of Lords." But it was easier to abolish the monarchy than to establish a new system of government acceptable to the people. Each of the three chief groups in the country—Parliament, the army, and the royalists—had its own ideas as to how the government should be run. The House of Commons was composed of middle-class landowners and merchants who opposed extreme forms of democratic government. The army, however, included a great many persons from the lower economic classes with advanced political ideas who demanded reforms, such as a written constitution and broadened suffrage. The royalists, on the other hand, wanted the monarchy restored.

Disgusted with all the quarrels, Cromwell took over more and more control of the government. In 1653 he abolished Parliament altogether and became Lord Protector of England under a written constitution called the Instrument of Government. Cromwell himself believed in a large measure of political and religious freedom, but the continued fighting among different factions forced him to rule England as a military dictator.

Cromwell was also forced to take other steps he considered unwise, such as closing theaters and alehouses, prohibiting mixed dancing and cockfighting, and ruling that games on Sunday were illegal. His chief supporters were the Puritans, who believed these idle amusements to be sinful.

When Cromwell died in 1658, there was no one strong enough to replace him.

Furthermore, most Englishmen had had their fill of Puritanism. In 1660 a new Parliament called on the son of Charles I, an exile in France, to become king, and he gladly accepted the invitation.

The so-called Puritan Revolution produced several important changes in the English government. It deprived the monarchy of arbitrary courts and the power to make laws by royal proclamation or to levy taxes without the consent of Parliament. The revolution also gave rise to democratic ideas—that the people should have a voice in the government, and that they should be granted religious liberty.

Section Review

1. In what way did the English monarchy under the Tudors differ from most of the monarchies in Europe?
2. Why did both James I and his son Charles I quarrel with Parliament?
3. Explain why personal rule by Charles I failed.
4. How and why did Oliver Cromwell become a dictator?
5. What were the chief results of the Puritan Revolution?

2 **England strengthened its democracy with a bloodless revolution**

Although the Puritan Revolution had limited the English monarchy, kings still had considerable authority. In effect, power was shared by king and Parliament.

Conflicts continued during the Restoration. In May 1660 royalty was restored to England in the person of Charles II, son of the unfortunate Charles I. Thirty years old at the time, Charles II was gay and fun-loving; his subjects called him the Merry Monarch. During his twenty-five year reign, known as the Restoration, the English went as far in the direction of

amusement as the Puritans had gone in the direction of austerity. For all his gaiety, Charles was clever and intelligent, with common sense and wit. He was lazy and cynical, however, and did not accomplish much for England.

Charles II favored the Roman Catholic religion and wanted to restore royal power. Mindful of his father's fate, he moved cautiously so as not to provoke Parliament. Nevertheless, some people suspected his plans, and once more the issues of religion and royal despotism began to emerge.

The controversy had two important results. One was the passage in 1679 of the Habeas Corpus Act, a safeguard against arbitrary imprisonment. Anyone who believed himself to be unjustly imprisoned could obtain a writ of habeas corpus (Latin for "you have the body"), which compelled the government to explain why the prisoner was being held. Another consequence was the beginning of modern political parties. The Whig party, which represented the middle class and the upper nobility, supported Parliament. The Tory party, representing the lesser nobility and the gentry, supported the king.

Since Charles II had no legitimate heirs, the issue between Whigs and Tories was reduced to the question of who would succeed Charles on the throne. The legitimate successor was Charles' brother James, an ardent Roman Catholic and proponent of divine right. Although the Whigs tried to have a law passed to keep him off the throne, the Tories defeated it; when Charles died in 1685, James became king.

The Glorious Revolution confirmed the power of Parliament. James II, intent on reasserting his own authority and that of the Roman Catholic Church, soon antagonized almost everyone. His open contempt for Parliament and his support of the Church of Rome alarmed even the Tories. His opponents were somewhat reassured by the fact that he was growing old. They were also aware that after his death the throne would pass to his two daughters by his first wife, who were Protestants. However, the king's second wife gave birth to a son in 1688, creating the possibility of a long line of Roman Catholic monarchs. Tories then joined with Whigs in offering the crown to James' older daughter, Mary, who had married William III of Orange, the ruler of the Dutch and a stanch Protestant.

In November of 1688, William and Mary landed in England at the head of a large army. James could offer little resistance, because his army commanders did not support him. He fled to France, and William and Mary were proclaimed the new rulers of England and Scotland. This reassertion of parliamentary authority is known as the Glorious Revolution, or Bloodless Revolution.

In order to safeguard the results of the Glorious Revolution, Parliament passed several important measures, usually called the Revolution Settlement. One of these, the Bill of Rights of 1689, guaranteed freedom of speech in Parliament, provided for frequent meetings of that body, and forbade the king to interfere with the election of its members. Other clauses guaranteed the right of the people to petition the government, forbade excessive bail, and protected the nation from the illegal use of the army. Another part of the Revolution Settlement, also passed in 1689, was the Toleration Act, which granted religious freedom to various Protestant groups, although those who were not members of the Anglican Church could not hold public office. A third measure, the Act of Settlement of 1691, provided that no Roman Catholic could be ruler of England, automatically excluding the descendants of James II by his second wife.

By making the king subordinate to Parliament, the Glorious Revolution was a striking victory for the principles of parliamentary government and the rule of law. It was also a victory for the principle of the right of rebellion against tyranny. After 1688, government in England was thought of as a sort of contract between king and people, with each having recognized responsibilities and obligations. The Glorious Revolution thus established a constitutional monarchy—that is, a democratic nation with a royal head.

Cabinet government developed under a new line of kings. Anne, the second daughter of James II, came to the throne in 1701. The last of the reigning Stuarts, she died in 1714 leaving no heirs. The Act of Settlement had stipulated that the throne was to go to the monarch's closest Protestant relative, who in this case was a German, the elector of Hanover. Although this ruler became George I of England and began the Hanoverian dynasty, his heart remained in his native land. He spoke no English and spent much time in Germany.

Unfamiliar as he was with English conditions, George I depended greatly upon his cabinet for advice and assistance. This institution had first taken shape under Charles II, when the most influential members of his Privy Council met with him in his private office, or cabinet. The cabinet members belonged to Parliament and most of them were ministers—administrative heads of governmental departments. Beginning with the reign of George I, the cabinet came to exercise true executive functions, such as policy formulation. This development owed much to Robert Walpole, the leader of the Whig party.

It so happened that for half a century after 1714 the Whigs controlled the House of Commons. Thus George I and his successor George II, who ruled from 1727 to 1760, chose their ministers from the Whig party. Walpole, who headed the party from 1721 to 1742, served during this time

The English Government underwent profound changes in the first 150 years after the Tudors. The monarchy lost much of its power as a result of the Puritan Revolution, satirized above as a fight between Cavalier and Roundhead dogs. Parliament asserted its supremacy in the Glorious Revolution, depicted in the cartoon below left. Fruit from an orange tree (representing the new ruler, William of Orange) knocks the crown from the head of James II and fells one of his officials. The cabinet assumed executive powers under the guidance of Robert Walpole, whose economic program drew criticism; he is shown below right as a fat tax collector on a barrel drawn by an angry British lion.

as the principal minister—a position that later came to be called prime minister.

Walpole was always careful to see that cabinet members were chosen from the majority party in the House of Commons. In this way he hoped to gain support for executive policies from the legislative arm, or Parliament as a whole. He carried this principle to its logical conclusion in 1742, when he resigned as prime minister because he lost his majority in the House of Commons. Walpole's actions firmly established the tradition that the executive branch of government in Great Britain must resign when its policies were no longer approved by the House of Commons. This principle removed the danger of conflict between the legislative and executive branches of the government, and meant that the actual executive—the prime minister and cabinet—came to represent the dominant party in Parliament.

Section Review

1. Describe two important developments that resulted from political conflicts during the reign of Charles II.
2. Why did Parliament force James II to abdicate? In what respects was the Glorious Revolution a victory for the principles of parliamentary government and the rule of law?
3. Why and how did cabinet government develop under the Hanoverian rulers?

3 **The American Revolution gave birth to a new nation**

While England was undergoing upheaval and change, its colonies in North America had grown and prospered. For over a century after the establishment of Jamestown in 1607, the colonists went their own way with little interference from the mother country and slight influence on the rest of the world.

The colonies and England grew apart. It has been said that the American Revolution really began when the first Englishman set foot on the soil of the New World. Certain conditions in America tended almost from the beginning to separate the colonists from their mother country.

To begin with, a new national type— the American—was created. Society in the New World differed from that in Europe. Social position and wealth counted for less. The opportunities for ambitious people to better themselves were greater, since the availability of cheap land enabled almost everyone to own some property. The rough life of the frontier added another new element. Englishmen became more self-sufficient, less inclined to follow tradition. The population differed not only because of changes among the English immigrants, but also because of the presence of other nationalities. Many hundreds of adventurous settlers emigrated from Scotland, Germany, the Netherlands, France, and Ireland.

Another factor that helped set the American colonies apart was the growth of democratic ideals. When settlers crossed the Atlantic, they carried with them the ideas of the Puritan Revolution. For example, thousands of Puritans who opposed the tyranny of Charles I moved to Massachusetts; as a result, many New Englanders were familiar with John Locke and his social contract theory.

Another important difference involved government. The American colonists enjoyed more self-government than any other colonists in the world. Every colony had a representative assembly of colonists. The first of these assemblies, the Virginia House of Burgesses, was established as early as 1619. Like their ancestors in England, colonial lawmakers soon discovered "the power of the purse." They exerted pressure on the royal governor by threatening to withhold funds. Local affairs, such as road building and repair and the enforcement of laws, were in the hands of the colonists themselves.

The English tightened their control. Like most European nations in the 17th and 18th centuries, England embraced the policy of mercantilism. According to this system, colonies were supposed to help the mother country by supplying raw materials and by buying finished goods. Starting about 1650, England passed a series of laws, the Navigation Acts, to control colonial trade. However, for more than a century, it did not enforce them strictly, and the American colonists, persistently ignoring the acts, carried on a profitable illegal trade.

After England defeated France in the French and Indian War in 1763, the English government initiated a new policy toward its North American colonies. The colonists had contributed very little to the war, which was won largely with British troops, ships, and taxes. Moreover, the constant threat from the Indians in the interior necessitated continued protection from British troops, since the colonists provided none of their own. England reasoned that the colonists should share in the financial burden. Therefore the English government took steps to enforce the old Navigation Acts and also passed a series of new laws to raise money.

The Quartering Act of 1765 required Americans to provide quarters, various supplies, and transportation for British troops in the colonies. The Stamp Act, passed the same year, required the purchase of stamps for newspapers, playing cards, and various legal documents. Although the tax was not very high and the practice was common in most of Europe, the colonists bitterly opposed the law as "taxation without representation." Opposition was so intense that in 1766 the act was repealed.

The next seven years were relatively calm. Then in 1773 Parliament tried to ease the financial distress of the East India Company, which had a surplus of Chinese tea, by granting the company the right to sell tea directly to local retailers in the colonies. This plan would have resulted in lower tea prices for the colonial consumer, but it would also have meant bypassing American importers. Colonists resented this monopoly and set up a boycott against the company's tea in all American ports. In Boston a group of citizens disguised as Indians threw a cargo of tea into Boston harbor—an incident known as the Boston Tea Party.

The British Parliament decided that the time had come to teach the colonists a lesson, and in 1774 it passed five so-called Intolerable Acts. These acts closed Boston harbor to shipping, ordered the colonists to cease their opposition, compelled them to pay for their acts of vandalism, and virtually revoked the charter of Massachusetts. The punishment was much too harsh, for closing the harbor meant economic ruin for Boston, and rescinding the charter ended local self-government. But King George III declared that "The die is cast. The colonies must either triumph or submit." Until this point the dispute had revolved around the problem of taxation; now the quarrel became a question of whether the colonists had the right to govern themselves.

American colonists won their freedom. In April 1775, British troops in Boston were ordered to confiscate munitions that the colonists were storing at Concord. On their way to Concord they met at Lexington a band of Minute Men, as the Massachusetts militia was called. Someone fired "the shot heard round the world," and fighting broke out. By the time the British returned to Boston, they had lost a third of their men.

At first, most American colonists did not want to break away from England. Only a determined minority of enthusiastic patriots argued for complete independence. As fighting continued, however, feelings grew more intense. The moderates gave way to the more radical patriots, especially since the British government seemed unwilling to compromise. The climax came on July 4, 1776, when representatives of the colonies, meeting in a Continental Congress, adopted the Declaration of Independence. This famous document was the work of a Virginian, Thomas Jefferson, who later became President of the United States. In stirring language, it set forth Locke's theory of natural rights to justify the colonists' right to revolt against British rule.

After that there was no turning back. What began as an American struggle for independence was almost immediately transformed into another world-wide conflict for empire among the European nations. During the next two years, the French secretly supplied the colonists with munitions. When the Americans won a decisive victory against the British in 1778 at Saratoga in New York, the French, anxious to strike back at the British, decided that the Americans were a good political risk and officially entered the war on the American side. A year later, Spain declared war on England, and both Spain and France sent strong naval forces to fight the English in the West Indies. The Netherlands joined the allies against England in 1780. England found itself fighting

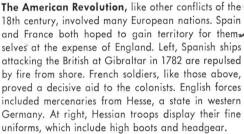

The American Revolution, like other conflicts of the 18th century, involved many European nations. Spain and France both hoped to gain territory for themselves at the expense of England. Left, Spanish ships attacking the British at Gibraltar in 1782 are repulsed by fire from shore. French soldiers, like those above, proved a decisive aid to the colonists. English forces included mercenaries from Hesse, a state in western Germany. At right, Hessian troops display their fine uniforms, which include high boots and headgear.

not only for its North American colonies but for its empire as well.

The aid of the French fleet and 6000 French troops was decisive. In 1781 George Washington, who commanded the American forces, accepted the surrender of the British general, Lord Charles Cornwallis, at Yorktown, Virginia. In 1783 a peace treaty was signed and England recognized the thirteen colonies as independent.

The English navy, in a striking comeback in the final year of the war, defeated the fleets of France and Spain, so that England did not lose any other colonies.

The American Revolution had important results. Although independence did not immediately give the new American nation a democratic system of government,

the seeds of democracy were well planted. The Revolution ended many reminders of the European class system, such as inherited titles. In its place was established the principle of equality before the law. Voting rights, at first confined to the property-owning classes, were soon broadened.

For the first time in modern history, a large nation established a republic of a federal type—that is, an organization of separate states having a central government, with the states yielding some of their sovereignty to unite into one nation. Heretofore a republican form of government had been thought practical only for small nations, such as the Netherlands or Switzerland. The Americans also developed a strong belief in written constitutions and the principle of limited powers of government. All thirteen states adopted written constitutions, each of which provided for the separation of legislative, executive, and judicial powers. In addition, each state constitution incorporated a bill of rights that repeated the philosophy of natural rights so eloquently stated in the Declaration of Independence.

Finally, the successful revolt of the American colonists and their statement in the great Declaration became a symbol and source of inspiration to all peoples seeking freedom, appealing to men in general, not just to Americans. It declared to the world at large that what the Americans had done, all peoples had the right to do. The American Revolution thus became an important factor in later independence movements.

Section Review

1. What factors made the American colonies grow apart from England?
2. Why did England change its trade policy toward the colonists after 1763? Name some events that led the colonists to proclaim their independence.
3. In what respects was the American War for Independence part of a worldwide conflict among European nations?
4. What were some of the results of the American Revolution?

4 **Growing dissatisfaction paved the way to revolution in France**

The French government had aided the Americans in their revolutionary struggle chiefly to harass the British. Many Frenchmen, however, sympathized deeply with the ideas of freedom and rebellion against tyranny for which the Americans fought. The success of the American revolt encouraged those Frenchmen who believed that far-reaching reforms were necessary for their own nation.

In some ways France at that time occupied an enviable position. With a population nearly triple that of England, a fine textile industry, and a flourishing export trade, France was probably the richest country in Europe. In all Western nations French was the language of the educated classes, and Paris was regarded as the cultural center of the Western world.

France was also the home of the Enlightenment. Through the writings of Montesquieu, Voltaire, and Rousseau, most educated Europeans came to believe in science, reason, and the inevitability of progress. They expected progress to come through government—provided there was enlightened leadership at the top. After about 1740, this faith became translated into a program of enlightened despotism as monarchs in most countries of Europe instituted reforms in an effort to make their governments more efficient. Ironically, France, the center of the Enlightenment, benefited least from enlightened despotism. Because the French monarchs failed to provide essential reforms, the despotism of the system was not tempered by enlightenment.

Inequality bred discontent. The root of the difficulty lay in the fact that French society was still legally organized along feudal lines, with unequal and unrealistic class divisions. Every person belonged to one of three classes, or "estates." The First Estate consisted of the clergy, the Second Estate was made up of the nobility, and the Third Estate included everyone else. Within this society, called the Old Regime, a person's status, civil rights, and privileges were determined by the estate to which he belonged. By the 18th century, people had become discontented with the old feudal arrangement of society.

Out of a total population of 24 million, the clergy numbered about 130 thousand or about one half of 1 per cent. Yet this relatively small group was the largest single landholder, owning 10 per cent of the land. The nobility, or Second Estate, had around 200 thousand members. By the late 18th century, the Second Estate monopolized all the best positions in the government and army.

The Third Estate was itself divided into three groups. The upper level consisted of the bourgeoisie—lawyers, doctors, merchants, and businessmen. They strongly resented the privileged position and political ambitions of the nobility. They considered themselves the backbone of the country and saw no reason why the useless and arrogant nobles should enjoy favored treatment and receive the best governmental offices. As men of energy, ideas, and ambition, growing in wealth and numbers, they felt they deserved a larger role in the affairs of state.

Below the bourgeoisie in the Third Estate was a small group of city wage-earners, consisting of skilled artisans, servants, and laborers. Their standard of living declined steadily in the 18th century as prices rose three times faster than wages. Some of these city dwellers lived close to starvation and were a dangerous source of mob violence.

Over 80 per cent of the French population was made up of peasants, the largest element of the Third Estate. However, while they owned 40 per cent of the land and serfdom had largely disappeared, most of them were still burdened by certain dues and obligations imposed on them by the nobility. The existence of outworn customs and privileges particularly irritated the peasants. They saw no justification for maintaining a group of absentee landlords who, unlike their ancestors in feudal times, performed no useful services.

Weak kings failed to promote tax reforms. Under these circumstances, the greatest single problem facing the govern-ment was the unfair tax system. Church, nobility, and bourgeoisie, the wealthiest elements of society, paid virtually no taxes; the First and Second Estates were exempted from most taxes by law, and the bourgeoisie could buy tax exemptions. The heaviest burden therefore fell on the peasants, who had the least money. As a result, France in the 18th century presented a strange spectacle. While the nation itself was prosperous, the government was constantly poor. The situation cried out for tax reforms, and since France was an absolute monarchy, vigorous leadership should have come from the king.

Unfortunately, Louis XV, who ruled from 1715 to 1774, and his grandson, Louis XVI, neither were vigorous nor were they natural leaders. Louis XV's chief interest was pleasure. He was aware of the unrest among the people, but he remained indifferent to it. When told how serious conditions had become, he is supposed to have replied, "Things will last in my time, but after me—the deluge."

Louis XVI, who was only twenty when he became king in 1774, sincerely wanted to govern well. However, he lacked a forceful personality, had no will power, and was afraid to offend people in direct contact with him.

Bankruptcy threatened the nation. During the reign of Louis XVI, the government of France rapidly approached bankruptcy. Fully three fourths of the total budget was devoted to military expenditures and to the payments on the public debt that had accumulated from previous wars. The debt increased even more sharply after 1778 when France joined the Americans in their struggle for independence. Actually, when compared to the public debt of other countries, that of France was not excessive, but the unbalanced tax system did not bring in enough revenue.

. . . the . . . Lords Spiritual and Temporal and Commons pursuant to their respective letters and elections, being now assembled in a full and free representative of this nation, . . . do . . . for the vindicating and asserting their ancient rights and liberties, declare

That the pretended power of suspending of laws or the execution of laws by regal authority without consent of Parliament is illegal.

That the pretended power of dispensing with laws or the execution of laws by regal authority, as it hath been assumed and exercised of late, is illegal. . . .

That levying money for or to the use of the crown by pretence of prerogative without grant of Parliament for longer time or in other manner than the same is or shall be granted is illegal.

That it is the right of the subjects to petition the king, and all . . . prosecutions for such petitioning are illegal.

That the raising or keeping a standing army within the kingdom in time of peace unless it be with consent of Parliament is against law. . . .

That election of members of Parliament ought to be free.

That the freedom of speech and debates or proceedings in Parliament ought not to be impeached or questioned in any court or place out of Parliament.

That excessive bail ought not to be required, nor excessive fines imposed, nor cruel and unusual punishments inflicted. . . .

And that for redress of all grievances and for the amending, strengthening, and preserving of the laws, Parliaments ought to be held frequently.

And they do claim, demand, and insist upon, all and singular, the premises as their undoubted rights and liberties and that no declarations, judgments, doings, or proceedings to the prejudice of the people in any of the said premises ought in any wise to be drawn hereafter into consequence or example. . . .

When in the Course of human events, it becomes necessary for one people to dissolve the political bands which have connected them with another, and to assume among the Powers of the earth, the separate and equal station to which the Laws of Nature and of Nature's God entitle them, a decent respect to the opinions of mankind requires that they should declare the causes which impel them to the separation.

We hold these truths to be self-evident, that all men are created equal, that they are endowed by their Creator with certain inalienable Rights, that among these are Life, Liberty and the pursuit of Happiness. That to secure these rights, Governments are instituted among Men, deriving their just powers from the consent of the governed, That whenever any Form of Government becomes destructive of these ends, it is the Right of the People to alter or to abolish it, and to institute new Government, laying its foundation on such principles and organizing its powers in such form, as to them shall seem most likely to effect their Safety and Happiness. Prudence, indeed, will dictate that Governments long established should not be changed for light and transient causes; and accordingly all experience hath shown, that mankind are more disposed to suffer, while evils are sufferable, than to right themselves by abolishing the forms to which they are accustomed. But when a long train of abuses and usurpations, pursuing invariably the same Object evinces a design to reduce them under absolute Despotism, it is their right, it is their duty, to throw off such Government, and to provide new Guards for their future security. Such has been the patient sufferance of these Colonies; and such is now the necessity which constrains them to alter their former Systems of Government. . . .

We, therefore, the Representatives of the United States of America, in General Congress, Assembled, appealing to the Supreme Judge of the world for the rectitude of our intentions, do, in the Name, and by the authority of the good People of these Colonies, solemnly publish and declare, That these United Colonies are, and of Right ought to be Free and Independent States; that they are Absolved from all Allegiance to the British Crown, and that all political connection between them and the State of Great Britain, is and ought to be totally dissolved. . . .

from the Declaration of the Rights of Man and of the Citizen, 1789

The representatives of the people of France, formed into a National Assembly, considering that ignorance, neglect, or contempt of human rights, are the sole causes of public misfortunes and corruptions of Government, have resolved to set forth in a solemn declaration, these natural, imprescriptible, and inalienable rights: that this declaration being constantly present to the minds of the members of the body social, they may be for ever kept attentive to their rights and their duties; that the acts of the legislative and executive powers of government, being capable of being every moment compared with the end of political institutions, may be more respected; and also, that the future claims of the citizens, being directed by simple and incontestable principles, may always tend to the maintenance of the Constitution, and the general happiness.

For these reasons, the National Assembly doth recognize and declare, in the presence of the Supreme Being, and with the hope of his blessing and favour, the following *sacred* rights of men and of citizens:

I. Men are born, and always continue, free and equal in respect of their rights. . . .

II. The end of all political associations, is the preservation of the natural and imprescriptible rights of man; and these rights are liberty, property, security, and resistance of oppression.

III. The nation is essentially the source of all sovereignty; nor can any individual, or any body of men, be entitled to any authority which is not expressly derived from it.

IV. Political liberty consists in the power of doing whatever does not injure another. The exercise of the natural rights of every man, has no other limits than those which are necessary to secure to every *other* man the free exercise of the same rights; and these limits are determinable only by the law.

V. The law ought to prohibit only actions hurtful to society. What is not prohibited by the law, should not be hindered; nor should any one be compelled to that which the law does not require.

VI. The law is an expression of the will of the community. All citizens have a right to concur, either personally, or by their representatives, in its formation. It should be the same to all, whether it protects or punishes; and all being equal in its sight, are equally eligible to all honours, places, and employments, according to their different abilities, without any other distinction than that created by their virtues and talents.

VII. No man should be accused, arrested, or held in confinement, except in cases determined by the law, and according to the forms which it has prescribed. . . .

IX. Every man being presumed innocent till he has been convicted, whenever his detention becomes indispensable, all rigour to him, more than is necessary to secure his person, ought to be provided against by the law.

X. No man ought to be molested on account of his opinions, not even on account of his *religious* opinions, provided his avowal of them does not disturb the public order established by the law.

XI. The unrestrained communication of . . . opinions being one of the most precious rights of man, every citizen may speak, write, and publish freely, provided he is responsible for the abuse of this liberty, in cases determined by the law. . . .

During the late 1770's and in the 1780's, government officials made attempts to solve the financial crisis by taxing the wealthy classes. They failed, however, because the king refused to stand up for his officials in the face of outraged opposition from the nobility. Finally, unable to collect taxes or to borrow money, Louis consented in 1788 to having the Estates-General meet in 1789. (The Estates-General, consisting of representatives from each of the three estates, had last met in 1614.) By insisting upon a meeting of this body, the nobles had forced Louis' hand, but in so doing they had unknowingly opened the door to revolution.

Section Review

1. Why did the social system of the Old Regime cause dissatisfaction?
2. What was the most important problem facing the French government in the 18th century? Why did efforts to solve it fail?
3. Why did Louis XVI summon the Estates-General?

5 The French Revolution brought drastic changes

In its traditional form, the Estates-General consisted of three "orders," one for each estate. Each order included the same number of representatives, who met together and voted on various issues. When the orders had all arrived at a decision, they had only one vote apiece in the Estates-General. When the representatives were finally recalled after 175 years, liberal reformers objected to this traditional form because it would allow the clergy and nobility to join forces against the Third Estate and carry the vote. The king yielded to their appeals and allowed the Third Estate to have as many representatives as the other two orders combined. The crucial question of voting procedure, however, remained unsettled.

Conflicts between the Estates-General and the king led to violence. When the Estates-General convened at Versailles in May 1789, the Third Estate refused to participate unless all three estates met as one body and voted as individuals. After weeks of argument, the Third Estate, joined by some members of the clergy, declared that they were the National Assembly representing the people. This was an act of revolution, for legally the members of the Third Estate had no authority to compose themselves as a sovereign legislative power. On June 20, 1789, on an indoor tennis court, they vowed never to disband until a new constitution had been written for France; their vow became known as the Tennis Court Oath.

Although the king at first tried to preserve the Estates-General in its traditional form, he finally gave in and ordered the clergy and nobility who had not already done so to join the Third Estate in the National Assembly. Thus the Estates-General no longer existed. However, Louis plotted against the Assembly in secret by ordering royal mercenary troops to surround Versailles and Paris.

Meanwhile, the peasantry in the country and the workers in the cities were suffering from bad harvests and depression. Food was scarce, prices were high, and unemployment was widespread. When the king made threatening moves against the Assembly, the people became apprehensive. Crowds in Paris roamed the streets in search of weapons, and on July 14, they besieged the Bastille, an old fort used as a prison. Although there were no weapons there, the crowd believed otherwise. A misunderstanding led to bloodshed, and the infuriated mob stormed the fortress and massacred the small garrison. (Ever since, the French have celebrated Bastille Day on July 14 as a national holiday.) The mob then marched upon the Town Hall, murdered the mayor of Paris, and set up a new municipal government. The king recognized the new government and ordered his royal troops to leave. In the rural areas the peasants, caught up in a wave of fear and hysteria, refused to pay taxes, attacked the manor houses of the nobles, destroyed the records of feudal dues, and in some cases burned the manors to the ground.

The National Assembly set up a constitutional monarchy. The National Assembly became alarmed by the spreading disorder and violence. On the night of August 4, it took a bold step and declared that feudalism was abolished and all manorial dues ended. The Assembly then set itself the task of establishing a new regime for France. As evidence of what it intended to do, it issued a Declaration of the Rights of Man and of the Citizen on August 27, 1789. Echoing the ideas of the Enlightenment, this famous document declared that government must be based on the fundamental principles of liberty, equality, and natural rights.

For the next two years the National Assembly (then located in Paris) labored to provide France with a constitution that would incorporate the principles of the Declaration. While the Assembly was working on the constitution, it tried to improve the financial situation in France, which had steadily grown worse. To raise money, the Assembly seized the vast land holdings of the Church, sold them, and used the money to pay off the public debt. The National Assembly then tried to place the Church under firmer government control by requiring public election of priests and bishops; all members of the clergy were supposed to take an oath to support this plan. The proposed system split the Church in France into two factions. One group took the oath; the other refused to do so and became bitterly opposed to the revolution.

As the revolution became more radical, it also aroused increasing opposition among the aristocracy. Louis XVI, becoming increasingly disturbed by the course of events, tried to escape from France with his family in June 1790, but was caught at Varennes, near the Luxemburg border. Louis had foolishly left behind a note denouncing the revolution, an action that encouraged the radicals to demand that the monarchy be abolished altogether.

Meanwhile, the Assembly had completely revamped the whole administrative structure of France. The constitution, completed by September 1791, declared France a constitutional monarchy. Laws were to be made by a Legislative Assembly, and while the king could delay legislation, he could not veto it absolutely. Although all privileges had been swept away and all men were equal before the law, the new government was designed primarily by and for the bourgeoisie. For example, election to the Legislative Assembly depended on property ownership, allowing only 50 thousand out of a total population of 24 million to qualify. After the king formally accepted the new constitution, the National Assembly was dissolved on September 30.

Foreign war led to a "second" revolution. The new constitution of France went into effect in October 1791 with the election of a Legislative Assembly, but this government lasted only eleven months, chiefly because of war with other countries.

The French Revolution was a source of increasing alarm to the monarchs of Europe, who feared that the universal principles of liberty, equality, and natural rights would undermine their own regimes. Their fears were intensified by the activities of the *émigrés*, French nobles who fled France and worked to persuade the kings of Europe to save the institution of monarchy by restoring it in France.

The French Revolution

The most dramatic of the events launching the Revolution was the fall of the Bastille, above. Successive waves of violence culminated in the Reign of Terror, one of whose first victims was Marie Antoinette; the sketch at left was made as she was carried to her execution. Meanwhile, France had gone to war, and citizen armies—like the one at right pulling cannon up the hill of Montmartre—had rallied to its defense. These commoners, dubbed sans-culottes (that is, those who did not wear knee breeches, like the aristocrats, but trousers instead), celebrated victories by dancing around Trees of Liberty that were decorated with emblems of the revolution.

The *émigrés* directed their frantic appeals to Emperor Leopold III of Austria because he was the brother of the French queen, Marie Antoinette. Leopold did not want to plunge his country into war, but in an effort to ease the almost unbearable pressure from the *émigrés*, he joined with the king of Prussia in August 1791 to issue the Declaration of Pillnitz, stating that it was the duty of *all* kings to "restore order in France." In other words, the rulers of Austria and Prussia were willing to move against the French revolutionaries only if the other rulers of Europe would move with them. Leopold knew full well, however, that neither Britain nor Russia was interested in war against France.

The *émigrés* seized upon the statement as the club they had been waiting for. They promptly warned the revolutionaries, who took them at their word, that they would soon be returning with all Europe behind them. The radicals in France, convinced that the revolution could never be safe unless monarchy were overthrown everywhere, became a war party and preached the necessity of international revolution. So strong did this war spirit become that on April 20, 1792, the Legislative Assembly voted overwhelmingly to declare war against Austria.

With war fever at a high pitch, suspicion against the king mounted. In August, when Louis XVI and his family were endangered by a Parisian mob, the Assembly suspended the monarchy, imprisoned the royal family, and shortly afterwards virtually destroyed its powers. Panic and hysteria gripped Paris. In September over 1000 royalists were dragged from prisons and executed by authority of a provisional government. The Legislative Assembly was abolished and a new National Constitutional Convention was elected on the basis of universal suffrage. Its purpose was to draw up a more democratic constitution. The uprising in August 1792 and the September Massacre were an outgrowth of war hysteria and popular dissatisfaction with the constitution of 1791, and represented a "second" French revolution.

France became a republic. Beginning in September 1792 and for the next three years, France was ruled by the National Constitutional Convention, usually referred to as the Convention. When it first met, it proclaimed France a republic and defied all royalty by announcing that it intended to spread the ideas of "liberty, equality, and fraternity" throughout Europe. French armies swarmed over the Austrian Netherlands (Belgium) and the area south of the Rhine; by 1793 France was at war with almost all of Europe, opposing a coalition that included England, Prussia, Austria, the Netherlands, Spain, Portugal, Sweden, and Sardinia.

As the war against this First Coalition proceeded, the revolution in France became more extreme. Louis XVI was tried for treason and convicted in December 1792. The following month he was sent to the guillotine.

During 1793 conditions approached a state of anarchy. French armies suffered several defeats; one of their best generals deserted to the Austrians. Food was scarce and prices high. Conservative peasants in the west, aided by returned *émigrés*, rebelled against the Convention, itself torn by quarrels between the moderate members, called Girondins, and the extreme radicals, the Jacobin party. In June a Parisian mob invaded the Convention and arrested the Girondin leaders, leaving the government in the hands of the Jacobins. When escaped Girondins incited revolts against the authority of the Convention in the large cities of the south, the situation grew even worse. To repress anarchy and counterrevolution and at the same time win the war against the First Coalition, the Convention took desperate measures.

Radicals instituted a Reign of Terror.
Executive authority was vested in a group of twelve members who were elected by the Convention and who were known as the Committee of Public Safety. Under the leadership of Maximilien de Robespierre, the committee launched a Reign of Terror to smash the menace of counterrevolution. All people suspected of hostility to the revolution were summarily tried on a charge of treason and executed. Between August 1793 and July 1794 more than 40 thousand persons died. Marie Antoinette was among the first to be sentenced and executed; the Girondist moderates soon followed. Thousands of others, regardless of class, were arrested and imprisoned.

Meanwhile, the war against the First Coalition had to be won. The Committee launched one program of price controls and another of national mobilization, called the *levée en masse*. In general the economic regulations were less successful than the *levée en masse*, which represented the first attempt in modern times to harness all the resources of a nation for the purpose of war. By the spring of 1794 France had the largest army in all Europe—800 thousand strong. Furthermore, unlike any other military force at the time, it was a citizen army with a strong spirit of nationalism. Frenchmen were not subjects fighting for a king but citizens fighting for a cause.

By the summer of 1794, this citizen army, commanded by vigorous young officers newly risen from the lower ranks, won a series of victories against the weak and divided Coalition forces, and, although the war against them was to continue until 1797, the nation was saved. There no longer seemed to be any justification for the harsh dictatorship of the Committee of Public Safety, and in July 1794 the Convention sent Robespierre and his followers to be "shaved by the national barber," the guillotine. Thus, the Reign of Terror was ended.

Conservatives set up the Directory.
Power again rested in the hands of the bourgeoisie, who wished to reëstablish a moderate republic. In October 1795 a new constitution ended the Convention and inaugurated a government known as the Directory. Under the new system, a two-house legislature was established which was responsible for electing a governing body of five men called Directors.

This new republic faced continuing inflation and other grave problems in addition to the war against the Coalition. Once again voting was restricted to the wealthiest property owners of the middle class and, as a result, neither royalists nor workers were satisfied. When free elections were held in 1797 and a great many royalist sympathizers were elected, the Directory called upon a successful young general named Napoleon Bonaparte for help. With the support of his army, the Directory violated its own constitution and declared the recent elections null and void.

After 1797 conditions in France became progressively worse. To be sure, Austria was forced to sign the peace treaty of Campo Formio—thanks largely to Napoleon's stunning victories in Italy. This treaty gave France the Austrian Netherlands and considerable territory on the Rhine and in northern Italy; it also signaled the end of the war against the First Coalition. Within France, however, people grew increasingly dissatisfied with the corrupt and inefficient Directory. A new threat arose in 1798 when Britain joined with Russia in a Second Coalition against France. The situation was ready-made for a strong man.

Section Review
1. By what steps was the National Assembly created from the Estates-General?
2. What were the chief reforms of the National Assembly?
3. Describe the conditions which led to the "second" French revolution.

4. What significant changes in government were made by the Convention?

5. What conditions led to the Reign of Terror? What did the Committee of Public Safety accomplish?

6. Why was the Directory unsuccessful?

6 Napoleon was a son of the revolution

As it turned out, a strong man appeared in the person of Napoleon Bonaparte, who had saved the Directory in 1797. Napoleon was born on the island of Corsica in 1769 and educated in the best French military schools. He became a lieutenant of artillery in the army of Louis XVI, but as a member of the lesser nobility, he could look forward only to a life of obscurity. The outburst of revolution opened the door to fame and power. Within four years Napoleon rose to the rank of brigadier general. By 1797 he was in command of a French army in northern Italy and, in a series of brilliant campaigns, he smashed the forces of Austria. When he dictated the terms of Campo Formio, he was then twenty-eight years old and already a hero.

Napoleon was a man of insatiable ambition. Well aware of the growing unpopularity of the Directory, he bided his time until a favorable opportunity arose for him to seize power. Meanwhile, he conceived a bold plan to cripple England by seizing Egypt and striking at India, the jewel of the British Empire. Napoleon invaded Egypt in 1798, but the English fleet destroyed his transport ships, isolating his army.

At this point Napoleon learned of the formation of the Second Coalition and the desperate position of the Directory. Abandoning his army, he eluded the British fleet and returned to France. He made his Egyptian adventure seem a great triumph and appeared to many people as the sav-

ior of the nation. Quickly he entered into a conspiracy and overthrew the Directory by force on November 9, 1799.

Napoleon became First Consul. A new government, the Consulate, was set up with Napoleon as First Consul. The man into whose hands France had fallen was only a little over five feet tall, but he was a leader among men. He had a sharp, incisive mind with a remarkable capacity to grasp problems and make decisions quickly. It was also a well-stocked mind, for Napoleon had read deeply in history and law as well as in military science. People were dazzled by his masterful qualities. Even Napoleon himself came to believe that he was the "child of destiny."

Although a product of the revolution, Napoleon intended to rule as a dictator. He wrote a new constitution for France, complete with a legislature and universal suffrage, but all real power lay with the First Consul, who claimed to represent the interests of the whole nation. Napoleon then turned his attention to military affairs and defeated the armies of the Second Coalition. Austria made peace in 1801 and England in 1802.

The Consulate lasted five years, a period during which Napoleon carried out a number of important reforms in France. He centralized the government and increased its efficiency and power. He offered stability and internal order to all willing to work for him—royalists and republicans alike.

In many ways Napoleon completed the work of the revolution. All remaining privileges were swept away once and for all. Promotion and rank, whether in government or in the army, were based on proven ability, regardless of social origin. Careers were "open to talent." The reformed tax system, which had been introduced in principle in 1789, became a matter of practice after 1799. Inflation was halted

THE COURSE OF THE FRENCH REVOLUTION

GOVERNMENT	PERIOD	CONTROLLED BY	
King and Estates General	May and June 1789	King	
National Assembly and King	1789-1791	Upper Middle Class	
Legislative Assembly and King	1791-1792		
National Convention	1792-1795	Parisian Masses / Robespierre	
Directory	1795-1799	Upper Middle Class	
Consulate	1799-1804	Napoleon	
Empire	1804-1815		

and the national debt stabilized. Probably the most famous of Napoleon's reforms was the modernization of French law in a series of five codes known collectively as the *Code Napoléon*. They firmly established throughout the land the principle of equality before the law.

Napoleon also ruthlessly suppressed all opposition, but despite his denial of political liberty and true representative government, his ability to provide order, stability, and efficiency made him popular. He had himself crowned Napoleon I, Emperor of the French, in 1804 and thus the Consulate gave way to an empire which lasted for ten years, longer than any French government since 1789.

Napoleon made himself master of Europe. Napoleon ruled France for fifteen years—five years as First Consul and ten as emperor. Driven by relentless ambition, he spent fourteen of those years at war. The short-lived peace of 1802 was broken in 1803; by 1805 a Third Coalition of Britain, Austria, and Russia had formed against France. With amazing speed, Napoleon defeated the armies of Austria and Russia in a series of brilliant military campaigns. Only England with its navy continued to defy the emperor. After Lord Horatio Nelson destroyed the French fleet at the Battle of Trafalgar in 1805, British naval supremacy was secure and England could not be invaded.

In the years from 1806 to 1812, Napoleon stood like a giant over Europe. He was emperor of France and king of Italy (having created a Kingdom of Italy from Austrian possessions in the north). In 1806 he dissolved the Holy Roman Empire and created the Confederation of the Rhine, an alliance of west German states that became a satellite of France. Through his brothers, Napoleon also controlled other states of Europe. Joseph reigned in the Kingdom of Naples and Sicily; Louis became king of Holland (the Netherlands had been overrun in 1794); and Jerome ruled the Kingdom of Westphalia in Germany. Napoleon took the pope prisoner and declared the Papal States to be part of France. French troops occupied Prussia; the grand duchy of Warsaw was created as a French protectorate; and Russia was an ally.

Since Napoleon could not defeat the British navy, he decided to ruin England through economic warfare. He reasoned that much of the wealth of England derived from its large export trade to Europe. He therefore declared all of Europe closed to British goods, and even persuaded Russia to comply with his edict. First imposed in 1806, the Continental System was a failure, largely because the British were able to develop other markets, particularly in Latin America. To control the ports of the Iberian Peninsula, Napoleon invaded Portugal, installed his brother Joseph on the Spanish throne, and stationed a French army in Spain. Using guerrilla tactics, the Spanish people fought desperately against the foreign troops. English forces under the Duke of Wellington took advantage of this revolt, invaded Portugal, then Spain, and by 1813 had driven the French army back into France.

European powers joined forces to defeat Napoleon. The people in the French satellite nations objected to Napoleon's demand that they furnish him with money and soldiers. In addition, the Continental System provoked a great deal of resistance because it limited trade and led to shortages of manufactured goods (formerly supplied by the British) that French industry could not supply. Moreover, the British in retaliation had imposed a naval blockade on all of Europe, limiting imports of such colonial products as cotton, sugar, and tobacco. Most important of all was the growth of nationalism, which Napoleon never understood, although it developed as a movement of resistance against French control. All countries experienced an upsurge of patriotic feeling against the hated French, but it was particularly significant in Germany after about 1800.

The climax came in 1812 when Napoleon resolved to crush Russia. The loss of trade with Great Britain had seriously injured the Russian economy, and Czar Alexander withdrew from the Continental System in 1810. His withdrawal angered Napoleon, who assembled a huge army of more than 500 thousand men and invaded Russia in the summer of 1812. Although he won several battles, he could not annihilate the Russian army. In September he reached Moscow, which the Russians had evacuated. Within a few days fire broke out and destroyed almost the entire city; shortly afterward the cruel Russian winter set in. After five weeks Napoleon finally ordered a general retreat. No more than 30 thousand of his army returned to France alive. The rest of his men perished in battles, blizzards, and snowdrifts.

This blow to Napoleon's power ruined him. From all directions his enemies rushed together to strike at the French tyrant—Russians, Prussians, Spaniards, Englishmen, Austrians, Italians. Russia and Prussia announced a War of Liberation and, joined by Austria, defeated Napoleon's forces at the Battle of Leipzig, or Battle of the Nations, in October 1813.

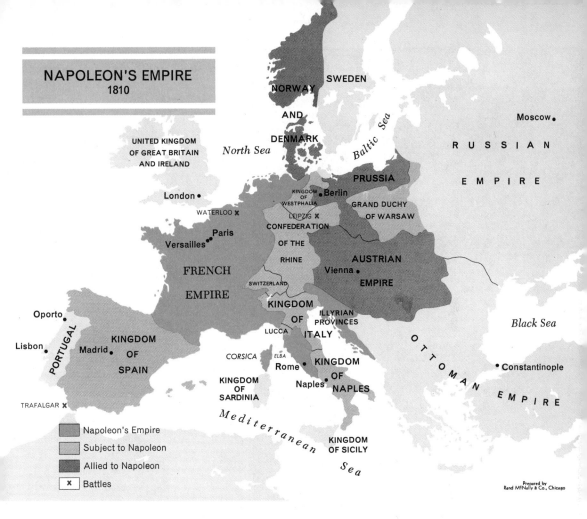

NAPOLEON'S EMPIRE
1810

SWEDEN

NORWAY

AND

DENMARK

North Sea

Baltic Sea

Moscow•

UNITED KINGDOM
OF GREAT BRITAIN
AND IRELAND

R U S S I A N

E M P I R E

PRUSSIA

London •

KINGDOM
OF
WESTPHALIA

•Berlin

GRAND DUCHY
OF WARSAW

WATERLOO X

LEIPZIG X

•Paris

CONFEDERATION

Versailles••

OF THE

AUSTRIAN

FRENCH

RHINE

Vienna •

EMPIRE

SWITZERLAND

EMPIRE

Oporto•

KINGDOM

Lisbon•

PORTUGAL

Madrid•

OF

ITALY

ILLYRIAN
PROVINCES

LUCCA

Black Sea

KINGDOM
OF
SPAIN

CORSICA

ELBA

Rome •

KINGDOM

Constantinople

KINGDOM
OF
SARDINIA

Naples•

OF

NAPLES

OTTOMAN

EMPIRE

TRAFALGAR X

Mediterranean

KINGDOM
OF SICILY

Sea

Prepared by
Rand McNally & Co., Chicago

■ Napoleon's Empire

☐ Subject to Napoleon

■ Allied to Napoleon

X Battles

Napoleon's empire crumbled rapidly and an allied invasion of France in 1814 forced him to surrender and abdicate as emperor. The victorious allies restored the Bourbon monarchy, and Louis XVIII, a brother of Louis XVI, ascended the throne.

The victors banished Napoleon to the little island of Elba off the west coast of Italy. But the exile's ambition still burned. Hearing that the victors were quarreling among themselves, Napoleon escaped from Elba and landed in France. For a period of one hundred days, he again reigned as emperor. His return united the allies, who determined to crush this "common enemy and disturber of the peace of the world." The end came at the little Belgian village

of Waterloo in 1815. Here the British Duke of Wellington, aided by a Prussian army under Gebhard von Blücher, destroyed the French army that Napoleon had hastily assembled. Napoleon was then banished to the lonely island of St. Helena in the south Atlantic. He died of cancer in 1821, brooding over the fame and glory which he had lost.

French reform influenced other nations. Although first and last a military adventurer, Napoleon could rightfully claim to be a son of the revolution. His soldiers and administrators spread the ideas and reforms of the French Revolution throughout Europe.

Napoleon said proudly, "I am no ordinary man," a boast borne out by his dazzling career. He is shown above in the full vigor of his youth after leading French troops to victory at Arcola, Italy, in 1797. Seven years later, energy and ambition gained him an emperor's throne. Although Pope Pius VII had been invited to officiate at the coronation, Napoleon placed the crown on his own head, above right. Napoleon's successes alarmed the other nations of Europe, who formed an alliance to end his power. At right, he stands lonely and defeated as he sails into exile. Of him a fellow Frenchman said, "He was as great as a man can be without virtue."

In all of the countries conquered by the French, constitutions were drawn up; the remnants of feudalism were wiped out; and the Napoleonic codes, with their principle of equality before the law, were established. Church lands were confiscated; the Church was made subordinate to the state; and religious toleration toward non-Catholics became the law. Taxes were reformed, the manorial system and medieval guilds were abolished, and the metric system of weights and measures was adopted.

The importance of these reforms lay in the fact that they streamlined government and society, and thereby helped modernize them. But in no instance was Napoleon interested in promoting the principle of political liberty. What he adopted from the revolution and gave to the rest of Europe was its emphasis upon reason, order, and efficiency. He thought these contributions of such universal significance that they would benefit everyone. In this sense he was the last of the enlightened despots, but he completely failed to understand the appeal of those other principles of the French Revolution, freedom and the desire of national groups to handle their own affairs. In the long run, this failure and his own boundless ambition brought about his destruction.

Section Review

1. What reforms did Napoleon make during the period of the Consulate?
2. Trace the steps by which Napoleon made himself master of Europe. Why did the Continental System fail?
3. What conditions created opposition to Napoleon? What were the most significant events that led to his banishment?
4. In what sense was Napoleon a son of the French Revolution?

Chapter 18   A Review

During the 17th and 18th centuries, revolutionary upheaval led to fundamental changes in three Western nations—England, the United States, and France. Though the national movements and their results differed in many ways, basically they all represented attempts to achieve more democratic forms of government.

In England, trouble began when the absolutist Stuarts came to the throne. James I challenged the power of Parliament and Puritanism, while the misrule of his son, Charles I, led to civil war. A great leader, Oliver Cromwell, brought victory to Parliamentary forces and the king was executed in 1649. Because the Commonwealth that replaced the monarchy was plagued with internal quarrels, Cromwell was forced to rule as a military dictator. He became Lord Protector, but failed to restore harmony, and his death brought a return of the monarchy. However, significant changes in the direction of more democratic government came as a result of the Puritan Revolution. It indicated that the English monarchy was not absolute. Charles II understood this situation and acted with caution in trying to extend royal power and the influence of the Roman Catholic Church. Two developments of his reign were the formation of modern political parties and the passage of the Habeas Corpus Act. His brother, James II, lacked Charles' wisdom and soon found himself deposed in the Glorious, or Bloodless, Revolution of 1688. By bestowing the crown on William and Mary and confirming the change in the Revolution Settlement, Parliament made it clear that the English ruler was henceforth to be the representative of a strictly limited constitutional monarchy. The next fifty years saw the development of a new kind of executive in the cabinet system, a uniquely English contribution to democratic government.

While England was achieving political stability at home, its colonies in North America began agitating for greater control over their own affairs. A lax English mercantilist policy gave way to stricter control after 1763, but the colonies proved unwilling to accept greater control from the mother country. Tempers rose, compromise grew more and more difficult, and war broke out in 1775. A year later, the colonists declared their independence, and with the help of France and other European nations, England was defeated and the Americans won their freedom.

One of the nations influenced by the American movement for liberty was France. It was a nation beset with growing discontent over the inequalities of the Old Regime and nearing bankruptcy because of an unrealistic tax structure. When King Louis XVI called a meeting of the Estates-General in 1789, the deep-seated dissatisfactions of the French erupted into revolution. The Estates-General transformed itself into the National Assembly and set about to reform the French government. A new constitution limited the monarchy, but other developments boded ill for the future of France—frequent mob violence in Paris, agitation by *émigrés,* a split in the Church, and the vacillation of the king. These elements played a part in the foreign war which began in 1792, soon putting an end to the existing government and to the institution of the monarchy itself.

In September of that year, a new ruling body, the Convention, established the first French Republic. Enemies within and without endangered the republic, and the revolution became more and more extreme, culminating in a Reign of Terror. When the tide of war turned in favor of France, the Convention gave way to the moderate Directory. Its weaknesses made it a prey to a strong man, the ambitious Napoleon Bonaparte.

Napoleon provided the leadership that France wanted, first as First Consul and then as emperor. He consolidated many of the revolutionary reforms in France, and by great military victories created a large European empire. But by 1814 it had crumbled under the combined onslaught of the other powers of Europe. However, Napoleon's most important legacy was the spread of the ideas of the French Revolution throughout Europe.

The Time

Some of the events named below are correctly placed under the period during which they occurred, and others are not. Rearrange the list so that all events appear in their proper time span.

1601-1650
Stuart dynasty began.
Habeas Corpus Act was passed.
Civil War broke out between the
   Cavaliers and Roundheads.
Petition of Right was passed.
French and Indian War ended.

1651-1700
Commonwealth was established.
Instrument of Government was drawn up.
Glorious Revolution took place.
Bastille was stormed.
Restoration began.

1701-1750
Virginia House of Burgesses
   was established.
Act of Settlement was passed.
English cabinet government took shape
   under Walpole.
Stamp Act was passed.
Hanoverian dynasty began.

1751-1800
Declaration of Independence was adopted.
Directory was established.
Battle of the Nations took place.
Boston Tea Party was staged.
Continental System was imposed.

1801-1815
Holy Roman Empire came to an end.
Declaration of the Rights of Man and of
   the Citizen was proclaimed.
First French Empire was established.
Battle of Waterloo took place.
First French Republic was proclaimed.

The Place

1. Where were the following battles fought and who were the victors and vanquished in each?

Naseby	Marston Moor
Yorktown	Saratoga
Leipzig	Waterloo

2. Why was the victory at Trafalgar of strategic importance to the British?

3. What was the Confederation of the Rhine? Name the countries or areas included in Napoleon's empire at its greatest extent.

The People

1. What contribution did each of the following persons make to the growth of democratic institutions or parliamentary government?

Robert Walpole   Napoleon Bonaparte
Thomas Jefferson

2. Who earned each of the titles listed below and why?

child of destiny   Merry Monarch
the wisest fool in Christendom

3. Name the country and a significant event associated with each of these rulers.

Louis XVI   William and Mary
Charles I   Charles II
Robespierre   James II
Leopold III   Oliver Cromwell

4. Identify each of the following men with a significant battle, indicating under what flag he fought and whether he won or lost.

Duke of Wellington   Gebhard von Blücher
Lord Charles Cornwallis Lord Horatio Nelson
Oliver Cromwell

Historical Terms

1. What safeguards for the individual did these documents or acts provide?

Declaration of the Rights of Man
  and of the Citizen
Petition of Right
Code Napoléon
English Bill of Rights

2. Political and religious issues in 17th-century England often overlapped. To what cause or principles did each of these groups give their support?

High Church party   Cavaliers
Puritans   Roundheads
Presbyterians   Tories
Separatists   Whigs

3. What is meant by the cabinet system of government as it developed in England under Robert Walpole?

4. How did the following parliamentary acts embitter the colonists against England?

Navigation Acts   Quartering Act
Stamp Act   Intolerable Acts

5. Define each of the following terms as it is applied to the period of the French Revolution.

Committee of Public Safety   émigrés
Reign of Terror   Girondins
Tennis Court Oath   Jacobins
First Coalition   Bastille
levée en masse   Old Regime
constitutional monarchy

6. Name one achievement or event associated with each of the following governments of the French Revolution.

king and Estates-General
National Assembly and king
Legislative Assembly and king
Convention
Directory
Consulate

Questions for Critical Thinking

1. How did a king's need for funds lead to the Puritan Revolution? to the French Revolution?

2. Was the Puritan Revolution a religious, social, or political revolution, or a combination of these? Explain.

3. In what respects did Oliver Cromwell both succeed and fail in advancing the growth of political liberties in England?

4. What do historians mean by the statement that the American Revolution began when the first English settlers came to North America?

5. Why did the colonists' success in winning the American Revolution have such a pronounced effect upon the thought and actions of other peoples?

6. What conditions, both domestic and international, led to the Reign of Terror?

7. To what extent were the principles of "liberty, equality, and fraternity" fulfilled during the French Revolution of 1789 to 1799? during the rule of Napoleon?

8. In what ways did Napoleon advance the cause of nationalism in Europe?

Nineteenth-Century Europe

The hundred years which followed the Napoleonic wars in Europe make up what has been called the "wonderful century." During this period of general peace from 1815 to 1914, Europe led the world in the arts and sciences. Important advances were made against disease, and illiteracy was greatly reduced. Industry forged ahead and wealth accumulated at an unprecedented rate.

To many people of the times, the 19th century was truly an age of peace and plenty, of optimism and hope. The history of the years from 1815 to 1914 is one of great change in politics, economics, and society. In large part, it is the story of the growth and development of four great forces or movements: nationalism, democracy, industrialism, and social protest.

The wars of Napoleon had produced a tide of nationalism which threatened to engulf the conservative rulers of Europe. After Napoleon's defeat, most of the former ruling dynasties returned to power. It was their aim to maintain the *status quo* and to prevent national groups under foreign rule from becoming independent nations. Divided people of the same nationality living in different lands were kept from uniting. Yet the history of the 19th century includes many successful nationalistic revolts which began as early as the 1820's. The century also witnessed the unification of two important nations, Italy and Germany.

The spread of democracy was closely tied to the growth of the European middle class. With their belief in the doctrine of *liberalism*, middle-class leaders championed greater economic opportunity and political participation for members of their own class. Although their principles did not constitute a strictly democratic program, middle-class liberals led the way to a fuller realization of basic rights, such as free speech, freedom of religion, and the protection of private property. In the latter half of the 19th century, many Western countries extended the right to vote to all adult males.

1800

Congress of Vienna   restoration of Bourbons
          Quadruple Alliance
Carlsbad Decrees   Peterloo Massacre
     revolts in Spain and Naples Congress of Verona

1820

          Greece independent
July Monarchy
Reform Bill of 1832   Belgium independent
          Chartism
     repeal of Corn Laws
revolutions of 1848 Louis Napoleon Frankfort Assembly

Zollverein   Victoria

1850

          Napoleon III   Cavour
Crimean War
                              unification of Italy
     Bismarck
          Seven Weeks' War   Dual Monarchy
Franco-Prussian War   unification of Germany
Disraeli   Third Republic of France

1870

Gladstone

     Reform Bill of 1884   William II

                              Dreyfus case

1900

Young Turks
          Parliament Act
                    Home Rule bill

1910

The third great force was industrialism, which first developed in England and then spread to the Continent. The wheels of industry ground out fortunes for the new capitalist class, but they also caught up millions of unfortunate workers. Working conditions were deplorable and wages, miserably low. Factory towns were overcrowded, grimy, and ugly. Shown in the aerial view at the beginning of this unit is such a town: Hanley, England. Although taken in the 1930's, the photograph speaks eloquently of how limited the chances for the good life were in towns like Hanley during the 19th century.

It was the factory system's "inhumanity to man" that stimulated the fourth important movement of the 19th century—social protest. The doctrine that society could be reformed by transferring the means of production and distribution from private to public control was known as *socialism*. The socialist movement took various directions. *Utopian socialists* advocated the establishment of model communities in which economic coöperation was supposed to produce harmony and happiness automatically. *Scientific socialists,* such as Karl Marx and Friedrich Engels, believed in the use of more direct and aggressive meth-

Chapter 21	Chapter 22	Date
spinning jenny / steam engine / power loom / cotton gin — macadamized roads — Jenner's vaccine — Romantic Movement / William Tell	The Wealth of Nations / laissez faire / Malthus	1800
storage battery / steamboat / Erie Canal — Dalton's atomic theory — Beethoven / Schubert	Owen / Ricardo	1825
steam locomotive / telegraph — reaper / dynamo — anesthesia — Dickens	Reform Bill of 1832 / Coöperative Movement / Communist Manifesto	1850
Bessemer steel / Koch / electric motors — The Origin of Species / Pasteur / Mendelyeev's Periodic Table — realism in the arts / Madame Bovary / Wagner / impressionism	First International / On Liberty / Das Kapital	1875
telephone / electric light / internal combustion engine / Diesel engine / wireless telegraph — X ray / Sullivan — Debussy / post-impressionism / Freud	German Social Democratic Party / Fabian Society / German social legislation / Rerum Novarum / Second International / Social Democratic Party in Russia	1900
	British Labour Party / British National Insurance Act / Menshevik-Bolshevik split	1915

ods for transforming society. They called for revolution and the destruction of the capitalist class. Moreover, they claimed to see an inevitable process in history by which class conflict would finally result in a victory of the *proletariat,* or the working class, over the *bourgeoisie,* or the capitalist class.

Despite Marx's pessimistic predictions that under capitalism the rich would become richer and the poor, poorer, the evils of industrialism gradually diminished. Writers and churchmen aroused the public to the need for reform. The growth of the labor union movement helped raise the standard of living for millions. Enlightened governments passed laws protecting workers from unemployment, accidents, and sickness. Most of the socialist parties in Europe gave up the idea of reform through violence, but the *Marxist socialists,* or *communists,* held out. Under Lenin and his followers, this revolutionary creed took root in Russia with significant consequences for the entire world.

Reaction and Revolt after Napoleon

CHAPTER 19   1815–1848

Since 1789, events in France had exerted a great influence on European politics. Just as the French Revolution had sparked the desire for liberty and self-government throughout the Continent, the revolutions of 1830 and 1848 kept the ideals of freedom flaming in the minds and hearts of men. The painting above depicts the street fighting in Paris in February 1848 that led to the abdication of King Louis Philippe and the creation of a new French republic.

It was March 1848. In an Austrian château not far from Vienna, an old man sat playing the violin, alone except for his host. Over and over again he played the "Marseillaise," the revolutionary French national anthem. The lonely old man was Prince Metternich, who until a few days before had been one of the most feared and hated men in Europe. Now, after more than forty years as the Austrian foreign minister, he had been toppled from power by a revolutionary uprising in Vienna. An era had come to an end and its chief symbol, Metternich, was to fade into obscurity.

The tide that swept Metternich out of office was only one dramatic episode in a Europe-wide upheaval. In Paris, Rome, Berlin, Prague, and Budapest, a wave of revolt burst forth to carry away existing regimes. Even though most of the governments were restored when the tide at last receded, it was the most significant revolutionary movement in Europe since 1789 when the French Revolution had destroyed the Old Regime.

Indeed, in many ways the events of 1848 were an outgrowth of the French Revolution, for it had given a great impetus to liberalism, which advocated governmental reform, and nationalism, which sought political independence. Although these twin forces had been severely repressed, every decade between 1815 and 1850 witnessed revolts of a liberal or national character, until Metternich himself, the chief architect of repression, became a victim of their relentless pressure.

The thirty-five years after Waterloo include a number of major themes. One was the attempt of the conservatives, led by Metternich, to restore and maintain royalist regimes as they had existed before the French Revolution. Another was the effort of liberals and nationalists, often working together, to realize the ideals of representative government, civil liberties, and the right of a people to choose their own government. A third theme underlying this struggle was the advance of industrialism, discussed in Chapter 21.

Chapter 19 shows how:

1. **The Congress of Vienna tried to restore stability.**

2. **The Great Powers opposed liberalism and nationalism.**

3. **Liberalism and nationalism made gains in the 1830's.**

4. **A great wave of revolutions swept Europe in 1848.**

1   **The Congress of Vienna tried to restore stability**

After their defeat of Napoleon in April 1814, the four allied powers—Austria, Prussia, Russia, and Britain—signed the first Treaty of Paris with France. It was a lenient peace, for the allies felt that a harsh settlement would create in France a desire for revenge and thus threaten the peace of Europe. They also believed that the balance of power would be upset if France were reduced to the status of a third- or fourth-rate power.

Sick of war and chaos, the people of Europe longed for continued peace and stability. The task of providing them fell to the victorious allies, who decided to convene at Vienna.

Four statesmen dominated the Congress. The Congress of Vienna met in September 1814 and lasted for eight months. Virtually every nation in Europe sent one or more dignitaries. Impressive as the public gatherings were, the hard work of negotiation went on privately among the four allies and France.

Four statesmen dominated the proceedings. The most clever and influential was

Prince Klemens von Metternich, the foreign minister of Austria. A vain and pompous man, he had once declared: "I say to myself twenty times a day how right I am and how wrong the others are. And yet it is so *easy* to be right." Metternich believed that in order to establish general stability in Europe, the revolutionary ideas born of the French Revolution should be stamped out. Another of his principal aims was to reconcile the conflicting interests of various states while making certain that Austria obtained a dominant position in Germany and Italy.

The British representative shared Metternich's general desire for peace and order. He was Viscount Castlereagh, the foreign secretary. Though shy and reserved in manner, he was a shrewd statesman who wanted to ensure a balance of power that would provide security for all.

Russia was represented by its czar, Alexander I. He was a difficult man to understand, an unstable person whose idealism and religious beliefs made him think of himself as the savior of Europe. His chief political objective was to secure for Russia as much Polish territory as possible.

Perhaps the most fascinating person at the Congress was the representative of France, Prince Charles Maurice de Talleyrand-Périgord, but known simply as Talleyrand. His life was a marvel of survival because of his knack for knowing when to change sides. Talleyrand began his career under the Old Regime, lived through the Revolution, served and betrayed Napoleon, and was at Vienna as an agent of the restored Bourbon King Louis XVIII. Talleyrand succeeded in convincing the allies that Napoleon, not France, was to blame for the problems faced by the Congress.

The Congress had two chief tasks. One was to restore the political equilibrium of Europe so that no one state would dominate the rest. The other was to provide a means of settling disputes peacefully among the great powers.

Victors redrew the map of Europe. More than two decades of revolution and war had led to radical changes in the map of Europe. The statesmen who met to redraw it faced an enormously complicated task.

There was, first of all, the matter of providing safeguards against France, which was still considered the principal threat to the peace of Europe. To guard against a possible resurgence of French power, buffers were created along its borders. In the north, Belgium (the Austrian Netherlands) was combined with the Dutch Netherlands. Farther east, Prussia received the Rhineland. In the south, Genoa and part of Savoy, which had been controlled by France, were added to the Kingdom of Sardinia. The rest of northern Italy, including Lombardy and Venetia, was placed under Austrian control. This partition was made to allow Austria to ward off any French attack on Italy and also to compensate Austria for the loss of Belgium.

Other territorial settlements were made by the Congress to restore prewar boundaries and dynasties and to compensate the victors. In Italy, the pope was reinstated in power in the Papal States while the House of Bourbon resumed control over the Kingdom of the Two Sicilies (Naples and Sicily) in the south.

In Germany, where Napoleon had created the Confederation of the Rhine with thirty-eight states, the Congress essentially accepted his work by establishing a German confederation with thirty-nine states. Farther north, Norway was taken from the Danes, who had sided with Napoleon, and placed under Swedish control. Sweden in turn lost Finland to Russia.

The thorniest problem was Poland, which Alexander I wished to place under Russian domination. Prussia had no objec-

EUROPE
After the Congress of Vienna

KINGDOM OF NORWAY AND SWEDEN

FINLAND (TO RUSSIA)

Christiania (Oslo)

Stockholm

UNITED KINGDOM OF GREAT BRITAIN AND IRELAND

North Sea

Copenhagen

DENMARK

HELGOLAND

Baltic Sea

Manchester

THE NETHER-LANDS

HANOVER Berlin

PRUSSIA

Warsaw

RUSSIAN EMPIRE

London

Amsterdam

KDM. OF

POLAND (TO RUSSIA)

BELGIUM (1830)

Frankfort

SAXONY

Paris

BOHEMIA

Cracow

UKRAINE

WÜRTTEM-BERG Troppau

BADEN

BAVARIA Vienna

Budapest

BESSARABIA

MOLDAVIA

ADYGE

KINGDOM OF FRANCE

SWITZER-LAND

AUSTRIAN EMPIRE

PARMA Verona

WALLACHIA

Black Sea

MODENA

SERBIA

KINGDOM OF SPAIN

Madrid

KDM. OF SARDINIA

TUSCANY PAPAL STATES

CORSICA

Rome

KDM. OF THE TWO SICILIES

MONTENEGRO

OTTOMAN

Constantinople

EMPIRE

Mediterranean Sea

GREECE (1829)

MALTA (BR)

Boundary of German Confederation

0   100   200   MILES

Prepared by
Rand McNally & Co., Chicago

tion provided it received Saxony. Austria and Britain, however, strenuously objected to any such arrangement. Both nations feared it would make Russia too strong and thus upset the balance of power in eastern Europe. Furthermore, Metternich was afraid that the addition of Saxony to Prussia would endanger the Austrian position in the German Confederation, where both Austria and Prussia were rivals for influence and prestige. This dispute grew so intense that in January 1815 the allies were on the verge of war. Only when Talleyrand threw the weight of France to the side of Britain and Austria did Prussia and Russia back down. A compromise awarded almost half of Saxony to Prussia and nearly all of Poland to Russia. Poland, though united with Russia, was granted a liberal con-

stitution and its own separate institutions, including an army.

Britain had no territorial ambitions on the Continent, but emerged from the Congress as the strongest naval power and the leading colonial nation of western Europe. During the wars against Napoleon, the English had captured such strategic areas as Ceylon, Cape Colony in South Africa, Malta, and Helgoland. The Vienna settlement allowed England to keep these territories.

The Congress set up a system of alliances. The statesmen at Vienna, well aware that no treaty can be a perfect guarantee of peace, sought some method by which disputes between nations could be resolved without conflict. While the Congress was meeting, joint action had been necessary to crush Napoleon during his Hundred Days' return to France, which had culminated in the Battle of Waterloo in June 1815. (A second, more severe, Treaty of Paris imposed on France an indemnity of 700 million francs and provided for the military occupation of its eastern territories.)

Czar Alexander's solution for a peaceful Europe was a union called the Holy Alliance. Its aim was to transform international relations so that they would be conducted in the spirit of true Christianity. No one knew quite what he had in mind. Castlereagh believed that the czar was mentally unbalanced, and rejected the proposal. Austria and Prussia, however, were reluctant to offend the Russian ruler. They signed the document, which declared that the members of the alliance would consider themselves delegates of Providence in the conduct of their foreign and domestic policies.

Much more practical was the Quadruple Alliance, signed by Austria, Russia, Prussia, and Britain in November 1815. Although directed primarily against France, this alliance also provided that the four signers would meet periodically to deal with any problems that might endanger the peace. In this way the four allies set themselves up as a kind of committee, the Concert of Europe, which planned to meet regularly to maintain the Vienna settlement and to preserve peace. (In 1818 France was admitted to the committee, making it a Quintuple Alliance.) The Concert of Europe, also called the Congress System, was the first attempt to regulate European affairs through an international organization.

Section Review

1. Why did statesmen meet at the Congress of Vienna? What were their chief tasks?

2. What were the principal territorial settlements made at the Congress of Vienna?
3. What was the purpose of the Holy Alliance? the Quadruple Alliance?

2 The Great Powers opposed liberalism and nationalism

In the generation after 1815, two forces —liberalism and nationalism—continually threatened to upset the arrangements made at Vienna. Both movements developed most strongly in the cities of Europe, where the Industrial Revolution stimulated the growth of commercial, industrial, and professional classes. The urban middle classes provided the chief leaders and the basic support for liberal programs and for nationalistic movements throughout the 19th century.

Liberalism and nationalism were important movements. The chief aim of liberals was to create constitutional governments with representative parliamentary assemblies. They wanted an extension of the right to vote, but only to men of property like themselves, whom they considered best qualified to have a voice in government. Liberals favored guarantees for individual liberties, such as the right to speak, write, and meet freely, and for the protection of private property. They believed that all persons should be treated as equals before the law. Liberals advocated either a monarchy based on a constitution that guaranteed certain rights to all citizens, or a parliamentary republic. In either case, the suffrage would be restricted to the wealthy classes.

Nationalists often favored liberal programs but were more concerned with political independence than with the form of government. They argued that every people who shared a common language, common customs, and a common culture had a right to form their own political institutions. In order to do so, they needed self-determination—that is, their own sovereign nation free from alien rule. Nationalists felt that all true patriots should work for liberation, or for unification in cases where a nation was divided. For example, nationalists in Hungary wanted independence from Austrian control, and German patriots were dissatisfied with the German Confederation, a loose union of rival states dominated by the most important member, Austria.

In 1815, the European ruling classes equated liberalism with revolution and therefore regarded it as a threat to peace and security. This antiliberal attitude was strongest where there was a weak middle class and little commercial and industrial progress. Thus, as one moved eastward across Europe, conservatism shaded into reaction. Russia had the most reactionary government of all, as discussed in Chapter 28.

The men who drafted the Vienna settlement almost completely ignored nationalistic sentiments; no one consulted the wishes of the Belgians, Danes, Norwegians, Finns, or Italians. Yet the sense of national consciousness, stimulated by the reaction against Napoleonic imperialism and the writings of propagandists, grew rapidly after 1815. Because many European countries included several national groups, the insistence on self-determination was bound to cause disturbances.

Several nations rebelled against the Congress System. Early in 1820 a revolt broke out in Spain. Basically it was an uprising of the army, but it soon gained popular support in a number of important Spanish cities. In an effort to quell the disturbances, King Ferdinand VII reinstated the liberal constitution that had been revoked in 1814. In July 1820 an insurrection in Naples forced Ferdinand I, king of the Two Sicilies, to grant a constitution.

Metternich was alarmed because the spirit of revolution threatened to spread throughout the entire Italian peninsula, endangering the Austrian position in the north. He therefore called a meeting of the Great Powers at Troppau in October. With the support of Russia and Prussia, Metternich issued a statement announcing that the Great Powers had the right to intervene to suppress the revolutions.

Lord Castlereagh, who refused to attend the conference, rejected the statement. Despite this rejection, the three eastern powers—Russia, Prussia, and Austria—authorized Metternich to send an Austrian army into Italy. The revolt in Naples was suppressed and the constitution revoked. When a similar revolt broke out in Piedmont in March 1821, Metternich again used the Austrian army for the same purpose.

Meanwhile, nothing had been done about the Spanish problem. In October 1822 Metternich summoned a conference at Verona in Venetia, Italy. Again Britain objected to intervention, and again it was overruled by the three eastern powers. This time they authorized France, fearful of a revolt so close to its borders, to restore order in Spain. In April 1823, 100 thousand French soldiers marched across the Pyrenees and within six months restored the reactionary regime of the Spanish king, Ferdinand VII.

There was one area in which the British were not overruled. Metternich and Alexander wanted to extend their authority across the Atlantic and to restore to Spain the Latin-American countries that had revolted against Spanish rule (see Chapter 23). The English resisted because they had developed important investments and a flourishing trade with the newly independent nations. Since Britain controlled the seas, the eastern powers could do nothing, and the Latin-American nations remained independent.

Nor were the members of the Holy Alliance any more successful in Greece. The Greeks had risen against Turkish rule in 1821 and had managed to stave off defeat for several years. Western Europeans who admired the culture of ancient Greece were sympathetic to the Greek cause and sent arms and money. (Lord Byron, the poet, fought and died for the Greek cause.) Greece also profited from the political and economic interests of the Great Powers in the Near East. Russia was interested in helping the Greeks, not because it supported nationalistic revolutions, but because it traditionally opposed Turkey and welcomed any opportunity to weaken the Ottomans. England and France did not want Russia to have a free hand in the Near East and thus secure control of the Dardanelles. Therefore in 1827 England, France, and Russia joined in an effort to secure Greek independence. Outnumbered by superior forces, the Turkish sultan finally acknowledged defeat. A peace treaty was signed in 1829, and the following year Greece became independent. This event represented the first significant change in the political map of Europe since the Congress of Vienna.

British Tories used repressive measures. The most conservative group of British society was the large landowning aristocracy that dominated Parliament through the Tory party from 1815 to 1830. When the Napoleonic wars ended in 1815, a sudden drop in the demand for manufactured goods produced a depression in industry. As wages fell and men were thrown out of work, radical agitation mounted. The Tories, anxious to preserve the high price of farm products, raised the protective tariff (the Corn Laws) against cheap imported grains. This move had the effect of keeping the price of bread high during a time of widespread unemployment. Riots broke out in various parts of the country. In 1819 some 80 thousand persons met at St. Peter's Fields outside Manchester in a huge protest meeting, demanding repeal of the Corn Laws and a drastic reform of the House of Commons. The jittery soldiers surrounding the field fired on the crowd; in the resulting panic, 11 people were killed and 400 wounded. Radicals called it the Peterloo Massacre.

The Tory government, badly frightened by the spreading disorder and violence, quickly passed the Six Acts. They sharply curtailed civil liberties and were the most repressive laws in British history.

During the 1820's economic conditions improved and radicalism subsided. Under these circumstances the Tories were willing to make some concessions to the demand for reform. In 1824 trade unions were made legal, although their members still did not have the right to strike. Four years later, Nonconformist Protestants were permitted to run for public office. The following year, 1829, Roman Catholics were granted the same right. Another reform was the liberalization of the criminal code; the death penalty was removed from 100 offenses. British conservatism thus took on a milder character and indicated some readiness to allow liberal changes through orderly methods.

The French monarchy became deeply conservative. Although the Bourbons returned to the French throne in 1814, they did not restore the despotic Old Regime. Louis XVIII was a constitutional parliamentary monarch pledged to protect individual rights. Fundamentally, his regime rested on the support of the upper middle class, who alone could vote. The liberals in France were willing to accept the monarchy provided it respected constitutional limitations on its power and worked through the French Chamber of Deputies.

Louis XVIII recognized this fact and tried to follow a conservative policy.

In 1820, however, the king's nephew was murdered by a fanatical workingman. A storm of protest arose from the extreme reactionaries, or ultraroyalists, who had never liked the constitution and who now demanded a sharp reduction in constitutional liberties. Louis gave in to their demands, and government policy became increasingly repressive. When Louis died in 1824, he was succeeded by his younger brother, the father of the murdered duke and the leader of the ultraroyalists.

The new king, Charles X, was a stubborn man with very little political intelligence. A firm believer in the theory of divine right, he seemed anxious to turn the clock back to 1789, as if nothing had happened in the meantime. His doggedly reactionary policy benefited only the clergy and nobility. It made the middle class hostile, creating a dangerous situation.

Austrian reaction dominated central Europe. Unlike England and France, which had homogeneous populations, the Austrian Empire was a sprawling state that included many peoples—Germans, Czechs, Slovaks, Poles, Magyars, Croats, Slovenes, Serbs, and Italians. Except for the Hapsburg ruling family, these peoples had little in common. The Germans were the dominant group, monopolizing the best positions in the government and in the army.

The two major classes were the wealthy landowning aristocracy, who controlled local government and local justice, and the peasants, who composed the bulk of the population. Most of the peasants were still serfs, bound to the land as their ancestors had been in the Middle Ages. Although there was some industry, the economy was largely agricultural. The Austrian government was one of the most reactionary in all of Europe, unwilling to make any reforms. Police spies were everywhere

(even Metternich's letters were opened), arbitrary arrest and secret trials were common, and censorship was harsh.

As the most powerful member of the German Confederation, Austria exerted a strong control over Germany. Metternich was concerned about the patriotic German student societies that advocated a united Germany, and in 1819 he forced the German states to adopt the Carlsbad Decrees. These laws abolished the patriotic societies, established government inspectors at all universities, and instituted a rigid censorship. The Carlsbad Decrees were enforced for many years. They checked the growth of liberalism and nationalism in Germany and central Europe.

Section Review

1. What were the aims of 19th-century liberals? of the nationalists?
2. Where and how did the Congress System succeed in crushing revolts during the 1820's? Where and why did it fail?
3. How did economic conditions in England after the Napoleonic wars lead to radical agitation? What repressive measures did the Tories take to counter this agitation? In what respects did Tory policy become more liberal during the 1820's?
4. Why did France become more reactionary after 1820?
5. In what respects was the Austrian government of the same period "one of the most reactionary in all of Europe"?

3 Liberalism and nationalism made gains in the 1830's

Except for those in Greece and Latin America, nationalist movements were effectively suppressed in the 1820's. Liberalism made advances only in those nations of western Europe that were becoming industrialized. In the 1830's, however, revolutions again erupted in Europe.

Political Cartoons of the early 19th century were powerful weapons in the hands of skillful artists. The English satirist George Cruikshank rendered a graphic denunciation of the Peterloo Massacre of 1819, left, showing fat blue-coated soldiers, their bloody axes upraised, charging into a crowd of terror-stricken civilians. To a cartoonist of the 1830's, the man in the French liberty cap, right, symbolized the revolutionary forces that toppled European rulers like so many flimsy playing cards. On the first card to fall is drawn a pear, a favorite symbol among cartoonists for jowly Louis Philippe of France. The discord between Belgium and the Netherlands was depicted as a domestic dispute, below left, with Belgium as a shrewish wife scolding her Dutch husband.

The French overthrew the Bourbon regime. Since 1824 opposition had been steadily building up against the ultraconservative government of Charles X. The climax came in July 1830 when general elections were held and a large number of liberals won. Knowing that they would repudiate his policies, Charles issued a series of decrees called the July Ordinances, which dissolved the Chamber of Deputies before it could meet, reduced the electorate by 75 per cent, imposed censorship on the press, and called for new elections.

The repercussions were immediate. Liberal politicians and journalists denounced the ordinances, and in Paris the workers joined the middle class in a revolution. After three days of fighting, with most of the army refusing to fire on the insurgents, Charles X fled to England as an exile.

The wealthy middle classes then took over the leadership of the revolution. They wanted to retain the constitutional monarchy and were opposed to the workers and students, who demanded a republic based on universal suffrage. They offered the crown to Louis Philippe, Duc d'Orléans, a relative of the deposed Bourbon, who promised to respect the constitution of 1814.

Louis Philippe's reign, called the July Monarchy, represented a triumph for the upper middle classes. Censorship was abolished, trial by jury was guaranteed, and the electorate was enlarged slightly. Voting, however, was limited to substantial property owners. The king himself had been a successful businessman in his own right, and he protected private property and encouraged business. While these policies satisfied merchants, bankers, and industrialists, radical democrats felt cheated. They became increasingly disillusioned with a regime that seemed to cater almost exclusively to the wealthy classes.

Belgium won its independence. The July revolution in Paris provided the impetus for revolutions elsewhere in Europe. The country most immediately affected was Belgium. The Belgians had never been happy with the Dutch union imposed upon them by the Vienna settlement. Differences in language and religion were aggravated by Dutch domination of Belgian affairs. Late in August 1830 Belgian nationalists and middle-class liberals rebelled against the Dutch and declared the complete independence of Belgium. National elections were held, and a constitution was drawn up that was more liberal than any other in Europe at the time.

Because the Belgian revolution violated the 1815 agreement, Russia, Prussia, and Austria prepared to intervene on behalf of the Dutch. The British and French, anxious to head off any intervention, summoned a conference of the Great Powers in London. In 1831 all five of the Great Powers signed the Treaty of London, which recognized the principle of Belgian independence and declared that Belgium must remain perpetually neutral. The treaty was finally confirmed in 1839 when the Dutch signed it.

Revolts failed in central Europe. Meanwhile, revolts broke out in the German states of Brunswick, Saxony, and Hesse-Kassel, where the rulers were forced to grant constitutions. Uprisings among Italians in Modena and Parma were suppressed by Austrian troops. Liberalism, continuing to flourish in Germany, soon became intolerable to Austria and Prussia. They quickly reimposed repressive measures, and by 1835 the conservatives were firmly in control.

Revolution also broke out in Poland in 1830. Encouraged by the success of the French and hoping for their aid, Polish nationalists rebelled against their king (the Russian czar, Nicholas I). They then set up a provisional government which tried to negotiate with the czar for reforms, but Nicholas opposed them all and sent a Russian army into Poland. The Polish rebels, divided among themselves, outnumbered by the Russians, and disappointed because Louis Philippe sent no aid, were easily crushed. Thousands of Poles fled into exile in western Europe as Nicholas abolished the 1815 constitution and imposed an oppressive military government.

Orderly reform progressed in Britain. Great Britain was the only major western European nation to escape violent revolution in the 1830's. It did so because reform was made possible through orderly means. During the 1820's even the Tories moderated their conservatism with a number of reform measures. None of these, however, changed the existing structure of the House of Commons, through which the Tories controlled the government and ruled the country. By 1830 the House of Commons was grossly out of balance. Candidates for office were elected from counties and districts known as boroughs, and no new borough had been created since 1688. This arrangement perpetuated the political power of the large landowners. Many new industrial towns in the north, which had grown rapidly in population during the 19th century, had no representation in the Commons, while boroughs in depopulated rural areas retained theirs. Some of these so-called rotten boroughs had no inhabitants at all; one, Dunwich, had been submerged by the sea.

Time after time in the years before 1830, the liberal minority party, the Whigs, introduced bills to reform the House of Commons, but they were always defeated by the Tories. This stubborn stand finally aroused public opposition and forced the Tories out of office in 1830. Lord Grey, leader of the Whigs, became head of the government and pledged reform. Twice the Whigs introduced a reform bill and twice it was defeated, the second time by the conservative House of Lords. When the House of Lords seemed ready to veto the measure a third time, riots broke out in several parts of the country, and Britain appeared to be on the brink of revolution. This situation, plus the king's threat to create enough new Whig peers to change the majority in the House of Lords, persuaded the latter to back down. In June 1832 the Reform Bill became law.

The Reform Bill accomplished two things. First, it lowered the property qualifications for voting and thereby increased the electorate by more than 50 per cent. Second, it redistributed the seats in the House of Commons to allow representation for the new industrial towns. Political power no longer belonged exclusively to the large landowners. From 1832 onward, it was shared by members of the upper middle class—merchants, manufacturers, businessmen, and professional people.

The Reform Bill of 1832 opened the way for a variety of other changes. Beginning with the abolition of slavery in the empire in 1833, Parliament went on to reform the system of poor relief, to modernize the local government of cities, and to regulate the finances of the Church of England. In 1833 it passed the first effective Factory Act, which prohibited child labor in textile mills. An act of 1842 forbade the employment of women and children in underground mines. Five years later, the daily working hours of women and children were limited to ten hours. This law soon applied to men also, and represented a great victory for the working classes.

Section Review

1. Why was the Bourbon monarchy overthrown in 1830? What kind of regime resulted?
2. Describe the conditions and the results of the 1830 revolts in Belgium and Poland.
3. What situation stimulated the English Reform Bill of 1832? Why was the bill important? What other reforms followed it?

4 A great wave of revolutions swept Europe in 1848

After the upheavals of the 1830's, Europe was changed. The new men of wealth had attained political power and advanced the cause of liberal constitutional, parliamentary government. This success was confined to western Europe, however. It was as if someone had drawn a line along the Rhine River. West of the line, industrialism and liberalism grew rapidly; east of the line, feudalism and autocracy continued with few changes.

Both west and east of the imaginary dividing line, many groups were discontented. In the West, especially in Britain and France, the bourgeoisie enjoyed a kind of golden age, but the lower classes resented their exclusion from political power and the unwillingness of middle-class governments to enact legislation to benefit them. In the east, nationalists and liberals were the principal discontented groups. In Germany and Italy, the desire for unification was stronger than ever, while in the sprawling Hapsburg Empire, Czechs, Magyars, and Croats all wanted independence. Liberals, frustrated in 1820 and again in 1830, still sought constitutional, representative government, civil liberties, and an end to serfdom.

These grievances were brought to a head by a business depression in the mid-1840's that caused large-scale unemployment from Britain to Silesia. In addition, potatoes and wheat—the staple foods of the lower classes—were in short supply and prices were high. A potato blight swept across Europe from Poland to Ireland in 1845 and again in 1846. In the latter year, the grain crops also failed and famine stalked the Continent. This combination of political discontent and economic distress caused a wave of revolutions in 1848.

France tried to create a republic. Once again Paris led the way. The regime of Louis Philippe catered especially to the interests of the richest members of the business community. Middle-class liberals became increasingly dissatisfied and wished to broaden the suffrage by reducing property qualifications for voting. The attitude of the government toward political reform was well expressed by the prime minister, François Guizot. To those who asked for the right to vote, he replied, "Get rich!"

Exasperation exploded in rebellion on the night of February 21, 1848, as barricades were hastily thrown up in the working-class districts of Paris. Soon rioting spread throughout the entire city. Guizot resigned. When the National Guard refused to fire on the people, Louis Philippe lost his nerve and on February 24 fled into exile. The July Monarchy ended as it had begun—in revolution.

The revolutionary leaders, a mixture of middle-class moderates and radicals from the industrial masses, proclaimed a republic (the second in French history) and set up a provisional government until a nationally elected assembly could draw up a new constitution. Meanwhile, the more radical leaders, led by the socialist Louis Blanc, demanded a bold program of social reform to alleviate the distress of the unemployed workers. Blanc proposed a scheme of government-financed factories managed by the workers, called national workshops. The bourgeois moderates disliked this socialistic system, but they needed the support of the workers. They therefore modified Blanc's original proposal, creating a program that was nothing more than a public-works project for unemployment relief. In a few months, one of every five Parisians depended on this relief for subsistence.

The Constituent Assembly, elected by universal manhood suffrage, met May 1848 and replaced the provisional government. Most members were moderates opposed to socialism. When they decided to abolish the national workshops, the workers again revolted. For three days in June, a savage civil war raged in the streets of Paris as insurgents fought against the troops of the Assembly. The workers were defeated, and 10 thousand Frenchmen lost their lives. These "June Days" left a legacy of bitter hatred between the workers and the middle class in France.

The June Days also frightened the Constituent Assembly into drafting a constitution with a strong president to be elected by universal manhood suffrage. When elections were held in December 1848, the nephew of Napoleon, Prince Louis Napoleon, was elected president by an overwhelming majority. An ambitious man, he set about carefully and methodically to build up his own power.

The Hapsburgs crushed opposition. Meanwhile, news of the February revolution in Paris had sparked outbursts throughout Europe. As one statesman put it, "When France sneezed, everybody else caught cold." On March 13, 1848, barricades mushroomed in the streets of Vienna, and students and workers surged into the imperial palace. Government leaders were stunned and terrified. Metternich hastily resigned and fled the city in disguise, while the government agreed to a popularly elected assembly.

The Magyars of Hungary, led by such nationalists as Louis Kossuth, had been agitating against Austrian rule for several decades. On March 15, 1848, the Hungarian Diet (assembly), meeting in Budapest, adopted the nationalists' program, known thereafter as the March Laws, which granted complete internal autonomy to the Hungarians. The Austrian emperor, Ferdinand, accepted these laws, and, when the Czechs revolted in Prague a few days later, he granted a similar status to the Kingdom of Bohemia. Serfdom was declared abolished in the Austrian Empire.

That same month revolutions exploded up and down the Italian peninsula. Austrian rulers were driven out of northern Italy. Venice declared itself a republic, as did Rome, and Pope Pius IX was forced to

Europe in 1848

Powerful reactionary leaders crushed many revolts in 1848, a year of social and political turmoil in Europe. However, the temporary victories achieved by the forces of liberalism and nationalism inspired patriots to continue their efforts. In France, a provisional government maintained order for several months after the inglorious end of the July Monarchy. Because of continued uprisings, a special police force was recruited from young bourgeois. A contemporary artist pictured a member of this *garde mobile* slouching at his post, right, his uniform in disarray. The year 1848 also marked the downfall of Prince von Metternich, who was a symbol of reaction and oppression. In the caustic caricature below left, he is shown fleeing Vienna, city of his past triumphs. Revolts led by Italian nationalists in 1848 failed when Austrian troops intervened to defeat the patriots. In the Italian cartoon below right, published in 1849, defenseless Italy is menaced by a double-headed eagle, the emblem of Austria.

flee. The king of Sardinia issued a constitution, declared war on Austria, and invaded the Austrian-held territories of Lombardy and Venetia.

The imperial government of the Hapsburgs, though stunned, was not destroyed. The army remained loyal and the tide began to turn in June. Early that month the Austrian commander in Prague, Alfred Windischgrätz, bombarded the city and chased out the radicals. In July, the Austrian commander in northern Italy, Joseph Radetzky, defeated the forces of the Sardinian king and restored Lombardy-Venetia to Hapsburg control. In September civil war broke out in Hungary when the Slavs refused to submit to Magyar rule and turned to Emperor Ferdinand for support. By this time, he felt that the liberal movement had gone too far, and saw that he could use the principle of "divide and rule" to suppress it. In October, Windischgrätz forced the liberals to surrender in Vienna.

By 1849 the Hapsburg monarchy had successfully crushed all opposition. The republics of Venice and Rome were destroyed and the pope was restored to his throne. Although the Hungarians put up a furious resistance, the end came when the Austrian emperor called on the Russian czar for help; 100 thousand Russian troops poured into Hungary, recapturing Budapest for the Hapsburgs in August 1849.

In the meantime, the old Emperor Ferdinand had abdicated in favor of his eighteen-year-old nephew, Francis Joseph. The new emperor felt that he need not be bound by any liberal promises that had been forced upon his uncle. After 1849 the imperial government, backed by the army, opposed with renewed vigor all forms of constitutionalism and nationalism.

Liberal movements failed in Germany. The contagion of the revolution in Paris also spread to Germany. Rioting broke out in Berlin on March 15, 1848, and the frightened king of Prussia, Frederick William IV, promised a constitution. Similar riots took place in the smaller German states, where governments collapsed one after the other. Elections were held for an all-German national assembly. Over 800 delegates met in Frankfort in May 1848 to draw up a liberal constitution for a united Germany.

From the beginning, however, the Frankfort Assembly exhibited serious weaknesses. For one thing, although it was popularly elected, it had no real power and could not force anyone to do its bidding. Second, the members of the Assembly were sharply divided over the question of the boundaries for the new Germany. Finally and most importantly, the delegates, coming mostly from the middle class, were liberals but not democrats. They therefore proceeded to write a constitution based on limited suffrage and the protection of private property. This action lost them the support of the German people who had elected the Assembly and without whom the revolutions of March would never have occurred in the first place.

Meanwhile, Frederick William had reasserted his authority with the help of his army, which had remained loyal. By the end of 1848, he regained the support of the peasants and workers by promising a program of economic security. He then called in the army and dispersed the Prussian legislative assembly. Rulers of other German states also succeeded in suppressing liberal movements in their domains.

The Frankfort Assembly had completed writing its constitution by April 1849 and, since it called for a constitutional monarchy, the delegates offered the new German crown to the king of Prussia. Frederick William turned it down, declaring that he could never accept a crown "created by an assembly born of revolutionary seed." This refusal was such a blow to the

Assembly that most delegates decided nothing further could be done and went home. A few doggedly remained in Frankfort and called upon the German people to rise again as they had done in March 1848. Some riots did occur, but the Assembly had lost its mass support. Prussian troops quickly suppressed the outbreaks and brought the Frankfort Assembly to an inglorious end.

Great Britain made peaceful changes. In spite of the reforms Britain had gained in the 1830's, many workingmen remained dissatisfied. Politically, they felt cheated by the 1832 Reform Bill, which denied them the right to vote. Economically, they felt exploited by the factory owners who kept their wages low, denied them the right to strike, and resisted social legislation. Two movements drew much support from them.

One was the Anti-Corn Law League, dedicated to the repeal of the protective tariffs that kept grain prices high. The organization was well run and financed, and its cause was aided by the business depression and crop failures of the mid-1840's. After much pressure, Parliament repealed the Corn Laws in 1846. Britain thus became committed to a policy of free trade. In effect, the nation had deliberately chosen to make itself dependent on imported foods, which it would pay for by exporting manufactured goods. This decision meant that more than ever Britain must control the seas for its very survival.

The second reform movement, known as Chartism, derived its name from the People's Charter (or petition), which was published in 1838. It demanded thorough reforms, including universal manhood suffrage, the secret ballot, and the abolition of property qualifications for membership in the House of Commons. The Chartists gathered over a million signatures and submitted their charter to the Commons.

When it was rejected, a wave of riots broke out in the country. In 1842 the Chartists collected more than 3 million signatures and again submitted their petition. Once more it was rejected.

The most dangerous phase of the movement came in 1848. Stimulated by the revolutions on the Continent, the Chartists not only collected over 2 million signatures for presentation to the House of Commons, but also prepared for an armed insurrection. The Commons for a third time turned down the charter. The plot for rebellion was betrayed by a government spy and the conspirators were quickly arrested. Henceforward, British workers concentrated their energies on trade unions and parliamentary change. Although Chartism died, the movement left its mark upon later political action and all but one of its reforms eventually became law.

The upheavals of 1848 had important results. By and large, the revolutions of 1848 failed to achieve their objectives; nevertheless, they had important results. One was the abolition of serfdom in Germany and the Austrian Empire. On the negative side was the realization that the revolutionaries failed not because their ideals were unworkable but because they lacked power. This situation was especially true in Germany. As a result, the years after 1848 saw a much greater emphasis upon military force and power politics as a means for obtaining desired goals.

Section Review

1. What conditions stimulated revolutionary movements in 1848?
2. What were the results of the revolts of 1848 in France? in the Austrian Empire? in Germany?
3. Why did the Frankfort Assembly fail?
4. How did the Anti-Corn Law League affect English economic policy? What reforms did the Chartists propose?

After Napoleon's defeat, European statesmen—led by Metternich, Castlereagh, Alexander I, and Talleyrand—met at the Congress of Vienna to restore the balance of power and redraw the map of Europe. They surrounded France with buffer states, reinstated the pope and the Bourbons in Italy, and made territorial adjustments in Germany, Scandinavia, and Poland. In addition, the Great Powers tried to work out arrangements to prevent conflicts. One, the Holy Alliance, was an idealistic and rather vague proposal. The other, the Quadruple Alliance, set up the Concert of Europe, or Congress System, dedicated to preserving peace by maintaining existing conditions.

In the years immediately following the Congress of Vienna, few basic political changes occurred. Liberalism and nationalism led to outbreaks against the Congress System in Spain, Naples, and Piedmont. These disturbances were quickly crushed, but a revolt of the Greeks against their Turkish rulers was eventually successful. Both England and France maintained a conservative policy during the 1820's, and the Austrian Empire ruled its subject peoples harshly.

In 1830 the French revolted against the reactionary Bourbon monarchy and placed Louis Philippe upon the throne. Inspired by this example, the Belgians revolted and secured their independence from the Dutch Netherlands. Less successful were outbreaks in several German and Italian states and in Poland. Great Britain escaped revolution by adopting such constitutional changes as the Reform Bill of 1832 and other liberalizing measures.

In 1848 liberal and nationalistic movements erupted in a great wave of revolutions, with the French again setting an example for the rest of Europe. After a bloody civil war, the middle class in France gained control and drafted a new constitution that called for a strong president.

The 1848 revolts inspired by the French had little success. The Austrian army quelled outbreaks in Vienna, Budapest, Prague, and Italy, and German revolutionaries fared little better. Frederick William of Prussia, though at first wavering under liberal pressure, reasserted his authority and put an end to the Frankfort Assembly and its attempt to unite Germany under a parliamentary system.

As in the 1830's, Great Britain made peaceful changes. Repeal of the Corn Laws was an important economic reform, and the nation avoided the violence spawned by the Chartist movement.

The Time

Arrange the numbered sentences below so that events appear in their correct time sequence.

(1) The Quadruple Alliance was formed to maintain peace. (2) Changing economic and social conditions in England led to the passage of the Reform Bill. (3) The repeal of the Corn Laws made British domination of the high seas more important than ever before. (4) Revolts in Spain, Piedmont, and Naples were successfully stopped by the Great Powers. (5) England, France, and Russia helped the Greeks win their independence from Turkish rule. (6) The Frankfort Assembly fell apart when it failed to unite Germany under a constitutional monarchy. (7) Metternich issued the Carlsbad Decrees to stifle student agitation for a united Germany. (8) The Bourbons were restored to the French throne. (9) The reactionary regime in France of Charles X was overthrown and replaced by the July Monarchy. (10) The Treaty of London guaranteed Belgian independence and neutrality. (11) Louis Napoleon was elected president of France.

The Place

1. Locate each of the following places and tell what country controlled it after the Congress of Vienna.

Belgium	Malta	Norway
Rhineland	Venetia	Finland
Genoa	Kingdom of	Cape Colony
Lombardy	the Two	Helgoland
Poland	Sicilies	Ceylon

2. In the 1820's, revolts broke out in Spain and on the Italian peninsula, and in alarm the Great Powers conferred at Troppau and Verona. Locate these cities.

3. Budapest, Prague, Sardinia, Berlin, and Frankfort were newsworthy in the revolutionary year 1848. Locate these places and tell what special events occurred in each.

The People

1. The Congress of Vienna was dominated by four men: Metternich, Castlereagh, Alexander I, and Talleyrand. Tell (1) what country each man represented, (2) what his aims were, and (3) in what ways each one was successful or unsuccessful in gaining his objectives.

2. Identify the following French leaders by citing an achievement or an event associated with each one.

Louis XVIII   Louis Blanc
Charles X   Louis Napoleon
Louis Philippe

3. Compare the attitudes of François Guizot and Lord Grey on extending the right to vote in their respective countries.

4. What action did each of the following rulers take in dealing with the problem of revolution within his own country?

Ferdinand I   Frederick William IV
Ferdinand VII   Francis Joseph
Nicholas I   Ferdinand (of Austria)

5. What part did the following men play in the revolutions of 1848?

Louis Kossuth   Joseph Radetzky
Alfred Windischgrätz

Historical Terms

1. Why was national self-determination, the goal held by many European peoples, a challenge to the settlements of the Congress of Vienna?

2. The Great Powers attempted to ensure stability in Central Europe by creating the German Confederation. What was it?

3. How were international relations to be regulated by the Holy Alliance? the Quadruple Alliance?

4. What was the Congress System, or Concert of Europe?

5. What agreements were reached at the conferences at Troppau and Verona?

6. In the generation after 1815, what were the main objectives of European liberals? of European nationalists?

7. The Corn Laws were an important issue in English politics. What were they? How did they lead to the Peterloo Massacre, the Six Acts, and the Anti-Corn Law League?

8. Why do each of the following terms denote an opposition to liberalism: rotten boroughs, ultraroyalists, Carlsbad Decrees, July Ordinances?

9. Tell why each of the following terms is associated with the idea of liberalism: July Monarchy, Frankfort Assembly, Reform Bill of 1832. What was Chartism?

10. What events in the French uprisings of 1848 are associated with the provisional government, the Constituent Assembly, and the June Days?

Questions for Critical Thinking

1. What principles for redrawing the map of Europe guided the statesmen at the Congress of Vienna? How were these principles applied in specific cases?

2. Why did the revolutions of 1848 generally fail to overthrow the ruling regimes or to bring about dramatic changes in their nature?

3. In the years between 1815 and 1850, what examples are there of the Congress System (or the Concert of Europe) in action? Would you say that national self-interest or a desire to preserve peace, or both, motivated the European diplomats and rulers of this period? Explain your answer with pertinent examples.

4. Compare and contrast the means by which liberal reforms were brought about in England and in France.

5. What examples of the triumph of nationalism are evident in the first half of the 19th century? Tell how each triumph came about.

6. Which of the revolutions of 1848 in France, in the German states, and in Hungary were primarily motivated by nationalism? by liberalism? Give reasons for your answers.

The Growth of Nationalism
and Democracy

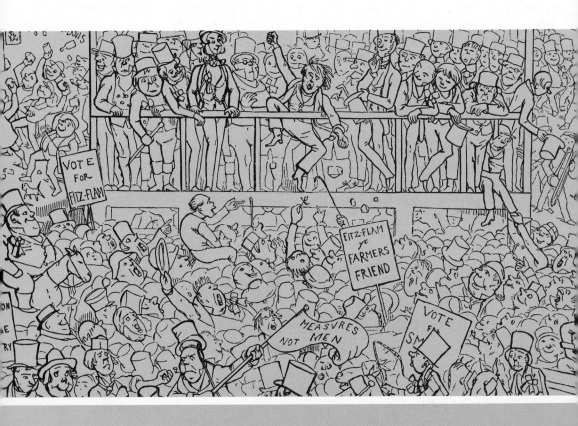

The right of every citizen to vote is considered a basic requirement for a modern democracy. One of the first European countries to grant universal manhood suffrage was England, where the tradition of democracy was so strong that social critics were free to lampoon some of its excesses. In the sketch above, the cartoonist pokes good-natured fun at the vigorous oratory of a vote-seeker.

On a July evening in 1870 in Berlin, three high-ranking Prussians sat gloomily eating their dinner. They were the prime minister, Otto von Bismarck; the war minister, General Albert von Roon; and the chief of staff, General Helmut von Moltke. Only the day before, Prussia had suffered a diplomatic defeat: France had forced the Prussian king, William I, to withdraw his support from a Hohenzollern prince (and distant relative) who had been asked to fill the vacant Spanish throne. Bismarck had advocated the candidacy in an effort to embarrass France, and now he felt so humiliated that he considered resigning.

At this moment a dispatch arrived from the king at the resort of Ems. The telegram described an interview with the French ambassador, who had demanded that William promise never to allow a Hohenzollern to accept the Spanish crown. Although irritated, the king had politely but firmly refused to make such a promise and had ended the interview.

Bismarck reflected a moment and then proceeded to condense this "Ems dispatch" so that it sounded as if the conversation between the Prussian monarch and the French ambassador had been discourteous. Then he released it to the press. The French public, in a warlike mood, regarded the telegram as an insult and demanded war. Prussia, with its powerful military machine, was only too happy to oblige.

Prussia won the Franco-Prussian War and much more besides, for out of it emerged a united German Empire under Prussian domination. Creation of this empire was Bismarck's greatest achievement, and the most significant nationalistic event in an age of rising nationalism. So strong was the tide of nationalism that by 1914 the political map of Europe was radically different from the map of 1815.

Along with the nationalistic tide ran the current of democracy. Considered revolutionary in 1815 and radical in 1848, by 1914 it was regarded as the most desirable form of government. Its progress was uneven, advancing fastest in western Europe and slowest in eastern Europe. Wherever it increased, however, it transformed political life and helped create a society based on active participation by the masses.

This chapter describes how:

1. **Several nations clashed in the Crimean War.**

2. **Continental Europe was politically reorganized.**

3. **Democracy advanced in western Europe.**

4. **Southern and eastern Europe made little progress.**

1 Several nations clashed in the Crimean War

Although in 1848 revolutions had swept through almost all of Europe, none of the major nations became involved in war with one another. This situation was due largely to England and Russia, the two powers that escaped revolution and followed a policy of careful restraint in their diplomacy. The revolutions, however, brought forward a new generation of politicians and statesmen who were willing to use any methods, including force, to advance their national interests. This new spirit in politics and diplomacy, known as *Realpolitik,* weakened the habits of coöperation among European nations, upon which the Concert of Europe had been based. An example of this new spirit was the Crimean War.

Disagreements arose over the Ottoman Empire. The first large-scale armed clash in Europe after 1815, the Crimean War, pitted France and Britain against Russia. All three nations had interests in the Near

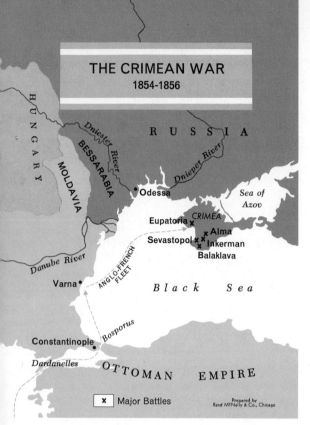

THE CRIMEAN WAR
1854-1856

HUNGARY

Dniester River

RUSSIA

BESSARABIA

MOLDAVIA

Dnieper River

•Odessa

Sea of Azov

Eupatoria ✗ CRIMEA

✗ Alma

Sevastopol ✗ ✗ Inkerman

Balaklava

Danube River

ANGLO-FRENCH FLEET

Varna •

Black Sea

Constantinople • Bosporus

Dardanelles

OTTOMAN EMPIRE

| ✗ | Major Battles

Prepared by
Rand M⁶Nally & Co., Chicago

Public opinion in Britain was thoroughly aroused and bent on teaching Russia a lesson. As for France, Napoleon III saw an excellent opportunity to enhance his prestige with a short, victorious war.

Almost all of the fighting took place in the Crimea, a peninsula jutting out from Russia into the Black Sea. In September 1854, thousands of English and French troops landed at Eupatoria and began to march on Sevastopol, a Russian city on the Black Sea. They defeated the Russians at the river Alma on September 20 and moved on toward the city. The allies were victorious again at the battles of Balaklava on October 25 and of Inkerman on November 5, but they could not break through the Russian trenches at Sevastopol. Cold weather, disease, and lack of food and fuel during the eleven-month siege cost the allies heavy losses. A small but well-trained army from Sardinia joined the French and English forces in the summer of 1855 and, after the French succeeded in capturing a strategic position in September, the city finally yielded. Czar Alexander II, who had come to the Russian throne in March, was ready for peace.

The war had important results. In March 1856 the nations involved in the war gathered at Paris for a peace conference. The treaty that resulted imposed a number of restrictions on Russia: the czar had to cede Bessarabia to Moldavia, thus losing control of the mouth of the Danube River; Moldavia and Wallachia were declared self-governing principalities and became the nucleus of a future Rumania; Russia yielded its claim as exclusive protector of Christians in the Turkish Empire.

The most humiliating provision of all was the requirement that Russia must not maintain warships on the Black Sea. Although this provision applied to every nation, it affected Russia more seriously because it left this great power with an

East and were seeking advantages in the Ottoman Empire. When a dispute arose over whether France or Russia had the right to protect Christians living in the empire and those visiting the Holy Land, Sultan Abdul Mejid I sided with the French. This decision angered the Russian czar, Nicholas I, who tried to intimidate the Turks by sending Russian troops into the Turkish-controlled principalities of Moldavia and Wallachia (now part of Rumania). The British viewed this action as a move to seize control of the Dardanelles. The czar refused to withdraw his troops and the Turks declared war on Russia in 1853. The Crimean War began in March 1854, when Britain and France, determined to prevent any Russian penetration of the Near East, took up arms in support of the Turks.

Nicholas realized that he had overplayed his hand and evacuated his troops from the Turkish provinces. It was too late.

undefended southern frontier. From then on the principal aim of Russian foreign policy was to revise the Black Sea clauses and regain military rights there. Russia could no longer be counted on to defend the existing balance of power as it had in the past, since this balance was not to its advantage.

Austria, which had wavered in its policy prior to the war, emerged weak and friendless. Britain had made a poor showing in the Crimea, and suffered a decline in military prestige. In such circumstances, ambitious men in France, Italy, and Prussia found opportunities to destroy the Vienna settlement of 1815.

Section Review

1. In what respect did the revolutions of 1848 bring about a change in international politics?
2. Why did the various powers clash in the Crimea?
3. What were the most important consequences of the Crimean War?

2 **Continental Europe was politically reorganized**

In the fifteen years following the Crimean War, the European political system was drastically reorganized. The changes were brought about by a remarkable group of vigorous and forceful statesmen, whose policies reflected the militant nationalism of the period.

France became a dictatorship. After his election as president of the Second Republic in 1848, Louis Napoleon worked to acquire greater and greater power for himself. He won the support of many Frenchmen by trading on the popularity of his uncle, Napoleon, and by stressing order and national prestige. He arranged a *coup d'état* in December 1851 to overthrow the constitution. The following year the people were asked to vote on whether he should be emperor. They responded with an overwhelming affirmative, and he became Emperor Napoleon III.

Unlike his uncle, Louis Napoleon was neither a military genius nor a brilliant administrator, but essentially a shrewd politician. Unscrupulous in his methods, clever in cultivating and manipulating public opinion, Napoleon III was a forerunner of 20th-century dictators. Although a parliament existed in France, it had no real power. The government controlled elections and rigidly enforced censorship.

Napoleon III sugared the pill of despotism with a program of economic advancement. Railroad construction expanded more than fivefold, iron ships were built to replace wooden ones, and in 1859 a French company began the ten-year task of building the Suez Canal. The French stock exchange did a brisk business. An energetic city planner, Baron Georges Haussmann, modernized Paris by creating broad, tree-lined boulevards, public squares and parks, and magnificent buildings and monuments. For the peasants Napoleon III established model farms, and for the workers he legalized strikes. Asylums and hospitals were built, and medicine was distributed free to the poorest classes.

Had Napoleon been content to concentrate on internal problems, he might have remained on the throne a long time. As the bearer of the Napoleonic name, however, he had a mystical belief in his destiny as a great figure in Europe and was determined to assert French power on the world political scene. In 1852 he had promised the French that the formation of the Second Empire meant peace, but by 1854 he had led France into the Crimean War, and other military adventures followed.

One of Napoleon's most disastrous projects was his intervention in Mexico. That

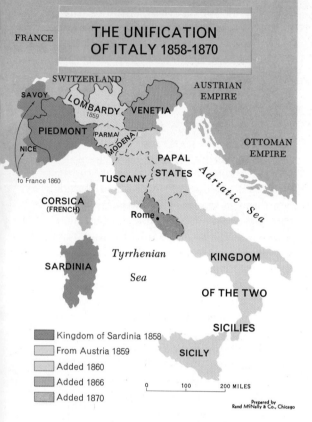

FRANCE

SWITZERLAND

SAVOY

LOMBARDY
1859

VENETIA

AUSTRIAN
EMPIRE

PIEDMONT

PARMA

MODENA

NICE

to France 1860

TUSCANY

PAPAL
STATES

OTTOMAN
EMPIRE

Adriatic Sea

CORSICA
(FRENCH)

Rome

SARDINIA

Tyrrhenian

Sea

KINGDOM

OF THE TWO

SICILIES

Kingdom of Sardinia 1858
From Austria 1859
Added 1860
Added 1866
Added 1870

SICILY

0   100   200 MILES

Prepared by
Rand M⁵Nally & Co., Chicago

ments there, and he deserted Maximilian, who in 1867 was captured and shot by Mexican soldiers.

Italy was unified. In 1859 Italy was still, as Metternich once remarked, a "geographical expression," divided into several large and small states. Ever since the French Revolution, however, Italian nationalism had been steadily growing. It expressed itself specifically in the writings of such ardent patriots as Giuseppe Mazzini and more generally in the *Risorgimento,* or resurgence, a movement among middle-class liberals who hoped for Italian unity.

The events of 1848 showed that brave men and noble dreams were not enough. Without the political, diplomatic, and military power to expel Austria, the dream of unity could not become reality. Count Camillo di Cavour appreciated this fact better than his countrymen. In 1852 he became prime minister of the Kingdom of Sardinia, politically and economically the most advanced state in Italy. A great admirer of England, he proceeded to make Sardinia a model of economic and political progress, and the natural leader in the movement for Italian unification.

Cavour was a shrewd political tactician who realized that Italy could not achieve unification without outside help. He deliberately involved Sardinia in the Crimean War, not because of any grievance against Russia, but because participation gave him a chance to publicize Italian grievances at the Paris peace conference.

Cavour then won the support of Napoleon III, who liked to think of himself as the champion of nationalism, and in 1859 cleverly maneuvered the Austrians into declaring war. The combined Franco-Sardinian armies easily overpowered the Austrians, and revolutions broke out all over northern Italy. Napoleon III, fearful that the movement had gone too far, infuriated Cavour by making a separate

nation, which had borrowed heavily from investors overseas, suspended payments on its foreign debt in 1861, and France, Spain, and Great Britain sent troops to compel President Benito Juárez to pay. Spain and Britain soon withdrew, realizing that Napoleon had ambitious plans. He sent additional troops to take Mexico City and in 1863 made the Archduke Maximilian of Austria, Francis Joseph's younger brother, emperor of Mexico. Maximilian, dependent on French troops to bolster his regime against a hostile populace, was little more than a puppet of Napoleon.

At that time the United States was involved in the War Between the States and could not protest effectively against the French. By 1866, however, the war was over and the Americans demanded that the French withdraw. Napoleon needed his forces in Europe because of involve-

peace with Austria. The revolutions continued, however, and in 1860 all of northern Italy except Venetia was united with Sardinia. Cavour in the meantime made peace with Austria.

There still remained the Papal States and the Kingdom of the Two Sicilies. At this point a fiery leader named Giuseppe Garibaldi took matters into his own hands. In May 1860, with a volunteer army of about 1100 men, he invaded the Kingdom of the Two Sicilies and conquered it. Then he prepared to march on Rome. Afraid that such a step would incur the wrath of both France and Austria, Cavour hastily sent a Sardinian army southward, which seized a large area of the Papal States and prevented Garibaldi from carrying out his attack. Cavour then persuaded Garibaldi to permit the unification of the Two Sicilies with Sardinia. In 1861, only a few months before the death of Cavour, the Kingdom of Italy was formally proclaimed with Victor Emmanuel of Sardinia as king. The final steps in the formation of modern Italy were taken in 1866 and 1870, with the addition of Venetia and Rome, respectively.

Bismarck became chancellor of Prussia. Politically, the Germany of 1862 was not much different from the Germany of 1815— a hodgepodge of states within the framework of the loose German Confederation. Socially and economically, however, important changes had taken place. Under Prussian leadership, the *Zollverein*, a tariff union to regulate and standardize trade duties, was established in 1834; it eventually included most of Germany outside of Austria. The Industrial Revolution stimulated the growth of cities, the expansion of the business and working classes, and networks of railroad and telegraph lines. To many German nationalists, the increasing economic unity pointed up the advantages to be gained through political unification. Furthermore, the failure of the Frankfort

Assembly of 1848 had demonstrated that force, not words, was needed to hammer Germany into a single nation. The necessary power was available only in Prussia.

Prussia, however, was indifferent to the larger question of German nationalism. It wanted to increase its own strength and importance within the Confederation, especially at the expense of Austria. This goal required a strong army. The question of a military buildup led to a constitutional deadlock in 1862. King William I wanted to reform and expand the army. The liberal-minded parliament, however, was suspicious of the aristocratic Junkers, the landowning class that dominated the army, and refused to approve the necessary expenditures. To break the deadlock, the king appointed Otto von Bismarck, a prominent conservative Junker, as his prime minister, or chancellor, in 1862.

It was a fateful move. Bismarck was a man of indomitable will. Clever and unscrupulous, he was oblivious to public opinion but passionately loyal to the Prussian monarchy. He was an opportunist who knew how to take advantage of each situation as it came along. Like Cavour, Bismarck was a believer in *Realpolitik*, carefully weighing every factor and unswayed by sentiment or by principles. He simply ignored the liberal Prussian parliament and went ahead with the army reforms, ordering taxes collected without consent of parliament. The people of Prussia, obedient to authority, did not revolt and parliamentary protests went unheeded. Bismarck announced that the issues of the day would be decided not by speeches and votes, but "by blood and iron."

Three wars helped form the German Empire. Bismarck showed what he meant in a series of three short wars. The first, in 1864, occurred when Denmark tried illegally to annex the duchy of Schleswig. Seeing a chance to enlarge Prussian territory,

THE UNIFICATION
OF GERMANY 1865-1871

SWEDEN

Baltic Sea

DENMARK

North

SCHLESWIG

EAST
PRUSSIA

Sea

HOLSTEIN

WEST
PRUSSIA

MECKLENBURG
SCHWERIN

P O M E R A N I A

Hamburg
Bremen

MECKLENBURG
STRELITZ

POSEN

OLDENBURG

KINGDOM
OF HANOVER

BRANDENBURG

RUSSIAN
EMPIRE

Berlin

NETHERLANDS

P R U S S I A

WESTPHALIA

BRUNSWICK
HANOVER

A N H A L T

K I N G D O M   *O F*

SAXONY

S I L E S I A

RHINE
PROV.
OF
PRUSSIA

HESSE-KASSEL

SAXON DUCHIES

KINGDOM
OF
SAXONY

BELGIUM

HESSE-
DARMSTADT

NASSAU

DARMSTADT

Frankfort

A U S T R I A N   *E M P I R E*

LUXEM-
BURG

BAVARIAN
PALATINATE

LORRAINE

GRAND DUCHY OF BADEN

KINGDOM

OF

······· Boundary, German Confederation of 1815

FRANCE

KINGDOM
OF
WÜRTTEMBERG

BAVARIA

Kingdom of Prussia 1865

ALSACE

Absorbed by Prussia 1866

Became member of Federation 1867

SWITZERLAND

Became member of Empire 1871

Prepared
Rand McNally & C

Bismarck invited Austria to join Prussia in a war against Denmark, presumably on behalf of the German Confederation. After defeating the Danes, Prussia took over Schleswig, and Austria seized the neighboring duchy of Holstein.

Friction then developed because of Prussian-Austrian rivalry. Confident that Prussia could easily defeat its rival in a military struggle, Bismarck first made certain that Austria had no friends. Russia and France promised to remain neutral, the former out of gratitude to Bismarck for

his offer of help in a Polish revolt in 1863, the latter because of vague suggestions of territorial rewards. Italy was won over by the promise of Venetia. In 1866 Prussia declared war on Austria, a war known as the Seven Weeks' War because Prussia won in that time.

The peace treaty ended the German Confederation and provided, among other things, that several states in northern Germany were to be incorporated into Prussia, and that all states north of the Main River would join in a North German Confederation under Prussian leadership. Austria was also forced to turn Holstein over to Prussia.

Bismarck next turned his attention to southern Germany, where there was much opposition to Prussia. He felt that only war with France would bring the southern states into a closer relationship with the north, first in a military alliance and later in a political union. When the Spanish throne became empty in 1870, the Prussian chancellor saw an opportunity to exert pressure on France. He deviously persuaded Spain to offer the throne to a member of the Prussian ruling family. The French, worried by growing Prussian power, protested vigorously and even outmaneuvered Bismarck for a time when they prevailed upon the Prussian king to withdraw his support from the Hohenzollern candidate. However, the French were not content with this diplomatic success and made further demands through their ambassador. When William rejected these demands, Bismarck took advantage of the king's dispatch from Ems to precipitate a war with France, known as the Franco-Prussian War.

Once again it was a brief conflict. Three German armies invaded Alsace-Lorraine in August 1870 and immediately won several battles against the poorly prepared French. In September, Napoleon III surrendered with his army at Sedan. News of his capture led to a revolution in Paris, which overthrew the Second Empire and proclaimed a republic. Paris resisted a German siege for 130 days, but finally fell in January 1871. Preliminary peace terms awarded Prussia an indemnity of 5 billion francs, as well as the territories of Alsace and Lorraine. The French never forgave the Prussians for the annexation of their frontier provinces.

The south German states had joined Prussia in the war against France. On January 18, 1871, while Paris was still under siege, the German Empire was formally proclaimed in the Hall of Mirrors at Versailles, with William of Prussia as emperor. The new empire, which included the south German states, soon became the strongest power in continental Europe.

Austria created the Dual Monarchy. In both Italy and Germany, nationalistic movements led to political consolidation. In the Austrian Empire, nationalism worked in the opposite direction, weakening the central regime. No other result was possible where various nationality groups clamored, not for complete independence, but for more local self-government. This was especially true of the Magyars, who comprised about one third of the population of Hungary. Bitter over their defeat in the 1848 revolution, the Magyars grew increasingly resentful as the predominantly German-speaking Hapsburg government tried to strengthen its autocratic rule.

The climax came in 1867. Weakened by war against Italy in 1859 and against Prussia in 1866, the Hapsburg government worked out a compromise with the Magyars. The result, in 1867, was a Dual Monarchy, with two kingdoms, one Austrian, the other Hungarian. Both had one ruler in common (the Hapsburg emperor). But each kingdom had its own parliament and enjoyed independence in internal affairs. Only in the fields of foreign affairs, finance, and war were there common ministries.

This reorganization was a clever device for preserving Austria-Hungary as a major power in international affairs, but it left unsatisfied the numerous Slavic groups that also wanted internal autonomy.

Section Review
1. Describe the chief features of the rule of Napoleon III.
2. What were the principal steps taken by Count Cavour in unifying Italy?

3. How did Prussia profit from the 1864 war with Denmark? the Seven Weeks' War? the Franco-Prussian War?

4. What conditions and events led Austria to form the Dual Monarchy? How were governmental functions divided between the two kingdoms?

3 Democracy advanced in western Europe

In the years between 1871 and 1914, from the end of the Franco-Prussian War to the outbreak of World War I, the nations of western Europe enjoyed phenomenal growth. Industry, transportation, and communications expanded rapidly, as did cities and the population. Externally its power and influence spread to the farthest corners of the globe in the great age of imperialism. These advances were accompanied by the extension of democratic constitutional government and social reforms. Ideas about the nature of democracy were also undergoing a change. The movement to extend voting privileges to ordinary people—not just the prosperous middle class—was gaining momentum, particularly in England. To be sure, pressing social, economic, and political problems existed. Yet the dominant tone in western Europe was one of continuing faith in progress and optimism about the future.

Britain adopted many reforms. The great model of material progress, orderly reform, and political stability in these years was once again Great Britain. For most of the period the reigning monarch was Queen Victoria, who became a symbol of an era characterized by far-reaching political power and great prosperity.

The Whig and Tory parties were transformed in the 1850's into the Liberal and Conservative parties, which were led by two outstanding figures, William E. Gladstone, a Liberal, and Benjamin Disraeli, a Conservative. The two alternated as prime minister from 1868 to 1880 and after Disraeli's death in 1881, Gladstone continued to dominate politics until he retired in

National Leaders

During the last half of the 19th century, national leaders used various methods to achieve power and prestige. Louis Napoleon hoped to re-create the grandeur that France had enjoyed under his uncle, Napoleon. His slogan, "The Empire is Peace," was mocked in an English cartoon, far left; the emperor is pictured as a porcupine, his body covered with bayonets. Chancellor Bismarck, left, was a skillful practitioner of *Realpolitik*, who found war to be a useful means of uniting Germany under Prussian leadership. The patriotic fervor of the revolutionist Garibaldi helped bring about Italian unity. In the cartoon below, he helps the new king, Victor Emmanuel, into a boot, the geographic symbol of Italy. Queen Victoria, during her long reign from 1837 to 1901, became the symbol of a stable and powerful British Empire. She is shown at right between the two political leaders on whom she depended for advice in most affairs of state: the Conservative Disraeli, above, and the Liberal Gladstone, below.

1894. Gladstone—deeply religious, eloquent, and serious—led a party composed chiefly of manufacturing and commercial interests. Witty and imaginative, Disraeli believed in the ruling mission of the landed gentry and aristocracy. He saw them as defenders of the common people against middle class business interests, and thus tried to promote a political alliance between the upper and lower classes.

Both parties, sensitive to continuing pressure to broaden the franchise, sponsored bills to extend voting rights, the Conservatives with the Second Reform Bill in 1867 and the Liberals with the Third Reform Bill of 1884. After 1884 most male adults had the right to vote. Under Gladstone and Disraeli, state-supported public education was adopted, the secret ballot was introduced, labor unions were given more freedom, and a workmen's compensation law was passed.

After 1900, important changes took place in British politics. The rise of the Labour party induced the Liberals, anxious to retain the working-class vote, to embark on a program of social welfare legislation. The Liberals, in control of the government from 1905 to 1916, and led by Herbert Asquith and David Lloyd George, enacted laws setting up old-age pensions, unemployment insurance, and minimum wages. In 1909, Lloyd George proposed a budget based on the idea that wealthy people should pay proportionately higher taxes than others, especially if their income was derived from rents. The House of Lords objected strenuously and in 1910 the House of Commons passed resolutions severely limiting the Lords' legislative functions. When it appeared that the Lords would defeat the resolutions, King George V threatened to create enough new peers to carry the vote. In 1911 the House of Lords reluctantly passed the Parliament Act abridging its own powers. Thereafter it wielded little real influence.

Southern Ireland became independent. Although England succeeded in bettering conditions for its own people, it could not seem to solve the so-called Irish Question. The Roman Catholic Irish objected to paying taxes for the support of the Anglican Church in Ireland. They also resented political control by England and a land system that kept them in perpetual poverty. Gladstone succeeded in abolishing tax support for the Anglican Church in Ireland with the Disestablishment Act of 1869. He also instituted a program of land reform, giving the peasants more rights in connection with the land they farmed. The passage of these economic measures benefited the Irish, but by this time agitation had shifted to political matters. The Irish responded enthusiastically to a strong nationalistic leader, Charles Parnell, who advocated Home Rule (self rule) for Ireland. Gladstone introduced two modified Home Rule bills, but neither carried Parliament.

Under Asquith, the Liberals again introduced a Home Rule bill, which was finally passed in 1914. This time the predominantly Presbyterian northern Irishmen of Ulster objected. During World War I the problem was put aside, but with the war's end violence broke out. In 1922 a compromise solution granted independence to southern Ireland (Eire) and allowed Ulster to remain within the United Kingdom.

A Third Republic was established in France. After the overthrow of the Second Empire and defeat in the Franco-Prussian War, the French held elections for a National Assembly, which would conclude peace with Germany and decide upon the form of government France would have. About one third of the deputies elected were republicans, the rest being monarchists of various kinds. Clearly the majority of the French still distrusted republicanism as being warlike and radical.

Paris, however, was a stronghold of republicanism. Unwilling to accept the harsh Prussian peace terms and deeply suspicious of the monarchist National Assembly meeting in Versailles, Parisians in March 1871 rose in rebellion against the Assembly and set up their own municipal council, the Commune. A bloody civil war raged in the streets of the capital for the next two months. The National Assembly finally subdued the Parisians and then carried out a fearful campaign of reprisal.

The fear of radical republicanism was so strong during this period that some form of monarchy could probably have been established if the monarchists had cooperated with one another. The two major factions, Bourbons and Orleanists, could not agree, however. The Assembly failed to adopt a constitution and instead passed three laws in 1875 which in fact amounted to the creation of a republic. The laws provided for a president and for a premier and cabinet responsible to the two-house legislature; the lower house (the Chamber of Deputies) was to be elected by universal manhood suffrage. This Third Republic, intended by the monarchists as a temporary expedient, lasted until 1940—longer than any regime since 1789.

Because of its irregular constitution and uncertain beginnings, the Third Republic was particularly vulnerable to attacks from its unreconciled opponents. Every scandal and revelation of corruption became a threat to the very existence of the regime. The 1880's and 1890's were filled with crises, the climax coming with the Dreyfus affair. A Jewish army officer, Alfred Dreyfus, was convicted of treason by a military tribunal in 1894. When evidence later indicated that the real traitor was an officer of aristocratic Catholic background, public opinion divided sharply. Foes of the Republic—the officer corps, monarchists, and the Church—strongly opposed reopening the case, arguing that to do so would undermine military authority. Pro-Republic forces finally prevailed, however. A civil court pardoned Dreyfus in 1906, thus asserting the power of the civil government over the army. The second verdict served also as a vindication of the principle that any citizen, regardless of race or creed, could obtain justice in a democracy.

By 1914 the Republic, although it still had enemies, had gained the support of the vast majority of Frenchmen. It had shown itself able to maintain peace, security, prosperity, and a respect for civil liberties. French politics, however, was in a confused state. The existence of many political parties showed that public opinion was divided. Although government policy remained fairly consistent, ministries rose and fell with chronic regularity; there were fifty between 1871 and 1914. Other problems developed as a discontented laboring class sought social legislation.

Social reforms were promoted in Germany. The destiny of the German Empire in the first twenty years of its existence rested largely in the hands of Chancellor Bismarck. He built the empire as a union of monarchies in which Prussia would have the strongest voice. Although there was a constitution and a lower house (Reichstag) elected by universal manhood suffrage, real power remained in the hands of the chancellor and the aristocratic upper house (Bundesrat).

Bismarck's intense nationalism made him suspicious of Germans who did not subordinate themselves completely to the state. During the 1870's he launched a campaign against the Roman Catholic Church in Germany. This *Kulturkampf*, or "battle of civilization," sharply curtailed Catholic education and freedom of worship. The Jesuits were expelled, Catholic bishops were arrested, and others fled into exile. After a few years, however, Bismarck abruptly ended the *Kulturkampf*.

Crises in European Politics involved almost all the major powers in the late 19th century. International rivalries broke out in the Crimean War, described by one historian as "entered into without necessity, conducted without foresight." The scene above left shows a British encampment near Sevastopol, where troops spent a harsh winter trying to capture the city. Dreams of imperial glory prompted the intervention in Mexico of Napoleon III. At left, in a painting by Edouard Manet, the puppet emperor Maximilian meets his death at the hands of a firing squad. The Irish Question disrupted the British Isles for decades. One problem was that English landowners ruthlessly evicted Irish tenant farmers, as shown above. France underwent several critical situations. Above right, national guardsmen execute Parisians after the Commune uprising in 1871. Below, Dreyfus hears testimony at his espionage trial in 1894.

He felt that the Catholic Church was no longer a threat, and that Catholic support would be useful in his next campaign, the drive against socialism.

The phenomenal expansion of German industry led to the growth of a large German working class. Many workers became interested in socialism—a movement which advocated, among other things, state ownership of all means of production and distribution. When they organized a Social Democratic party in 1875, Bismarck became alarmed. Beginning in 1878, Germany passed law after law against socialism. Designed to exterminate the movement, these laws succeeded only in driving it underground. In the 1880's Bismarck tried to lure the workers away from socialism by initiating a comprehensive state program of social insurance covering sickness, accident, and old age. It was the most advanced program of its kind in Europe, but it did not kill socialism. In 1890 the chancellor quarreled with the new emperor, William II, about antisocialist legislation, which the latter considered too extreme. On the surface, it appeared that the breach between the two men was motivated by issues. But in reality, the clash was one of two strong-willed personalities. Bismarck, after almost thirty years of service, was forced to retire.

William II, who was twenty-nine when he became emperor in 1888, reigned until 1918. An ambitious man with exalted ideas about his own power, he instituted an aggressive foreign policy. In domestic affairs he abolished the antisocialist laws and broadened the system of social insurance, but refused to extend political democracy. The Social Democrats continued to gain strength, in 1912 becoming the largest single political party in the Reichstag.

Smaller countries shared in the reform movement. Of the smaller nations in western Europe, Belgium came closest to paralleling developments in Britain. A constitutional monarchy, Belgium in the 1890's adopted universal manhood suffrage, initiated factory legislation, and instituted a program of social insurance. The Netherlands, less industrially advanced, moved more slowly toward political democracy. In the 1890's, less than 15 per cent of the population could vote, and universal manhood suffrage was not adopted until 1917.

The most advanced democracy in continental Europe was Switzerland, a federal union of cantons with a two-house legislature. Universal manhood suffrage was adopted in 1874 and was reinforced by a large measure of direct democracy, including the initiative and referendum. The former was the procedure by which people could propose new laws; the latter allowed them to pass on legislation already in existence.

In northern Europe, the constitutional monarchy of Denmark granted the right to vote to all men and most women in 1915. Norway and Sweden, united at the Congress of Vienna, separated peacefully in 1905. Both were constitutional monarchies and soon adopted universal suffrage. In 1907 Norway became the first sovereign state to grant women the right to vote.

Section Review

1. What groups made up the English Conservative and Liberal parties? Name some reforms adopted from 1867 to 1911? Name the chief steps by which Southern Ireland gained its independence.
2. Why did Parisians set up the Commune? Describe the kind of government that was established after its fall. What were the strengths and weaknesses of the Third Republic by 1914?
3. What steps did Bismarck take to strengthen Prussian nationalism in the German Empire and to combat socialism? In what respects did William II reverse Bismarck's policies?

4. Discuss the progress toward democracy made by Belgium, the Netherlands, Switzerland, and Scandinavia in the late 19th and early 20th centuries.

4 Southern and eastern Europe made little progress

Beyond the inner industrial core of western Europe was an outer zone of less economically advanced nations, including Spain, Portugal, Italy, Austria-Hungary, the Balkans, and the Ottoman Empire. The economy of this outer zone was chiefly agricultural. Compared to the advanced industrial nations, this region had fewer large cities, railroads, and factories, and more extensive poverty, illiteracy, and disease. Class divisions between rich and poor were sharp, the middle class was small, and political life tended to be unstable.

Spain and Portugal lacked stability. Spain during the later 19th century was in a state of near anarchy. A revolution in 1868 deposed the corrupt Queen Isabella II, but there was no agreement on her successor. Monarchists were split into opposing factions, republicans sought to abolish the monarchy altogether, and both the army and the Roman Catholic Church continually intervened in politics. When the crown was offered to a Hohenzollern in 1870, it became an excuse for the Franco-Prussian War.

After a confused period, Spain in 1876 became technically a constitutional monarchy. The right to vote was limited to the propertied classes, however, and parliamentary rule was a sham. The government remained corrupt and ineffective. An unfortunate war with the United States, the Spanish-American War of 1898, resulted in a diminished empire and an empty treasury. Within Spain increasing discontent among peasants and workers led to the growth of radical social doctrines. As the 20th century opened, Spanish political life was beset by a rising wave of violence, terrorism, and assassination.

Nor was violence any less marked in the neighboring monarchy of Portugal. Between 1853 and 1889 the country seemed to make some progress toward parliamentary government, but in the following twenty years government again reverted to the traditional pattern of reactionary absolutism. A revolution in 1910 overthrew the hated monarchy and Portugal became a republic. Instability continued, however, as political parties vied with one another for power.

Italy had serious problems. Unification did not automatically eradicate the traditional problems of Italy—sectional hatreds, widespread illiteracy, a backward educational system, an unjust land system and tax structure, and a lack of any strong tradition of self-government.

Although Italy was a constitutional monarchy, voting was restricted to men of education and property. Out of a population of 20 million, only 150 thousand had the right to vote. Elected politicians were more interested in gaining office than in enacting reforms. Economic distress became so acute in the 1890's that riots broke out in several Italian cities. In 1911 suffrage was granted to all men over age thirty, but this act merely stimulated the growth of mass-supported extremist parties. To escape the stifling economic and political conditions, thousands of young Italians emigrated to other countries.

Minority groups threatened Austria-Hungary. The greatest single problem facing Austria-Hungary in the years after 1870 was that of nationalities. In an empire of such diverse national groups, it was difficult, with nationalism on the rise, to find a common policy acceptable to all. The

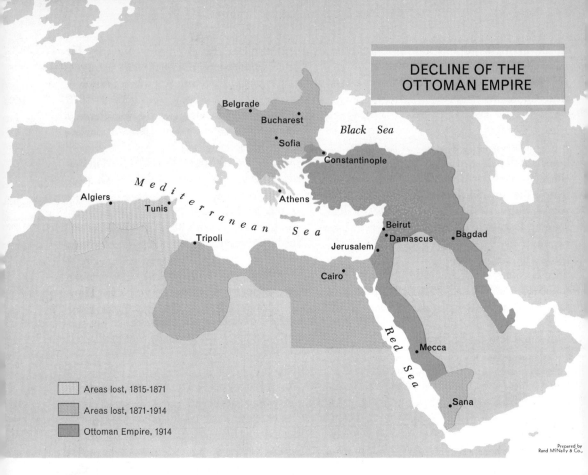

DECLINE OF THE OTTOMAN EMPIRE

Belgrade
Bucharest
Sofia
Black Sea
Constantinople
Mediterranean Sea
Algiers
Tunis
Athens
Tripoli
Beirut
Damascus
Jerusalem
Bagdad
Cairo
Red Sea
Mecca
Sana

☐ Areas lost, 1815-1871

▨ Areas lost, 1871-1914

▨ Ottoman Empire, 1914

Prepared by
Rand McNally & Co.,

unique compromise of 1867—the Dual Monarchy—had only temporarily satisfied the Magyars of Hungary. By the end of the century they began to agitate for complete independence from Austria. At the same time, their own policy within Hungary— where they constituted less than half the population, but controlled politics—was one of unremitting hostility toward the other subject nationalities, such as Rumanians, Slovaks, and Serbs.

In Austria, Germans dominated political, economic, and cultural life. Although universal manhood suffrage was adopted in 1907, it did not solve the nationality problem. The Czechs in particular demanded autonomy for themselves, conscious of their proud history, cultural development, and rapid economic growth. But Emperor Francis Joseph was a weak-

willed man who never faced up to this problem. His failure to do so ultimately led to the collapse of the empire.

The Ottoman Empire grew weaker. The Ottoman Empire was even more complex than Austria-Hungary in its composition, being multireligious as well as multinational. The great majority of its people were Moslems, but there were also Jews and Christians, both Roman Catholic and Greek Orthodox. Turks and other Moslems were the privileged groups, monopolizing army and government posts.

Lagging far behind western Europe in economic and political development, the Ottoman Empire for over two centuries had been the "sick man of Europe." In the 16th century, it ruled an area from Algeria to the Persian Gulf and northward to southern Russia and the Balkans. Internal weakness led to declining political control, and gradually peoples on the outer fringes of the empire broke away from Turkish rule, beginning with Hungary in 1699. This long process of territorial disintegration led to the so-called Eastern Question, which agitated European nations throughout the 18th and 19th centuries. In truth, the problem revolved around the rival ambitions of the Great Powers, each seeking to gain advantages for itself at the expense of the crumbling Ottoman Empire. The empire lasted as long as it did only because the competing European nations felt that its existence was necessary to maintain the balance of power.

By the end of the Crimean War, the Turks had lost effective control over southern Russia, the Crimea, Rumania, Serbia, Greece, Arabia, Egypt, and Algeria. Defeat in war glaringly revealed Turkish weakness and demonstrated the need for reform and reorganization. In 1856 the Turkish government issued an edict called the *Hatt-i Humayun,* the most important Turkish reform of the 19th century. It promised equality before the law, abolition of torture, a more equitable tax system, and the elimination of graft and corruption among public officials. In 1876 a con-

stitution was proclaimed providing for parliamentary government. These changes, however, encountered powerful resistance. Moreover, the ruling sultan from 1876 to 1909, Abdul Hamid II, was fiercely opposed to reform. He dissolved parliament and introduced a reign of terror.

In 1877 war broke out between Turkey and Russia, this time over Turkish possessions in the Balkans. Although the Turks were defeated, and lost more Balkan territory, Abdul Hamid's rule did not soften, and outbursts among the nationalistic peoples of the Balkans continued. A revolution in 1908 brought a reforming group, the Young Turks, to power. They restored parliament, but could not stem the rising tide of nationalism in the Balkans. (See Chapter 26.)

Section Review

1. What conditions in Spain led to political instability?
2. Why was it difficult for parliamentary government to function well in Italy?
3. What was the most serious single problem confronting Austria-Hungary in the late 19th century?
4. What was the Eastern Question? What efforts were made to better conditions in the Ottoman Empire?

Chapter 20   A Review

The late 19th and early 20th centuries brought many political changes in Europe. Two chief factors behind these changes were militant nationalism and the growth of democratic institutions. The ideal of coöperation, fostered by the Concert of Europe, gave way to a new concept of power politics known as *Realpolitik.* An example of this spirit in action was the Crimean War.

Adroit leaders schemed to take advantage of international rivalries and realize their nationalistic ambitions. Emperor Louis Napoleon fostered prosperity within France but entangled his nation in unfortunate foreign

schemes, including an ill-advised attempt to rule Mexico through a puppet emperor. Count Cavour, as prime minister of Sardinia, directed the movement for Italian unification and almost single-handedly created the Kingdom of Italy. Another accomplished statesman, Otto von Bismarck, led his beloved Prussia through wars with Denmark, Austria, and France; from these conflicts emerged a new German Empire. Within the Austrian Empire, nationalistic movements led to the formation of the Dual Monarchy.

Beginning about 1870, several progressive nations of western Europe made great social and economic progress. Victorian England, particularly under Gladstone and Disraeli, broadened the suffrage and adopted other democratic reforms; in the early 20th century, further liberal measures were enacted. One troubled area, southern Ireland, eventually gained its independence. Although politically unstable, France under the Third Republic provided peace and security for its people and managed to withstand pressures from internal enemies. Germany was unsuccessful in campaigns against the Roman Catholic Church and the socialists, but did confer many social benefits on its growing working class. Belgium, Switzerland, and Scandinavia grew increasingly democratic.

Other European nations fared less well during this period. Corruption and oppression prevented Spain and Portugal from equaling the progress made in countries to the north, while Italy found it difficult to overcome serious economic and social problems. Austria-Hungary did little to appease the dissatisfied nationalities within its borders. In the decaying Ottoman Empire, an inept central government seemed helpless in the face of growing tension in the Balkans.

The Time

Indicate the period in which the events described in the following statements occurred.

(a) prior to 1848   (d) 1871-1890
(b) 1848-1860   (e) 1891-1910
(c) 1861-1870   (f) after 1910

1. The Crimean War was fought.
2. The Franco-Prussian War began with the invasion of Alsace-Lorraine.
3. The *Zollverein* was established.
4. Southern Ireland was granted its independence.
5. The Third Republic of France was created.
6. The Young Turks came to power in Turkey.
7. Louis Napoleon became Emperor Napoleon III of France.
8. The Kingdom of Italy was proclaimed.
9. Louis Napoleon was elected president of the Second Republic of France.

10. Bismarck was appointed chancellor of Prussia.
11. The Seven Weeks' War broke out.
12. The German Empire was proclaimed.
13. The Dual Monarchy was formed.
14. Archduke Maximilian was made emperor of Mexico.
15. Cavour became prime minister of Sardinia.
16. The Third Reform Bill was passed in England.
17. William II became emperor of Germany.

The Place

1. Locate the site and tell what important defeat took place at Sedan, Alma, Balaklava, Sevastopol.
2. Locate each of the following places and tell which became part of the Kingdom of Italy in 1861: Kingdom of Sardinia; Kingdom of the Two Sicilies; Venetia; Rome. Locate each of the following places and tell when it came under the rule of the king of Prussia: Schleswig; Holstein; Alsace-Lorraine.
3. How were each of the following places affected by the outcome of the Crimean War: Moldavia; Wallachia; Bessarabia?
4. What part of Ireland became Ulster? Eire?
5. Locate each of the following places that had become virtually free of Ottoman control by 1856: Rumania; Egypt; Serbia; Algeria; Arabia.

The People

1. What steps did each of the following men take to enhance the power and prestige of his nation?
Bismarck   Nicholas I
Napoleon III   Camillo di Cavour
2. Explain the role of each of the following men in the unification of Italy: Giuseppe Mazzini; Giuseppe Garibaldi; Victor Emmanuel.
3. For what particular policies or achievements is each of these leaders noted?
William E. Gladstone   Benjamin Disraeli
Herbert Asquith   David Lloyd George
Charles Parnell
4. Name the country and a significant fact associated with each of these rulers.

William I

Abdul Mejid I

Alexander II

Maximilian

Victoria

George V

William II

Abdul Hamid II

5. What was Georges Haussmann's contribution to France during the Second Empire? Why is Alfred Dreyfus a significant figure in the history of the Third Republic of France?

Historical Terms

1. What were the origins of the Conservative and Liberal parties in Britain? Name an outstanding leader of each party.

2. What did the British Parliament accomplish in passing the following reform legislation?

Home Rule Bill of 1914

Second and Third Reform bills

Parliament Act

Disestablishment Act

3. Explain what is meant by *Realpolitik.*

4. Describe the role of the National Assembly and the Commune in the establishment of the French Third Republic. Identify the monarchists and republicans.

5. What was Bismarck's *Kulturkampf* policy and why did he abandon it?

6. What was the *Zollverein?* How did it aid in the unification of Germany under Prussian domination?

7. The political machinery of the German Empire included the Reichstag and Bundesrat. Explain these terms.

8. What was the *Risorgimento?*

9. What were some of the provisions of the *Hatt-i Humayun?* Who were the Young Turks?

Questions for Critical Thinking

1. Why did the *Hatt-i Humayun* fail to bring about lasting reform in Turkey?

2. Compare and contrast the problems of Bismarck and Cavour in unifying their respective countries. Which country do you think faced the greatest problems? Explain.

3. How did the Crimean War affect the balance of power in Europe?

4. Although both Germany and Italy completed unification at approximately the same time, and had approximately the same number of inhabitants, Germany immediately rose to the position of a great power, whereas Italy quite evidently lagged behind. How would you explain this?

5. What were the accomplishments of the Second French Empire? For what reasons did it ultimately collapse?

6. What problems faced those who tried to establish a republican form of government in France after the downfall of Emperor Napoleon III?

7. What were some of the factors which worked against the achievement of stability in 19th-century Spain? in Portugal? in Austria-Hungary?

8. How did Ireland achieve independence from England during the years from 1869 to 1922?

The Industrial Revolution, Science, and The Arts

CHAPTER 21   1700–1900

During the 19th century, Western civilization underwent tremendous changes. They were sparked by developments in industry so far-reaching as to be termed an Industrial Revolution. Textile manufacturing provided a dramatic example. In the late 18th century, a home weaver (in a painting at left by Van Gogh) worked many hours to produce a single bolt of cloth. A century later, a factory employee operating a bank of machines could make fifty times as much cloth.

Not all the great changes of the 19th century took place at the barricades, on the battlefield, or around the conference table. While violent revolutions, military conflicts, and political rearrangements occupied the center of the stage, powerful forces were quietly at work behind the scenes transforming the very nature of western civilization.

One of the most important single figures in this transformation was a Scottish instrument maker named James Watt. In 1763 a fellow faculty member at the University of Glasgow asked him to repair a model steam engine. Watt, good Scotsman that he was, noticed that the engine wasted a great deal of fuel. He discussed the matter with several professors at the university, but no one could think of any practical solution. For months Watt pondered the problem. Even after he hit upon a solution in 1765, it took him four years to iron out the technical difficulties before he could finally take out a patent on his greatly improved steam engine.

The adoption of this invention by the workaday world had far-reaching consequences. The efficient steam engine was destined to limit or replace traditional energy sources—horses, oxen, the water mill, and human muscle power. By 1819, when James Watt died, machines powered by his device were supplanting hand tools in much of British industry, and goods produced in factories were competing with articles made in the home. Industrialization spread to the rest of western Europe during the 19th century and across the seas to the United States and Japan.

The advance of industrialism was accompanied by new discoveries in science and medicine. Scientific progress not only made life healthier and more comfortable, but also changed men's ideas about their origins, their development, and their relations to one another. Literature, art, music, and architecture reflected the profound changes of the 19th century in a burst of creative activity.

This chapter tells how:

1. **The Industrial Revolution began in England.**

2. **The development of technology spurred industrial growth.**

3. **Science and medicine progressed rapidly.**

4. **The arts displayed great vigor.**

1 The Industrial Revolution began in England

There was a time when historians viewed the industrialization that began in the late 18th century as *the* Industrial Revolution. It was interpreted as a "cataclysm followed by a catastrophe"—that is, as the sudden appearance of new machines that transformed production, created the factory system, and resulted in the cruel exploitation of men, women, and children. All of these things were supposed to have happened within a few decades.

It is now known that this picture is grossly exaggerated. The essence of the so-called Industrial Revolution was the process by which power-driven machinery came to take the place of hand tools in the manufacture of various goods. As such, it is a movement that had no precise beginning and has not yet ended. Many new inventions appeared in the 18th and 19th centuries, but not suddenly. They were preceded by centuries of trial-and-error experimentation in many countries. The search for new machines and new sources of power to run them still continues. Nuclear energy and atomic reactors are only examples from the latest stage of a continuous development.

Still, the idea of an Industrial Revolution is a useful one because it signifies that in a relatively short period of time—about two centuries—there occurred an exceedingly rapid acceleration of economic growth. This dramatic speed-up was first seen in England between about 1760 and 1830. It did not become evident in Germany until the 1860's, in the United States until the 1870's, and in Russia until the 1890's. Many areas of the world have yet to experience an industrial revolution.

Several conditions favored industrialization. In 18th-century England, a number of factors combined to produce a favorable setting for industrial development.

One important factor was a supply of natural resources. England was fortunate in possessing rich deposits of coal and iron. Short, swift rivers furnished the water power to keep machines whirring, and ample harbors helped in shipping the products of British industry around the world. Native wool and cotton from the colonies provided the raw materials for a flourishing textile industry.

Another condition aiding industrialization was a large labor force. A phenomenal increase doubled the population of Great Britain in the 18th century. Because of improvements in sanitation and hospital care and advances in medicine, the death rate was reduced. New methods of farming required fewer people to produce food; thus many farm laborers were free to take up other kinds of work. Because the British were leaders in developing mechanical inventions and in training people to use them, their labor force was skilled and well educated compared to its counterpart on the Continent.

Resources and an ample labor supply were organized by businessmen who supplied capital, bought the new machines, and built the new factories. For centuries, Englishmen had been accumulating capital from farming, handicrafts, and overseas trade. They had invested in joint-stock companies. Successful businessmen and landowners reinvested their profits to an even more marked degree after 1750. The men who developed business enterprises provided the equipment which the army of new workers needed.

Businessmen would not have made goods unless there was a demand for them. In Britain it sprang from several sources. The rapid rise in population created an enormous need for food, clothing, and housing. Colonies abroad provided additional incentives for increased production. The Napoleonic wars of the late 18th and early 19th centuries spurred demand for home-grown foodstuffs and iron and steel products.

The government of 18th-century England encouraged the growth of industrialism. During the 17th century, trade was sluggish and the English government felt that any radical business changes would endanger the economy. It closely regulated businesses, taxed profits heavily, and opposed any inventions that threatened to throw people out of work.

In the 18th century, however, markets expanded and foreign and domestic trade increased rapidly. Many restrictions were relaxed, taxes on profits were reduced, and the manufacture of new machines was actually encouraged. The English Parliament stimulated economic growth by permitting far-reaching changes in the landholding system, authorizing the building of roads and canals, and issuing patents to protect the work of inventors. The British navy safeguarded merchantmen around the globe, while at home an efficient legal system kept the roads free of bandits and assured justice for businessmen in the courts.

British society was relatively mobile—that is, a poor man who worked hard and saved his money might rise to wealth and arrange for his daughter to marry into the gentry or the nobility. This circumstance helped encourage enterprise because it

The Industrial Revolution in Europe during the 18th and 19th centuries may be better understood by noting the locations of European coal fields, iron ore deposits, and avenues of transportation. The combination of these geographic factors helped to provide a favorable environment for the growth of the Industrial Revolution.

In northern and north-central England, for example, great industrial cities such as Newcastle, Manchester, Sheffield, and Birmingham grew up around sources of coal and iron and transportation facilities. Coal was necessary in the manufacture of iron and steel, and was also used to provide power for industrial machinery. Since coal is bulky and costly to transport from mines to factories, many industrial centers were built near coal fields to reduce shipping costs.

Some iron ore and other raw materials, however, had to be transported from ocean ports or from inland areas to the centers of industry, and manufactured products had to be shipped to domestic and overseas markets. Thus, a low-cost system of transportation was needed to link port cities such as Liverpool and London with the industrial cities. To meet this need, canals and, later, railroads were constructed. By 1830 England had more than 3000 miles of canals. By 1850 the country was served by more than 6600 miles of railroads. (In proportion to population, England had more than twice the railroad mileage of any country in Europe.) In that same year England produced half of all the iron in the world. The favorable location of its coal and iron resources and transportation facilities had important consequences. England was able to gain an early lead in industrialization.

France and Germany also had resources which favored the development of industry. Both countries possessed extensive deposits of coal and iron ore, which were linked by a network of rivers, canals, and railroads. These two countries became the industrial leaders in continental Europe.

Certain other European countries lacked one or more of the resources which favored the growth of industry. It is an important geographic fact that there is almost no coal in the Mediterranean region of Europe. This circumstance helps to explain why Mediterranean countries such as Spain and Italy failed to achieve the degree of industrialization experienced by England, France, and Germany in the 18th and 19th centuries.

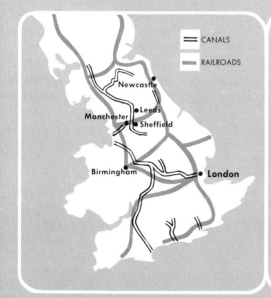

CANALS
RAILROADS

Newcastle
Leeds
Manchester
Sheffield
Birmingham
London

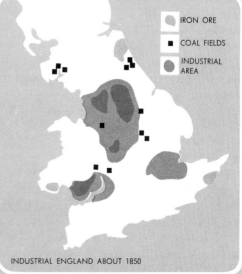

IRON ORE
COAL FIELDS
INDUSTRIAL AREA

INDUSTRIAL ENGLAND ABOUT 1850

467

gave opportunities for talented men to better themselves. Another encouraging factor was the example set by the upper classes. Some noblemen spent their lives at creative labor on their land; the Duke of Bridgewater built one of the first modern canals in England. Even George III loved to inspect his estate in high boots and thought of himself as a "farmer king." The upper classes had long engaged in trade. Only the eldest son of a noble line became noble, and since the younger sons often turned to business, working lost its social stigma.

A revolution in agriculture preceded that in industry. The 18th century witnessed an enormous increase in food production, an increase so rapid that it has sometimes been termed an Agrarian Revolution. This development consisted of two broad, interrelated movements. One was a series of technical improvements in methods of farming; the other represented changes in the system of landholding. England led the way in both.

Early in the 18th century, Englishmen began seeking ways in which to increase the efficiency of their farms. Most of them were well-to-do landlords who were free to experiment with new and sometimes costly techniques. Among the first was Jethro Tull. Experimenting on his father's estate early in the 18th century, Tull proved that he could obtain larger crops with less seed if he planted the seed in rows instead of scattering it over the fields. He devised a mechanical contrivance called a seed drill, the direct ancestor of modern planters.

One of Tull's contemporaries was Viscount Charles Townshend, who had an estate in Norfolk. Much of his land was sandy. Using a technique he had observed in the Netherlands, he treated the soil with a mixture of clay and lime called marl and obtained excellent results. Instead of letting fields lie fallow regularly, he worked out a four-phase rotation system by adding turnips and clover to the traditional crops of wheat and barley. Planting clover improved the soil by transferring nitrogen from the air to the ground (although this chemical action was not understood at the time) and since turnips required constant hoeing, cultivating them killed weeds and kept the soil loose. (Townshend became such an advocate of using turnips that he was nicknamed "Turnip" Townshend.) Another advantage of clover and turnips was that they could be stored and fed to livestock during the winter. Fewer animals had to be slaughtered in the fall and, as a consequence, there was an increase in their numbers.

The quality of livestock, however, was still inferior. A farmer named Robert Bakewell improved the size and health of his animals through careful selection and inbreeding. Thanks to his work and that of other men, England tripled its meat supply in the 18th century and gave the world such famous breeds as Shorthorn, Hereford, and Devon cattle, Leicester sheep, and Berkshire hogs.

The second basic element in the agricultural revolution consisted of changes in the system of landholding. Most English farms in the 18th century were composed of strips leased to tenants and open fields used for common pasture. Farming as a business enterprise could not be conducted efficiently on small, widely separated plots of ground. Nor could the small farmers afford drills or expensive fertilizers. English landlords were anxious to reap the benefits from a rise in farm prices and from an increasing demand for food. Landlords, who dominated Parliament, secured laws that enabled them to consolidate their holdings into compact farms and enclose them with hedges or fences. By the 1870's, half of all the land in England was owned by fewer than 2500 persons.

The enclosure movement made agriculture more efficient and stimulated productivity. It created social problems, however. Tenant farmers were forced to give up their rights to the land they worked. Many were compensated for their losses, but others received nothing and became either paupers or agricultural laborers. The small farmers of England, its "bold peasantry," decreased in number. A large new class of wage earners arose. Long before the coming of the factory, there existed in England as nowhere else a source of mobile labor ready to move where jobs were available and wages attractive.

Section Review

1. Explain the meaning of the term Industrial Revolution as it applied to a period beginning in the late 18th century.
2. What conditions favored rapid industrialization in 18th-century England?
3. Describe the contributions of Tull, Townshend, and Bakewell to the Agrarian Revolution.
4. What was the enclosure movement? How did it affect the Agrarian Revolution? the Industrial Revolution?

2 The development of technology spurred industrial growth

Economic growth is a seamless web; all parts of the process fit together. In 18th-century England, several conditions favored rapid industrialization. Changes in agriculture freed laborers from farms and simultaneously produced additional food to sustain them as urban workers. Against this background, a series of new inventions helped transform economic life.

The industrialization of the textile industry helped create the factory system. Most industry prior to the late 18th century —with the exception of mining, shipbuilding, and sugar refining—was carried on with hand tools in small shops or in people's homes. This method, called the domestic system or cottage industry, was especially common in textile manufacture. Managers supplied the raw materials, and workers spun the yarn and wove the cloth at home.

Early in the 18th century, the demand for cotton cloth from new city dwellers and from markets abroad became so great that old methods of production could not keep pace. In 1733 an English weaver named John Kay developed a "flying shuttle," which cut weaving time in half. Within a few years, his invention was widely adopted all over the land. This development created a new problem: spinners could not supply enough yarn.

For several years no solution was found, and then in 1769 two important inventions were patented. One was James Hargreaves' mechanized spinning wheel, the spinning jenny, which used eight bobbins instead of one; its chief drawback was that it produced a rather weak yarn. The other was Richard Arkwright's water frame, a water-powered device capable of producing fine, strong yarn. By 1779 a jenny spinner named Samuel Crompton found a way to combine the best features of both spinning jenny and water frame into a single machine. His "spinning mule" made excellent yarn that was the envy of his fellow spinners. At first the mule was driven by water power, but by 1830 it was adapted to steam.

These inventions ended the "famine in yarn" and for awhile transferred the bottleneck back to the weavers. A fortune awaited anyone who could devise a faster loom. In 1785 Edmund Cartwright patented a successful power loom, and by 1800 it was widely adopted throughout England.

The new machines were used primarily in making cotton cloth. Supplies of raw cotton were limited because cleaning seeds from the cotton bolls took a long time.

Changes in Technology

Hardly an industry or occupation was untouched by the technological advances of the Industrial Revolution. At an English coal mine of the 18th century, top left, a Newcomen engine in the rear lifts loads of ore from mine shafts at left and right while workers collect the coal in wheelbarrows. The railroad industry itself was a product of the Industrial Revolution. A drawing of the Liverpool and Manchester Railway, middle left, compares the luxury of first-class coaches (above) to open third-class cars (below). Virginia farmers and their slaves gather to witness a demonstration of the McCormick reaper, bottom left. In a single day, such a machine could harvest six times as much grain as a man with a scythe. The scene below, drawn in 1912, depicts workers constructing one of the giant locks of the Panama Canal. Among man's most notable engineering achievements, the canal opened in 1914 and cut in half the sailing distance from New York to San Francisco. To the right is the munitions plant of the great Krupp steelworks in Germany. Alfred Krupp inherited a mill employing only four workers in 1848. He introduced the steam engine and enlarged his operations so that over 16 thousand men were employed by 1873. His method of casting steel was a family secret for years.

When a New Englander, Eli Whitney, went to Georgia in 1793 and learned of the problem facing Southern planters, he built a machine in ten days that could clean cotton as fast as fifty men working by hand. Whitney's cotton gin made possible a fiftyfold increase in the American cotton crop within twenty years. By 1820 cotton led all exports from the southern United States; in addition, it was the chief import of Great Britain.

With the introduction of mechanical power, employers found it more economical to group expensive machines together in factories close to convenient sources of power. This arrangement saved time and money, for instead of carrying material to the workers, manufacturers had the workers come to them. Employers could also make certain that their workers observed regular hours and did not waste raw materials. By centralizing production through the so-called factory system, employers could control the quality of goods more effectively and be assured of a steadier rate of production. They could also take advantage of new techniques such as mass production—that is, production in standard sizes and large numbers—which required a division of labor not possible in the domestic system.

Iron and steel manufacture was improved. Building many new mechanical devices required increased amounts of iron. The supply seemed limited, however, because most smelting was done with charcoal, which was not only slow and costly, but was also depleting English forests. In 1735 Abraham Darby began smelting ore with coke instead of charcoal; because of his success, the iron industry shifted from forest areas to the coal regions. In the 1780's Henry Cort, a contractor for the British navy, found that by "puddling," or stirring, molten iron with long rods in a furnace, he could quickly burn off many

impurities and produce a large amount of wrought iron. He also developed a system of passing hot iron through heavy rollers, squeezing out further impurities and producing iron sheets that could be used for boiler plate and armor.

The manufacture of steel—stronger and generally more useful than iron—was aided by Sir Henry Bessemer, who in 1856 introduced a process for burning off impurities in molten iron to make steel. Ten years later another Englishman, Sir William Siemens, and two French brothers, Émile and Pierre Martin, developed the open-hearth furnace for smelting iron. Their system was widely adopted because it could make a greater range of steels.

Such technical advances made possible abundant supplies of cheap iron and steel, without which modern mechanized civilization would be impossible. Great steel centers grew up in areas blessed with stores of coal and iron ore, such as northern England, the Ruhr valley in Germany, and the Pittsburgh area in Pennsylvania. As iron and steel became more available, they were utilized to make machines of increasing size and complexity. In the sparsely populated western United States, for example, farmers were helped by machines developed to take advantage of plentiful rich soil. Cyrus McCormick demonstrated a horse-drawn reaper for grain in the 1830's. Hiram and John Pitts invented a threshing and winnowing machine in 1837. John Deere constructed an all-steel plow in 1847. In the 1880's the reaper and thresher were combined in a single machine, the combine. These mechanical improvements in farming helped open up the vast plains of America and, later, of Europe.

Transportation became faster and cheaper. In this field, as in farming, the early 18th century presented a picture little different from that of the Middle Ages. Roads were bad and travel by horseback or stagecoach was slow and uncomfortable. Some improvements were made when private companies began building roads in the early 18th century. Stone was used to pave these so-called toll roads. They were also called turnpikes because they were blocked by pikes, or gates, that were turned aside upon payment of a fee. As late as 1760, however, it still took two weeks to travel the 400 miles from London to Edinburgh. Greater advancements resulted after 1770 with the work of two Scottish engineers, Thomas Telford and John McAdam. Both advocated better drainage of roads and the use of layers of crushed rock; McAdam's economical method, known as macadamizing, became the basis for all modern road building.

Waterways also underwent change. Rivers were dredged to make them more easily navigable and in 1761 one of the first modern canals was dug. Built by the Duke of Bridgewater to link some of his coal mines with the city of Manchester, this seven-mile waterway was so successful that the price of coal in Manchester dropped over 80 per cent. A canal-building craze resulted. By 1830 England had one of the best inland waterway systems in the Western world. The mania spread to other countries, particularly the United States, where the Erie Canal was completed by the year 1825.

Meanwhile, there had appeared the steam engine. Building on experimentation of the 17th century, an English ironmonger named Thomas Newcomen invented a steam engine. From about 1705 onward, Newcomen engines were widely employed for pumping water out of mines. It was a model of one of these that James Watt was asked to repair in 1763. His new engine, patented in 1769, was over four times as efficient as its predecessor. After Watt found a way to adapt it to rotary motion in 1781, it could be used for purposes other than pumping water.

In the mid-1700's, iron rails—over which donkeys pulled carts—were in common use around English coal mines. It occurred to Richard Trevithick, an English mining engineer, that a steam engine on wheels would be more efficient than animal power. Trevithick built two such engines in the early 1800's, but they were used only at mines. In 1825 another mining engineer, George Stephenson, succeeded in constructing a locomotive that could do the work of forty teams of horses. When a group of businessmen decided to build a railway between Liverpool and Manchester, they offered a prize for the best locomotive. In a competition held in 1829, Stephenson won with his *Rocket,* which pulled a train thirty-one miles at an average speed of fourteen miles an hour. Stephenson's achievement set off a railroad building boom in England that reached its peak in the 1840's. By 1850 the most important routes were built and freight trains operated regularly. Western Europe and the United States began building railroads in the mid-1800's, and had almost completed their rail networks before the century was over.

The steam engine also had a drastic effect on water transportation. Robert Fulton, an American inventor, bought an engine from the firm of James Watt for use on a ship. In 1807 his *Clermont* steamed 150 miles from New York City up the Hudson River to Albany in only thirty-two hours. Fulton's was not the first steamboat, but it was the first to be a practical and financial success. In the next few decades steamboats came into common use on island waterways and short coastal journeys.

Ocean voyages presented more formidable problems. Until about 1880, the maritime world remained predominantly one of wind and sail. A good supply of wood from the Americas and, after the 1830's, the use of iron hulls, kept construction costs so low that sailing vessels could offer very low rates. In 1838 a British ship, the *Sirius*, crossed from Liverpool to New York entirely under steam in eighteen days. By 1850 oceangoing steamships were firmly established in mail and passenger traffic because of their speed and regularity. Only after such inventions as the screw propeller, however, did steamships begin to displace sailing vessels for carrying cargo.

All the improvements in transportation reduced shipping costs, brought town and country within easy reach of one another, and knit nations more closely together.

Capitalism changed. The mercantile capitalism of the Commercial Revolution had been based essentially on trade and commerce. As industrialism grew in the 18th century, capitalism adapted to new kinds of enterprises. Called industrial capitalism, it was usually based on small companies managed directly by their owners (either one man or a group of partners).

Some industries, however, required extremely large amounts of capital because the equipment needed was so expensive. This was especially true of railroads and iron and steel manufacture. Since no one individual could supply this capital, some form of joint enterprise was necessary. The joint-stock companies that had come into existence during the Commercial Revolution had generally been confined to the field of overseas trade and colonization; they were also strictly limited by government charters. During the 19th century, there evolved a more flexible organization, the corporation. Unlike the joint-stock company, it was recognized legally as a distinct being, and so was able to own property, bring and defend suits at law, and maintain a continuous existence despite changes in shareholders or directors.

By the end of the 19th century, corporations had become the usual form of organization in the business world. They were managed not by their owners but by sala-

ried executives who used other persons' money. The role of banks and financiers became increasingly important because of the large amounts of capital needed; thus the economic organization of the period after 1850 is known as finance capitalism.

Section Review

1. Summarize the chief steps in the mechanization of the English textile industry.
2. Explain why the introduction of mechanization led to the factory system.
3. What developments made iron and steel cheaper and more abundant? Show by example how increased use of iron and steel led to increased mechanization.
4. Describe some of the improvements in transportation that took place during the 18th and 19th centuries. How did these improvements affect society?
5. How did capitalism change as the pace of industrialization increased?

3 **Science and medicine progressed rapidly**

An increased willingness to adopt new ways of doing things helped spur the growth of industrialism; it also led to remarkable advances in science and medicine. In the 19th century, the great majority of Europeans became more science-minded than ever before. They were confident that science was the key that would unlock nature's secrets and open the door to limitless material progress.

Chemists and physicists made important discoveries. Chemistry was put on a new footing with the work of John Dalton, an English schoolteacher of the early 19th century. Dalton, like the Greek philosopher Democritus, believed that all matter is composed of invisible particles called atoms. He theorized further that all the atoms of any one chemical element are alike and differ in weight from those of any other. Dalton said that in chemical compounds, atoms combined into units (now called molecules), and he devised a type of chemical formula to describe them. During the next fifty years, chemists discovered more elements and refined their methods of combining them. In 1869 a Russian, Dmitri Mendelyeev, drew up the Periodic Table, in which he classified in families all known elements (at that time sixty-two were known) according to their atomic weights. This classification enabled him to indicate gaps where other elements might be—and later were—found, and to describe these elements in advance with remarkable accuracy.

Important discoveries in physics helped establish the close relationships among electricity, magnetism, heat, and light. In 1800 Alessandro Volta of Italy, working on the principle that electric current can be produced by chemical action, made one of the first batteries. Hans Christian Oersted of Denmark discovered electromagnetism in 1820 when he found that current flowing through a wire would move a compass needle lying parallel to it. Further investigation of the connections between electricity and magnetism were carried on by an English scientist, Michael Faraday. In 1831 he showed that electric current could be produced by moving a wire through the lines of force of a magnetic field. Faraday's discovery, the first dynamo, was the basis for the electric generator.

Faraday's experiments inspired the Scottish scientist James Clerk Maxwell, who in the 1860's formulated exact mathematical equations to explain them. Maxwell theorized that light too was electromagnetic in nature. Using Maxwell's equations, physicists demonstrated the existence of other electromagnetic waves. It soon became clear that not only electric current and visible light, but also radiant heat and other invisible kinds of radiation were all electromagnetic waves of different lengths. In 1885 Heinrich Hertz of Germany proved the existence and measured the velocity of what were later called radio waves. Another German, Wilhelm Roentgen, in 1895 discovered rays that could penetrate solid substances; he called them X rays. In searching for similar rays, Pierre and Marie Curie of France isolated the element radium in 1898. Their discovery of this radioactive element was a milestone in the new field of atomic physics that was to revolutionize 20th-century science.

Increased scientific knowledge stimulated inventions. Many of the discoveries of pure science helped to solve problems posed by industrialism. During the 19th century, chemists analyzed nearly 70 thousand chemical compounds and developed portland cement, vulcanized rubber, synthetic dyes, nitroglycerin explosives, and celluloid. A German scientist, Justus von Liebig, discovered in the 1840's that the chemical composition of the soil had a direct bearing on plant life. His discovery explained why Townshend's rotation plan had worked, and opened the door to the development of commercial fertilizers.

Building on the work of Faraday and others, inventors improved electric generators so that they would provide steady supplies of electricity at a reasonable cost. The first electric motors were constructed in the 1870's, and it soon became possible to use electricity to propel trolley cars, trains, and ships. Engineers quickly adapted electric motors to power machines in factories.

In 1832 Samuel F. B. Morse of the United States made the first electric telegraph. Another American, Alexander Graham Bell, patented the telephone in 1876, and a fellow-countryman, Thomas A. Edison, developed the first practical electric light in 1879. A young Italian, Guglielmo Marconi, developed a wireless telegraph which was put into operation across the English Channel in 1898; three years later, messages were transmitted across the Atlantic. All these inventions linked together the new world-wide economy and aided the growth of cities.

Other advances tapped rich natural resources as new sources of power. Fuel gas, although known since ancient times, was first manufactured and given a practical application in the late 18th century, when English and French scientists experimented with it for lighting. London, in 1807, became the first city to light streets with gas. As its use grew more widespread, natural gas reserves in America and Europe proved of great value. Another resource, petroleum, gave rise to a new industry in the middle 1800's, with the United States soon taking the lead. At first petroleum was in demand chiefly for lubrication and as a source of kerosene. In the 1860's and 1870's, however, scientists in France, Germany, and Austria began building internal combustion engines, the more advanced of which used gasoline for fuel. From then on, this by-product of petroleum became its most important use. As these engines were made lighter, the foundation was laid for the development of the automobile. Another type of internal combustion machine, the Diesel engine, was patented in 1892. It was designed to run on fuel oils instead of gasoline and found wide use in ships and locomotives, for though the engines were heavier than gasoline engines, they operated more cheaply.

Medical research lengthened the human life span. Modern medicine advanced greatly with the work of an English physician, Edward Jenner, who developed vaccination as a preventive against smallpox, for centuries a dread and often fatal disease. In 1796 he inoculated a boy with the virus of cowpox (a mild disease related to smallpox). When the boy was later inoculated with smallpox, he did not fall ill.

The field of surgery benefited from new developments in chemistry. Until the mid-19th century, surgeons operated on patients who shrieked with pain as they were held down by force. In the 1840's several Americans experimented successfully with various anesthetics; in 1846 W. T. G. Morton, a Boston dentist, publicly demonstrated the value of ether during an operation at Massachusetts General Hospital. News of this event prompted experiments by Sir James Simpson, an English professor of medicine at the University of Edinburgh, who discovered chloroform. The use of anesthetics resulted in painless surgery, and also made it possible to perform medical research on living animals.

Although operations grew less fearsome, they were still very often fatal. Infection was quite common because sterilization was unknown. Surgeons wore their operating coats for years without washing them. One problem was that the cause of infection was not understood. It was a great French scientist, Louis Pasteur, who proved conclusively that infectious diseases are caused by microscopic organisms. In the 1850's, Pasteur began a study of fermentation and, finding that it was caused by certain bacteria, invented a heating process (later named pasteurization) to retard it. In the 1870's Pasteur worked with another scientist, Robert Koch of Germany, in studying the infectious disease anthrax. Koch isolated the organism that caused the disease, and Pasteur in 1881 developed a vaccine to prevent it. Pasteur went on to investigate rabies; in 1885 he successfully inoculated a little boy who had been bitten by a mad dog. Koch meanwhile discovered the individual organisms that caused eleven diseases, including tuberculosis and cholera.

Profiting from the new germ theory of disease, Joseph Lister, an English surgeon,

Scientists had a great impact on 19th-century intellectual life. Above left, Pasteur records experimental data on rabbits. Darwin gathered a wealth of evidence for his theories; above right, he observes a giant tortoise. Madame Curie, right, stands in her laboratory. Freud and a diagram of the psychological system he devised are shown below. Unconscious impulses arising from the id are modified by the ego (conscious self) and the superego (like the conscience).

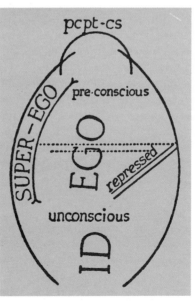

began to search for a chemical antiseptic that would destroy bacteria and make surgery safe as well as painless. In the 1860's he hit upon a mild carbolic acid solution as the best agent for sterilizing hands, instruments, wounds, and dressings. Lister's antiseptic methods are said to have saved more lives than were lost in all the wars of the 19th century.

Like the development of modern agriculture and industry, these discoveries in medicine increased mankind's life span and made possible the growth of urban communities where men could live healthy and prosperous lives.

Biology was revolutionized. In ancient Greece, some thinkers had held that the earth and living organisms were not changeless but had developed from simple to complex forms through a process of evolution. Several 19th-century scientists advocated the idea of continuous development and change from past to present, but no one could explain satisfactorily how the evolutionary process worked in nature.

Charles Darwin, an English naturalist, became interested in why there was such a great variety of plants and animals, and why some types had become extinct while others lived on. After much reading and study, he reasoned as follows: Most animals tend to increase faster than the available food supply, so that there is a constant struggle for existence. Those that survived must have some advantage over those that perished, making them better adapted to their environment. Hence only the fittest survived and lived to produce offspring with the same characteristics. This, nature's way of choosing, Darwin called the principle of natural selection.

These three ideas—the struggle for existence, the survival of the fittest, and natural selection—became the basis for Darwin's theory of evolution. For more than twenty years he carefully gathered data to support it, and in 1859 published his findings in *The Origin of Species by Means of Natural Selection.* The implications of Darwin's theory were that all living things developed through evolution, that they all evolved from simpler forms over eons of time, and that they probably had a common ancestor. In *The Descent of Man* (1871), Darwin theorized that human beings and apes were probably descended from a common ancestor.

Like the heliocentric theory of the 16th century, Darwin's theory of evolution had repercussions throughout European intellectual life. The churches in particular were aroused by it, for Darwin's theory seemed to contradict the Biblical account of creation. For half a century a heated controversy raged between the defenders and opponents of Darwinism. Eventually, however, many persons, including churchmen, came to feel that science dealt with certain aspects of human life and religion with others. Thus, they concluded that no real conflict existed between Darwinism and Christianity.

Another objection to Darwin's theory was that it did not sufficiently explain how characteristics were actually passed on from one generation to another. Pioneering work in the field of heredity was done by an Austrian monk named Gregor Mendel. After careful experiments with plants, he found that inherited characteristics are carried by minute particles (now called genes). Although Mendel's laws of heredity did not receive wide recognition when first formulated in the 1860's, they were later regarded as the foundation of the science of genetics.

Psychology became a science. Modern psychology, the science of human behavior, grew from the work of physicians who studied men's conscious experiences, especially the operation of the senses. In the 1890's a Russian, Ivan Pavlov, went much further. In a series of experiments, he gave food to a dog while ringing a bell. Food and bell became so closely linked that the dog eventually watered at the mouth when a bell was rung, even if no food were present. Pavlov's experiments with dogs influenced scientists' attitudes toward human beings. Many of them took the view that man's reason was not responsible for his actions, but that many human responses were the result of mechanical reactions to stimuli.

Most important of all was the work of a Viennese physician, Sigmund Freud. He believed that men often act in response to unconscious needs and desires. In the 1890's, he devised psychoanalysis as a method of revealing unconscious motives and developed a complex theory to explain how they worked. By making men aware of the powerful emotional impulses that determine their behavior, Freud provided new insights in understanding human beings and new methods for treating mental illness.

Section Review

1. What contribution to chemistry was made by Dalton? by Mendelyeev?
2. Describe at least six discoveries in physics that were made in the course of the 19th century.
3. What were some of the practical inventions in transportation, communication, heating, and lighting that resulted from important scientific discoveries of the 19th century?
4. What advances in medical research during the 19th century helped to lengthen man's life span?
5. Explain the basic principles of Charles Darwin's theory of evolution. What additional contribution in biology was made by Gregor Mendel?
6. Describe briefly the work of Ivan Pavlov and Sigmund Freud in the field of psychology.

4 The arts displayed great vigor

The 19th century was a period of tremendous activity in the world of literature and the fine arts. Here, too, the impact of industrialism was evident. Some writers and artists deliberately turned their backs on the confusion and bustle of contemporary life in favor of fantasy, the exotic, or the past. Others tried to understand and describe the forces that were changing society. As the middle class grew in size and influence, it became increasingly important as an audience for creative works. Artists, writers, and musicians were no longer dependent on the patronage of the wealthy for their support. As a result, they enjoyed greater freedom to express their own ideas in a variety of different art forms.

Romanticism dominated the early 19th century. Toward the end of the 18th century, there developed a reaction against the excessive emphasis on reason that characterized the Enlightenment. Several artists and thinkers adopted a different outlook, called romanticism; a forerunner of the movement was Jean Jacques Rousseau, a French social philosopher. Romantics argued that man must take account of emotion, intuition, and imagination. Feelings of love and responses to beauty and religion, they said, could not be explained exclusively in rational terms. As artists, romantics wished to free themselves from rigid neoclassical forms and models, which had allowed little scope for personal feelings. They believed above all that art must reflect the artist as a distinct and unique expression of his own being. Romanticism also represented a reaction against the ugliness and materialism of an increasingly industrial society.

In literature, there was a great diversity of themes as writers let their imaginations roam freely. One was a stress on liberty. A

Painting of the 19th Century was dominated by French artists. Claude Monet was an outstanding impressionist. In his painting of a park scene entitled "The Frog Pond," left, the shimmering water almost seems to move. One reason for this vibrancy is that the colors, instead of being blended on the canvas, are "mixed" in the viewer's eye. Another notable impressionist was Edgar Degas. In his painting of two laundresses, below left, he has caught a fleeting moment at the ironing table. Paul Cézanne, a post-impressionist, was more interested in exploring three-dimensional reality than in portraying surface effects. Bands of rich color create a feeling of depth in his portrait of a friend, Victor Chocquet, shown at right.

German movement known as *Sturm und Drang* (Storm and Stress) glorified individualism and a defiance of authority. Among its members were Johann Schiller, whose drama *William Tell* dealt with the Swiss struggle for independence, and Johann Wolfgang von Goethe, author of the epic drama of human striving, *Faust* (Part I, 1808; Part II, 1833). A spirit of rebellion also characterized two great English poets, Lord Byron and Percy Bysshe Shelley.

Another aspect of the Romantic Movement, a belief in beauty as a fundamental standard superior to ethical ones, is best exemplified in the work of another English poet, John Keats. Two famous lines from his poem, *Ode on a Grecian Urn*, express this attitude:

"Beauty is truth, truth beauty,"—that is all
Ye know on earth, and all ye need to know.

An important romantic theme was nature, treated not as the orderly, mechanical system pictured by 18th-century thinkers, but as having a mystical beauty, especially in its wild state. The English poet William Wordsworth discarded the artificial poetic expressions of neoclassic writers and used instead what he termed the "very language of men" to express his love of nature. Wordsworth and other romantics, following Rousseau's example, regarded primitive men—and the common people at home—as noble and virtuous because they were unspoiled by the artificialities of civilization. Thus, romantics developed a great interest in myths, fairy tales, and folk songs. Some of the great collections of this material, such as the folk tales of the Grimm brothers, are products of the Romantic Movement.

Believing as they did in the inadequacy of reason, some romantics turned for inspiration to dreams, fantasies, and the supernatural. Examples of this approach are *Rime of the Ancient Mariner* (1797) by Samuel Taylor Coleridge, an Englishman, and the poetry of the American Edgar Allan Poe. Interest in the exotic also led the romanticists into rediscovering the Middle Ages, shunned by 18th-century thinkers as barbaric. The romantics regarded the medieval period as the golden age of chivalry, justice, romance, and adventure. Such feelings are reflected in the novels of Sir Walter Scott of Scotland and Victor Hugo of France.

Painting, like literature, reflected romantic attitudes. Eugène Delacroix of France, a master of color, painted exotic scenes as well as subjects inspired by the political revolts of the 1820's and 1830's. The painters of England, like its poets, found inspiration in nature. The work of John Constable and J. M. W. Turner had a fresh, dramatic quality considered revolutionary by the other landscape painters of the time.

Architecture exhibited the influence of romanticism primarily as a renewed interest in the Gothic style of the Middle Ages. In France and Germany much work was done in restoring medieval buildings that had fallen into decay. In England, when the old Westminster Palace burned down in 1834, new Parliament buildings were constructed completely in Gothic style. Churches, houses, and public buildings bristled with pointed arches, flying buttresses, and turrets.

Romanticism in music, as in the other arts, represented a break with tradition. Composers expanded 18th-century forms to make them more varied and expressive;

for example, the symphony became much longer and more complex. Technical improvements also broadened the range of musical expression. The orchestra grew in size, and many instruments were made easier to play. The harpsichord was replaced by the piano, which had greater flexibility. All of these changes are evident in the music of Ludwig van Beethoven, whose great symphonies and chamber music served as a bridge between classicism and romanticism.

Romantic composers used music to portray personal emotions. The hundreds of songs written by Franz Schubert covered a wide range of lyric expression. Other trends that characterized romantic music were the use of folk themes and the importance of the virtuoso performer. Both trends are evident in the careers of two composer-pianists: Frédéric Chopin of Poland and Franz Liszt of Hungary.

Later movements reacted against romanticism. By the mid-19th century, the exaggerations of some romantic art stimulated a reaction against its principles. Much of it had become merely sentimental and, in an age that admired *Realpolitik*, its otherworldliness seemed out of date. Romanticism did not disappear completely, but it was no longer the dominant tone of the arts.

In literature, the reaction against romanticism frequently took the form of realism. Realists, like the romantics, were aware of the harsh social conditions of their times. But while romantics sought escape from them, realists wanted to present life as it actually existed. In avoiding romantic idealism, realists tended to stress the sordid aspects of life and to emphasize the evils of society. Even the English poet Alfred, Lord Tennyson, while predominantly a romantic, expressed in some of his work the troubled attitudes of his contemporaries toward their changing world.

One group of literary realists wanted to stimulate public awareness of various problems, educating their readers as well as entertaining them. One of the greatest of these was the Englishman Charles Dickens. Although he was romantic enough to enliven his novels with sentiment, whimsy, and melodrama, he was also a severe social critic who portrayed the poor and downtrodden to call attention to needed reforms. *Oliver Twist* (1837-1839) depicted the abuses of children in workhouses and slums; *Nicholas Nickleby* (1838-1839) and *David Copperfield* (1849-1850) exposed the injustices of education; and *Bleak House* (1852-1853) dealt with the social evils of the legal system. In France, Honoré de Balzac wrote a panoramic series of over ninety novels, *The Human Comedy*, which presented a searching picture of lower- and middle-class French life. Many of his novels attacked greed and social climbing.

Mark Twain described with humorous accuracy life in the American Midwest and on the frontier. At the same time his writings underscored the evils of slavery and other social injustices. A Norwegian, Henrik Ibsen, developed a new form of realistic drama through which he presented many problems previously considered too controversial to discuss in public. In his best-known play, *A Doll's House* (1879), he attacked loveless marriage as immoral.

Other realistic writers particularly excelled in portraying character. In *Madame Bovary* (1857), Gustave Flaubert of France described with objectivity the downfall of a weak woman obsessed by romantic love. Russia produced two great novelists whose work shows penetrating psychological insight—Feodor Dostoevski, who wrote *Crime and Punishment* (1866) and Leo Tolstoy, author of *War and Peace* (1862-1869) and *Anna Karenina* (1875-1877).

In England, William Makepeace Thackeray wrote with detachment about human foibles and created unforgettable characters in his *Vanity Fair* (1847-1848). A similar interest in character—although with more emphasis on traditional moral values —motivated the work of the woman novelist George Eliot. Subtle analysis of human personality through poetry was the great achievement of Robert Browning in his "dramatic monologues" such as "My Last Duchess" and "Fra Lippo Lippi."

Another group of writers, the naturalists, tried to be as objective as scientists in describing a "slice of life." They felt that writers should tell their stories without comment or any expression of their own emotions. The outstanding representative of this school was the French novelist Émile Zola, who wrote about various members of a family in books that are almost clinical case histories.

In painting, realism had its spokesman in Gustave Courbet, the son of a French peasant. He believed in painting people and places as they were, and once remarked that he did not paint angels because he had never seen one. Courbet, by inspiring other painters to break with the romantic tradition, helped stimulate a movement known as impressionism. The impressionists developed new techniques for depicting light and color on canvas and tried to present an impression of a scene at a given moment, undistorted by subjective feelings. Famous painters in this style—all of whom were Frenchmen—included Claude Monet, Edgar Degas, and Auguste Renoir. Impressionism, however, by emphasizing fleeting moments, brought its own reaction. Paul Cézanne of France, a leader of the post-impressionist school, concentrated on the elements of space and solidity. A Dutch artist, Vincent van Gogh, used vivid colors and bold outlines to convey his heightened emotions about people and places.

Creative Personalities brought new and often controversial ideas to the literature and music of the 19th century. Lord Byron of England, above, rebelled against conventional social standards and became a symbol of the poet in revolt. The German composer Richard Wagner is cartooned above right, conducting amid a welter of bruised notes. One critic called his music an "inflated display of noise and extravagance." Playwright Henrik Ibsen of Norway, center right, also drew indignant criticism. His "problem plays" were designed to provoke thought rather than entertain. The realistic novelist Leo Tolstoy, lower right, hated inequality and believed that everyone should earn his living by physical labor. In his later years, he renounced his Russian title and worked in the fields among the peasants.

Architecture felt the impact of a realistic approach as architects abandoned Gothic imitations in favor of more original styles. One reason for the change was a variety of new structural materials such as steel, reinforced concrete, and stronger glass. In the United States, Louis Sullivan developed the doctrine of functionalism, based on the principle that buildings must be constructed to suit their functions. A modern bank, he said, should not look like a Greek temple, nor a warehouse like a medieval castle. Sullivan was a pioneer builder of skyscrapers, which combined new materials and new designs.

Music in the late 19th century reflected various trends. The German composer, Johannes Brahms, continued the romantic tradition in his symphonies, as did the Italian Giuseppe Verdi, who composed such great operas as *Rigoletto*, *La Traviata*, and *Aida*. Strong nationalist feeling inspired the work of Richard Wagner of Germany. Using Germanic folklore as the basis of his "music dramas," he integrated plot, poetry, music, and stagecraft to create a unified impact. Russia produced an entire school of nationalist composers, including Modest Moussorgsky and Nikolay Rimski-Korsakov, who drew upon Russian folk themes in their compositions. More romantic was Peter Tschaikowsky, whose gift for melody made his works among the most popular of all classical compositions. The French composer Claude Debussy, like the impressionists in painting, used unusual techniques to gain brilliant, shimmering effects.

Section Review

1. What were the chief characteristics of romanticism? Show, with specific examples, how they were reflected in literature.
2. How was romanticism expressed in painting? architecture? music?
3. Describe the following movements: literary realism; naturalism; impressionism; functionalism.

Chapter 21 ▰▰▰▰▰ A Review

The Industrial Revolution, a dramatic speed-up in Western economic life, consisted of a vast number of interrelated discoveries, inventions, and processes. It began in England, where conditions were particularly favorable. The development of industrialism was aided by an Agrarian Revolution, which increased food production and freed laborers from farms to swell the urban labor force.

Economic life was changed by a series of developments in technology. In a pivotal industry, that of textiles in England, a rapid shift from hand to machine methods stimulated the factory system in this and other fields. Of special significance were innovations in iron and steel manufacture and mechanized farming. Improvements in transportation—better roads, networks of canals and railroads, and the displacement of sailing vessels by steamships—knit regions more closely together.

Capitalism itself adapted to new conditions; old methods of business organization were replaced by industrial and, later, by finance capitalism.

Meanwhile, the scientific spirit flowered to produce an ever increasing stream of new discoveries that broadened man's knowledge of the world. Beginning with the work of Dalton, a chain of developments in chemistry and physics wrought profound changes within a few decades. Inventors like Morse, Bell, Edison, and Marconi made contributions in the field of communications that further united the world. Men found and exploited new power sources, such as gas and petroleum. In medicine, one of the greatest advances was Pasteur's germ theory of disease, which aided in the conquest of such age-old enemies as rabies and tuberculosis. Knowledge of new chemicals helped in developing painless surgery and antiseptics. The theories of Darwin, Mendel, and Freud opened up entire new fields of scientific investigation.

The dynamic changes of the period were naturally reflected in literature and the other arts. The ordered neoclassicism of the Age of Reason gave way to romanticism, which pervaded most of the arts until the mid-1800's. As the century progressed, it brought a bewildering variety of forms and movements— among them the literary realism of Dickens, Flaubert, and Zola; the shimmering impressionistic painting of Monet and Renoir; the functional architecture of men like Sullivan; and the nationalism of such composers as Wagner and Moussorgsky.

The Time

Indicate the period in which each invention, discovery, or book listed below appeared.

(a) 1751-1800   (c) 1851-1900
(b) 1801-1850

1. Coleridge's *Rime of the Ancient Mariner*
2. Deere's all-steel plow
3. Stephenson's *Rocket*
4. Edison's electric light
5. Fulton's *Clermont*
6. Pasteur's anthrax vaccine
7. Morse's telegraph
8. Flaubert's *Madame Bovary*
9. Watt's steam engine
10. Hargreaves' spinning jenny
11. Bessemer's steel-making process
12. Dickens' *Oliver Twist*
13. Faraday's dynamo
14. Darwin's *The Origin of Species by Means of Natural Selection*

The People

1. What contribution did each person named below make to his field?

AGRICULTURE

Tull	Townshend	McCormick
Deere	Pitts brothers	Bakewell

TEXTILE INDUSTRY

Kay	Arkwright	Crompton
Whitney	Cartwright	Hargreaves

IRON AND STEEL PRODUCTION

Darby	Siemens	Martin brothers
Cort	Bessemer	

TRANSPORTATION

Watt	Trevithick	Stephenson
McAdam	Fulton	

COMMUNICATION

Morse	Bell	Marconi

MEDICINE

Jenner	Koch	Simpson
Lister	Morton	Pasteur

CHEMISTRY AND PHYSICS

Hertz	the Curies	Liebig
Dalton	Faraday	Roentgen
Oersted	Mendelyeev	Volta

BIOLOGY AND PSYCHOLOGY

Darwin	Mendel	Pavlov	Freud

2. Classify the following writers as romanticists, realists, or naturalists and explain why each is so classified.

Dickens	Keats	Flaubert
Schiller	Ibsen	Browning
Balzac	Wordsworth	Coleridge
Goethe	Grimm brothers	Hugo
Twain	Zolá	Thackeray

3. Which of the following painters were romanticists? realists? impressionists? post-impressionists?

Delacroix	Courbet	Constable
Cézanne	Renoir	Monet

4. What kind of music did each of the following men compose?

Beethoven	Schubert	Wagner
Tschaikowsky	Moussorgsky	Verdi
Brahms	Liszt	Chopin

Historical Terms

1. How did the domestic system differ from the factory system?
2. Explain the terms industrial capitalism and finance capitalism. How did the corporation differ from the joint-stock company?
3. Define each of the following terms and give an example to illustrate the trend in liter-

ature or the arts that it represents: romanticism, *Sturm und Drang*, realism, naturalism, impressionism, functionalism.

Questions for Critical Thinking

1. Why did the Industrial Revolution begin in England and not in Germany or Russia?

2. What changes took place in industry between 1700 and 1890 with respect to the following: (a) production method; (b) tools and machinery; (c) transportation; (d) ownership and financing? Give specific examples to illustrate your answer.

3. What ideas and attitudes are revealed in the literature, art, architecture, and music of the 19th century?

4. From the standpoint of their impact on society, what were the advantages and disadvantages of the following developments of the Industrial Revolution: (a) speedy transportation; (b) large business companies; (c) specialization of labor; (d) the factory system; (e) large cities?

5. Why did Charles Darwin's theories provoke controversy during the 19th century? Explain in detail.

6. What factors promoted the growth of population in Europe and America between 1750 and 1900?

7. Is the Industrial Revolution still going on today? If so, what are some recent revolutionary developments?

Movements of Social Protest

CHAPTER 22   1800–1900

In transforming the Western world, industrialism produced ill effects as well as good. One of these ills—the exploitation of labor—is reflected in the grim mood of the discontented workers shown above (a lithograph by Käthe Kollwitz). Protests against industrial evils came from social reformers of many different types. Some called for government help to correct the abuses, while others advocated new systems of organizing and governing society.

It was a town of red brick, or of brick that would have been red if the smoke and ashes had allowed it; but as matters stood it was a town of unnatural red and black, like the painted face of a savage. It was a town of machinery and tall chimneys, out of which interminable serpents of smoke trailed themselves for ever and ever, and never got uncoiled. It had a black canal in it, and a river that ran purple with ill-smelling dye, and vast piles of buildings full of windows where there was a rattling and a trembling all day long, and where the piston of the steam-engine worked monotonously up and down, like the head of an elephant in a state of melancholy madness. It contained several large streets all very like one another, and many small streets still more like one another, inhabited by people equally like one another, who all went in and out at the same hours, with the same sound upon the same pavements, to do the same work, and to whom every day was the same as yesterday and tomorrow, and every year the counterpart of the last and the next.

This description of a drab and ugly industrial town and the deadly monotony of the lives of its inhabitants appeared in the novel *Hard Times* (1854) by Charles Dickens. He deplored the evils of industrialism as he saw them in the England of his day. Through his novels he protested against a social and economic system which seemed to be cruelly indifferent to human life and dignity.

Charles Dickens was one of the more gifted writers who succeeded in arousing the social conscience of his fellow countrymen. He was not alone. There were many others—social critics, religious leaders, political leaders, and philanthropists—all of whom spoke out against the social evils of their time. To a greater or lesser degree they all demanded reforms. The more radical among them called for revolution.

This outpouring of social protest was not confined to England, nor was it caused exclusively by the advance of industrialism. The movement was European-wide in scope, and it had its roots in the 18th century. Unless these factors are kept in mind, it may be difficult to understand why the 19th century became such an era of social dissent. After all, the lot of the common man had been harsh for centuries. When oppression became too great to bear, popular uprisings and peasant revolts had occurred. But the leaders of those earlier outbursts did not seek to overturn the established social order, which they accepted.

By the 19th century this attitude was changing. Three great revolutions brought about the change. One was the intellectual movement known as the Enlightenment, which introduced the idea that social institutions must be analyzed to determine whether they helped or hindered man in his natural right to pursue life, liberty, and happiness. The second was the French Revolution, which provided an example of direct action by the people in the destruction of the old feudal system and its replacement by a republican government.

The third great revolution that brought about a new attitude toward the structure of society was the Industrial Revolution. In the long run the steam engine, the factory, and the railroad transformed society even more radically than had the French Revolution. Europe changed from a rural, agrarian, sparsely populated area based on an economy of scarcity to an urban, industrial, densely populated area based on an economy of plenty. The relative swiftness with which these conditions came about created staggering problems. Age-old peasant ways of life were ill-suited to the crowded conditions of the new factory towns. And while the new technology produced greater wealth, in the opinion of many people that wealth was distributed unfairly. The problem of the distribution of wealth generated bitter criticism and intensified social protest.

As a result of these three revolutions, the 19th century, and particularly its first half, was agitated by a tumult of ideas and programs for change. In one way or another all of them were critical of a social system that permitted poverty to exist in the midst of growing prosperity. All of them insisted that the capitalist system should be reformed, and some that it be abolished.

This chapter is divided into the following sections:

1. **The new industrialism presented grave problems.**

2. **Socialists proposed far-reaching changes.**

3. **Conditions for the workers improved.**

1 **The new industrialism presented grave problems**

Unsanitary and dangerous factories, inhumanly long working hours, child labor, exploitation of women, low wages, slums, and recurring unemployment—these conditions were considered the seven deadly sins of the Industrial Revolution by its most violent critics.

The growth of cities caused a variety of problems. In 1800 Europe was a vast farming community. No city anywhere had as many as a million inhabitants. By 1900, however, the majority of western Europeans lived in great urban areas. Five cities had populations of over a million; London alone had more than 6½ million people.

The sudden growth of old cities and the emergence of new cities created many problems. Streets in many sections of the cities were unpaved, lighting was poor, and water supplies were insufficient. London did not have a police force until 1829, and in 1838 the industrial city of Birmingham still used pigs as scavengers to get rid of garbage from its 170 thousand residents. Tuberculosis and epidemics, especially of typhoid fever, took their toll of lives.

Few cities had adequate building codes to require safe housing for the increasing population. Houses were built close together, in long rows, one against another, side to side and back to back. The workers lived crowded together in the damp, cold, and unsanitary rooms, from the attic lofts down to the cellars. In the tenement districts, fire was a constant danger.

From the standpoint of present-day standards, there can be no doubt that living conditions in the great industrial towns a century ago were deplorable. But it is essential to keep the problem in perspective. Recent researches have shown that compared to the mid-18th century, urban conditions had probably improved. And compared to the great nonindustrial towns of other countries, English industrial towns of the mid-19th century were actually less crowded and no more unsanitary. Indeed, it was the iron pipe, a product of the Industrial Revolution, which made it possible for large numbers of people to live together in towns under sanitary conditions. Part of the blame for the prevalence of disease in cities can be traced to the laws of the time. Legislators put a tax on windows, bricks, and tiles. Such taxes discouraged the provision of light and air for buildings, and hampered the construction of drains and sewers.

Factory and mine workers labored under harsh conditions. Working conditions in the factories, mills, and mines were unsanitary and dangerous. In writing about an English cotton mill, one man declared that it was a "sight that froze my blood. . . . The heat was excessive and the stink pestiferous. . . . I nearly fainted." With almost no safety devices on machines, accidents were common. An injured worker seldom received compensation for loss of a leg or an arm on the job.

Men, women, and children were required to work from twelve to fifteen hours a day. Mothers who had to work to supplement their husbands' incomes left their children at home without proper attention or else brought them to the unhealthful and dangerous factories. Orphaned children were often forced to work in factories or mills. In 1835 about one third of the factory workers in the cotton industry in England were young people, half of whom were under fourteen years of age. They worked from five-thirty in the morning until eight at night with only forty minutes off for their meals.

Here again, the picture must not be exaggerated. Much that was wrong was the result of obsolete laws, customs, and forms of organization from earlier periods. Women and children, for example, were commonly employed in farming and in cottage industries. The worst forms of exploitation took place in remote villages in the countryside, not in the growing manufacturing towns. In the towns themselves, the worst working conditions were in small workshops located in cellars or garrets, not in factories using steam power.

As for wages, they were lowest among the domestic workers, not among factory employees. Although real wages did remain low for unskilled factory workers, they rose substantially for the large and growing sections of skilled workers. This development was reflected in the changing diet of English workers. Meat was a rarity in the 18th century. By 1830 meat and potatoes were staples for the artisan, and wheat took the place of coarser rye and oats. By then, too, many workers were buying and wearing the new, cheap and abundant textiles which were easily washable and thus more sanitary.

The significant improvement in diet and clothing does not obscure the fact that much privation and poverty existed. But it should be remembered that the harsh conditions were not new and were not the exclusive result of the advance of industrialism. What was new was an aroused public awareness that deplorable conditions existed, and a quickening social consciousness that demanded something be done about them. This attitude was felt first and most strongly in England.

The middle class favored the laissez-faire system. The Industrial Revolution created its own leaders—the enterprising middle-class men, the owners of the railroads, mines, and factories which were transforming the life of the times. These men were known as industrial capitalists, because they owned the means of production themselves and usually managed their own business affairs. They believed that government should place no restrictions on business, and they subscribed to the principles of *laissez-faire capitalism*. (*Laissez faire* is French for "let do," and it came to mean "let them do as they please" when referring to businessmen.)

Adam Smith, a Scottish professor, was the first influential advocate of laissez-faire capitalism. In his book *The Wealth of Nations* (1776), he promoted the idea of freedom for commerce. Under the mercantile system, a government maintained strict controls over its economy in order to increase its own wealth and power. Smith believed that nations would gain wealth by removing trade restrictions such as tariffs so that supply and demand could govern the exchange of goods.

A generation later Thomas Malthus, an English clergyman and economist, greatly strengthened the laissez-faire argument with *An Essay on the Principles of Population* (1798). Malthus placed the blame for poverty on the laws of population growth. Population, he said, grew in geometrical ratio (1, 2, 4, 8, 16) while food

supply increased in arithmetical ratio (1, 2, 3, 4, 5). Unless something were done to prevent population growth from outstripping food supply, misery was bound to increase. Malthus' answer was that individuals should marry later in life and have fewer children. Furthermore, he believed that social reform was no solution because it would simply encourage the further growth of population. He was so gloomy and pessimistic that many people came to think of economics as "the dismal science."

Both Thomas Malthus and Adam Smith wrote at a time when English society was still predominantly agricultural. It was an English banker and economist named David Ricardo who, in the early 19th century, combined Smith's argument for free trade and Malthus' theories of population and applied them to the new industrial society. Those who complained about low wages, said Ricardo, did not understand that wages would always remain near the subsistence level. Wages were governed by an "Iron Law." According to this "law," when population increased, the labor supply would increase also; this increase would create competition among workers for jobs and keep wages from rising. If the labor supply declined and wages did rise, workers would produce more children and the labor market would again become glutted. Therefore, government efforts to improve the lot of factory workers were bad

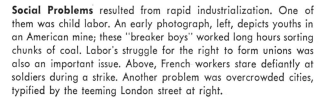

Social Problems resulted from rapid industrialization. One of them was child labor. An early photograph, left, depicts youths in an American mine; these "breaker boys" worked long hours sorting chunks of coal. Labor's struggle for the right to form unions was also an important issue. Above, French workers stare defiantly at soldiers during a strike. Another problem was overcrowded cities, typified by the teeming London street at right.

for two reasons: first, because these efforts would only make the conditions worse for the workers; second, because government intervention would interfere with the law of supply and demand. Economists believed that supply and demand operated in similar fashion to the natural laws governing the universe as explained by Newton in the Age of Reason.

The members of the new industrial capitalist class eagerly adopted and strongly supported the laissez-faire theory. Supply and demand, they said, would automatically control the production of goods and their selling prices, ensure fair prices and improved goods for the consumer, and guarantee good profits for the businessman.

It made little difference that in practice laissez faire did not always result in fair wages or just prices. The important point is that for most of the 19th century these ideas became the accepted social philosophy of the rising middle class.

Many voices spoke out for reform. Nevertheless, as industrialism advanced and as more people became aware of bad conditions in towns, factories, and mines, criticism.mounted. In England a group of young Tories, anxious to make reforms, came into prominence. This group included men such as Lord Palmerston and a brilliant young capitalist named Robert Peel. In the 1820's, largely through their efforts, labor unions were made lawful, tariffs on imported grain were lowered, the harsh criminal code was revised, and Roman Catholics and Nonconformists were permitted to hold political office.

The most important piece of political legislation in 19th-century England was the Reform Bill of 1832. It gave representation in the House of Commons to the new industrial towns of the north. Of greater consequence, this act extended the right to vote, thus granting a share of political power to the new business class. The "Reform Parliament" then went on to abolish slavery in the British Empire (1833), to revise the poor laws (1834), and to liberalize municipal government (1835).

Since most of these reforms benefited the Whig industrialists, the Tories championed the cause of the industrial workers. They set up parliamentary commissions to investigate conditions in the factories and mines. Their reports aroused public indignation. In 1833 they pushed through the first effective factory legislation of the industrial era, an act which regulated the employment of children in factories. In 1842 an act was passed which prohibited the use of women, girls, and young boys in underground mines. With the passage of the Ten Hours Act in 1847, the principle of ten hours as a normal working day was established.

The drive toward reform involved popular English writers like Charles Dickens, who attacked the ugliness and misery of industrialism in many of his novels. Other prominent reformers were the philosophers Jeremy Bentham and John Stuart Mill. Bentham, who popularized the phrase "the greatest happiness for the greatest number," was the most important figure in the development of the doctrine of Utilitarianism. He argued that the true test of any institution was its usefulness to society. The efforts of the Utilitarians led to reforms in law codes and in the treatment of prison-

ers. Bentham's disciple, Mill, was one of the great champions of personal liberty. His essay *On Liberty* (1859) is a defense of individual freedom. He did not accept the extreme policy of laissez faire and argued that some form of social legislation was necessary. For him the key issue was the protection of the individual's rights and the adoption of the best means to preserve those rights. He rejected the gloomy implications of Malthus and Ricardo and stressed the need for positive, practical remedies for the ills of industrialism. Mill's ideas on liberty and his humane, practical approach to problems have had a continuing influence down to the present day.

Section Review

1. Identify the three great revolutions that were responsible for a new attitude toward social change in the 19th century. How did each of these revolutions help shape this attitude?
2. What were some of the problems created by the quick growth of cities? by the factory system?
3. In what ways did the ideas of Adam Smith, Malthus, and Ricardo contribute to the middle-class belief in laissez faire?
4. What were the key ideas of John Stuart Mill? How did the social legislation passed by the British "Reform Parliament" contribute to the reform movement?

2 **Socialists proposed far-reaching changes**

Throughout the 19th century, many plans were proposed to help workers and society in general. Some thinkers believed that the ownership, management, and control of all means of production should be placed in the hands of the workers. Others advocated government ownership of the means of production. These systems of social organization came to be called *social-*

ism, and the persons who proposed them were known as *socialists.*

Many schools of socialism arose in the early 19th century, each proposing its own plan for remaking society. While the specific schemes differed from one another, they were all based on a common belief, inherited from the 18th century, that only a good society could produce good men. The implication of this belief was that the organization of society was bad and that it must be completely modified. The problem was how to bring about this transformation of society.

Utopian socialists hoped to build a better world. The first to deal with the problem of transforming society were the *Utopian socialists,* named after *Utopia,* the title of Sir Thomas More's 16th-century description of an ideal society. Active in England and France, the Utopian socialists dreamed of a harmonious community based upon the principles of coöperation and economic planning. They rejected all forms of class violence and class dictatorship. They hoped that by establishing model communities, all people would discover the merits of socialism and would want to imitate them. Utopian socialists wished to bring about the good society through persuasion, not through revolution. As it turned out, many of their schemes were impractical.

The first important Utopian socialist was a French nobleman, Count Henri de Saint-Simon, who lived from 1760 to 1825. He believed that industry should be operated to benefit the masses and that captains of industry'and technicians were best qualified to do so. Although the latter idea seemed to favor the middle-class industrialists, who were trying to gain political power, Saint-Simon was a sincere socialist who wanted to reorganize society. He expressed the principle that people should be compensated "from each according to his capacity, to each according to his work."

Later on, this statement became a popular slogan for socialists.

Another French reformer, François Fourier, who lived from 1772 to 1837, thought that society should be broken up into units of self-sufficient communities of about 5000 acres. Each unit would be composed of approximately 1600 to 1800 people who would live and work together for the common good. His plans were not put into practice in Europe, but in the United States, where land was cheap, a few coöperative communities were set up. None of them proved successful.

Fourier's ideas influenced the most effective of the Utopian socialists, the Englishman Robert Owen. The textile mills he owned in New Lanark, Scotland, employed 2000 persons, 500 of whom were children. When Owen took charge of the mills in 1800, he was determined to improve the living and working conditions of the workers. In addition, he wanted to test his theories regarding human relationships and community living. He raised the wages of the workers, built schools and new houses, and employed no children under eleven years of age. The improved environment wiped out almost all crime and disease. Furthermore, Owen's mills continued to make a profit.

In 1825 Owen set up another colony which he called New Harmony, near Evansville, Indiana. Owen's model community was intended to prove that liberal employers could educate workers to form ideal social groups. The community failed after two years, however, when disagreements arose among the inhabitants.

Owen's ideas led to the founding of the Coöperative Movement. In 1844 a group of linen workers at Rochdale, England, collected a sum equal to $140 and started a store. Members shared the profits of this enterprise in proportion to their purchases at the store. Other coöperative stores, or consumer coöps, were formed elsewhere in Europe. Coöps grew particularly strong in England and in Scandinavia, where they assumed ownership and operation of factories as well as retail stores. In the United States, storage and marketing coöps became important among farmers.

Although Utopian socialism and coöperatives benefited some workers, these movements were not major trends. The middle class was opposed to them and did not lend their support. The workers were not fired by idealistic schemes that had few lasting effects. The importance of the Utopian socialists stems not from their specific schemes but from the influence of those ideas in promoting social reforms. Those ideas also stimulated the whole socialist movement, which in later years deeply affected the modern industrial world.

Karl Marx introduced a new kind of socialism. Karl Marx dismissed the Utopians as completely impractical and offered what he believed was a solution to man's ills. *Scientific socialism* was the name he gave to his brand of socialism.

Marx's father was a well-to-do lawyer in Germany, and Marx himself studied law and philosophy at the universities of Bonn and Berlin. After graduation he became a journalist and then a newspaper editor, but his radical views on political and economic reforms led him into trouble with government authorities in Germany, and he fled to France. In Paris he met Friedrich Engels, the son of a wealthy manufacturer in England, who became his lifelong friend. In 1848 they published the *Communist Manifesto,* a pamphlet which embodied most of the principles of Marxian socialism and set forth a complete strategy for social revolution. The *Manifesto* created little stir when it first appeared, but it was to become one of the most important documents of modern history.

In 1848 Marx played an active role during the February revolution in Paris and in the uprisings in Germany. When these uprisings failed, Marx fled to London. There he began the three volumes of *Das Kapital* (Capital), his major work. The first volume was published in 1867. Before he could finish the third volume, he died, and Engels completed the work for him.

Marx believed that revolution was inevitable. Basically, Karl Marx was a revolutionary who believed that the capitalistic system was doomed. The destruction of capitalism, he believed, would come about in a revolution during which the workers—whom Marx called the *proletariat*—would seize control from the *bourgeoisie,* or middle class. Moreover, Marx claimed that the socialist revolution was inevitable and that it was "the wave of the future." Although thoughtful people wondered why Marx urged people to work for a revolution that he felt was inevitable anyway, Marx dodged the issue and concentrated on proofs to bolster his prophecy.

Basic to Marx's thinking was his belief that changes occur in history primarily because of economic factors, which form the foundation of society. Marx believed that the way in which goods are produced ultimately determines the character of society. Marx further maintained that those groups controlling the production of goods also control the society itself, and therefore its laws, government, religion, and culture. When the form of production changes, the ruling group changes. Furthermore, he maintained that all significant changes come about through class struggle. In a famous passage the *Communist Manifesto* proclaimed:

The history of all hitherto existing society is the history of class struggles. Freeman and slave, patrician and plebeian, lord and serf, guildmaster and journeyman, in a

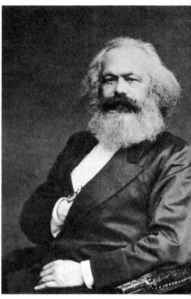

Reform Movements proposed various methods to remedy the hardships that accompanied industrialism. The Salvation Army, a religious organization founded in England in 1865, provided food and shelter for the poor. Above, Salvation Army workers distribute coffee and bread in a mission. Members of the Amana coöperative community in Iowa held all property in common. Below, Amana residents say grace before a meal; men and women ate separately "to prevent silly conversation and trifling conduct." Karl Marx, above right, urged laborers to use force in taking over governments.

word, oppressor and oppressed, stood in constant opposition to one another, carried on an uninterrupted, now hidden, now open fight, a fight that each time ended either in a revolutionary reconstitution of society at large, or in the common ruin of the contending classes.

According to Marx, just as the middle class had replaced the feudal aristocrats, so the oppressed proletariat was destined to replace the middle class after gaining control of the means of production. At this point, a classless society would be born, and class struggle would cease.

Another element in Marx's "proof" that capitalism was doomed stemmed from his analysis of the capitalistic system in *Das Kapital*. This analysis was based on the labor theory of value. According to this theory, the value of any product depends upon the amount of work necessary to produce it. For example, making a piano might require 1000 man-hours of labor. If the laborers had been paid at the rate of $1 an hour, the real value of the piano would be $1000. If the manufacturer sold it for $2000, the extra thousand dollars was *surplus value* and really belonged to the workers because they had created the real value of the product through their labor. Instead, this surplus value went into the pocket of the manufacturer.

The logical result of this system, Marx argued, was that the poor would become poorer and the rich richer as wealth became concentrated in fewer hands. Meanwhile, goods made in increasing amounts under the capitalistic system would pile up in warehouses because the workers would not be able to buy them. Then businesses would fail, factories would close, and millions of persons would lose their jobs. Eventually, after a series of depressions, capitalism would collapse. At this point the workers would seize control, destroy the capitalistic system, and impose socialism upon their society.

Marx's ideas were vulnerable to attack. In his theories about changes in history, Marx succeeded in making many people aware of the importance of economic forces. Until then history had been written with the emphasis largely on military and political developments. Furthermore, the late 19th and early 20th centuries did witness a concentration of wealth, the growth of ever larger industrial units, and varying periods of economic depression. Yet the events of history have shown that Marx was a poor prophet. In addition, his theories suffer from basic weaknesses in his logic.

In his own day, and long afterwards, Marx's ideas have been widely attacked. Most historians believe that Marx's interpretation of historical forces is oversimplified. Events do not result only from economic causes nor are people shaped solely by them. Many factors must be accounted for—patriotism, religious zeal, and political loyalties are among the strong motives which move men to action.

Class struggle as a theory of historical change has serious shortcomings. Ordinarily, people do not think of themselves only in terms of economic class. Numerous examples in history show that men of many classes fight together against a common enemy. The world wars of modern times have shown nationalism as a force stronger than class feelings. In addition, many reputable historians maintain that it was not the capitalistic system that caused the laboring class to be exploited but the misuse of power and authority on the part of certain individual capitalists. Capitalism was young at the time of Marx, and evils of industrialism were obvious, but as time advanced, many of these evils diminished or were corrected.

Economists have demolished Marx's labor theory of value. The cost of making a product includes not only the labor required to make it but the contribution of a manufacturer, who must provide raw materials and maintain the factory and its equipment and pay for its upkeep. Furthermore, the price of a product is affected by the general conditions in the market; for example, an oversupply of a particular item can lead to a decrease in the selling price—sometimes even below the cost of the labor that went into it.

Marx also exhibited a blind spot about labor. He did not recognize the importance of creative abilities and managerial talents. Physical labor is not the only ingredient creating values in a product. Many workers do not produce material goods at all but supply skills essential to the manufacture of a product.

History did not bear out Marx's prophecies. With the growth of trade unions, which began late in the 19th century, workers were able to bargain effectively with their employers for higher wages and shorter working hours. The advance of political democracy and the spread of universal manhood suffrage meant that workers could elect their own government representatives and that they, in turn, would strive for social reforms. In the final years of the 19th century, conditions for the workers improved. Wages advanced, and workers could afford to buy the products made in the factories and mills. To be sure, some of the rich did become richer, but most of the poor did not become poorer. Instead, the general standard of living rose to heights never before attained in history.

Marxists created international associations. In 1864 Karl Marx helped organize the First International Workingmen's Association in an effort to bring together radicals of every country. The First International had a stormy career and lasted a brief twelve years. Despite its estimated 5 million supporters scattered through Europe, the First International was weak and ineffective. Quarrels between Marx and the other radicals were so bitter and persecution by hostile governments increased so much that by 1876 it went out of existence.

In 1889, six years after Marx died, the Second International was organized. It was composed of the Marxist socialist parties which, as discussed in the next section of this chapter, were developing in the major countries of Europe. At its height the Second International had representatives from twenty-three nationalities. But like its predecessor, it was plagued with internal dissension and also proved ineffective. The two great issues around which controversy raged were whether socialists should accept office in nonsocialist governments and whether socialists should support their government in time of war. Moderates said yes to both questions; extremists said no. When the crucial test came in 1914, all but a handful of extremists loyally supported the war efforts of their countries, and it was clear that nationalism was far stronger than socialism. The Second International died with the First World War.

Section Review

1. What were the aims and the methods of the Utopian reformers? To what degree was Utopian socialism successful?
2. Why did Marx believe that the socialist revolution was inevitable?
3. What were some of the arguments used to attack Marx's logic? In what respects did his predictions prove incorrect?
4. What was the purpose of the First International? What problems did the Second International face?

3 **Conditions for the workers improved**

If a revolution had not occurred in Russia in 1917, bringing to power a group of self-proclaimed Marxists, the name of Karl Marx would probably be known today only to a few scholars. Even Marx himself in the late years of his life (he died in 1883) recognized that, contrary to his earlier predictions, the general standard of living for European workers was rising.

Two broad movements helped refute the prophecies of Marx. One trend dealt with technical matters. While discoveries in science and medicine and improved sanitation reduced death rates, stepped-up farming and industrial production provided people with more food, more clothes, and more houses. The other trend concerned political and social developments. As the right to vote was extended to all men, as political leaders became sensitive to the wishes of masses of new voters, as workers gained greater freedom to organize trade unions and political parties, the pressures rose for government to take a more active role in dealing with the social and economic problems created by industrialism. In the years between 1870 and 1914, significant changes took place in political and social life, and the idea of a laissez-faire state slowly gave way to the idea of a social welfare state.

Many countries adopted universal manhood suffrage. From a political point of view, the most noteworthy development of the half century before the First World War was the granting of the right to vote to all men regardless of property qualifications. The movement toward universal manhood suffrage was strongest in the countries of western and northern Europe. As discussed in Chapter 20, the right to vote was granted to most men in Britain, France, and Germany before 1890. By 1917 it had also been adopted in Belgium, the Netherlands, Switzerland, and the Scandinavian countries.

A few countries permitted women to vote before the First World War: Norway, Australia, and New Zealand. Also, some Western states in the United States granted women the right to vote. In 1903 a women's suffrage movement was organized in Great Britain by Emmeline Pankhurst and her two daughters. But for fifteen years the British government held firm, relenting only after a prolonged campaign of unladylike violence by the suffragettes and the intervention of World War I. Englishwomen gained their goal in 1918, and American women, in 1920.

Governments enacted social reforms. The advance of democracy soon expressed itself in the kinds of reforms that the governments of western Europe enacted in the years after 1870. In fact, the politics of all European states became increasingly concerned with social problems. As big towns grew rapidly and industry became more mechanized, more voters were drawn from the industrial wage-earning classes. These voters were the very people who demanded that government take a more active role in social affairs. Events in England can serve as a good example of the trend of the times.

The British government, which had already passed considerable legislation regulating working conditions in factories, mines, and mills, extended its activities to new fields. In the 1870's laws were enacted governing housing and public health; in the 1890's infants' welfare centers were set up to provide free milk to poor mothers; in 1902 the Education Act was passed as the climax of a long effort to build up a national system of primary and secondary education. When the Liberal Party came to power in 1905, it moved even more vigorously in the field of social legislation. Pushed by the new Labour Party, the Liberals outlawed sweatshop conditions after 1909, introduced a legal weekly half holiday with pay in 1911, and, most important of all, passed the National Insurance Act in 1911. The act insured the whole working population against losses suffered due to sickness, provided them with free medical attention, and gave certain kinds of workers unemployment insurance.

In many ways Germany set the pace in systematic social legislation. Unlike Britain, Germany did not emphasize factory legislation or unemployment insurance. Guided by Bismarck, German legislation aimed at the three most common problems of urban industrial life—sickness, accident, and incapacity in old age. Laws tackling these problems were passed in 1883, 1884, and 1889. (It was ironic that these laws were sponsored by the conservative-minded Bismarck, who wished primarily to weaken the appeal of socialism by strengthening his own political position.) Eventually free medical and hospital care was provided, but factory codes and child labor laws were not added until 1914. Germany's pioneering efforts in welfare legislation meant that by the outbreak of the First World War, German workers were better protected against the dangers and uncertainties of industrial society than the workers of any other country.

In France, where the movement toward industrialization and urbanization developed more slowly, social legislation also came more slowly. In the 1890's laws were passed limiting women to a ten-hour workday and making partial provision for pensions and accident insurance. The ten-hour workday was made general in 1900, and in 1906 a six-day work week was established.

Many other countries followed the examples of Britain, Germany, and France. By 1914 nearly every European country except Russia and the Balkan states had well-developed factory codes and labor legislation. There were also minimum standards for the building of houses and streets and the preparation of food and drink.

In addition, between 1871 and 1914 every Western nation created a system of public education. On the primary level, education was made compulsory as well as free, for only by this means could mass illiteracy be wiped out. At the same time high schools, technical institutes, and universities were greatly expanded to supply the growing need for engineers, doctors, teachers, technicians, and administrators. In most countries, but particularly in France and Germany, bitter struggles between church and state broke out over the control of education, but eventually the state won out. The movement toward public education developed so rapidly that Prussia spent thirty times as much on primary education in 1901 as it had in 1871, and England twice as much in 1914 as it had in 1900. Public education did more than make great inroads against illiteracy. It also became the greatest single force in shaping public opinion and teaching people how to live in an industrial civilization.

Trade unions won concessions. The use of the ballot in pressing for social legislation was only one way in which workers tried to improve their position. They also resorted to other methods. One was to organize trade unions and seek concessions directly from employers. Although labor unions had existed before 1870, their most rapid expansion came after that date. In the 1880's France granted trade unions legal recognition and the right to strike; Germany did likewise in the 1890's.

In the 1880's trade unions entered a new phase of organization. Prior to that time unions were basically craft unions, composed primarily of skilled workers. They concentrated on winning benefits through negotiations with employers. After the mid-1880's large masses of semiskilled and unskilled workers in one industry, such as the steel industry, banded together to form huge industrial unions. These so-called new unions came into existence after a series of long and bitter strikes of the less skilled workers in the 1880's and 1890's in Belgium, England, France, and Germany.

Most notable was the great London dock workers' strike of 1889, which shut down the port of London for the first time since the French Revolution. The success of the strikes proved that organized opposition was a useful tool in winning concessions from employers. Hence, unlike the craft unions, the larger industrial unions came to rely more heavily on strikes than on negotiations. As a result, in the years before the First World War, the whole union movement became more aggressive in its methods.

Socialists formed political parties. Another method by which workers tried to improve their position was through the organization of political parties that sought to change the capitalistic system. By and large it was the socialists who took the lead in this development. The first of these parties was the German Social Democratic Party, founded in 1875. Soon afterward similar socialist parties were formed in most countries of western Europe. Despite their Marxist inspiration, for all practical purposes these socialist parties were not revolutionary. Wherever the tradition of representative government and democracy was strong, workers used their political parties to elect candidates who would work for reforms within the existing system.

Great Britain is a good example. In 1883 a group of intellectuals, which included writers like George Bernard Shaw and H. G. Wells, formed the Fabian Society. Although critics of capitalism, the Fabians were moderates who believed in gradual, piecemeal reforms. (The Society was named after Fabius Maximus, the cautious Roman dictator whose tactics frustrated Hannibal of Carthage.) In 1900 the Fabians joined with a small Marxist group and the major trade unions to found the British Labour Party. Through the influence of the Fabians, the British Labour Party was content to work patiently for specific practical reforms through orderly parliamentary channels.

Even on the Continent, revolutionary Marxism was tamed into parliamentary socialism. Moderates like Jean Jaurès in France and Eduard Bernstein in Germany argued that in the light of the obvious improvement in the workers' standard of living, Marxist doctrine had to be revised. Socialists should drop the notion of revolution and class dictatorship and concentrate instead on gaining their ends through orderly legislation. In most countries of western Europe, social democratic parties followed the program of the so-called revisionists.

In the countries of eastern Europe, where parliaments did not exist, political parties and trade unions were outlawed, and strikes were considered a crime against the state. In short, in the nations in which orderly channels for reform were totally lacking, Marxism retained a strong revolutionary fervor. In Russia, for example, the Social Democratic Party was founded in 1898. It was a Marxist group and, of necessity, it was a secret organization, as were all other political parties in czarist Russia. In 1903 the Russian Social Democrats split into two factions, the *Mensheviks* (meaning "minority") and the *Bolsheviks* (meaning "majority"). The Mensheviks argued that Russia was not yet ready for a Marxist revolution. They wanted to coöperate with middle-class liberals and democrats. The Bolsheviks, led by Lenin (Chapter 28), vehemently denounced both the revisionists and Mensheviks as class traitors and declared that the primary goal was the revolution of the proletariat. Ultimately, the chaos of the First World War gave Lenin and the Bolsheviks an opportunity for seizing power in Russia, but in 1903 they were considered insignificant.

In general the working class as a whole had come a long way by 1914. Between 1870 and 1900, their real wages in the industrialized countries rose by 50 per cent. Clearly the revisionists were right and Marx was wrong. The European working class was in no mood for revolution. To be sure, they continued to demand a greater degree of social justice, but they were confident that the rise in their own living standards was proof that their goals could be obtained through powerful unions, through political parties, and through voting. To destroy a government from which workers and all other citizens as well could expect to benefit was considered extreme foolishness.

Middle-class attitudes changed. By 1914 the developments discussed in this chapter brought about an important change in the strong laissez-faire attitude that had prevailed in the early 19th century. That older attitude may be described as *classical liberalism.* It rested on the belief that each individual is a free human being; that governments should be limited in power and based on majority rule; that the right to vote should be restricted to men of property; that government had no right to interfere in the natural operation of the economic and social system; that, in accordance with the law of supply and demand and the Darwinian principle of struggle and survival, individuals should be left free to compete with one another.

The advance of democracy and industrialism greatly modified liberal beliefs. The key principle, faith in the freedom, dignity, and worth of the individual, still remained. But the idea grew that the preservation of the key principle in a complex industrial society required a changed attitude toward the proper role of government. The state came to be thought of as having a responsibility for the welfare of its citizens. While businessmen looked to the state for subsidies and tariff protection, labor unions, socialist parties, and masses of new voters demanded factory codes, social

insurance, a system of free public education, and regulation of the purity of food and drugs.

The change in attitude could be seen in the position of the Catholic Church. In 1891 Pope Leo XIII issued a major statement of Catholic social doctrine in the form of an encyclical entitled *Rerum Novarum* (of modern things). It defended private property as a natural right but criticized capitalism for its failure to provide social justice to the working class. Poverty, insecurity, and degradation were declared to be unjust and unchristian. To the extent that socialism sought to remove these evils, socialism was Christian. It was the atheism of socialism that was unchristian. *Rerum Novarum,* therefore, encouraged Catholics to form their own socialist parties and labor unions in order to seek a greater measure of social justice.

Politicians became more sensitive to the demands of the electorate and heeded their demands for social and economic reform. As political leaders increasingly intervened in social and economic matters, the idea of a social welfare state began to gain acceptance among middle-class liberals.

Section Review

1. What countries adopted universal manhood suffrage most readily?
2. In what ways was Germany a pioneer in social legislation? Compare German social legislation with that in Britain and in France.
3. What significant changes took place after 1880 in the organization of trade unions and in the methods they used to gain their objectives?
4. What political parties in Europe represented the moderate socialist position? How did Mensheviks and Bolsheviks differ in their doctrines?
5. What ideas made up classical liberalism? How had those ideas been modified by 1914?

Three great revolutions—the Enlightenment, the French Revolution, and the Industrial Revolution—led men to analyze 19th-century social and economic conditions and to suggest ways to eliminate injustices. Although these suggestions varied, the main goal was the reform of the capitalistic system so that poverty would be abolished. The fact of poverty itself was not new, but public awareness of deplorable living and working conditions represented a trend new to history. Early in the 19th century, England took the lead in passing important reform legislation.

The rapid spread of industrialism disrupted the lives of many people. Workers flocked from the farms to cities and towns. Crowded, unsanitary housing, the threat of epidemics, and insufficient water supply were among the problems of urban dwellers. In factories and mines, too, harsh conditions often existed. Men, women, and children were forced to work long hours for little pay. However, in some respects, the lot of the worker in the 19th century was an improvement over 18th-century conditions. Wages for skilled workers rose, and better food and clothing became available.

The middle class favored laissez-faire capitalism. The proponents of this system held that any restrictions on business would only cause problems worse than those already in existence. The economists Adam Smith, Thomas Malthus, and David Ricardo contributed ideas which supported the laissez-faire theory. The influential thinker, John Stuart Mill, argued that personal liberty could best be achieved through the modification of laissez-faire policies and the adoption of social legislation.

Some reformers proposed drastic changes for society. Socialists wanted all means of production turned over to the workers or to the government. Utopian socialists experimented with model communities based on principles of coöperation and economic planning. The Coöperative Movement involved the establishment of worker-owned stores and factories, the profits of which were shared. A more radical form of socialism was that proposed by Karl Marx. In the *Communist Manifesto* (1848), he and Friedrich Engels predicted that the workers would revolt against the middle class and forcefully seize control of industry and government. The revolution, they said, was inevitable because the capitalistic system was doomed.

Marx's prediction that conditions for the worker would grow worse did not come true. Instead, in the years after 1870, the general standard of living rose higher than ever before. Medical discoveries reduced the death rate, and technological advances produced new and better consumer products. Democracy took great strides forward as universal manhood suffrage was extended and compulsory public education became widespread. Labor unions were given legal recognition and increased in membership and power. Socialists coöperated with governments to reach their goals through reform legislation. Only in countries where democratic government was weak or nonexistent, as in Russia, did revolutionary Marxism remain strong.

The Time

Some of the following events and movements occurred during the time spans designated. Others did not. Rearrange the items on the list so that all events appear in their proper time spans.

1751-1800
> First International was formed.
> Thomas Malthus' *An Essay on the Principles of Population* was published.
> Russian Social Democrats split into two factions, Mensheviks and Bolsheviks.
> First volume of Karl Marx's *Das Kapital* was published.
> French and German labor unions won recognition and the right to strike.

1801-1850
> New Harmony experiment took place.
> British Labour Party was formed.
> Social Democratic Party in Russia was organized.

Coöperative Movement began in Rochdale.
Communist Manifesto was published.

1851-1900
Adam Smith's *The Wealth of Nations* was published.
Bismarck inaugurated social legislation in Germany.
Charles Dickens' *Hard Times* appeared.
John Stuart Mill's essay *On Liberty* was published.
German Social Democratic Party was founded.

1901-1915
London dock workers' strike shut down the port of London.
Second International was formed.
Fabian Society was organized.
Pope Leo XIII issued his *Rerum Novarum*.
National Insurance Act was passed in Britain.

The People

1. How did the ideas of the following economists strengthen the argument for laissez-faire capitalism: Adam Smith, Thomas Malthus, David Ricardo?

2. How did the following people contribute to the reform of 19th-century industrial society?

Lord Palmerston	Jeremy Bentham
Robert Peel	John Stuart Mill
Charles Dickens	Pope Leo XIII

3. In what ways did each of the following men contribute to the development of moderate socialism: H. G. Wells, George Bernard Shaw, Jean Jaurès, Eduard Bernstein?

4. What were the views of each of these Utopian socialists: Count Henri de Saint-Simon, François Fourier, Robert Owen?

5. With what socialist group was Lenin associated?

Historical Terms

1. Give a simple definition of the term socialism. What goals and principles did all socialists—moderate, Marxist, and Utopian—have in common? What characteristics distinguished each of these kinds of socialism from the other?

2. What does Karl Marx mean by his use of each of the following terms?

bourgeoisie	proletariat
surplus value	class struggle
classless society	

3. What is the meaning of laissez faire as applied to an economic theory?

4. Explain each of the following terms as it applied to efforts to improve conditions for the working classes.

Utilitarianism	labor unions
Coöperative Movement	Ten Hours Act
National Insurance Act	*Rerum Novarum*
social legislation	

5. What is meant by parliamentary socialism?

6. Which of the following organizations or groups promoted moderate socialism? revolutionary socialism?

First International	Second International
Russian Social Democratic Party	Fabian Society
	Mensheviks
German Social Democratic Party	Bolsheviks
	revisionists
British Labour Party	

Questions for Critical Thinking

1. Laissez faire and scientific socialism were extreme solutions to the problems of industrial society. Explain why by 1900 most of the countries of Western Europe, as well as the United States, had rejected these extremes.

2. Compare the achievements of the Utopian socialists with those of the moderate socialists. Which group was more successful?

3. What are the shortcomings of Marx's belief that changes occur in history primarily because of economic factors?

4. By the turn of the 19th century, to what extent had social legislation corrected the evils of industrial society? Explain your answer.

5. Why is it incorrect to attribute the 19th-century problems that accompanied the emergence of large cities entirely to the Industrial Revolution?

Growth and Expansion Outside Europe

During most of the world's history, the non-Western peoples were the most advanced in government, military power, economic development, learning, and the arts. Civilization itself originated in the river valleys of the Near East and Asia. Up to about 1500 A.D., the non-Europeans had been in the vanguard of human progress. But after 1500 western Europe forged ahead. Its people were endowed with boundless energy and confidence, with military power, and with a vigorous economy. The non-Western peoples, on the other hand, were in decline. In the smug belief that they enjoyed a superior civilization, they withdrew from the new currents of world history and fell far behind the progressive West. In time, the whole world came under Western control, whether imperial control by the mother continent of Europe or settlement by its sons and daughters who migrated abroad.

In the temperate zone of the Americas, South Africa, and Australia, relatively underpopulated lands attracted people of all types. A tremendous tide of humanity flowed from Europe, constituting one of the greatest mass movements of people in all history. During the 19th century and the early years of the 20th century, 40 million people sought new homes across the seas. By 1914 the people of European stock in the new lands totaled 200 million, as many people as there had been in all Europe in 1815.

The United States in particular was regarded as a land of opportunity and freedom. The ports along its eastern seaboard teemed with ships from which throngs of excited immigrants disembarked. They came from all classes—the peasant, the small shopkeeper and trader, the artisan, and the well-educated professional man. However, the majority were poor and needy, seeking a better life and a new chance at fortune. The painting reproduced on the opposite page shows the arrival in 1847 of Irish immigrants in New York harbor.

The immigrants brought with them their social customs, religious faiths, and political ideas. In short, they brought their "culture" with their baggage. The nations in which they settled were truly "New Europes." The United States was the world's leader in the development of great natural resources and the establishment of stable, democratic government. Canada, Australia, New Zealand, and South Africa also made notable progress. Latin America lagged behind, hindered by political instability, illiteracy, and backward economic practices.

The growth of New Europes made up one aspect of European expansion; the other was imperialism. The superior technology of the West, the need for markets and for raw materials, and the sincere wish to aid backward peoples—these factors were all part of Europe's quest for colonial empires. The immense wealth of the tropical lands—cotton, tea, rubber, ivory, and palm oil—lured traders. In Africa, India, Southeast Asia, and the islands of the South Seas, backward societies offered little resistance to European penetration. Colonial governments were established and natural resources were developed by enterprising businessmen.

Imperialism reached its height in the 19th century when it is estimated that 283 million Europeans controlled over 900 million non-Western peoples. Britain built the largest colonial empire; its imperialistic rule encompassed 13 million square miles inhabited by 470 million people. India was the greatest single colony, and Africa was the largest continental area to be partitioned by European colonial powers. In 1914, from the shores of the Mediterranean to the Cape of Good Hope, only two African states retained their independence— Liberia and Abyssinia (now Ethiopia). In the Far East several small pieces of territory were chipped away from China by the imperialistic West. More important, European nations exercised indirect control of China through treaties and other agreements. Of all the great Asian powers, only Japan succeeded in avoiding Western imperialism. Latin America experienced the pressures of imperialism, particularly in economic matters.

Many different views of imperialism exist. Some people emphasize positive aspects—the reduction of disease, the ending of tribal warfare, the spread of Christian principles by dedicated men and women of God. Critics have seen in imperialism only evil and the pursuit of riches at the expense of backward peoples unable to protect themselves. Yet the most important result of imperialism cannot be denied. This dynamic movement transmitted over the earth the powerful ideas of nationalism and democracy and the tangible benefits of science and technology. All these forces taken together stirred the rest of the world and reawakened its people.

Canada became British possession
Captain Cook
Quebec Act
American Revolution

Articles of Confederation

Constitution of the United States   Australia colonized
Washington President

Seven Years' War
India became British possession

India Act of 1784

Netherlands East Indies

1800

Louisiana Purchase   Haiti independent

Cape Colony a British possession   Bolívar
San Martín

British expansion in India

1820

Brazil independent
Monroe Doctrine   Mexico independent
Spanish South America free

Texan secession

Durham Report

Algeria became French colony

1840

New Zealand colonized   Dom Pedro II
Mexican War

Voortrekkers

China opened to trade

Japan opened to trade

Sepoy Rebellion
India ruled by British government

1860

War Between the States
Maximilian emperor of Mexico
Dominion of Canada formed

Russia acquired Chinese territory

Meiji Restoration   Suez Canal
Europe's golden age of imperialism   Rhodes
Stanley and Livingstone

Russian expansion in mid-Asia

1880

gold found in Transvaal

Boer War

partition of Africa
Egypt became British protectorate
Indian National Congress
French Indo-China formed
European "spheres of influence" in China
Sino-Japanese War
Spanish-American War   Fashoda incident
Open Door Policy

1900

Commonwealth of Australia formed

New Zealand became British dominion

Union of South Africa created

Republic of Panama
Roosevelt Corollary   Russo-Japanese War
Moslem League
"dollar diplomacy" in Latin America
Panama Canal

The Emergence of New Nations

European colonists who settled overseas carried with them the ideals of nationalism and freedom. Their dedication to these principles helped shape the character of the new nations they established. Simón Bolívar was a great figure in the movement to liberate Latin America from colonial control. He is shown on a white horse in the foreground above, leading his men to victory over the Spanish.

In 1805 a dashing young man of twenty-two, accompanied by his old tutor, climbed to the top of the Aventine Hill in Rome. There, among the ancient ruins, he fell to his knees and made a solemn vow: "On my life and honor, I swear not to rest until I have liberated America from her tyrants!" The young man was Simón Bolívar of Venezuela. Twenty years later Spanish rule in Central and South America had ended, thanks in large part to his efforts.

It was significant that Bolívar made his vow in one of the oldest cities of Europe, for in a sense the event symbolized the interconnection of the Old World and the New. In the centuries after the epic voyages of the Age of Discovery, millions of Europeans settled and colonized territories overseas, carrying with them the traditions and customs of their home countries. In this way, European civilization was transplanted to the Americas, to Africa, and to the distant shores of Australia and New Zealand.

Until the 19th century the vast majority of colonists emigrated from western Europe. This was the region which had experienced most fully the Renaissance, the religious upheavals of the 16th century, the impact of scientific thought, and the ideals of the Enlightenment. Thus, the culture established in the overseas colonies was not only essentially that of western Europe, but also one in which the tradition of individualism was growing.

Life in the colonies strengthened this attitude. As each colony matured, colonial-born generations came to resent the restrictions that kept them under the control of the mother country. Late in the 18th century, resentment had flared into open revolution in the thirteen British colonies of North America. The outcome of the Revolutionary War modified the colonial policy of Great Britain and thus helped prepare the way for a greater degree of freedom in many of its overseas possessions. The liberal spirit also sparked revolts in the vast colonial empire of Spain. By the end of the 19th century, a wider world of European civilization had come into being, encircling the globe with a band of free, sovereign nations.

This chapter describes how:

1. **The United States grew strong.**

2. **New nations developed within the British Empire.**

3. **Latin America gained its independence.**

1 **The United States grew strong**

When Americans in the thirteen colonies became the first Europeans overseas to achieve independence, many thoughtful persons in the Old World wondered whether they could succeed as a nation. The French statesman Turgot thought Americans "should be an example of political, religious, commercial, and industrial liberty," but he had some doubts about whether they could achieve the unity essential to nationhood. After all, he shrewdly observed, the American states were "only an aggregation of parts, always too much separated and preserving always a tendency to division by the diversity of their laws, their manners, their opinions." Clearly, the new nation had to overcome some grave problems.

Americans established a new government. The most immediate problem was to establish a new government. In 1781, two years before the peace treaty with Britain which ended the Revolutionary War, the thirteen colonies ratified the Articles of Confederation, creating the first national American government. Coming as they did after a decade of protest against strong central authority in London, the Articles established a loose union and created a central government with no authority to levy taxes, regulate commerce, or control western lands. Because the government had little power, it commanded little respect. The obvious deficiencies of the Articles convinced many persons that reforms were needed. In May 1787, fifty-five delegates met at Independence Hall in Philadelphia to consider revising the Articles of Confederation. They decided to abandon them altogether and finally devised a new constitution.

The Constitution of the United States represented a compromise between an excessively strong central authority and the weak national government of the Articles. The men who wrote it discarded the idea expressed in the Articles of Confederation—that the United States was a league of sovereign independent states. Instead they proclaimed the nation to be a union of individuals subject to the Constitution as the supreme law of the land. Mindful of the dangers of tyranny, however, the framers of the Constitution constructed an ingenious set of safeguards. They followed the principle of federalism and carefully distributed power between the states and the national government. At the same time they built a system of checks and balances into the federal government by organizing it into three separate units— executive, legislative, and judicial. As another safeguard, a series of ten amendments were added to the Constitution. Known collectively as the Bill of Rights, they guaranteed to all Americans basic civil liberties, such as freedom of speech, of the press, of assembly, and of religion.

The new United States Constitution stirred the imagination of Europe and became a model for the world at large. By combining the principles of constitutionalism, federalism, and limited government in a workable fashion, it stimulated belief in the practicability of self-government. And by stating certain rights as belonging to all men, it encouraged others to seek them also.

The young nation expanded. The Constitution establishing the United States of America went into effect in June 1788, and the first President of the new nation, George Washington, was inaugurated in April 1789. The next eighty years were a period of remarkable territorial expansion for the young republic.

The vast areas west of the Allegheny Mountains were both fertile and sparsely inhabited, and therefore attractive to settlers. In addition, no great power directly bordered the United States to thwart westward movement. Indeed, conflicts among European nations during the early years of the republic created opportunities for the United States to acquire new territory. In 1803 Napoleon was preparing to resume war against Britain. In need of money and fearful that he could not resist an attack against the Louisiana territory, owned by France, he sold the entire area that year to the Americans for only $15 million. With a stroke of a pen, the size of the United States was almost doubled. In 1819, Spain, weakened by upheaval at home and in its overseas possessions, ceded Florida to the Americans.

Meanwhile, restless pioneers pushed westward. In the 1820's and 1830's farmers moved into the Mexican province of Texas. The Texans seceded, or broke away, from Mexico and declared their independence in 1836 and, after almost a decade of independence, joined the United States in 1845. Mexico refused to recognize the Texan secession, and eventually the dispute led to war with the United States in 1846. Mexico was defeated in 1848, and in the resulting treaty gave up a vast territory; from this were later formed all of California, Utah, and Nevada and parts of Colorado, Wyoming, Arizona, and New Mexico.

Other hardy pioneers crossed the Great Plains to the fertile valleys of the Oregon Territory in the Pacific northwest. When the United States purchased Alaska from Russia in 1867, the process of continental expansion which had begun in 1783 was completed. The new nation had become a sprawling giant of 3 million square miles. Its population had grown from less than 4 million in 1790 to over 38 million in 1870.

Democracy was extended. A fundamental democratic principle—that governments derive their powers from the consent of the governed—was stated in the Declaration of Independence, incorporated in the federal constitution, and reasserted in all of the state constitutions. In practical political terms, democracy meant the right to vote and the right to hold public office. When the new American nation came into being, these rights were generally restricted to men who were white Protestant property owners.

The growing West provided the pressure to extend these rights. Tennessee and Ohio, admitted to the Union in 1796 and 1803 respectively, adopted constitutions which in effect granted suffrage to all white men. Thereafter, every new western state followed the same procedure. In time the older eastern states liberalized their constitutions. By 1830 property and religious qualifications for voting and officeholding had been abolished for white men in almost every state.

During the next few decades, educational opportunities were increased and public welfare improved. However, reformers were troubled by the continued existence of Negro slavery in the southern United States. Since its beginnings early in the 17th century, slavery had become a vital element of the Southern economy, especially on the cotton plantations of the deep South. Conservative Southerners, dominated by an aristocratic landed gentry,

felt that slavery was an economic necessity. However, in the growing industrial cities of the North, where change was rapid and society more democratic, public opinion became increasingly opposed to slavery as a moral wrong.

Abraham Lincoln, representing a party opposed to the extension of slavery in new territories, was elected President in 1860. Thereupon, seven Southern states withdrew from the United States and created the independent Confederate States of America. Lincoln insisted that the Union was indivisible and secession illegal. He therefore ordered troops to enforce the laws and defend federal territory in the South. Four more Southern states then joined the Confederacy. The civil war that followed lasted from 1861 to 1865 and was one of the bloodiest struggles of the 19th century.

The North won the War Between the States, and by doing so decisively settled two great issues: (1) slavery was abolished, and (2) the United States was established firmly as an indivisible national state. These principles were made part of the Constitution with the adoption of the Thirteenth and Fourteenth amendments. Many problems remained, however, especially those involving the economic condition of the South and the position of the freed Negroes.

Economic growth prepared the United States for world leadership. During the first fifty years after the War Between the States, the most significant development in the United States was its rapid economic growth. The war itself did much to accelerate this development, especially in the North; in the decade between 1860 and 1870, the value of manufactures doubled. As in England a century earlier, the American industrial revolution was made possible by a combination of favorable circumstances. Among these conditions

The United States was the first large nation to be established as a republic. As the country matured, the right to vote was gradually extended to all men, regardless of wealth or religion. States west of the Alleghenies were among the first to broaden the suffrage, and frontier areas gained a reputation for rough-and-tumble politics. The scene above shows the first state election in Michigan in 1837. Near the old city hall in Detroit, citizens gather to discuss candidates and election issues.

The appeal of a free and prosperous society lured many immigrants across the Atlantic in the 19th century. Most of these transplanted Europeans, proud of their new home, quickly adopted national customs. In "Patriots in the Making," left, a drawing by William Glackens, immigrants in a crowded city slum enthusiastically celebrate the Fourth of July. Flags fly from tenement windows and people gather on fire escapes to watch the noisy street below. The fire engine (rear) and ambulance (left) are reminders of the constant danger from fireworks that characterized the "old-fashioned Fourth."

were rich natural resources, coupled with inventions and techniques for converting them into finished products; a network of railroads, rivers, and canals capable of meeting the transportation needs of an expanding economy; a huge national market unobstructed by state barriers; a growing population at home and abroad; the incentives of tariff protection, low taxes, and generous subsidies provided by a business-minded government; and a labor supply that was constantly renewed through immigration. By 1914 the United States produced more iron, steel, coal, and electricity than any other nation.

One factor in particular—the huge tide of European immigration that poured into the United States throughout the 19th century—was of great significance in shaping the United States. Although immigration had been proceeding steadily since the first days of the republic, it assumed gigantic proportions in the 1840's, when famine and unemployment stalked through Europe. In that decade alone, over 1,700,000 persons entered the United States, more than had come in the fifty years following the ratification of the Constitution. Thereafter, immigrants continued to arrive by the millions in every succeeding decade. By 1914, a total of 35 million persons had made their way to American shores.

To "Americanize" so large and varied a group proved to be a problem, but, on the whole, one that was solved with relatively few difficulties. It was accomplished through such means as public schools and political organizations. Important too was the eagerness of many immigrants to participate in the affairs of a nation that offered them individual liberty, freedom of religion, and boundless economic opportunity. Without their skills and labor, the United States would not have achieved the phenomenal growth that so astonished Europe.

An additional reason for the rapid progress of the United States was its geographical isolation, which freed it from international involvements. The nation did not have to test its strength in any serious or prolonged foreign wars, nor divert needed resources for large standing armies or heavy armaments. Untroubled by any major threats to their national security, Americans came to consider isolation from world affairs a positive virtue.

Section Review

1. Why were the Articles of Confederation inadequate? What were the chief features of the Constitution that replaced them?
2. Why was the United States able to expand its territory so rapidly after 1789?
3. How did the United States become more democratic between 1789 and 1865?
4. Describe the chief factors enabling the United States to become an industrial nation in a comparatively short time.

2   **New nations developed within the British Empire**

The American Revolution left the British Empire with little more than Canada and the West Indies. British settlers continued to emigrate overseas, however—both to these regions and to other areas far from the homeland, such as Australia, New Zealand, and South Africa. Like the thirteen colonies that became the United States, the communities they formed were colonies of settlement, and the people who moved there carried with them strong traditions of self-government. British statesmen came to believe that colonies of this type would eventually seek independence, as in the case of the United States. This consideration, plus the fact that the 19th century was generally an age of liberalism in western Europe, transformed British imperial policy and led to

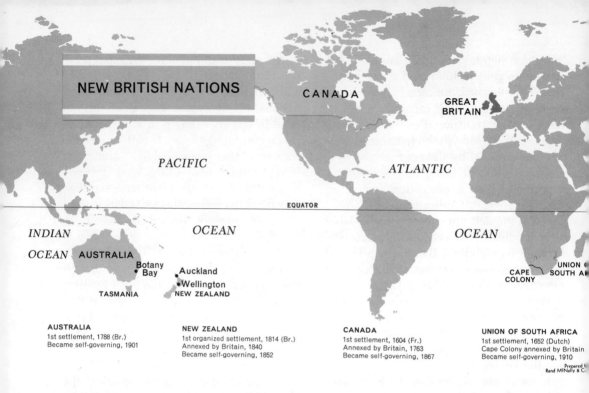

NEW BRITISH NATIONS

CANADA

GREAT BRITAIN

PACIFIC

ATLANTIC

EQUATOR

INDIAN OCEAN

OCEAN

OCEAN

AUSTRALIA

Botany Bay

Auckland

Wellington

NEW ZEALAND

TASMANIA

CAPE COLONY

UNION OF SOUTH AFRICA

AUSTRALIA
1st settlement, 1788 (Br.)
Became self-governing, 1901

NEW ZEALAND
1st organized settlement, 1814 (Br.)
Annexed by Britain, 1840
Became self-governing, 1852

CANADA
1st settlement, 1604 (Fr.)
Annexed by Britain, 1763
Became self-governing, 1867

UNION OF SOUTH AFRICA
1st settlement, 1652 (Dutch)
Cape Colony annexed by Britain
Became self-governing, 1910

Prepared b
Rand McNally & C

the emergence of four new independent English-speaking nations: Canada, Australia, New Zealand, and South Africa.

Canada moved toward independence. Originally explored and settled by the French, Canada came completely under British control in 1763, after the Seven Years' War. Although there were some English settlers in Newfoundland and Nova Scotia, they were greatly outnumbered by the French Canadians, about 65 thousand of whom lived along the St. Lawrence Valley from below Quebec to beyond Montreal. The British government treated them leniently. The Quebec Act of 1774 recognized French civil law and the use of the French language, and granted toleration to the Roman Catholic Church.

Friction developed when 40 thousand loyalist settlers from the thirteen colonies fled to Canada during the American Revolution and settled in Nova Scotia and the upper St. Lawrence Valley. The French

Canadians were worried about this large influx of English-speaking Protestant settlers. The loyalists, on their part, did not wish to live under French institutions. The British Parliament tried to solve the problem with the Constitutional Act of 1791, which created two distinct provinces: an English one, Upper Canada (later Ontario), and a French one, Lower Canada (later Quebec). Each was granted limited powers of local self-government and had its own governor, legislative council, and elected assembly.

Trouble again developed after 1815. In Lower Canada the French, suspicious of the English minority that dominated the government, business, and commerce, demanded greater political power. In Upper Canada, where British settlement was increasing, newcomers resented the way in which the older aristocrats controlled political and economic affairs. Grievances also developed between the two Canadas, for Lower Canada blocked Upper Canada's outlet to the sea.

In 1837 both Canadas experienced minor rebellions. Although they were easily suppressed, the Whig government in London, pursuing a general policy of reform at home, decided to carry out reforms in Canada as well. A prominent Whig, Lord Durham, was sent out as the new governor general to investigate conditions. In 1839 he published his *Report on the Affairs of British North America,* which became a classic in British imperial affairs. Durham argued that Canada should be a united nation with common citizenship, and that the country should have self-government. The British government accepted Lord Durham's recommendations. It united Upper and Lower Canada in 1840 and in the years from 1846 to 1848 granted the nation self-government in internal matters.

The new system worked well. However, large-scale immigration from the British Isles beginning in the 1840's greatly swelled the English-speaking population. The French felt their position threatened. Many Canadians decided that the only solution was confederation—each province to control its local affairs but all to act together on national issues. Canadians of all parties worked together to draw up a proposal for confederation. In 1867 the British Parliament passed the proposal as the British North America Act, which created the Dominion of Canada. The Dominion included Upper and Lower Canada as the provinces of Ontario and Quebec, as well as Nova Scotia and New Brunswick. It had a common parliament, composed of a Senate and a House of Commons, and, following the British model, cabinet ministers chosen from the majority party. Each province had its own legislature to govern internal affairs. Like the United States Constitution, that of Canada allowed for the easy admission of new territories. Manitoba became a province in 1870 and British Columbia a year later. Both were linked solidly to the rest of the nation when the Canadian Pacific Railway was completed in 1885. The railroads also opened to settlement the vast prairies of Saskatchewan and Alberta, both admitted in 1905.

Canadians thus solved their greatest political problem in a unique federal arrangement somewhat similar to that of the United States. The British North America Act represented the first orderly and successful transfer of political liberty by an imperial power to one of its colonies. If Great Britain had adopted a similar policy a century earlier, as men like Benjamin Franklin had urged, the thirteen American colonies would probably have remained loyal to the mother country. In the years after 1867, Canada gradually gained control over its external affairs. As the country became more independent, the term *dominion* came to signify a self-governing nation. The Canadian example set a precedent whose principles Britain learned to apply with great success elsewhere.

Australia became a nation. Explorers from the Netherlands discovered Australia in the 17th century, but the northern, western, and southern shores they visited were so barren that the Dutch made no efforts to colonize. Captain James Cook headed an English scientific expedition to the South Seas from 1768 to 1771 and discovered the fertile eastern shore of Australia, which he called New South Wales. The British government decided to establish a penal colony there after losing its thirteen American colonies. (Georgia, for example, had been used as a place of settlement for debtors and other convicts.) In 1788 an expedition of 1100 persons, including over 700 convicts of both sexes, landed at Botany Bay on the southeast coast. Within a week the city of Sydney had been founded. Several other penal colonies were set up, including one on the large island of Tasmania.

Since very few free settlers migrated to New South Wales, the colony grew slowly and in 1821 numbered only 30 thousand inhabitants, one fourth of whom were ex-convicts. Nevertheless, a colonial-born generation had grown to maturity and wanted political reform. In 1823 Parliament granted the colony limited powers of self-government. Convicts continued to make up the majority of immigrants until 1830. After that date free settlers became dominant, attracted by the sale of cheap land. Although much of the interior consisted of vast deserts, there were many ranges of pasture suitable for grazing sheep, and wool production soon became the principal activity of the colonists. In search of more land, they explored the interior to the north, west, and south, establishing the colonies of Queensland, South Australia, Western Australia, and Victoria. Self-government was granted to all of them in 1850.

The discovery of gold in New South Wales and Victoria in 1851 led to a rush of immigration such as no British colony had ever witnessed before. Within a decade the total population of the Australian colonies jumped from 400 thousand to over a million. (Australians protested against the continued use of their territory as a penal colony because of the high crime rate, and Great Britain landed the last convicts in 1867.) Railroads and telegraph lines were built, and once the gold fever subsided, many newcomers turned to farming and sheep raising. By the early 20th century, Australia had become one of the world's chief exporters of wheat, wool, and meat.

For many years the Australian colonies delayed the formation of a federation because, unlike Canada, there were no strong pressures to drive them in that direction. Nor was there any vigorous neighboring power ambitious to expand. The situation changed with the outburst of European imperialism in the late 19th century. When France and Germany moved into the South Pacific, the Australians decided to unite for their own security. In 1901, with the approval of the British Parliament, they formed an independent dominion, the Commonwealth of Australia. The government blended British, Canadian, and American features. Each colony became a state with its own legislature. The Commonwealth Parliament, composed of an elected Senate and House of Representatives, chose the cabinet from the majority party.

New Zealand joined the empire. A thousand miles southeast of Australia lie the islands of New Zealand, discovered in 1642 by a Dutch sea captain, Abel Tasman. In 1769 Captain Cook rediscovered the islands and noted the fertility of the soil. Colonization there proceeded very slowly at first because the British government had no great interest in the area. In 1840 the New Zealand Company, a privately owned investment and colonization enterprise, sent out the first British settlers, who founded the cities of Auckland and Wellington. This move forced the British government to lay claim to the islands. Thereafter, the population—mostly from Britain—rose steadily; by 1867 it totaled more than 170 thousand. Farming, stock raising, and dairying became important occupations, with wool, meat, and butter the chief exports.

Unlike Australia, which was largely uninhabited before the arrival of Europeans, New Zealand was the home of more than 100 thousand natives, the Maoris. They were a strong, proud, intelligent people with a well-developed culture. They were warlike, however, and firmly attached to their lands. In defending them, they clashed savagely with the British. The Maori Wars lasted from 1843 to 1870, when peace was made and the Maoris were

The British Empire united a variety of peoples. In Canada, both French and British colonists preserved their own traditions. Above, at the site of Winnipeg in 1821, white settlers and Indians fish through the ice. Many of the colonists of Australia were English convicts, who found pioneering difficult. Below right, "basket boats" are used to cross an Australian river. Although Dutch and British settlers in South Africa differed in many ways, they combined to form one commonwealth in 1910. Pretoria, capital of the Transvaal, is shown below left around the time of the Boer War.

granted political rights and allowed to keep more than half the area of North Island.

The colonists of New Zealand gained self-government over local affairs in 1852. Over the years, New Zealand, of all the dominions, became the most typically British in attitude and manner, chiefly because most of its settlers were British. Like the mother country, it adopted many progressive reforms. In 1893 it became the first British colony to give women the vote. During the late 1890's New Zealand provided for arbitration of labor disputes, an eight-hour day, and old-age pensions. It became a fully self-governing dominion in 1907.

South Africa was united. In the 17th century the Dutch established Cape Colony in South Africa to grow and supply food for its Indies-bound ships. During the Napoleonic wars early in the 19th century, the British seized the colony for strategic reasons because they wanted a good naval station on the route to the East. By this time the white population numbered 26 thousand; farming, based on the slave labor of African natives, was the chief occupation. The Treaty of Paris in 1814 allowed the British to keep the territory.

The British position in South Africa after 1814 resembled that in Canada after 1763. The English controlled a colony of alien Europeans—Dutch settlers, called Boers— who differed in language, religion, and attitude. A further problem was the fact that the colonists were greatly outnumbered by a large, often warlike, native population. In addition, the existence of slavery on colonial farms disturbed English missionaries, who were determined to stamp it out.

The British abolished slavery throughout the empire in 1833. Shortly afterward some 10 thousand Boers, angered by British policy and anxious to obtain new land, embarked on the Great Trek, an overland journey northeastward into the interior. There the British permitted these so-called *Voortrekkers* to establish the two republics of the Transvaal (1852) and the Orange Free State (1854). Meanwhile, in 1852 Britain granted limited self-government to the Cape Colony. By that time a predominantly British colony, Natal, had also developed on the east coast; it was given the right to elect its own assembly in 1856.

All four colonies followed different policies regarding the natives, which led to much confusion. Influenced by the example of Canada, the London government urged federation, but the colonists rejected the idea. Matters became acute when diamonds were discovered in the Orange Free State in 1867 and gold was found in the Transvaal in 1886. These discoveries brought a great influx of British immigrants; they soon outnumbered the Boers in the Transvaal. Distrustful of the newcomers, the Boers refused to grant them equal political rights.

Tension mounted rapidly between the two groups. In 1899 the Boer War broke out between the two Boer republics and the British. After three years of fighting, the Boers were defeated. The British treated the Boers leniently and though their two republics were made British colonies, in 1906 they were given limited self-government. However, the need for common policies toward tariffs, railroads, and the natives continued. These factors led to the formation in 1910 of a new dominion, the Union of South Africa.

Section Review

1. What political problems disturbed Canada after the American Revolution? in the early 1800's? after the union of Upper and Lower Canada? How did the British try to solve each one?
2. How was the development of Australia affected by the American Revolution? by the discovery of gold in New South Wales

and Victoria? by European imperialism in the 19th century?

3. How did the population of New Zealand differ from that of both Canada and Australia? What reforms were adopted in New Zealand between 1852 and 1907?

4. Describe the problems that made South Africa difficult for the British to govern. How did these problems lead to the Great Trek? to the Boer War? For what reasons was the Union of South Africa created?

3 Latin America gained its independence

The colonies of Spain and Portugal were the oldest in the New World. By the time the first small band of English colonists landed at Jamestown in 1607, 250 thousand Spaniards and Portuguese had already crossed the Atlantic to make their homes and fortunes in the region that came to be called Latin America. For over three centuries, Spain and Portugal governed their New World empires, controlling much larger areas than any other nation of the period even attempted. The Spanish and Portuguese have been criticized, with some justice, for the harshness and despotism of their rule. However, their comparative success in transplanting their religion, culture, and languages to a vast region populated by alien peoples can hardly be overestimated. For both good and ill, the traditions they imparted lasted long after their colonial peoples had become independent.

Spain kept its colonies under strict control. At its height, the Spanish empire in America stretched from Chile to California. For many decades, this region far surpassed the rest of the New World in population and development. In the mid-17th century, when New York (still the Dutch village of New Amsterdam) consisted of only 2000 persons, Mexico City was a thriving metropolis of 150 thousand, and Lima, Peru, had a population of 40 thousand. Other important centers were Potosí (with the richest silver mine in the world), Quito, Bogotá, Cuzco, Santiago, and Buenos Aires. These towns were bustling centers, with arsenals, workshops, warehouses, and mints. Beautiful homes and churches displayed the wealth of the rich colonists. Mexico City and Lima boasted the two oldest universities in the Americas, both chartered in 1551.

In governing its vast empire, Spain followed absolutist policies current in 16th-century Europe, when its chief conquests were made. The king, who possessed supreme authority, appointed a Council of the Indies to help him rule his far-off provinces. The Council, a kind of legislature for the colonies, had charge of all branches of colonial administration, and its decrees carried the force of law. Under weak kings, it had almost absolute power.

During the 16th century Spain divided its empire into two viceroyalties. One, the Viceroyalty of New Spain, with its capital at Mexico City, included all Spanish possessions in North and Central America and the West Indies, as well as the Philippine Islands. The other, the Viceroyalty of Peru, had its capital at Lima and included all Spanish possessions in South America. In the 18th century, Spain divided the Viceroyalty of Peru and created two more viceroyalties: New Granada, with its capital at Bogotá, and La Plata, with its capital at Buenos Aires. Each viceroyalty was subdivided into various provinces and districts. All the officials, from the viceroy to minor subordinates, were appointed rather than elected. Many were corrupt and used their offices chiefly to enrich themselves.

Like other European maritime nations after the Age of Discovery, Spain followed a mercantilist policy, which regarded

VICEROYALTIES OF SPAIN

VICEROYALTY
OF
NEW
SPAIN

Havana

Atlantic Ocean

Mexico City

San José • Panama • Caracas

Bogotá • VICEROYALTY OF NEW GRANADA

Pacific Ocean

Lima • VICEROYALTY OF PERU

VICEROYALTY
OF
LA PLATA

Santiago •

• Buenos Aires

Prepared by
Rand M⁹Nally & Co., Chicago

to grow sugar, tobacco, coffee, cocoa, and tea for export. They also made grants of *encomiendas,* which were rights to the labor of a certain number of natives. The semifeudal encomienda system was a disaster for the Indians, many of whom died from the effects of forced labor and new diseases. Because of the Indians' high death rate, the Spanish began to import large numbers of Negro slaves from Africa early in the 16th century. Although encomiendas were abolished in the 18th century, the system of peonage—by which workers were tied to the land they farmed —had already developed in their place.

Probably the single most important factor in extending and maintaining Spanish rule was the Roman Catholic Church. To it was entrusted the task of teaching new ways to the Indians, who numbered between 15 and 20 million at the time of the Spanish conquests (North America had only about a million native inhabitants). Priests and monks converted the Indians to Christianity, taught them loyalty to the Spanish monarch and his representatives, instructed them in the building of churches, and did much to protect them from the harshness of mine and plantation owners. Spain rewarded the services of the Church with grants of land, revenues, and encomiendas. By 1800 the Roman Catholic hierarchy controlled almost half the wealth of Latin America.

Discontent grew. Over the years, Spanish colonists became increasingly dissatisfied with conditions in Latin America. For one thing, they resented the restrictions which mercantilism imposed on trade and manufactures.

Another grievance arose out of Latin-American society itself. Unlike the English in North America, the Spanish had brought very few of their own countrywomen with them. They therefore intermarried with the Indians and to a lesser extent with the

overseas colonies as existing chiefly for the benefit of the mother country. Because mercantilist theory measured a nation's wealth chiefly in terms of precious metals, the gold and silver mines of Mexico, Peru, Bolivia, and Colombia were of tremendous importance. From them a constant stream of metals poured into Spain, and through Spain into Europe. This influx of bullion helped promote the Commercial Revolution of the 16th and 17th centuries.

According to mercantilist policy, colonies were important as markets for home manufactures and as sources of raw materials. The Spanish monarch granted explorers and noblemen large tracts of land in order

Negroes. By the beginning of the 19th century, the population of Latin America was estimated at 45 per cent Indian, 42 per cent mixed, 19 per cent white, and 4 per cent Negro. Class divisions based on birth and background were of great importance.

At the top level were the Spanish-born officials, the *peninsulares,* who held all the important political and military positions. Below them was a colonial-born white aristocracy, the Creoles, who lived like feudal nobles on the income from their estates. At the bottom of the social pyramid were the millions of Indians, Negroes, and mixed peoples—mestizos (white and Indian) and mulattoes (white and Negro). Most of them lived in a state of serfdom or slavery, and performed all manual labor, which the Europeans looked upon as degrading.

Of these groups, it was the Creoles who were most dissatisfied. Although they were of pure Spanish descent, their colonial birth made them ineligible for the highest government posts. Wealthy and well-educated, many of them were familiar with the works of Locke, Voltaire, and Rousseau and thus with the political liberalism of the Enlightenment. They were eager to take control of their own affairs, but the colonial system kept them frustrated and impatient.

At times discontent flared into open revolt: outbreaks occurred in Mexico during the 17th century and in Paraguay early in the 18th century. In the 1780's, encouraged by the example of Britain's North American colonies, colonists rebelled unsuccessfully in Peru, Colombia, Ecuador, and Venezuela. One reason for their failure was that—unlike the North Americans, who received help from France —the isolated Latin-American insurgents fought without aid.

The only successful uprising of the 18th century occurred in Haiti, a French colony on the western part of the island of Hispaniola. There Toussaint L'Ouverture, a freed slave, commanded a Negro rebellion against the French in 1794. Toussaint was captured and later died in a French prison, but his successor, Jean Jacques Dessalines, led the Haitians to independence in 1803.

Successful revolts freed South America. In 1808 a radical change in the international situation gave the Creoles their big chance. In that year Napoleon seized control of the Spanish government. The Spanish-American colonists refused to recognize the new French regime. When the deposed royal government informed the colonists that "your fate . . . is in your own hands," spontaneous revolts swept through the empire from Mexico to Argentina. Although the deposed king, Ferdinand VII, returned to the throne in 1814 determined to restore Spanish control, the drive toward independence had already gone too far.

The greatest leader of this movement was Simón Bolívar, born in 1783, who is called "the Liberator" and "the Washington of South America." The son of a wealthy Creole of Caracas, Bolívar was studying in Madrid when Napoleon's troops overran Spain. He hurriedly returned home, and, after commanding unsuccessful revolts in 1810 and 1811, succeeded in taking Caracas in 1813. During the next twenty years, Bolívar organized and fought many engagements. In the end he gained freedom for what are now the countries of Venezuela, Colombia, Panama, Bolivia, and Ecuador.

Another great hero of this period was José de San Martín, who was born in 1778 in what is now Argentina. He was fighting in Spain against the French when he learned that Buenos Aires had revolted in 1811. San Martín returned home to recruit and train an army, which he led over the

Andes Mountains to victory in Chile in 1817. By the next year San Martín had cleared Chile of Spanish soldiers. He then began to build an army to subdue Spanish troops in Peru, the last stronghold of the Spanish in South America. In 1821, San Martín entered Lima, where he and Bolívar conferred on how best to drive the Spanish from the rest of Peru. The two men disagreed and San Martín unselfishly turned his army over to Bolívar and voluntarily withdrew to France. By 1826, Bolívar had made all Spanish South America free.

Men like Bolívar, inspired by the example of the United States, dreamed of forging a great federal union embracing all of Spanish America. This dream of confederation, however, was never realized. Shortly before Bolívar died, he remarked sadly, "I have been plowing the sea."

Foreign powers maintained interests in Latin America. Among the problems disturbing the Concert of Europe in the years after 1814 were those involving the recent outbreaks in Spanish America. Most European nations wanted either to restore the colonies to Spain or appropriate them. Two powers opposed both alternatives. The United States had sympathetically watched Latin America win its freedom. Great Britain was interested in trading with the newly independent areas that were now freed from mercantilist restrictions. The British favored a joint declaration warning against European intervention in America. United States President James Monroe, however, acted independently and proclaimed the Monroe Doctrine in 1823. Monroe warned that the United States would oppose any European attempt to interfere in the affairs of the Western Hemisphere. All Europe accepted this warning, knowing that the British navy stood ready to enforce the American position.

Although the Monroe Doctrine prevented Spain from retaking its colonies, it was not always effective in controlling foreign intervention. Later in the 19th century, as discussed in Chapter 24, imperialistic powers interfered and exploited Latin-American resources for their own profit.

Mexico struggled to win and maintain independence. In Mexico, Father Miguel Hidalgo led Indians and mestizos in revolt in 1810. Although he was soon captured and executed, the movement he led continued to flourish under a lieutenant, Father José Morelos. The latter seized several cities and in 1813 called a congress that declared Mexico free. Morelos, however, was captured and shot in 1815. After a liberal revolution in Spain, a reactionary Spanish officer, Agustín de Iturbide, seized power in Mexico and declared it independent in 1821. He had himself made emperor a year later but was deposed after an eleven-month reign. Mexico then became a republic, in 1824.

The years that followed were difficult. A dictator, Antonio Lopez de Santa Anna, seized power in 1834. During his rule Mexico was defeated by the United States in the Mexican War and lost half its territory to its northern neighbor. Liberal Mexicans gained strength during the 1850's and in 1860 their leader, Benito Juárez (a full-blooded Indian), became president. He planned to weaken the power of the Roman Catholic Church and to increase the political rights of Indians and mestizos. However, economic difficulties forced Mexico to suspend payment on foreign debts in 1861, and European intervention resulted (Chapter 20). Juárez again became president in 1867 but died a few years later, before many of his reforms could take effect. Mexico then fell under the control of Porfirio Díaz, who set up a dictatorship that was to last until 1911.

Latin-American Society has been influenced by the presence of many different peoples—Indian, Spanish, Portuguese, and Negro. The painting above depicts Uruguayan Negroes performing the *candombe,* a dance that originated in Africa. In Mexico, political disorder has often been intensified by discrimination against mestizos and Indians. Under the dictatorship of Porfirio Díaz, Indians suffered many injustices. Below, the Mexican national police capture a foe of Díaz. The prisoner's sombrero is jammed over his eyes so he cannot see where he is being taken.

Brazil achieved its freedom peacefully.
Portugal had claimed lands along the northeastern coast of South America after the voyage of Cabral in 1500. A much smaller nation than Spain, Portugal had fewer colonists to send abroad, and they settled along the Atlantic coast. For many years, the colony of Brazil which they established remained almost entirely agricultural, its chief crops being cotton and sugar cane. Beginning in the early 16th century, large numbers of African Negroes were imported to work on the plantations, and in some areas they soon outnumbered the Portuguese twenty to one. Three races —white, Negro, and Indian—intermingled more thoroughly in Brazil than anywhere else in Latin America. As elsewhere, the Church was important in educating and controlling the Indians.

Because Brazil apparently had no precious metals or other mineral resources, Portugal took little interest in the colony. However, the colonists themselves, particularly those of São Paulo, were an aggressive and restless group. Against the wishes of the Portuguese authorities, the so-called *Paulistas* pushed westward into the interior in search of gold and slaves. Although they came into conflict with the Spanish colonists of Argentina and Paraguay, these Brazilian pioneers tripled the area under Portuguese control so that Brazil came to occupy more than half of the South American continent. *Paulistas* discovered gold late in the 1600's and diamonds in 1728. Their discoveries greatly stimulated immigration.

When Napoleon's troops invaded Portugal in 1807, the Portuguese royal family fled to Brazil, which became the seat of the Portuguese Empire. Soon afterward the king made Brazil a self-governing dominion. After he returned to Portugal in 1821, however, the mother country tried to return Brazil to its colonial status. But the king's son, Dom Pedro, who had stayed in Brazil as its ruler, declared the nation an independent empire in 1822. His successor, Dom Pedro II, instituted many reforms when he became emperor in 1840. Rail lines were built and industry and trade greatly expanded. However, when the slaves were freed in 1888 without compensation to their owners, much dissatisfaction resulted. In 1889 Brazilians, after forcing the emperor to abdicate, set up a federal republic.

Internal problems hindered progress.
In general, the Creoles who led revolts in South America were more interested in seizing authority for themselves than in radically altering the social or political structure. Thus, the basic pattern of life did not change, especially for the lower classes. In contrast to the United States, which became a rich and powerful nation in a comparatively short time, the Latin-American republics made painfully slow progress. They struggled against several obstacles.

For one thing, Spain and Portugal had not permitted self-government in their colonies. Because of this background, people lacked political training. Very few Latin-American republics found it possible to maintain stable democratic governments. In many, corrupt dictatorships resulted. Power changed hands rapidly as ambitious men—often military leaders—seized office from one another.

Political instability was accentuated by sectional, racial, and class divisions. The 18 million Latin Americans were dispersed over an area of 8 million square miles and were separated by the Isthmus of Panama, the Andes Mountains, and the rain forests of the Amazon region. At the time of independence, four fifths of the total population consisted of poor, illiterate Indians, Negroes, mestizos, and mulattoes; many of them knew neither Spanish nor Portuguese. Jealousy and distrust prevented effective coöperation among them and among the whites.

In the late 19th century, some Latin-American nations, particularly the "ABC countries" (Argentina, Brazil, and Chile), began to wrestle more forcefully with the problems of poverty, illiteracy, and economic and social backwardness. However, much remained to be done in overcoming massive social injustice as Latin America moved into the 20th century.

Section Review

1. Discuss some of the chief characteristics of the Spanish colonies from the standpoint of their population, land area, and religion. How did Spain maintain a strict control over its colonies?

2. Why did Spanish colonists become dissatisfied with the rule of the mother country? What were the chief steps in the liberation of Spanish South America? of Mexico?

3. Describe how Brazil gained its independence. How did Haiti win its independence from France?

4. What was the Monroe Doctrine? What situation led to its proclamation by the President of the United States?

5. Why did Latin America progress more slowly than the United States after achieving independence?

Chapter 23 ⬛⬛⬛⬛⬛⬛⬛⬛⬛⬛ A Review

During the 19th century, many European settlements overseas emerged into full-fledged nationhood, so that "new Europes" came into being around the globe.

Many of the new nations were settled by the British. The North American colonies had won their independence from Britain in the Revolutionary War. After a few years of weak government under the Articles of Confederation, statesmen drafted a Constitution establishing a strong new state, the United States of America. This document became a model for many other democratic nations. In the years after ratification, the young nation expanded its territory and became more democratic; suffrage was extended and slavery abolished. During the War Between the States, the United States began to undergo its own industrial revolution. Rapid material progress was aided by a flood of immigration and by isolation from foreign conflicts.

Its experience with the thirteen colonies helped liberalize the colonial policy of Great Britain. Many problems were settled with the passage of the British North America Act in 1867, which created the Dominion of Canada. Australia developed more slowly because of the inhospitable terrain and the unsuitable background of many of its early colonists. Cheap land and the discovery of gold encouraged settlement, although the Australians delayed the formation of a commonwealth until 1901. In New Zealand, fertile land drew a fairly steady stream of immigrants. The colony, noted for its progressive social legislation, became a dominion in 1907. South Africa presented a different picture. A sizable group of non-English settlers (as in Canada), together with a large native population (as in New Zealand), led to difficulties that were complicated by rivalries between the four individual colonies and by the discovery of gold and diamonds. After an outbreak of violence, the Boer War, the Union of South Africa was created in 1910.

The overseas empires of Spain and Portugal were the oldest and largest of any European nation. Although Spain maintained a strict control, its New World colonies revolted after the Napoleonic invasion of Spain, and eventually succeeded in achieving their freedom. Brazil, meanwhile, grew slowly and emerged as an independent nation only late in the 19th century. Although both the United States and Britain favored the Latin-American cause, many internal problems hindered progress in the area—unstable governments, class and racial divisions, illiteracy, and poverty.

The Time

Indicate the time period in which each event described below occurred.

(a) 1751-1800   (c) 1851-1900
(b) 1801-1850   (d) 1901-1925

1. The Durham Report recommended that Canada be united and given self-government.

2. The Boer War broke out between Dutch and English settlers in Africa.

3. The Articles of Confederation were ratified.

4. New Zealand became a fully self-governing dominion.

5. San Martín's army entered Lima.

6. The Treaty of Paris permitted the British to keep Cape Colony.

7. The War Between the States was fought in the United States.

8. Dom Pedro declared Brazil an independent empire.

9. The first British settlement in New Zealand was founded.

10. The Constitution of the United States went into effect.

11. The Union of South Africa was formed.

12. Mexico achieved independence.

13. President James Monroe declared the Monroe Doctrine.

14. The Dominion of Canada was created by the passage of the British North America Act.

15. Haiti won independence from the French.

16. The independent Commonwealth of Australia was formed.

17. Mexico and the United States fought the Mexican War.

18. Bolívar took Caracas for the Spanish-American colonists.

19. The first British colonists landed in Australia.

20. Britain abolished slavery throughout the empire.

The Place

1. Locate each nation listed below and tell what European power controlled it before it became independent.

Union of South Africa	New Zealand
Australia	Brazil
Canada	Haiti

2. Which of the following British colonies or provinces were a part of the Union of South Africa? of Australia? of Canada?

New South Wales	Nova Scotia	Quebec
Orange Free State	Queensland	Ontario
New Brunswick	Saskatchewan	Alberta
British Columbia	Victoria	Manitoba
Cape Colony	Transvaal	Natal

3. Locate the viceroyalties of New Spain and Peru and name the capital city of each. Which viceroyalty was later divided into New Granada and La Plata? What was the capital city of each of these new viceroyalties?

4. Under what circumstances and in what order did each of the areas listed below become part of the United States: (a) Louisiana territory; (b) Alaska; (c) Florida; (d) Texas?

The People

1. What was the role of each of the following leaders in freeing Latin America from European control?

Toussaint L'Ouverture	Simón Bolívar
José de San Martín	Miguel Hidalgo
Jean Jacques Dessalines	José Morelos
Agustín de Iturbide	

2. What part did Captain James Cook play in the history of Australia and New Zealand?

3. Who was the first ruler of independent Brazil? What developments took place in Brazil during the rule of Dom Pedro II?

4. What famous document was issued by President James Monroe? by Lord Durham?

Historical Terms

1. What was the encomienda system? How did it affect the Indians? What system replaced the encomiendas when they were abolished? How did the Roman Catholic Church come to hold encomiendas?

2. Describe each of the following groups of people. Which groups formed the social classes in Spanish South America?

Maoris	*Voortrekkers*	Boers
Paulistas	mestizos	Creoles
peninsulares	mulattoes	

3. What was the Council of the Indies?

4. Discuss the purpose of each of the following documents.

(a) Constitution of the United States; (b) British North America Act; (c) Bill of Rights;

(d) Quebec Act of 1774; (e) *Report on the Affairs of British North America;* (f) Monroe Doctrine; (g) Constitutional Act of 1791; (h) Thirteenth and Fourteenth amendments; (i) Articles of Confederation.

What was the major difference between the Articles of Confederation and the Constitution of the United States?

5. For each of the following wars, describe the issue involved and name the combatants and the victor: the Maori Wars; the Mexican War; the Boer War; the War Between the States.

Questions for Critical Thinking

1. How does the principle of federalism apply to the Constitution of the United States? to the British North America Act?

2. Why did mercantilism and the structure of Latin-American society cause discontent in the Spanish colonies?

3. In what ways did the winning of independence in Canada differ from that in Australia?

4. What racial, religious, and economic factors were common to both Spanish and Portuguese territories in South America?

The Triumph of Imperialism

European interest in overseas possessions revived in the late 19th century. Many nations adopted a new policy of expansion called imperialism, which extended Western rule the world over. Great Britain was the leading imperialistic power of the period, with holdings in so many regions of the globe that it was said, "The sun never sets on the British Empire." Above, a British governor general of India, Lord Canning, visits the maharajah of Kashmir.

A young French army officer stepped aboard a British ship anchored far up the Nile River near the Sudanese town of Fashoda, and was greeted politely by an English general. The situation was delicate. The Frenchman, Captain Jean Baptiste Marchand, had marched into the small settlement in July 1898 with 120 African troops and had hoisted the French flag over the fort there. It was now September, and British General Horatio Herbert Kitchener had just steamed up the river with 25 thousand troops fresh from a victory over the Sudanese at the Battle of Omdurman.

The upper Nile territory, Kitchener said, belonged to Egypt—a protectorate of Britain—and the French had no business there. Marchand replied that he was acting on orders from his government and could not retreat without authorization. Although British forces were far superior in number, Kitchener contented himself with raising the Egyptian and British flags on some ruined bastions south of the fort. Then the two men referred the problem back to their home governments.

It was a time of intense rivalry among European nations, and Britain and France came close to open warfare in negotiations over the so-called Fashoda Incident. One British official blustered: "There are worse evils than war, and we shall not shrink from anything that may come." Eventually, however, both sides grew more moderate. France backed down and ordered Marchand to evacuate his troops. Thus armed conflict was avoided.

Why were two of the great powers of Europe willing to risk a war over this steaming little town on the upper Nile? What brought them to Africa in the first place? The answers to these questions depend on an understanding of imperialism, which flourished between 1870 and 1914. During this period, many nations competed with one another in acquiring influence over and control of overseas territories.

The rule of one country by another was nothing new to the 19th century. Previous chapters have described how the nations of Europe built up huge colonial empires in the 16th and 17th centuries and fought to keep them. However, except for the British in India and the Dutch in the East Indies, Europeans lost interest in overseas possessions late in the 18th century. The expense of maintaining and protecting them hardly seemed worth while, since these efforts were often rewarded by independence movements and revolts, as in North America. Furthermore, with the waning of mercantilism and the growth of free trade, political control did not seem necessary to promote commerce.

After about 1870, however, interest in colonies revived, due to several factors. Increasing industrialism and a rising standard of living stimulated the need for raw materials—many from tropical areas. Competition among industrial nations led each country to raise its tariffs for protection against foreign competitors and to look abroad for new markets. The "backward" areas of the world offered not only markets for goods but also possibilities for investment. Many Europeans and Americans had surplus capital, and were attracted by opportunities abroad. Stock in Algerian railways or Dominican sugar plantations might yield profits as high as 20 per cent a year, compared to the average 6 per cent paid on domestic stocks. Businessmen wanted protection for their investments, which usually meant outside control.

Economic factors were reinforced by political pressures. The years after 1870 saw intense nationalistic rivalry among the states of the Western world. Two new European nations—Germany and Italy—were especially eager to compete for possessions. The control of faraway islands or outposts sometimes seemed necessary in the interests of national security, if only to be sure they did not fall into the hands of a potential enemy. Pride and prestige were also involved, for the greatness of a nation came to be measured largely in terms of its colonial possessions. Conflicts between nations over imperialistic claims were an important factor leading to World War I, as discussed in Chapter 25.

Pride in turn was mixed with religious and humanitarian motives. Westerners thought of their civilization as superior to those of Asia and Africa. They felt duty-bound to uplift and enlighten those whom they considered the more backward peoples of the earth. Missionaries, physicians, and administrators went forth to carry what the English poet Rudyard Kipling called "the white man's burden." This attitude did promote reforms. Westerners helped abolish slavery and torture, relieve famine, improve health and education, and introduce humane standards of justice. Too often, however, they aroused antagonism because of their superior attitude toward native peoples. And many who talked of noble purposes were more interested in motives of profit and gain.

This chapter tells how:

1. **India lost its independence.**

2. **Foreign powers exploited China.**

3. **Japan became a world power.**

4. **Many nations acquired influence elsewhere in the East.**

5. **Africa was carved into many colonies.**

6. **Imperialism flourished in Latin America.**

1 India lost its independence

Mogul power in India reached its height in the 17th century. Aurangzeb, the great-grandson of Akbar, brought virtually all of India under Mogul control. Aurangzeb was a religious fanatic, however, and bitterly persecuted the Hindus. When he died in 1707, the Mogul Empire was torn with unrest. His sons quarreled among themselves and the Persian king invaded India and sacked Delhi. Less than forty years after Aurangzeb's death, his empire had fallen into complete chaos.

The British won control. By this time England and France had acquired commercial interests in India. Recognizing the advantages that could be derived from trade, Mogul rulers during the 17th century had allowed the English East India Company to establish small settlements at Calcutta and Madras on the east coast, and at Surat on the west coast. In 1661 the English also obtained the island of Bombay off the west coast. These settlements, called factories, were rented to the English. They were fortified and used chiefly for storage and as posts for trading with the nearby inhabitants.

The French East India Company had established trading posts along the east coast in the late 1600's. Pondichéry, the strongest, lay only 100 miles from Madras. Competition between the two groups of traders was strong. It increased when India lapsed into chaos in the 18th century, a situation that seemed to invite interference.

When the War of the Austrian Succession broke out in 1744, with England and France on opposing sides, the conflict inevitably spread to the East. The French governor in India, Joseph Dupleix, was an able, ambitious, and resourceful man. With help from Indian troops, he fought a series of brilliant battles against the British and captured Madras. When a general European peace was signed in 1748, however, the French government—with little interest in India—returned the town to the British. Dupleix then plunged into native Indian affairs in an effort to oust the British, but was recalled to France in 1754.

Two years later the Seven Years' War broke out in Europe and again the conflict spread to India. At that time English forces were led by a brilliant young Englishman, Robert Clive, who had gone to India in 1743 as a Company clerk. In 1756 the Nawab of Bengal, who favored the French and detested the British, attacked Calcutta and imprisoned 146 Englishmen overnight in a small windowless dungeon. By morning most of them had died of suffocation in the Black Hole of Calcutta. Clive was in Madras when the attack occurred. He quickly loaded his forces on ships, sailed northward to Calcutta, and won a smashing victory over the Nawab at Plassey. Pondichéry surrendered to the English in 1761. When the Seven Years' War was over in 1763, the English, thanks to Robert Clive and superior sea power, had put an end to French rule in India and found themselves masters of Bengal. This region became the cornerstone of the British Empire in India.

Company rule was limited. The British government disapproved of a commercial organization having extensive political power, and determined to supervise the East India Company more closely. The India Act of 1784 gave authority over the Company to a Board of Control, whose president was to be a Cabinet member. The British government appointed the highest Company official in India, the governor general. In 1814 Parliament revoked the Company's commercial monopoly, except for the China trade; this monopoly was in turn revoked in 1833.

However, the East India Company continued as an administrative agency under government supervision. Faced by threats from local Indian princes and by the anarchy that followed the end of the Mogul Empire, it extended British control over more and more territory. Company representatives either conquered lands directly or arranged alliances with local rulers who accepted the protection of the Company. By the mid-19th century the entire subcontinent of India had come under English control.

The final blow to the authority of the East India Company came in 1857 as the result of a mutiny among the native troops, or sepoys, serving the British. Dissatisfaction had been growing for some years. Indians resented British missionary activity and modernization policies, and were alarmed by the aggressive policy of expansion followed by the Company in the mid-1800's. Then in 1857 a rumor spread among the sepoys that new rifle cartridges—the ends of which had to be bitten off— would be greased with beef and pork fat. Hindus regarded cows as sacred and Moslems considered pigs unclean. Both groups were outraged, rose in mutiny, and slaughtered many Europeans. The Sepoy Rebellion lacked mass support, however, and the British were able to suppress it by the end of 1858.

As a result of the Sepoy Rebellion, the British Parliament abolished the East India Company in 1858 and transferred all of its authority and holdings to the British crown. The government created a new Cabinet post, Secretary of State for India, and appointed a viceroy to rule in India itself. It established a clear division between the provinces governed directly by the British (British India) and the native princely states (Indian India); the latter controlled their own internal affairs.

By and large, the British government retained the administrative and financial system developed by the East India Company. The viceroy had full authority. In 1861 legislative and executive councils, including Indian representatives, were created to assist him. All the members, however, were appointed rather than elected. An efficient Indian civil service was developed and although the British did monopolize the top positions, Indians eventually filled most of the posts in the intermediate and lower ranks.

British administration had mixed results. Probably the single most important contribution of the British in India was unification; never before had the entire subcontinent come under one authority. Political unity was strengthened by the introduction of English as the official language. Prior to this time, there had been no single language which all educated Indians could speak.

The British in India also suppressed organized bands of robbers, reduced the dangers of travel, and provided protection for life and property. They outlawed suttee (the suicide of widows on their husbands' funeral pyres) and the killing of infant girls. Other improvements included increased medical facilities, miles of railroads and telegraph lines, and extensive irrigation works that watered over 30 million acres of land.

The picture had a dark side, too. Because of better sanitation and the restoration of law and order, the population increased rapidly. Food supplies could not keep up with this growth, so that living standards for large numbers of people actually declined. Millions lived so close to the starvation level that a single bad season was enough to create famine. Poverty was an old story in India and the British did try to relieve it, but without great success. A heavy blow was the end of the village handicraft system, which for centuries had been a vital part of the Indian economy. With the growth of British industry, India became a great market for cheap manufactured goods, especially cotton textiles. The Indians' handwoven cloth could not compete with the imported textiles at home, and they were forbidden to sell it to other countries. Thus Indians were forced to depend more and more on agriculture for subsistence.

Problems also arose in the field of education. In 1833 the British government inaugurated a new educational system. It was based on British models, and all instruction was in English. Little was done to set up schools in the villages, and illiteracy actually increased in the population at large. However, a small group of Indian intellectuals, trained in the new schools in the cities, absorbed English history as well as the English language. What they learned about the liberal traditions of 19th-century Europe intensified their own desire for self-government. In 1885 Hindu leaders formed the Indian National Congress; in 1906 a group of educated Moslems formed the Moslem League. Both organizations had as their common aim representative self-government for India. Indian nationalism grew steadily in strength.

Section Review

1. How did the following affect British-French rivalry in India: Mogul decline; the War of the Austrian Succession; the Seven Years' War?
2. In what respects did the end of the Seven Years' War mark the beginning of a new era for India?
3. Why and how did the British government reduce the powers of the East India Company?
4. What was the Sepoy Rebellion? Why was it important?
5. What were some of the accomplishments of British rule in India? some of the shortcomings?

2 Foreign powers exploited China

In the mid-17th century, when Mogul power was at its height in India, the Manchus established a new dynasty in China. For many years they controlled a vast and prosperous empire. However, decline set in about 1800. Population grew rapidly,

The Chinese, who looked upon other peoples as barbarians, resisted Western influence. For many years, European and American merchants were allowed to carry on only limited trade and were forbidden to mingle with the Chinese people. Merchants in Canton were confined to a small area of the harbor, shown above, until military pressure from the West forced China to liberalize its policy. At right, a Chinese caricature depicts a British sailor as a hideous creature with tobacco smoke pouring from his mouth. The Chinese writing warns that: "Soldiers should shoot it with fire-arms, for bows and arrows are unable to injure it. . . . When it meets anyone it forthwith eats him. It is truly a wonderful monster."

and agriculture did not advance fast enough to keep pace. Insufficient food and increasing poverty caused discontent. Sectional differences also developed because the Manchus discriminated against the southern Chinese. By the mid-19th century, Manchu leadership was in serious decline. Rebellions were breaking out in various parts of the country, and secret societies were being organized against the regime.

Europeans used force to win trading rights. Unfortunately for China, with its government deteriorating and internal discontent growing, Europeans appeared on the scene to complicate matters further.

Europeans had begun carrying on some commerce with Ming China in the mid-16th century, but the Manchu government restricted it severely. Foreign merchants were permitted to trade only at Macao and Canton, tariffs were high, and the Chinese imported very few Western products. With the advent of industrialism in Europe, however, Westerners sought to increase the volume of trade with China. Friction developed as the two civilizations, with different conceptions of law and justice, came into greater contact with one another.

Discord burst into open warfare in 1839. Basically, the war grew out of the Manchu refusal to allow the British to establish regular commerce with China. The immediate cause, however, was opium, which the English East India Company had been importing in exchange for Chinese tea and silk. Although there was a law against the practice, the Manchus had not enforced it for years. Suddenly a Cantonese official seized quantities of the drug and destroyed it. The British protested, but negotiations failed and the two countries went to war.

Although the Opium War lasted three years, the Chinese, who had no navy, were no match for the British. The conflict ended with the Treaty of Nanking in 1842, by which the Chinese ceded Hong Kong to the British, paid damages for the opium cargoes they had destroyed, and agreed to a uniform and moderate tariff on trade. Most important of all, the Chinese were forced to open five port cities to trade. The Treaty of Nanking signaled the real opening of China, for soon afterward other Western nations received similar rights.

Foreigners, aware of the weakness and corruption of the Chinese government, abused their privileges and friction developed. In 1856 war again broke out. This time a combined English-French fleet sailed upriver to the capital, Peking, forced the emperor to flee, and burned the beautiful summer palace. In treaties signed in 1858 and 1860, the Manchus opened eleven additional ports, legalized the opium trade, agreed to receive diplomatic representatives, and promised to protect Christian missionaries. China also granted foreigners the privilege of extraterritoriality—that is, they were released from the jurisdiction of Chinese courts and subject only to their own.

China was divided into spheres of influence. For the next fifty years the history of China was a dismal tale of continued governmental decline, internal rebellions, and foreign encroachment. As explained in Section 4, Russia gained control of the entire Asian seacoast north of Korea, France acquired Indo-China, and Britain seized Burma. China regarded all these neighboring areas as protectorates. That is, they were under the protection of, and partly governed by, China. Another such region, the Korean peninsula, was the object of Japanese interest. China resented the growth of Japanese influence there, and in 1894 the two countries went to war. Japan easily defeated China in the eight-month Sino-Japanese War. The Treaty of Shimonoseki in 1895 provided for the independence of Korea. Japan gained the island of

Formosa, the Pescadores Islands, and a large indemnity.

The utter helplessness of China was now clear to all, and foreign powers quickly moved in to carve up the "Chinese melon" by establishing spheres of influence—that is, regions where their economic interests were supreme. Within its sphere of influence, each nation had rights to specific tracts of land called concessions, which they more or less controlled and where they enjoyed extraterritoriality. In the rich Yangtze valley, for example, British businessmen were allowed to build railroads, establish factories, and open mines. No other foreigners could operate in this area. In return, the British promised not to interfere in other spheres of influence. Russia had concessions in the north, Germany on the Shantung peninsula, and France in the south.

The scramble for concessions from the Manchus prompted the United States to announce its Open Door Policy in 1899. Fearing that China might be completely divided up into exclusive spheres that would shut out American trade, the United States proposed that nations having such spheres should permit businessmen of all nations to compete on equal terms. Several nations agreed to the plan, which ultimately helped keep China intact territorially and assured American businessmen an opportunity to compete on equal terms with those from Europe.

The Chinese deeply resented the exploitation of their country by foreigners. Conservative interests dominated the Manchu court, which clung more fiercely than ever to traditional Chinese customs. Many of the people joined a secret organization, the Society of Harmonious Fists (dubbed "Boxers"), which opposed all Westerners. The Boxers revolted in 1899, destroying railroads, burning bridges, and killing Europeans. The Boxer Rebellion was quickly put down by a combined force

of Europeans, Americans, and Japanese, and even more stringent controls were placed upon the Chinese government. Meanwhile, a group of progressive Chinese, convinced that change was necessary, began a revolutionary movement that spread rapidly throughout the country.

Section Review

1. How did China by the mid-19th century show evidence of Manchu decline? Describe the conditions and events that led to the Opium War. How did Britain profit from it? What further concessions to foreign powers were the Manchus forced to grant in the treaties of 1858 and 1860?
2. What were spheres of influence as applied to China? How were they affected by the Sino-Japanese War? the Open Door Policy?
3. How did the Manchu rulers react to Western intervention in China? How did other groups react? What was the outcome of the Boxer Rebellion?

3 **Japan became a world power**

About forty years before the Manchus became all-powerful in China, the Tokugawa clan had won control of the shogunate in Japan. Under their vigorous leadership, Japan was unified under a stable political system. After foreigners were expelled and Christianity outlawed in the 17th century, Japan enjoyed a long period of peace, prosperity, and orderly government in virtual isolation from the rest of the world.

Tokugawa rule, however, was based on the strict division of social classes. The samurai warriors and feudal nobles (daimios) enjoyed many privileges while the peasants, who were the vast majority of the population, endured harsh exploitation. In the 18th century, internal trade flourished, prices increased, and merchants and traders in the cities prospered. However,

the nobles, in order to meet the rising cost of living, went heavily into debt. As they did so, they increased the rent paid them by the peasants. Conditions became so intolerable that peasant uprisings broke out frequently in the mid-18th century. By the mid-19th century, discontent had reached a dangerous point. The peasants were desperate and the nobles were mired in debt. Powerful daimio families were jealous of the Tokugawas, and many Japanese intellectuals had begun to raise doubts about the feudal system of shogunate.

The United States opened Japan to trade. Since the early 19th century, American whaling ships had been operating in the northern Pacific, and clipper ships sailed near Japan in trading with China. American shippers were interested in Japan because they needed stations where their vessels could stop for food, fuel, and water.

They also wanted protection for their sailors; those who had been shipwrecked on Japanese shores had been harshly treated.

In 1853 the American government sent Commodore Matthew Perry and a squadron of four ships to ask the Japanese to open their ports and trade with the outside world. Perry delivered a message from President Millard Fillmore, requesting that the Japanese open their country to foreign trade. Then he left, promising to return the following spring for an answer.

In February 1854 Perry returned with ten ships. He carried many presents for the Japanese officials—books, rifles, revolvers, clocks, perfume, sewing machines, and even a small locomotive. The Japanese were impressed by the gifts and by Perry's dignity and show of force. They agreed to the Treaty of Kanagawa, which opened two ports and provided better treatment

The Japanese opened their ports to American and European merchants in the late 19th century, ending a traditional policy of isolation. However, several powerful nobles were opposed to allowing Westerners in Japan. Only after the British bombarded the Japanese port of Kagoshima in 1863 were these nobles convinced of the impossibility of continued isolation. In the scene at left, drawn a few years after the arrival of Admiral Perry in 1853, Westerners and Japanese gather together in a merchant's house at Yokohama, a major trading port.

for shipwrecked sailors. In 1858 a second treaty opened additional ports, established diplomatic relations between the United States and Japan, and granted extraterritoriality to American citizens in Japan. Soon afterward, other Western nations negotiated similar treaties. The way seemed to lie open to foreign exploitation on a large scale.

The Japanese adopted new ways. Japan, however, did not go the way of China. Unlike the Chinese rulers, the Japanese decided that their country could survive only by adopting some Western ways. One of the first changes involved the shogunate itself. Antiforeign riots had followed the Treaty of Kanagawa. The Tokugawas were blamed for these uprisings, as well as for the poor conditions of the preceding hundred years. In 1867 powerful daimio leaders forced the shogun to surrender his

powers. The next year the emperor was restored to a position of authority and the capital was moved from Kyoto to Tokyo. Emperor Mutsuhito, a youth of fifteen, adopted *Meiji* (meaning "enlightened peace") as the name of his reign; his accession to the throne is known as the Meiji Restoration.

During the forty-five years of the Meiji Era, Japan was transformed into a powerful modern state, the first industrialized nation of Asia. However, the revolutionary changes in political, social, and economic affairs were carefully controlled and directed. Japanese leaders sent delegations to study the techniques and institutions of all the major Western powers, and then adopted only what they thought suitable for Japan.

In 1871 the emperor abolished feudalism. In 1889 he issued a constitution modeled on Bismarck's constitution for the German Empire. Although it provided for a two-house legislature, the emperor remained supreme. Only the lower house was elected, and voting was limited to about 1 per cent of the population. Military leaders wielded great power in the government, which was in no sense a democracy. The army and navy were reorganized and strengthened, the former based on the German model and the latter on the British. Compulsory education was introduced and illiteracy virtually abolished. The government adopted a new legal code and judicial system, patterned after Western ones, so that all foreign powers gave up their rights of extraterritoriality by 1899.

Perhaps even more remarkable than the political changes were those in economic life. Aware that the strength of the Western nations was based on industrial power, Japanese leaders pushed ahead with an intensive program of industrialization. Because capital was in short supply, the government not only granted loans and subsidies to private industrialists but also entered directly into the building of railroads, factories, shipping facilities, and telegraph and telephone systems. Many of these enterprises were eventually turned over to private capitalists, but the government never relinquished its control over railroads and communications. Japan thus developed an unusual industrial system. For one thing, it was a "mixed" system of private and governmental enterprise. For another, it was dominated by a few wealthy families that made up an economic ruling class.

A third significant feature of Japanese industrialization was its rapidity. At the time of the Meiji Restoration, there were practically no factory workers in Japan. By 1900 there were half a million.

Foreign aggression furthered Japanese ambitions. In becoming a modern industrial nation, Japan also became imperialistic. A rapid rise in population had resulted from improved sanitation and better medical services. In the Meiji Era alone, population expanded from less than 30 to over 50 million. The nation could not produce enough food for its people. It also lacked raw materials and needed markets for its manufactures. Japan looked to the Asian mainland as a solution for its difficulties. As early as 1876 the Japanese obtained commercial privileges in Korea. It was such transactions that irritated the Chinese and precipitated the Sino-Japanese War of 1894-1895. By defeating China, Japan made its first significant acquisition of territory beyond its own borders.

The Treaty of Shimonoseki granted Japan not only Formosa and the Pescadores but also the Liaotung Peninsula of Manchuria, which jutted southward into the Yellow Sea. The Russians, pursuing their own vigorous policy of imperialist expansion in Manchuria, had long desired Liaotung because at its southern tip lay Port Arthur, one of the finest year-round harbors in the Far East. Backed by France and Germany, Russia forced Japan to return Liaotung to China, and shortly afterward leased the peninsula and harbor for itself through a treaty with China. This move angered the Japanese, as did Russian intrigues in Korea.

Negotiations between Japan and Russia over Korea and Manchuria broke down in 1904. Fighting began when Japan, without a formal declaration of war, attacked the Russian fleet at Port Arthur. Much to the surprise of the West, Japan won the Russo-Japanese War. This was the first time in modern history that an Asian country had defeated a great European nation. In the Treaty of Portsmouth (1905), Japan regained Liaotung and Port Arthur, obtained a definite sphere of influence in Korea, and won the southern half of the Russian island of Sakhalin. Five years later Japan openly annexed Korea. Almost over-

EUROPEAN HOLDINGS IN THE FAR EAST: 1914

British
Dutch
French
German
Portuguese

Prepared by
Rand McNally & Co., Chicago

night Japan had become a first-class power among the nations of the world.

Section Review

1. What internal conditions in Japan led to dissatisfaction with rule by the Tokugawa clan?
2. Why did the United States wish to establish closer contacts with Japan? How was this aim accomplished?
3. What was the Meiji Restoration? How was Japanese life transformed during the forty-five years that followed?
4. Why did Japan become imperialistic? What territories did Japan gain as a result of the Treaty of Shimonoseki?

5. Describe the background and results of the Russo-Japanese War.

4 **Many nations acquired influence elsewhere in the East**

When old and proud civilizations, such as those of India and China, proved unable to withstand European penetration, it was not surprising that smaller nations in Asia, as well as the scattered islands of the Pacific Ocean, should also come under Western domination. In the Pacific region, the imperialistic nations of Europe found a new rival, the United States.

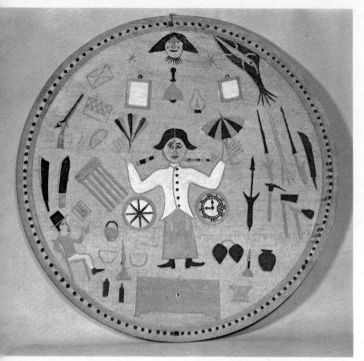

Through Native Eyes, Europeans often appear strange. A native of New Caledonia, an island northeast of Australia, made the amusing drawing below, showing French soldiers holding huge rifles. The Aleutian Islands, located off Alaska, were exploited by Siberian fur traders. At bottom, two Aleuts paddle a stern Russian in a kayak. The wooden plaque at left was made in the Nicobar Islands, a British possession in the Bay of Bengal. The central figure, a native god, is surrounded by European objects that symbolize the power of the white man, including a spoked wheel, a clock, a rifle, mirrors, and hatchets.

European powers expanded into several regions of Asia. In northern Asia, Russia had for generations been building up its settlements in Siberia. When China became vulnerable to Western exploitation in the mid-19th century, the Russians—always in search of warm-water ports—took advantage of the situation to secure a large coastal area north of Korea, where they founded Vladivostok in 1860. Later they won concessions in Mongolia and Chinese Turkestan. In 1890 Russia began building the Trans-Siberian Railroad, and obtained permission from China for the line to cross Manchuria. The Russians failed to hold the Liaotung Peninsula, however, and their defeat in the Russo-Japanese War was a serious blow to their imperialistic plans in this area.

Meanwhile, Russian imperialists were advancing into southwestern Asia—particularly the Caucasus and the steppes east of the Caspian Sea. Both advances worried the British. Russian influence extended into Persia, and the British feared that the Russians might reach the Persian Gulf and menace the British route to India and the East. In mid-Asia the Russians reached the borders of Afghanistan, a position that also threatened India. In 1907 Britain and Russia signed an agreement promising to refrain from seizing Afghanistan; Persia was divided into spheres of influence, with Russia controlling the north and Britain the south.

In southeast Asia, Britain and France were the two chief rivals for territory. The French first moved into the area in the late 18th century, and peaceful relations were maintained for many years. In the mid-19th century, however, hostile feelings resulted in the persecution of French missionaries. A French naval expedition attacked and captured Saigon in 1860. During the next twenty years France established protectorates over Cochin-China, Cambodia, and Annam. These areas had traditionally paid tribute to China, which tried unsuccessfully to eject the French by force in the 1880's. In 1893 the French took over Laos. They grouped all these areas together to form the French colony of Indo-China, an area nearly 50 per cent larger than France.

Burma meanwhile had come under British influence. Conflicts along the Indian border touched off small wars which enabled the viotorious British to seize more and more territory. Burma was formally annexed to India in 1885. Other possessions of the British in this area were Ceylon, Singapore, and northern Borneo.

One other European power of importance in this region was the Netherlands, which controlled the East Indies. As was the case with the British in India, a private trading company (the Dutch East India Company) ruled for many years. Then in 1798 the home government took over and made the territory a colony, called the Netherlands East Indies. The Dutch reaped handsome profits from their colony. They built schools, but insisted that instruction be given in native languages. This system had the effect of preserving native cultures and—more important from the Dutch viewpoint—also delayed the spread of disruptive European ideas like nationalism and democracy.

Pacific islands fell under foreign domination. The Pacific Ocean became increasingly significant in the late 19th century as a vast international waterway for the nations that ringed its shores. With the rapid development of ocean transportation, trans-Pacific commerce developed with amazing suddenness. And just as suddenly, the thousands of islands that lay scattered across the Pacific became important as refueling stops.

Under these circumstances it was natural that Great Britain, the most important naval power, acquired the largest number of Pacific islands, beginning with its annexation of the Fiji Islands in 1874. Ten years later Britain proclaimed southeast New Guinea a protectorate, and in the 1890's added the Gilbert Islands and southern Solomons to its domain.

The Germans colonized northeastern New Guinea and acquired the northern Solomon Islands in the 1880's. In 1899 they purchased from Spain the Marshall, Caroline, and Mariana Islands. These islands were valuable chiefly as coaling stations. French possessions in the Pacific were less extensive than those of the British and Germans. The French made protectorates of Tahiti and the Society Islands in 1842 and annexed New Caledonia in 1853. Later in the century, they established joint rule with the British over the New Hebrides. Economically the most valuable island was New Caledonia, which became an important source of chromium in the 1900's.

The United States too was interested in Pacific possessions. During the 19th century, Americans and Europeans settled in the Hawaiian Islands and developed a thriving export trade in sugar. By the 1880's resident Americans dominated the government, although Hawaii was technically independent. In 1890 the McKinley Tariff destroyed the favored position enjoyed by Hawaiian sugar on the American market. To regain a preferred status, local sugar planters urged annexation to the United States. When the strong-willed Queen Liliuokalani refused, she was overthrown in 1893. The provisional government, controlled by Americans, asked for annexation, which Congress finally granted in 1898.

The islands of Samoa were the object of keen rivalry among the United States, Germany, and Great Britain. In 1899 Britain withdrew from Samoa entirely, Germany received two of the largest islands, and the United States obtained Tutuila with its excellent harbor of Pago Pago, which was promptly turned into a naval base.

Meanwhile, in the Spanish-American War of 1898, the United States had acquired Guam and the Philippines, Spanish possessions in the Pacific. When the war ended, the United States decided to keep the islands because of their economic and strategic value. The Filipinos wanted complete independence but, after three years of stubborn guerrilla warfare, were finally subdued. Military government was replaced by civil government in 1902, when the United States initiated a policy of preparing the Philippines for self-government and eventual independence.

Section Review

1. Name the chief areas of Russian imperialistic penetration in the 19th century. How were resulting conflicts resolved?
2. Describe the imperialistic ventures of Britain, France, and the Netherlands in southeast Asia.
3. Why did the islands of the Pacific become important in the late 19th century? How did the United States gain possession of Hawaii? of the Philippines?

5 **Africa was carved into many colonies**

Nowhere did imperialism proceed with such speed as in Africa. Only one tenth of its huge land mass was under European control in 1875. Within twenty years only one tenth was free of such control.

France and Britain gained control of North Africa. Africa north of the Sahara Desert had been conquered by the Turks in the 15th century and incorporated into the Ottoman Empire. By the 19th century, Turkish power was waning and the nations of Europe saw an opportunity to extend their influence.

The first important European penetration was made by the French, who invaded

Algeria in 1830, both for prestige and to avenge the attacks of Algerian pirates. For many years no other European state showed much interest in North Africa. Then in 1869 a French company under Ferdinand de Lesseps finished building a canal across the Isthmus of Suez. The Near East again became, as it had been in ancient times, a great crossroads of world trade.

The Turkish khedive (governor) of Egypt, Ismail Pasha, owned a large bloc of shares in the Suez Canal Company. However, in trying to modernize Egypt, he had borrowed a great deal of money from European banks and had gone deeply into debt. In 1875 he sold his stock in the canal company to the British government. From then on Britain had a direct interest in the canal, a vital link in its lifeline to India, Australia, and New Zealand. When internal disorders broke out in Egypt in 1882, Britain sent in a military expedition and reduced the country to the status of a British protectorate. Although Egypt was technically an autonomous province of the Turkish Empire, the Turks were too weak to resist.

The British, hoping to acquire a solid belt of territory from Cairo in the north to Cape Town in the south, then moved into the Sudan. (Their immediate goal was to put down a native revolt.) The first expedition ended in disaster when General Charles George Gordon was killed by Sudanese forces at the battle of Khartoum in 1885. Thirteen years later General Kitchener avenged Gordon's death by defeating the Sudanese at Omdurman. The following year Britain and Egypt made the Sudan a condominium—that is, an area to be jointly ruled by both countries. Actually, of course, Britain was the dominant power.

Meanwhile, France had been active developing Algeria and extending its influence over Tunisia and Morocco. It had also made settlements farther south throughout the Sahara region. The French had dreams of establishing a solid belt of territory across the top of Africa, from Dakar on the west to French Somaliland on the east. It was one step in realizing this plan, Captain Marchand's expedition, that precipitated the Fashoda Incident. Although blocked in the upper Nile region, the French continued to penetrate central and western Africa.

European explorers opened up the "Dark Continent." For centuries only the coasts of sub-Saharan Africa—the "Dark Continent"—were known to Europeans. Exploration of the interior began late in the 18th century with Mungo Park, a young Scottish doctor who explored the Niger River. In the 1830's Richard Lander, an Englishman, further investigated this area, so that by 1840 the entire course of the river was known. The first accurate descriptions of the Lake Chad region were made by Heinrich Barth, a German who explored the area in the 1850's. In East Africa, two English explorers, Richard Burton and John Speke, made important discoveries in 1858—Burton of Lake Tanganyika, Speke of Lake Victoria. Six years later Speke proved that the Nile had its source in Lake Victoria.

The greatest, and certainly the most famous, of all African explorers was David Livingstone, a Scottish medical missionary. He explored southeast Africa, making several great journeys between 1851 and 1873. He was the first white man to cross the Kalahari Desert and to see Victoria Falls. His writings, even more than his explorations, had significant results. Livingstone's reports on the horrors of the slave trade, for example, speeded up its abolition in East Africa. By stressing the point that Africa should be opened to "commerce and Christianity," he created widespread interest in the continent.

Livingstone began his third journey in 1866 and was not heard from for several years. The belief spread in Europe and America that the greatest living explorer was lost. In 1869 the New York *Herald* sent its best reporter, Henry M. Stanley, to Africa with orders to "find Livingstone." Stanley underwent great hardships in his search. Finally, one day in 1871, he wandered into a village on Lake Tanganyika. There stood a lone white man. In Stanley's words:

> As I advanced slowly toward him I noticed he was pale, looked wearied, had a grey beard, wore a bluish cap with a faded gold band around it, had on a red-sleeved waistcoat, and a pair of grey tweed trousers. I would have run to him, would have embraced him, only I did not know how he would receive me; so I walked deliberately to him, took off my hat, and said: "Dr. Livingstone, I presume?" "Yes," he said with a kind smile, lifting his cap slightly. "I thank God, Doctor, I have been permitted to see you."

Stanley tried to persuade Livingstone to give up his work and return to civilization, but Livingstone refused. Instead he traveled west to explore further and died two years later.

Meanwhile, Stanley became an explorer in his own right and made the dangerous trip down the Congo River from its source to its mouth in the Atlantic. In the course of his explorations he became convinced that Africa offered vast possibilities for commercial exploitation. He went to Europe to seek financial backing and found it in the person of Leopold II, king of Belgium. In 1878 they founded a private company called the International Congo Association.

Western powers partitioned Africa. The formation of the International Congo Association represented the beginning of the rapid partition of sub-Saharan Africa. This region was inhabited by hundreds of Negro tribes who lived by primitive farming or cattle raising. Although they varied widely in culture, none had developed a written language or strong political system. They were virtually helpless against the superior technology of the Europeans.

Stanley returned to the Congo in 1879 and within a few years made over 400 treaties with native chiefs. The latter did not understand that, in placing their marks on bits of paper in exchange for trinkets and cloth, they were turning over their land to the Congo Association. Stanley acquired enormous tracts by these methods.

Other explorers adopted Stanley's techniques and obtained huge areas for their countries. Pierre de Brazza of France worked in western Africa and enabled France to claim a vast territory along the right bank of the Congo River. A German, Karl Peters, concentrated on eastern Africa, and was instrumental in acquiring German East Africa for his nation. From their base in Angola (the oldest colony in Africa), the Portuguese explored southern Africa. Italians made claims along the Red Sea.

In a class by himself was the great British empire builder, Cecil Rhodes. Rhodes went to South Africa in 1870, where he soon made a fortune in the diamond and gold mines. One of his ambitions was a Cape-to-Cairo railroad, and he worked ceaselessly to extend British territories so that it would be possible. Rhodes was instrumental in getting Britain to declare a protectorate over Bechuanaland in 1885. He gained settlement and mining rights to vast areas north of it—named Rhodesia after him—which also became British territory.

By 1914 all of Africa had been partitioned, with only Liberia and Abyssinia (now Ethiopia) remaining independent. In addition to Egypt and the Sudan, Rhodesia and Bechuanaland, Britain had acquired Nigeria, the Gold Coast, Uganda, Kenya, Nyasaland, and British Somaliland.

Imperialism in Africa disrupted the lives of the natives. Well before the imperialistic era, slave traders had begun taking people from their villages. The diagrams below show how the Negroes were packed into ships. (The top view is a ship as seen from above, and the lower one is a cross section.) In the 19th century, white explorers seized and exploited vast regions of Africa. Above, natives fall before the guns of men accompanying Henry Stanley. Some Europeans, including missionaries and doctors, tried to improve conditions in Africa. A carving of a French nun, below right, was made by a West African.

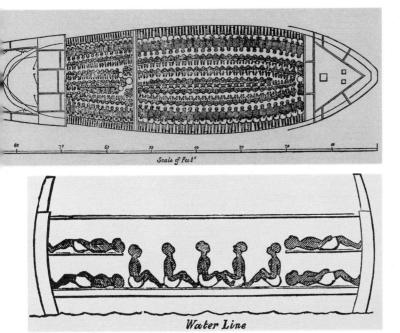

AFRICA IN 1914

EUROPE

ASIA

Black Sea

Caspian Sea

Mediterranean Sea

Rome

Madrid

Athens

Tangier
Gibraltar
Tunis
Algiers
Oran
SPANISH
ZONE
TUNISIA

Casablanca
MOROCCO

Madeira Is.
(Port.)

Tripoli
Bengazi

ALGERIA

Agadir
IFNI

Alexandria
Cairo
Port Said
Suez Canal

Canary Is. (Sp.)

LIBYA

RIO
DE ORO

SAHARA

DESERT

EGYPT
(BRITISH PROTECTORATE)

Aswan

Persian Gulf

Red Sea

FRENCH WEST AFRICA

ANGLO-

EGYPTIAN

SUDAN
(CONDOMINIUM)

Khartoum

Blue Nile River

ERITREA

Asmara

ADEN

FRENCH SOMALILAND

Timbuktu

Niger River

Lake Chad

Dakar
Bathurst
GAMBIA
PORT. GUINEA
Bissao

Senegal River

Nile River

BRITISH
SOMALILAND

Djibouti

Fashoda

Freetown
SIERRA
LEONE
LIBERIA
IVORY
COAST

GOLD
COAST
TOGOLAND
DAHOMEY

NIGERIA

Lagos

Upper Nile

ABYSSINIA
Addis Ababa
(ETHIOPIA)

ITALIAN SOMALILAND

Soc

Monrovia

Accra

CAMEROONS
Buea

FRENCH EQUATORIAL AFRICA

Ubangi River

Lake
Rudolf

Mogadisc

Fernando Po (Sp.)
RÍO
MUNI

Gulf of Guinea
Principe (Port.)
St. Thomas (Port.)

UGANDA

BRITISH
EAST AFRICA
(KENYA)

EQUATOR

FRENCH
CONGO

Stanleyville

Congo River

Entebbe

Nairobi

Annobon (Sp.)

Lake
Victoria

Mt. Kilimanjaro

ATLANTIC

BELGIAN

Brazzaville
CABINDA
Léopoldville
Boma

CONGO

GERMAN
EAST AFRICA
(TANGANYIKA)

Pemba
Zanzibar
Dar es Salaam

Amiran
(Br.

Ascension
(Br.)

Lake
Tanganyika

Loanda

Lake
Mweru

OCEAN

Benguela

ANGOLA
(PORT. WEST AFRICA)

NORTHERN
RHODESIA

NYASALAND

Lake
Nyasa

Comoro Is.
(Fr.)

Mozambique

St. Helena
(Br.)

Zambezi River

Blantyre
Salisbury

PORTUGUESE

Victoria
Falls

SOUTHERN
RHODESIA

EAST

Beira

AFRICA

MADAGASCAR
Tananari

GERMAN
Windhoek
WALVIS BAY

SOUTHWEST

BECHUANALAND

Limpopo River

TRANSVAAL

Pretoria
Johannesburg

Lorenço Marques
SWAZILAND

AFRICA

UNION

ORANGE
FREE STATE

NATAL

Bloemfontein
OF

Orange River

Durban
BASUTOLAND

SOUTH AFRICA

Cape Town

Port
Elizabeth

INDIAN

OCEAN

Cape of
Good Hope

Legend

France
Italy
Great Britain
Germany
Portugal
Belgium
Spain

0   250   500   1000 MILES

Prepared by
Rand McNally & Co.

France by 1900 had gained control of the largest colonial empire in Africa. It included most of the Sahara and large areas adjacent to it; on the east the French ruled Madagascar and French Somaliland. Germany had obtained German East Africa, the Cameroons and Togoland, and German Southwest Africa. Least successful were the Italians. They gained Eritrea, Italian Somaliland, and Libya, but none of these regions was of much value. They were defeated decisively by the Abyssinians in 1896 when attempting to occupy their country.

The coming of the white man brought mixed results in sub-Saharan Africa. On the one hand, it led to the eventual abolition of slavery and tribal warfare. European help was invaluable in fighting disease and illiteracy and in building cities, railroads, and industries. On the other hand, Europeans wanted African labor above all and exploited the natives cruelly in order to obtain it. Many Africans were uprooted from their tribal and village societies, taxed heavily, and compelled into forced labor. Some of the worst barbarities occurred in the Belgian Congo, where European overseers inflicted brutal punishments in order to increase rubber production. Execution, whipping, and torture were common.

Conditions gradually improved in the 20th century, and a small Westernized class of Africans slowly emerged. Resentful of their treatment at the hands of Europeans, they formed the core of a nationalistic movement that gathered strength as the century advanced.

Section Review

1. How was North Africa affected by the decline of the Turks? the construction of the Suez Canal?
2. How did Britain extend its control over Egypt and the Sudan? Why did it clash with France?

3. Describe the work of Livingstone, Stanley, and Rhodes in opening up the "Dark Continent."
4. What were the chief African possessions of Great Britain, France, and Germany in 1914?
5. How did imperialism affect the peoples of Africa?

6 Imperialism flourished in Latin America

Foreign interference in Latin America generally involved its economic affairs. Actual colonization and direct control were less common than in Africa and Asia.

Foreign investments led to difficulties. Latin America in the latter part of the 19th century offered fertile ground for imperialism. Its resources—including silver, gold, oil, rubber, platinum, tin, and copper— were underdeveloped. At the same time, most countries were poorly governed, offering little resistance to foreign penetration. Revolutions were common, many government officials were dishonest, and social welfare was neglected.

American and European businessmen were quick to take advantage of these circumstances. They spent billions of dollars to dig mines, sink oil wells, and build railroads and public utilities. Their developments yielded a high rate of return and helped the countries in which they were located, but they also caused serious problems. Some promoters bribed corrupt officials to sign agreements that robbed the people of resources that rightfully belonged to them. Huge profits went into the pockets of promoters and officials, while the majority of the population remained desperately poor.

Trouble also arose because of unstable governments. A new ruler, anxious to enrich himself, might refuse to honor agreements entered into by the previous government. Foreign property was seized without compensation in times of revolutionary upheaval. When foreign businessmen found their investments threatened, they sought help from their home countries.

The United States intervened. The possibility of large-scale European interference in Latin America worried the United States, which felt that its security was endangered. The Monroe Doctrine was a valuable statement of principle. However, as imperialism in Latin America increased, further United States action seemed necessary. An important modification of the Monroe Doctrine was made in 1895, as the result of a border dispute between Venezuela and British Guiana. Secretary of State Richard Olney, announcing that "the United States is practically sovereign on this continent," declared that Britain must submit the problem to international arbitration. Thus the United States not only opposed European intervention, but also stated its intention to act as a negotiator in Latin-American international disputes.

The Monroe Doctrine, from the point of view of Latin Americans, was a two-edged sword. Although it offered protection against intervention from Europe, it provided no such guarantees against interference by the United States. This situation was made very clear after a war with Spain.

During the late 19th century, Cuba and Puerto Rico—the last remnants of the once-mighty New World empire of Spain —were swept by revolutionary agitation aimed at independence. Americans were highly sympathetic toward these aspirations, and their indignation was aroused by Spanish severity toward the rebels. Their sympathies were reinforced by other considerations: Americans had invested some $50 million in Cuba; Cuba was the largest supplier of American sugar; and the island was strategically important because it controlled the entrance to the Gulf of Mexico. An unstable, unfriendly Cuba threatened all these interests. When the American battleship *Maine* exploded in Havana harbor under mysterious circumstances in 1898, the United States went to war and defeated Spain in less than five months.

As a result of the Spanish-American War, the United States annexed Puerto Rico, as well as the Philippine Islands. Cuba, for whose freedom the conflict had presumably been fought, was permitted to set up an independent government. However, the United States imposed several restrictions on Cuba. It reserved the right to supervise the foreign relations of Cuba, intervene in its internal affairs, and establish naval bases on the island. In effect, Cuba became an American protectorate. In the next twenty years, the United States actively intervened there several times. Not until 1934 did the American government give up all rights of intervention, and even then it retained a naval base at Guantanamo Bay.

Dollar diplomacy characterized the early 20th century. In the thirty years following the Spanish-American War, American investments in Latin America reached new heights. The American government worked closely with business interests to obtain favorable terms for investors. The coördinated efforts of government and business are often called "dollar diplomacy."

Theodore Roosevelt, President from 1901 to 1909, was a dominant figure in this phase of Latin-American relations. The United States planned to build a canal across the Isthmus of Panama, which belonged to Colombia. Roosevelt became irritated because the Colombian legislature delayed ratifying a long-term lease on the territory. When revolution broke out in Panama in 1903, he sent American marines to the scene and prevented Colombian troops from suppressing the rebels. Two weeks later the United States formally recognized the new Republic of Panama and negotiated a perpetual lease on a zone ten miles wide. Panama, like Cuba, became essentially an American protectorate. The Panama Canal, of great strategic value to the United States, was finished in 1914.

In 1904, Roosevelt proclaimed his famous corollary to the Monroe Doctrine. The United States, he announced, would be forced to assume the duties of an international policeman in the Western Hemisphere whenever "brutal wrongdoing, or an impotence which results in a general loosening of the ties of civilized society may finally require intervention by some civilized nation." This was Roosevelt's way of informing the world that the United States regarded itself as responsible for seeing that Latin-American nations met their foreign obligations.

During the era of dollar diplomacy, the Roosevelt Corollary served to justify repeated American intervention in Central America and the Caribbean. In 1905, when unstable Santo Domingo went bankrupt and could not pay off its European bondholders, the United States took over customs collections and assured payment to all creditors. The United States also intervened in Nicaragua and Honduras to set chaotic finances in order and protect American investments. In 1915 internal disturbances erupted in Haiti. American marines, sent to restore order, remained in the country almost twenty years.

Many Americans opposed imperialistic ventures. Their opposition, together with growing Latin-American resentment toward the "Colossus of the North," helped modify dollar diplomacy by the 1930's.

Section Review

1. What conditions in Latin America invited imperialism? Why did United States intervention in Latin America increase during the latter 1800's?
2. How was the Monroe Doctrine modified in 1895? in 1904?
3. What were the factors behind United States entry into the Spanish-American War? How did the United States maintain control over Cuba after the war?
4. Explain how the United States maneuvered to control the Panama Canal.
5. What was dollar diplomacy? Give three examples of this policy in action.

Chapter 24   A Review

Between about 1870 and 1914, many Western nations were active in extending their rule over foreign territories, particularly underdeveloped areas. This movement, known as imperialism, had several causes and took many different forms.

Earlier, in India, the English had defeated the French in the 18th century and had gained a free hand to enlarge their territories at the expense of the declining Moguls. Rule by the East India Company was replaced by government control after the Sepoy Rebellion of 1857.

China under the Manchus had grown poor and weak by the 19th century. Beginning with the Opium War in 1839, the country fell more and more under foreign influence. Its defeat in the Sino-Japanese War signaled a scramble for concessions, which left China virtually helpless at the hands of Britain, France, Germany, and Russia. Although the Open Door Policy of the United States helped stave off total collapse, the Boxer Rebellion and revolutionary agitation heralded future trouble.

The Japanese were brought into closer relations with the outside world by the United States. Instead of succumbing to Western domination, however, Japan undertook a modernization program of tremendous proportions. The feudal shogunate was abolished, a constitution adopted, and reforms instituted in education and law. Most far-reaching was the rapid transition from an agricultural to an industrial economy. Japan itself turned to imperialism; its fruits were territorial acquisitions and recognition as a first-rate power.

Imperialism was also at work elsewhere in Asia. Manchuria and Mongolia came under Russian influence, as did central and southwestern Asia. Indo-China became a French protectorate, and Burma was added to British possessions. The Dutch ruled a scattered island empire in the East Indies. Pacific islands were snapped up by Britain, Germany, France, and the United States.

Africa was quickly partitioned. While the French and British were dividing North Africa between them, explorers penetrated the "Dark Continent" below the Sahara. In the last few decades of the 19th century, all but two areas lost their independence. Britain and France won the lion's share, but sizable portions went to Belgium, Germany, and Portugal, and even Italy established claims.

In Latin America, foreign investments reached a high level, and the United States asserted a dominant rôle to protect its security. Especially after the Spanish-American War, its own investments in the region were sizable. A policy of dollar diplomacy led to intervention in Panama, Nicaragua, and Haiti, and earned much dislike for the "Colossus of the North."

The Time

Indicate the period in which the events described in the following statements occurred.

(a) 1751-1800	(e) 1881-1890
(b) 1801-1850	(f) 1891-1900
(c) 1851-1870	(g) 1901-1910
(d) 1871-1880	(h) 1911-1920

1. The Panama Canal was completed.
2. Roosevelt proclaimed his corollary to the Monroe Doctrine.
3. The International Congo Association was formed.
4. The Treaty of Kanagawa opened Japan.
5. The Seven Years' War ended.
6. Japan won the Sino-Japanese War.

7. France invaded Algeria.
8. The Sepoy Rebellion resulted in the abolishment of the English East India Company.
9. Hawaii was annexed by the United States.
10. The Suez Canal was completed.
11. The United States announced the Open Door Policy.
12. The Spanish-American War resulted in the annexation of Puerto Rico and the Philippines by the United States.
13. The Treaty of Nanking opened Chinese ports.
14. The Republic of Panama was formed.
15. The Netherlands East Indies was created.
16. Egypt became a British protectorate.
17. The Meiji Restoration began in Japan.
18. The Russo-Japanese War broke out.

The Place

1. During the period of imperialistic expansion, nations gained possessions in Asia, Africa, and the Pacific. Name and locate at least two possessions that the nations listed below gained within the area named.

Britain, France, Japan . . . . Asia
Britain, France, Germany, Italy . . . . . . Africa
Britain, Germany, United
   States . . . . Pacific islands

2. Which imperialistic nations were rivals for control or influence in each of the following areas: southwestern Asia and mid-Asia, Samoa, southeast Asia, Liaotung Peninsula?

3. In what part of China was a sphere of influence established by Russia? by Britain? by France? by Germany?

4. Locate the places named below. Of what value was each one to the imperialistic nation that controlled it?

Pago Pago	Isthmus of Suez
Port Arthur	Vladivostok
Cuba	Isthmus of Panama

5. Locate the following places where frictions from imperialism arose: Khartoum, Fashoda, Omdurman, Calcutta, Pondichéry. Who were the opponents of the British at each place?

6. On a map of Africa, locate the following places and name one man associated with the discovery and/or exploration of each one.

Niger River   Kalahari Desert
Victoria Falls   Lake Tanganyika
Congo River   Lake Victoria
Lake Chad

The People

1. Describe one action by each of the following men that directly or indirectly extended the influence of an imperialistic nation.

Henry M. Stanley   Ismail Pasha
Theodore Roosevelt   Leopold II
Cecil Rhodes   Richard Olney
Pierre de Brazza   Karl Peters

2. What American naval officer persuaded the Japanese to open their ports to trade? Why were the Japanese impressed with him?

3. In what military incident were each of the following men involved?

Joseph Dupleix   Robert Clive
Jean Marchand   Charles Gordon
Horatio Kitchener

4. What contribution did each man make to the development of an overseas territory: David Livingstone, Ferdinand de Lesseps?

5. With what significant change in Japan is Emperor Mutsuhito associated?

Historical Terms

1. What circumstances led to each of the following movements: Moslem League, Indian National Congress, Sepoy Rebellion, Society of Harmonious Fists?

2. What were the terms of each of the treaties listed below? Name the wars that ended in three of the treaties.

Treaty of Nanking   Treaty of Shimonoseki
Treaty of Kanagawa   Treaty of Portsmouth

3. Describe three major accomplishments —one social, one political, and one economic— of the Meiji Restoration.

4. Explain each of the following terms as applied to imperialism in the Americas, in China, and in Africa, respectively: dollar diplomacy, spheres of influence, International Congo Association.

5. What were the purposes of these United States policies: the Open Door Policy, the Roosevelt Corollary?

6. What was extraterritoriality as applied to imperialistic nations in China?

7. Give an example of a protectorate and name the nation which controlled it.

Questions for Critical Thinking

1. Why did Latin-American nations use the phrase "Colossus of the North" in resentment rather than in gratitude?

2. Compare the methods used by European powers to gain control in Africa with the methods used in China. Why do you think the European nations gained control so easily in Africa?

3. Do you think the imperialistic nations were actually concerned with taking up "the white man's burden"? What evidence in this chapter justifies your answer?

4. Why did imperialism in Latin America primarily involve economic affairs, rather than colonization and direct control?

5. Why do you think Japan succeeded in becoming a modern industrial nation by the end of the 19th century?

6. In what respects are the factors which inspired colonial expansion during the 16th and 17th centuries similar to those that inspired imperialism during the late 19th century? In what respects are they different?

National Rivalries and World War I

Europe in the 19th century was the cultural, political, and industrial center of the world. From the famous capital cities of London, Paris and The Hague, its aggressive leaders controlled huge colonial empires the world over. The people of Europe enjoyed steadily improving living conditions and material well-being.

The year 1914 marked an abrupt end to the peace and plenty of the 19th century. It was in August that the Great War, subsequently known as World War I, broke out. For four years, Europe endured the tramp of marching armies, the thunder of cannon, and the spit of machine guns. World War I was a new kind of war, more deadly than men had ever imagined. It was fought under the sea by submarines, on the surface of the waters by giant battleships, in the air by airplanes, and on the land by huge mechanized armies. The glamour of conflict was obliterated by the horrors of machine warfare. Human beings had little chance against a barrage of shells, the fumes of poison gas, or the entanglements of barbed wire. Soldiers became almost like the machines that now dominated their lives. In the painting on the opposite page, "La Guerre," by the French artist Marcel Gromaire, the sinister quality of modern war is depicted. The French soldiers, the *poilus,* look less like men than automatons.

The First World War was fought in many areas—in western Europe, eastern Europe, the Balkans, the Near East, Russia, tropical Africa, and on the seas. Some of the most bitter fighting took place in the trenches on the Western Front in Belgium and northern France. The eerie, nightmare aspects of trench warfare are described in the following passage:

> In and near the front several millions of men lived like moles, fearing even to show their steel helmets above the sandbagged parapets. . . . In time, after [the front-line trenches] had been fought over a good deal, almost all sense and direction were lost to them and they became murderously confused, interconnected in haphazard new ways, astounding labyrinths in

which the men moved warily and felt little security. Sometimes British and German troops occupied what was in effect the same trench, separated from each other only by a bomb barrier and an unspoken agreement. . . .

And finally in the intricate, molelike maze of the Western Front were the dugouts, in their most primitive form merely extra-large holes scooped into the side of a trench for the personal use of one man. But many caverns were minor marvels of crude engineering ingenuity that housed dozens of troops. Here in the fetid smell of unwashed bodies and dank earth the men lived when not on active duty, made coffee in brown pots, dried their stockings, played chess, warmed potatoes, dozed, argued, cleaned their rifles, wrote letters, waited for morning, or guard duty, or a bit of action, and shuddered . . . under the pounding of enemy artillery exploding overhead with dull, harmless thuds. Candles flickered (far back in the dugout the air was so bad they often went out), the rats prowled, but there was no peril even from the direct hit of a 15-inch railway shell. The sound of war was muffled almost to extinction. . . .

Between the lines was No Man's Land, above which nightly hung the star shells thrown up to probe the stripped, blasted wasteland with a nightmarish glare. Machine guns in set patterns raked the desolate ground, searching for enemy patrols. . . . every man knew the whiplash crack of a rifle bullet near the direct line of fire, and the melancholy whine of a ricochet.

As for men, they were seldom to be seen. For this was the peculiarity of the Western Front: the uproar seldom ceased and the number of men involved was countless, but the terrain seemed deserted. Nothing moved in the lethal zone where the great armies brushed against each other. Nobody appeared to be fighting. . . .

How did this nightmare come about? Its causes, courses of development, and outcome are discussed in the two chapters of this unit. In the closing decades of the 19th century, many Europeans believed that a widespread, general war between the great powers was unthinkable. This view was supported by the conviction that wars settled nothing and had no place in a civilized world. Peace societies were organized to spread and popularize this belief. Wealthy industrialists contributed large sums to encourage the cause of peace and the growth of internationalism. Businessmen pointed to the growing interdependence of nations being fostered by international trade. Governments coöperated in establishing international agencies to supervise world postal, telegraph, and cable services.

The forces working for harmony were offset by those creating discord. One of the chief factors was the growth after 1871 of two powerful military alliance systems in Europe. On the one side were Germany, Austria-Hungary, and Italy; on the other, Russia, France, and Great Britain. The members of these alliances were rivals in the race to build up their armed forces. Their imperialistic ambitions clashed as they sought colonies for strategic bases, raw materials, and markets for their surplus manufactured goods.

The Balkans was an explosive area. Russia was determined to expand its influence by strengthening Serbia and weakening Austria. Germany, equally determined to prevent the extension of Russian influence, lent its support to its only reliable ally—Austria. Britain and France stood on the diplomatic sidelines. In the event of a showdown in the Balkans, the major nations of Europe would be drawn into a war. The fatal event took place in June 1914 at Sarajevo, when Archduke Francis Ferdinand, heir to the Austrian throne, was assassinated by a Serbian terrorist. Austria declared war on Serbia and inevitably all the members of the two rival alliances were drawn into the conflict.

In the opening months of the war, it seemed as if victory might go quickly to one side or the other. German forces almost reached Paris; and Russian armies threatened Berlin by the "back door" of East Prussia. These moves were averted, however, and the war settled down to a dreary, agonizing stalemate. Great attacks were launched only to conquer a few square miles of shell-pocked land. Striving to end the deadlock, Germany stepped up its submarine warfare only to bring the United States into the conflict on the side of the Allies. Following a last unsuccessful drive for victory by Germany, the Allied armies, strengthened by the arrival of American troops, forced a surrender of their exhausted foes.

At Paris, the victors met. Hopes were high for the establishment of permanent peace by "the war to end all wars." However, wide gulfs separated the national aims of the peacemakers. It soon became painfully clear that making the right kind of peace was as difficult as waging a victorious war.

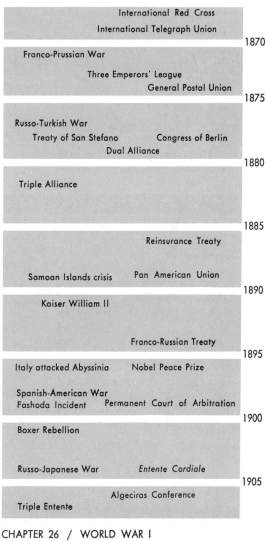

CHAPTER 25 / DRIFTING TOWARD WAR

International Red Cross
International Telegraph Union
1870
Franco-Prussian War
Three Emperors' League
General Postal Union
1875
Russo-Turkish War
Treaty of San Stefano   Congress of Berlin
Dual Alliance
1880
Triple Alliance

1885
Reinsurance Treaty

Samoan Islands crisis   Pan American Union
1890
Kaiser William II

Franco-Russian Treaty
1895
Italy attacked Abyssinia   Nobel Peace Prize

Spanish-American War
Fashoda Incident   Permanent Court of Arbitration
1900
Boxer Rebellion

Russo-Japanese War   Entente Cordiale
1905
Algeciras Conference
Triple Entente

CHAPTER 26 / WORLD WAR I

Austria annexed Bosnia and Herzegovina
1910
1st Balkan War
2nd Balkan War
Sarajevo
Germans invade Belgium, France   Tannenberg
1915
Gallipoli campaign   Lusitania
Russian Revolution   United States enters war
Treaty of Brest-Litovsk   Argonne   Armistice
Paris Peace Conference   Versailles Treaty
1920

Drifting Toward War

Militant self-interest dictated the policies of European nations during the late 19th century. In the Spanish cartoon above, national leaders play billiards using rifles and swords as cues. Bombs are stacked beneath the table, which is covered with a map of Europe and presided over by a snake-haired figure identified as Diplomacy. Played for ever higher stakes, the deadly game of international power politics was ultimately to result in the First World War.

In 1862 appeared a slim volume by a Swiss businessman entitled *A Memory of Solferino.* The author was Jean Henri Dunant, who had been an eyewitness to the Battle of Solferino. Within fifteen hours on that fateful day of June 24, 1859, the Austrians and their opponents, the French and the Sardinians, together lost 40 thousand men. After the defeated Austrians withdrew, Dunant himself helped carry the wounded to makeshift hospitals in the villages of the countryside surrounding Solferino. He observed a pitifully small corps of doctors and orderlies fighting fatigue as they toiled to relieve their patients. He watched men die for lack of adequate medical supplies and was haunted by the cries of the wounded lying helplessly on the battlefield, many for as long as a week. *A Memory of Solferino* was both a stirring account of the tragic aftermath of the battle and a passionate appeal for the prevention of the suffering caused by war. Dunant proposed the organization of relief societies as stand-by units ready for immediate assistance to war victims, regardless of nationality. The societies were to be governed by a neutral board of "honorable reputation" and staffed with crews of "zealous, devoted and thoroughly qualified" volunteers. He urged that ambulance units be set up and medical supplies stocked in advance of emergencies.

Dunant worked tirelessly for the adoption of his proposals. Neglecting his business, he took his case to the heads of states in Europe and to the officers of influential associations. Finally, in 1864, his efforts were rewarded. At a meeting in Geneva, Switzerland, delegates from twelve nations voted for the creation of an organization which they named the Red Cross. It was intended to provide care for war victims, whether they were friend or foe. Also adopted at Geneva were rules which guaranteed the neutrality of Red Cross personnel.

One of Dunant's most widely quoted statements was the simple declaration that "all men are brothers." The establishment by 1900 of Red Cross societies in thirty nations showed that the humanitarian sentiments which united men were strong and enduring. And yet the forces which divided nation from nation, and man from his fellows—imperialism, militarism, and nationalism—were powerful and menacing.

Chapter 25 tells how:

1. **Imperialism threatened peace.**

2. **Europe split into two armed camps.**

3. **Some conditions favored peace.**

4. **Strong forces led to war.**

1 Imperialism threatened peace

By the 1870's the major European nations were highly industrialized. To keep factories humming, raw materials and new markets were needed. As shown in Chapter 24, Great Britain, France, Germany, and other European nations, along with Japan, moved into underdeveloped areas in Africa and Asia. Imperialistic ambitions led to situations which threatened world peace. But major conflicts were avoided at first, largely through the efforts of the Concert of Europe, created after the Napoleonic wars. A system of balancing power prevented the emergence of one predominant nation or coalition of nations. At the close of the 19th century, national rivalries became more intense as the race for colonies continued. The present chapter shows how the delicately maintained balance of power began to break down.

Imperialism in Africa and Asia incited wars and rebellions. The unification of Italy in the latter half of the 19th century brought this Mediterranean nation into the race for colonies after most of the European powers had already staked out their claims. French occupation of Tunis in 1881 infuriated the Italians, who had hoped to obtain for themselves this North African area, formerly a province of Turkey. (In ancient times, Tunis had been the site of Carthage in the Roman Empire.) In 1896, without provocation, Italy attacked Abyssinia, but the untrained Africans completely defeated the poorly led Italian army at Adowa. More than three decades later this defeat was avenged when an aggressive Italian nation led by Benito Mussolini conquered Abyssinia (Chapter 29).

Imperial rivalry in Africa brought France and Britain to the verge of war in 1898. Both nations wished to control the waters of the Upper Nile in the Sudan, and conflict was avoided only when France backed down after the Fashoda Incident. In South Africa, where Dutch settlers and British fortune seekers clashed, imperialism was one of the basic causes of the Boer War, from which Britain emerged the victor in 1902. In Morocco in North Africa, both in 1905 and in 1911, Germany threatened French authority. The first Moroccan crisis resulted in a diplomatic victory for France after a conference of European powers at Algeciras, Spain, in 1906. Six years later the Germans again challenged the French when a German gunboat attempted to back up the kaiser's protest against French activity in Morocco. Britain's support of France, however, forced Germany to yield again.

In 1889 imperialist ambitions led to intense rivalry among Germany, Britain, and the United States over the Samoa Islands in the Pacific. The three nations sent battleships to the area under dispute, and war was averted only when a fierce hurricane destroyed nearly all the vessels. Common danger had drawn the rivals together and tempers cooled. The dispute was temporarily settled at a conference in Berlin where a three-power protectorate was created. When this arrangement proved unsatisfactory, Great Britain gave up its claims and the Samoan archipelago was divided between the United States and Germany.

The rebellion of native peoples was another aspect of imperialism that darkened international relations near the turn of the century. After the United States had extended the Spanish-American War of 1898 to Spain's Philippine Islands, President William McKinley decided to take them over. A Filipino patriot, Emilio Aguinaldo, who had fought with the Americans against Spain, felt that his country had been betrayed when the United States failed to give the Filipinos their independence. He led a rebellion against the Americans which lasted more than two years and which proved more costly to the United States than the original campaign against the Spanish. In 1900 anti-foreign feeling in China led to the bloody Boxer Rebellion. The Chinese resented Western economic and political encroachments. False reports of Christian rites in which Chinese children were sacrificed added to their anger. Only after desperate fighting did an international army save the besieged legation personnel at Peking and force China to sue for peace in 1901. A heavy indemnity was imposed on China, but in keeping with traditionally good relations between the United States and China, a substantial part of the American award was set aside for educating Chinese students in the United States.

Great Britain and Japan resisted Russian expansion. The Russian Empire commanded an enormous land area, but its coasts were blocked by ice most of the year. For centuries Russian rulers had tried to obtain an outlet to the sea that would be open all year round. In 1877 Russia

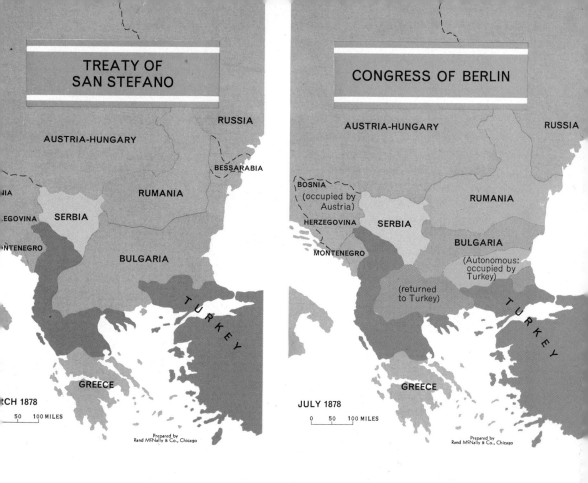

TREATY OF
SAN STEFANO

AUSTRIA-HUNGARY

RUSSIA

BESSARABIA

RUMANIA

?IA

?EGOVINA   SERBIA

?NTENEGRO

BULGARIA

T U R K E Y

GREECE

?CH 1878

50   100 MILES

Prepared by
Rand McNally & Co., Chicago

CONGRESS OF BERLIN

AUSTRIA-HUNGARY

RUSSIA

BOSNIA
(occupied by
Austria)

HERZEGOVINA   SERBIA

MONTENEGRO

RUMANIA

BULGARIA
(Autonomous:
occupied by
Turkey)

(returned
to Turkey)

T U R K E Y

GREECE

JULY 1878

0   50   100 MILES

Prepared by
Rand McNally & Co., Chicago

declared war on Turkey in hopes of gaining control of the Dardanelles. Russia justified aggressive action by declaring to the world that it was rescuing its fellow Slavs in the Balkan portion of the Ottoman Empire from Turkish cruelties. After months of hard fighting, Russia won the Russo-Turkish War and dictated the peace in March 1878. The resulting Treaty of San Stefano established Montenegro, Serbia, and Rumania as independent nations and made Bulgaria an autonomous state. With these Balkan countries in its sphere of influence, Russia was in a position to gain access to the warm water ports of the Mediterranean Sea.

Great Britain was alarmed at the Russian gains which threatened British sea power in the Mediterranean and brought Russia close to the Suez Canal, the sea route to India which was a lifeline of the British Empire. To protect the canal, the British prime minister, Benjamin Disraeli, sought the coöperation of other European nations. Since the Austrian emperor, Francis Joseph, was equally concerned with Russian encroachments in the Balkans, Austria agreed to help Great Britain. In July 1878, acting as the Concert of Europe, representatives from Russia, Germany, Austria, Great Britain, France, Italy, and Turkey met at the Congress of Berlin. The brilliant assemblage of statesmen included Chancellor Bismarck of Germany, who, by failing to support Russia as the latter had hoped, assured the British and Austrians a great diplomatic victory. As a result of this meeting, Bulgaria was reduced in size, and about one-third of its land was returned to Turkey. Austria was

THE TRIPLE ALLIANCE
and TRIPLE ENTENTE

GREAT BRITAIN

North Sea

Baltic Sea

GERMANY

RUSSIA

FRANCE

AUSTRIA-HUNGARY

Black Sea

ITALY

Mediterranean

Sea

Triple Alliance—formed 1882
Triple Entente—formed 1907

Prepared by
Rand McNally & Co., Chicago

made protector of the Ottoman provinces of Bosnia and Herzegovina, and Rumania was enlarged at Russian expense. The most important result of the Congress was the frustration of Russian designs. Russia's aim of advancing to the Mediterranean through control of its Balkan allies was blocked.

The actions taken at the Congress of Berlin, however, did not halt Russia in its drive for greater empire. Blocked in Europe and the Near East, Russia turned to the Far East, where it attempted to gain a port in Manchuria. This move clashed with the imperialistic designs of Japan, which considered Manchuria as its special source of raw materials and markets. Rivalries there, as well as in Korea, led in 1904 to the Russo-Japanese War (Chapter 24) in which the Russians were defeated by Japan. Although Japan made significant gains in the peace treaty which ended the war, many Japanese felt that American

mediation of the conflict had saved the Russians from paying a huge money indemnity to Japan. This settlement was merely one incident in a series of events which undermined the friendship between the United States and Japan in the early 20th century. The newly emerged Far Eastern nation had entered the imperial race and was determined to pit its growing strength against the West.

Section Review

1. Why did Italy attack Abyssinia in 1896? What was the result of the war which followed?
2. Why did the powers of Europe call the Congress of Berlin in 1878? What were the results of this meeting?
3. Did the United States participate in imperialism? Explain.
4. What brought on the Russo-Japanese War? What were its results?

2 Europe split into two armed camps

The Franco-Prussian War of 1870-1871 completed the unification of Germany—a keystone in Bismarck's policy of increasing German power. He looked forward to a long period of peace in which his country could consolidate its gains. Because France smarted under its defeat, Bismarck feared it might seek allies in a war of revenge. Therefore, he began to make alliances, primarily to isolate the French.

Bismarck formed a series of alliances favorable to Germany. The German chancellor first made an alliance with Russia. In 1873 the two nations agreed to help each other in case of attack. Austria also agreed to aid Germany. These agreements became part of the *Three Emperors' League,* which proved to be a failure as an alliance. Austria and Russia disagreed over Balkan matters, and by 1875 relations between Germany and Russia had cooled. This relationship was further strained when Bismarck allowed Austria and Great Britain to block Russian demands at the Congress of Berlin in 1878.

In 1879 Bismarck negotiated the *Dual Alliance* with Austria. Three years later Italy joined Germany and Austria, thus establishing the *Triple Alliance.* Although Italy and Austria had long disagreed over territory that Italy wanted—the Trentino in the Alps and the region around Trieste at the head of the Adriatic—the latter agreed to halt anti-Austrian propaganda. The members of the Triple Alliance promised that if any one of them should be attacked, all three would wage warfare together against the aggressor.

Through skillful diplomacy Bismarck was able to bring Germany and Russia together again in the so-called *Reinsurance Treaty* of 1887. Germany pledged its support to Russia in certain matters relating to the Balkans while Russia assured Germany of its neutrality in the event of a French attack on Germany. These agreements succeeded in furthering Bismarck's basic plan: the isolation of France.

The kaiser changed German policy. In 1888 the young and brash Kaiser William II came to the German throne. He dismissed old Chancellor Bismarck, considering him too cautious and old-fashioned. Contrary to Bismarck's policy of friendship with Russia, the German emperor stopped making loans to the czar. The treaty between Germany and Russia was allowed to lapse, and the kaiser joined Austria in a program to defend their common interests in the Balkans against the Russians.

Snubbed by Germany, the Russians looked to other great powers for alliances and loans. France eagerly grasped the opportunity to ally itself with Russia. Common fear of Germany fostered the alliance. France had made an amazing recovery from its defeat of 1871, had built a strong army, and was again prosperous. It loaned Russia millions of francs which Russia used for the purchase of arms and for building the Trans-Siberian Railroad. In 1894 France and Russia signed a treaty of military alliance. This treaty not only helped forestall German supremacy in Europe but also split Europe into two armed camps.

Great Britain began to seek allies. Great Britain was in neither camp. Protected by its great navy, this island empire practiced what it called "splendid isolation." Its rich colonies circled the earth and its strong navy brought a feeling of security to the home islands and colonies. Great Britain preferred not to meddle in European affairs so long as no European nation threatened its interests. By 1900, however, Great Britain decided that it needed allies. The British were afraid of being left outside the two power blocs in Europe. They also feared that a growing rivalry with France for colonies might bring war.

The British first turned to Germany as a logical ally against the French. The idea of Anglo-Saxon kinship seemed to support Anglo-German friendship in the eyes of some prominent British statesmen. However, when the kaiser began to build a merchant fleet and a navy to outstrip English sea power, the British were roused to action. Without control of the sea, and in the event of an enemy blockade, the people of Great Britain would be in danger of starvation, for they had to import most of their food. To keep control of the seas, Britain needed to build twice as many ships as Germany. The British grimly prepared to achieve this costly goal. Other developments in Germany gave Britain added cause for worry. German industry rivaled that of Great Britain, and the two nations competed in world markets. Kaiser William's warlike speeches disturbed the British as much as his actions. The British ambassador to Germany said "[the kaiser was] like a cat in the cupboard. He may jump out anywhere."

The two rivals, France and Great Britain, were brought together because of mutual distrust of Germany and because of French desire to regain the provinces of Alsace and Lorraine, which Germany took in 1871. The Fashoda Incident had indicated the growth of better understanding between the two great powers. In 1904 the British and French signed an agreement called the *Entente Cordiale* (French for "friendly understanding"). Then France worked to bring Russia and Great Britain closer together. This task was made easier because of Russian and British opposition to Germany's growing influence in the Near East. The German kaiser had helped the Turkish sultan organize and equip his army, and a Berlin-to-Bagdad railway was being planned by German and Austrian financiers. Thus, in 1907, France, Great Britain, and Russia became partners in the second of the great European systems, the *Triple Entente*. The world viewed with growing concern the possibility of a clash between the two sets of rivals.

Section Review

1. Why did Bismarck seek allies for Germany after 1871? How did his alliances isolate France?
2. How did the actions of Kaiser William II lead Russia and Britain to turn to France as an ally?
3. Why was the formation of the Triple Alliance and of the Triple Entente a threat to the peace of Europe?

3 **Some conditions favored peace**

In many respects the 19th century had been a "wonderful century." Mankind could look back at it with some pride. Winston Churchill, the famous British statesman and writer, described the century as a period when " . . . accumulation of health and wealth had been practically unchecked. . . ." By 1900 conditions for the working man were greatly improved. Many countries had achieved universal manhood suffrage, and education had been extended to the lower classes. Science and medicine had made tremendous gains along with industry and technology. Civilization, many persons thought, had attained a new height.

Economic interdependence fostered peace. By the early 20th century, the nations and peoples of the world had become economically interdependent. European capital and know-how had helped speed the economic growth of Asia, Africa, and the Americas. For example, money borrowed from Britain helped finance the American railway system, as well as railroads in Argentina and eastern Europe. As late as 1914, total European investments in the United States were triple the American national debt.

Peace meant that industrial leaders could locate raw materials throughout the world and sell their products in a world market. Large companies could establish offices, factories, and plantations in foreign countries, with telephone, telegraph, and cables providing quick communication. Railroads and steamships could carry products without hindrance in peacetime. Prosperity built on international trade would be destroyed by war. Because peace meant prosperity, many businessmen and statesmen worked for world harmony.

Philanthropists urged peace. Some of the great industrialists of the world made noteworthy contributions to the cause of peace. The Swedish millionaire Alfred Nobel, who had invented dynamite in 1866, established the Nobel Peace Prize in 1896. The prize was awarded to persons or organizations making outstanding contributions to the maintenance of peace. One of the first recipients was Theodore Roosevelt, who was instrumental in mediating the Russo-Japanese War at Portsmouth, New Hampshire, in 1905.

Andrew Carnegie, the Scottish immigrant whose rags-to-riches career was one of the greatest 19th-century American success stories, gave funds to build the Palace of Peace at The Hague in the Netherlands. In 1899 and again in 1907, international conferences met there to discuss plans for the reduction of armaments and the peaceful settlement of disputes.

International organizations furthered understanding. Coöperation through diplomatic activity and world organizations helped foster peace. In the 19th century, the Concert of Europe had operated to preserve peace. In the Balkan controversy of 1878, it had arranged a settlement which temporarily prevented war. In 1884 the Concert laid down rules for the peaceful partition of Africa. Compromises and agreements resulted in the allocation of vast areas to one nation or another. It was agreed that any country wishing to annex territory in Africa was required to notify the other powers of its intentions.

In the Western Hemisphere, the Pan-American movement encouraged coöperation among the American nations. At one of the early meetings in 1889, seventeen countries met in Washington, D.C., and set up a bureau which became known as the Pan American Union. Its chief purpose was to promote trade. (In 1948 the Union became part of a larger agency called the OAS, or Organization of American States.)

In 1868 twenty nations established the International Telegraph Union, and in 1874 the General Postal Union was formed. International agreements were reached also on such matters as weights and measures, the laying and operation of cables, the navigation of international rivers, and the protection of wildlife. The Greek Olympic games were revived in 1896. This event, held every four years, brings together participants from nearly every country of the world.

The International Red Cross, founded through the efforts of Jean Henri Dunant, helped lessen the hardships of war. The Geneva Convention of 1864 was a set of agreements reached at the first meeting of the International Red Cross. It became the forerunner of other international agreements covering victims of warfare at sea, prisoners of war, and civilians during wartime. National Red Cross societies also offered aid during times of peace to disaster victims and other unfortunates.

Peace movements were organized. The idea of peace through international federation goes back many hundreds of years. In 1623 a French monk, Emeric Crucé, published a pamphlet proposing his scheme for perpetual peace. Reacting against the horrors of the Thirty Years' War, he suggested a plan of union which included not only European countries, but also China, India, and Persia. The "Grand Design" of the French king, Henry IV, described in 1634 by his minister, the Duc de Sully, contemplated the division of Europe into fifteen nations which would coöperate through a common council similar to that of the ancient Greeks. Toward the close of the 17th century, the English Quaker William Penn, the founder of Philadelphia, suggested the creation of an all-European parliament called the Great Diet, in which representation would be based on national wealth. Early in the 18th century, the Abbé Saint-Pierre proposed an alliance of states meeting in a permanent assembly which could impose penalties by force on nations guilty of violating agreements. In 1761 the French philosopher Jean Jacques Rousseau in his essay, *A Lasting Peace Through the Federation of Europe,* advanced the idea of a permanent Congress of Europe in which the combined military force of all members would be applied against aggressors. The English philosopher and reformer Jeremy Bentham published his treatise on the principles of international law in 1789. The union of states he proposed would achieve common peace through application of moral laws rather than force. Bentham pointed to economic rivalries, armaments, and the struggle for colonies as causes of war. In his famous essay, *Toward Eternal Peace* (1795), the eminent German philosopher Immanuel Kant based his hopes for peace on republicanism as a universal form of government. He also advocated world citizenship and the gradual abolition of standing armies.

Practical statesmanship, rather than visionary schemes, was characteristic of 19th-century international relations. However, the modern organized peace movement produced devoted leaders in the first half of the century and attracted a significant following. In the United States and Great Britain, private organizations played an important part in molding public opinion. Two of the early peace groups in the United States were the New York Peace Society and the American Peace Society. In an essay written in 1840, William Ladd, the founder of the latter group, proposed the establishment of a congress of ambassadors from all Western nations and a voluntary international court of arbitration. In England, two well-known philosophers, James Mill and his son John Stuart Mill, also suggested plans for international arbitration through establishment of a European court federation. From 1848 to 1850, international peace congresses met in important European cities. In 1849 Victor Hugo, the celebrated French author, delivered a notable address in Brussels, Belgium, in which he urged the formation of a United States of Europe.

Arbitration was used to settle international disputes. In the last half of the 19th century, arbitration as a means of settling international disputes became more widespread. In arbitration, the disputing countries agree in advance to abide by the decision of the judge or judges chosen to consider the case. This practice, which originated in Greek and Roman times, was used to compose important differences between the United States and Great Britain. For example, in the claims arising from British help to Confederate sea raiders in the War Between the States, an arbitral commission in 1872 awarded the United States $15,500,000. A boundary dispute between Canada and the United States in the Alaskan Panhandle was settled in 1904 by a joint commission of British and Americans.

The Permanent Court of Arbitration was established in 1899 at The Hague in the Netherlands. Contesting states could avail themselves of arbitrators furnished by the Court from an official panel. Arbitration agreements were concluded by many countries, and by 1914 the Court had rendered decisions in fourteen international disputes.

Section Review

1. Why were the businessmen of the early 20th century eager to maintain peace among nations? How did Nobel, Carnegie, and Dunant make important contributions to the cause of peace?
2. What international organizations helped foster harmony among nations?
3. Name four thinkers who, previous to the 19th century, proposed methods for establishing world peace. Briefly summarize the plans of each.
4. What is arbitration and how did it help settle international disputes?

4   Strong forces led to war

Some people believed that the principal cause of war was nationalism. They felt that if an international authority could be established with power to enforce its decisions, peace would be maintained. Others held that such an authority was uncalled for and that it might be a threat to national loyalties and well-being.

Nationalism threatened peace. Spurred on by intense national pride, the people of some nations believed that they were superior to their neighbors. War, they thought, was a legitimate and excellent means of proving superiority. Demagogues and unscrupulous nationalists urged their followers to press for war in order to avenge fancied insults, to take territory claimed as their own, or to "liberate" fellow nationals living under foreign rule. Persons who favored these aggressive policies became known as *jingoes*. The term came from a song that was popular in England near the turn of the century:

> We don't want to fight;
>   But by Jingo if we do,
> We've got the men, we've got the ships,
>   We've got the money, too.

There were many pockets of discontented nationals in Europe. In Austria-Hungary two ruling nationalities, German and Hungarian, governed unhappy Czechs, Poles, Serbs, and Italians. In other areas, French, Poles, and Danes were under German rule. These "submerged nationalities" plotted secretly and dreamed of the day when they would form their own independent governments or combine with fellow nationals to create a new nation.

The Irish were displeased with being tied to England. In the early years of the 20th century, they organized the *Sinn Fein* movement, which stressed national self-reliance. Irish leaders, such as Eamon De Valera and Arthur Griffith, insisted that the people rely on their own actions and not on the British Parliament to gain reforms.

Extremists glorified war. Many important intellectuals and statesmen considered war a worthwhile activity. Social Darwinists, who derived their ideas of national struggle from Darwin's biological theories, saw war as the supreme principle producing social progress. They pictured an international competition in which nations were pitted against each other in a struggle for existence. As with biological species, this struggle would result in the survival of the fittest.

Extreme German nationalists, such as Heinrich von Treitschke, popularized ideas glorifying expansionism and militarism.

On the Brink of War

The rivalries among European nations drew caustic comment from cartoonists. The English cartoon at left mocks the 1907 peace conference. Germany, France, Russia, and England, all heavily armed, politely invite each other into The Hague. In a German cartoon of 1912, above, Winston Churchill (then First Lord of the Admiralty) urges John Bull, symbol of England, to shoulder more naval expenditures. The English stepped up their shipbuilding program to maintain supremacy over the fast-growing German fleet.

Imperialistic conflicts and military alliances were also subjects for lively cartoons, as shown on the opposite page. At top left, a German eagle and a British lion eye one another suspiciously as each claims a portion of prostrate China. Below, Germany is ridiculed for not resisting French penetration of Morocco. A wily Frenchman eats his way through a cake identified as "Marokko" (Morocco), while a passive German sheep holds a banner marked "Algesiras" (Algeciras); a 1906 conference in this Spanish city supposedly assured Moroccan independence. Below right, France and Britain refuse to give a musical instrument to Germany, at right, who wants to join their concert. The trio above right represents the Triple Alliance. Germany, center, robustly leads the singing while Austria at left and Italy at right lend only half-hearted support.

Treitschke was an ardent defender of the Prussian ruling class and a bitter enemy of Great Britain. His ideas had a great impact on German youth in the latter 19th century. Treitschke declared:

> The grandeur of war lies in the utter annihilation of puny man in the great conception of the State, and it brings out the full magnificence of the sacrifice of fellow-countrymen for one another. In war the chaff is winnowed from the wheat.

Militarism was a strong factor for war. In the three wars that Bismarck fought in order to unify Germany, he proved the value of military conscription, or the draft. Under this system, military service was compulsory. Other nations copied this practice, each trying to build the strongest armed force.

Military strength was no longer concentrated only on defense. Military leaders whose careers were furthered by international instability became spokesmen for preparedness. They argued that quick mobilization and early action were matters of life or death for any nation. In the United States, Alfred T. Mahan, a naval officer and historian, focused attention on the importance of sea power in the life of a nation. He helped influence Americans to build a powerful navy. One of his disciples was Theodore Roosevelt, a vigorous nationalist and exponent of the military life.

Fear and suspicion endangered peace. Under the influence of imperialism, nationalism, and militarism, the two armed camps of Europe faced each other in conditions sometimes described as international anarchy. The system of international order, which had managed to prevent a major conflict in the 19th century, appeared to be breaking down. The Concert of Europe was being replaced by rival alliance systems. National sovereignty, or independence, far outweighed the respect for international obligations.

Statesmen and diplomats used their wiles to threaten and confuse rival countries. Secret agents and spies were employed to secure information about the military strength of other governments and their attitudes toward war. In the atmosphere of fear and suspicion that marked European international relations from about 1900 to 1914, it was not improbable that sooner or later something would happen to set off a reaction which would bring the sensitive alliance system into play.

Section Review

1. Why were discontented national minorities a threat to peace?
2. How did the ideas of the Social Darwinists contribute to the glorification of war?
3. What were the basic ideas of Mahan? of Treitschke?

Chapter 25 ▬▬▬▬▬▬ A Review

In the 19th century Western nations were building empires the world over in order to obtain raw materials and markets. In the latter part of the century, imperialism led to many rivalries among the Great Powers. Some of the conflicts were settled peaceably; but others resulted in wars, such as the Russo-Japanese War and the Boer War. These wars, however, were localized, or restricted in scope. A kind of balance was maintained which prevented a major conflagration.

Another factor which worked against the outbreak of war was the increasing economic interdependence of nations. Their prosperity depended on the exchange of raw materials and finished goods. Other forces for peace included the activities of philanthropists such as Nobel and Carnegie and the agreements reached by various international organizations. In the 19th century, the organized peace movement continued. It attracted many well-known proponents and involved various societies and congresses which helped to influence public opinion.

It was the European alliance system which finally threatened to bring on a world-wide disaster. Under the shrewd guidance of Bismarck, the German Empire set up a complex network of alliances including the Triple Alliance with Austria-Hungary and Italy. To protect themselves, France, Russia, and Great Britain formed the Triple Entente. The formation of alliances, the military build-ups they fostered, and the fear and suspicion which they fomented led to unease and unrest in Europe. By 1900 the world watched anxiously as these two armed camps faced each other.

The Time

Place the events named in the list below in their correct chronological sequence.

Russo-Japanese War began.

Algeciras Conference met.

Congress of Berlin met to discuss Balkan problems.

Franco-Prussian War ended.

Spanish-American War broke out.

Triple Entente was formed.

American nations created a bureau.

Triple Alliance was established.

Treaty of San Stefano ended the Russo-Turkish War.

Boxer Rebellion ended.

The Place

1. What political changes were made in the Balkans by the Treaty of San Stefano? Why were these changes of particular advantage to Russia? How did the decisions of the Congress of Berlin impede the Russian advance to the Mediterranean Sea?

2. In which of the major alliances were the member nations joined together in one continuous land mass?

3. On a map of the world, locate the following places and cite one important event which occurred at each place during the period from 1871 to 1914.

Morocco   Samoa Islands
The Hague   Manchuria
Abyssinia (now Ethiopia)

The People

Indicate the importance of the following figures in the history of international relations.

Jean Henri Dunant   Alfred Nobel
William Penn   Alfred T. Mahan
Andrew Carnegie   Jeremy Bentham
Heinrich von   Jean Jacques Rousseau
  Treitschke   Otto von Bismarck
William II   Theodore Roosevelt

Historical Terms

1. Identify each of the following alliances.

Three Emperors' League   Reinsurance Treaty
Dual Alliance   *Entente Cordiale*
Triple Alliance   Triple Entente

2. Define the following terms: submerged nationalities, jingoes, conscription.

3. What was the purpose of each of the following groups?

International Red Cross   Concert of Europe
American Peace Society   Olympic games
International Telegraph   *Sinn Fein*
  Union   Pan American
Permanent Court of   Union
  Arbitration

Questions for Critical Thinking

1. What is the significance of the late unification of Italy and Germany in the imperialist race for colonies?

2. Of the trends toward peace and those toward war from 1871 to 1914, which seemed stronger? Give reasons for your answer.

3. Why did the Concert of Europe after 1900 cease to function effectively as a "policeman" or "balancer" in maintaining the peace of Europe?

4. From the standpoint of geography, what military advantages and disadvantages did the nations of the Triple Alliance have? the nations of the Triple Entente?

5. To what degree did the actions of Kaiser William II weaken the position of Germany on the continent of Europe? Had he continued Bismarck's foreign policies instead of pursuing his own, would the danger of war have decreased by 1914? Explain.

World War I

Extreme nationalism, entangling alliances, and imperialistic rivalries plunged Europe into a grim, bloody war in 1914. Hope for a quick settlement soon vanished as armies found themselves fighting for months over possession of a few miles of mud, trenches, and barbed wire. Dangerous new weapons multiplied the horrors of combat. When hostilities ended four years later, the victors were torn between a longing for peace and their desire to punish Germany.

A friend came to see me . . . he thinks it was on Monday, August 3 [1914]. We were standing at a window of my room in the Foreign Office. It was getting dusk, and the lamps were being lit in the space below on which we were looking. My friend recalls that I remarked on this [scene] with the words: "The lamps are going out all over Europe; we shall not see them lit again in our time."

These sorrowful words of Sir Edward Grey, the foreign secretary of Great Britain, echoed the sentiments of many men and women in the dark days of August 1914. Europe was plunging into a long and deadly conflict, a Great War which eventually drew into it not only the major powers of Europe, but of America and Asia as well.

The Great War, or World War I, as it was later known, was to make a mockery of the peace and abundance prophesied by the statesmen and scientists of the 19th century. No longer could the consequences of imperialistic ambitions, rival alliances, rabid nationalism, and the race for armies and armaments be averted. Nor could the threat of the new and deadly instruments of war devised by modern technology be pushed aside. Enlisted in the services of warfare were the noteworthy advances which had been made during the 19th century in the fields of invention, manufacturing, transportation, and communication. Indeed, the lamps were going out for the "wonderful century." When they came on again in the autumn of 1918, few men doubted that the world had passed into a new era.

Chapter 26 describes how:

1. **A crisis arose in the Balkans.**

2. **The powder keg exploded.**

3. **The world went to war.**

4. **The victors tried to build a lasting peace.**

1 A crisis arose in the Balkans

By the early 20th century, five Balkan countries—Greece, Serbia, Montenegro, Rumania, and Bulgaria—had freed themselves from Turkish rule. Proud of their freedom, the Slavs in these countries were determined to free other Slavs who remained under foreign control. Serbia, for example, had a large Slavic population, and it had long dreamed of creating a Greater Serbia. This ambition was aimed chiefly against Turkey and Austria, both of which governed many Slavic people.

The rivalries of the great European powers centered in the Balkans. In the mid-1800's the desire of the Slavs for freedom found expression in Pan-Slavism, a nationalistic movement to unify the Slavic peoples. Pan-Slavism gained strength during the next fifty years, especially in Russia, which had assumed the role of protector of its "little Slavic brothers" in the Balkans. By encouraging unrest in the Balkans, Russia hoped to weaken Austrian and Turkish power there and gain for itself two straits—the Bosporus and the Dardanelles. With these waterways under its control, Russia would then realize its ambition to have a warm-water outlet to the Mediterranean and to the profitable Near Eastern trade.

Germany also wanted to increase its strength in the Balkans and to enlarge its Near Eastern trade. To gain influence in the area, Kaiser William II made diplomatic visits to Turkey in 1898. Another move was German financial support for a "Berlin-to-Bagdad" railroad. Parts of the railway had been built by the turn of the century.

For its part, Great Britain was opposed to an increase of either German or Russian power in the Balkans. Although allied with Russia in the Triple Entente, Britain particularly feared Russian control of the straits. It was a direct threat to the British sea route to India and the Far East through the Suez Canal.

The Balkan situation was most crucial to the interests of the Austrian Empire, made up as it was of many different peoples, including Germans, Hungarians, Poles, Italians, Czechs, and Serbs. If the Serbs should break away from Austria, other nationality groups might do the same, thereby bringing about the collapse of the whole empire.

The Congress of Berlin in 1878 had given Austria the right to "protect" Bosnia and Herzegovina. These two Slavic Balkan provinces formerly had belonged to Turkey. In 1908 Austria annexed the provinces as part of a secret arrangement with Russia, and in return, Russian warships were to be allowed to use the Dardanelles and the Bosporus. When the British objected strongly to Russia's claim on the straits, Austria denied all knowledge of an agreement. This betrayal angered the Russians, for Austria kept the two Balkan provinces while Russia got nothing.

Austrian seizure of Bosnia and Herzegovina also angered the Serbs, because their plan for a Greater Serbia had included the absorption of these two Balkan provinces.

The Balkans became the most dangerous spot in Europe. The Greater Serbia movement was weakened by two basic factors. First, no one of the great powers involved in this area could be counted upon to support Serbia. Although Russia avowed its sympathies with the Serbs after the Bosnia and Herzegovina incident, it could offer the Serbs no direct help because it had been badly battered in the war with Japan in 1904 and 1905. Nor were the appeals that Russia made to its partners in the Triple Entente (Britain and France) of any avail.

A second and even greater deterrent to the Greater Serbia movement was the lack of coöperation among the Balkan peoples themselves. Dissension, distrust, and intrigue weakened them even when they appeared united in a common cause. In 1912 the First Balkan War broke out when Bulgaria, Greece, Montenegro, and Serbia attacked Turkey, intending to drive it from Europe and to free Albania, Macedonia, and Thrace. Turkey was defeated, but the great European powers, meeting in London, kept the victors from dividing the spoils among themselves. A blow to Serbia was the establishment of Albania as an independent nation. Thus Serbia was prevented from acquiring this seacoast area as an outlet to the Adriatic.

Denied Albania, the Serbs joined the Greeks in an alliance against Bulgaria, hoping to gain territory in Macedonia. In 1913, Bulgaria attacked Serbia and Greece, and the Second Balkan War began. Bulgaria was in turn attacked by Turkey and Rumania and defeated. Bitterness in the Balkans increased, but Serbia, growing in power and prestige, was more than ever determined to unite the Slavs.

By 1914 Serbian-Austrian relations were approaching a breaking point. More dangerous, these relations involved Austria and Russia. These two great powers—one trying to maintain its conglomerate empire and the other promoting Pan-Slavism—were members of rival alliances. The interaction of these opposing systems could have dangerous consequences to the peace of Europe. Small wonder that the Balkan Peninsula was considered the "powder keg of Europe."

Section Review

1. How did the Balkan interests of European powers conflict?
2. How did relations between Russia and Serbia add to the unrest in the Balkans?
3. Why were Russian and Austrian inter-

NORTH
Sea

EUROPE IN 1914

FINLAND

NORWAY

SWEDEN

Christiania

Stockholm

Glasgow

*North
Sea*

DENMARK

*Baltic
Sea*

Copenhagen

Dublin

GREAT BRITAIN

RUSSIA

lantic

London

THE
NETHER-
LANDS

Hamburg

Berlin

Warsaw

POLAND

Ocean

Brussels
BELGIUM
Sedan

Cologne
LUXEM-
BURG

GERMAN EMPIRE

Paris

Prague

UKRAINIA

Munich

Vienna

FRANCE

SWITZER-
LAND

Budapest

Lyons

AUSTRIA-HUNGARY

Bordeaux

RUMANIA

Black Sea

Genoa

Bucharest

Marseilles

Belgrade

ANDORRA

Sarajevo

SERBIA

BULGARIA

Madrid

MONTENEGRO

Sofia

Constantinople

SPAIN

Rome

ALBANIA

THE BALKANS

TURKEY

Valencia

OTTOMAN EMPIRE

Mediterranean

GREECE

ALGERIA

Athens

0 100 200 MILES

Sea

Prepared by
Rand McNally & Co., Chicago

TUNIS

ests in the Balkans especially dangerous to the peace of Europe?

2 The powder keg exploded

During the tense days of June 1914, Archduke Francis Ferdinand, heir to the Austrian throne, visited Sarajevo, the capital of Bosnia. As he rode through the streets in an open automobile, a young man sprang forward, fired a revolver, and killed both the archduke and his wife.

The murder of the archduke furnished the spark. The crime set off events that brought on a world war within a month. The killer was identified as a young Bosnian student named Gavrilo Princip.

(Only later was it learned that Serbian officials who belonged to an anti-Austrian society were plotting to kill the archduke during his visit. Whether Princip was a member of their group has never been definitely proved.)

Count Leopold von Berchtold, the Austrian foreign minister, suspected that the crime was of Serbian origin. Immediately, he went into action to remove Serbia as a center for anti-Austrian propaganda. In a letter to Kaiser William II of Germany, which was signed by the Austrian emperor, Francis Joseph I, Berchtold asked for German help. Eager to keep Austria as an ally and in the belief that the conflict could be confined to the Balkans, the kaiser assured the Austrian emperor of his support. His reply, placing no limits on the amount of help Austria could expect from Germany, became known as the "blank check."

Berchtold thus had all the assurance he needed, and on July 23 he sent an ultimatum to Serbia. He insisted that all anti-Austrian activities in Serbia cease; that Austro-Hungarian officials be assigned to suppress such activities; and that all Serbian government officials guilty of anti-Austrian propaganda be dismissed.

Austria declared war on Serbia. Count von Berchtold gave the Serbs forty-eight hours to reply. Should they refuse his ultimatum, he was confident that Austria could defeat Serbia in a local war. Furthermore, with Germany as an ally of Austria, he believed other nations would be afraid to help Serbia.

The Serbs agreed to some of the Austrian demands, but considered others as violations of Serbian sovereignty. They suggested the dispute be placed before the World Court at The Hague for arbitration. When Austria refused, Serbia called on Russia for help. The Russians pledged support, and thus a world war—not a local one—threatened. As tension mounted in the capitals of Europe, Sir Edward Grey, the British foreign secretary, tried to arrange a conference between Serbia and Austria. While the diplomats worked for peace, Berchtold convinced the Austrian emperor that war was the only way to deal with the Serbs. He paid no attention to Grey's proposals for peace nor to the warning from the German chancellor, Theobald von Bethmann-Hollweg, that Germany refused "to be drawn into a world conflagration." German militarists, whose interests often conflicted with those of the diplomats, encouraged Berchtold. On July 28 Austria declared war on Serbia.

Alliances brought other nations into the war. Even at that critical stage, increased pressure from the German chancellor might have opened a path for a peaceful settlement. However, on July 30 Russian mobilization began and prevented further attempts at negotiation.

Because of Russian kinship with the Serbs and because a Serbian defeat would endanger Russian designs on the straits, Russian generals urged the immediate mobilization of the army. Czar Nicholas II of Russia was at first reluctant to follow this advice, but he yielded when France assured him of support.

News of Russian mobilization and French support caused alarm in the German capital, for Germany would have to fight on two fronts: France on the west and Russia on the east. Germany immediately demanded that Russia halt war preparations and that France stay neutral. These nations refused, and on August 1 Germany declared war on France and demanded of Belgium that German troops be allowed to cross its frontiers on their way to the French front. Belgium refused to grant permission, although its independence had been guaranteed, and appealed instead to Britain and France. Germany thereupon ignored the refusal and sent its troops across Belgium.

Great Britain, as a member of the Triple Entente, was not bound to help France or Russia in a war. However, in entering Belgium, Germany had violated a treaty by which both Germany and Britain were pledged to respect Belgian neutrality. The violation not only angered the British but made them fearful lest Germany gain control of the North Sea coast and thus threaten the British Isles. Therefore, on August 4, Great Britain declared war on Germany.

Section Review

1. After the murder of the archduke, what were the steps Austria took to crush anti-Austrian influences in Serbia? How did Germany help Austria?

2. Following the ultimatum from Austria, what steps were taken to prevent a war?
3. How did alliances bring European nations into war?

3   The world went to war

In August 1914, at the outset of the war, only six nations were involved. On one side were the Allies—Great Britain, France, Russia, and Serbia. Opposing them were the Central Powers—Germany and Austria. The strength of the Central Powers was increased when Turkey joined them in October 1914 and Bulgaria a year later.

Although Italy was an ally of Germany and Austria in the Triple Alliance, it felt no real friendship for Austria. When the war began, Italy declared its neutrality, and for several months afterward the Allies and the Central Powers each sought to win Italy to its side. In April 1915, after receiving promises of territory in Austria and an extension of its African colonies, Italy joined the Allies.

Japan had joined the Allies in 1914, and in 1917 China declared war against Germany and Austria. Eventually, thirty-one countries including the United States were engaged in the conflict. The war was to last four years and to draw more than 61 million men into military service.

German aggressiveness shocked the world. No major European nation could escape some of the blame for conditions leading to war. Ever since the Franco-Prussian War of 1870-1871 when Germany had acquired the two valuable French provinces of Alsace and Lorraine, France had nursed a bitter hatred of Germany. Great Britain feared German colonial, naval, and industrial strength, and neither these two nations nor Russia trusted the kaiser, William II. Tensions in Europe had been increasing ever since William

had come to the throne and proclaimed his intentions to make Germany the most powerful nation in the world. In the Allied nations, many of the people felt that Germany was chiefly at fault for the outbreak of World War I.

When German troops marched into Belgium, thousands were shocked at such disregard of international law. Their anger and dismay increased when the German chancellor justified the invasion by saying, "Necessity knows no law. . . . We shall try to make good the wrong we have thus committed as soon as we shall have reached our military goal." This frank acknowledgment of bold self-interest put Germany in the wrong as a treaty-breaker, a position that lost it support and sympathy throughout the world.

The Allies held firm. By striking fast through Belgium, Germany tried to deal France a lightning blow. The highly trained German troops almost reached Paris before the French under Marshal Joseph Joffre stopped them. His hastily assembled army forced the Germans back at the Marne River, ending German hopes for a quick victory. The Germans, however, occupied northeast France and almost all of Belgium. In a race for the Channel ports, the Germans destroyed the main British force at Ypres, and Britain was not able to regain its full strength on land until 1917.

From 1915 to 1917, bitter fighting on the Western Front raged back and forth. The Allies and the Germans built trenches, ranging for hundreds of miles from the English Channel to the Swiss border, but neither side made significant advances. For days and weeks at a time cannons bombarded the trench-bound soldiers. The fire of machine guns, the menace of poison gas, and the shelling of big guns added to the constant danger of the men in the trenches.

The Deadly Weapons of Modern Warfare revolutionized combat tactics during World War I. The surprise element of land attacks was reduced by aerial reconnaissance flights, but ships at sea had no warning against submarines prowling the ocean waters. Above left, Allied airplanes (marked by circles) battle German aircraft in a "dogfight." Moored in a German harbor, the submarine at right takes on supplies. The German soldier above right wears a gas mask as protection against the newly developed poison gases, which were used by both sides. He carries a hand grenade, an effective weapon in trench warfare. British tanks, like those below, terrified German troops when first used in 1916. The British had developed the tank secretly under the pretext of constructing water tanks, thus giving the new vehicle its name.

In 1916 French soldiers under General Henri Pétain held the Germans back at Verdun, and at the Somme River the Allies made a small gain. During these two battles, it is estimated that each side lost nearly a million men.

Technology provided both sides with deadly weapons. Science, invention, and manufacture combined to make weapons more effective and more frightful than ever before in history. Battles were fought in the air and under the sea as well as on land and sea. Germany countered the British battleships with submarine attacks. Early in the war both Germany and the Allies used airplanes for reconnaissance and photography. By 1917 both had developed fighter and bomber squadrons that bombed targets hundreds of miles from their bases.

The British introduced tanks, and later the Germans adopted them. Internal-combustion engines powered land, air, and sea transportation systems. Sea and land mines, torpedo boats, hand grenades, flame throwers, machine guns, and many other devices for war were created or improved by technological advances. Giant guns, such as the German "Big Bertha," lobbed shells more than seventy-five miles.

The Central Powers achieved victories in the East. On the Eastern Front, the Russians kept a large segment of the German army occupied. The Russian invasion of East Prussia in 1914 drew German divisions from the Western Front. However, after the Germans under General Paul von Hindenburg made a successful counterattack in the East Prussian battles of Tannenberg and the Masurian Lakes, the Russians drew back. Further defeats and losses demoralized them. Although they continued to resist the Germans and Austrians, for the most part they fought only a defensive war.

In 1915 the British and French attempted to capture the Dardanelles and to send supplies through the straits to Russia, but their plans ended in failure. The Allies then landed troops on the Gallipoli Peninsula in Turkey, but this campaign also failed and more than 200 thousand men were lost. Later in 1915 Austria and Bulgaria defeated Serbia and occupied the country. This victory gave the Central Powers control of an unbroken line from Berlin to Constantinople.

Germany stepped up naval warfare. During the first months of the war, heavy damage had been inflicted on Allied shipping by the German navy. However, by December the British had destroyed the German fleet in the Pacific. Of greater consequence in the conflict, the British had begun to lay mines in the North Sea. As a result, on February 4, 1915, Germany announced that all the waters surrounding the British Isles would be considered a war zone and that any enemy ship—including merchant ships—would be attacked. Britain retaliated by ordering a blockade of Germany, seizing all goods destined for German ports.

By 1916 the British naval blockade of the Continent had resulted in a drastic reduction of food supplies in Germany. In the battle of Jutland, also in 1916, German battleships engaged the British. During the struggle, both sides lost an equal number of ships but the British lost a greater tonnage. Later in the year, Germany increased the number of its submarines, and its light cruisers slipped through the blockade to raid Atlantic shipping. Although Britain speeded up shipbuilding and developed depth bombs, German naval warfare—especially submarine warfare—was very effective. By the early part of 1917, supplies of food in England were running low and the country was brought close to starvation.

On the Home Fronts, World War I affected the lives of civilians more than any previous conflict. Public support was aroused by the effective use of propaganda. In the American poster at right, a plea for contributions to the war effort, a young girl protects a baby from the menacing "Hun." Women eased the labor shortage by taking jobs in factories; below, a group works at an American assembly line. Because of an Allied blockade which cut off foreign food supplies, the Central Powers faced starvation late in the war. In the scene above, German city dwellers strip a dead horse for its meat.

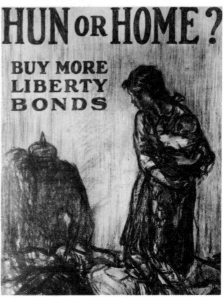

HUN OR **HOME?**

BUY MORE LIBERTY BONDS

The Allies faced collapse. In April 1917 a large-scale attack by the French on the German lines was beaten back with horrible losses. Two months later the British launched several offensives in Belgium and lost 400 thousand men. War weariness among British soldiers, a growing spirit of mutiny among the French, and lack of cooperation between British and French commanders weakened the Allies.

In March 1917 the people of Russia had revolted against the czar and had set up a new government. It tried to carry on the war, but from that time on Germany had little to fear from Russia.

Late in 1917, a German-Austrian army defeated the Italians at Caporetto, capturing 300 thousand men while more than that number deserted. An Allied victory seemed more and more remote.

The United States joined the Allies. Several weeks after the war began, President Woodrow Wilson said in a message to Congress:

The United States must be neutral in fact as well as in name . . . . We must be impartial in thought as well as in action, [we] must put a curb upon our sentiments. . . .

Nevertheless, as the war advanced, strict neutrality was difficult to maintain. Some Americans were angered by the British search of vessels on the high seas and by its naval blockade of Germany. Others were strongly pro-Ally. When German submarines sank merchant ships carrying American passengers, sentiment for the Allied cause increased.

On May 7, 1915, a German submarine sighted the British liner *Lusitania* in the war zone and torpedoed it. Almost 1200 lives were lost, including more than a hundred Americans. Wilson demanded reparations and assurance from Germany that such disasters would not occur again, but

in 1916 more Americans were involved in the sinking of another vessel, the French *Sussex*. As a result, Wilson threatened to break off diplomatic relations with Germany, and received the promise that merchant vessels would not be attacked without warning. He also continued his attempts to end the war through negotiation and at the same time urged nations to organize "some definite concert of power" to make war impossible.

In the meantime, other factors turned sentiment in the United States predominantly toward Great Britain and France. British propaganda for the Allied cause was handled skillfully. More than 350 newspapers in the United States were supplied with daily news releases, and stories of German atrocities against Belgian civilians were distributed by various Allied agencies. Although a great number of the atrocity stories were false, the effect on public opinion was far-reaching. In widely circulated cartoons, the Germans were pictured as bestial Huns and brutal war-lovers.

The immediate causes of the United States entry into the war were the German submarine campaign and the Zimmermann telegram. On January 31, 1917, Germany announced unrestricted submarine warfare, and in the next two months several American ships were sunk. Late in March, British agents intercepted a note sent to Mexico by Alfred Zimmermann, the German foreign secretary, suggesting that Mexico ally itself with Germany and help fight the United States. In addition to financial aid, Germany promised that Mexico should recover Texas, New Mexico, and Arizona when the Allies were defeated.

German submarine warfare and the exposure of the Zimmermann telegram raised public opinion in the United States to a fever pitch. President Wilson urged immediate entry into the war, and on April 6, 1917, Congress declared war on Ger-

WORLD WAR I IN EUROPE

Central Powers

Allied Powers

x Battle

many. By that time, most people in the United States were eager for the fight and, under the spell of Wilson's idealistic speeches, thousands enlisted, as the President said, "to make the world safe for democracy."

Germany gambled for a final victory. In March 1917 after the government of Czar Nicholas II of Russia had been overthrown, a provisional government was established. In November the radical Bolsheviks incited a second revolution. Led by Nikolai Lenin, they offered to make peace with Germany, and on March 3, 1918, at Brest-Litovsk, the Bolsheviks signed a treaty in which Russia lost one third of its people, nine tenths of its coal mines, and the great Caucasian oil fields to Germany. As a re-

sult, Germany not only increased its power, but, of greater strategic importance, it no longer needed to fight on two fronts.

While Russia was crumbling, the first troops from the United States landed in France. German leaders sought to win the war before this new army could go into action. Following the Brest-Litovsk treaty, General Erich von Ludendorff sent almost every German soldier to the Western Front and in a massive offensive, his troops drove ahead. But at Château-Thierry, American and French troops, under the command of General Ferdinand Foch of France, stopped the Germans. Ludendorff then launched one final, desperate offensive, which was countered by Foch. Under the force of the combined Allied drive, the German attack was decisively smashed.

The tide turned for the Allies. By the time of Ludendorff's last offensive, American troops were arriving in France by the thousands. Under General John J. Pershing, the commander of the American Expeditionary Force (AEF), they carried out brilliant offensives at St. Mihiel and in the Argonne Forest. In the autumn of 1918, Allied morale soared as it became clear that German strength was spent. One by one Germany's allies quit. Bulgaria, overwhelmed by Allied forces advancing from Greece, sued for peace in September; the British, after conquering Turkish lands along the eastern Mediterranean, forced Turkey to sign an armistice on October 30; Austria-Hungary, besieged by Italian troops, surrendered on November 3. That same day German sailors mutinied at Kiel, and four days later a revolution broke out in Germany. A republic was founded, and the kaiser fled to Holland. Thus ended the Hohenzollern government and the Second German Reich.

Officials of the new German government agreed to an armistice, requesting that the peace settlement be based on the Fourteen Points that President Wilson had set forth in a speech before Congress on January 8, 1918. Wilson had recommended an end of secret agreements; freedom of the seas in peace and in war; reduction of armaments; the right of nationality groups to form their own nations; an association of nations to keep the peace. In other speeches Wilson called for a negotiated peace with reasonable demands on the vanquished. He proposed as a peace aim, "No annexations, no contributions; no punitive indemnities." The Allies agreed somewhat reluctantly to model the peace settlement on the Fourteen Points.

Early in the morning of November 11, 1918, in a railroad car in the Compiègne Forest in northern France, two German delegates met Allied officials to sign the armistice. The Allies demanded that Germany vacate all Allied territory; allow Allied forces to occupy Germany west of the Rhine River; give up thousands of its locomotives, freight cars, and trucks, and large numbers of its submarines and warships. The Germans signed the armistice, and the fighting ceased.

Section Review

1. With what success did the opposing powers fight from 1914 to 1917? What was achieved in the outstanding offensives?
2. What action did Britain take for control of the seas? How did the British response affect Germany?
3. What made the United States abandon its policy of neutrality?
4. How did the Bolshevik revolution affect the course of the war in Russia?
5. What factors led to victory for the Allies?

4 **The victors tried to build a lasting peace**

No previous war in the world's history had been responsible for such widespread horror. More than 10 million men were killed in battle; 20 million more were wounded; and 13 million civilians died from famine, disease, or war injuries. In addition, the cost of the war was estimated to have totaled more than $350 billion.

Gathering momentum during the wartime years was the belief in a league of nations, whereby governments could discuss differences and avoid war. The organization of such a league was a major concern of President Wilson. Indeed, he considered it the most important of his Fourteen Points. After the armistice was signed, the Allied Nations met at Paris to discuss peace terms. Although many of the delegates hoped to build a permanent peace, each delegation also had the interests of its own nation to advance.

Three men played the leading roles at the Paris Peace Conference. Contrary to Wilson's wishes, the Central Powers were denied representation at the peace conference, and the so-called Big Three dominated the meeting. They included President Wilson, David Lloyd George, prime minister of Great Britain, and Georges Clemenceau, premier of France.

Woodrow Wilson was an idealist who was handicapped by his unwillingness to compromise his principles and by his inability to negotiate skillfully. Yet he expressed the hopes of people everywhere that the conflict had been "a war to end war." At the conference Wilson upheld the idealistic peace conditions outlined in his Fourteen Points and insisted on an association to keep the peace.

David Lloyd George was a clever politician and skillful diplomat. He had aroused audiences in England with his promise to secure the "squeezing of the German lemon until the pips squeaked." Committed to carry out the pledge of his political party, the Liberals, Lloyd George was determined that Great Britain should take over the German colonies, that the German navy be destroyed, and that Germany pay the cost of the war.

Georges Clemenceau, known as the "Old Tiger," had led France during its darkest hours. At seventy-seven years of age, he was interested primarily in the security of France. He wanted to prevent at all costs a resurgence of German strength so that France would never again be invaded. The French Chamber of Deputies supported his announcement that France would rely for its security upon its alliances and the traditonal balance of power. Clemenceau placed little faith in a league of nations.

The League of Nations Covenant became part of the Versailles Treaty. Once the conference began, the Allies forsook Wilson's idealism in favor of secret agreements made during the war. For example, Turkish and African territories had been pledged to Italy; Japan had been promised German concessions in China; Rumania was to receive portions of Austria-Hungary; Britain had made vague promises of independence to the Arabs; and France and Britain had agreed between themselves on the division of Turkish Iraq and Syria.

Wilson gave in to the Allies on many details so that he could direct his main effort toward the acceptance of an association of nations. Finally, the participants agreed to embody the Covenant of the League of Nations in the treaty. The Covenant outlined the organization, purpose, and powers of a new world league, dedicated to the maintenance of peace among the nations of the world.

Germany lost territory and wealth. When the German delegation arrived to sign the treaty, they found its terms harsher than they had anticipated. For example, Article 231 stated:

The Allied and Associated Governments affirm and Germany accepts the responsibility of Germany and her allies for causing all the loss and damage to which the Allied and Associated Governments and their nationals have been subjected as a consequence of the war imposed upon them by the aggression of Germany and her allies.

The Germans were angered at this war-guilt clause, which placed the entire blame for the war on Germany. In addition, they were disappointed to find that many of Wilson's Fourteen Points were missing or were weakened by changes. The first delegates from Germany refused the treaty, but rather than subject Germany to Allied occupation, a second delegation signed it on

June 28, 1919, five years to the day after the Sarajevo incident.

In the peace settlement Clemenceau of France won back the provinces of Alsace-Lorraine. He also wanted the German territory west of the Rhine, a strip of land about 10 thousand square miles in extent, to become a buffer state under French control. Lloyd George and Wilson, opposing this idea, worked out a compromise whereby the area was to be occupied by Allied troops for at least fifteen years. Wilson and Lloyd George also promised to guarantee France against German aggression. France was given the rich coal mines of the Saar, but the territory itself was to be administered by the League of Nations. After fifteen years, the Saarlanders could vote to have their region restored to the German government or remain under the French. (In 1935 they voted to be a part of Germany.)

In March 1917 Poland had become independent of Russia and, through the Versailles Treaty, it won a broad stretch of land from Germany. This region, known as the Polish Corridor, gave Poland an outlet to the Baltic Sea. The Polish Corridor also divided Germany, isolating its province of East Prussia.

The Versailles Treaty gave German possessions in Africa and in the Pacific to the League of Nations, which in turn placed them under the control of the Allied nations. These lands, known as mandates, were allocated mainly to Great Britain and France, but also to Japan, South Africa, Australia, and New Zealand. The Allied nations commissioned to administer the laws of the mandates were subject to rules established by the League and had to submit a detailed report annually.

The Allies also insisted that Germany pay the cost of the conflict and demanded an immediate payment of $5 billion in cash. Two years later, they billed Germany for $32 billion, plus interest.

Determined to reduce German military power, the diplomats in Paris permitted Germany an army of not more than 100 thousand men. The navy was allowed only six warships and some other craft. No submarines or military airplanes were permitted.

Allied demands on Germany had left its statesmen stunned, but they were not alone in thinking the peace terms unjust. Even David Lloyd George was in doubt about the justice of the Versailles Treaty. President Wilson was disappointed that his Fourteen Points had been modified, but he was encouraged by the agreement to form the League of Nations. He hoped it could keep the peace, and that after a few years the unjust features of the treaty could be eased.

New independent nations were formed. Four empires had collapsed in the course of World War I—the German, Austro-Hungarian, Turkish, and Russian. The Allies concluded a series of peace treaties with the Hapsburg and Turkish empires and reorganized the land lost by Russia to Germany in the Brest-Litovsk Treaty. From the western portion of old Russia, five new nations were created: Poland, Finland, Latvia, Lithuania, and Estonia.

After the defeat of Austria-Hungary in 1918, nationalist groups proclaimed their independence of Austria and established republics. Austria and Hungary also became two independent republics. Their boundaries and those of the other new republics—Yugoslavia and Czechoslovakia—were redefined by the Allies when peace terms were negotiated. Most of the former Austrian territory was awarded to Poland, Italy, Yugoslavia, and Czechoslovakia. Hungarian lands were given to Rumania, Yugoslavia, and Czechoslovakia.

The Turkish Empire was also dismembered. Syria, Iraq, and Palestine became mandates, the first administered by

The Versailles Treaty was signed in the Hall of Mirrors of the great palace. It represented the hard work of delegates from about thirty nations. Leader of the American delegation was Woodrow Wilson, seated at the table fifth from left. He was the first American President to visit Europe while holding office. Seated at his left are Georges Clemenceau of France and David Lloyd George of England. Across the table, two German officials sign the document. Germany had not been invited to participate in the peace conference, and the first German representatives resigned when they read the harsh provisions of the treaty. However, a second delegation reluctantly signed it, realizing that the German government actually had no choice in the matter.

France, and the last two by Britain. These mandates were promised independence at a future time. The independent kingdom of Hejaz was recognized in Arabia.

One of Wilson's Fourteen Points, that of self-determination, or the right of peoples to form their own nations, had been partially fulfilled in the creation of new states. However, the changed political boundaries again brought nationality groups under foreign control. For example, Austrians living in the Tyrol came under the rule of Italy, while other German-speaking Austrians (the Sudetens) were placed under Czechoslovakian rule. Some Germans lived in the new Polish Corridor, and certain Hungarians came under Rumanian control.

Few of these peoples were completely reconciled to the changes made in their lives. Their discontent was an ominous sign of troubled times for the future of Europe.

Section Review

1. How did the aims of the countries represented by the Big Three differ?
2. What factors prevented all Fourteen Points of Woodrow Wilson from becoming a part of the Versailles Treaty?
3. In what ways did the Versailles Treaty satisfy each of the Big Three?
4. What were the chief effects of the peace terms on Germany? on its allies?
5. How were nationality groups affected by the treaties?

Chapter 26 ▨▨▨▨▨▨▨▨ A Review

In 1914 Serbia dreamed of building a Greater Serbia that would include neighboring Slavic groups in the Balkans. Its ambition menaced the Austro-Hungarian Empire, which was the home of many Slavs. Russia encouraged Serbia, hoping to gain an outlet to the Mediterranean Sea through two Balkan straits that were ruled by Turkey. Germany also wanted influence in the Balkans in order to extend its economic interests in the Near East. However, Britain objected to Germany or any other country posing a threat to its route to India and China.

In 1914 at Sarajevo, a member of a Slavic secret society murdered Archduke Francis Ferdinand of Austria, creating a war between Austria and Serbia. The war immediately involved Russia, a friend of Serbia, and Germany, a partner of Austria. France and Great Britain joined Russia, and ultimately twenty-seven Allied nations, including Italy and the United States, fought against the Central Powers headed by Germany, Austria, and Turkey.

From 1914 to 1917, France and Britain fought bitterly with Germany on the Western Front. The British blockade in the North Sea prevented trade between Germany and neutral nations and reduced food supplies in Germany. In turn, German submarines sank so much Allied shipping that England was brought almost to starvation.

In 1917 Bolshevik Russians made a separate peace with Germany. In 1917 also the United States declared war on the Central Powers after Germany opened unrestricted submarine warfare and encouraged Mexico to attack the United States. In 1918 thousands of American soldiers joined the French and British in France. Together the Allies pushed the Germans back toward the French-German border and forced the Central Powers to ask for peace.

In his Fourteen Points, President Wilson had set forth a basis for peace, but few of Wilson's proposals were acceptable to the other victorious powers. Agreement was reached, however, on Wilson's proposed new concert of nations, the League of Nations.

The major portion of the treaty deprived Germany of territory, wealth, and military strength. Other treaties with the Central Powers defined boundaries of new states formed from former empires. Some nationality groups gained independence, but others were unhappily placed under foreign control.

The Time

Place these events of the World War I period in their correct chronological sequence.
Lusitania was sunk.
Archduke Francis Ferdinand was murdered.
Treaty of Brest-Litovsk was signed.
Austria annexed Bosnia and Herzegovina.
Armistice ending World War I was signed.
First Balkan War broke out.
United States declared war on Germany.
Treaty of Versailles was signed.
England declared war on Germany.
Austria issued an ultimatum to Serbia.

The Place

1. Locate each of the places named below and describe its part in the Balkan crisis leading to World War I.

Dardanelles Bosnia   Rumania
Herzegovina Albania   Bulgaria
Sarajevo   Serbia

2. Locate the site and tell the outcome of each of the following battles of World War I.

Château-Thierry Marne River Verdun
Masurian Lakes Tannenberg Jutland
Argonne Forest Gallipoli Ypres
Somme River   Caporetto

3. From what empires were all or parts of the following independent countries created after World War I?

Czechoslovakia Estonia
Yugoslavia   Finland
Lithuania   Hejaz
Poland   Latvia

4. By the terms of the peace treaties after World War I, which country gained and which lost the following areas? Polish Corridor, Alsace-Lorraine.

5. What agreement was reached about the Saar?

The People

1. Describe the role of each of the following men in the 1914 Austrian-Serbian crisis that led to World War I.

Francis Ferdinand   William II
Leopold von Berchtold Edward Grey
Francis Joseph I

2. Cite one military achievement of each of the following generals of World War I and the country for which he fought.

Erich von Ludendorff Henri Pétain
Paul von Hindenburg Joseph Joffre
John J. Pershing   Ferdinand Foch

3. State the major objectives of each of the Big Three at the Paris Peace Conference.

Historical Terms

1. Show how each of the following terms applied to events leading to World War I.

Berlin-to-Bagdad railroad "blank check"
Greater Serbia   mobilization
Pan-Slavism   ultimatum

2. Use each of the following terms in a sentence that describes one or more events that occurred during World War I.

Central Powers   Allies
Eastern Front   AEF
Western Front   armistice
naval blockade   neutrality
Zimmermann note

3. Define each of the following terms as applied to the peace settlements after World War I.

covenant   self-determination
war-guilt clause   Fourteen Points
mandates

Questions for Critical Thinking

1. Why were the Balkans prior to World War I called the "powder keg of Europe"?

2. For what reasons were the major European powers unable to bring about a settlement of the dispute between Austria and Serbia and thereby prevent a general European war?

3. Explain why the Germans continued unrestricted submarine warfare even when they realized that it might bring the United States into the war.

4. For what reasons did Italy withdraw from the Triple Alliance in 1914 and join the Allies in 1915?

5. What did President Wilson mean when he said that the war was "a war to end war"?

6. In your opinion, were the immediate and long-term effects of World War I more disastrous than those of any previous war? Why or why not?

7. Were the Germans justified in resenting the war-guilt clause of the Treaty of Versailles? Explain your answer carefully.

Introduction to Unit 10

Challenges to Democracy and World War II

The painting on the opposite page by the contemporary American artist Jack Levine is entitled "1932." It portrays one event in the period between World War I and World War II which had a marked influence on world history. In that fateful year Germany was suffering from the effects of a world-wide depression. The German people were confused and restless, and the unemployed were in an ugly mood. No statesmen of high caliber emerged to help guide the nation. Instead, politicians, adventurers, and militarists schemed for power.

The three figures in the painting are actors in a sordid drama. In the center is Paul von Hindenburg, the president of Germany, who was over eighty years old, doddering, and almost senile. An officer in the Franco-Prussian War and a hero of World War I, he once confessed that he had read nothing but military literature since his cadet days. Receiving a baton, a symbol for governmental power, is the newly appointed chancellor, Adolf Hitler,

who wears the uniform of the Nazi party. An embittered veteran of World War I, he had attained success as a politician and a fanatical rabble rouser. To the left, eying the scene through his monocle, is a third man. Although Mr. Levine, the artist, has declared that no specific person is intended, the figure could be said to represent the elegant aristocrat and wealthy industrialist, Franz von Papen. It was the wily von Papen who was responsible for Hindenburg's selection of Hitler. With hopes of becoming the "power behind the throne," von Papen influenced Hindenburg to agree that Hitler should become chancellor even though the Nazi party did not hold a majority of votes in the Reichstag. Von Papen planned to use Hitler for his own ends, but the plan misfired completely. Hitler himself gained control of Germany and kept a firm grasp on the reins of power.

The scene depicted in the painting took place about midway in the period from 1919 to 1945, which is discussed in the four chapters of this unit. This period is

CHAPTER 27 / THE LEAGUE OF NATIONS AND THE SEARCH FOR PEACE	CHAPTER 28 / THE RISE OF COMMUNISM IN RUSSIA	
	Decembrist Revolt	
		185•
	Crimean War serfs emancipated	
		190•
Chinese revolution revolution in Mexico Arab revolt Balfour Declaration League of Nations Gandhi Weimar republic	Russo-Japanese War "Bloody Sunday" First Duma Bolshevik Revolution Lenin provisional government Period of Militant Communism civil war Comintern	192•
Washington Conference Sun Yat-sen Little Entente Egypt a sovereign state Corfu incident Mustapha Kemal Ruhr invaded Dawes Plan	New Economic Policy U.S.S.R. established Treaty of Rapallo Stalin eliminated Trotsky	192
Locarno treaties Kellogg-Briand Pact Chiang Kai-shek	Stalin's first Five-Year Plan	193
Iraq independent Commonwealth of Nations Saudi Arabia established	United States recognized U.S.S.R. U.S.S.R. admitted to League	193
Indian provinces given self-government	"Stalin Constitution" reign of terror Hitler-Stalin nonaggression pact	194
		194

crowded with interesting personalities, dramatic events, and important movements. During the 1920's, a time of hope and growing prosperity, the world seemed to be on the verge of solving many difficult problems. The League of Nations included most of the important countries of the world. Although limited in its powers, it worked to maintain peace. The worldwide depression of the 1930's destroyed the optimism of the preceding decade. Hunger and want were widespread. Men out of work were desperate. Hard times offered would-be dictators the chance to gain power by preying on the fears of the people. Many of the new democracies set up after World War I became dictatorships.

In the older and stronger democracies—the United States, Great Britain, and France—democratic methods of rule were maintained. However, the preoccupation of the more stable democratic nations with problems of the depression gave dictators the opportunity for aggression and expansion. In 1931 Japan invaded the rich Chi-

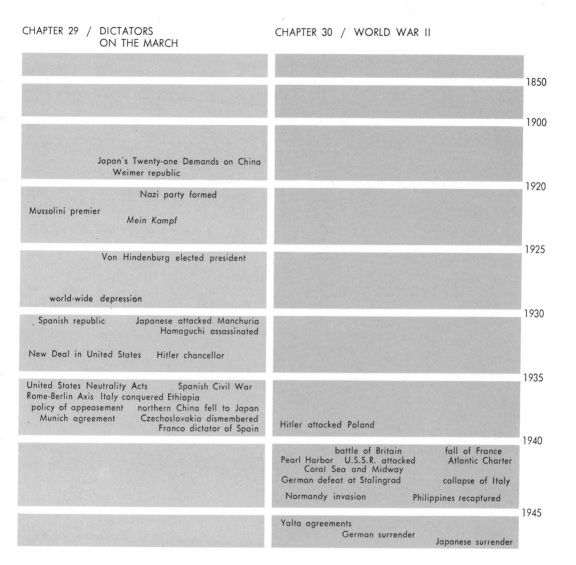

1850

1900

Japan's Twenty-one Demands on China
Weimer republic

1920

Nazi party formed

Mussolini premier

Mein Kampf

1925

Von Hindenburg elected president

world-wide depression

1930

Spanish republic   Japanese attacked Manchuria
Hamaguchi assassinated

New Deal in United States   Hitler chancellor

1935

United States Neutrality Acts   Spanish Civil War
Rome-Berlin Axis Italy conquered Ethiopia
policy of appeasement   northern China fell to Japan
Munich agreement   Czechoslovakia dismembered
Franco dictator of Spain

Hitler attacked Poland

1940

battle of Britain   fall of France
Pearl Harbor   U.S.S.R. attacked   Atlantic Charter
Coral Sea and Midway
German defeat at Stalingrad   collapse of Italy

Normandy invasion   Philippines recaptured

1945

Yalta agreements
German surrender
Japanese surrender

nese province of Manchuria. In 1935 Italy seized defenseless Ethiopia. In 1938 Hitler invaded Austria and, in the autumn of the same year, he and his fellow dictator, Mussolini, dismembered Czechoslovakia. By 1939 it became crystal clear to Britain and France that they would have to make a stand against fascist aggression or be themselves conquered.

When Hitler invaded Poland, Britain and France declared war. With Germany's attack on the Soviet Union and Japan's treachery against the United States at Pearl Harbor, the conflict became world-wide. The United States, the U.S.S.R. and Britain made up *the Grand Alliance* against fascism. Fierce fighting took place in Europe, the South Pacific, Southeast Asia, North Africa, and the Mediterranean. In June 1944 the Allies invaded France and, after almost a year of bitter warfare, Germany surrendered. Victory in the Pacific came in August 1945 when Japan capitulated after two atomic bomb attacks. Battered and weary, the world then turned to the serious problems of peacemaking.

The League of Nations
and the Search for Peace

"This hammer works for peace," reads the caption of a French cartoon that reflects the faith in disarmament shared by many diplomats in the 1920's. Shown are the foreign ministers of three European nations. Aristide Briand of France demolishes a rifle while Sir Austen Chamberlain of Great Britain, left, and Gustav Stresemann of Germany, center, await their turns to destroy weapons of war.

I think I ought to tell you," said a British colonel in the Grenadier Guards, "that we were not consulted at all on the matter of your coming to join us." He was speaking to Major Winston Churchill, who had just joined the army and was reporting to the colonel in France. A few months before, on May 27, 1915, Churchill had resigned from his cabinet post as First Lord of the Admiralty in disgrace. A campaign that he had sponsored on the Gallipoli Peninsula against the Turks early in 1915 had ended in failure, and Churchill was blamed for the death of thousands of British soldiers. Although later developments indicated that the campaign could have been successful had Churchill's course of action not been overruled, the fact remained that in 1915 the British people wanted no more of him.

After several months at the front lines in France, Churchill regained a measure of public esteem, and he also returned to his seat in the House of Commons. In the fall of 1916, he was again in the cabinet, this time as Minister of Munitions, one of the highest positions in the government. From then on to the end of the war, Churchill experienced seasons of tragedy and triumph, both in his personal and public life. After the close of the conflict, he wrote his war memoirs, entitled *The World Crisis,* and in a final passage of this great narrative, Churchill said:

The curtain falls upon the long front in France and Flanders. The soothing hands of Time and Nature, the swift repair of peaceful industry, have already almost effaced the crater fields and the battle lines which in a broad belt from the Vosges to the sea lately blackened the smiling fields of France. The ruins are rebuilt . . . . Only the cemeteries . . . assail the traveller with the fact that . . . millions . . . shed their blood or perished . . . . Merciful oblivion draws its veils; the crippled limp away; the mourners fall back into the sad twi-

light of memory. New youth is here to claim its rights, and the perennial stream flows forward. . . .

Is this the end? Is it to be merely a chapter in a cruel and senseless story? Will a new generation in their turn be immolated to square the black accounts of Teuton and Gaul? Will our children bleed and gasp again in devastated lands? Or will there spring from the very fires of conflict that reconciliation of the three giant combatants, which would unite their genius and secure to each in safety and freedom a share in rebuilding the glory of Europe?

Chapter 27 describes the different ways in which statesmen and ordinary people the world over faced the difficult and complex problems of the postwar era of the 1920's. Their successes and failures are described in the five sections entitled:

1. **The League of Nations began its work.**

2. **Statesmen sought to solve problems of peace.**

3. **Democracy faced new trials in Europe.**

4. **The American nations faced contrasting social problems.**

5. **Nationalism developed in Africa, in the Near East, and in Asia.**

1 The League of Nations began its work

To a world facing many grave problems, the League of Nations represented a force for peace. Its headquarters were established in imposing white buildings overlooking Lake Geneva, Switzerland, and the city of Geneva was regarded as the peace capital of the world. By 1920 League membership had reached a total of forty-two nations. (In 1937, when Egypt became the last nation to join, sixty-three nations were included on the League roster.)

The United States refused to join the League. Although the League of Nations was regarded as the inspiration of President Woodrow Wilson, the United States Senate refused to ratify the Treaty of Versailles, which included the Covenant of the League of Nations. Wilson's political opponents argued that the concept of the League ran counter to the Founding Fathers' advice against "entangling alliances" with foreign nations. Moreover, they believed that the provisions of the treaty violated the Monroe Doctrine. Article 21 of the Covenant stated that the Monroe Doctrine would remain in force, but the United States Senate refused to ratify the treaty.

Leading the opposition to the League was Senator Henry Cabot Lodge of Massachusetts, who succeeded in turning public opinion against ratification. The rejection by the Senate, Wilson felt, disgraced the nation in the eyes of the world. The American people, he warned, had "to learn now by bitter experience just what they have lost." Yet Wilson himself refused most of the compromises offered by the opposition, thus contributing to the failure of his program. In the presidential elections of 1920, the Democratic party was defeated at the polls, and the victorious Republican candidate, Warren G. Harding, viewed the ratification of the treaty as a dead issue. The refusal by the United States to join the League was a damaging blow to the newborn organization.

The League had three main parts. The Assembly, the Council, and the Secretariat made up the major divisions of the League. The Assembly, or the parliament of the League, was composed of representatives from all member nations. It carried on the business of the League: the admission of new members, the establishment of the annual budget, and the amendment of the League constitution, or Covenant. Any matter endangering the peace of the world could be taken up by the Assembly. Somewhat unwieldly because of its size, it became the forum for lengthy debates.

The Council, a smaller body, served as the board of directors of the League. At first, it was composed of representatives from eight nations—Great Britain, France, Italy, and Japan, which held permanent seats, and four others elected annually. Later on, both Germany (admitted to the League in 1926) and the USSR (admitted in 1934) held permanent seats on the Council. A unanimous vote by Council members was required on important decisions.

The Secretariat was the office force of the League, and its international civil service was pledged to serve the interests of all members.

The purposes of the League were to serve world peace. The League had three chief functions: (1) to prevent war; (2) to carry out the provisions of the peace treaties; (3) to assist in the improvement of social and economic conditions.

In order to prevent war, the League gave constant attention to the task of securing a reduction of armaments. It sought also to abolish secret diplomacy, insisting that all treaties and international agreements be registered with the League. Members agreed to submit to League arbitration any dispute that could not be settled peaceably and to abide by the decision handed down. They agreed also to take joint action against any member that ignored a League decision. One of the weapons permitted by the League took the form of *economic sanctions,* by which League members would sever all financial and commercial relations with a defiant nation and, in effect, isolate it. The League had no military troops of its own to enforce its decisions, but if sanctions failed to prove effective, the Council could then request members to supply military forces against the outlaw nation. The judges of the Permanent Court of International Justice, or World Court, were selected by the League, and the majority of League members were pledged to accept court rulings concerning questions of international law.

In fulfillment of its second function—the maintenance of the peace treaties—the League arranged plebiscites (direct votes by the people) in Poland and Germany to determine boundaries. It administered Danzig, an international seaport on the Baltic, and the rich coal and iron basin of the Saar. To supervise the operation of the colonial mandates system, a Permanent Mandates Commission was set up.

The final task of the League was to help improve economic and social conditions the world over. The International Labor Organization (ILO) collected a wealth of valuable statistical information and sought to improve working conditions and wage levels. The reforms suggested by the ILO were often used as a charter of rights for labor groups in individual member nations. The League attacked many problems spawned by the war and its aftermath. Some 400 thousand prisoners of war were repatriated and thousands of refugees were resettled. Loans to new nations, such as Hungary and Austria, were arranged. In the field of education, the League encouraged coöperative research projects and gave attention to rebuilding schools and restocking libraries. In the realm of public health, the League helped control epidemics, standardize serums and drugs, and establish international standards of nutrition. Its success in these fields encouraged the establishment of similar agencies when the United Nations was organized in 1945.

The League scored successes but suffered defeats. During its first ten years of existence, more than thirty serious disputes were brought before the League;

the majority were settled peaceably. A number of these controversies involved boundary claims, such as those between Greece and Bulgaria in 1925 and between Yugoslavia and Albania in 1927.

In contrast to these successes, some discouraging setbacks occurred. In 1922 a majority of the people in the city of Vilna, on the borders of Lithuania and Poland, voted for union with Poland. The district was duly united with Poland, but the two nations remained in a state of war for another five years. Peace was restored only when Lithuania abandoned its claims. League mediation attempts were fruitless.

The most serious failure came in 1923. While serving in Greece on an international boundary commission, an Italian general and four members of his staff were murdered by unknown assassins. Despite lack of evidence, Benito Mussolini, who had been recently granted dictatorial powers by the king of Italy, blamed the government of Greece and proceeded to exploit the incident to give his new Fascist regime an easy military triumph. Italian warships bombarded the island of Corfu and took possession of the port, while the League Council hesitated to intervene.

Italian troops were withdrawn from Corfu after the Council meekly approved a decision which ordered Greece to pay a cash indemnity demanded by Mussolini.

The Corfu incident revealed the fatal weaknesses of the League. Conflicts between small nations had presented no real challenge to League authority. In the Corfu affair, involving a major power, the League shirked the challenge.

Underlying the failures of the League were these factors: (1) the rule of unanimity on important decisions tended to block action; (2) the League had no standing military force of its own; (3) the League could recommend the use of military force, but members were not obligated to supply arms.

1. What were the duties of the League Assembly? the Council? the Secretariat?
2. What were the chief purposes of the League? What steps could member nations take against a nation that defied an order of the League?
3. In what respects did the League fail? In what respects did it succeed?

2 Statesmen sought to solve problems of peace

While the League of Nations was trying to strengthen peaceful relations, opposite forces were at work. The war had left a legacy of mistrust and fear, and hidden tensions were ever likely to disrupt the work of the League.

The French relied on defensive alliances. At the Paris Peace Conference, Great Britain and the United States had promised aid to France in the event of a German attack. After the United States Senate, in accordance with its mood of isolationism, refused to ratify this agreement, Britain also withdrew its promise. As a consequence, France began to seek allies in an attempt to circle Germany. In 1920, France signed a treaty with Belgium and, two years later, with Poland. French strength in central Europe was increased by the military and financial support it offered the Little Entente, a bloc formed in 1920 and 1921 by Rumania, Yugoslavia, and Czechoslovakia. A few years later, France signed separate agreements with each member of the bloc.

During the 1920's France and its allies were the military masters of Europe; no other alliance system challenged this supremacy. France and its allies did not encircle Germany completely, however. This geographical fact was a major check upon the strategic value of the alliance.

The reparations issue posed serious problems. In 1921 the Reparations Commission, which was not controlled by the League of Nations, fixed the total German debt to the Allies at $32 billion, an amount intended to compensate for civilian property losses incurred during the war. France was to get the lion's share, 52 per cent; Britain, 22 per cent; with the remainder to be parceled out among the other Allies, except the United States. It had waived all claims on reparations but demanded that war debts incurred by the Allies be paid.

The German payment in 1921 strained national resources to the limit, causing a dangerous decline in the value of its currency. As a result, Germany was permitted to delay its next payment. By July 1922, however, German gold reserves were exhausted. Britain was sympathetic to the plight of Germany, but France was determined that Germany meet its obligations. In addition, France believed that French dominance in Europe would be ensured for many years if the recovery of the German economy were retarded.

Following the German default of payments and rejecting British attempts to lighten the burden, France and Belgium (in January 1923) marched troops into the German Ruhr, an area of coal mines and steel mills. The French planned to use the income from the industries as part payment for reparations. But the German workers resorted to passive resistance, with the result that production in the mines and factories ceased. Because they were unfamiliar with the German equipment, the French had little success running the industries. Their occupation of the Ruhr was a failure: German resources were further strained and France received no reparations.

The year 1924 witnessed two events which offered hopes for a solution to the reparations problem. The Ruhr fiasco resulted in a new French government which

EUROPE
After World War I

ICELAND

NORWAY
SWEDEN
FINLAND

Oslo
Helsinki
Stockholm
Tallinn
Leningrad
(Petrograd)

Baltic
Sea
ESTONIA

GREAT
BRITAIN

North Sea

DENMARK

Copenhagen
Riga
LATVIA

Moscow

MEMEL
LITHUANIA

THE
NETHERLANDS

Danzig
EAST
PRUSSIA
Kaunas

Vilna

SOVIET UNION

London

The Hague
Berlin
*POLISH
CORRIDOR*

Brussels
BELGIUM
GERMANY
Warsaw

Versailles
Paris
LUXEMBURG
Weimar
POLAND

Kiev

SAAR

FRANCE
Prague
CZECHOSLOVAKIA

LIECHTEN-
STEIN
Vienna

Bern
SWITZ.
AUSTRIA
Budapest

Geneva
Locarno
HUNGARY
Odessa

UGAL

ANDORRA

YUGOSLAVIA
Belgrade
RUMANIA
Bucharest

TRANSCAUCASIA

Madrid
on
SPAIN

ITALY
Adriatic Sea

Black Sea

CORSICA
(Fr.)

Rome

BULGARIA
Sofia

BALEARIC IS.
(Sp.)

SARDINIA
(It.)

Tirana

ALBANIA

Constantinople
(Istanbul)

PANISH
AREA

CORFU
GREECE
Ankara

M e d i t e r r a n e a n

SICILY

*Aegean
Sea*

TURKEY

OCCO

MALTA
(Br.)

Athens

DODECANESE
IS. (It.)

SYRIA
(Fr. Mandate)
IRAQ
(Br. Mandate)

ALGERIA
TUNIS

CRETE
CYPRUS
(Br.)
Damascus

S e a

PALESTINE
(Br. Mandate)

00   200   300 MILES

Prepared by
Rand McNally & Co., Chicago

LIBYA

EGYPT

TRANS-
JORDAN
(Br. Mandate)
ARABIA

was more friendly toward Germany. And Charles G. Dawes, an American businessman and later Vice President of the United States, presented the report of a commission which had been formed to study the problem of reparations. Dawes and his associates recommended the French evacuation of the Ruhr, a system of graduated payments adjusted to the ability of Germany to pay, a loan to Germany, and the creation of a supervised German central bank to strengthen and direct finances. The Dawes plan was accepted in April 1924 by both Germany and its creditors, and the economic recovery of Germany began. With the aid of loans from the United States, the payments called for in the years immediately following were duly paid. In 1929, another commission headed by Owen D. Young, an American lawyer, further reduced the amount of German reparation payments.

Nations continued efforts toward disarmament. During the winter of 1921 and 1922, the United States invited representatives from eight nations to Washington, D.C., to discuss naval disarmament. There, Secretary of State Charles Evans Hughes outlined a bold plan to which the delegates finally agreed. An equal tonnage of battleships was allotted to the United States and to Britain, with proportionately lower allocations to Japan, Italy, and France. In addition, the representatives agreed that construction of large naval craft was to cease for ten years.

Further conferences on naval disarmament in London in 1927 and in Geneva in 1930 were marred by disagreements between the United States and Britain and between France and Italy. Nevertheless, the United States, Britain, and Japan were able to agree on the relative strengths of their cruiser and submarine fleets. (Japan had reached the status of a formidable power, and as such was allowed a fleet comparable to those of the United States and Britain.)

While limited progress had been achieved in the reduction of naval strength, the attempt to reduce land and air forces was a failure. From 1925 the League wrestled with this problem but ran into solid disagreement. Meanwhile, Germany, deprived of large military forces by the Treaty of Versailles, was becoming increasingly impatient over the failure of other European nations to disarm. The Germans felt at the mercy of their neighbors.

A resurgence of optimism appeared in Europe. International relations appeared to take another step forward in 1925 at a meeting held in the Swiss town of Locarno and attended by representatives of Germany, France, Britain, Belgium, Italy, Czechoslovakia, and Poland. Representatives signed a series of agreements in which their nations were pledged to settle disputes peaceably. One of the Locarno treaties guaranteed the existing frontiers between France and Germany and between Belgium and Germany, and it established the Rhineland as a neutral zone. The Locarno treaties heralded a new expectation of peace, and Germany accepted an invitation to join the League.

In 1928 the Kellogg-Briand Pact, or the Pact of Paris, furnished evidence of the optimism among world leaders. The French foreign minister Aristide Briand and the United States Secretary of State Frank Kellogg drew up this document, which renounced war. Over sixty nations signed it. However, this pact was simply a pledge on the part of the signatories not to use force in any international dispute; it contained no means of enforcing its provisions.

The years between 1925 and 1929 have been called the high period of Europe. Hope was in the air. At Locarno, Briand had declared:

> Peace for Germany and for France. That means that we have done with the long series of terrible conflicts . . . which have stained the pages of history. . . . Away with rifles, machine-guns, cannon! Clear the way for conciliation, arbitration, peace!

But his hopes were exaggerated. Under the apparently calm surface of the European diplomatic sea ran deep and dangerous currents of suspicion and fear. There were strong doubts of League ability to ward off armed attack, based on its failure to secure reduction in air and land forces. The Locarno pacts were little more than a gesture on the part of old foes who later proved not to have the courage of their convictions.

Section Review

1. What steps did France take to increase its power at the expense of Germany?

2. List the events in the years between 1924 and 1928 which gave promise of world peace.

3. To what degree were the disarmament conferences of the 1920's successful?

3   Democracy faced new trials in Europe

In 1919 men indeed believed that the Great War had been fought "to make the world safe for democracy." The map of Europe was transformed as old empires were carved up to establish new democratic states. Many people had their first opportunity to live under governments of their own choosing. But in the new democracies, serious political and economic problems—coupled with the lack of experience in democratic methods—threatened the growth of stable governments. The old democracies, such as Britain and France, faced crucial issues also, but their representative systems of government were deeply rooted and the people were accustomed to solving problems by democratic methods.

Britain experienced political and social changes. Much of the overseas trade upon which British prosperity depended had been captured during the war by the United States and Japan. Mines, factories, and shops in Britain went into debt or shut down entirely and, after the war, unemployment became widespread. About a million people, including many men recently released from the armed forces, were out of work—a state of affairs which continued throughout the 1920's. One measure designed to ease the problem was the grant to the unemployed of an insurance payment known as the Dole. In 1926 discontent in the coal mines triggered a general strike of trade-union members. Although the strike lasted for only a few weeks and was settled peaceably, conditions still did not improve for the workers.

The close of the war had seen the rise of the Labour party which more or less took over the role of the old Liberal party. Under James Ramsay MacDonald, the first Labour government followed a mild socialist policy which made little headway against unemployment. A Conservative government that followed, led by Stanley Baldwin, had no more success. Despite ineffective leadership, Britain preserved its democratic institutions, while its governments "muddled through" the years following World War I.

During this time important political changes occurred in the relationship between Britain and its empire. In the 19th century a desire for self-government had been growing in colonies populated by European stock, such as Canada. By 1914 Canada, Australia, New Zealand, and the Union of South Africa had gained self-government, but Britain remained in control of foreign affairs. In theory, the British Parliament was still superior to the colonial assemblies. During World War I, troops from these four colonies fought in large numbers beside those from Britain. Having shouldered equal responsibility, the colonials felt they deserved the status of independent nations. Each one sent representatives to the Paris Peace Conference, and all were admitted to the League of Nations. In 1926 recognition of the equality between Britain and its dominions was given at an imperial conference in London when it was stated that these nations were "autonomous communities within the British Empire, equal in status, in no way subordinate to one another."

Again in 1931 the British Parliament expressed this equality in the Statute of Westminster by creating a Commonwealth of Nations completely free of British parliamentary control. Members of the Commonwealth became voluntary partners, held together by loyalty to the British crown and by common traditions. Advantageous trade agreements also strengthened the unity of the Commonwealth.

Instability marked the French government. Serious financial problems arose in France when German reparations were not paid, but the country as a whole was prosperous. Industry boomed and the people enjoyed full employment. With its military allies, France was supreme on the Continent until the early 1930's. However, serious flaws marred the pattern of French politics.

First of all, numerous political parties in France made the formation of a stable government difficult. The events of the 1920's and the decade following seemed to bear out the truth of an old saying, "One Frenchman—intelligence; two Frenchmen —debate; three Frenchmen—anarchy." In order to gain the support of a majority in the legislature, the premier had the difficult task of securing the backing of several other parties as well as his own.

Another factor contributing to political unrest was the French mode of changing leadership. In Britain, members of Parliament were wary of voting out a government without strong reason. Ever since the early 18th century, when the first prime minister took office, he also became leader of the majority party in the House of Commons. From that time whenever a prime minister resigned—willingly or otherwise —the whole government fell. The people then had to elect a new parliament, and members of the House of Commons had to campaign against new candidates to regain their seats in parliament. In France, members of the National Assembly of Deputies (which is roughly comparable to the House of Commons) had security of tenure. They could force a premier and his cabinet to resign without risk of losing

their own places in the assembly, and a vote of "no confidence" by the assembly did not bring on a general election. As a result, before a premier had time to carry through his policies, he could be voted out of office. Then a new premier would be in power, leading a new political line-up with different policies. From 1919 to 1937, thirty-four governments held office.

In Germany the Weimar Republic was established. Germany began the years of reconstruction with a new national assembly which met at Weimar in January 1919. The new constitution, adopted in July 1919, included many democratic features: freedom of speech and religion was guaranteed, compulsory education of children was recognized, and labor unions were protected by the right of free association. However, other aspects of the constitution proved to be serious defects to democracy. The president was granted certain emergency powers which made it possible in 1933 for a dictatorship to take over the government by legal means. Another serious defect was a complicated system of allocating seats in the legislative assembly according to the votes of the people. This system led to the development of many small political parties, which prevented any one party from gaining a majority in the assembly and led to the kind of political instability which prevailed in France. Extremists on the Right and on the Left threatened the new government. They blamed the ruling group—a coalition of socialist parties—for accepting the hated Treaty of Versailles and regarded the socialists as traitors to their fatherland. The power of the extremists grew stronger as the German economy wavered.

The Weimar Republic hoped to convince the world of German good faith by the prompt payment of Allied reparation claims. But the intolerable burden of these payments was a central factor in the

Postwar Problems impeded the recovery of European nations. When Germany fell behind in paying its huge war debt, the French and Belgians seized German industries in the Ruhr in 1923. Above, French soldiers man a German locomotive. Britain was plagued by labor troubles. Below left, British police and workers clash during the general strike of 1926, which involved about 2½ million men. That same year, political disputes in Poland led to a revolution and street fighting, below right.

wild inflation of 1922 and 1923. People saw their life savings wiped out as prices skyrocketed upward. At the end of the war, a United States dollar was worth about four German marks. Four years later 7000 marks equaled one dollar. In 1923 the exchange between dollars and marks was measured in millions, and then billions, of marks. Finally, in 1924, the Weimar government set up a new currency system, increased taxation, and secured large loans from the United States. These measures, along with the adoption of the Dawes plan and the evacuation of the Ruhr, aided the recovery of the economy.

Between 1925 and 1929, the Weimar Republic enjoyed an increase in popular support. Industrial production was restored to prewar levels and in time was second only to that of the United States. However, democracy in Germany remained a fragile force. It was feared that a return of unemployment or inflation would strengthen the extremists who were eager for any opportunity to overthrow the government.

Democracy fared poorly in most of eastern Europe. A number of factors worked against the growth of strong democratic states in eastern and southern Europe. Many of the people in this area were illiterate, and in addition, the existence of many quarrelsome nationality groups obstructed lawmaking in the legislative assemblies. Economic factors were also important. The lack of modern industry and the backwardness of agricultural methods kept standards of living low, while wealthy landowners blocked urgently needed reforms in order to preserve their traditional privileges.

Poland, which had been wiped off the map at the end of the 18th century, was reëstablished as a nation and proclaimed a republic in 1918. The building of a strong state was hampered, however, by reactionary aristocrats who prevented land reform and social progress. In 1926 a Polish general, Marshal Jósef Pilsudski, took over the government and, little by little, assumed dictatorial powers. South of Poland lay Austria, reduced to a small state about the size of Maine. Many Austrians felt that only *Anschluss,* or union with Germany, could solve the nation's economic problems, but this move was forbidden by the terms of the peace. Neighboring Hungary had also lost territory and population. In 1918 the Hungarian republic fell prey to a Communist government which in turn was ousted by a new regime in 1919. Although Hungary was formally a monarchy, the throne remained vacant. The real ruler was Admiral Miklós von Horthy, who ran the government with an iron hand.

Only one of the postwar democracies established in eastern Europe was considered a success: Czechoslovakia. This new nation benefited from the enlightened leadership of its president, Thomas G. Masaryk. Businessmen prospered because foreign trade was encouraged and industry boomed.

In southern Europe, the newly created state of Yugoslavia was an unhappy combination of Serbs and Croats whose rivalries caused continual strife and dissension. Before the end of the 1920's, a dictatorship was set up—a pattern all too typical of most of the other Balkan nations. Italy, the strongest power in southern Europe, succumbed to Mussolini and his Black Shirts in 1922, as discussed in Chapter 29.

The record of democracy on the European continent was not all dismal. The Low Countries, Switzerland, the neutral nations of Scandinavia—Norway, Sweden, Denmark—and the new state of Finland prospered and enjoyed good government.

Turkey made progress under a benevolent dictatorship. Situated on the fringe of Europe but closely associated with it throughout history was Turkey. Having opposed the Allies in World War I, Turkey was obliged not only to accept drastic reductions in its territory, but also to surrender its independence. Although the government and the sultan remained in Istanbul, the capital, Turkey was placed largely under the control of the Allies. Aroused nationalists began a campaign in 1920 to keep Turkey from being entirely dismembered, and, led by Mustafa Kemal, a patriot and military genius, they set up a government at Ankara. In 1922 they overthrew the sultan and established a republic. The next year the Allies were forced to conclude a treaty with Kemal, restoring some of the lost territory to Turkey and recognizing its independence.

Mustafa Kemal, elected president in 1923, wielded supreme power in the new Turkish republic, but his rule was benevolent. It was his plan to carry out badly needed reforms and prepare his people for self-government. In addition, his measures were intended to Westernize the land and its people. Kemal abolished polygamy, forbade men to wear the fez and women the veil, introduced the Western alphabet and calender, made notable improvements in education, and required everyone to choose a surname. For himself Kemal chose the name Atatürk, meaning "father of all the Turks."

Section Review

1. How did postwar conditions in Britain lead to unemployment and labor unrest?
2. What political changes in the British Empire resulted as movements for independence increased?
3. How did the numerous political parties in France contribute to instability in government?
4. What threats faced the democratic movement in Germany?
5. What success did other new democratic nations have?

4 **The American nations faced contrasting social problems**

While Europe struggled to regain its prewar well-being, the United States experienced rapid economic development and prosperity. Latin-American nations did not share this boom in living standards, but significant social and economic changes took place within them during the war years and afterward.

The United States adopted an isolationist policy. The massive industrial expansion of World War I had made the United States a great economic power, and by 1919 it had been transformed from a debtor nation to the richest creditor in the world. Though the country was an acknowledged leader among nations, the people in the United States preferred to be free from entanglement with European problems. They were weary from the restrictions and emotions of the war, and President Harding correctly gauged popular sentiment. In his campaign, he had promised a return to "normalcy," and after his election he signed peace treaties with the Central Powers that eliminated any possibility of United States membership in the League of Nations. During his administration and also that of his successor, Calvin Coolidge, the United States followed a policy of isolationism. Except for the Washington Conference in 1922, the Dawes and Young plans for reparations, and the Kellogg-Briand Pact, the United States chose to have little to do with international affairs.

The Congress concerned itself chiefly with domestic problems. Among its significant laws was the Volstead Act of 1920, providing for the enforcement of the Eighteenth Amendment, which prohibited the manufacture, sale, and transportation of intoxicating liquor. The structure of the Volstead law was weak, however, and violators could escape conviction. During its existence, racketeers and corrupt politicians built a crime syndicate on bootlegging and gambling that threatened ordinary citizens and gave rise to violence and terror. (Not until 1933, in the first term of Franklin D. Roosevelt, was Prohibition repealed.)

Other significant legislation included the ratification in 1920 of the Nineteenth Amendment, by which suffrage was granted to women. In 1924 the National Origins Act placed limiting quotas on immigration, which benefited labor groups by restricting the flow of cheap labor into the United States.

During the decade of the 1920's Congress raised tariff rates to a degree higher than ever before in United States history. In retaliation, foreign nations enacted high tariffs also. Farm produce from Canada, Argentina, and the Soviet Union glutted the world market, and in the United States farmers found the sale of their products blocked in world commerce. The decline in food prices in the United States after the war also reduced farm income, and many farmers were forced into bankruptcy.

On the other hand, industrial production boomed, helped by government subsidies, lowered taxes, and high tariffs. Assembly-line methods, improved machinery, inventions born during the war, and electric power made household appliances, gadgets, and innumerable other products available. Of great importance was the production of automobiles, which in turn encouraged new and improved roads and suburban real-estate developments. Jobs increased in the cities and wages were high. The public, buying on the installment plan, indulged in an orgy of spending. Foreign trade was lively also, but here appearances were deceptive, for a great amount of the trade was sustained by United States loans to corporations and nations abroad.

In this atmosphere of apparent prosperity, speculation on the stock market became contagious, and the prices of stocks began to rise rapidly. In his book *Only Yesterday*, the American social historian, Frederick Lewis Allen, said:

> Stories of fortunes made overnight were on everybody's lips. One financial commentator reported that his doctor found patients talking about the market to the exclusion of everything else and that his barber was punctuating with the hot towel more than one account of the prospects of Montgomery Ward. Wives were asking their husbands why they were so slow, why they weren't getting in on all this, only to hear that their husbands had bought a hundred shares of American Linseed that very morning. Brokers' branch offices were jammed with crowds of men and women watching the . . . ticker tape . . . whether or not one held so much as a share of stock, . . .

Prices on stocks soared up and up, and financial analysts threw out mild warnings as business grew less active and farmers became more hard pressed. As long as prosperity seemed secure, however, the danger signals were ignored. Complacent and prosperous, many Americans looked to Wall Street for leadership instead of to the White House; they remained largely indifferent to world affairs.

Latin Americans demanded reforms. In the twenty republics of Latin America, business booms had resulted during the war from the heavy demand for products, such as wheat, beef, rubber, copper, nitrates, and oil. New industries in Buenos Aires, Santiago, São Paulo, Rio de Janeiro, Havana, and other cities brought thousands of workers to factories and increased the number of merchants and businessmen in these localities.

The city masses and the new middle classes demanded reforms and a greater voice in government Many evils, such as widespread illiteracy (in some countries it was more than 75 per cent) and a tragically high death rate, needed correction. Dysentery, tuberculosis, smallpox, and malaria were common, and as a result of the vast inequality of wealth, too many of the people were hungry most of the time. A few rich landowners controlled the large estates and farms, on which the laborers lived little better than medieval serfs. Some large plantations, oil fields, and mines were owned by foreign investors, who took their profits out of the country and provided few benefits for the native workers.

Mexico was the standard bearer in the attack on these evils. A revolution in 1911 had been followed by six years of disorder, but in 1917 a new constitution, representing reformist and nationalist views, was adopted. Gradually the government secured control over the vast foreign oil properties and restricted the power of the Church, one of the great landowners. Later, the Mexican government made compensation for some of the property it seized. The government also promoted universal suffrage, a minimum wage, an eight-hour working day, and schools for rural villages.

The Mexican revolution stirred the people of Latin America to demand political and social changes. Between 1919 and 1929, seven nations adopted new, liberal constitutions. Governments took over some of the educational and charitable functions of the Church. Not all changes were permanent, however, and many of the basic causes of dissatisfaction remained.

Section Review

1. After World War I, what was the position of the United States among nations? Why did the people of the United States favor a policy of isolationism? List some of the chief developments in internal affairs of the United States during the 1920's.

2. What effect did the war years and the 1920's have on Latin-American countries? How did the Mexican revolution stimulate a demand for reform throughout Latin America?

5 Nationalism developed in Africa, in the Near East, and in Asia

Elsewhere in the world, the powerful force of nationalism was growing, especially among groups dominated by European powers. The wide publicity given the concepts of democracy, freedom, and self-determination at the Paris Peace Conference influenced many peoples who lived under colonial rule.

Independence movements for Africans began. Until World War I, Africa was a vast preserve of European colonies, except for the two independent states of Ethiopia and Liberia. European government had provided noteworthy benefits for the natives including the suppression of tribal warfare, the introduction of public-health measures, the establishment of transportation and communication systems, and the development of education. On the other hand, some Europeans seized African lands and made huge profits without adequate provision for native peoples.

While the Paris Peace Conference was in session, a Pan-African Congress also convened in Paris. Its delegates, composed largely of American Negroes, sought to raise the status of the Negro race. They opposed colonial rule and exerted pressure on the negotiators at Versailles to place the former German colonies in Africa under the protection and rule of the League.

The Peace Conference decided on the mandate system, in which the former German colonies were to be administered by various European nations, but with League protection and with the assurance that the

LEAGUE OF NATIONS MANDATES

SYRIA AND LEBANON
(Fr.)

IRAQ
(Br.)

PALESTINE
(Br.)

TRANSJORDAN
(Br.)

BRITISH CAMEROON

FR. TOGO-
LAND

BRITISH TOGOLAND

FRENCH CAMEROON

RUANDA-URUNDI
(Belg.)

TANGANYIKA
(Br.)

SOUTH-WEST AFRICA
(U. of S. Afr.)

Prepared by
Rand McNally & Co., Chicago

MARIANA IS.

CAROLINE IS.

PALAU

MARSHALL IS.
(Japan)

(Austl.)
NEW GUINEA

NAURU
(Austl.)

SAM
(N.

TURKEY

LEBANON

SYRIA
(Fr.)

IRAN

AUSTRALIA

PALESTINE
(Br.)

IRAQ
(Br.)

TRANS-
JORDAN
(Br.)

EGYPT
(Br. Prot.)

ARABIA

NEW
ZEALAND

native peoples would be prepared for self-government. Tanganyika was placed under the control of Britain; Ruanda and Urundi under Belgium; South-West Africa under the Union of South Africa, while Togoland and the Cameroons were divided between France and Britain.

The Arabs demanded independence. The Arabs in North Africa and the Near East were united by a common religion (Islam) and a common language (Arabic). They shared also a desire to be free of foreign control. After World War I, the Arab world—as this area is often called—was troubled by dissension and revolt.

During the 1920's, several underground movements in Tunisia and Morocco threatened French rule. In Algeria, where a large European group had settled, Arabs began a long struggle to win French citizenship and a greater voice in the government. It was in the British protectorate

of Egypt, however, that nationalism burst forth as a hot flame. After a delegation of Egyptian nationalists had been denied permission to attend the Paris Peace Conference, the Nile valley rose in revolt. Order was not restored until 1922, when the British agreed to terminate the protectorate. Although Egypt became a sovereign state, Britain retained the right to keep troops there, to conduct Egyptian foreign affairs, and to defend the Suez Canal. The Egyptians accepted this agreement and proclaimed a constitution in 1923.

In the Near East, Arab pressure against the corrupt rule of the Ottoman sultans had long been a source of disquiet. When Turkey entered World War I on the side of Germany, Britain courted the favor of the Arabs in order to undermine Turkish power. In 1915 and 1916 Britain made vague promises of independence to the Arabs to spark a rebellion against the Turks. Before the end of the war, in June 1916, the revolt began. Under the brilliant leadership of T. E. Lawrence, a young British officer, the Arabs rose up against the Turks.

When the war ended, the Arab leaders claimed self-government as their reward, but it soon became clear that Arab independence was a victim of European power politics. During the war, Britain and France had concluded a secret agreement to divide the Near East between them. With the war over, the Allied powers then agreed that certain Arab territories formerly in the Ottoman Empire were to be administered as mandates. Syria and Lebanon were mandated to France, and Iraq to Britain. To the Arabs the mandates were a poor substitute for independence, and hostility toward the Europeans grew. However, the British, by their more enlightened policies in Iraq, were able to avoid the conflicts encountered by the French in Syria and Lebanon. In 1930 an Anglo-Iraqi treaty recognized the full independence of Iraq, subject to military limitations similar to those made by the British in Egypt. Meanwhile, the French appeared both unable and unwilling to guide their charges to self-government.

The collapse of the Ottoman Empire in 1918 brought independence to several states in the Arabian peninsula. The most important, the newly created kingdom of Hejaz, was conquered by Ibn Saud, an Arab warrior who consolidated nearly all of the peninsula under his rule by 1926. In 1932 Ibn Saud changed the name of his vast domain to Saudi Arabia, and in that year the discovery of fabulously rich oil reserves added to his power and prestige. Another strong man emerged in the Near East after World War I. In 1921, Riza Shah Pahlavi took over the reins of power in Persia, a Moslem but not an Arab nation, which became known as Iran, or Land of the Aryans. A strong nationalist, the shah rid the land of foreign controls and determined to modernize his country as Mustafa Kemal Atatürk had modernized Turkey. Schools were built and national resources were developed. But as the years passed, the shah became a despot. Not until 1941 was his regime overthrown.

A source of continual strife in the Near East was the state of Palestine. In 1917 the British statesman Arthur Balfour indicated, in a statement known as the Balfour Declaration, that a national home for the Jews would be established in Palestine. In 1920 Palestine was made a British mandate, and Jewish immigration began. The skill and ingenuity of the Jewish immigrants amazed the world as modern cities were built and farms and industries prospered. Although the Arabs constituted the larger part of the population in Palestine, they were alarmed, for they viewed the Jews as "intruders" and feared possible economic and political domination. As refugees fled from Nazi Germany in the 1930's and Jewish immigration swelled, the Arabs resorted to guerrilla warfare. The British tried to bring peace to the area, but their recommendations were not accepted by either the Arabs or the Jews, and enmity between the two peoples continued.

India demanded freedom. During World War I, India loyally supported Britain. Wealthy princes made large financial contributions, and almost a million Indian soldiers fought on the side of the British. Indians hoped their loyalty and support would be rewarded by self-government, for in 1917 Britain had pledged itself to give self-rule to India in successive stages. At the end of the war the Government of India Act of 1919 established a diarchy, or double government, which gave certain powers to provincial legislatures but reserved others, more important, to Britain. The act disheartened most Indians, and chances for its acceptance were entirely swept away by the outbreak of a struggle between the British and

20th-Century Nationalists championed the cause of independence for their countries. Mohandas Gandhi, above left, guided the people of India in a campaign of nonviolent resistance to British rule. Sun Yat-sen, above right, led the struggle to unify China and cast off foreign influence. The two Moslem leaders below, Mustafa Kemal Atatürk of Turkey, left, and Riza Shah Pahlavi of Iran, right, worked to modernize their countries along Western lines, but wanted no interference from European powers.

the Indian nationalists. Early in 1919, the British passed the Rowlatt Acts, allowing the police extraordinary powers in ferreting out subversive activity. Although the acts were never enforced, they were deeply resented and disgruntled nationalists demanded sweeping changes.

The widespread dissatisfaction found a spokesman in Mohandas K. Gandhi, who came forward to champion the cause of freedom. This remarkable nationalist leader had been educated in England as a lawyer and had set up a successful practice in South Africa, where the plight of his fellow Indians attracted his attention. Gandhi returned to India during World War I and stanchly supported the British. At the same time, he was the champion of the oppressed and lowly. Millions worshiped him as a holy man, or *mahatma*, for he understood their problems and honored their ancient traditions. Gandhi strongly opposed the Government of India Act and introduced a campaign to force the British to grant India self-rule. Advocating nonviolent disobedience, he coined a term to describe his methods: *Satyagraha*, meaning "the force of truth."

Despite Gandhi's pleas for nonviolent resistance, many of his supporters became lawless. In April 1919, a month after the passage of the Rowlatt Acts, a wave of murder, looting, and arson reached its climax at Amritsar where soldiers were ordered to open fire on demonstrators with a heavy toll in dead and wounded. Gandhi and his followers in the Indian National Congress were shocked by this incident and became determined to win complete freedom.

During the 1920's and 1930's Gandhi launched several campaigns of nonviolent resistance against British authority. One of his methods to force the British to meet Indian demands was the economic boycott of British-made goods, and for his various activities he was imprisoned from time to time. While striving for the independence of India, Gandhi sought to end excessive drinking among the Indian people, to erase the stigma attached to the untouchables, and to bring about coöperation between Hindus and Moslems. He was convinced that injustices could be wiped out only through love, unselfishness, and patience.

In 1929 the British opened a series of round-table conferences with Indian leaders to prepare India for dominion status, and in 1937 the British Parliament passed a law which gave the provinces self-government. In the central government at New Delhi, the capital, all power was handed to Indian members of the legislature except for that relating to defense and foreign affairs.

Revolution in China brought about important political changes. During the late 19th century China had been forced to cede some territory to Japan. At the same time European powers were establishing spheres of influence in China and obtaining special economic privileges. Young Chinese who resented this foreign influence organized secret societies to combat it. Among these nationalists was Sun Yat-sen, who had lived in Honolulu for three years and had graduated from a medical college in the British colony of Hong Kong. For many years he made plans to overthrow the tyrannical Manchu dynasty, and his activities forced him to flee China. For fifteen years he worked among Chinese communities abroad to organize the Kuomintang, or Nationalist Peoples Party, and received financial support from the overseas communities to begin a revolution.

In October 1911, Chinese rebels succeeded in overthrowing the government, and in the spring of 1912 the Manchus abdicated. An imperial army led by Yüan Shih-k'ai had been sent to put down the revolt, but instead Yüan bargained with the rebels in the north and became their leader. Sun, who had been in London at the outbreak of the revolution, returned at once to his homeland, took over the leadership of the rebels in the south, and was elected president of the United Provinces of China in December 1911. Yüan, hoping to restore the monarchy, set up a capital at Peking.

Since the United States and other powers extended diplomatic recognition and economic and military aid to Yüan, Sun Yat-sen was soon obliged to compromise with the northern leader. Yüan was made president of China in 1913.

In 1915 Yüan tried to have himself made emperor, but his plans were opposed by warlords as well as by Sun Yat-sen. Yüan died in 1916, without having reached his goal, and after his death Sun fought the warlords who wanted China divided among themselves. After a long conflict, Sun was elected president of China in 1921 and made plans to unify the country. Unable to obtain aid from the Western powers, whose imperialistic aims he had denounced, Sun turned to the new communist government in Russia which offered him money, arms, and advisers. Prominent among the latter was General Michael Borodin, who greatly influenced Sun and persuaded him to adopt a program similar to that of the Russian Communist party.

Sun died in 1925. Although he was unable to lead his followers successfully, he was a source of inspiration to them and his writings became guides for reform. One book, *Three Principles of the People*, became the manual of the Kuomintang. It advocated nationalism and freedom from foreign control, government by the people and for the people, and economic security for all the Chinese.

Sun's place was taken by his disciple, Chiang Kai-shek, a brilliant military officer. In 1926 Chiang led his army north-ward, and two years later he captured the government at Peking and united China. During this campaign, Chiang encountered growing opposition from the communist wing of the Kuomintang party. It had hitherto been content to coöperate with the revolutionary movement in order to seize power at an opportune moment. Realizing this danger, Chiang instituted a purge which resulted in the execution of many communist sympathizers and also of many liberals. Borodin and his group of Russian advisers left China for Moscow. A small group of communists remained in China, but from that time the Kuomintang became increasingly conservative.

Chiang built factories, railroads, and new highways. From the new national capital of Nanking, a vigorous educational program was set in motion to teach millions of Chinese to read. This nationalist government was recognized by the Western powers in 1928 as the official government of China, and a start was made toward removing the special privileges enjoyed in China by foreign nations.

Section Review

1. What was the purpose of the Pan-African Congress? In what respect was the mandate system, as applied to the former German colonies in Africa, a forerunner of self-government for the African native peoples?
2. What changes in the Near East after World War I were the result of French and British influence?
3. What changes in the Near East were chiefly the result of nationalism?
4. How did Gandhi's method of gaining independence differ from the methods employed in many other countries? What steps toward Indian freedom did the British take between 1917 and 1937?
5. Name some of the outstanding political changes that took place in China between 1911 and 1928. What three principles of Sun Yat-sen became a guide for China?

Chapter 27 ▰▰▰▰▰▰ A Review

The League of Nations held out the hope that nations of the world could live together in peace. The organization did solve a number of disputes, and its influence was especially strong in the realm of social and economic reform. If the United States had become a member, its influence might have made the League more effective. However, the basic weaknesses in the structure of the League were a major cause of its failure, and they became apparent after the Corfu incident.

The atmosphere of mutual suspicion that persisted in Europe after World War I was not relieved by idealistic pronouncements or high-flown phrases, which had marked the Locarno Conference. The older democracies also encountered serious internal difficulties, while the new nations of eastern Europe struggled to establish democratic institutions, and for the most part were unsuccessful.

As Europe groped with its problems, important changes were occurring elsewhere in the world. The United States had emerged as the world's most powerful nation, but it chose to remain isolated from international entanglements and to concern itself chiefly with internal affairs. A rising middle class in Latin America demanded a greater voice in government. Influenced by the Mexican revolution, they agitated for land reform, improved labor laws, and liberal constitutions.

Nationalism was a powerful force following World War I. Inspired by President Wilson's efforts in behalf of self-determination, Africans won a measure of independence through the mandate system. Among the Arabs in North Africa, efforts to throw off foreign control were most successful in Egypt. In the Near East conflicting British and French promises, made during the stress of war, earned the hostility of the Arabs. Their demand for independence was only partially fulfilled, and a new source of dissatisfaction arose when a national home for the Jews was established in Palestine. In India, Mohandas K. Gandhi advocated passive resistance in the people's fight against British rule. Although India won a degree of self-government during the 1920's, the fight for complete freedom continued into the next decade.

In China, the revolution differed from the revolts in other countries. No foreign power was ousted, but a corrupt and backward regime was overturned. After a long struggle, Sun Yat-sen succeeded in establishing a republic. His successor, Chiang Kai-shek, routed communist groups and united the nation.

The era of the 1920's brought into the open some of the basic problems of the world: the lack of mutual trust among nations; the extremes of wealth and poverty existing in some areas; the need for political and economic reform; and the desire for freedom from foreign control.

The Time

Indicate in which of these four periods the following events occurred.

(a) 1900-1920   (c) 1926-1930
(b) 1921-1925   (d) 1931-1935

1. Mustafa Kemal Atatürk became president of Turkey.

2. The Mexican revolution broke out.

3. France and Belgium invaded the Ruhr.

4. The Kellogg-Briand Pact was signed in Paris.

5. The Washington Conference on naval disarmament was held.

6. The Locarno treaties were signed.

7. The Government of India Act was passed.

8. The Manchu government in China was overthrown.

9. The Commonwealth of Nations was created.

10. Sun Yat-sen was made president of the the Chinese republic.

11. The Italians bombarded the island of Corfu.

12. The Dawes plan was accepted.

13. The constitution of the Weimar Republic was adopted.

14. The Arabs revolted against the Ottoman sultans.

15. Chiang Kai-shek captured the Peking government and united China.

The Place

1. The League of Nations assumed much of the responsibility for the administration of the *Saar* and *Danzig*. Locate these places and tell what made them important.

2. The places named below were set up as mandates under the League. Indicate to which nation each of these places had belonged before the war and to what country they were mandated.

Tanganyika	South-West Africa	Syria
Ruanda	Togoland	Lebanon
Urundi	Cameroons	Iraq

3. Explain how these places came to be trouble spots after World War I: Vilna, Ruhr, Palestine.

4. In what countries are these Latin-American cities located: Buenos Aires, São Paulo, Rio de Janeiro, Havana?

5. Locate each of the following cities and tell why it is associated with nationalism: Ankara, New Delhi, Nanking, Amritsar.

6. Name and locate areas of the Arab world in which postwar nationalistic movements were developing.

7. Tell why hopes for a lasting peace were raised at these cities: Geneva, Washington, Locarno, Weimar.

8. Movements for the independence of Africa began after World War I. What two countries were already independent?

The People

1. How did each of these men further the cause of nationalism?

Mustafa Kemal Atatürk	Mohandas K. Gandhi
T. E. Lawrence	Sun Yat-sen
Ibn Saud	Yüan Shih-k'ai
Riza Shah Pahlavi	Chiang Kai-shek

2. How did these men work for peace?

Woodrow Wilson	Aristide Briand
Charles Evans Hughes	Frank Kellogg

3. Identify these national leaders by country and give one fact about each man.

Henry Cabot Lodge	Stanley Baldwin
Warren G. Harding	Jósef Pilsudski
Benito Mussolini	Miklós von Horthy
James Ramsay MacDonald	Thomas G. Masaryk

4. How did Charles G. Dawes and Owen D. Young help ease the reparations problem?

Historical Terms

1. How did the Assembly carry on the business of the League of Nations? What was the purpose of the Council? the Secretariat?

2. In what ways were the Permanent Court of International Justice (World Court), Permanent Mandates Commission, and the International Labor Organization supposed to carry out the aims of the League?

3. The plebiscite was one of the League tools for enforcing the peace treaties; economic sanctions were a means by which the League might maintain peace. Explain these terms.

4. What were some of the decisions of the Reparations Commission? How were these changed by the Dawes and Young commissions?

5. What was the Little Entente? Explain its role in the French system of alliances.

6. The Locarno treaties and the Kellogg-Briand Pact raised hopes for a lasting peace. What were the provisions of each? What were some agreements reached at the Washington Conference?

7. Explain each of these terms by showing how it applies to British efforts to cope with problems within the empire.

the Dole	Statute of Westminster
Labour Party	Commonwealth of Nations
Rowlatt Acts	Government of India Act

8. What was the purpose of each of the following enactments in the United States?
Volstead Act
Eighteenth Amendment
Nineteenth Amendment
National Origins Act

9. What structural weaknesses were apparent in the National Assembly of Deputies (France) and in the Weimar Republic?

10. Indian nationalism was guided by a policy of nonviolent resistance, a faith in Satyagraha, and a leader called Mahatma. What do these terms mean?

11. What were the roles of the Kuomintang and of the *Three Principles of the People* in the emergence of China as a sovereign state?

12. How did the Pan-African Congress and the mandate system attempt to promote self-rule for the African native peoples?

13. What was the Balfour Declaration?

Questions for Critical Thinking

1. What forces in the period from 1924 to 1928 were a threat to lasting peace?

2. How did World War I and the peace treaties stimulate the surge of nationalism in Asia and Africa?

3. Why did democracy fail to establish a permanent hold on the new countries of eastern Europe after World War I?

4. Compare the challenge to democracy in postwar England with that in postwar France. In which country was the challenge more serious? Support your answer with specific examples.

5. In what respects did the United States, during the 1920's, fail to provide strong leadership for the rest of the world? What steps did it take during this period to promote better international relations?

6. Compare and contrast the revolutionary movements in Turkey, Mexico, and China from the standpoint of (1) the underlying causes of each revolution and (2) reforms that came about as a result of each revolution.

7. What do you think was the most serious danger to democracy in Germany after World War I? Explain.

8. Do you think that the British, after World War I, maintained an enlightened policy in dealing with rising nationalism in the Near East and India? Support your answer with specific examples.

The Rise of Communism in Russia

Popular discontent with the autocratic rule of Russian czars was voiced early in the 19th century. However, revolts met with little success before 1917. In that year, the czar was overthrown and power was seized by the revolutionary Bolsheviks, who proposed an entirely new system of government based on Marxist socialism. Above, their leader, Lenin, addresses a crowd of Bolsheviks in the early days of the revolution. Behind him stand Stalin and Trotsky.

Dear comrades, soldiers, sailors, and workers! I am happy to greet in your persons the victorious Russian revolution, and greet you as the vanguard of the worldwide proletarian army. . . . Any day now the whole of European capitalism may crash.

The speaker was Vladimir Ilyich Ulyanov (better known under his assumed name, N. Lenin), and the occasion was his arrival in Petrograd, the Russian capital, on April 16, 1917. Lenin, a mild-mannered, nondescript little man, had for over a decade led the Bolsheviks, the radical group within the Social Democratic movement. After many years of exile in Switzerland, he had been transported to his homeland by the German High Command. The Germans hoped that Lenin and his followers could undermine the provisional government of Russia, which had been set up in March after the abdication of Czar Nicholas II. This tactic, designed to obstruct the Russian war effort, was to have consequences far beyond those concerned with the final outcome of World War I.

Within seven months of his arrival in Petrograd, Lenin and his followers had wrecked the provisional government and established their own rule. This *coup d'état,* the Bolshevik Revolution of November 1917, was an event of world-wide significance. Established for the first time in history was a state founded on the principles of Marxist socialism.

The new regime was dedicated to the overthrow of the property-owning class the world over. In their attempts to achieve this objective, the Bolsheviks, or Communists, assisted the growth of parties outside Russia, modeled on their own. Their members also infiltrated other radical groups in order to spread the doctrines of communism. The Communists held firm to the idea that the principles of communism would some day be accepted by all mankind. Throughout his lifetime, Lenin was a vigorous foe of capitalist civilization, and his memory is revered in the Soviet Union and in other communist-controlled countries as the prophet of a new social order.

To understand how communism gained control of the Russian government, the czarist past must be examined, and to understand the influence of communism in the modern world, the purposes and effects of communism must be studied.

Chapter 28, which is divided into four main sections, shows how:

1. **Autocratic rulers weakened Russia.**

2. **Bolsheviks seized control of Russia.**

3. **Stalin established a despotic regime.**

4. **Relations with the West were unfriendly.**

1 Autocratic rulers weakened Russia

The political ideas and economic changes that transformed European society in the 18th and 19th centuries had little effect upon Russia. To other Europeans of the time, the vast domain of the czars seemed remote, mysterious, and backward. A despotic system of government choked off the deep longing of the Russian people for a better life. An economy largely confined to agriculture remained stagnant.

The majority of the population were peasants—ignorant, impoverished, and debased. Most of them were bound to the soil as were the serfs in western Europe during the Middle Ages. Occasionally they were moved to violent but futile outbreaks against the nobility, their landlords. The nobles objected strenuously to reforms that might weaken their power and privileges, while the czars were usually as conservative as the nobles and failed to provide energetic leadership. Political and economic reforms were granted so slowly and reluctantly that the great upheaval of 1917 came as a long-delayed answer to the accumulated grievances of the past.

Czars suppressed democracy in Russia.

After the death of Catherine the Great in 1796, her son came to the throne as Paul I. An eccentric tyrant, he made many enemies among the court nobility. In 1801 he was assassinated in a conspiracy led by the military governor of St. Petersburg.

Paul was succeeded by Alexander I, the most complex and baffling figure of all the Russian czars. Despite his intellectual gifts and his charming manner, he lacked strength of character. He professed sympathy for democracy and a hatred of despotism, yet he could hardly be termed a benevolent ruler. His early attempts at reform were interrupted by the Napoleonic wars, and during the last decade of his reign he cruelly disappointed the hopes of his early liberal admirers and turned increasingly for advice to outspoken reactionaries. For example, he founded "military colonies" in which peasant families were placed under strict army discipline.

Widespread dissatisfaction with Alexander's rule led to the formation of secret revolutionary societies. The small membership of these societies was confined largely to army officers who had been influenced by Western ideas, especially during the occupation of France after Napoleon's defeat. When Alexander died suddenly in December 1825, these officers rebelled against the government. They had very little support from the people and the uprising was easily suppressed. Yet the so-called Decembrist Revolt inspired later revolutionary movements in Russia and showed how ideas from the outside could spark a demand for reform.

Throughout his life, memories of the bloodshed that had opened his reign haunted the new czar, Nicholas I. Unlike Catherine the Great and Alexander I, Nicholas frankly proclaimed autocracy the first and best principle of government. As one of his officials stated, "The czar is a father, his subjects are his children, and children ought never to question their parents. . . ." Nicholas held stubbornly to his faith in the efficiency of a centralized and regimented government under his personal control. His officials were burdened with mountains of reports, rules, and regulations. The press was rigidly censored, and academic freedom in the universities was severely restricted. Police spies ferreted out enemies of the regime and had them packed off to exile in Siberia.

The corruption and incompetence of the czar's bureaucratic system made the outcome of the Crimean War almost inevitable, and the Russian war effort was strangled (Chapter 20). Nicholas, a bitter and disillusioned man, died before the end of the war.

Alexander II introduced reforms.

Alexander II, who succeeded his father in 1855, was by nature as conservative as his predecessor. But the humiliation of Russia in the Crimean War led Alexander to try reform. As he told an assembly of nobles in Moscow, "It is better to abolish serfdom from above than to wait until it begins to abolish itself from below."

In 1861, by an imperial decree known as the Act on the Emancipation of the Peasants from Serfdom, the serfs were granted personal liberty and promised portions of land as their own. The land was not given them outright, however, but was placed under the jurisdiction of the local village, or *mir*. The landlords were allowed to retain the parts of their estates formerly set aside for their own use—usually about half—and were compensated for the portions turned over to the *mir*. This compensation came through a "redemption" tax from the freed serfs to be paid over a period of forty-nine years. Though no longer in bondage to their landlords, the peasants discovered that in some respects they were little better off than before. In many cases, the land they received was poor or the landlord exerted undue influence on the village officials. Well-to-do peasants, called *kulaks*, had been able to buy or lease the more fertile land while less fortunate peasants were forced to work as farm laborers at pitifully meager wages.

Many injustices arose in the gradual process of redistributing the land, and the life of the peasant continued to be a hard one. Yet the emancipation of the serfs stands out as the most important single event in 19th-century Russian history. It was the beginning of the end of power for the landed aristocracy. Emancipation brought a supply of free labor to the cities; industry grew and a middle class arose.

Other measures followed the emancipation decree: greater academic freedom for the universities, local self-government, and a reorganization of the judicial system. Even though these measures were often thwarted by meddling bureaucrats, they aroused hopes for a greater degree of freedom. However, many young people, particularly idealistic students, were unwilling to wait for gradual reform. They founded revolutionary societies and tried to overthrow the government by striking directly at the throne. After escaping several assassination attempts, Alexander II was killed by a bomb in 1881. His murder solved nothing. Russia simply acquired another autocrat, and the czarist system was preserved intact.

The czarist system grew more reactionary. The last two czars—Alexander III, who reigned until 1894, and Nicholas II, who was czar until 1917—made no serious effort to introduce responsible government or to recast the social order to fit the needs of a modern state. In fact, both rulers attempted to turn back the clock by reinstat-ing repressive measures and curtailing the reforms of Alexander II. Censorship became more severe, and academic freedom in the universities was stifled. Religious persecution was allowed to go unchecked; many Jews were either terrorized or murdered in terrible drives called *pogroms*. Secret agents of the czar were instructed to infiltrate revolutionary groups and to incite them to murder government officials; the agents then exposed the rebels to the police.

Low wages, long hours, and poor working conditions led to a wave of strikes in the 1890's. Since labor unions were illegal and strikes prohibited, the frustrations of the workers mounted.

Russia lost a war with Japan. Russian imperialism in the Far East brought on a clash with the Japanese. By 1900 Russia dominated Manchuria and was eager to include Korea in its sphere of influence. Because Japan was considered a weak rival, Russia did not try to avoid a test of arms. As an official of the Russian government expressed it, a "little victorious war to stem the tide of revolution" was not unwelcome.

In February 1904, without a formal declaration of war, the Japanese fleet struck at Port Arthur, the Russian naval base on the tip of the southern Manchurian coast. In the conflict that followed, Russia was shown to be—as in the Crimean War—a giant with feet of clay. Its army and navy suffered an unbroken series of defeats, and the government ended the Russo-Japanese War with an unfavorable peace treaty signed in September 1905.

The 1905 revolution served a warning to the czar. In the meantime, a revolution had broken out which was touched off by the notorious "Bloody Sunday" incident on January 22, 1905. A large procession of workers, bearing a petition to the czar, was fired on by troops in St. Petersburg.

Czarist Russia was a despotic state. These illustrations from Soviet textbooks stress the brutality and backwardness of the regime. Pugachev's revolt, a peasant uprising of 1773-1774, was ruthlessly suppressed. Above, a man is hanged by a rib and a woman is buried alive. Unrest increased in the 19th century. On the opposite page, top, a prisoner is forced to run the gantlet between two rows of soldiers. Center right, the political writer Nikolay Chernyshevsky is chained to a post and punished for advocating revolution; he was later exiled to Siberia. Serfs, center left, plead for mercy from a landlord who has evicted them. Peasant conditions improved somewhat after 1864, when a new law established local councils, called *zemstvos*, where peasants had an equal voice with the middle class and gentry. A typical *zemstvo* is shown at bottom.

Russia has the longest coast of any country in the world, yet for centuries it has been handicapped by the lack of usable seaports. Murmansk, in northwestern Russia, is the only ocean port which is open and ice-free the year round. Waters along the rest of the vast northern Russian coast are frozen over for nine to ten months of the year. The eastern coast of Russia on the Pacific Ocean also is blocked by ice for several months each year. On the south, the straits (the Bosporus and the Dardanelles) leading from the Black Sea to the Mediterranean have been controlled for centuries by the Turks and by international agreements. On the west, however, the Baltic Sea affords an open route to western Europe and the Atlantic. Therefore, the Baltic has been of prime importance in Russia's search for ice-free ports.

One of the most important Baltic ports was the city of Riga, located on the Gulf of Riga, an arm of the Baltic Sea. Medieval land routes linked Riga with Europe and the Mediterranean Sea. The Western Dvina River linked Riga with the interior of Russia. From its source near the upper Volga River, the Western Dvina flows 650 miles northwest to the Baltic. It is navigable by barges and commands a considerable river traffic. By gaining control of the river and its mouth near the port of Riga, Russia could link its internal trade routes with the Baltic Sea. Czar Ivan IV declared that the Dvina was worth its weight in gold.

From 1557 until 1582 Ivan IV attempted to conquer Riga and Narva, another port on the Baltic. After some initial successes he was defeated by Polish and Swedish forces. Further attempts to win control of Baltic ports were made by Czar Peter the Great during the early 1700's. In 1703 he built the city of St. Petersburg on the Gulf of Finland, in hopes of opening a new avenue to the west. As a result of the Great Northern War with Sweden (1707-1721), Russia became master of the eastern shores of the Baltic, including Riga, Narva, and St. Petersburg.

Throughout the 19th century Russia maintained control of the ice-free Baltic ports. When Finland was acquired from Sweden in 1809, more outlets to the Baltic were gained.

During World War I, Germany conquered the eastern Baltic region. After the war this area was formed into the independent states of Estonia, Latvia, and Lithuania. Russia reoccupied these states during World War II, however, once more establishing access to ice-free ports on the Baltic Sea.

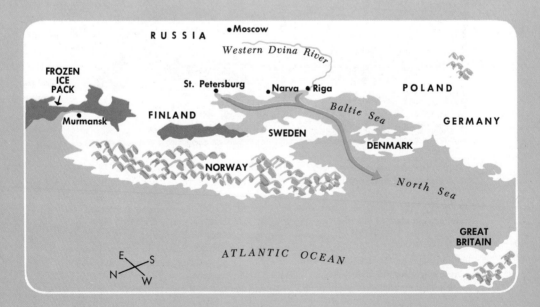

Several hundred unarmed workers were killed, and news of this act aroused fierce hostility against the government. A spontaneous wave of strikes broke out that finally paralyzed the railroads, the telegraph system, government offices, and most public functions in the large cities. Councils of workers called *soviets* sprang up in the cities to direct the rebellion. Crowds carried red banners and posters demanding political reforms. (Red was the traditional color of revolutionary socialism.) Active in the St. Petersburg outbreak were both Lenin and another revolutionary who was destined to become world famous, Leon Trotsky.

Shocked and dismayed by the fury of the popular outcry, Nicholas reluctantly granted a constitution in October 1905. Civil liberties were guaranteed and a national parliament, which was known as the Duma, was set up. Russia had at last apparently become a constitutional monarchy. But the Duma, which might have operated as a safety valve for popular discontent, was severely restricted in its powers. The first Duma, which met briefly in 1906, was dismissed by the czar because of its aggressive demands for reform. A similar fate befell the second Duma in 1907. Responsible for inaugurating some moderate reforms were the third and fourth Dumas, but they represented only a small part of the population. To some observers, the passions released in the 1905 revolution seemed to have subsided, and on the surface it appeared that political and economic stability had been achieved.

The apparent stability was deceptive, however. Further industrial development, much of it financed by the government, created new jobs for workers and new economic opportunities for middle-class businessmen. But peasants remained discontented and factory workers were disturbed by the indifference displayed by the government toward their working and living conditions. Both classes were potentially dangerous to the established order.

Section Review
1. In what respects was 19th-century Russia a backward country compared to the other great powers of Europe?
2. Discuss the results of the abolition of serfdom.
3. What conditions and events led to the 1905 revolution? To what degree did the revolution succeed? fail?

2 Bolsheviks seized control of Russia

World War I placed the autocratic system of the czars under a severe strain. The shock of military defeat and the acute shortages of food and other consumer goods produced among the masses a rebellious mood similar to that in 1905. In 1917, after more than 300 years of unbroken rule, the Romanov dynasty was swept from power.

The czarist government fell. Russia had entered the war in 1914 in a burst of patriotic fervor. The people's ardor quickly cooled, however, as the toll of dead and wounded mounted. Food and fuel stocks decreased and goods skyrocketed in price. Mismanagement and graft added to the woes of a government already overwhelmed by the problem of waging a major war. Irresolute as always, the czar showed little capacity for leadership, yet he stubbornly refused to allow the Duma any share in the affairs of state.

In March 1917 food shortages led to street demonstrations in Petrograd, the capital. (St. Petersburg had been renamed Petrograd in 1914.) At first, the crowds were orderly and good natured, but when police, soldiers, and special Cossack units were called out against them, they fought back. Within a few days the armed forces in the city mutinied and added their strength to that of the crowds. The uprising had become a revolution. Czar Nicholas, isolated at army headquarters near the front, was forced to abdicate.

A special committee of Duma members chose one of their number, Prince George Lvov, as prime minister. They organized a cabinet of middle-class liberals and set up a provisional government. Meanwhile, workers and soldiers in Petrograd formed soviets, as had been done in the 1905 revolution. Later on, soviets in other cities and towns followed the lead of the capital and took over the functions of government in their own localities.

The provisional government in Petrograd removed all restrictions on civil liberties and promised elections to a constituent assembly which would organize a permanent democratic government. It planned to continue the war, a decision that proved highly unpopular in the army and in most of the soviets. A program to distribute land to the peasants was postponed until the constituent assembly could meet. Lenin was unalterably opposed to continuing the war; he argued for peace with the Central Powers and the immediate redistribution of the land. The peasants, unwilling to wait, began to seize the estates of the landowners and to divide the land among themselves.

In July 1917 Alexander Kerensky, a lawyer with moderate socialist views, succeeded Lvov as prime minister. He was sincere and conscientious, but he failed to rally the people to the support of the provisional government.

The Bolsheviks took over the government. Mounting unrest and the growing unpopularity of Kerensky's provisional government played into the hands of Lenin, Trotsky, and their followers. Presented with an opportunity to seize power, they planned their moves skillfully.

Opportunity came in the autumn of 1917. The Bolsheviks were still a small party, but their slogan, "Peace, Land, and Bread," had a broad appeal to a nation exhausted by the prolonged ordeal of World War I. They took control of the Petrograd and Moscow soviets, and organized a workers' militia called the Red Guard. They then prepared to take over the central government by force. On the night of November 6 and in the early morning hours of the following day, the Red Guard, joined by pro-Bolshevik soldiers and sailors, captured strategic buildings in the capital and stormed the Winter Palace, the site of the provisional government. All the ministers were arrested except Kerensky, who escaped and attempted to organize resistance to Lenin. He failed and eventually fled the country.

Lenin's *coup d'état* was an amazing feat. But when free elections were held to form a constituent assembly to frame a new constitution, the Bolsheviks received less than a quarter of the votes. With the bayonets of the Red Guard, Lenin dissolved the assembly. Thus ended Russia's last free parliament in January 1918. The Bolsheviks proceeded quickly to set up a party dictatorship and adopt the name Communist.

The new regime faced many enemies. As the unchallenged leader of the Communist party, Lenin became chief of state with virtually limitless power. He devoted his life to making Russia communistic and acted ruthlessly whenever he considered it necessary in the interests of communism. He began his rule by applying Marxist principles to the organization of Russian society. All private property was abolished, and strategic industries, the banking system, railroads, and shipping were placed under government ownership. The Orthodox Church, long a tool of the czars, was shorn of its landholdings, and its officials and doctrines came under attack. To ease the food-supply problem, the peasants were allowed to farm the land they had already confiscated. The early years of the regime, from 1918 to 1921, were known as the Period of Militant Communism.

In March 1918 Lenin made peace with the Central Powers. The terms of the Treaty of Brest-Litovsk were harsh (Chapter 26), but Russia was out of World War I. Two months before the treaty, in January 1918, Lenin's plans for a period of peaceful reconstruction were shattered by an uprising against the Communist government which began in the Ukraine, the southern part of European Russia. Generals who had served under the czar led the revolt, and fighting spread to other parts of Russia. Many anti-Communists, from socialists to monarchists, joined in the struggle. Soon the country was involved in a civil war between the "Reds," or Communists, and the "Whites," or anti-Communists, a conflict that lasted until 1920 and was more savage and destructive to Russia than World War I. Famine and disease killed hundreds of thousands, and atrocities committed by both sides added to the ghastly toll of human life. Among the casualties were the ex-czar, his wife, and their five children, who were shot by the Reds.

Before the Bolshevik Revolution, the Allies had shipped war matériel to various Russian ports. To protect these supplies and to uphold the eastern front, Britain and France intervened on the side of the Whites. The United States also sent troops but attempted with some success to maintain neutrality. Japan, seeking to dominate eastern Siberia, occupied Vladivostok and other Pacific ports. Beset by the civil war and Allied intervention, the Communist government seemed likely to fall at any moment. But the Reds defeated their enemies. The anti-Communist armies were widely scattered and were unable to coordinate their efforts or to inspire confidence in the peasants, who distrusted the pro-landlord policy of the White generals. The Bolshevik regime also built up a superior military force under Trotsky, then Commissar for War. In addition, Allied intervention aroused Russian nationalism. By late 1920 Communist rule was secure against internal threat, though it enjoyed no great degree of popularity.

The Soviets modified Marxist economic and political principles. To ease the strain of long years of hardship and privation and to restore the Russian economy to its prewar levels, the government retreated from militant communism by introducing the New Economic Policy (NEP) in 1921. Although the state retained its ownership of basic industries, private enterprise in retail trade and small business was encouraged. "Nepmen" (as small businessmen were called) prospered under the new regulations. Also pacified were the peasants, who had been required previously to sell their grain at fixed prices and from whom grain had been seized with no payment during the civil war. Except for a tax on surplus grain, the peasants were free from government interference; they were allowed to cultivate their farms and to dispose of their produce as they saw fit.

The Communist leaders, as followers of Marx, believed that they had established a "dictatorship of the proletariat." Once capitalism had been wiped out and communism created, Communists believed the state would "wither away" because it would no longer be needed. But in practice the theory proved incorrect. Far from weakening, the state grew more powerful and coercive. The government was controlled by the party, and the national legislature—the Congress of Soviets—met infrequently and played little more than a ceremonial role. It approved the cabinet— the Council of People's Commissars—and passed without debate the legislation submitted to it.

In 1922 the Union of Soviet Socialist Republics became the official name of Russia and its federated republics: the Ukraine, White Russia, and Transcaucasia. In theory, the old Russian Empire had become a federal union.

Stalin eliminated Trotsky. The death of Lenin in 1924 brought on a bitter struggle for power between Leon Trotsky and Joseph Stalin. Trotsky, a brilliant writer and speaker, was as well known as Lenin, and most observers expected that he would become the new party leader. Stalin was an obscure figure, even to most Russians. While less intellectually gifted than Trotsky, he was a shrewd politician who had used his post as party secretary to place his supporters in key positions. The trend of the times also favored Stalin, for the world revolution that Trotsky so confidently predicted had failed to take place. Stalin advocated "building socialism in a single country." If Russia were to become a workers' paradise, then perhaps communist ideas might become more attractive to non-Russians.

Stalin's policy was accepted at the Fourteenth Party Congress in 1925, and Trotsky was expelled from the party in 1927. Two years later he was exiled, and in 1940 he was murdered in Mexico, apparently by an agent of Stalin.

Section Review

1. What conditions led to the revolution of March 1917? Why did the provisional government fall?
2. Describe the steps by which Lenin seized power. How did he make Russia communistic? Give reasons why the "Reds" won the civil war against the "Whites."
3. What was the NEP? Tell why it was established.
4. How did Stalin defeat Trotsky in the struggle for political power after the death of Lenin?

3 Stalin established a despotic regime

By the late 1920's Stalin had clearly emerged as Lenin's successor. Yet the traditions and customs of the party placed restrictions on one-man rule, and until the mid-1930's Stalin was careful to consult his associates and to conduct himself in a modest manner. His position at the head of the government was entirely unofficial. His only title until 1941 was general secretary of the Communist party. (In 1941 he became premier as well as party secretary.)

In 1928 the NEP came to an end. The economy had recovered to prewar levels, but the Marxist dream of a classless society was farther removed than ever. Party propagandists charged that the Nepmen and kulaks were profiteering at the expense of the workers and poor peasants. It was decided to renew the "socialist offensive." As Stalin explained the new policy:

> We are fifty to a hundred years behind the advanced countries. We must make up this lag in ten years. Either we do this or they will crush us.

Stalin's two major goals were rapid industrialization and the collectivization of agriculture. It was his belief that only by eliminating private use of land and enforcing dictatorial governmental controls on a massive scale could the objectives of his program be achieved.

Stalin began the Five Year Plan. In 1928 the government launched a gigantic program of industrialization known as the Five Year Plan. It emphasized the production of steel, hydroelectric power, locomotives, tractors, and other heavy goods. Food rationing was introduced, the production of consumer goods was curtailed, and living standards were allowed to fall. With only a few exceptions, all private enterprise was abolished.

Stalinist Russia was characterized by rigid control of all aspects of life. Political conformity was enforced by a series of purge trials, like the one shown above. Economic activity was carefully regulated by the Five Year Plans; below right, workers operate an oil rig. The regime molded public opinion through a massive propaganda program. A poster of Stalin, below left, dominates a busy city street.

A second major goal of the Plan was the collectivization of agriculture. Large-scale mechanized farms were designed to replace the small plots of the individual peasants. Many poor farmers joined the new collectives, but the kulaks, with a great deal more to lose, resisted the surrender of their land. As a final act of defiance, many of them burned their grain and killed their livestock rather than have them confiscated. Determined to crush the kulaks as a class, the government shipped them to less fertile areas, where many starved to death. Other kulaks were shot or taken by force to work in labor camps. Stalin called a halt to these methods in 1930, and thereafter propaganda and economic pressure were substituted for brutality. By 1936 about 90 per cent of the peasants belonged to nearly a quarter million collective farms.

In 1933 a second Five Year Plan began. Waste, inefficiency, and a severe shortage of technicians and skilled workers handicapped the government, yet in the short span of twelve years, Russia became a first-class industrial power. A third Five Year Plan was curtailed by World War II.

Some conditions improved but culture was regimented. Despite a low standard of living and the absence of civil liberties under the Stalin regime, the Russian citizen made some social gains. The planned economy provided full employment and productivity grew steadily. A drive to wipe out illiteracy and to develop educational facilities enabled ambitious and capable citizens to take advantage of free tuition and scholarships at the university level. State medical care, old-age pensions, and illness and accident insurance were put into effect. Women also achieved almost complete economic and social equality with men. They were encouraged to enter the professions, especially the field of medicine.

For the Russian intellectual, these gains for the masses scarcely made up for the steady "Stalinization" of Soviet culture. In the early years of the Communist regime, writers, artists, and scholars had been able to pursue their work without government interference so long as they were not outspokenly anti-Communist. But by the mid-1930's the party leaders demanded that the intellectuals contribute to the building of a Communist society. Thus, historians were required to glorify Russian heroes of the past, novelists to portray all Communists as pure-minded idealists, and composers to write melodies that the musically untrained could enjoy.

Marxist theory, which had previously stressed economic equality, was revised to fit the needs of the state. The Communist motto, "from each according to his ability; to each according to his needs," was scrapped. Training and skill were rewarded with salary increases, bonuses, and increased social prestige. Soviet patriotism was lauded, and the ideal of internationalism and the solidarity of the working class was de-emphasized. The family assumed a new importance: child-bearing was encouraged and divorce laws were tightened. Atheism remained the official Communist position on religious matters, and the government continued to harass the Orthodox Church, an attitude that was repeatedly attacked by world public opinion.

Stalin's drive for power was insatiable. In 1936 the "Stalin Constitution" was adopted. At face value it was an extremely liberal document, and Communists everywhere boasted that the Soviet Union was the most democratic country in the world. In actual operation, the new constitution did not protect the basic freedoms of the individual, and those who expected some relaxation of Soviet totalitarianism were bitterly disappointed. Although the structure of government was altered somewhat,

THE SOVIET UNION
In 1939

ARCTIC OCEAN

Bering Sea

Archangel

Leningrad
(Petrograd)

RUSSIAN SOCIALIST FEDERATED SOVIET REPUBLIC

ARCTIC CIRCLE

Lena River

Sea of Okhotsk

SAKHALIN

Nikolaevsk

ESTONIA
LATVIA
LITHUANIA
Minsk
WHITE RUSSIAN S.S.R.
Kiev
UKRAINIAN S.S.R.
Odessa
Moscow
Volga River
URAL MOUNTAINS
Ob River
Yenisei River

Black Sea
GEORGIAN S.S.R.
Tiflis
ARMENIAN S.S.R.
Erivan
AZERBAIJAN S.S.R.
Baku
Caspian Sea
Rostov
Sea
Aral Sea
KAZAKH S.S.R.
Lake Balkhash
TANNU TUVA
Lake Baikal
Amur River
Vladivostok
JAPAN

MONGOLIA
MANCHURIA
Port Arthur

TURKMEN S.S.R.
Ashkhabad
Tashkent
UZBEK S.S.R.
Frunze
KIRGHIZ S.S.R.
Alma-Ata
Stalinabad
TADZHIK S.S.R.

Annexed by Soviet Union in 1940

Prepared by
McNally & Co., Chicago

0   500   1000 MILES

the Communist party monopoly of political power was unchanged; and behind the party stood Stalin. No longer content to be first among equals, his thirst for absolute power became insatiable. His portrait appeared everywhere, and hardly a speech was made or a book published without some flattering reference to Stalin, the "Great Marxist-Leninist."

Suspicious of many of his old comrades, Stalin had scores of party leaders tried and convicted of treason in a series of public trials staged in Moscow from 1936 to 1938. Most of the defendants were executed. In addition, thousands of army officers, government officials, managers, technicians, and party members were arrested and held without trial by the secret police. Some were shot; others were sent to forced labor camps, already crowded with kulaks, alleged Trotskyists, and other "enemies of the people." The reign of terror eased in

1938, but Stalin's morbid suspicions and despotic rule remained a distinguishing feature of his regime.

Section Review

1. Why did Stalin launch the Five Year Plans? What methods were used in dealing with the kulaks?
2. What social gains did Soviet citizens make?
3. How was Soviet culture "Stalinized"? In what respects was Marxist theory revised during the 1930's?
4. Why did Stalin conduct a reign of terror against his political opponents in the 1930's?

4   **Relations with the West were unfriendly**

Although the non-Communist world was not uniformly hostile toward the Soviet government, relations were seldom cordial in the 1920's and 1930's, especially with the Western democracies. The Soviet leaders were convinced that the capitalist nations were bent upon crushing the Communist state. Many politicians and businessmen in the democratic countries regretted the failure of Allied intervention after the Bolshevik Revolution. They were also deeply alarmed over Marxist notions of world-wide revolution, but no government was prepared to wage a war of aggression against the Soviet Union.

The Russians themselves constantly tried to incite revolution abroad by means of propaganda, funds, and agents. Communist parties were founded during the early 1920's in most countries of the world. These parties became members of the Communist International ("Comintern" for short), an organization that was founded in Moscow in 1919. By the late 1920's the Soviet Communist party completely dominated the foreign parties through its control of the Comintern. The activities of the Communist groups outside the Soviet Union did not conflict with Stalin's policy of building socialism in a single country. Although he was skeptical of the Marxist idea of world revolution, Stalin used the Comintern as a propaganda tool.

The U.S.S.R. was isolated. In the 1920's Germany was the only friend of the Soviet Union in western Europe. Both countries were outcasts in the European community —Germany because it was a defeated power, Russia because of its Communist principles. In 1922 they formed a political partnership by signing the Treaty of Rapallo and by arranging secret military collaboration. German officers were sent to help train the Red Army, and in exchange Germany used Soviet munitions factories to rearm, an act that was in violation of the Versailles Treaty.

During the next few years, Russia gained the diplomatic recognition of most of the major powers. Britain and France restored relations in 1924, but the United States did not grant recognition until the year 1933.

In the Far East, the most significant aspect of Soviet policy was the assistance given Sun Yat-sen's Kuomintang, or National People's party, in its effort to unify China. Beginning in 1923 the Russians also sent advisers and arms to Sun, and later to his successor, Chiang Kai-shek, to help defeat the militarists of north China and unify the country. Communists had been allowed to join the Kuomintang as part of the bargain with Moscow. In 1927 Chiang suddenly turned on the Communists and drove them from the party. Many thousands were killed, and the Soviet aim of revolutionizing China received a sharp setback.

Stalin sought collective security. The 1930's saw a change in the direction of Soviet foreign policy as new and dynamic totalitarian regimes arose in Germany and Japan. The important events of this period are described at length in the next chapter; it is necessary to mention them briefly here, however, in order to understand the position of the Soviet Union during this troubled decade.

By 1934 Adolf Hitler and his Nazi party had consolidated their power in Germany and the "Rapallo spirit" of the 1920's was wholly extinguished. Hitler did not conceal his hatred of communism and of the Soviet Union; he had Communists arrested and suppressed their activities thoroughly. The imperialistic designs of the Japanese on the Asiatic mainland also worried the Russians. Faced by these dangers and convinced that he must seek the good will of the democracies in western Europe, Stalin advocated a policy of collective security. That is, he tried to coöperate with the peace-loving states against the militaristic dictatorships.

In 1934 Russia was admitted to the League of Nations, and the Comintern, long a source of irritation to the West, ceased its revolutionary role. Communists abroad were ordered to support any party or government that would join in a common struggle against the aggressive dictators. This so-called Popular Front policy enjoyed temporary success in France in 1936 and 1937. Russia also furnished military advisers and supplies to China in its struggle with Japan and to the anti-Franco forces in the Spanish Civil War, which broke out in 1936.

Britain, suspicious of Soviet intentions, preferred to avoid the risk of war. Fearful of losing British friendship, France likewise avoided measures that might offend Hitler and his fellow dictators. During the Munich crisis of 1938, the Soviet government was completely ignored by Britain and France. Already disillusioned by the weakness of the Western powers, Stalin decided to change his strategy. Soviet foreign policy reversed its course when Stalin and Hitler signed a nonaggression pact in 1939. Soon after this agreement, World War II began.

Section Review

1. What was the Comintern? How was it used by Stalin for the advantage of the Soviet Union?
2. What were the aims of Soviet foreign policy in the Far East? How did Chiang Kai-shek block the Communists?
3. Why did the rise of Adolf Hitler destroy the "Rapallo spirit"?
4. Why did Stalin abandon his policy of "collective security"?

Chapter 28 ▰▰▰▰▰▰▰▰ A Review

Although Russia was an important military and political force in 19th-century Europe, it remained outside the stream of Western civilization. The backward Russian economy and government were controlled by an autocratic czar and mishandled by a decadent nobility. The majority of the peasants were ill-treated and counted for very little in the society.

The reign of the energetic Catherine the Great was followed by a succession of troubled regimes. Her son, Paul I, was assassinated in 1801. The erratic Czar Alexander I succeeded him and made half-hearted attempts at reform. But Russian involvement in the Napoleonic wars and his fear of revolution were responsible for the reactionary policies he fostered. At his death in 1825, an unsuccessful revolution foreshadowed unrest for the reign of his successor, Nicholas I. Autocracy, orthodoxy, and nationalism were the keynotes of Nicholas' rule. He governed with an iron hand, suppressed all liberal movements, and did little to ease the hardships of the downtrodden peasants, who continued to agitate for the abolition of serfdom.

Alexander II, who came to the throne in 1855, freed the serfs. The emancipation, however, did not materially help the peasants. In 1881 the czar was assassinated. Under succeeding rulers, Alexander III and Nicholas II, the international as well as domestic position of Russia deteriorated. Revolution followed an ignominious defeat by the Japanese in 1905. In the period leading up to Russian entry into World War I, some feeble attempts were made to reform the society and government, but discontented revolutionaries, including militant Marxists, fanned the flames of discontent.

Russian participation in World War I brought out the basic shortcomng of the czarist system. Disorganized and defeated, the czar surrendered his power to a provisional government of middle-class liberals. In 1918 the Romanov dynasty ended with the murder of the czar and his family. The provisional government was followed by the advent of Communist rule under the Bolshevik leader,

N. Lenin. After the Treaty of Brest-Litovsk, Russia left the war and prepared to create a socialist society.

Lenin introduced a strict Marxist program while faced with a counterrevolution and the intervention of foreign powers. In the early years of Communist rule, Russia was also bedeviled by famine and disease. In 1921 Lenin made a temporary retreat from communism and introduced the New Economic Policy, in which the government retained control of basic industries but allowed private enterprise in other areas of the economy.

Lenin's death in 1924 brought on a struggle for power within the Communist party. The two chief rivals were Trotsky and Stalin. The victor was Joseph Stalin, who used his position as general secretary to gain power. To the rigors of Marxism, Stalin added his own personal despotism. In 1928 he abandoned the New Economic Policy and began the first of the famous Five Year Plans. Factory workers were regimented and peasants were forced to work on collective farms. The kulaks lost their land and were eliminated as a class. By the middle of the 1930's, the Soviet Union had made important economic gains. Its people, however, were subjected to the hardships of a police state, and Soviet cultural activities were watched carefully by special government officials.

In the area of international relations, the U.S.S.R. moved from a position of relative isolation in the 1920's to one of political recognition and acceptance in the 1930's. The Soviets were admitted to the League of Nations in 1934. With the rise of Mussolini and Hitler, the Soviet Union searched for allies in a system of collective security. When his bid for a defensive alliance with Britain and France was rejected, Stalin signed a nonaggression pact with Hitler in 1939.

The Time

In each group below arrange the events in their correct time sequence.

PRE-REVOLUTIONARY MILESTONES
1. The Act on the Emancipation of the Peasants from Serfdom was decreed.
2. The Russo-Japanese War began.

3. The Decembrist Revolt took place.
4. The "Bloody Sunday" massacre occurred.
5. The first Duma held a meeting.

THE REVOLUTIONARY ERA
1. The Treaty of Brest-Litovsk was signed.
2. The provisional government was set up.
3. Russia entered World War I.
4. Kerensky became prime minister.
5. Lenin staged a successful *coup d'état*.
6. Street fighting began in the city of Petrograd.

THE ESTABLISHMENT OF THE U.S.S.R.
1. Civil war broke out between the "Whites" and the "Reds."
2. Trotsky was expelled from the Communist party.
3. The "Stalin Constitution" was adopted.
4. The New Economic Policy was introduced.
5. The Treaty of Rapallo was signed.
6. The first Five Year Plan was launched.
7. Lenin died.
8. Hitler and Stalin signed a nonaggression pact.
9. Russia was admitted to the League of Nations.
10. Moscow treason trials took place.

The Place
1. Locate the following cities, and name an event that took place in each one: Petrograd, Vladivostok, Port Arthur.
2. In what part of Russia was each of these federated republics located: Ukrainian S.S.R., White Russian S.S.R., Georgian S.S.R.?

The People
1. Identify these rulers of czarist Russia by giving the years of their reigns and by stating one significant fact about each man.

Paul I   Alexander II
Alexander I   Alexander III
Nicholas I   Nicholas II

2. Explain the part each of the following men played in the transformation of czarist Russia into the Soviet Union.

N. Lenin   Alexander Kerensky
Prince George Lvov   Joseph Stalin
Leon Trotsky

Historical Terms

1. Explain the function of each of the following:

provisional government   soviets
constituent assembly   Duma
Congress of Soviets   Comintern
Council of People's Commissars

2. Describe these milestones of Russian history: Decembrist Revolt; Act on the Emancipation of the Peasants from Serfdom; "Bloody Sunday."

3. As Russia was being transformed from a czarist to a Communist state, what historical role was played by each of the following elements of Russian society?

kulaks   Red Guard
Bolsheviks   Reds
Nepmen   Whites

4. What was the Popular Front in Soviet international relations? the "Rapallo Spirit"?

5. Explain the objectives of Lenin's New Economic Policy and Stalin's Five Year Plans. What was the "Stalin Constitution"?

6. Explain what is meant by the "Stalinization" of Russian culture.

Questions for Critical Thinking

1. The Revolution of 1905 has been considered a "dress rehearsal" for the 1917 revolution. Do you agree with this statement? Use pertinent examples to support your answer.

2. Why was the czarist government able to survive the upheaval of 1905 but not that of 1917?

3. In your opinion, what possibilities existed for a democratic regime to succeed after the downfall of the czarist regime? What factors favored democracy and what factors made its survival difficult?

4. Describe the steps by which Russia under the Communists became a totalitarian society.

5. Evaluate the "Stalinization" of Russian society in the 1930's in terms of: (a) material gains; (b) personal liberties; (c) social gains; (d) political stability.

6. What were Lenin's goals during the Period of Militant Communism? In what respects did Stalin attempt to realize these goals?

7. In what ways was the position and power of the czar prior to 1905 similar to that enjoyed by Stalin in 1939? In what ways was it different?

8. To what extent did the Soviets succeed in establishing a "dictatorship of the proletariat"?

Dictators on the March

CHAPTER 29   1929–1939

A bitter economic depression gripped the world in the 1930's. Unemployment and hunger plagued Europe and America. A lithograph by the Mexican artist José Orozco, above left, portrays the despair of jobless workers. Quick to take advantage of widespread discontent, fascist dictators like Benito Mussolini and Adolf Hitler gained power by promising better conditions for their people.

Ours is a land rich in resources, stimulating in its glorious beauty, filled with millions of happy homes, blessed with comfort and opportunity. . . . I have no fears for the future of our country. It is bright with hope.

When President Herbert Hoover spoke these words at his inaugural in 1929, the future did look bright to many Americans and to the world. But eight months after Hoover took office, a stock market crash set off the worst and longest depression in American history. During the three years following the crash, factories became idle, people lost their jobs, business confidence was destroyed, banks closed, and the savings of many Americans were swept away.

In the United States election of 1932, voters chose Franklin Delano Roosevelt for President, the candidate who had pledged "a new deal for the American people." In his inaugural speech he said:

This great Nation will endure as it has endured, will revive and will prosper. So, first of all, let me assert my firm belief that the only things we have to fear is fear itself. . . . I am prepared under my constitutional duty to recommend the measures that a stricken nation . . . may require . . . to wage a war against the emergency, as great as . . . if we were in fact invaded by a foreign foe.

International trade declined sharply as the depression spread around the world. Unemployment, hunger, and mass unrest threatened the stability of all governments. In the older democracies, such as Great Britain, France, and the United States, economic reforms were initiated without the loss of democratic rule. In some of the nations where democracy had been introduced after World War I, governments were unable to meet the economic crisis. Desperate and confused, the people were ready to trade liberty for livelihood. Ruthless leaders rose to power with eloquent promises of full employment and a better life for all. Chapter 29 tells how:

1. **Fascist leaders took control of weakened governments.**

2. **Aggressive dictators defied the democracies.**

3. **Democratic nations tried to maintain peace.**

4. **Appeasement failed to block the dictators.**

1 Fascist leaders took control of weakened governments

A dictatorship is a modern form of absolutist government, and a dictator is a person who seizes control of a government although he has no claim to rule through inheritance or a free election. After World War I, several countries came under the rule of dictators. In Russia after the Bolshevik Revolution of 1917, a dictatorship developed according to communist political ideas. It advocated common ownership of property and capital under the control of a group that supposedly represented the people. Another type of dictatorship, called fascism, permitted private ownership of property and capital, but imposed rigid government regulations upon the people. Fascism arose first in Italy, later in Japan and Germany. Both communism and fascism suppressed opposing political parties, practiced rigorous censorship, denied civil liberties, and assumed absolute control of the people. Communism and fascism became the strongest antidemocratic movements in the world.

Mussolini gained followers in Italy. After the war, unemployment brought social unrest to Italy, and workers demanded reforms. The government in

Italy was organized as a democracy, with a parliament elected by the people. In the 1919 elections, the Socialist party won the greatest number of seats in the Chamber of Deputies, which was the more powerful of the two houses of parliament. Extreme socialists, influenced by the Bolshevik Revolution in Russia, tried to stage a similar revolution in Italy. They called a strike, and workers seized the factories.

The strike and the attempt to make Italy a communist state failed, but the crisis continued. Leaders in parliament quarreled among themselves and were virtually powerless to cope with the situation. They proposed no satisfactory way to improve conditions. So Benito Mussolini, leader of the small Fascist party, decided that the time was right for him to seize power.

Mussolini, born in Dovia, Italy, in 1883, had been attracted to politics as a young man and had become successful as a rabble rouser. As editor of a socialist newspaper in 1912, he posed as a pacifist and attacked Italy's entrance into World War I. Later he changed his attitude and demanded that the country join the Allies. After the armistice, Mussolini organized the Fascist party. He adopted the name *fascist* from the Latin *fasces*, the bundle of rods bound around an ax that had been the symbol of authority in Imperial Rome.

At first, Mussolini pretended to champion the masses, especially the army veterans. He promised to improve working conditions and impose heavy taxes on the rich. Then, as the working classes leaned increasingly toward communism, Mussolini shifted his principles. He attacked communism and developed a following among wealthy landowners, professional people, intellectuals, and high-salaried members of the middle class. In the belief that Mussolini could save them from communism, these groups accepted him as a kind of superman and hailed him as *Il Duce,* or

"the leader." Mussolini took this expression as his title. To break up strikes, he hired black-shirted toughs. By beatings and overdoses of castor oil, Fascist thugs forced political opponents to "agree" with Mussolini's views.

The socialists, who blamed all the woes of Italy on those who had favored participation in the war, comprised the largest party in Italy. They strongly opposed the Fascists. Trade unions also tried to rouse the country to the menace of the Fascists and to the threat of one-man rule and dictatorship. By 1921 the Fascists had won only twenty-two seats in parliament, a mere 4 per cent of the membership. This situation led Mussolini to fear that his movement would lose ground if the discontent in the country were allowed to subside. Therefore he issued an announcement that unless the government was turned over to the Fascists, there would be violence.

Mussolini won control of the government. On October 24, 1922, Mussolini addressed a huge rally of Fascists at Naples. Before the meeting was over, there were thunderous cries of "On to Rome!" Sparked by this rally, thousands of militiamen converged on the capital and occupied it four days later. In view of this demonstration, Italian government officials questioned whether any opposition to the Fascists would be safe or possible. The king of Italy, Victor Emmanuel III, fearful of communism and a civil war, made Mussolini premier. At first Mussolini ruled according to the constitution, but slowly, through a policy of terror, he gained control of parliamentary elections. In 1924 his party won 65 per cent of the votes, which entitled it to 375 seats in parliament.

The year 1924 brought Mussolini a temporary setback in his drive for power. A non-Fascist member of parliament, Giacomo Matteotti, was murdered after he had exposed the terror tactics used by the Fascists. When evidence showed that a gangster employed by Mussolini had killed Matteotti, the people were roused to indignation. Mussolini denied that he had anything to do with the murder and imposed strict censorship of the news. With the press silenced, Il Duce regained popularity. In January 1926 he was authorized to govern by decree if necessary.

Il Duce worked to consolidate his power. Between 1926 and 1931 fascism in Italy took on all the features of despotism. While the monarchy was retained, it served as mere window dressing for a dictatorship. Mussolini declared, "There is no room for an opposition." He made the Fascist party the only legal political party. He allowed men over twenty-one to vote, but gave them only a choice of candidates selected by the Fascists. He used parliament merely to rubber-stamp his own policies.

Mussolini liked to think of himself as the successor to the imperial Caesars of ancient Rome. He declared that Italy should extend its borders and that the whole Mediterranean area should be controlled by Rome. He referred to the sea as *Mare Nostrum* ("our sea").

As a part of a plan to make Italy self-sufficient in case of war, Mussolini set up a great public works program. His government built roads, stadiums, hydroelectric power stations, houses, and schools; reclaimed land from marshes; improved industry and farming. These enterprises furnished work for thousands of men. Wages for workers, however, were lower than in any other European country. Mussolini also enlarged the armed forces, thereby ending unemployment for several more thousands. At the same time he encouraged an increase in population, thus eventually adding to the number of unemployed and their dependents. Parents of large families were praised by state officials, and

Italians living in other countries were urged to return to Italy.

A firm believer in the strength of propaganda, Mussolini used all means of communication to spread Fascist ideas. Schools became institutions to teach party doctrine. Textbooks were rewritten to glorify the "mission" of Italy, to preach the invincibility of Il Duce, and to promote soldiering as the noblest of careers.

By 1930 the depression that had begun in the United States spread to Europe. It increased the internal problems in Italy, and Mussolini's attempts to improve the economy were largely ineffective. With the growing scarcity of food and lack of raw materials, standards of living fell and discontent increased. Mussolini believed that only some gigantic gamble, some successful military exploit, could enable him to maintain his hold on the Italian people.

Japan made demands on China. In 1868 Japan began a far-reaching program of modernization along Western lines. Industry needed new sources of raw materials and tariff-free markets. Living space was becoming a crucial problem for the increasing population. In 1914 Japan entered World War I to fulfill these needs.

As soon as Japan had declared war on Germany, it invaded areas in China that had been leased to Germany. After these areas had been conquered, China asked Japan to withdraw, but in January 1915 Japan replied with an ultimatum, known as the Twenty-one Demands. In this ultimatum, Japan insisted that the rights Germany had held in Shantung be turned over to Japan; that Manchuria and Mongolia be given to Japan; and that China yield control of its military, financial, and commercial affairs. The United States protested against these demands because, if granted, they not only would put China under the control of Japan but also would deny rights to other nations as well.

Fascist Governments skillfully manipulated public opinion in order to maintain police states. Censorship was common. At right, Italian Black Shirts supervise the burning of socialist books, considered subversive to Mussolini's regime. Military training in fascist countries began at an early age and children were taught to admire war. Below, uniformed Japanese boys raise their rifles in a salute to Emperor Hirohito. At massive Nazi rallies, like the one at Nuremberg, left, Hitler's oratory—against a background of searchlights, bands, and massed troops—aroused his hearers to a fever pitch of excitement and thunderous acclaim.

Japan withdrew some of its demands, but the president of China, Yüan Shih-k'ai, was forced to accept others when the Allies showed no further disposition to support China. The Chinese kept their independence, but the Japanese threat remained. At the end of the war, Japan was granted some former German-held islands in the Pacific, but these islands promised no economic benefits. For expansion, Japan continued to eye Chinese territory.

Military leaders won control in Japan. In the 1920's the Japanese government pursued a moderate policy toward China. Democratic forces were making some progress in Japan, but serious obstacles to democracy existed. Parliament had little power, and the prime minister was responsible only to the emperor. Military leaders were virtually independent of the government, and these war lords were eager for more power. They disliked the trend toward democracy, and they disagreed intensely with the moderate policy toward China. After 1926 the militarists gained strength in the parliament, largely through the support of the peasants, who had come to associate democracy with their poor living conditions.

By 1930 the world depression had caused economic hardships throughout Japan. Export trade was cut in half as the United States and other countries drastically reduced purchases. Widespread unemployment, wage cuts, and strikes gave the militarists an opportunity to seize more power, while fanatics organized secret societies to further their aims.

In November 1930 the liberal prime minister, Yuko Hamaguchi, was assassinated. Two years later, militarists were in control. Their every effort was directed toward building an army and a navy second to none in the Far East, and they murdered statesmen in order to intimidate all political opposition. Their support came

largely from industrialists who had interests in Manchuria and from young men whose careers had been blighted by the depression. The military leaders preached the idea of the glorious destiny of Japan to justify their aggressive actions.

The Weimar Republic encountered storms. During the 1920's, events in Germany were taking an ominous turn. The constitution of the Weimar Republic, adopted in 1919, was democratic in many respects. However, it empowered the president to rule by decree in the event of a serious threat to the public safety. Three chancellors before 1933 made brief use of this provision—a dangerous precedent for the future. The existence of many political parties and the necessity for coalition governments made it difficult to get laws passed and to rule efficiently. An ever present threat to democracy was the strength and influence of the militarists. Their power was apparent in 1925 when Paul von Hindenburg was elected to the presidency. This famous general of World War I was a friend of the monarchy and a symbol of the old militarism. He had never liked democracy.

Radical groups, such as communists and ultra right-wing factions, strongly opposed the Weimar Republic. Fanatical nationalists wanted revenge for the treatment Germany had received at Versailles. The most stable element in the German population, the middle class, had been all but ruined by the inflation following World War I, and the younger generation, disillusioned by the chaos, blamed their problems on the way their elders ran the country. Militarists blamed their defeat in World War I on liberals, pacifists, and Jews. There had long been deep-seated envy—and even hatred—of the Jews, who controlled much of the nation's wealth. The depression provided further unrest. The people were willing to listen to one who echoed their own frustrations and bitterness. His name was Adolf Hitler.

Hitler founded Naziism in Germany.

Adolf Hitler was born in an Austrian village in 1889. As a young man, he worked occasionally as a draftsman or as a colorist of post cards. Much of the time Hitler lived in poverty. After World War I began, he enlisted in the German army and served on the Western Front. While in a hospital recovering from poison gas injuries, news of the armistice and of the German defeat reached him. The anger and shame he felt for his adopted country mingled with the bitterness and frustrations resulting from his own failures. His political attitudes became saturated with hatred for the new German government, for Jews, and for anyone associated with the Versailles Treaty.

In April 1920 the National Socialist German Workers' party, or Nazi party, was formed. Its program, drawn up in part by Hitler, was designed to appeal to all discontented persons, to whatever class of society they belonged. Hitler proclaimed his political beliefs later that year at the first mass meeting of the party in a Munich beer hall. He had discovered the effectiveness of his oratory and delighted in spellbinding his audiences. His favorite themes were as follows:

The army was never defeated in 1918. Germany was stabbed in the back by traitors at home and betrayed by the Allies. Most of the woes of Germany were caused by the Jews, who had manipulated finances to the ruin of Germany and who could never be loyal to Germany or to any other government. Germany had to become strong again. The country must be cleansed of traitors, and the Versailles Treaty must be scrapped.

The value of the German mark began to fall drastically in 1921, and by July 1923 it was practically worthless. At a mass meeting in Nuremberg the following September, Hitler denounced the Weimar Republic. The enthusiasm with which the speech was received by the thousands of his followers who were present led Hitler to consider attempting the overthrow of the German government. As a first step in overthrowing the government, Hitler planned an uprising in Bavaria. This attempt failed, and he was imprisoned. During his months in prison, he wrote the story of his life, which he called *Mein Kampf* ("My Struggle").

In October 1928 the Nazi party had only twelve representatives in the Reichstag, the lower house of the national legislature. By September 1930, when the depression hit Germany, the Nazis had increased their number to 107, becoming the second largest group in the Reichstag. Hungry, desperate people turned to Hitler's brand of fascism, and industrialists saw it as a bulwark against communism. By 1932 the Nazis were the largest party in Germany.

Hitler became Führer of Germany.

On January 30, 1933, President Hindenburg made Hitler chancellor of Germany, and on that date the Third Reich was born. (The First Reich, or empire, was begun by Charlemagne in 800, renewed by Otto in 962, and abolished in 1806 by Napoleon. The Second Reich began in 1871 with the unification of Germany and continued until 1918 when Germany was defeated in World War I.)

Through the Enabling Act of March 23, 1933, the Reichstag gave Hitler dictatorial powers. The next year, Hitler stripped the Reichstag of all power. He also dissolved opposition parties; outlawed trade unions; established labor camps; discarded laws not convenient to the Nazi authorities; nationalized business; and, as President Hindenburg lay dying in 1934, abolished the office of President. Three hours after

Geopolitics may be defined as the study of government and its policies as affected by physical geography. The word *geopolitics* came into common usage in Germany during the 1920's and 1930's, chiefly because of the efforts of Dr. Karl Haushofer, a retired general who was a professor of geography at the University of Munich. One central thesis was basic to Haushofer's theories of geopolitics. He believed that the nation which controlled eastern Europe would be able to control the Heartland, the area extending from southeastern Russia to Mongolia. Command of the Heartland would lead to control of the World-Island, consisting of Europe, Asia, and Africa.

Haushofer believed that under German leadership, eastern Europe, with its mineral and agricultural resources, would become a great industrial region. The economic and military power of German and eastern European industry would then enable Germany to control the Heartland. According to Haushofer, the Heartland provided space for withdrawal of vital industries beyond range of possible attack. It was also a base from which armies could attack any country on the rim of the Heartland. Thus, invulnerable to attack and

with great economic and military resources, Germany would rule the World-Island. Command of the World-Island, which made up two thirds of the land surface of the earth, would result in German domination of the entire world, he concluded.

Karl Haushofer's ideas on geopolitics influenced the thinking of Adolf Hitler, who agreed that control of eastern Europe and the Heartland was a necessary step toward world domination. During World War II, Hitler tried to conquer the Heartland by sending armies into the Ukraine and southwest Russia. Hitler's failure, together with the association of German geopolitics with Nazi aggression, caused geopolitics to fall into disrepute.

Some geographers attacked Haushofer's theories by stating that air power and modern missile technology rendered the Heartland vulnerable to attack. Other geographers showed that the Heartland's mineral and agricultural resources were insufficient to achieve world domination. Today, geopolitics is used chiefly as a tool by social scientists to help explain foreign policies of governments. They understand that geography, though important, is only one element in the record of nations.

Hindenburg's death on August 2, Hitler became *Führer* (the leader) and Reich Chancellor of Germany. Hitler immediately demanded that each member of the armed forces take an oath of loyalty not to Germany, but to Hitler. The military forces thus came under the control and direction of Hitler.

The Nazis preached the idea of a "super race." According to the Führer, Germans were Aryans and were the "master race," or "super race." The Nazis began a carefully planned program to eliminate Jews from German national life. In 1935, by the infamous Nuremberg Laws, Jews were deprived of citizenship rights and relegated to a position of social inferiority. Intermarriage of Jews and gentiles was prohibited. A national boycott of Jewish businesses and professional services was introduced, forcing Jews to give up their property and leave Germany.

Hitler's insistence on the idea of the Germans as a "super race" instilled in the German people a sense of prestige. They felt that Hitler was giving Germany strength, importance, and prosperity in place of weakness, defeat, and depression. They enthusiastically accepted him as their leader. Unemployment was ended. Germans, young and old, were made members of organizations that provided various attractions, from showy uniforms for boys to athletic events and inexpensive vacations for workers. Hitler's growing popularity was shown in the Saar where, after fifteen years of management by the League of Nations, the Saarlanders voted in 1935 by an overwhelming majority to join Germany.

The Third Reich was organized for war. As they did in Italy and Japan, fascists in Germany immediately sought to mold the minds of the citizens by a program that glorified war. Textbooks were rewritten and the press and radio were censored as

steps toward the mastery of Europe. Declaring that Germany must have *lebensraum,* or "living space," Hitler began massive preparations for the expansion of Germany. Strict food-rationing laws were put into effect to make Germany self-sufficient in the event of war. These laws regulated the amount of food each person could have and where he could buy it. The Third Reich was short on raw materials, and rules were set up so that nothing was wasted. Shopkeepers were allowed a specified amount of wrapping paper for each package; housewives were forbidden to dispose of such items as empty toothpaste tubes, waste fats, paper, or anything that might be useful in warfare. Such waste items had to be kept until authorized collectors inspected them. Barbers even had to preserve hair clippings. Synthetic, or *ersatz,* products took the place of rubber, wool, butter, flour, and other essentials. Imports could rarely be paid for in money. They had to be paid for chiefly in products not needed for warfare, such as canaries or harmonicas. The highway system of *Autobahnen* was constructed to permit rapid movement of troops, and an enormous stockpile of munitions was accumulated.

Businessmen and industrialists, who in 1932 thought they could control Hitler, found too late that Germany was being conquered by the master mind of fascism. Outside of Germany, many people believed that their nations could deal with Hitler, that he wanted only to restore Germany to prosperity and to its rightful place among nations. Ultraconservatives in the democracies tended to admire Naziism for its discipline, efficiency, and hostility to communism.

Section Review

1. What conditions in Italy after World War I paved the way for dictatorship? How did Mussolini gain control of the Italian government? As Il Duce, what steps did

he take to consolidate his power and to transform Italy into a fascist nation?

2. What were the motives of the Japanese for expansion in China? Explain how military leaders succeeded in gaining control of the Japanese government.

3. What problems of the Weimar Republic contributed to the rise of fascism in Germany? How did Hitler succeed in becoming Führer of Germany? Describe the developments which took place in Germany as Hitler transformed it into a Nazi nation.

2 Aggressive dictators defied the democracies

After the fascists had consolidated their power in Germany, Italy, and Japan, they concentrated on expansion.

Japan attacked China. Japanese militarists were determined to control China, but each aggressive step only made the Chinese increase their resistance. In September 1931 Japanese troops seized several provinces in Manchuria, using as a pretext an explosion on a railroad owned by the Japanese. They accused the Chinese of blowing up the track. The Japanese, in turn, were accused by the Chinese, who appealed to the League of Nations. The League appointed a commission under Lord Lytton to investigate the situation. Late in 1932 the Lytton Commission reported that although Japan had rights in Manchuria, it was chiefly at fault in the dispute and should withdraw its troops. The commission also recommended ways to settle the conflict and to restore Chinese sovereignty. In the meantime, the Japanese had transformed Manchuria into their puppet state of Manchukuo and indicated that they had no intention of giving up the territory, which was rich in natural resources. Therefore, Japan rejected the rec-

ommendations of the Lytton Commission, withdrew from the League of Nations, and in May 1933 forced a truce with the Chinese. Nevertheless, guerrilla fighting continued.

From the start of hostilities in 1931, the Chinese boycotted Japanese goods and cut imports from Japan by 94 per cent. Japan tried to install local governments in China that would be favorable to Japan, but constant friction resulted. In 1937 Japan again began open warfare in China. Shanghai, Nanking, and other large cities fell to the Japanese, but the Chinese did not surrender. Instead, 50 million of them fled to the western part of China, taking machinery, farm equipment, and furniture in carts or on their backs. They set up a new capital for China at Chungking late in 1938.

The League of Nations condemned the Japanese aggression. Its members—as well as the United States—continued to protest Japanese actions. But they were unwilling to use military force against Japan, for most of them were still suffering from the depression. They feared that their domestic economic problems would be increased if they antagonized Japan. This failure to act against Japan dealt a heavy blow to the prestige of the League.

Mussolini also humbled the League of Nations. In Italy, Mussolini was motivated by two main desires. He was anxious to obtain raw materials for Italy's industries, and he was eager to win military glory.

As a first step to military glory, Mussolini turned toward Ethiopia. In October 1935 he invaded Ethiopia, claiming that the Ethiopians were attacking the Italian colony of Somaliland. The Italian forces were equipped with poison gas, heavy artillery, air force bombing squadrons, and other modern weapons against which the Ethiopians had no defense.

Although Britain and France took the lead in demanding League action against

By League of Nations Mandate 1919

GROWTH OF JAPAN
1851–1939

PACIFIC OCEAN

EQUATOR

Japanese Empire
1851–1931

1932–1933

1936–1939

0   300   600 MILES

Prepared by
Rally & Co., Chicago

Italy, the League imposed only a few economic sanctions against Mussolini. Because the sanctions did not include a prohibition on sale of all war materials and because the United States (which was not a member of the League) imposed no sanctions, League opposition had little effect. By 1936 Mussolini's victory was complete.

Hitler and Mussolini scrapped treaties. In 1933, after Japan had withdrawn from the League, Germany also announced its withdrawal. In March 1935 Hitler denounced the Versailles Treaty, declaring that he was rearming Germany on the grounds that other nations had failed to disarm in accordance with peace treaties. (Germany had actually been training military personnel in Russia ever since the Treaty of Rapallo in 1922.) The League formally condemned Hitler's denunciation of the Versailles Treaty, but Hitler did not take this censure seriously. In March 1936, one year after denouncing the treaty, Hit-

ler sent troops into the Rhineland, thus completely violating treaty provisions.

Neither France nor Britain wanted to become involved in a war with Hitler. Furthermore, the British had a feeling of guilt about the Versailles Treaty with respect to its provisions affecting Germany. "Why should not Hitler have the right to fortify his own territory?" many Englishmen asked. "If this demand can be satisfied, Germany will likely become a good neighbor." History was to prove that this hope was unjustified, but it was not obvious in 1936.

Until that year, France, Britain, and Italy usually stood together against Germany. In fact, Mussolini in 1934 had forced Hitler to retreat from a move against Austria. In the spring of 1935, England, France, and Italy had met in Stresa, Italy, to establish mutual defense measures. However, when Britain and France opposed his attack on Ethiopia early in October, Mussolini scrapped the agreements made at the Stresa Conference and turned to Germany.

Between World Wars, small-scale conflicts occurred in many places. In 1931, Japan defeated the Chinese in Manchuria; the Japanese tank on the opposite page, above, patrols a captured Manchurian city. Below it, Ethiopian soldiers march toward a front-line clash with Italian troops, who invaded their country in 1935. Italy and Germany used Spain as a training ground for their troops when they intervened on Franco's side during the fascist uprising of 1936-1939. At left, Loyalist refugees flee Spain. Below, in a cartoon by the famous English cartoonist David Low, Hitler and Mussolini flank a passive Franco and proclaim, "Honest, mister, there's nobody here but us Spaniards"; their thin disguise disturbs Daladier of France and Chamberlain of England, who were committed to a policy of neutrality. The cartoon on the opposite page mocks the peace efforts of diplomats, whose cannon-barrel heads reveal their insincerity and mutual distrust.

On October 27, 1936, Mussolini and Hitler formed an alliance known as the Rome-Berlin Axis.

Fascism gained control in Spain. In 1931 the Spaniards overthrew their monarch and set up a republic. For five years afterward the nation struggled against problems of poverty, illiteracy, and social unrest. The Spanish republic introduced many reforms, but failed to control a strong fascist group that blocked the attempts to improve conditions. Led by General Francisco Franco, military chiefs revolted against the republic in 1936, and the Spanish Civil War began. Franco's forces were joined by the fascists and extreme nationalists.

Thousands of people, known as Loyalists, rushed to the defense of the republic. They were aided by a communist group, who felt their best interests would be served by fighting fascism. Volunteer contingents from other nations arrived in Spain to help the Loyalists, and for a while they were successful, but they lacked arms.

As in the Rhineland crisis, Britain, France, and other European states wished to avoid involvement in a war. Therefore they adopted a policy of strict neutrality. The United States had also passed strong neutrality laws to keep out of conflicts. Such policies and laws prevented these nations from helping the Loyalists.

Mussolini and Hitler, however, sent arms and troops to aid Franco's fascists. In March 1939 the capital city, Madrid, was captured by Franco, and the republic ceased to exist. The neutral policy of the democratic nations was largely responsible for the appearance of yet another fascist dictatorship in Europe.

Section Review

1. What steps did the League of Nations take to stop Japanese aggression in China? With what results?

2. Why did League action fail to prevent Mussolini's conquest of Ethiopia?
3. Describe the British reaction to Hitler's seizure of the Rhineland.
4. How did the neutrality of Western powers serve to further the cause of fascism in Spain?

3 Democratic nations tried to maintain peace

While fascism was taking over in Italy, Japan, Germany, and Spain, the governments of France, Britain, and the United States retained their democratic forms. Noisy minorities of fascists who admired Hitler and a scattering of communists who believed Russia was a Utopian state gained little ground in these older democracies, but they remained a serious threat. While unemployment, depression, and social unrest called for solutions, governments tried to keep out of war.

France faced many crises. For ten years after World War I, France enjoyed a flood of free-spending tourists. For a time employment levels were so high that foreign workers had to be imported to fill jobs. The chief worry among the French was the possibility of another war, and this fear centered on Germany.

At the beginning of the 1930's, the depression brought an end to prosperity. France lost many of its markets, as well as most of its tourists, who also were hit by the depression. Unemployment became serious, and budget deficits mounted. Public dissatisfaction and unrest increased, and government after government came to power. The changing of governments became so ludicrous that an American wit, Will Rogers, likened the comings and goings of the French cabinets to the changing of the guard at the gates of Buckingham Palace in London.

The confidence of the French in their government was shaken by the instability of political life and also by a number of scandals. The most notorious was the affair of Alexandre Stavisky, an unscrupulous promoter who robbed French investors of millions of francs. Yet the government seemed unwilling to prosecute the swindler or to take action to stop corruption among high officials. Public anger exploded in 1934 when irate citizens rioted before the French parliament building.

At the same time, totalitarian movements menaced the republic. On the extreme right were the fascists, who believed that a dictator for France was the only solution. On the left were the communists, who schemed for a violent revolution. French democracy was in serious danger, and a patriotic coalition, the National Union, was formed. It demanded stronger powers for the prime minister as a means of halting the changes of governments.

A champion of reform, Leon Blum, came to power in June 1936. He was supported by a number of liberal parties, including the French communists. This alliance of parties, formed to curb fascism in France, was called the Popular Front. It also sought to root out corruption, strengthen national finances, and improve conditions for workers. While Blum's government struggled with these problems, the civil war began in Spain in July, and fascism threatened France from both inside and outside the country. Unable to achieve its goals at home and fearful of becoming involved in a war, the Blum government was forced to resign in June 1937. A second Popular Front government was formed in 1938, but it lasted only a few months. Meanwhile, strikes continued and unrest grew. While Frenchmen quarreled among themselves, German factories, staffed by disciplined and regimented workers, rapidly built armaments for Hitler and strengthened Germany.

Britain sought reconciliation among nations. Great Britain emerged from World War I with a domestic and foreign debt ten times as great as it had been before the war. Unemployment, strikes, and a desperate need for better education, health, and housing staggered British statesmen. During the hectic postwar years, the country was alternately ruled by two political organizations: the Labour party, led by James Ramsay MacDonald, and the Conservative party, led by Stanley Baldwin. Neither these leaders nor their parties showed much energy or vision. When the depression worsened conditions after 1929, the government began strenuous economies and introduced tariffs to protect home markets, but most of Britain's domestic problems were only partially solved. While Britain muddled along, the aggressions of the dictators continued to challenge British interests. Japan threatened British holdings in the Far East; Mussolini was a disturbing element in the Mediterranean; and the rise of Hitler presented a menace even closer to home.

When Baldwin retired in 1937, Neville Chamberlain became prime minister. He had strong hopes that world peace could be gained by agreements among nations. British statesmen had championed reconciliation with Germany in the 1920's and had sought to reduce armaments. Even in the face of increasing fascist strength, they advocated disarmament. The British people themselves were strong supporters of pacifism. With each fascist demand, Chamberlain doubled his efforts to settle difficulties through agreements. His policy was one of appeasement.

The United States introduced a bold program of social reform. During the 1920's the United States had been an economic oasis with its high wages, prosperity, and general optimism. With the onslaught of the depression, the unemployed numbered nearly 13 million. In 1932 Franklin D. Roosevelt was elected to the presidency. As Chief Executive, he pledged himself to restore prosperity to the country. His plan, called the New Deal, consisted of relief for the needy, recovery for business, and basic reforms for the nation's economic system.

In a comprehensive program of direct relief, the federal government assumed a large part of the responsibility for feeding, clothing, and sheltering needy Americans. This was accomplished through allocation of funds by the federal government to the states. Hope was rekindled for many who could perform "socially useful" work through the Works Progress Administration (WPA). Although some critics described such tasks as cleaning streets and parks and performing certain clerical jobs as "boondoggling" or "made work," these jobs furnished regular pay checks and helped restore self-respect to millions. The Civilian Conservation Corps (CCC) enrolled young workers, who would otherwise compete with older men for jobs, to aid in reforestation and prevention of soil erosion. Other youths were encouraged to remain in school by the National Youth Administration (NYA), which created part-time jobs for students in educational institutions. Farmers and home owners who were in danger of losing their property because of failure to meet mortgage payments were aided through federal loans.

Roosevelt's program of recovery included strengthening of the Reconstruction Finance Corporation (RFC), which loaned billions of dollars to business and industry. After public confidence in banks had been shaken by thousands of failures, Roosevelt closed the nation's banks and quickly reopened those which were declared sound after inspection. A major effort was made to revive industry and give labor unions more recognition through the National Recovery Administration (NRA). This agency organized businesses through national codes of fair practices and gave workers the right to engage in collective bargaining. Congress attempted to help farmers by passing the Agricultural Adjustment Act (AAA), which regulated the production of farm goods.

The New Deal also took steps toward long-range reform. A Federal Deposit Insurance Corporation (FDIC) was created to safeguard bank deposits. Laws to protect the public against worthless stocks were enforced by the Securities and Exchange Commission (SEC). An extensive program of social security was begun through a law which furnished unemployment insurance to those who lost jobs, provided old age pensions to workers over sixty-five, and aided needy unemployables. In an experiment which had no parallel in American history, the Tennessee Valley Authority (TVA) undertook to furnish cheap electricity and many other services to millions of Southerners by the creation of huge public power projects. In the field of international trade, the Roosevelt administration encouraged reciprocal tariff agreements which resulted in lowering of duties and increased trade.

Although New Deal measures helped improve business and reduce unemployment, an economic decline in 1937 proved that prosperity could not easily be guaranteed by government. Better times returned in 1938, but a rapidly growing population made the task of creating full employment very difficult.

People argued violently over the New Deal. Some asserted that it gave too much power to labor unions, introduced too much government control, and encouraged too much public spending at the expense of the taxpayer. On the other hand, its defenders argued that it had saved the capitalistic system, and that it was an essential compromise between the old economic ways that had led to depression and the totalitarian system of absolute control wielded by the dictators.

The United States strengthened its ties in the Western Hemisphere. When the international situation became threatening in the 1930's, the United States made determined efforts to stay out of war. From 1935 to 1937, Congress passed neutrality laws to insulate the nation from foreign dangers. The sale of arms and munitions to nations at war was prohibited, but the President was given authority to designate certain other goods to be paid for in cash by warring countries, provided these goods were transported in foreign ships.

The United States also began to strengthen friendly relations with its neighbors—Canada and the Latin-American countries. Generally speaking, relations with Canada were cordial. Much American capital had been invested in this northern neighbor, and the frontier between the two countries was the longest undefended border in the world.

Relations "south of the border" were more complex and difficult. Frequent revolutions and strife in Latin America had prompted the United States on a number of occasions to bring pressure on its southern neighbors. Troops from the United States had occupied areas in the Caribbean —among them Haiti and Nicaragua—in order to maintain order and protect United States interests. Latin Americans resented these acts, which they called Yankee imperialism. During the late 1920's, the United States began to change its policy toward Latin America. In his inaugural address in 1933, President Roosevelt spoke of the need for a Good Neighbor Policy. In 1935 at Buenos Aires and again in 1938 at Lima, the United States agreed with Latin-American countries that no one nation should intervene in the affairs of another; that there was to be peaceful settlement of all disputes; and that a threat to the peace,

security, or territorial integrity of any American republic was the concern of all. By this agreement the United States gave up the right it had formerly claimed to intervene in Latin-American affairs, and in so doing it gained the good will of all twenty Latin-American republics.

In a real sense, the United States strove to isolate itself from affairs overseas by cementing ties in the Western Hemisphere. But the menace and challenge of hungry, ambitious fascist nations increased, and President Roosevelt and the State Department tried to rouse Americans to the danger. In 1937, in a speech in Chicago, the President said:

> The peace-loving nations must make a concerted effort in opposition to those violations of treaties and those ignorings of humane instincts which today are creating a state of international anarchy and instability from which there is no escape through mere isolation or neutrality.

Americans loathed the racial persecution in Nazi Germany and the sword rattling in Italy and Japan, but they wanted to avoid actual conflict. Isolationist sentiment in the United States remained strong.

Section Review
1. What conditions in France during the 1930's created unrest and lack of confidence in the government?
2. How did the British, under the leadership of Neville Chamberlain, hope to establish world peace?
3. What measures did the New Deal take to cope with the problems of the depression?
4. How did the United States attempt to insulate itself from European entanglements?
5. What efforts did the United States make to strengthen its ties with the other nations of the Western Hemisphere?

4 Appeasement failed to block the dictators

The failure of the League of Nations as an agency of collective security had become obvious by 1935. The memory of World War I was still vivid to the British and French, and they were reluctant to become involved in another war. They adopted a policy of appeasement in the belief that if the dictators were allowed to achieve some of their aspirations, they might be satisfied. Thus conflict would be averted.

Germany seized Austria. The policy of appeasement gave Hitler the chance he needed to plan for large-scale territorial expansion. In 1936 a German-Japanese agreement, followed by an agreement between Italy and Japan, united the three fascist powers. On the surface the alliance was a defensive agreement against Russia; in reality it was designed for aggression and expansion.

Hitler first planned to annex Austria. So in February 1938 he invited the Austrian chancellor, Kurt von Schuschnigg, to his mountain hideaway at Berchtesgaden in southern Germany. There, Hitler threatened the Austrian chancellor, who agreed to include Nazis in the Austrian cabinet. Hitler followed this meeting with an invasion of Austria by his armed forces on March 12 and 13. His secret police, the Gestapo, took over Vienna and began repressive measures against liberals and Jews. Thousands of persons, especially scientists, writers, and artists, fled the country to find safety elsewhere.

By means of the *Anschluss* (as the union of Austria and Germany is commonly called), Hitler was able to gain for the Reich $100 million in gold, 7 million additional citizens, and rich resources in timber. Neither France nor Britain did anything more than protest this aggressive act.

Hitler moved into Czechoslovakia. Czechoslovakia was Hitler's next victim. For some time Hitler had courted the support of about 3 million German-speaking people who lived in an area of Czechoslovakia called Sudetenland. In the summer of 1938, a torrent of Nazi propaganda was directed against the Czech government. The Nazis claimed that the Sudetenland Germans were being oppressed by the Czechs. Hitler denounced the Czech president and thus brought on another crisis.

British Prime Minister Neville Chamberlain was determined that no war should result. He argued that because the Sudetens were Germans, Germany naturally wanted to bring them into the Third Reich. Chamberlain held a conference with Hitler at Berchtesgaden on September 15, 1938, where the prime minister agreed to the incorporation of Sudetenland into the Third Reich. Both France and Russia, who had previously guaranteed the frontiers of Czechoslovakia, failed to support the Czechs in their hour of need. Another meeting between Hitler and Chamberlain followed a week later, this time at Godesberg. Confident of success, Hitler made a further demand: the immediate surrender of all Sudeten districts. At this meeting Hitler also supported the claims of Poland and Hungary for parts of Czech territory.

Chamberlain refused to accept the new terms and returned to London. He appeared to take a firm stand against Hitler. Then Hitler announced, "This is the last territorial claim I shall make in Europe." He asked Chamberlain and the French premier, Edouard Daladier, to meet with him and Mussolini at Munich on September 29, 1938. They agreed. Representatives from neither Czechoslovakia nor Russia were present at the meeting.

The conference arranged for the transfer of Sudetenland to Germany, with the frontiers of Czechoslovakia to be fixed by an international commission. Hitler and

AXIS ACQUISITIONS
March 1936–April 1939

Rhineland annexed by Germany
March 1936

Austria annexed by Germany
March 1938

Sudetenland annexed by Germany
September 1938

Czechoslovakia annexed by Germany
March 1939

Albania annexed by Italy
April 1939

Prepared by
Rand McNally & Co., Chicago

Chamberlain signed a statement denouncing war, and France and Britain guaranteed the new Czech frontiers set at the conference. Immediately following the Munich Conference, Poland and Hungary pressed their claims for Czech territory, and these demands were settled by Germany and Italy.

The result of the Munich Conference was that Czechoslovakia surrendered 16 thousand square miles of territory and 5 million of its population. Nazi Germany increased its territory by more than 10 thousand square miles, added 3½ million people, and took over large supplies of arms. The Third Reich thus became the largest nation in area in western Europe.

Section Review

1. Why did the people of England and France support Chamberlain's policy of appeasement?
2. Describe Hitler's seizure of Austria.
3. Summarize the negotiations leading to the Munich Conference and describe the results of the meeting.

In Italy, Benito Mussolini became premier in 1922 and within a few years established himself as a Fascist dictator. Fascism also gained ground in Japan, where militarists, using consequences of the depression to further their aims, gained complete control by 1932. Adolf Hitler, leader of the Nazi party, became chancellor of Germany in 1933. He suppressed all opposition and brought business, labor, and the armed forces under his control. The Reichstag was shorn of authority, laws were rewritten, and systematic persecution of the Jews was begun.

In 1931 Japan was censured by the League of Nations for aggression in China. Thereupon, Japan withdrew its membership and continued its military advances. Members of the League hesitated to take further steps against Japan and thus dealt a fatal blow to the League.

Mussolini, who realized the weakness of the League, successfully attacked Ethiopia in 1935. Hitler then allied his nation with Italy, and together they aided fascist forces in the Spanish Civil War (1936-1939).

Great Britain, France, and the United States, the three strongest democracies, managed to retain democratic ways of life through the depression years. President Roosevelt introduced sweeping reform legislation in the United States. As international problems mounted, the United States strengthened ties in the Western Hemisphere and passed neutrality laws to avoid becoming involved in Europe's quarrels. Great Britain and France adopted a policy of appeasement toward aggressive dictators as a means of avoiding war. In 1938 Hitler moved against Austria, annexed it to Germany, and demanded large areas of Czechoslovakia. Determined to keep peace in Europe, Britain and France allowed Hitler to have his way at the Munich Conference.

The Time

Indicate the period in which each event described in the following statements occurred.

(a) 1916-1920   (d) 1931-1935
(b) 1921-1925   (e) 1936-1940
(c) 1926-1930

1. Hitler invaded Austria.
2. Popular Front government came to power in France.
3. Mussolini invaded Ethiopia.
4. World-wide depression began.
5. Mussolini became premier of Italy.
6. Chinese set up a new capital for China.
7. Hitler and Mussolini formed the Rome-Berlin Axis.
8. Hitler became chancellor of Germany.
9. Fascists revolted in Spain.
10. Japanese troops invaded Manchuria.
11. Franklin D. Roosevelt was elected President of the United States.
12. Neville Chamberlain became prime minister of Britain.
13. Nazi party was formed.
14. Four-power conference was held in Munich.
15. Japanese prime minister, Yuko Hamaguchi, was assassinated.

The Place

1. Locate each of the following places and tell which fascist power gained control over it: Manchuria; Sudetenland; Ethiopia.

2. Name one event of the 1920's or 1930's associated with each of the following cities:

Madrid	Munich	Godesberg
Chungking	Stresa	Berchtesgaden
Nuremberg	Vienna	

The People

Identify the following political leaders by country and give one fact about each man.

Benito Mussolini	Giacomo Matteotti
Neville Chamberlain	Paul von Hindenburg
Adolf Hitler	Leon Blum
Franklin D. Roosevelt	Francisco Franco
Kurt von Schuschnigg	Edouard Daladier

Historical Terms

1. Explain the meaning of each of the following terms as it applied to Naziism in Germany.

Führer	*Mein Kampf*
Enabling Act	Third Reich
lebensraum	Gestapo

2. Name the country and one policy with which each of the following groups or movements was associated: National Union; New Deal; Popular Front; Loyalists.

3. What were some of the provisions of Japan's Twenty-one Demands on China? What were some of the recommendations of the Lytton Commission?

4. What was the Good Neighbor Policy?

5. Identify the following government agencies of the United States and describe the purpose of each:

NRA	AAA	TVA
FDIC	NYA	RFC
CCC	SEC	WPA

Questions for Critical Thinking

1. How did the fascist dictatorships of Germany and Italy differ from the communist dictatorship of the Soviet Union?

2. Why did fascism succeed in Germany and Italy but not in England and France?

3. In what respects was the dictatorship of Mussolini similar to that of his Roman predecessor, Julius Caesar? In what respects was it different?

4. Why has the world-wide depression of the 1930's been called "the match that lighted the flames of war"?

5. Why was the League of Nations powerless to stop fascist aggression?

World War II

Only twenty-one years after "the war to end all wars," the world was engulfed by the most devastating conflict in the history of mankind. At least 17 million men were killed in battle, and 18 million civilians lost their lives behind the lines. A painting, "The Martyrdom of Warsaw," depicts the heroic resistance of civilians to enemy occupation. At right, intact above the ruins of Dresden, Germany, a statue symbolically extends a comforting hand of pity.

Soldiers, sailors and airmen of the Allied Expeditionary Force: You are about to embark upon a great crusade, toward which we have striven these many months. The eyes of the world are upon you. The hopes and prayers of liberty-loving people everywhere march with you. In company with our brave allies and brothers in arms on other fronts you will bring about the destruction of the German war machine, the elimination of Nazi tyranny over the oppressed peoples of Europe, and security for ourselves in a free world.

Your task will not be an easy one. Your enemy is well trained, well equipped and battle-hardened. He will fight savagely.

But this is the year 1944. Much has happened since the Nazi triumphs of 1940-41. The United Nations have inflicted upon the Germans great defeats in open battle, man to man. Our air offensive has seriously reduced their strength in the air, and their capacity to wage war on the ground.

Our home fronts have given us an overwhelming superiority in weapons and munitions of war, and placed at our disposal great reserves of trained fighting men.

The tide has turned. The free men of the world are marching together to victory. I have full confidence in your courage, devotion to duty and skill in battle. We will accept nothing less than full victory. . . .

This message was the order of the day issued June 6, 1944, by the supreme commander of the Allied Expeditionary Forces, General Dwight D. Eisenhower. It signaled the invasion of France, which became known as "Operation Overlord." On that day the greatest amphibious operation in history reached the coast of Normandy. It was the climax of months of coöperation and planning among countries which had united to fight the fascist hordes of Hitler and Mussolini. Such coöperation and unity had not been present in the democratic countries of western Europe in the dark days of 1938 when Czechoslovakia was cut apart by Hitler and Mussolini. Nor had there been any resist-

ance to Mussolini's invasion of Albania in 1939. Only when Hitler struck in Poland were the democracies shocked into direct action.

Chapter 30 tells how:

1. **The Axis powers sought to master the world.**

2. **The Allies defeated the Axis.**

1 The Axis powers sought to master the world

Prime Minister Chamberlain had returned to England after the Munich Conference of 1938 with the promise of "peace in our time." Although a wave of relief swept over millions of apprehensive Europeans, it was not, as Winston Churchill pointed out, the end of fear. It was, he declared, "only the first sip, the first foretaste of a bitter cup. . . ."

Danzig and the Polish Corridor were trouble spots. The Treaty of Versailles had given Poland a corridor through Prussia to provide it with an outlet to the Baltic Sea. Danzig, the port city of the corridor, was declared a free, or independent, city under the protection of the League of Nations. Although 90 per cent of the corridor's population was Polish, almost all the inhabitants of Danzig were German.

On March 23, 1939, Hitler demanded that Danzig be ceded to Germany and that the Nazis be allowed to occupy a narrow strip of the corridor connecting Germany with East Prussia. Poland was suspicious of these demands and appealed to Britain for support. Hitler's demands on Poland convinced Chamberlain that his efforts to appease Hitler had been futile. Therefore, England abandoned the policy of appeasement and began to take steps toward preparedness. Conscription was introduced and, in a short time, British military

WORLD WAR II OFFENSIVES
1939-1942

ALASKA

SOVIET UNION

ATTU
KISKA   ALEUTIAN IS.
• Dutch Harbor

San Francisco

CHINA   JAPAN
                         • Tokyo

Chungking   • Shanghai   MIDWAY IS.
                                           ✗
INDIA   June 1942
        Canton   Pearl Harbor
BURMA   • Hong Kong   WAKE I.   ✗   HAWAIIAN IS.
        PHILIPPINE IS.   To Japan   Dec. 1941
    Manila•   To Japan   Dec. 1941
             May 1942   • GUAM
                                           MARSHALL IS.
    Prince of Wales   PACIFIC   OCEA
    and Repulse   CAROLINE IS.
    Sunk Dec. 1941
    ✗
    Singapore   NEW GUINEA
    To Japan   •Rabaul
    Feb. 1942   SOLOMON IS.
DUTCH EAST INDIES   ✗ GUADALCANAL
                                May 1942

INDIAN OCEAN   Coral Sea
                    ✗
                    May 1942   NEW CALEDONIA
                                (Fr.)
        AUSTRALIA

                • Sydney   ☐ Allies
                Auckland•   ▨ Territory controlled by
                Wellington •   Axis powers, late 1942
                        NEW   ▨ Non-Belligerents
                        ZEALAND
                                           ▨ Areas of German
                                             Submarine Concentration

                                           ☒ Battle

expenditures soared to $5 million a day. Similar preparations occurred in France. Both nations warned Hitler that, in the event of action threatening Polish independence, they would come to the aid of Poland.

The position of the Soviet Union was critical. In the months following their declaration about Poland, Britain and France competed with Germany for an alliance with Russia. Britain suggested that a united front, including the U.S.S.R., be formed against Nazi aggression. Stalin, who had been ignored in the Munich crisis

of 1938, was not eager to join the democracies, who had long been antagonistic toward his regime. He also distrusted Hitler, who had persecuted German communists. However, he came to feel that Hitler as a friendly enemy would be far better than Hitler as a fighting enemy. When the German leader suggested a military pact with Russia, Stalin was receptive. The Nazi-Soviet pact was signed on August 23, 1939. Hitler's real motive was to secure his eastern flank from Russian attack when Germany would be at war with Poland. The pact appealed to Stalin

GREENLAND

ICELAND

× H.M.S. Hood
Sunk May 24, 1941

Murmansk

NADA

Battle of
Britain
Aug.–Oct.
1940

Leningrad
× Siege 1941–43

Bismarck ×
Sunk May 27, 1941

Berlin • Warsaw

• Moscow

Stalingrad
Sept.–Nov. 1942
×

O STATES
New York
Washington

New
Orleans

Battle of the Atlantic
1940–1943

Dunkirk ×
Fall of France
June 1940

× Taranto
Nov. 1940

Casablanca •

Oran
Algiers

El
Alameın
•

ATLANTIC

Allied invasion
of Africa
Nov. 1942

Oct. 1942 ×

Panama Canal

OCEAN

• Dakar

ITALIAN
EAST AFRICA
Br. Occupied
Nov. 1941

INDIAN

OCEAN

• Natal

BRAZIL

MADAGASCAR
British Occupied
May 1942

• Rio de Janeiro

• Montevideo
×
Graf Spee
Scuttled Dec. 1939

Cape Town •

Prepared by
Rand McNally & Co., Chicago

because it gave the Soviet Union time to build up its military strength.

Hitler attacked Poland. Early in the morning of September 1, 1939, without a declaration of war, Nazi troops crossed the Polish frontier. The assault moved in by land, sea, and air. On September 3 Britain demanded that the invasion be halted immediately. Hitler did not bother to answer the ultimatum. That same day Britain and France declared war on Germany.

The Nazi technique was a *blitzkrieg*, or lightning war, which depended upon the

speed of mechanized armies following the infiltration of fifth columnists, or undercover agents, who created fear and dissension among intended victims. The German panzer, or mechanized, divisions rolled through towns and villages and across the open country, crashing through barricades and destroying everything in their paths. The planes of the *Luftwaffe* (air force) bombed civilians and military alike. The Poles, who met the enemy with an outmoded horse cavalry, were overwhelmed.

Meanwhile, Russian forces advanced into Poland from the east. Poland did not receive direct aid from the Allies. England and France discovered that they had very little to send and that it was already too late to help the Poles. Resistance lasted less than a month. By the end of September the two invaders had conquered the country. Then, without any hesitation, Germany and the Soviet Union divided Poland between them.

Along the Franco-German border the British and French failed to take the offensive. They believed that Nazi Germany could be defeated by a naval blockade and by firm Allied defensive action along the Maginot Line, the entrenched fortifications built by the French. For almost seven months, from September 1939 until the end of March 1940, almost no fighting took place along the western front. This period was known as the time of the "phony war," or *Sitzkrieg*.

Russia attacked Baltic nations. The Soviet Union took advantage of the time it had gained by signing the Nazi-Soviet pact. With German troops busy in Poland and French and British troops concentrated on the Maginot Line, Russia forced Latvia, Lithuania, and Estonia to sign treaties granting the Soviets naval and air bases. The Soviet Union then ordered Finland to surrender some of its territory near Leningrad. When the Finns refused, the Russians launched a brutal attack against Finland in November 1939. Finland met the attack with stiff resistance, but the Russians, far outnumbering the Finns, broke through their defenses in March 1940. The Finns were forced to surrender land and to lease important military bases to the Russians.

Stalin, who was becoming increasingly distrustful of his German ally, began to build a buffer zone between Russia and the German frontier. In June 1940 Russian troops moved into Rumania to occupy almost 20 thousand square miles of that country. In August, the Soviet Union an-

nexed the countries of Latvia, Lithuania, and Estonia.

Hitler seized Denmark and Norway. When the conquest of Poland had been completed, Hitler and his generals took advantage of inaction in the west to plan another blitzkrieg. He turned to the Scandinavian countries. On April 9, 1940, without warning, Hitler's paratroopers (disguised in uniforms of other nations) prepared the way for ground forces which invaded Denmark and Norway. Denmark surrendered without much resistance. Norway proved more stubborn, but its resistance had been softened in advance by fifth columnists. Foremost among them was the Norwegian fascist Vidkun Quisling, whose name became synonymous with a traitor. After months of secret collaboration with the Nazis, his followers opened the way for the Germans. Allied forces sent to aid Norway were driven out by the firmly entrenched invaders.

Hitler moved into Belgium and the Netherlands. Through the conquest of Norway and Denmark, Hitler gained new air bases, additional food supplies, and valuable natural resources. With Germany's economy bolstered, Hitler was ready to begin a lightning war through the Low Countries—Belgium, Luxemburg, and the Netherlands—and France.

On May 10, 1940, the Nazi armies launched a blitzkrieg on the Western Front. The Germans encountered little immediate resistance to their mass invasion of the Low Countries. Merciless bombings of such civilian centers as Rotterdam brought the surrender of the Dutch on May 14. French and British soldiers quickly moved northward into Belgium in an attempt to halt the enemy. At the same time, a second Nazi force, bypassing the French Maginot Line, rushed through the gap that had been opened when the Allied troops went to the aid of Belgium. This German force swept through northwestern France and pushed on toward the English Channel. Suddenly, hundreds of thousands of British and French soldiers realized that they were trapped between the German armies in the Low Countries and the second German force and the English Channel.

No help for the Allied troops was forthcoming from Belgium, for King Leopold had decided that his country's position was hopeless. On May 28 Belgium surrendered to Hitler. The Allied forces then had no choice but to retreat to the coast at Dunkirk, where their capture and destruction seemed inevitable. However, in one of the most amazing events of the war, England called into service more than 600 civilian yachts, tugs, barges, motorboats, and various other types of marine craft. These civilian craft crossed the Channel to Dunkirk under cover of darkness to rendezvous with 200 British naval vessels. With the aid of the Royal Air Force, or R.A.F., which provided air protection, this hastily assembled fleet, "in a miracle of deliverance," evacuated more than 335 thousand soldiers to England by June 4.

France fell to the Nazis. The French had placed so much confidence in the Maginot Line that they were otherwise militarily unprepared to defend their country. Furthermore, Nazi fifth columnists with their propaganda methods had weakened the French people psychologically. Thus, when the Nazi army arrived, many French soldiers had little will left to resist the Germans. Early in June 1940, after an all-out Nazi attack, the French army collapsed. French government officials and thousands of terrorized French civilians and military personnel fled to the south of France. Deserted and lifeless, Paris was easily captured on June 14. Marshal Henri Pétain signed an armistice with the Germans on June 22 in the same railroad car in

which Germany had signed the agreement ending World War I. The terms of the armistice split France into two zones. One zone, known as Occupied France, included northern France and the Atlantic coastline. This zone was governed by Germany. The second zone became known as Unoccupied France and was administered by Marshal Pétain at Vichy. The Nazis, however, actually controlled Pétain's Vichy government. For this reason it was opposed by many patriots who refused to give up hope for French liberty. These patriots were represented in London by an exile government known as the Free French government, headed by Charles de Gaulle. The Free French government sponsored an underground group in France, the Maquis, which proved to be an effective guerrilla force against the Nazis during the rest of the war.

When the German defeat of France became certain, Mussolini believed that the war would soon be over. On June 10, 1940, he declared war on France and Britain in hopes of gaining benefits for Italy at a future peace settlement.

The Battle of Britain began. The conquest of France made Hitler the master of the western European continent. Only the British Isles remained unvanquished. Britain had not been invaded since 1066, when William the Conqueror had done so. In the light of Hitler's successes on the continent of Europe, Britain realized the extent of its unpreparedness. This feeling produced great alarm because Hitler seemed poised to order a mass invasion of the island.

The English prepared to fight, and Prime Minister Chamberlain, by now a broken man, resigned. On May 10, 1940, King George VI asked Winston Churchill to form a new government. In the face of almost hopeless odds, Prime Minister Churchill defied Hitler and his armies.

Early in the War, Axis victories stunned the world. Above, a German panzer division occupies a Polish city after a blitzkrieg attack. Allied morale reached a low ebb when Anglo-French forces were trapped at Dunkirk in May 1940; on the opposite page, above, Allied troops await evacuation from the beach. In the Pacific, the Japanese also used blitzkrieg tactics. A Japanese aerial photo, center left, shows the prime target on December 7, 1941—the American fleet at Pearl Harbor. Grim resistance finally slowed the Axis onslaught. At center right, Australian soldiers in the Sahara Desert drop to the ground as a captured German tank suddenly explodes. Below, a dead horse and an abandoned German vehicle testify to fierce fighting in the snows of Russia.

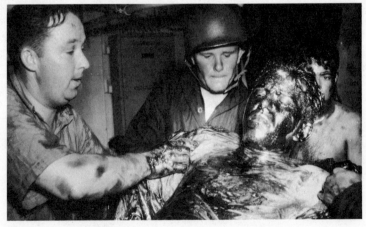

Challenges to Democracy and World War II

The Allied Offensive

Late in 1942, Allied forces began a series of offensives against the Axis powers. American and British troops landed in North Africa in November and, after six months of fighting, freed it from German control. Below left, American Coast Guardsmen peel oil-soaked clothing from a seaman rescued from the water off the African coast. A major Allied move was the D-Day invasion on June 6, 1944, which broke the solid German front in western Europe. At left, troops disembark from ships at a beach in Normandy.

In the Pacific, the American fleet won decisive victories over the Japanese navy, beginning with the battles of Midway and the Coral Sea in early 1942. As their empire disintegrated, the Japanese resorted to desperate methods. One was the use of suicide planes called *kamikazes*, which dove at warships, as shown at right. On the Asian mainland, Allied soldiers battled malaria and typhus as they cut roads through thick jungles. Below, Chinese troops carry supplies along a jungle trail in Burma.

He rallied Britain and the entire free world to the defense of liberty. Following the successful evacuation at Dunkirk, Churchill declared:

> We shall defend our island whatever the cost may be. We shall fight on the beaches, we shall fight on the landing grounds, we shall fight in the fields, and in the streets, we shall fight on the hills; we shall never surrender. . . .

Although Hitler began to strengthen his navy, the invasion by sea never materialized. Hermann Goering, commander of the *Luftwaffe,* had convinced Hitler that the battle against Britain could be won by aerial warfare, thus making the risk of invasion by sea unnecessary.

On August 8, 1940, the first of Germany's nightly bombing missions droned over Britain. The *Luftwaffe* concentrated its bombs on English cities in hopes of quickly breaking Britain's will to resist. By the end of October, thousands of civilians had lost their lives and large areas of Britain had been destroyed. But British morale was far from broken.

The battle in the air was by no means one-sided. With the help of a new device called radar and a splendid fighter plane named the Spitfire, the R.A.F. gradually gained superiority over the *Luftwaffe.* At the end of three months, the British had destroyed almost twice the number of planes that they themselves had lost. Hitler was then forced to abandon his plan of bombing Britain into submission.

The United States abandoned neutrality. Immediately after the evacuation of Dunkirk, President Roosevelt signed an executive order that allowed the United States to send arms to Britain. At the same time, the United States began to look to its own military preparedness. An immense armament program that included plans for a two-ocean navy was launched. In exchange for fifty "overage" destroyers, the British gave the United States the right to establish military bases in Newfoundland and the West Indies. A Selective Service Act was passed in 1940 to draft men for the armed forces. In 1941 the Lend-Lease Act gave the President the power to sell, exchange, or lease arms to a country whose defense was considered vital to the safety of the United States. President Roosevelt declared to the world that the United States was rapidly becoming the "arsenal of democracy."

United States sea and air patrols were established for both the North and South Atlantic. As 1941 progressed, the United States ceased to be a neutral and became a full-fledged but non-shooting member of the Allies.

In August President Roosevelt and Prime Minister Churchill met on a British battleship off the coast of Newfoundland. There they drew up a document known as the Atlantic Charter, or Pact. The pact stated the peace aims of the Allies and emphasized the unity of purpose shared by Britain and the United States. It declared that the Allies sought no territorial changes that did not accord with the freely expressed wishes of the peoples concerned and that all peoples had the right to choose their own forms of government. The charter assured the world that "after the final destruction of Nazi tyranny," all nations should live in peace, free from fear and want; and that all nations "must come to the abandonment of the use of force."

As evidence of the expanding role of the United States in the war, its navy began to convoy merchant vessels to a point in the Atlantic south of Iceland. By locating Nazi underwater craft, United States patrol forces helped bring about the destruction of many German submarines. Germany retaliated by ordering its U-boats to attack American ships. In November

1941 the Congress of the United States voted to arm American merchant ships.

The Battle of the Atlantic was won. The struggle for control of the seas had begun with the British naval blockade of Germany at the outset of the war. Britain planted mines from Scotland to Norway and across the English Channel. Since the British navy had nine times the tonnage of Germany's, Hitler realized the futility of challenging Allied supremacy at sea by the use of surface craft.

Although the Germans planted magnetic mines near the approaches to British harbors, British naval experts learned how to neutralize the magnetic fields of their ships and render them safe. The Germans then resorted to a familiar alternative: U-boat warfare. As in World War I, it was hoped that Britain's life line could be cut by persistent, unrelenting attack. During the early months of the war, more than 65 Allied ships were destroyed by submarines. The British countered by organizing a convoy system with covering aircraft which protected vessels near shore. The Nazi U-boats inflicted considerable damage to Allied shipping, but by May 1943 the antisubmarine campaign, which was greatly aided by the United States, had succeeded in stemming German efforts to cripple Britain.

The Axis overran the Balkans. In September 1940, following the fall of France, Hitler and Mussolini made an alliance with Japan. This agreement, the Tripartite Pact, called for mutual aid. Allied military analysts felt that Axis strategy aimed at the penetration of the Near East so that their armies could join forces with those of the Japanese.

In November 1940 Hungary and Rumania were pressured into endorsing the Tripartite Pact, and Bulgaria followed suit the following March. However, not all the Balkan countries were ready to submit so easily to Axis authority. In October 1940 Italian troops moved into Greece and demanded its surrender. The Greeks answered by driving the Italians back into Albania. In March 1941 Hitler demanded that Yugoslavia join the Rome-Berlin axis. The Yugoslavs refused, virtually daring Hitler to attack. Swiftly and mercilessly, Nazi panzer divisions knifed into Yugoslavia and Greece. On April 17, twelve days after the invasion began, Yugoslavia capitulated. Greece surrendered three days later.

The next month Germany conducted the first large-scale airborne invasion in history against the island of Crete. Nazi paratroopers routed the British from their air and naval bases there. The eastern Mediterranean area was almost within Hitler's grasp.

The war spread to Africa and to the Near East. Mussolini believed that Britain would be unable to defend its possessions in Africa. In August 1940, Italian troops successfully invaded British Somaliland in eastern Africa. However, this victory was short-lived. In January 1941, much to Mussolini's surprise, the British took the offensive. By June the Italians had surrendered almost all of their territories in eastern Africa.

Nor was the war going well for the Italians in northern Africa. In April 1941 Hitler sent three Nazi armored divisions to reinforce the Italians in Libya. The long distance along which the Axis powers stretched their supply lines was a disadvantage, but the Nazi *Afrika Korps,* under the command of Field Marshal Erwin Rommel, proved effective in desert fighting. By June 1941 the *Korps* had driven the British to the Egyptian frontier. When Rommel's forces came within 200 miles of Alexandria, Egypt, German seizure of the Suez Canal seemed imminent.

**OFFENSIVES IN EUROPE
1943-1945**

Neutral Countries

Land Area Held by Allies in July 1943

Allies in Jan. 1944

Allies in July 1944

Allies in Sept. 1944

Allies in Jan. 1945

Allies in May 1945

Held by Germans in May 1945

0   100   200   300 MILES

Prepared by
Rand McNally & Co., F

Hitler attacked the Soviet Union. Despite the warnings of his generals, who recalled Napoleon's fatal invasion of Russia in 1812, Hitler decided to turn on his Soviet ally. On June 22, 1941, Germany launched its attack on Russia, opening up a battle front 1800 miles long from the Baltic to the Black Sea. The Nazis swept through the buffer zone that Stalin had established and pushed onward into the Soviet Union. The Russian troops were forced to retreat.

As they fell back, the Russians carried out Stalin's scorched-earth policy, burning everything that might be of use to the advancing German army. The Germans continued their steady advance to the suburbs of Moscow, and the Soviet Union seemed on the verge of collapse. In October 1941, confident of success, Hitler boasted that victory was his.

However, Hitler, like Napoleon, had underestimated the severity of the Russian winter. Snow soon blocked the roads to Moscow, and the long German supply lines bogged down in the intense cold. German soldiers, who were inadequately clothed for the climate, suffered miserably in the freezing weather. Winter had brought the German army to a standstill.

The Russians, on the other hand, showed no signs of surrendering. Indeed, accustomed to the cold weather, they slowly prepared to counterattack. Before spring arrived in 1942, the Russians had made important gains against the invaders.

Japan bombed Pearl Harbor. Meanwhile, the Japanese had been quietly extending their influence in the Pacific. They had joined the Tripartite Pact in September 1940; the following April they signed a separate pact with the Soviet Union. In July 1941 Japan exerted pressure on the Vichy government and gained permission to station troops in French Indo-China.

Although the United States warned the Japanese against any territorial expansion by force, the Japanese occupied Indo-China on July 24. President Roosevelt immediately froze Japanese credits in the United States and placed an embargo on war materials to Japan. The Japanese government demanded that trade between the two countries be resumed. The United States replied that trade would return to normal if the Japanese would support the principle of noninterference in the affairs of other countries.

A special Japanese peace envoy arrived in Washington, D.C., in November 1941 for the apparent purpose of reaching a peaceful solution to the trade problem. However, this move was only a camouflage for the preparation of a treacherous strike against the United States. On Sunday, December 7, without a declaration of war, Japanese planes attacked the United States naval base at Pearl Harbor in Hawaii. The invaders sank five American battleships and severely damaged three more. Approximately 2500 soldiers, sailors, and civilians were killed. With United States striking power in the Pacific knocked out for months to come, Japan formally declared war on the United States and Great Britain. By December 11, the United States had declared war upon all of the Axis powers.

Section Review

1. Why were the Polish Corridor and Danzig trouble spots prior to World War II?

2. Why did Russia seek German friendship before World War II?

3. Describe the background of the Dunkirk evacuation.

4. How many governments did France have during Nazi occupation? What was the role of each?

5. What steps did the United States take to aid the Allies prior to the Pearl Harbor attack?

6. What major areas of disagreement between the United States and Japan were under discussion when the Japanese struck at Pearl Harbor?

2 The Allies defeated the Axis

In January 1942 in Washington, D.C., twenty-six nations, headed by the United States, Great Britain, and the Soviet Union, pledged themselves to fight together until the Axis powers were defeated. These countries referred to themselves formally as the United Nations, although they were still popularly known as the Allies, or Allied nations.

The United States, with its great industrial capacity, was the main hope for halting the Axis march to victory. After Pearl Harbor the United States engaged in the most gigantic production effort in history. Factories producing consumer goods were rapidly converted into war plants. Americans, including hundreds of thousands of women, worked around the clock turning out ships, planes, guns, and tanks in unprecedented quantities. The "arsenal of democracy" began to supply its allies with the arms, munitions, and equipment so badly needed to halt the Axis.

Axis power reached its greatest extent. While the Allies were organizing their forces, the Japanese continued their expansion in the Pacific. In the month of December 1941, Manila, Wake Island, Guam, and Hong Kong were captured. By the spring of 1942 Singapore, the Dutch East Indies, Malaya, and Burma were conquered. Japanese raids on the Philippines wiped out American resistance and forced United States troops on Bataan to surrender.

In Russia the Germans made important gains in the spring and summer of 1942. In Africa Rommel's *Korps* continued to score victories over the British. By July 1942 the Nazis were 250 miles inside Egypt and only 70 miles from Alexandria. These Axis advances of 1942 were perhaps the most awesome of the war, but they also proved to be the most difficult to sustain.

In the Pacific the Allies won two significant victories. In May 1942, in the Battle of the Coral Sea, Japan suffered heavy naval losses at the hands of a United States fleet. As a result, the Japanese were prevented from cutting the Allied supply route to Australia. In June, American carriers scored a decisive victory in the Battle of Midway. This battle was one of the most important in the war because it restored the balance of naval power in the Pacific.

The tide turned against the Axis. In August 1942 the German army in Russia began a strong attack on Stalingrad, an important industrial center. Although the Nazis entered the city, they were unable

to capture it. Russian counterattacks in September and October forced the Germans to retreat to the surrounding countryside. In the spring of 1943 the Nazi position on the Russian front was desperate. Hitler lost the entire army that had attempted to fight through the winter at Stalingrad.

Elsewhere in the world, Allied victories became more frequent. In November 1942 Field Marshal Bernard Montgomery's British armies began a powerful attack on Rommel's forces. The *Afrika Korps* was forced to flee from the gates of the Nile. Synchronized with this British offensive was an Anglo-American invasion of North Africa commanded by General Dwight D. Eisenhower. After landing in French Morocco and Algeria, the troops speedily captured Casablanca, Oran, and Algiers from the Vichy French forces. In retaliation for the North African invasion, the Germans attempted to seize French warships interned at Toulon in southern France. However, the crews on the French ships scuttled the vessels.

Between January and May 1943 the Allies succeeded in completely defeating the Axis armies in North Africa. Eisenhower's forces advanced from the west toward Tunis while Montgomery's Eighth Army closed in from the east. Rommel's forces, retreating up the coast of Tunisia, collapsed in May 1943.

Italy declared war on Germany. After their North African victory, the Allies invaded Sicily in July 1943. Within two weeks Mussolini was forced out of office and imprisoned. A new government, formed by Marshal Pietro Badoglio, signed an armistice on September 8, surrendering unconditionally to the Allies one day before the Allied invasion of Italy was scheduled to begin.

Shortly afterward, Nazi forces rescued Mussolini from prison and took him to

Behind the Lines, World War II caused widespread death and suffering. On Bataan peninsula in the Philippines in April 1942, the Japanese forced thousands of American and Filipino soldiers to march eighty-five miles without food. Above, prisoners await orders to continue the Death March. Below left, a woman and child stare numbly at wreckage in Chungking, the Chinese wartime capital, after a Japanese bombing raid. Piles of bodies at Belsen concentration camp, below right, are grim evidence of Nazi inhumanity. During the war, 6 million Jews perished, as well as thousands of political prisoners and other "undesirables."

OFFENSIVES IN THE PACIFIC: 1943-1945

MONGOLIA
MANCHURIA
SOVIET UNION
Peiping
KOREA
JAPAN
Tokyo
Hiroshima
Nagasaki
Shanghai
CHINA
Chungking
Yellow River
Yangtze River
Ledo
Myitkyina
Kunming
BURMA
Rangoon
THAILAND
FRENCH INDO-CHINA
Hong Kong
Okinawa
Iwo Jima
PACIFIC OCEAN
Formosa
Lingayen Gulf
Philippine Islands
Manila
Leyte
Wake
Tinian
Saipan
Guam
Eniwetok
Kwajalein
Peleliu
Truk
Singapore
Morotai
Tarawa
Gilbert Is.
Netherlands East Indies
Hollandia
Los Negros
New Guinea
New Britain
Bougainville
Guadalcanal
FARTHEST JAPANESE ADVANCE JULY 1943
Fiji I.
New Hebrides

Allied Advance in Jan. 1944
Allied Advance in July 1944
Allied Advance in Jan. 1945
Allied Advance in April 1945
Held by Japan in April 1945

0   500   1000 MILES

Prepared by
Rand McNally & Co., C.

northern Italy where he was installed by Hitler as head of a makeshift government. On October 13, Badoglio's government declared war on Germany. Stout German resistance hindered the Allies. Finally, on June 4, 1944, the Allies entered Rome. However, the Germans continued to hold northern Italy until the spring of 1945.

Allied leaders planned strategy. The leaders of the Allied nations conferred frequently during the war to coördinate activities and plan for the future. In January 1943 Roosevelt and Churchill agreed at Casablanca in Morocco that unconditional surrender of the Axis was the Allied goal. It was here that Churchill termed the three largest Allied nations—the United States, Great Britain, and the Soviet Union—*the Grand Alliance.*

In December 1943 the three leaders met again at Teheran in Iran. Roosevelt and Churchill presented Stalin with plans for the invasion of Europe through France. Stalin agreed that, after the defeat of the Nazis, the Soviet Union would join in the fight against Japan. Finally, the leaders of the Grand Alliance agreed that a strong international organization was needed to replace the League of Nations which had lost its influence by 1939.

The Allies invaded France. Plans for the invasion of France had been one of the major considerations of the Allies since 1942. Preparations for the assault neared the final stages early in 1944. A million and a half trained Allied troops massed in Great Britain; ships and landing craft collected at British ports. Utmost secrecy was maintained. Diversionary raids along the Channel coast put the Germans off guard; the Nazis did not expect the Allies to invade the Normandy coast, for this part of the French coast lacked natural ports and had extreme tidal variations. Furthermore, it was defended by Hitler's "Atlantic Wall," which included many miles of underwater obstacles.

"Operation Overlord," under the supreme command of General Eisenhower, moved across the Channel on June 6, 1944. The Germans were subjected to a blitzkrieg, Allied style. Six hundred ships battered German beach emplacements while paratroopers were dropped behind the German coastal defenses. Allied fighter planes outnumbered the *Luftwaffe* 50 to 1. After a week of fighting, the invasion army held a sixty-mile strip of the Normandy beach. In July the Allied armored divisions broke through the German lines, opening the door to the rest of France. By August, Paris was liberated.

Germany was invaded. In October the advancing Allied columns entered Germany near Aachen. Two months later, in the Battle of the Bulge, Hitler's last counteroffensive, the German attack bent the Allied lines back for fifty miles. This counterattack delayed the Allies only a month. The advance of the Russians toward Berlin forced Hitler to dispatch most of his troops and equipment to the eastern front, which removed the last obstacle in the west.

As the Allied soldiers moved farther into Germany, they uncovered the horrifying truth of the Nazi concentration and extermination camps where Hitler's executioners had destroyed more than 10 million persons —Jews, Poles, Czechs, Russians, and others —whom the Nazis considered racially inferior.

Germany surrendered to the Allies. By February 1945 victory in Europe was in sight for the Allies. The three leaders of the Grand Alliance met at Yalta in southern Russia to discuss peace terms. Agreements on territorial arrangements and postwar control of Germany constituted the main business of this meeting. In later years, this conference became a controversial subject because of the number of concessions granted to the Soviet Union.

A few weeks after the Yalta Conference, Russian troops entered Berlin. German forces in Italy gave way to the Allies late in April. The final surrender of Germany occurred on May 8, 1945.

A few days earlier, Hitler had committed suicide. In Italy, Mussolini had already been captured and shot by Italians. The Allied nations, too, had lost a leader. President Roosevelt died on April 12.

The Allies tightened the ring around Japan. In October 1944 the United States, prepared to launch a full-scale attack to recapture the Philippine Islands, landed the Sixth Army on Leyte. This attack, if successful, could give the Allies the foothold needed to retake the islands. The Japanese, therefore, were determined to hold Leyte. For a month a fierce battle raged, but on December 25, 1944, General Douglas MacArthur, Allied commander in the Pacific, declared that the island had been secured by United States forces. With Leyte as a base for air and sea operations, most of the Philippines were taken by May 1945.

As the war progressed in the South Pacific, United States planes bombed the Japanese home islands, and American submarines inflicted immense damages on Japanese shipping. By 1945 Tokyo was in ruins. Still the Japanese refused to respond to American warnings of total destruction. A planned invasion of Japan by land was made unnecessary by the dropping of the atomic bomb. On August 6, 1945, the destructive force of 20 thousand tons of dynamite struck Hiroshima, destroying three square miles of the city and killing more than 160 thousand persons.

On August 9 the Soviet Union declared war on Japan, and Russian troops invaded Korea and Manchuria. On the same day a second atomic bomb was dropped on Nagasaki after the Japanese refused to surrender. President Harry S. Truman warned that more bombs would follow unless an immediate surrender was secured. With no choice remaining, Japan agreed to United States demands. On September 2, 1945, the Japanese signed the surrender document, ending a war that had lasted six years and one day.

Section Review

1. Describe the Allied African campaign.
2. What was the significance of the Normandy invasion?
3. What agreements were reached at the Casablanca, Teheran, and Yalta conferences?
4. Explain the importance of the battles of the Coral Sea, Midway, and Leyte.

Chapter 30   A Review

Although Great Britain and France allowed Czechoslovakia to be sacrificed, they refused to stand by idly when the Nazis threatened Poland. Stalin, failing to reach an agreement with Britain and France, concluded a pact with Hitler.

Germany's attack on Poland in 1939 started World War II. Great Britain and France immediately declared war on Germany. The Russians took advantage of the preoccupation of the powers in order to gain land in Finland and the Baltic countries. After the fall of Poland, Hitler turned to the Scandinavian nations. Denmark was easily defeated, and Norway's surrender came soon after. Next, Hitler attacked the Low Countries. Allied forces were trapped on the French coast at Dunkirk but were miraculously rescued by a fleet of civilian craft. Outflanking the Maginot Line, the Germans poured into France. In June 1940 the demoralized and defeated French accepted armistice terms which split the country in two.

With the western European continent under Nazi control, Hilter began the Battle of Britain. He met stiff resistance. In the Battle of the Atlantic the German submarine menace was brought under control by the Allies. In the Balkans and eastern Europe the Axis gained early successes, although the Italians were thrown back in Greece. Mussolini also suffered reverses in North Africa, but by June 1941 Hitler's *Afrika Korps* threatened the Suez Canal. On June 22, 1941, Hitler attacked the Soviet Union. Steadily advancing toward Moscow, the Germans were stopped by a severe Russian winter and a strong counterattack.

Japan had become a member of the Axis in September 1940. On December 7, 1941, it attacked the United States at Pearl Harbor and brought the Americans officially into World War II. But the United States had already proven an invaluable friend to the Allies in Europe by scrapping its policy of neutrality and materially aiding the Allies. United States war production reached new heights as Axis expansion continued. In crucial battles fought in the Coral Sea and at Midway, the American navy dealt severe blows to the Japanese. The Germans suffered the most disastrous defeat of the war at Stalingrad early in 1943 and by May were defeated in North Africa also. Sicily was invaded in July.

At Casablanca and at Teheran, the Allied leaders met to discuss war plans and postwar questions. By 1944 Allied strength was beginning to tell. France was invaded in June, and Paris was liberated in August. As Allied troops moved into Germany, they unearthed the horrors of Nazi concentration camps. With the victory in Europe in sight, Roosevelt, Churchill, and Stalin met at Yalta in February 1945. A few weeks later, Russian troops entered Berlin. German forces in Italy also fell before the Allies, and on May 8 victory in Europe was proclaimed. In the Pacific, the United States recovered most of the Philippine Islands by May 1945. Japan was subjected to severe bombings and surrendered after President Truman decided to use the atomic bomb on Hiroshima and Nagasaki. World War II ended on September 2, 1945.

The Time

Arrange the following possible newspaper headlines in chronological order.
1. Allies Invade Normandy
2. Nazis Sign Pact With Russia
3. Japs Bomb Pearl Harbor
4. Fighting Rages in Battle of the Bulge
5. Japan Surrenders
6. Germans Capture Paris
7. Britain, France Declare War on Germany
8. United States Enters War
9. Allied Leaders Meet at Yalta
10. Jap Fleet Routed in Coral Sea
11. Hitler Moves Into Poland
12. Churchill Forms Government in England
13. Italy Surrenders to Allies
14. Atomic Bomb Levels Hiroshima
15. War in Europe Ends

The Place

1. Locate Danzig and the Polish Corridor and tell their significance to events prior to World War II.
2. Why did Great Britain especially fear German advances in North Africa?
3. Locate the sites of the following conferences and tell what was discussed at each: Casablanca, Teheran, Yalta. What was the Atlantic Charter and where was it signed?
4. Locate Pearl Harbor and tell its significance to World War II.

5. Name three important Allied victories in the Pacific and locate the site of each.
6. What events of World War II occurred at Dunkirk; Stalingrad; Leyte; Hiroshima? Locate each of these places.

The People

1. Who were the leaders of the countries of the Grand Alliance?
2. What role did each of the following military leaders play during World War II? Dwight D. Eisenhower

Erwin Rommel   Douglas MacArthur
Hermann Goering   Bernard Montgomery
3. Who replaced Mussolini when Italy surrendered to the Allies?
4. For what has Vidkun Quisling's name come to stand?
5. What roles did Marshal Philippe Pétain and General Charles de Gaulle play in France's participation in World War II?

Historical Terms

1. Define the following German terms as applied to World War II: *blitzkrieg*, panzer, *Luftwaffe, Afrika Korps*.
2. What were fifth columnists?
3. The Free French government and the Maquis resisted German occupation of France. What were they?
4. With what countries were the terms "scorched-earth" policy and "arsenal for democracy" associated during World War II? What was meant by each term?
5. What was the Maginot Line? "Operation Overlord"? the Battle of the Bulge?
6. Who were the signers of the Tripartite Pact?

Questions for Critical Thinking

1. Why were Hitler's troops so successful at the beginning of the war?
2. If the Japanese had not bombed Pearl Harbor, do you think the United States would have entered the war? Explain your answer.
3. What lesson could Hitler have learned from Napoleon's experience in Russia?
4. Describe the work of fifth columnists. How successful were they?

The World Today

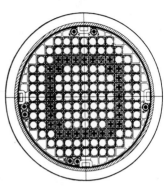

Following the flash there was a blast of heat and wind. The large majority of people within 3,000 feet of ground zero were killed immediately. Within a radius of about 7,000 feet almost every Japanese house collapsed. . . . Persons in the open were burned on exposed surfaces, and within 3,000–5,000 feet many were burned to death while others received severe burns through their clothes. In many instances clothing burst into spontaneous flame and had to be beaten out. Thousands of people were pinned beneath collapsed buildings or injured by flying debris. . . . Shortly after the blast fires began to spring up over the city. Those who were able made a mass exodus from the city into the outlying hills. There was no organized activity. The people appeared stunned by the catastrophe and rushed about as jungle animals suddenly released from a cage. Some few apparently attempted to help others from the wreckage, particularly members of their family or friends. Others assisted those who were unable to walk alone. However, many of the injured were left trapped beneath collapsed buildings as people fled by them in the streets. Pandemonium reigned as the uninjured and slightly injured fled the city in fearful panic. . . .

This account, taken from the records of the United States Strategic Bombing Service, describes what happened after the atomic bomb was dropped on the Japanese city of Hiroshima. The development of the atomic bomb—a break-through in scientific knowledge—had ushered in the horror of atomic warfare. The need to establish a peaceful world became more imperative than ever before in history.

In 1945 great excitement filled the meeting halls at San Francisco where the new United Nations Organization drafted a charter. The fifty sponsoring nations planned hopefully for the reduction of arms and armies, the peaceful settlement of disputes, the improvement of living conditions in all nations, and greater understanding among the peoples of the world. Basic to the success of the new world organization was the need for the coöperation of the major powers, particularly the Soviet Union and the United States. The friendship born of World War II, however, languished in peacetime. Freed of the anxieties of survival, the Soviet Union launched a campaign to spread communism and extend its own power. A Cold War resulted with the United States taking the lead in bolstering the security of the Free World through a system of defensive alliances. When the Soviet Union succeeded in exploding an atomic bomb in 1949, the problems of regional security became secondary to the need for international control of nuclear weapons. As the number of nations with atomic bombs increases, the agreement over controls for nuclear weapons becomes more difficult to achieve.

Another crucial problem has been brought into focus by the birth of new and independent nations in Africa, Asia, and the Middle East. The political and economic growth of these underdeveloped areas is complicated by an unprecedented population explosion. Indeed, the challenge of raising living standards while mankind's numbers rapidly increase is one of the greatest dilemmas facing the contemporary world.

The uncertainties and complexities of the 20th century sometimes appear overwhelming, but they should not be overmagnified. Many encouraging signs are apparent. The postwar recovery of western Europe has been miraculous. Out of the rubble of bombed cities have emerged the most prosperous communities which Europe has seen in its long history. Very promising also has been the growth of economic unity among European nations and the long-awaited reconciliation between the old enemies, France and Germany. The political unity of Europe is becoming a possibility. The United Nations, although it has not lived up to its more optimistic expectations, has succeeded in preventing the outbreak of world conflict by furnishing a forum in which disputing nations may meet together. In addition, UN agencies have aided the work of economic and social reform.

The accumulation of knowledge and the advance of technology have made living more challenging and more satisfying for millions of people. The picture reproduced at the beginning of this unit is a contemporary painting entitled "Electronics Industry." The painting attempts to show the relationship of man to the complex technology he has created. Scientific developments hold both promise and menace depending on the human capacity to understand and to control them.

Throughout his long existence, man has been not only a *problem maker* but also a *problem solver*. This is the most important lesson of world history. Problems will appear; they will be resolved; others will take their place; they in turn will be solved. The process is inevitable and without end. It is the way of human progress and civilization.

1900

Law of Radiation Wright brothers' flight
Special Theory of Relativity

Cubism

Schönberg
Stravinsky

The Decline of the West

radio broadcasting

insulin *Ulysses*

Lindbergh's flight *Strange Interlude*
penicillin

Empire State Building
Brave New World
Study of History

Wright

1940

streptomycin Abstract Expressionism

atomic bomb

UN Charter war crimes trials
Philippines independent Fourth French Republic
Truman Doctrine India/Pakistan
Marshall Plan OAS Berlin airlift
Nineteen Eighty-Four NATO Communist regime in China

1950

Korean police action

Libya independent

Austrian peace treaty

polio vaccine Eisenhower Nasser

Nautilus SEATO Indo-China divided
Atoms for Peace Geneva Conference Afro-Asian Conference
Doctor Zhivago Suez Canal crisis

Malaya independent
Sputnik I International Geophysical Year European Common Market De Gaulle Khrushchev
Explorer I Euratom Castro coup d'état CENTO

1960

Republic of the Congo

first manned space flight Kennedy elected Berlin Wall
Telstar United States blockade of Cuba

Assassination of Kennedy

Twentieth-Century Science and The Arts

CHAPTER 31 1900—

The 20th century has been characterized by breakthroughs in transportation, communications, nuclear power, space research, and medicine. Yet primitive ways of life persist in nonindustrialized areas. The contrast between the old and new is symbolized above by oxen plodding across an airstrip in southeast Asia. As the benefits of modern science become more widespread, it is hoped that the gap between "have" and "have-not" nations will lessen.

"The Italian navigator has reached the New World," telephoned a scientist in Chicago to a colleague in Boston one day in December 1942.

"And how did he find the natives?" asked the man in Boston.

"Very friendly," replied the Chicagoan.

This brief conversation referred, not to Christopher Columbus, but to a modern-day compatriot of his who had just completed one of the most momentous scientific experiments of the 20th century.

In October 1942 a group of physicists at the University of Chicago went to work in an unused squash court under the west stands of Stagg Field, the university stadium. Using blocks of wood and graphite bricks in which chunks of uranium were embedded, they built, layer by layer, a sphere some twenty-six feet in diameter. After six weeks, on December 2, the structure—an atomic pile, or reactor—was completed and a small group of men gathered to witness an experiment.

Enrico Fermi, the "Italian navigator" in charge, directed a fellow physicist, who pulled a cadmium rod a few inches out of the pile. As he did so, a mechanical pen traced a rising line on a graph, then leveled off and stopped. Several hours passed as the rod was drawn out bit by bit. Each time, the pen rose and then stopped. Finally, at 3:20 in the afternoon, the rod was pulled out past a certain point and the moving pen climbed steadily without leveling off. Everything went exactly as Fermi and his colleagues had predicted. They had produced the first controlled atomic chain reaction—a series of splittings (fissions) in uranium atoms that transformed matter into energy. Late in the afternoon, the cadmium rod was pushed back into the pile to stop the reaction, and the experiment was concluded.

The success of Fermi's experiment meant that man for the first time could harness the energy of atoms, the minute particles that make up the universe. At that time, the United States was at war—hence the coded message from Chicago to Boston—and the first use of atomic power was in the bombs that demolished Hiroshima and Nagasaki, Japan, in 1945. The new force, however, was not to be just another weapon of destruction. President Harry Truman said, "The fact that we can release atomic energy ushers in a new era in man's understanding of nature's forces." Enrico Fermi on that wintry day in 1942 had indeed reached a "New World"—the Atomic Age.

The 20th century has witnessed a series of revolutionary changes, not only in science but in almost every branch of knowledge and creative expression. As a growing sense of anxiety and responsibility gripped the world, men everywhere felt the need for a clearer understanding of their rapidly changing environment.

This chapter tells how:

1. **Great discoveries were made in science.**

2. **Technological change was rapid.**

3. **The arts reflected a changing world.**

1 Great discoveries were made in science

No abrupt break divided 20th-century scientific thought from that of the 19th; many of the discoveries of the 1800's laid the foundations for those of the 1900's. However, most scientists no longer seemed to have the supreme confidence in progress that had inspired 19th-century thinkers. As men learned more about the universe, they realized how little they knew. Still, scientists worked with a consciousness of the beauty and complexity of the world around them. Said a noted 20th-century astronomer, "It is a magnificent universe in which to play a part, however humble."

New theories revolutionized physics. At the beginning of the 20th century, it was commonly believed that scientists had discovered all the important natural laws that governed the universe, and that little remained to be done in the field of basic physics. Several 20th-century discoveries soon disproved this idea.

For many years, scientists had held that radiant heat and other forms of electromagnetic energy flowed in a continuous stream. In 1901 a German physicist, Max Planck, published his *Law of Radiation,* which showed that radiant heat travels irregularly in so-called "energy packages." He labeled these packets "quanta" ("quantum" in the singular), and his revolutionary idea became known as the quantum theory. It was eventually to be extended to all the various forms of electromagnetic radiation.

The year 1905 was one of the most momentous in the history of modern science. In that year a young German, Albert Einstein, published three papers of great significance. In one, he extended Planck's quantum theory to light; his conclusions resulted in the photoelectric cell (electric eye). In a second paper, Einstein related matter to energy in a famous formula: $E = mc^2$ (energy equals mass times the velocity of light squared). The central meaning of this equation is that mass and energy are equivalent, and that a small amount of matter can be transformed into a huge amount of energy.

The third and most famous of Einstein's three papers of 1905 was the one in which he outlined his Special Theory of Relativity. The young scientist stated that time and space, even gravity and motion, are relative to the observer. No longer was the world limited to Newton's classical ideas of length, breadth, and thickness as the only dimensions of matter. Einstein challenged the world to think in terms of a new dimension, time.

Meanwhile, other scientists were exploring the structure and behavior of atoms. Dalton had held that they were indivisible, but research in the late 19th century indicated otherwise. The discoveries of Roentgen and the Curies led to the idea that electricity is composed of particles (called electrons) that are integral parts of atoms. In 1911 Ernest Rutherford of England published findings on atomic structure in which he showed that each atom has a core, or nucleus, which is positively charged. Scientists then went on to describe the atom as a kind of miniature solar system with the nucleus at the center and the negatively charged electrons whirling about it. It thus became clear that atoms were not solid particles, but could be split apart.

In 1925 a German physicist, Werner Heisenberg, announced findings that further amplified Planck's quantum theory. Because of their importance, they created a new field of physics known as quantum mechanics. Two years later Heisenberg published a revolutionary theory known as the "uncertainty principle." His research led him to the belief that it is impossible to determine with equal certainty both the position and momentum of a given particle: the more learned about the one factor, the less that can be known about the other. Succeeding experiments demonstrated the proof of Heisenberg's formulas. His principle almost single-handedly overturned long-held ideas of certainty in science. What had previously been definite rules became instead statements of probability.

In 1938 Otto Hahn and Fritz Strassmann of Germany succeeded in splitting the atom of uranium; the following year two Austrian physicists, Lise Meitner and Otto Frisch, explained the process as fission and predicted that it could release large amounts of energy if properly controlled. Building on these discoveries and on Einstein's formula of 1905, Fermi's team of scientists were able to carry out their successful experiment in 1942.

Research in chemistry and biology had important results. Late in the 19th century, several scientists began an intensive study of human nutrition. In 1906 Frederick Hopkins of England announced that certain previously unrecognized substances in foods were necessary for human growth and the maintenance of normal health. These substances were named vitamins by a Polish scientist, Casimir Funk, who isolated vitamin B. Biologists isolated several other important vitamins and made it possible to synthesize and manufacture them. As a result, the incidence of such vitamin-deficiency diseases as rickets and pellagra was greatly reduced by the 1940's.

Other scientists investigated basic substances within the human body. One particularly important field involved hormones, the secretions of the endocrine glands that control growth and development. Adrenalin was isolated in 1901. Another hormone, insulin, was discovered in 1921 by Frederick Banting and Charles Best of Canada. The following year they successfully administered it to a patient suffering from diabetes and proved that this previously fatal disease could be controlled. Two other hormones, cortisone and ACTH, were first produced from animal sources during the 1940's and were found to be particularly effective against rheumatism, rheumatic fever, and severe burns.

Drugs played an important role in the never-ending war on disease. A vital group, the sulfonamides (or sulfa drugs), was first developed in Germany during the 1930's by Gerhard Domagk. They were used successfully in the treatment of meningitis, pneumonia, and blood poisoning. Another group, the antibiotics, came from molds and bacteria found in the soil. The first of these, penicillin, was discovered by British biologist Sir Alexander Fleming in 1928, although several years passed before its effectiveness was realized. It later proved invaluable in treating such diseases as diphtheria, scarlet fever, and pneumonia. In 1944 Selman Waksman, an American, discovered streptomycin, widely used against tuberculosis. Other antibiotics included aureomycin and terramycin.

The antihistamine drugs, developed in the early 1940's by French chemists, helped sufferers from hay fever, skin rashes, and motion sickness. Tranquilizer drugs not only reduced tensions in normal persons but also brought relief to the seriously disturbed in mental hospitals.

A long-awaited breakthrough involved poliomyelitis. Two Americans made important contributions toward the prevention of this widespread illness, which often reached epidemic proportions. Jonas Salk announced his development of a polio vaccine in 1953, and mass immunization with this first safe and effective preventive began in the United States the next year. An oral vaccine produced by Albert Sabin was widely tested in Mexico and Russia, and came into general use in the United States in the 1960's.

Of great importance not only to medicine but to all biological studies was research into cell structure. Scientists worked with a substance known as DNA (deoxyribonucleic acid), which all cells contain and which plays a vital role in the complex processes of inheritance. Research in the 1950's and 1960's indicated that it might be possible for scientists to control such hereditary diseases as diabetes. Also, because DNA was so closely connected with cell growth, biologists believed they might eventually solve the riddle of cancer.

Psychology broadened in scope. Psychologists of the 1900's tried to discover more about man's learning and thinking processes, especially as they involved mental illness. Freud continued his pioneering work into the 1930's, although other thinkers modified his theories. Carl Jung, a Swiss, studied psychological disturbances in the light of myths and religion. Alfred Adler of Austria founded the school of Individual Psychology, which emphasized the uniqueness of every person. Adler originated the idea of the inferiority complex as a powerful force in human behavior, stating that "To be a human being means to possess a feeling of inferiority which constantly presses towards its own conquest."

Psychology was applied to many fields. Its findings were used in studying alcoholism and drug addiction in an attempt to limit their spread. Business and industry devised psychological tests to evaluate personnel. One important application of educational psychology was programmed learning, or the use of teaching machines. In this system, the material to be taught, called a program, is broken down into detailed items of information. They may be presented in many different ways, from the simplest printed sheets to large electronic machines. All operate under the same principle: the student is tested constantly and cannot continue the program without giving an answer.

Section Review

1. Describe briefly some of the discoveries that revolutionized 20th-century physics.
2. What discoveries in chemistry and biology helped in the conquest of disease?
3. What developments took place during the 20th century in the field of psychology?

2 **Technological change was rapid**

No sooner did laboratory science make important discoveries about nature and man than technicians put them to work in the everyday world. Technological change during the 20th century proceeded at a dizzying pace. One reason for its rapidity was team research, stimulated by World War II. Governments and private industries set up great research and development centers for groups of technicians and engineers, who had previously worked alone or in small groups. Many of their projects were specialized, focusing on immediate short-term goals of commercial or military application. In 1960, for example, the United States spent $10 billion on scientific and technological research, but only 8 per cent of this amount went toward genuinely basic, or pure, research that was not directed toward a specific aim.

Improved transportation and communications shrank distances. Manufacturers of the 20th century adapted the internal combustion and Diesel engines to wheeled vehicles, and within a few years were turning out automobiles, buses, and trucks in a steady stream. Henry Ford, an American pioneer in mass production, began making his Model T automobile in quantity in 1910. Roads were improved. Engineering progress, stepped up by two world wars, stimulated automobile development. By midcentury, auto manufacturers of the United States and western Europe were producing more than 9 million automobiles yearly, in a wide range of prices and designs. The increased use of automobiles brought people closer together, encouraged the growth of sprawling suburban communities, and tended to break down regional barriers.

Travel time was cut even more drastically with the development of aviation. For centuries men had dreamed of flying; the dream was first realized in 1903 at Kitty Hawk, North Carolina, when Wilbur and Orville Wright successfully tested the first full-sized power-driven airplane.

World-wide air travel soon became feasible. In 1926, a famous American polar explorer, Richard E. Byrd, became the first man to fly over the North Pole. A year later, Charles A. Lindbergh of the United States made the first nonstop solo flight across the Atlantic. The decade of the 1930's saw the first nonstop flight across the Pacific, the first solo round-the-world flight, and the inauguration of regular transoceanic passenger service.

Aircraft production was stimulated by World War II, and many improvements resulted. Powerful engines, durable metals, and better instrumentation and design increased speed and maneuverability so that planes could fly longer, higher, and more safely than ever before. In the 1950's, jet engines, pioneered in Great Britain, began to replace the piston engines of earlier aircraft. They were lighter and more compact than piston engines, and could fly faster at high altitudes. By the 1960's, jet-propelled planes dominated long-range passenger service throughout the world. Military jets attained tremendous speeds and altitudes; in 1962 an experimental American plane, the X-15, flew to an altitude of 58.7 miles and faster than 4100 miles per hour.

The first successful helicopter was flown by Louis and Jacques Bréguet of France in 1907. These light and extremely maneuverable aircraft did not become commercially successful until the 1940's.

Air transportation made it possible for men and goods to travel with previously undreamed-of speed. In 1900 the fastest trip from New York City to the west coast of the United States (by train) took four days; in the 1960's the same distance could be covered by jet plane in slightly more than four hours. Aviation also linked previously isolated areas—for example, the rain forests of Latin America and the arctic tundra—with the rest of the world.

In the field of communications, inventions followed each other with bewildering speed. One innovation, first developed by Edison in the late 1800's, was the motion picture. The first films lasted only a few minutes, but soon studios in the United States and Europe began making longer "movies" that told a story. Modern movie making is said to have started with the American film *Birth of a Nation* in 1915. Motion pictures became an important medium of entertainment and were also widely used in education.

Of special importance in the 20th century was the field of electronics—the science dealing with the action of electrons in vacuums and gases. One of the earliest electronic devices was the radio, based on the findings of such 19th-century scientists as Faraday, Maxwell, and Hertz. The first voice transmission took place in 1900, and the first radio broadcasting in the United States began in 1920. Radio, like aviation, brought far-flung communities closer together; installed in ships and aircraft, it vastly increased safety.

Electronic research made possible sound motion pictures. (Those produced prior to 1927 had all been silent, with printed dialogue shown in separate frames.) It also led to the invention of radar, a device that "bounced" radio waves off objects so that men could "see" hundreds of miles away. Radar, first developed in the 1920's, was widely used during World War II. Another invention was the radio telescope, which receives radio waves from outer space. A new group of specialists, radio astronomers, make use of these waves to locate stars and planets beyond the reach of ordinary telescopes. The largest radio telescope, at Jodrell Bank, England, has a saucer-shaped antenna 250 feet across.

Television—using electromagnetic waves to transmit both sound and pictures—grew out of a long series of inventions perfected in the 1950's. Like motion pictures, television found wide use not only as entertainment, but also in education and industry.

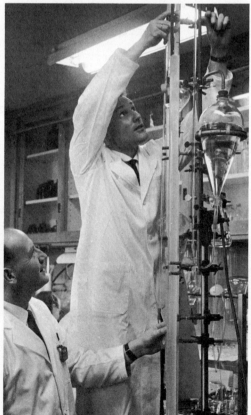

Science and Technology have made tremendous strides forward during the 20th century. Giant radio antennas, like the "dish" at far left, enable man to communicate with satellites spinning around the earth. This structure, located near Barstow, California, stands fifty-five feet high. The intricate device above left is called a MASTIF—multiple axis space test inertia facility. In it, astronauts experience the same degree of "tumbling" that occurs in a space craft in flight. Important research in biology has involved DNA, a substance governing cell reproduction. Below left, medical scientists experiment with DNA in the field of cancer prevention. Automation has become vital to many industries. Above, a technician checks the inner workings of a computer which records flight information. Atomic energy has been adapted for peaceful purposes. Below, two men investigate the effects of radiation in an atomic reactor test-station.

An improvement that spurred further developments in electronics was the transistor, a minute device that performed many of the tasks of vacuum tubes. First used in the 1940's, the transistor was adapted to many communications systems, making possible, for example, portable radios no larger than a person's hand.

Men explored space. Closely allied to 20th-century developments in aviation and military technology was the exploration of space, the area beyond the earth's atmosphere, which extends upward about a hundred miles. Early in the century, scientists began intensive work on rockets—projectiles driven by the pressure of burning gases. Robert H. Goddard of the United States, a pioneer in the field, discussed the principles of using rockets for space flights in a scientific paper of 1919, and launched the first liquid-fuel rocket in 1926. (Rockets burning solid fuels, such as skyrockets, had been known for centuries, but were not generally suitable as high-altitude projectiles.) Germany and the Soviet Union were the first nations to sponsor governmental research programs in the new field of rocketry.

Most early work on rockets was directed toward military goals. Near the end of World War II, the Germans perfected a rocket-propelled guided missile, the V-2, with an electronic "brain" and "eye" to follow orders and "see" its target. German V-2 missiles, launched from the Baltic coast of Germany against London and Antwerp in 1944, could travel 200 miles at a peak speed of 3600 miles an hour. They inflicted great damage because, traveling faster than the speed of sound, they could not be effectively intercepted. After the war, the major powers continued their work on rockets with the help of German scientists. Technicians produced a great variety of guided missiles launched from the ground, from ships, and from airplanes (including

antimissile missiles designed to prevent enemy attacks). Some rocket-powered weapons, the intercontinental ballistic missiles, had a range of over 5000 miles.

The Space Age officially began on October 5, 1957, when Russia, using rocket power, launched the first artificial earth satellite. Sputnik I (the Russian word means "traveling companion") was an aluminum ball 23 inches in diameter and weighing 184 pounds, which sent radio signals from a height of 558 miles. On November 3, the Russians sent up Sputnik II. It weighed 1120 pounds and carried a live dog, the world's first passenger into outer space.

Increased efforts were made to step up the American space program. In January 1958, the Americans launched their first satellite, Explorer I. It was a slim, pencil-shaped device weighing eighteen pounds. In March, Vanguard I went up, and was still transmitting data back to the earth five years later.

The launching of artificial satellites by Russia and the United States was the most spectacular achievement of the International Geophysical Year, an eighteen-month period from July 1, 1957, to December 31, 1958. During this time, scientists from more than sixty nations on all continents united in unprecedented coöperation to learn more about the earth, the seas, and space. Specific fields of study included earthquakes, weather, tides, glaciers, and cosmic rays.

Another milestone in space exploration occurred on April 12, 1961, when Russia sent its first "cosmonaut," Yuri Gagarin, orbiting the earth in the first manned space vehicle. That same year two American "astronauts" made brief suborbital flights into space. Another Russian cosmonaut circled the earth for twenty-five hours in August 1961, while the United States made additional space flights in February and May 1962. In June 1963 the Russians sent into orbit the first space ship containing a woman.

Space Age research involved not only earth satellites and orbital flights, but also probes and satellite devices that orbited other planets and the sun. Late in 1959, a Russian space probe successfully photographed the dark side of the moon. In 1962 the American probe Mariner II traveled more than 181 million miles from the earth to within 9000 miles of the planet Venus.

On July 10, 1962, an experimental American communications satellite, Telstar, was rocketed into orbit around the earth. Telstar circled the globe once every two and a half hours at a speed of more than 11 thousand miles per hour. As it flew, it relayed radio, television, and telephone messages back and forth between the United States and Europe. Never before had television been beamed across the Atlantic.

Intense competition between the United States and Russia led to a so-called space race. Both nations announced their determination to be the first on the moon. Although the Soviet Union demonstrated superiority in manned space flight, the United States launched more satellites and probes and received and made available more useful scientific information. Space research yielded valuable data on electromagnetic waves, gravitational fields, and the weather. For example, Explorer I revealed the existence of a series of belts containing radioactive particles thousands of miles in the air. James Van Allen, who was instrumental in their discovery (and for whom they were named), warned that they might constitute an extreme danger to humans attempting to penetrate them on missions to distant space.

Atomic energy was harnessed. The release of a vast amount of energy by atomic fission was first demonstrated to the world through military weapons. On July 16, 1945, the first atomic bomb was tested near Alamogordo, New Mexico; the following month saw the devastating explosions over Hiroshima and Nagasaki. The United States went on to develop more powerful bombs, which it tested both in the United States and in the Pacific Ocean. One of these was a hydrogen bomb hundreds of times more powerful than the atomic bombs that fell on Japan. (The hydrogen bomb is based on the principle of atomic fusion—uniting atoms, rather than splitting them. Fusion produces more power than fission.)

Russia tested its first atomic weapon, a hydrogen bomb, in 1953, and the ensuing arms race eventually also involved Great Britain and France. Many peoples were apprehensive about the effects of widespread testing, which released radio-active debris, called fall-out, into the atmosphere. They felt that fall-out would eventually cause serious radiation damage to humans.

The peaceful uses of atomic energy (also called nuclear energy) received increasing attention. Scientists constructed atomic reactors, similar to the one built by Fermi and his associates in Chicago, where they could conduct controlled reactions. (Atomic bombs represented uncontrolled atomic reactions; at present, only fission can be controlled.) In December 1951, atomic energy was used to produce electricity for the first time. Power generated in a reactor at Arco, Idaho, lit four 200-watt bulbs. Scientists then refined reactors for use under water, where they are particularly adaptable because they do not require oxygen. In 1954 an American submarine, the *Nautilus,* became the first nuclear-powered vessel in the world. In 1959, an American nuclear-powered merchant ship, the *Savannah,* was launched.

The use of nuclear power to produce electricity was of special interest to Europe, where power shortages threatened to become an acute problem. On October 17,

1956, the world's first full-scale nuclear power station opened at Calder Hall, England. Similar installations were later built in the United States and the Soviet Union.

International coöperation helped further research in the field of atomic energy. The United States Atoms for Peace program was organized in 1955 to help other nations set up nuclear reactors by supplying them with uranium. In 1958 France, Belgium, West Germany, Italy, Luxembourg, and the Netherlands formed the European Atomic Energy Community (Euratom), designed to facilitate the construction of large power reactors.

On June 29, 1961, atomic power was first used in outer space, when an atomic battery weighing only five pounds provided power for radio transmitters sending messages from a satellite back to the earth. Technicians were also at work developing plans for atomic-powered rockets, airplanes, and space stations.

Atomic energy was found to have uses in fields other than weapons and the production of power. In medicine, radioactive materials have been used to diagnose disease and to treat cancer. They have also been used in industry to measure density and friction, and in agriculture to trace growth and study heredity.

Industry benefited from new products and processes. The improved technology of the 20th century affected almost every aspect of life, particularly in the United States, which enjoyed the highest standard of living in the world.

Some inventions helped man cope with his environment. Air-conditioning machines cooled and cleaned the air in homes, factories, public buildings, and even automobiles. Airplanes "seeded" clouds with dry ice and other substances to make rain fall in periods of drought. Other improvements affected the food supply. Crop production was increased through hybridiza-tion, chemical fertilizers, and the use of such pesticides as DDT. Food products were dehydrated and frozen to preserve them longer and simplify preparation.

A new industry of great importance was that of man-made materials called synthetics. One of the first of these was a fabric, rayon, patented by Hilaire Chardonnet of France in 1885 and first manufactured in the United States in 1910. It was made from cellulose fiber in wood pulp or cotton. Early in the 20th century, Leo H. Baekeland of the United States made one of the earliest plastics, Bakelite. These substances were produced, through complicated chemical processes, from raw materials that included coal, water, air, and natural gas. They could be manufactured in sheets, rods, tubes, and fibers, and boasted special properties such as flexibility and resistance to wear, water, and acids. By the mid-1900's, plastics and other synthetics had found hundreds of uses—machine parts, furniture, fabrics of all sorts, dishes, and even artificial blood vessels.

One of the basic innovations of the 20th century was automation—the use of machines that regulated themselves and performed complex tasks with little human guidance. It was found that many new industrial operations demanded automatic control because processes had become too fast, too complex, or too dangerous for control by hand. Automation, in wide use by midcentury, took several forms, the most important being information-handling machines called computers. These instruments, often electronic, receive information on cards or tapes and use it to solve difficult problems or to perform time-consuming clerical work. Computers have been utilized in almost every kind of business. They make surveys, keep inventories and bank balances, figure pay rolls, and handle railroad and airline seat reservations. They have even been used to translate scientific documents from one language into another.

Automation has also taken the form of automatically controlled machine tools; these can be run with high precision from directions fed into them on plastic tape "etched" with magnetic impulses. Automatic materials-handling systems are used to carry materials from one machine to another; the automobile industry has utilized them to assemble engine parts. Control systems have been developed for chemical and steel industries. For instance, blast furnaces in steel mills are monitored, or checked, by electronic equipment, which "reads" gauges and then "decides" how to run the furnace.

Many persons feel that automation is as important to the 20th century as mechanization was to the 19th. Where mechanization freed man from physical labor, automation frees him from mental labor. However, like the Industrial Revolution of the 1800's, automation has brought with it many social problems. Although it relieved people of many routine and tiring jobs, it threw thousands out of work and called for drastic reorganization in many areas of business and industry.

Section Review

1. Summarize developments in automobile and air transportation in the 20th century. How did they affect ways of living?
2. Describe four electronic devices that improved 20th-century communications.
3. Explain the significance of the following in space exploration: V-2 missiles, Sputnik I, Explorer I, Telstar. How did the achievements of the United States in space compare with those of Russia?
4. Describe six milestones in the development of atomic energy that occurred between 1942 and 1959.
5. What new products of the 20th century helped raise the standard of living of people in the United States?
6. What is automation? Give examples of ways in which it is used.

3 The arts reflected a changing world

Although the progress of 20th-century science and technology was an exciting adventure for many people, others found it confusing and even alarming. Writers and artists reflected these feelings. A deeply pessimistic tone characterized many literary works, and distortions in painting and sculpture seemed to turn the visible world upside down. In an age of increasing mechanization, creative persons stressed individual expression—to such an extent that much of what they produced was obscure in meaning and left the public feeling bewildered and irritated.

Ironically, while writers and artists retreated into private worlds, science and technology made it possible for them to reach more people than ever before. Original works of art could be purchased not only in galleries but also through widely circulated mail-order catalogues. Reproductions of famous paintings and sculptures sold well. Phonographs were in common use, and millions of records brought music, drama, and poetry into homes and schools. Modern publishing techniques mass-produced magazines and paper-backed books at low cost. Motion pictures, radio, and television presented musical and theatrical productions to audiences in the millions.

Some critics felt that the fine arts would be cheapened by being exploited through the mass media. Others, however, pointed out that such distribution helped raise the general level of taste by making available many works of value, from Plato's *Republic* in a paper-back edition to a television version of Mozart's *Don Giovanni*.

Literature expressed a wide range of ideas. A major trend in 20th-century literature was the exploration of inner states of mind through experimental techniques.

Painting of the 20th Century has played havoc with the human form. Picasso's "Three Musicians," below, is an example of Cubism, a technique involving the reduction of natural shapes to geometric designs. Three masked players, resembling cutouts, are interlocked like a jigsaw puzzle. The "Spanish Physician," right, was painted by the Surrealist Max Ernst. As if in a nightmare, a ghostly woman in a tattered dress flees a beast and a sinister figure that seem to be formed from red coral. In "Woman V," below right, Abstract Expressionist Willem de Kooning uses bold strokes of color to suggest an overpowering and somewhat menacing female figure.

Writers were influenced by the psychological theories of Sigmund Freud, with their emphasis on subconscious fears and desires.

James Joyce of Ireland used a technique called "stream of consciousness" in which he wrote of both outward events and individual reactions and memories almost simultaneously. His first novel, *A Portrait of the Artist as a Young Man*, appeared in 1916. Joyce's masterpiece, *Ulysses* (1922), dealt with several Dubliners during a twenty-four-hour period. His difficult but brilliant style—with invented words, fragments of foreign languages, and parodies of other writers—had a profound effect on 20th-century literature.

William Faulkner of the United States also made use of the stream-of-consciousness technique. He wrote a series of novels about the American South, where he saw poverty, corruption, and delusion. Faulkner's major works included *The Sound and the Fury* (1929), *As I Lay Dying* (1930), and *Absalom, Absalom!* (1936).

Poet T. S. Eliot, an Englishman born in the United States, was strongly influenced by Joyce. His works also combined obscure quotations with vivid imagery describing feelings and events. *The Waste Land* (1922) reflected the despair that characterized much of the writing in the period immediately following World War I. Eugene O'Neill, an American dramatist, brought to the theater the psychological insights of experimental novels and poetry. In *The Great God Brown* (1926), characters wore masks to distinguish their artificial selves from their real personalities. Other notable O'Neill plays included *Strange Interlude* (1928), *Mourning Becomes Electra* (1931), and *The Iceman Cometh* (1939).

Several 20th-century writers continued in the realistic tradition of the late 19th century. American novelist Ernest Hemingway used the terse, almost flat language of everyday American speech to create a world peopled by tough, disillusioned men of action. *The Sun Also Rises* (1926) described the aimless life of Americans in Europe. *A Farewell to Arms* (1929) took place during World War I, while *For Whom the Bell Tolls* (1940) dealt with the Spanish Civil War. In *The Old Man and the Sea* (1953), Hemingway presented the age-old theme of the individual's struggle against the forces of nature.

Poet Robert Frost of the United States wrote of New England and its people with a disarming simplicity and power. In poems dealing with ordinary incidents—"Stopping by Woods on a Snowy Evening," "The Death of the Hired Man"—he challenged man to look within himself for the strength needed to meet the 20th century.

Another group of contemporary authors, in the tradition of Dickens, criticized social evils in their writings. The American novelist John Steinbeck was deeply concerned with the plight of poor farmers. *In Dubious Battle* (1936) described a strike of fruit pickers in California. Steinbeck's most famous work, *The Grapes of Wrath* (1939), portrayed dispossessed Dust Bowl farmers forced to become migrant laborers during the depression.

Two English writers created unforgettable pictures of future societies which they felt might result from 20th-century tendencies toward totalitarianism. In *Brave New World* (1932), Aldous Huxley portrayed tranquilized, pathetic, and lonely men enslaved by their elaborate technology. George Orwell's *Nineteen Eighty-Four* (1949) pictured a nightmare state where individualism is dead and people have been brainwashed by slogans: "War Is Peace," "Freedom Is Slavery," and "Big Brother Is Watching You."

Russian novelist-poet Boris Pasternak caused a sensation with *Doctor Zhivago* (1956), a novel about a physician during and after the Bolshevik Revolution. Pasternak's hero took little interest in politics and, in fact, criticized Communist hypocrisy and oppression. Such realism proved unacceptable to the rulers of the Soviet Union, who forced the author to decline the 1958 Nobel prize for literature.

Another trend in 20th-century writing was the use of fiction to convey philosophical ideas. Thomas Mann of Germany was particularly concerned with the impact upon modern man of centuries of civilization. He upheld traditional moral values, but approached them through a study of myths and Freudian psychology. Mann's most famous work, *The Magic Mountain* (1924), is set in a tuberculosis sanitarium, where the patients represent many facets of contemporary European life.

In France, a philosophical movement known as existentialism became the basis of a literary school under the leadership of Jean-Paul Sartre. Existentialists held that "existence precedes essence"—meaning that the actual day-to-day life of an individual is more important than any abstract thoughts about abstract man. Sartre wrote a series of four novels known collectively as *The Paths of Liberty* (the first published in 1945) and a number of plays, including *The Chips Are Down* (1947). In them he made clear his belief that, although the world is ridiculous, man must take an active role as a responsible person. Albert Camus was influenced by existentialism but had a more hopeful attitude toward life. He sympathized with the masses of men and their sufferings in the political upheavals of his time, and explored these feelings in his novels *The Stranger* (1942) and *The Plague* (1947).

Historians compared civilizations. Two historians launched major studies of modern civilization in the light of developments in the 20th century. In 1918 the German scholar Oswald Spengler published the first volume of *The Decline of the West*. After a detailed comparison of eight historic civilizations, Spengler concluded that all had proceeded, like biological organisms, through the same steps of growth and decay. Western civilization, he declared, had begun its final phase in the 20th century. A succession of wars and a dwindling of creativity would lead to eventual collapse. He wrote:

> . . . the future of the West is not a limitless tending upwards and onwards for all time towards our present ideals, but a single phenomenon of history, strictly limited and defined as to form and duration, which covers a few centuries. . . . We cannot help it if we are born as men of the early winter of full Civilization, instead of on the golden summit of a ripe Culture, in a Phidias or Mozart time. Everything depends on our seeing our own position, our *destiny*, clearly, on our realizing that though we may lie to ourselves about it we cannot evade it.

Arnold J. Toynbee, an English historian, began publishing his multivolume *Study of History* in 1934. Only slightly more hopeful than Spengler, Toynbee traced the decline of earlier civilizations to moral weakness and predicted that Western culture would suffer the same fate. He felt, however, that religion was a key factor and that Western civilization, even as it died, could benefit the world by stimulating a new religious tradition.

Painters experimented with line and color. In 1905 an exhibition of paintings in Paris included several considered so radical that they were isolated in a separate room and their creators dubbed "Les Fauves" (French for "wild beasts"). Fauvism, as their art came to be called, was characterized by brilliant colors and decorative surface effects. Foremost among the Fauves was Henri Matisse, whose deceptively simple canvases communicated a sense of gaiety and enjoyment through rhythmic lines and bright colors. Matisse said that he dreamt of "an art of balance, of purity and serenity . . . which might be for every mental worker . . . something like a good armchair in which to rest from physical fatigue."

Georges Rouault, another Fauve, used rich colors separated by black lines to create paintings that somewhat resembled medieval stained glass. A devout man, Rouault expressed his feelings not only through religious subjects but also in sympathetic portraits of sad clowns and laboring peasants. His greatest single body of work was a series of etchings, *Miserere*, attacking war and man's inhumanity to man.

Closely related to Fauvism was a movement known as Expressionism, which flourished in Germany from the early 1900's until the period of World War II. Expressionists distorted visual reality in order to express their emotions freely. According to one, "The exterior art form is the artist's interior feeling." The works of some Expressionists were abstract—that is, they contained recognizable elements that had been exaggerated or simplified (for example, a human figure indicated by only a few daubs of color). Russian-born Vasili Kandinski, who believed that color and line alone could arouse emotions, created in 1910 the first nonobjective painting— one that completely eliminated recognizable elements. Most of his later works were also nonobjective, either planned arrangements called "Compositions," or freer "Improvisations."

Other Expressionists retained recognizable forms, but contorted them to express feelings of melancholy or horror. Emil Nolde's twisted figures and clashing colors conveyed a mood of religious exaltation. George Grosz was sickened by the brutalities of the First World War, and he graphically attacked militarism, the greed of war profiteers, and moral decay.

Meanwhile a quite different school of painting, Cubism, had grown up in France. It was launched around 1907 by Pablo Picasso, a Spaniard living in France, and the French painter Georges Braque. Two important influences were African sculpture and the work of Cézanne, with its emphasis on structure. Cubism, a form of abstract painting, derived its name from the charge of critics that Braque had reduced all form in his paintings to "jumbles of cubes." There was some truth in this statement. The Cubists, approaching painting from an intellectual point of view, developed theories on how to reduce natural forms to their essential geometric structures. Picasso explained, "In my case, a picture is a sum of destructions."

Cubists explored the possibilities of their approach for a few years, but it soon began to seem limited and sterile, and most of them modified their techniques. Picasso developed a number of different styles, some tender and lyrical, others violent and contorted. Some artists influenced by Cubism worked out an analytical style of nonobjective painting. Piet Mondrian of the Netherlands wrote that, "for the modern mentality, a work which has the appearance of a machine" is the most effective. His paintings—rectangles of primary colors separated by black lines on a white ground—had a great influence on modern design.

Other nonobjective artists stressed free and spontaneous creation. Abstract Expressionism (also called "action painting") flourished in the United States after World War II. Jackson Pollock created dense webs of pigment by dripping and throwing paint against the canvas, sometimes leaving cigarette butts and old paint tubes where they fell. Willem de Kooning, though he "smuggled" recognizable human images into some of his paintings, produced a similar feeling of chaos through his use of forms and colors.

Various movements rejected the trend toward nonobjective art. One was Surrealism, which used realistic techniques to portray a world of subconscious fantasies. Max Ernst of Germany painted real objects in dream landscapes, giving the results such provocative titles as "Two Children Are Threatened by a Nightingale" and "Princes Do Not Sleep Well." Another Surrealist was Salvador Dali of Spain. In a famous work, "The Persistence of Memory," he painted huge limp watches in a deserted seaside landscape. Paul Klee of Switzerland was influenced by Surrealism, although his delicate fantasies have been compared to Japanese prints in style.

Other artists rejected completely abstract art in favor of paintings with greater social significance. Two leaders of this trend, both from Mexico, were Diego Rivera and José Clemente Orozco. They displayed great talent as muralists, and often chose themes glorifying the Indians of their native country and attacking the rich who exploited them. In the United States, Ben Shahn treated a variety of subjects, including war and atomic testing. Another American, Jack Levine, used a loosely expressionistic technique in such paintings as "Gangster Funeral," in which the mourners include the mayor, governor, and police chief.

Sculptors and architects created new forms. Sculptors worked in a variety of styles, many of them related to those of painters. (In fact, many painters—including Matisse, Picasso, and Ernst—also created sculpture.) American-born Jacob Epstein, who lived in England most of his life, developed an agitated, expressionistic technique for his sculptured portraits. They were notable for their rough surfaces and distortions influenced by African sculpture. The English sculptor Henry Moore was known for his large-scale, stylized human figures and for the holes and hollows he shaped in them to emphasize volume.

More abstract than Moore's sculpture was that of Constantin Brancusi of Rumania, who created "Bird in Space" from one slender, irregularly tapered shaft of polished bronze. Although it was not representational, its form did suggest a bird's sudden upward movement in the air. An American, Alexander Calder, produced completely nonobjective work that achieved wide popularity. He invented ingenious and entertaining "mobiles"—jointed metal constructions suspended in the air, which moved and shifted balance with the slightest current.

In architecture, constantly improved materials, such as reinforced concrete, made experimentation relatively easy. Skyscrapers in the United States reached ever greater heights. The Empire State Building, built in New York City in 1930-1931, had a total of 102 stories and reached 1250 feet to become the tallest building in the world.

Architects continued the functional trend initiated by Louis Sullivan in the 19th century. One expression of this ideal was the International Style, which was launched in Europe after World War I. It owed much to Walter Gropius, a German architect who established the Bauhaus, a school of architecture and related arts. The buildings he designed for the school expressed in visual form his belief in geometrically precise structures. One architect of this group, Le Corbusier of France, defined a house as "a machine for living," and it was this spirit that stimulated the building of severe rectangles of steel, concrete, and glass throughout Europe and the United States. Ludwig Mies van der Rohe, a German-American architect, coined the phrase "Less is more"—a fitting motto for this disciplined style.

The United Nations Secretariat Building in New York City, constructed in 1951,

20th-Century Architecture broke away from 19th-century styles. Frank Lloyd Wright, the "prairie architect," designed long, low homes to blend with the flat terrain of the Midwest. At top is one of these—the Robie house, built in Chicago in 1909. Directly above are buildings designed about 1925 by Walter Gropius for the Bauhaus, an architectural school in Dessau, Germany (photograph courtesy of the Museum of Modern Art, New York). The straight walls of concrete and glass contrast with the curved columns of the Palace of the Dawn at Brasília, Brazil, right, designed in the 1950's by Oscar Niemeyer.

represented a triumph of the International Style. A rectangle of glass, its surface was relieved only by reflections of clouds and nearby office buildings. According to one architect:

> In its size and elegant slimness it represented the full bloom of the box. . . . This plain slab was, excepting a few minor imperfections, the ultimate rectilinear form—one image, unornamented, windowless (while being all glass). It was a monument to technology and impersonal technique, and stated in a language which the everyday architect could easily adopt.

Many critics, however, objected to the glass "boxes" of the International Style. Foremost among them was Sullivan's outstanding pupil, Frank Lloyd Wright. Although many of Wright's early buildings had inspired the International Style, he himself became increasingly opposed to its unrelieved plainness.

Wright stressed an "organic" architecture, growing out of function and location, rather than a formal set of rules. According to him, "When man builds 'natural' buildings naturally, he builds his very life into them." His houses blended with the natural scenery surrounding them, and even his factories and offices included unusual and dramatic decorative elements. One of his last buildings, the Solomon R. Guggenheim Museum in New York City, was designed as a spiral ramp within a concrete drum.

Another architect who modified the rigid forms of the International Style was Oscar Niemeyer, a Brazilian. The many structures he created for the capital city of Brasília fused functionalism with elements of Portuguese colonial buildings common in his country.

Music blended traditional and modern elements. Musical romanticism in the tradition of Brahms continued into the early part of the 20th century. Richard Strauss of Germany was particularly noted for his tone poems, elaborate orchestral compositions based on literary themes—*Till Eulenspiegel's Merry Pranks* (a German folk tale), *Don Quixote* (Cervantes' novel), and *Thus Spake Zarathustra* (a work by the German philosopher Friedrich Nietzsche). Gustav Mahler, an Austrian, enlarged the orchestra and often combined it with voices to create richly dramatic effects. His *Song of the Earth* blended the two elements with panoramic grandeur.

Another Austrian, Arnold Schönberg, at first showed the influence of Mahler but soon developed an individual approach that greatly influenced 20th-century music. Because he felt that traditional scales had "said" all they could musically, Schönberg devised a new twelve-tone scale. For each composition, he arranged the twelve tones of the octave into a different pattern, called a tone row. The result was extremely dissonant music that has been compared to Expressionism in painting. Schönberg wrote a number of chamber works, as well as compositions combining an orchestra with a reciter.

Schönberg's music is called atonal because it has no fixed key. Atonality was adopted by other composers, as was polytonality—the use of two or more keys at the same time. Many were influenced by such techniques, even though they did not accept them wholly. The most important of such composers was the Russian-American Igor Stravinsky. In his early ballets, such as *Petrouchka, Firebird,* and *The Rite of Spring,* written before World War I, Stravinsky adapted Russian folk melodies to a dissonant, brilliantly rhythmical style of his own. Later he turned to neoclassicism in such works as *Oedipus Rex,* an oratorio. Late in life he wrote a twelve-tone ballet, *Agon.*

Several other composers followed Stravinsky's lead in combining native traditions with the technical innovations pioneered by Schönberg. Béla Bartók of Hungary, an authority on the folk music of his country, used it as the foundation for his harsh, vigorous style. He wote a great deal for the piano, including a series of teaching pieces, *Mikrokosmos,* that illustrated his unusual harmonies.

The American composer Aaron Copland became well known for his ballet music based on traditional American themes— *Billy the Kid, Rodeo,* and *Appalachian Spring*—and for his opera, *The Tender Land.* In England, both Ralph Vaughan Williams and Benjamin Britten incorporated native folk melodies in their symphonic and vocal music. Sergei Prokofiev, a Russian, wrote a popular musical version of the Russian folk tale *Peter and the Wolf,* music for the Russian films *Alexander Nevsky* and *Ivan the Terrible,* and ballets that included *Romeo and Juliet.*

Section Review

1. How did 20th-century science and technology make the arts available to mass audiences?
2. Describe, with examples by specific authors, the following trends in 20th-century literature: experimentation to reveal inner states of mind; realism; social criticism; the use of fiction to convey philosophical ideas.
3. Summarize the chief characteristics of the art movements represented by the following artists: Matisse, Nolde, Picasso, Pollock, Dali.
4. What is nonobjective art? Name two painters who adopted this style.
5. How did the International Style of architecture differ from that of Wright?
6. Give examples of 20th-century composers who made use of the following styles or elements: romanticism, atonality, folk melodies.

Chapter 31

A Review

Scientific progress was perhaps the keynote of the 20th century. The discoveries of Planck, Einstein, Heisenberg, and others were milestones in the field of physics. Biological research revealed the importance of vitamins and hormones and led to such new drugs as the sulfas, antibiotics, antihistamines, and tranquilizers. Men learned how to prevent polio and investigated cell reproduction. Psychology increased in importance.

Technology developed rapidly, too. Automobiles and airplanes created vast transportation networks, and communications were furthered by motion pictures, radio, radar, and television. Rocket research paved the way for daring exploits in space—artificial satellites, manned space vehicles, and probes to distant planets. The potential of atomic energy was explored for both military and peaceful purposes. New industries, such as synthetics, and the new process of automation transformed the everyday life of millions.

Reflecting the far-reaching changes of the period were revolutions that made the arts vastly different from what they had been a century earlier. In literature, experimental work by Joyce, Faulkner, Eliot, and O'Neill explored man's subconscious. Although employing more traditional techniques, writers like Huxley, Orwell, Mann, and Camus communicated ideas of particular urgency and applicability.

Painting took many different directions: the brilliant color and free forms of Fauvism and Expressionism, the intellectual approach of Cubism, the nonobjective abandonment of reality, and the fantasies of Surrealism. Sculpture discarded the traditions of the 19th century, while architects created varied new forms in steel, glass, and concrete. In music, experimentation produced the dissonances of Schönberg, who in turn influenced the varied work of Stravinsky, Bartók, Copland, and Prokofiev.

Indicate the period in which each event described in the following statements occurred.

(a) 1901-1920   (c) 1941-present
(b) 1921-1940

1. First full-scale nuclear power station was opened.
2. Jonas Salk announced his development of a polio vaccine.
3. Albert Einstein published his Special Theory of Relativity.
4. Frederick Banting and Charles Best discovered insulin.
5. Sputnik I was launched.
6. Max Planck published his *Law of Radiation.*
7. Empire State Building was built.
8. Radio broadcasting in the United States began.
9. Sir Alexander Fleming discovered penicillin.
10. Wright brothers made their first successful flight.
11. James Joyce's *Ulysses* appeared.
12. American communications satellite Telstar was rocketed into orbit.
13. First controlled atomic chain reaction was produced.
14. International Geophysical Year was held.
15. George Orwell's *Nineteen Eighty-Four* was published.

The People

1. Planck, Einstein, and Heisenberg each developed theories that altered previously held ideas about the universe. What were their theories?
2. What contribution did each of the following make to man's health and well-being?

Domagk   Waksman   Sabin   Salk
Hopkins   Funk   Fleming
     Banting and Best

3. How did these scientists contribute to the study and use of atomic energy: Hahn and Strassmann; Meitner and Frisch; Fermi?
4. With what milestones in transportation are the following persons associated?

Goddard   Bréguet brothers   Lindbergh
Byrd   Wright brothers   Gagarin

5. Name one achievement in literature or the arts for which each of the following persons was noted.

O'Neill   Rouault   Gropius
Pasternak   Rivera   Schönberg
Sartre   Calder   Bartók

Historical Terms

1. What were the following advances in physics and which scientist developed each: quantum theory; formula $E=mc^2$; Special Theory of Relativity; "uncertainty principle"?
2. The field of atomic physics has added many new words to the 20th-century vocabulary. Define these: nucleus; electron; atomic reactor; fission; fusion; fall-out.
3. Describe the following substances important in biological research: vitamins; hormones; sulfonamides; antibiotics; DNA. Name at least one disease affected by research in each of these fields.
4. What are transistors? To what uses are they put?
5. What was the stream-of-consciousness technique? Name two 20th-century writers who used it. What was existentialism?
6. Describe the following art movements, and name a painter representative of each: Fauvism; Expressionism; Cubism; Abstract Expressionism; Surrealism.

Questions for Critical Thinking

1. It has been said that, whereas science prior to 1900 dealt with certainties in the visible universe, 20th-century science concentrates on probabilities in a world of invisible phenomena. Explain.
2. What is the difference between basic and applied research? Which, in your view, is more important?
3. Some persons feel that the destructive forces unleashed by modern science offer no appreciably greater threat to mankind than did the invention of the spear in prehistoric times or the introduction of gunpowder in the Middle Ages. Do you agree?
4. Do you think that automation is a benefit or an evil? Give reasons for your answer.
5. Using their quoted statements, contrast the attitudes toward art of Matisse and Mondrian. Which point of view do you prefer?

The World Since 1945

CHAPTER 32   1945—

In 1945 the United Nations was established "to save succeeding generations from the scourge of war." Since then, the organization has attempted to maintain a delicate balance of peace in a divided world. At UN headquarters in New York City, diplomats assemble to seek peaceful solutions to international problems. Above, the Secretary-General presides at a meeting of the General Assembly.

A hush fell over the General Assembly of the United Nations, meeting in September 1960, as the delegate rose to speak. He was Kwame Nkrumah, president of the African nation of Ghana. To his fellow delegates from all over the world, Nkrumah spoke as follows:

The great tide of history flows, and as it flows it carries to the shores of reality the stubborn facts of life and men's relations one with another. One cardinal fact of our time is the momentous impact of Africa's awakening upon the modern world. The flowing tide of African nationalism sweeps everything before it and constitutes a challenge to the colonial powers to make a just restitution for the years of injustice and crime committed against our continent.

The presence of Nkrumah of Ghana in the United Nations symbolized the growing unity of the world. Never before in history had so many people of different races and creeds been brought together in an international organization. Since 1945 the halls of the UN have resounded with debates on all of the grave problems confronting modern man in his search for security and well-being.

The UN can only reflect the still imperfect world it tries to improve. Thus, the UN mirrors the views, rivalries, and relationships of its members. The UN is not a supergovernment, but it has acted to cushion international conflicts by keeping its members in contact with one another. As a kind of "town meeting" of the world, the UN makes it possible for serious problems to be ventilated.

A record of the debates and actions of the UN makes up a chronicle of world history from 1945. Since that year history has been made at an incredible pace. This chapter does not discuss all the complicated facts of recent world history. It does, however, seek to identify basic historical trends that will affect the shaping of a new world

in the remaining decades of the 20th century.

Chapter 32 shows how:

1. **The end of war brought new challenges to nations.**

2. **The Cold War began.**

3. **The Free World sought peace, liberty, and prosperity.**

4. **The Communist World was dominated by the Soviet Union.**

5. **An unstable Third World was formed.**

1 The end of war brought new challenges to nations

Early in the war the Allied nations foresaw the need of a new international organization which would effectively maintain world peace. The first big step toward creation of such an organization was taken in June 1945, at San Francisco, when representatives of fifty nations drafted the Charter of the United Nations.

The United Nations began its work. The Charter describes the operation of the international organization. The most important working bodies of the UN are the General Assembly and the Security Council. All member nations are represented in the General Assembly, where members have the right to discuss any matter that affects international affairs or the general welfare of the world's peoples. The Security Council has eleven members, five of which hold permanent seats. The permanent members are the United States, the Soviet Union, the United Kingdom, France, and Nationalist China. The six nonpermanent members are elected for two-year terms. The Security Council deals with problems threatening world peace. Each of the permanent members has the right

POSTWAR EUROPE
Territorial Adjustments

NORWAY

SWEDEN

FINLAND

Baltic

ESTONIA

LATVIA

LITHUANIA

SOVIET

UNION

North

Sea

DENMARK

Sea

EIRE

GREAT

BRITAIN

Danzig •

EAST
PRUSSIA

WHITE

RUSSIA

NETHERLANDS

·American
·Enclave

British Zone

Soviet
Zone

EAST

• Berlin
(Joint Occupancy)

POLAND

BELGIUM

WEST

GERMANY

LUXEMBURG

French
Zone

GERMANY

American Zone

CZECHOSLOVAKIA

RUTHENIA

FRANCE

French
Zone

SWITZERLAND

French
Zone

Amer.
Zone

Soviet
Zone •

British Zone

AUSTRIA

Vienna •
(Joint Occ.)

→To Czech.

HUNGARY

BUCOVINA

BESSARABIA

RUMANIA

Black Sea

(To France)

Trieste •
(Free City)

Zadar •

YUGOSLAVIA

SPAIN

ITALY

PELAGOSA IS.
(To Yugoslavia)

SAZAN
I.
(To Albania)

ALBANIA

GREECE

BULGARIA

TURKEY

DODECANESE IS.
(To Greece)

Soviet Union

Poland

Yugoslavia

Bulgaria

Bdy. of Allied Occupation Forces
Withdrawn 1955

0   100   200   300 MILES

Prepared by
Rand McNally & Co., Chicago

to veto discussion or action on any Council matter not of a routine nature.

The Secretariat, which is headed by the Secretary-General, is the permanent staff of the UN. To perform the numerous tasks assumed by the UN, many agencies have been set up. Some of the most important are the International Labor Organization; the UN Educational, Scientific, and Cultural Organization (UNESCO); and the World Health Organization.

The UN was not established as a world government. Each member retained national sovereignty, and purely domestic affairs were outside the scope of the UN. The early years of the postwar period made it clear that the success of this body depended largely on Big Power harmony.

The Charter of the UN provided for the creation of military contingents and for a Military Staff Committee to advise the Security Council and direct the UN forces. Although "teeth" were thus provided for enforcement of UN decisions, Soviet use of the veto continually blocked action.

The defeated nations were occupied. At the end of the war, Germany was divided by the Allied powers into four occupation zones: the Soviet Zone in eastern Germany; and the American, British, and French zones in western Germany. Berlin, the German capital, which lies far within the Soviet Zone, was also divided into occupation zones. The Russians were assigned the eastern sector; the Western powers were given the western sectors, which could be reached through a ten-mile-wide corridor through the Soviet Zone. All rail and road transport had to pass through this corridor, which was under Soviet control.

Japan was occupied by the armed forces of the United States under General Douglas MacArthur. United States officials and Japanese leaders planned a democratic constitution, which was adopted in 1946.

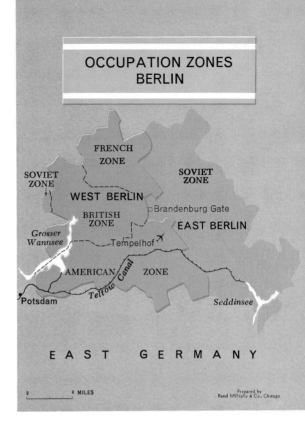

OCCUPATION ZONES BERLIN

FRENCH ZONE
SOVIET ZONE
SOVIET ZONE
WEST BERLIN
Brandenburg Gate
BRITISH ZONE
EAST BERLIN
Grosser Wannsee
Tempelhof
AMERICAN ZONE
Teltow Canal
Potsdam
Seddinsee
EAST GERMANY

0 4 MILES

Prepared by
Rand McNally & Co., Chicago

To provide the people of Germany and Japan with a decent standard of living, the occupation authorities helped farmers put their lands back into cultivation and encouraged the rebuilding of industrial and transportation facilities. Rehabilitation was carried on at a cost of many millions of dollars, most of which the United States assumed.

The victorious nations set up war crimes courts in Germany and Japan to try the men who were accused of crimes against humanity and world peace. Nineteen of the twenty-two top German leaders who were tried were sentenced either to death or to long prison terms. In Japan the wartime premier, Tojo, was convicted along with other war criminals and was hanged.

The U.S.S.R. rejected its former allies. As final victory over the Axis powers approached, a widening gulf appeared between the Soviet Union and its wartime allies. In 1946 Stalin introduced a new Five-Year Plan that had as its basic objective the buildup of Soviet military power. While Britain and the United States were reducing their armed forces, the Soviet government continued to maintain a huge land army. In 1947 a new organization, the Cominform, replaced the Comintern, which had been discontinued in 1943. The objectives of both organizations were identical: to spread Communist propaganda throughout the world.

Other evidence of the Soviet Union's coolness toward the West soon emerged. The Soviet government forbade its citizens to marry foreigners. It jammed foreign radio programs and censored all books, magazines, and news from the outside world. These acts led Winston Churchill to declare in 1946: "From Stettin in the Baltic to Trieste in the Adriatic, an iron curtain has descended across the Continent."

Even more serious in Western eyes was the manner in which the Soviet Union disregarded its Yalta pledges to allow the liberated peoples in eastern Europe and the Balkans to set up governments of their own choosing. Between 1945 and 1948 Communist regimes were imposed on Rumania, Bulgaria, Poland, Hungary, and Albania. Czechoslovakia, which had been a successful democracy between World Wars I and II, was seized and overrun by the Communists in 1948.

Section Review

1. What is the function of the General Assembly? the Security Council? the Secretariat? What nations are permanent members of the Council?
2. What problems faced the occupation authorities in Germany and Japan?
3. In what ways did the Soviet Union indicate its hostility toward the Western nations?

2 The Cold War began

By 1947 the Western nations had no doubt of the Soviet Union's plans for expansion. Faced with the possibility of a new war, western Europe could not concentrate on regaining normal production. Inflation and black market operations undermined the people's faith in their governments' abilities to meet postwar needs. Communist parties took advantage of the situation to stir up further unrest.

The Truman Doctrine and the Marshall Plan blocked communism. The task of blocking the ambitions of communism fell largely upon the United States. In the spring of 1947, President Harry S. Truman declared: "I believe that it must be the policy of the United States to support free people who are resisting attempted subjugation by armed minorities or by outside pressures." This pronouncement became known as the Truman Doctrine. Under this policy the United States gave economic and military aid to Turkey which enabled the Turks to resist Soviet pressure. The legal Greek government also received support in defeating Communist-sponsored rebels. The enforcement of the Truman Doctrine made it clear that the period of international rivalry known as the Cold War had begun.

Under the leadership of the United States Secretary of State, George C. Marshall, the European Recovery Plan, better known as the Marshall Plan, was launched in 1948. This plan made available a total of $11 billion to supply European nations with food, machinery, and raw materials. The success of the Marshall Plan and the Truman Doctrine contributed to the "containment" of the Soviet Union by preventing the spread of communism.

Differences developed over Germany. Soon after the occupation, serious dis-

Aid Programs have promoted welfare and relieved hardships in many regions of the world. The United Nations Relief and Rehabilitation Administration aided needy countries after World War II; below right, Greek children receive lunch from an UNRRA official. The United States and Britain organized a massive airlift to transport supplies to West Berlin during the Russian blockade of 1948-1949; at bottom, a relief plane soars over the city. At a rural school in British Honduras, below left, an American teacher in the Peace Corps instructs a class in arithmetic.

KOREA

U.S.S.R.

Vladivostok

C H I N A

Yalu River

NORTH
KOREA

S E A

Pyongyang

O F

38TH PARALLEL

Panmunjom

Seoul

J A P A N

Inchon

SOUTH
KOREA

Pusan

Korea Strait

Hiroshima

J A P A N

0   50   100 MILES

Prepared by
Rand M?Nally & Co., Chicago

Nagasaki

many separate from East Germany by uniting the American, British, and French zones. To prevent this plan from succeeding, Soviet authorities in 1948 imposed a blockade upon West Berlin, whereupon the Western powers organized an airlift of cargo planes to transport food, coal, and other supplies to the 2½ million people of the city. The Berlin airlift succeeded. In the spring of 1949 the Russians lifted the blockade.

NATO was born. By 1949 it was clear to most statesmen in the West that there was an urgent need for defensive alliances against the Soviet threat. The Russians had succeeded in creating an atom bomb, thus destroying the United States' monopoly. In April twelve nations under the leadership of the United States formed the North Atlantic Treaty Organization (NATO). Its first military head was General Dwight D. Eisenhower. Members of NATO declared that an attack on any one of its group would be considered an attack on all.

China became Communist. Soon after the defeat of Japan, full-scale civil war broke out between the Nationalist government and the Chinese Communists. The U.S.S.R. supported Mao Tse-tung and the Communists by turning over to them weapons and supplies taken in Manchuria from the defeated Japanese. The United States supported Chiang Kai-shek and the Nationalist government. Much of the matériel given to Chiang's government by the United States was sold by corrupt Nationalist leaders and fell into the hands of the Chinese Communists. In 1945 General Marshall was sent to China to attempt a reconciliation of the two forces, but his suggestion of a coalition government was turned down.

Manchuria was overrun by the Communists in 1948, and the cities of Nanking, Shanghai, and Canton fell to Mao's forces

agreements arose over the treatment of Germany. At the Potsdam Conference of 1945, the victors agreed that the Russian-controlled zone, which was mainly agricultural, would exchange food for the industrial products of the western zones. When the Soviets demanded huge payments of reparations and refused to help feed the people of the western zones, the United States and Great Britain were obliged to ship food in to prevent starvation.

Reluctantly, the Western occupation authorities began to organize a West Gerthe following year. In October 1949 the Communists proclaimed the birth of the People's Republic of China, while Chiang and a remnant of his forces fled to the island of Formosa. The Chinese Communists sought to destroy Chiang's new regime, but they were blocked by the United States, which protected the Nationalist government on Formosa.

The Korean "police action" broke out.
At the end of World War II, differences arose between Russia and the United States over the future of Korea. The Soviet Union controlled the northern part of the country, and the United States controlled the south. The Russians would not permit a UN-sponsored commission to supervise free elections in the northern zone. In June 1950 Communist North Korean troops, equipped with Russian arms, invaded South Korea. The UN recommended the use of force to halt this aggression.

Led by the United States, fifteen UN members sent troops under the command of General Douglas MacArthur to Korea. Since there was no declaration of war, the UN operation was termed a "police action." The fighting was fierce and increased in intensity when Communist China sent in its troops in November 1950. Almost three years later, in July 1953, an armistice was signed and the fighting came to a halt. The agreement divided Korea much as it had been before the Communist attack began.

The significance of the Korean police action could not be denied. The independence of South Korea had been preserved, but the burden had been carried by a minority of UN members, the United States making the heaviest sacrifice in men and money. Furthermore, the initial action against Communist aggression had been possible only because of the absence of the Russian delegate in the Security Council. (The Soviets had boycotted the council when other council members refused to grant UN membership to Communist China.) Fearful of Russian intervention to aid China, and with it the prospect of a third world war, UN forces did not punish China for its attack. Yet, imperfect as international action was, a UN military force had been employed, establishing a precedent that could be important for the future.

Defense pacts were established in Asia and in the Middle East.
In Asia, as in Europe, Communist threats and attacks led the endangered areas to combine for defense. In 1951 the Japanese government signed a security pact permitting the United States to maintain military bases in Japan. In 1952 Australia and New Zealand joined the United States in forming another defensive alliance; two years later a larger organization was formed: the Southeast Asia Treaty Organization (SEATO).

To meet the Soviet challenge in the Middle East, five nations—Great Britain, Turkey, Iran, Iraq, and Pakistan—signed a treaty forming the Middle East Treaty Organization (METO) in Bagdad in 1955. Though it did not join this pact, the United States lent its support. In 1958 a revolution in Iraq threatened the collapse of the pact, whereupon the United States became a full member. After Iraq withdrew from the alliance in 1959, the name was changed to Central Treaty Organization (CENTO).

Mutual assistance pacts were concluded also by the Soviet bloc. In 1950 Communist China and the Soviet Union signed a thirty-year treaty of friendship. In May 1955 Soviet-controlled nations of eastern Europe were placed under Russian military command by the Warsaw Treaty.

The Cold War changed.
After the death of Stalin in 1953, Communist Russia showed signs of becoming more coöperative in world affairs. In the spring of that year, after ten years of stalling, the Soviet Union agreed to an Austrian peace treaty.

Other signs of a thaw in the Cold War included Soviet encouragement of travel by Western tourists in Russia and satellite countries and the establishment of diplomatic relations between West Germany and the U.S.S.R. By 1955 it appeared that a stalemate had been reached in the Cold War.

In Geneva, in 1955, occurred the first meeting of Russia and the Western powers since the Potsdam Conference ten years earlier. At the Summit Conference of 1955, the United States, Great Britain, France, and the Soviet Union discussed disarmament, German reunification, and the reduction of barriers to trade, travel, and information between East and West. Although little progress was made on specific issues, many observers felt that the danger of a hot war had receded considerably.

Section Review

1. How did the Truman Doctrine and the Marshall Plan "contain" Soviet expansion?
2. What was the significance of the Korean "police action"?
3. Name the chief defensive alliances established by anti-Communist nations, and tell when they were set up.
4. What events showed that a thaw had occurred in the Cold War?

3 **The Free World sought peace, liberty, and prosperity**

The nations of the Free World were, generally speaking, those with democratic constitutions, freely elected legislatures, and executive branches responsible to the will of the people. These nations guaranteed the basic rights of the individual and supported what is referred to as a *Free Society*. They opposed the spread of communism, and most of them were members of one or more of the Western alliance systems, such as NATO.

The United States led the Free World. Foremost of the nations of the Free World was the United States. In the Presidency, Truman was followed by Eisenhower, who was elected in 1952 and again in 1956. Despite sharp differences in some areas, both Democratic and Republican party leaders agreed on the basic objectives of government, such as coöperation with Free World nations, support of the UN, and full employment.

In 1961, John F. Kennedy became President. He was the first Roman Catholic to be elected to the nation's highest office. Almost three years later, in November 1963, the country was grief stricken when he was assassinated. Lyndon B. Johnson, his successor, continued Kennedy's programs, especially in the area of civil rights.

Following the Supreme Court decision of 1954, which called for the desegregation of public schools, a period of tension began for whites and Negroes. Violence occurred in both the North and the South as "freedom riders" and "sit-in" demonstrators sought to end discrimination in transportation, employment, and public accommodations. In the area of civil rights, as well as in the promotion of economic security, the role of the federal government became more and more prominent.

Social change, wherever it takes place, is usually a difficult and complex process. Other nations in the world, especially those in Africa and Asia, were prone to criticize the handling of racial matters in the United States. Yet the American people were attempting to solve this important problem. They did not deny its existence or confuse world public opinion with propaganda.

Britain adopted socialist measures. Although it had suffered much during World War II, Great Britain remained one of the important Western powers. For almost ten years the "tight little isle" was plagued by a variety of economic problems. In 1945 the British Labour party had come into power. Much of the economy was nationalized, including the Bank of England, the railways, airlines, and the coal, electricity, and gas industries. Social legislation passed by the Labourites included the National Insurance Act, which broadened existing benefits, and a National Health Service Bill, which provided free medical, hospital, and dental care. Most of these measures were retained by the Conservatives when they returned to power in 1951.

In foreign policy, the greatest achievement of postwar Britain was the peaceful breakup of its empire. Nearly all of the colonies were granted independence and welcomed as equals into the British Commonwealth.

France was a divided nation. During the German occupation, many Frenchmen had collaborated with their conquerors. The trial and punishment of these traitors resulted in great bitterness. Another serious problem for France was the drain on its economy caused by costly colonial wars, particularly in Indo-China and North Africa. General Charles de Gaulle, who had been the spirit of French resistance during World War II, was elected president of France, but resigned in 1946 because he was not given the power he wanted. In the fall of that year a new constitution, setting up the Fourth French Republic, was adopted. The new government, however, was not able to cure the country's ills.

In 1957 France teetered on the brink of disaster. The revolt in Algeria (Section 5) cost $1 million a day. Other problems included labor unrest and a decline in the value of the franc. The next year France faced civil war. Army leaders in Algeria and Corsica revolted and called for their great war hero, De Gaulle, who was asked to form a new government. His patriotism,

honesty, and character rallied the people. They responded to his demand for a stronger government to replace the worn-out Fourth Republic. A new constitution drawn up for the Fifth Republic gave De Gaulle as president greater powers than his predecessors and made it difficult for the legislature to overthrow the government of France.

West Germany made outstanding gains. From a beaten, devastated nation, West Germany emerged during the 1950's as the most prosperous country in Europe. Under the leadership of Konrad Adenauer, a strong democratic government was established with its capital at Bonn. West Germany became a NATO member and earned the friendship of the Free World. Combining free enterprise with an extensive program of social legislation, the West Germans achieved an amazing prosperity. Many observers found it difficult to evaluate the success of the program of denazification and democratization begun by the Allies after the war, but they reported that the West Germans showed no enthusiasm for rearming. Perhaps the most serious issue confronting the nation was the problem of reunification of East and West Germany.

Economic conditions in Europe improved. Elsewhere in Europe, the signs of economic advances and governmental stability were encouraging. Italy made unexpected progress in its industries. The great city of Milan became studded with skyscrapers and busy factories. Italians were happy to be rid of Mussolini and Fascism. Yet some anxiety existed because of the strength of the Italian Communist party.

The smaller European states, such as Belgium, Switzerland, Sweden, Norway, and Denmark, were reasonably prosperous and maintained democratic governments.

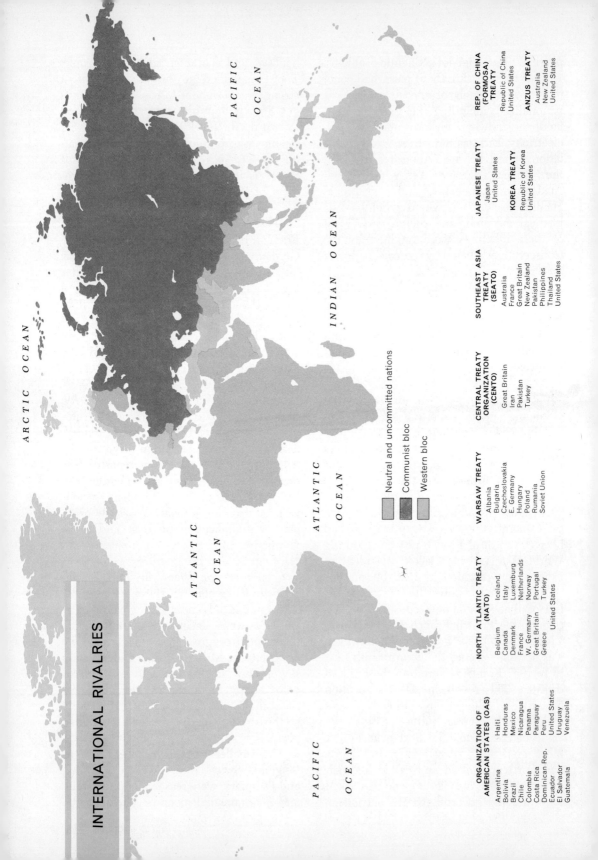

INTERNATIONAL RIVALRIES

ARCTIC OCEAN

PACIFIC OCEAN

INDIAN OCEAN

ATLANTIC OCEAN

ATLANTIC OCEAN

PACIFIC OCEAN

Neutral and uncommitted nations
Communist bloc
Western bloc

ORGANIZATION OF AMERICAN STATES (OAS)

Argentina	Haiti
Bolivia	Honduras
Brazil	Mexico
Chile	Nicaragua
Colombia	Panama
Costa Rica	Paraguay
Dominican Rep.	Peru
Ecuador	United States
El Salvador	Uruguay
Guatemala	Venezuela

NORTH ATLANTIC TREATY (NATO)

Belgium	Iceland
Canada	Italy
Denmark	Luxemburg
France	Netherlands
W. Germany	Norway
Great Britain	Portugal
Greece	Turkey
	United States

WARSAW TREATY

Albania
Bulgaria
Czechoslovakia
E. Germany
Hungary
Poland
Rumania
Soviet Union

CENTRAL TREATY ORGANIZATION (CENTO)

Great Britain
Iran
Pakistan
Turkey

SOUTHEAST ASIA TREATY (SEATO)

Australia
France
Great Britain
New Zealand
Pakistan
Philippines
Thailand
United States

JAPANESE TREATY

Japan
United States

KOREA TREATY

Republic of Korea
United States

REP. OF CHINA (FORMOSA) TREATY

Republic of China
United States

ANZUS TREATY

Australia
New Zealand
United States

Throughout most of western Europe the general trend was toward better living standards. In Spain and Portugal, however, where the one-man regimes of Franco and Salazar prevailed, the masses were underprivileged and had little to say in the government.

The most dramatic movement in Europe was progress toward unity. In 1958 the European Economic Community was formed with six states as members: France, West Germany, Italy, Luxemburg, Belgium, and the Netherlands. The goal of this organization was to create a Common Market in which goods would flow tariff-free throughout these countries. Remarkable economic gains were registered.

Under the leadership of Great Britain, another trade group was formed. This became known as the Outer Seven (in contrast to the Inner Six of the Common Market) and included Great Britain, Sweden, Denmark, Austria, Switzerland, Norway, and Portugal. Its success did not compare with that of the Common Market countries.

For a decade and a half following World War II, Europe was content to follow the lead of its stronger partner, the United States. With the revival of power and prosperity, however, Europe displayed a new mood. It wanted to be its own master. This spirit was revealed by De Gaulle, who opposed control and monopoly of nuclear weapons by the United States. The French leader wanted France to be a nuclear power on its own and, with West Germany, the leader of a Europe independent of the United States. In 1962 De Gaulle vetoed the application of Great Britain for entry into the European Common Market, an act which greatly disappointed many statesmen of the Free World. Another action of De Gaulle's that was disappointing to Western statesmen was his refusal in 1963 to join the United States, Great Britain, and the Soviet Union in a treaty banning above-ground testing of atomic weapons.

Democracy was challenged in Latin America. Latin America also felt the effects of World War II. In 1945, under the Act of Chapultepec, the republics of the Western Hemisphere agreed that an act of aggression against any American country was a matter of concern to all. Three years later a new regional system, called the Organization of American States (OAS), was created and proceeded to set up a security zone for the Americas.

The postwar period saw serious challenges to democracy develop in some of the Latin-American nations. Even before the end of the war, Argentina fell to nondemocratic elements. In 1943 a group of army officers sympathetic to the Axis powers seized the government. Emerging as leader of this group was Juan Perón, who became a fascist dictator. Not until 1955, when Perón's brutalities, excesses, and his attacks on the Roman Catholic Church brought about his downfall, did Argentina take steps to become a democratic nation. In other Latin-American countries, such as Brazil, Mexico, and Chile, the democratic basis of government was stronger; and these nations, for the most part, were relatively stable. With the inauguration in 1961 of the Alliance for Progress program by the United States, those Latin-American countries which were capable of organizing self-help projects were given economic assistance.

Section Review

1. What basic objectives of United States policy did Presidents Truman and Eisenhower share?
2. Describe the changes instituted by the Labour party after it won control of the government in Great Britain.
3. What was the goal of the European Economic Community?

United Nations Intervention has aimed at settling armed conflicts. UN troops representing several member nations prevented Chinese and North Korean Communists from seizing South Korea in 1950-1953. At right, a UN patrol trudges up a Korean hill. The UN played a vital role in the Suez Canal crisis of 1956; a UN force was recruited to maintain peace on the Israeli-Egyptian border, and UN technical advisers helped clear the canal of sunken ships, shown below. The UN aided in restoring order to the Congo in 1960, when this newly independent country was torn by tribal warfare. At bottom, Malayan soldiers of the UN force hack through a Congolese jungle.

4 The Communist World was dominated by the Soviet Union

While the United States was assuming leadership of the Free World, the Soviet Union became the undisputed leader of the Communist World. Included in this bloc of nations were Communist China and the satellite states of the Soviet Union. In varying degrees, the governments of the Communist World were totalitarian, exerting direct control over the lives of their people.

The Soviet Union changed under Khrushchev. In spite of staggering losses from war damage, the Soviet Union emerged from World War II as the second most powerful nation in the world. Stalin, whose rule continued to be as despotic as that of the czars, remained dictator until his death in 1953. In 1958, after successfully ousting his rivals, Nikita Khrushchev came to power.

Stalin had ruled by terror; his victims could be counted by the tens of thousands. Khrushchev, however, avoided these excesses and inaugurated a kind of "totalitarianism without terror." The power of the dreaded secret police was reduced, and the prison population of the U.S.S.R. was diminished appreciably. Within the Communist party some opportunity was allowed for criticism of policies in order to expose administrative incompetence.

Some of the most notable gains in the Soviet Union have taken place in the economic and scientific fields. Between 1952 and 1959, it was claimed that steel production rose 70 per cent and that in the same period Russia became the world's greatest producer of coal. Although the economic growth of the Soviet Union has been estimated to be about twice that of the United States, the total output of the Soviet economy in 1961 was only half that of the United States. Furthermore, Russian production was concentrated on industrial, rather than consumer, goods. The standard of living of the Russian people was well below that of Americans. One of the most important problems of the Russian economy has been the lag in agricultural production. While Khrushchev promised that Soviet farm output would exceed that of the United States by 1960, this goal was not achieved. Significant food shortages continued to exist.

Advances in the field of science reflected the great improvements made in education. The Soviet government encouraged and sponsored promising students with high scholastic averages. Greater opportunity was granted to women, who could enter many of the professions ordinarily reserved for men. Technical and scientific education was stressed. It was claimed that many more engineers and doctors were being trained in Russian schools than in American schools. Another feature of Soviet education was the method of combining school studies with work on farms and in factories. That Russian education was of high quality could be seen in the amazing accomplishments of their scientists in space exploration and rocketry.

Soviet satellites were tightly controlled from Moscow. Officials of the Soviet Union never tired of attacking "Western imperialism." Yet the satellite nations of the U.S.S.R. were, in effect, colonies, and the Russians exerted significant political and economic control over them. In spite of these tight controls, rebellions in the satellite countries broke out, and some were successful. Yugoslavia broke away from Moscow in 1948. It remained a Communist nation under its dictator, Tito, but managed to steer its own course without Russian interference. The example set by the Yugoslavs stirred other satellites to revolt. In 1953 serious rioting broke out in East Germany and in Czechoslovakia. The riots were crushed quickly, but they gave an indication of what satellite peoples thought of "workers' democracies." Other uprisings occurred in 1956—in Poland and in Hungary. Although these rebellions were unsuccessful, they forced the Soviets to give the satellite peoples some independence of action and better living conditions.

Still, defections from Communist-controlled lands continued. Especially significant was the steady stream of refugees from East to West Germany through West Berlin. To stem this flow, the East Berlin government erected the Berlin Wall in August 1961. This wall became a symbol of Communist oppression to free people throughout the world.

China sought leadership in the Far East. In the Far East, the largest nation of the Communist World was the People's Republic of China, with some 600 million inhabitants. At first China appeared to be just another satellite at the beck and call of the Soviet government. But by the end of the 1950's, China began to "feel its oats." Although still dependent on the Soviet Union, Red China adopted a more independent policy.

China's leader, Mao Tse-tung, initiated a program that sought to undermine family loyalties and other Confucian traditions and to replace them with rigid Marxism. Opponents of the new regime were dealt with severely. Land was taken from the landlord class and put into the hands of the state. Industrialization was pushed with ruthless energy. All of this activity was accomplished by driving and regimenting the people.

The gains registered in industry were made at the expense of farm production, however. To increase crop levels, Communist leaders established agricultural *communes,* or regimented communities, where workers were herded together and closely supervised. Often, members of the same

family were separated. The peasants, overworked and underfed, were furnished with inadequate means of production. Bad weather and floods also affected farm output, and serious food shortages continued to exist.

Important ideological differences arose between the Russian and Chinese Communists. While the Russians spoke of "coexistence" with the Western world and, at times, softened their belligerence toward the United States, the Chinese Communists took a "hard line." They insisted that conflict with the capitalist world was inevitable and carried on a "Hate America" campaign.

Cuba became a hotbed of communism. In 1959 the Cuban dictator Fulgencio Batista was overthrown by the revolutionary forces of Fidel Castro. Castro's victory was hailed in the United States, because it was believed he would establish a democratic regime. Admiration soon shifted to pained surprise when Castro ordered the execution of thousands of his opponents with only a bare pretense of legal proceedings. He ruled out elections, muzzled the press, and imprisoned his critics. Leading Communists were given important posts in the government. Thousands of refugees fled to the United States, and Castro began to seize American properties without compensation. By the end of 1960 there were more than 100 thousand Cuban refugees in the United States.

In April 1961, an attempt by Cuban refugees to invade their native country failed. Some critics of United States policy claimed that the Kennedy administration shared responsibility for this failure since inadequate military support was given the invaders. On the other hand, many felt that greater United States involvement might have led to a new world war.

At one point the Communist buildup in Cuba threatened to involve the world in

Communist Power was extended and strengthened after 1945. Above, Communist troops occupy Nanking in 1949, one of the final steps in setting up a Communist government in China. Russia sometimes used force to maintain its hold over European satellite nations, as in the Hungarian revolt of 1956; a Hungarian refugee weeps for her homeland, right. Cuba became part of the Communist World after Fidel Castro took over the country in 1959. Below, his officers conduct one of the many war crimes trials that followed the revolution.

war. Air reconnaissance by United States planes in 1962 revealed that Soviet missile bases had been erected on the island and that Cuba was being supplied with offensive weapons threatening the security of the United States and other American nations. President Kennedy thereupon declared a naval blockade of Cuba and demanded the removal of the missiles. This action was supported by the Organization of American States. As pressure mounted, Soviet Premier Khrushchev finally announced his intention to withdraw the missiles and bases. Although the emergency ended, Cuba continued to pose a threat to the peace and security of the Western Hemisphere.

Section Review

1. What changes in Russia's domestic policy came as a result of Khrushchev's rise to power?
2. How did satellite countries indicate their opposition to the Soviet Union?
3. What basic difference in ideology divided Russia and Communist China?
4. Show how the attitude of the United States toward Cuba changed after Castro took over.

5   **An unstable Third World was formed**

The Third World is the term used to identify the nations and peoples who prefer to remain neutral in the conflict between the Free World and the Communist World. The Third World includes nations in Africa, the Middle East, and southern Asia. World War II marked the beginning of the end of imperialism in these lands. During the war, Britain and France needed the aid of their colonial peoples and promised them many reforms, including self-government, in order to obtain their support. The end of the war brought increased demands by the colonial peoples for quick independence. More than forty new nations, with a total population of nearly one billion people, made their appearance on the world scene.

The new nations achieved their freedom in a complex and unsettled world which was split by the Cold War and threatened with atomic annihilation. To avoid involvement in Big Power rivalry, they tried to follow a policy of *nonalignment* or *neutralism.* Concentrating on their own urgent problems, the Afro-Asian nations remained outside the defensive alliances of powers engaged in the Cold War. The policy of neutralism had its shortcomings, however. India discovered this fact when its borders were attacked by the Chinese Communists in 1962. Indian leaders then turned desperately to both the Free World and the Soviet Union for aid in pushing back the Chinese invaders.

Statesmen of the Third World nations met together in order to solve common problems. They formed an Afro-Asian bloc in the United Nations and were represented by such spokesmen as Nehru of India, Sukarno of Indonesia, Nkrumah of Ghana, and Nyerere of Tanganyika. From time to time, these neutralist nations called conferences. One of the most famous was the meeting at Bandung, Indonesia, in 1955. There the delegates recommended independence, self-determination, and United Nations membership for all Afro-Asian nations.

The Arabs led the march to nationhood.
In 1944 the French mandates of Syria and Lebanon became independent. Two years later the British mandate of Jordan also became free. In 1948 Britain surrendered its control over troubled Palestine, where both Jews and Arabs made territorial claims. War ensued, with the new Jewish state of Israel facing seven Arab countries. After severe fighting, a truce was achieved

with the aid of the United Nations, and Israel continued its existence as an independent state.

Egypt was an especially important area of British colonial control. At the end of the war Britain still retained some troops in Egypt to guard the Suez Canal. Egyptians not only resented having foreign troops on their soil, but also were disgusted with the corrupt and inefficient regime of their king. The result was the revolution of 1953, which declared Egypt a republic and placed a strong military leader, Gamal Abdel Nasser, at its head. Nasser saw to the evacuation of British troops.

In 1956 Egypt seized control of the Suez Canal. At the same time, Israel claimed violation of its borders by Egypt. Great Britain, France, and Israel combined in an attack on Egypt which was denounced as an aggression by the UN. The three powers withdrew their forces and a contingent of UN troops was dispatched to patrol the Israeli-Egyptian border in hopes of preventing further trouble.

Arab nationalism also developed in North Africa. Libya, a former Italian dependency, gained its freedom in 1951. French-controlled Morocco and Tunisia were granted independence in 1956. In Algeria, however, the situation was more complicated. Of 10 million inhabitants, 1 million were *colons,* or colonials, of European (chiefly French) background. The preponderant Arab population occupied the lowest economic position since most of the best land and nearly all of the business establishments were in French hands. With the Algerian French opposing separation from their homeland and Arabs clamoring for independence, the country was tragically divided. A civil war, waged with shocking cruelty, broke out in May 1958. A long period of terrorism followed, which was ended when President de Gaulle made peace with rebel leaders in 1962 and Algeria was given its independence.

India and Pakistan became self-governing. The most populous nation to be affected by the movement for independence was India. At the end of World War II, India was a land of 430 million people, divided into Hindu and Moslem groups. British offers of independence were complicated by the fact that Moslems, who made up 25 per cent of the population, refused government under the Hindus. The outcome, in 1947, was the formation of two nations. One was Pakistan, chiefly Moslem, with its capital at Karachi. It was made up of two areas separated by a thousand miles. The other nation was the Union of India, chiefly Hindu, with its capital at New Delhi.

A serious quarrel between India and Pakistan arose over the region of Kashmir, which was peopled largely by Moslems. Kashmir had been expected to join Pakistan. Its Hindu ruler, however, sided with India. Although unable to resolve the dispute, the UN managed to bring about an uneasy truce. India and Pakistan continued their independent paths, both concerned with the ever present problem of raising the miserably low living standards of the masses.

Southeast Asia was a target for communism. Southeast Asia, made up mostly of new nations created from former colonies, has a strategic location and is rich in natural resources. As such, it became one of the chief targets of Communist expansion. By 1954 the Communists were in control of North Vietnam and had taken a small section of the kingdom of Laos. The United States resolved to make Laos (which has been called a "revolving door" into Burma, Thailand, Cambodia, and South Vietnam) a bulwark against communism. Although the Laotians were given great amounts of United States aid, internal dissension and Russian support of the Communists weakened the democratic cause. In 1961, when it appeared that an international crisis was brewing in Laos, a fourteen-nation conference met at Geneva, Switzerland, and a cease-fire was proclaimed. This agreement, however, did not halt Communist expansion.

Two other nations in Southeast Asia, the Philippines and Burma, gained independence peacefully. The United States granted the Philippines independence on July 4, 1946, and Burma gained its freedom from Britain in 1948. In both of these new nations, Communists waged guerrilla warfare against the new democratic governments. However, as a result of the vigorous leadership of President Ramón Magsaysay in the Philippines and Prime Minister U Nu in Burma, the rebels were defeated. Communist guerrilla warfare also plagued Malaya until 1957, when Britain granted that area its independence but retained responsibility for its defense.

Indonesia did not gain its independence peacefully. After World War II the Dutch, who had been ousted from the Netherlands East Indies by the Japanese, tried to reëstablish their rule. Nationalist forces demanded their independence, which the Dutch refused to grant. Fighting then broke out. After four years of conflict, the UN negotiated a cease-fire, and the Dutch reluctantly recognized the independence of Indonesia in 1950.

The spirit of freedom spread to sub-Saharan Africa. In Africa south of the Sahara desert, a new feeling of nationalism emerged. During World War II Negro soldiers from this area had seen other parts of the world, and American troops stationed in Africa had been bearers of new ideas. A group of nationalist leaders, educated abroad in the 1930's, came to the forefront. One of them, Kwame Nkrumah of the Gold Coast, gained independence for his country, which became known as Ghana. This event in 1957 opened up the floodgates to the current of African nationalism. In quick succession, more than thirty former colonies became independent.

The former Belgian Congo was a symbol of the magnitude of the problems in the Third World. Although its people were not adequately prepared for self-government, this former Belgian colony was granted its independence in 1960. Civil war broke out, and the Congolese faced starvation. Only the intervention of UN armed forces averted catastrophe.

Major obstacles faced the new nations. While the Afro-Asian people planned to establish democracies, their leaders soon found that self-government was a difficult task. There was an absence of trained civil servants, a general lack of experience in government, and many corrupt and self-seeking politicians. With the notable exception of India, dictatorship became a prevailing pattern in these new Afro-Asian countries. Although people of the Western democracies criticized this development, Afro-Asian leaders claimed that only by strong, dictatorial government could basic problems in underdeveloped nations be solved.

These problems included runaway populations which threatened food supplies, inefficient farm methods, lack of industry, poor health conditions, and inadequate educational facilities. In Africa the average annual income per person was not much more than $50, compared to a figure of $2700 in the United States. The majority of the new nations set in motion crash programs for economic development. Such programs required financing by the richer nations or they were doomed to failure.

The Afro-Asian countries had many problems of their own making to solve. The rivalry of India and Pakistan over Kashmir was an example of a festering internal crisis. In the Middle East, instability of government and intermittent revolutions plagued the area, and the need for social reform was urgent. The hostility of the Arab nations toward Israel also complicated matters in the Middle East. The new Jewish nation had made remarkable progress but was unwelcome and unrecognized by the Arabs.

In Africa, friction existed in many areas where white minorities strongly opposed self-government. In Kenya and the Central African Federation, European minorities resisted African independence movements. The British, however, recognized the right of Kenya to independence and also granted freedom to two of the three countries of the Central African Federation, Nyasaland and Northern Rhodesia. Although slow to develop, nationalism arose in the Portuguese territories of Angola and Mozambique and brought savage uprisings. It was evident that isolated areas of European rule would be difficult to maintain in emerging Africa.

All things considered, it was likely that the Third World would face great challenges from within and without. While this group of nations sought to remain detached from the great powers, separation was impossible. Not only was science making the world one unit, but also the new nations were, by necessity, dependent on the more advanced nations for help in improving conditions of life.

Section Review

1. What is meant by the term "Third World"? What are the other two "Worlds"?
2. Discuss the growth of Arab nationalism in the postwar period.
3. What is meant by the policy of neutralism? Why was it difficult for Afro-Asian countries to follow this policy?

Chapter 32   A Review

Created in 1945, the United Nations has served as a meeting place for the world's statesmen and has helped ease international tensions. However, a basic weakness in the structure of the UN has been the necessity for unanimous decisions by the Security Council.

The Soviet Union, freed of the threat of German domination and no longer in critical need of Allied assistance, took advantage of postwar instability to increase its political control in eastern Europe and to spread the Communist philosophy. The Cold War became a reality when the United States met growing Soviet pressure with the Truman Doctrine and the Marshall Plan. With its Western allies, the Americans resisted Russian attempts to take over in Berlin and West Germany. In 1949 the North Atlantic Treaty Organization was formed to promote the collective security of the Western community. This organization was followed by other regional arrangements intended to halt Communist penetration. In the Far East, Mao Tse-tung defeated the National-

ists in 1949 and set up a Communist regime. Because of American aid, the Chinese Communists failed both to dislodge Chiang Kai-shek from Formosa and to tip the balance in favor of a Communist takeover of Korea. The policy of the U.S.S.R. toward the West softened considerably after the death of Stalin in 1953 and the emergence of Nikita Khrushchev. Soviet possession of the atomic bomb made the need for disarmament undeniable, but little progress was registered in East-West talks on this matter and on other international questions.

The Free Nations were involved with many internal problems. The postwar prosperity of the United States, while heartening, was uneven during both Democratic and Republican administrations. Despite serious economic and social problems, however, the United States maintained a strong and stable democracy. Britain's government and economy took a socialist path in the postwar period, and a large part of its empire was surrendered. After a decade of disunity and discord, France regained internal stability under the leadership of Charles de Gaulle. It became a leader in the Common Market and installed a more stable form of government. West Germany joined NATO and experienced great prosperity. In Italy and in most of the other western European countries, living standards improved. Latin America continued to lag behind the United States and western Europe in economic progress. The United States offered its neighbors a program called the Alliance for Progress, which combined self-help and foreign aid.

In the Communist World, the Soviet Union emerged as the world's second strongest power. Although its economic growth lagged behind that of the United States, it made significant advances in science and technology. Soviet success in space travel and rocketry was evidence of progress in education. Control of satellite countries by the Russians was threatened by uprisings in East Berlin, Hungary, and Poland. China, no longer a sleeping dragon, became the leader of the Communist movement in the Far East. Marxist leaders inaugurated a program which altered the traditional home life of the Chinese peasant and plunged the vast country into the arena of international politics. Important ideological differences arose between the Russian and Chinese Communists. A new Communist force appeared in the Western Hemisphere with the victory in Cuba of Fidel Castro, who initiated a Marxist revolution. In 1962, the United States forced the withdrawal of Soviet missiles and equipment from Cuba after one of the most explosive exchanges of the postwar period.

Newly independent nations of Asia and Africa formed a Third World, which tried to remain neutral in the Cold War. Included in this group were millions of Arab peoples to whom independence was only the first step in a struggle toward economic and political progress. India and Pakistan became independent but quarreled over the status of Kashmir. Newly created countries of Southeast Asia became objects of Communist expansion. There, as in the rest of the world, the United States tried to counter Communist penetration

with military and economic aid. In North and sub-Saharan Africa a new spirit of revolt brought freedom to many former colonies. A corps of aggressive African leaders was critical of the armaments race and Big Power rivalry. As in much of the Third World, however, these emerging nations found it impossible to solve their vexing internal problems without foreign aid. Despite conflict and crisis, interdependence seemed to hasten the coming of One World.

The Time

Some of the events listed below are correctly placed under the time span during which they occurred; others are not. Rearrange the list so that all events appear in their correct time span.

1946-1950

President Kennedy was assassinated.
Communist regimes were imposed in Hungary and Poland.
People's Republic of China was proclaimed.
UN took "police action" in Korea.
Batista government in Cuba was overthrown by Castro.

1951-1955

Fourth French Republic was proclaimed.
NATO was formed.
Belgian Congo was granted independence.
Dutch recognized Indonesian independence.
SEATO was formed.

1956-1960

India and Pakistan became self-governing.
Marshall Plan was launched.
European Economic Community was formed.
Berlin airlift began.
Philippines were granted independence.

1961-

Cease-fire was proclaimed in Laos.
Algeria was given independence.
Chinese Communists attacked India.
Egypt seized control of the Suez Canal.
United States imposed a blockade on Cuba.

The Place

1. Name and locate the areas of eastern Europe that the Soviet Union controlled by 1948.

2. Locate the American, British, French, and Soviet zones of occupation in Germany and in the city of Berlin.

3. Locate Korea, the 38th parallel, the Yalu River, and Seoul.

4. Name and locate the countries that are members of NATO; SEATO; the Warsaw Treaty group.

5. Which areas benefited most from the Marshall Plan? from the Truman Doctrine?

6. Locate the following countries which are part of the neutral bloc:

India   Ghana
Indonesia   Tanganyika

7. Locate the nations that are included in the Outer Seven; those which are included in the Inner Six.

8. The following nations became independent in the postwar era. Locate each.

Israel   Pakistan
The Congo   Philippines
Algeria   Burma

The People

1. Name four leaders of the Third World. Why have they maintained a neutral position?

2. Who are the leaders of the "two" Chinas? What political philosophies do they follow?

3. What have been the results of dictatorial government under the following leaders?

Tito   Francisco Franco
Fulgencio Batista   Juan Perón
Fidel Castro   Gamal Abdel Nasser

4. What roles did Douglas MacArthur and Dwight Eisenhower play in the reconstruction of a war-torn world?

5. Identify each of these leaders of the postwar world.

John F. Kennedy   Nikita Khrushchev
Charles de Gaulle   Joseph Stalin
Konrad Adenauer   George C. Marshall

Historical Terms

1. What is the function of each of the following organs or agencies of the United Nations?

General Assembly   Secretariat
Security Council   UNESCO
International Labor Organization
World Health Organization
Military Staff Committee

2. What is meant by the concepts of "containment" and "hard line"?

3. How did the following contribute to the policy of containment?

Truman Doctrine   SEATO
Marshall Plan   METO
NATO   CENTO

4. What is the purpose of the Cominform? What organization did it replace?

5. What is meant by the terms "Third World" and "nonalignment"?

6. How have the following organizations contributed to an economic union of Europe: European Economic Community; Outer Seven; Inner Six.

Questions for Critical Thinking

1. What major problems faced the Allied powers after their victory in World War II? How did they attempt to solve them? Which of these problems remain unsolved?

2. What was the purpose of creating the United Nations? In what respects has the UN succeeded in fulfilling its original purposes? In what respects has it failed?

3. Where has the policy of containment been successful since 1945? Where has it failed? What other policies are possible?

4. What are the major problems of the Afro-Asian nations in the 20th century? What progress has been made toward the solution of these problems?

5. What is the purpose of the Common Market? Is it likely that there will be a United States of Europe in the near future? Explain your answer.

Atlas of the Contemporary World

The color maps in this reference section have been prepared especially for use in *Living World History*. They are authoritative, up-to-date, and designed to present essential information clearly and concisely. Correlation has been maintained with the appropriate chapters in the textbook. For example, the place names and physical features referred to in the chapters on 20th-century history will be found on one or more of the maps in this section.

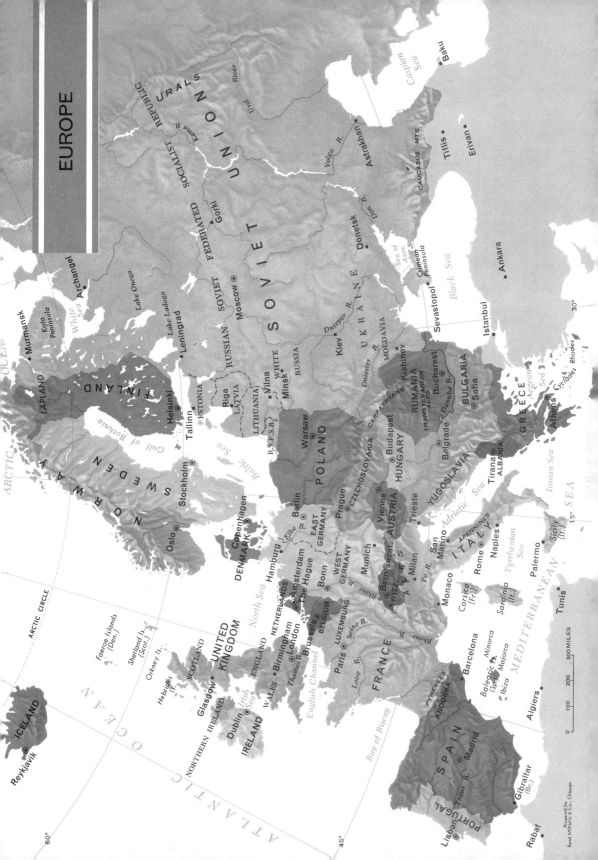

EUROPE

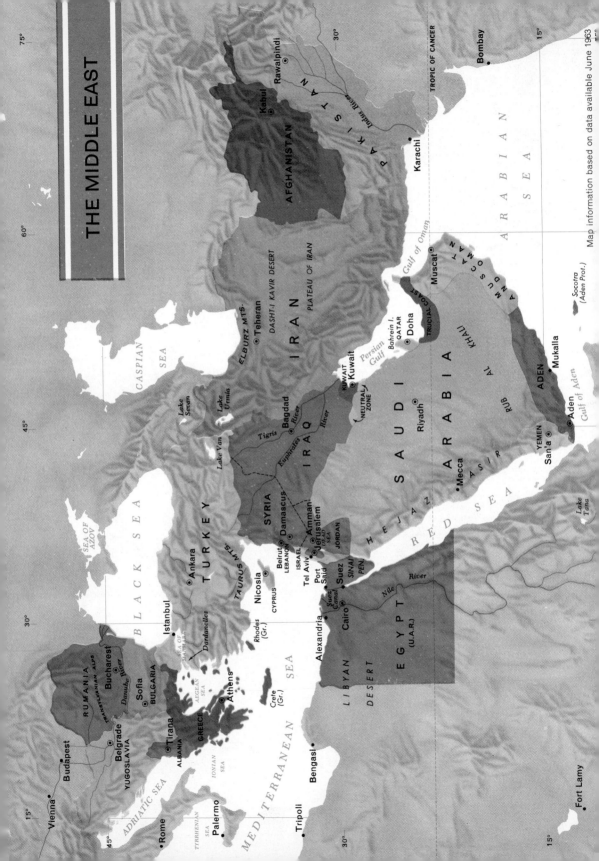

THE MIDDLE EAST

Map information based on data available June 1963

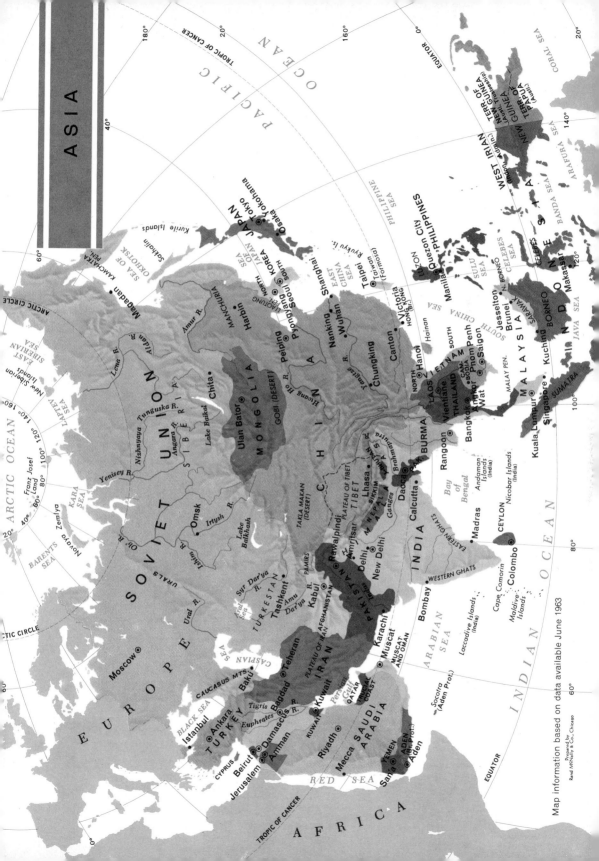

A S I A

Map information based on data available June 1963

Prepared by
Rand McNally & Co., Chicago

PACIFIC OCEAN

TROPIC OF CANCER

ARCTIC OCEAN

BARENTS SEA

KARA SEA

LAPTEV SEA

EAST SIBERIAN SEA

SEA OF OKHOTSK

BERING SEA

SEA OF JAPAN

YELLOW SEA

EAST CHINA SEA

PHILIPPINE SEA

CORAL SEA

ARAFURA SEA

BANDA SEA

CELEBES SEA

SULU SEA

SOUTH CHINA SEA

JAVA SEA

Bay of Bengal

INDIAN OCEAN

ARABIAN SEA

RED SEA

BLACK SEA

CASPIAN SEA

MEDITERRANEAN SEA

Persian Gulf

EUROPE

AFRICA

SOVIET UNION

SIBERIA

TURKESTAN

URALS

CAUCASUS MTS.

MONGOLIA

MANCHURIA

CHINA

GOBI (DESERT)

TAKLA MAKAN (DESERT)

PLATEAU OF TIBET

TIBET

PAMIRS

NORTH KOREA

SOUTH KOREA

JAPAN

NORTH VIETNAM

SOUTH VIETNAM

LAOS

CAMBODIA

THAILAND

BURMA

MALAYSIA

INDONESIA

BORNEO

SUMATRA

SARAWAK

N. BORNEO

PHILIPPINES

LUZON

WEST IRIAN (West New Guinea) (Indon.)

TERR. OF NEW GUINEA (Austl.)

NEW GUINEA

TERR. OF PAPUA (Austl.)

INDIA

NEPAL

SIKKIM

BHUTAN

PAK.

PAKISTAN

AFGHANISTAN

IRAN

PLATEAU OF IRAN

TURKEY

SAUDI ARABIA

YEMEN

MUSCAT AND OMAN

QATAR

KUWAIT

ADEN (Br. Prot.)

CYPRUS

CEYLON

MALAY PEN.

EASTERN GHATS

WESTERN GHATS

TROPIC OF CANCER

ARCTIC CIRCLE

EQUATOR

Moscow

Ankara

Istanbul

Beirut

Jerusalem

Amman

Damascus

Baghdad

Tehran

Baku

Kuwait

Riyadh

Mecca

Sana

Aden

Muscat

Karachi

Kabul

Tashkent

Omsk

Chita

Ulan Bator

Harbin

Peiping

Pyongyang

Seoul

Tokyo

Yokohama

Osaka

Shanghai

Nanking

Wuhan

Chungking

Canton

Hong Kong

Victoria (Br.)

Hanoi

Vientiane

Bangkok

Phnom Penh

Angkor Wat

Saigon

Rangoon

Kuala Lumpur

Singapore

Kuching

Jesselton

Brunei

Manila

Quezon City

Taipei

Madras

Colombo

Bombay

New Delhi

Delhi

Amritsar

Rawalpindi

Lhasa

Dacca

Calcutta

Makassar

Magadan

Yenisey R.

Lena R.

Ob R.

Irtysh

Ishim

Ural R.

Tigris R.

Euphrates R.

Amu Dar'ya

Syr Dar'ya

Aral Sea

Lake Balkhash

Lake Baikal

Amur R.

Aldan R.

Angara R.

Nizhnyaya Tunguska R.

Hwang Ho R.

Yangtze R.

Si R.

Ganges R.

Brahmaputra R.

Indus R.

Mekong R.

Salween R.

Irrawaddy R.

Kurile Islands

Sakhalin

Kamchatka Pen.

New Siberian Islands

Wrangel I.

Novaya Zemlya

Franz Josef Land

Zemlya

Hainan

Ryukyu Is.

Taiwan (Formosa)

Andaman Islands (India)

Nicobar Islands (India)

Laccadive Islands (India)

Maldive Islands (India)

Cape Comorin

Socotra (Aden Prot.)

Malabar Coast

180°

160°

140°

120°

100°

80°

60°

40°

20°

0°

20°

40°

60°

80°

100°

120°

140°

160°

NORTH AMERICA

SOUTH AMERICA

90°   75°   60°   45°

West Indies

CARIBBEAN   SEA
Curaçao (Neth.)

NICARAGUA   Caracas   Trinidad
Barranquilla
COSTA RICA Colón   Lake
        Balboa   Maracaibo
  PANAMA   VENEZUELA   Georgetown   Paramaribo
                            BRITISH   Cayenne
          Bogotá   GUIANA   SURINAM
Buenaventura COLOMBIA   (NETH.)   FRENCH
                                                GUIANA

Quito   Rio Negro   EQUATOR   0°
Galápagos ECUADOR   River
Islands   Amazon   Manaus   Belém
(Ecuador) Guayaquil   Napo R.
          Iquitos

                              B R A Z I L
        P   Madeira R.   Recife
        E   MATO GROSSO
        R   Ucayali R.   São Francisco R.   Salvador
        U   Brasília
        Lima   Lake   BOLIVIA   15°
                     Titicaca   La Paz
        Arequipa   Sucre
                                                 Bello Horizonte
                        GRAN   PARAGUAY
                        CHACO   Paraná R.   São Paulo
TROPIC OF CAPRICORN Antofagasta   Rio de Janeiro
                          Asunción   Santos   30°
        PACIFIC   Tucumán A
                        R
                        G   Paraguay R.
                        E
                        N
                        T   Córdoba   Santa Fé
        Valparaiso   C I   Mendoza Rosario   URUGUAY
                     H N   Montevideo
        Santiago   I A   Salado R.   30°
                     L   Buenos Aires   Rio de la Plata
        OCEAN   E

        Valdivia   Colorado R. Bahía Blanca   ATLANTIC

                     Chubut R.
                PATAGONIA   OCEAN
                A
                N
                D   PATAGONIA
                E
                S   45°

        Magallanes   Falkland Is.
        (Punta Arenas)   (Br.)
                     West Falkland East Falkland
                     TIERRA DEL FUEGO
                        Cape Horn

90°   75°   60°   45°   30°   15°

AFRICA

EUROPE

ASIA

ATLANTIC OCEAN

MEDITERRANEAN SEA

RED SEA

INDIAN OCEAN

ATLANTIC OCEAN

Lisbon
Rome
Athens

Tangier
Algiers
Tunis
Rabat
TUNISIA
ATLAS MOUNTAINS
Tripoli
Bengasi
Alexandria
Cairo
Sinai Pen.

Sidi Ifni
IFNI (Sp.)
MOROCCO

Madeira Is. (Port.)
Canary Is. (Sp.)

Villa Cisneros

ALGERIA
LIBYA
LIBYAN DESERT
EGYPT (U.A.R.)

Mecca
ARABIAN PENINSULA

TROPIC OF CANCER

SPANISH SAHARA
S A H A R A
Nile

MAURITANIA
Nouakchott
MALI
NIGER
TIBESTI MASSIF
CHAD
Lake Chad
Omdurman
Khartoum

SUDAN

ERITREA
Lake Tana
Djibouti
FR. SOMALILAND
Gulf of Aden

Dakar
SENEGAL
Gambia R.
BATHURST
GAMBIA
PORT. GUINEA Bissao
GUINEA
Conakry
Freetown
SIERRA LEONE
LIBERIA
Monrovia

Senegal R.
Timbuktu
Gao
Niamey
Bamako
UPPER VOLTA
Ouagadougou
Niger R.
Niger River
Volta
GHANA
TOGO
DAHOMEY
Lome
Porto-Novo
Lagos
Accra
Abidjan
IVORY COAST

NIGERIA
Fort-Lamy

CENTRAL AFRICAN REPUBLIC
Bangui
CONGO BASIN
CONGO Ubangi
Congo River

KORDOFAN PLATEAU
Blue Nile
White Nile
AMHARA PLATEAU
Addis Ababa
ETHIOPIA
SOMALI REPUBLIC
Mogadiscio

15°

CAMEROON
Yaounde
Fernando Po (Sp.)
Principe (Port.)
Bata
RIO MUNI (Sp.)
Libreville
St. Thomas (Port.)
GABON
Annobon (Sp.)
Brazzaville
CABINDA (Ang.)
Léopoldville

Gulf of Guinea

UGANDA
Kampala
Lake Rudolf
KENYA
Nairobi
Lake Victoria
Kigali
RWANDA
Usumbura
BURUNDI
Lake Leopold II
Lake Tanganyika
Lake Kivu
THE CONGO
TANGANYIKA
Zanzibar Is.
Dar es Salaam

EQUATOR

Ascension (Br.)

Luanda

ANGOLA (Port.)

NYASALAND (Br.)
Lake Nyasa
Aldabra Is. (Br.)
Comoro Is. (Fr.)

St. Helena (Br.)

NORTHERN RHODESIA (Br.)
Lusaka
Zomba
Victoria Falls
Zambezi River
MOZAMBIQUE (Port.)
Tananarive
MALAGASY REPUBLIC
Madagascar

SOUTH-WEST AFRICA (S. African Mand.)
Windhoek
Okovanggo Swamp
Salisbury
SOUTHERN RHODESIA (Br.)
Mozambique Channel

TROPIC OF CAPRICORN

Walvis Bay (S. Africa)
BECHUANALAND (Br. Prot.)
KALAHARI DESERT
Mafeking
Pretoria
SWAZILAND
Lourenço Marques
BASUTOLAND (Br.)
DRAKENSBERG MOUNTAINS

SOUTH AFRICA

Cape Town
Cape of Good Hope

Delagoa Bay

Prepared by
Rand McNally & Co., Chicago

THE AIR AGE

Air Distances shown in Statute Miles

Prepared by
Rand McNally & Co., Chicago

Bibliography

REFERENCES AND GENERAL READING

An Atlas of African Affairs, by Andrew Boyd and Patrick Van Rensburg. Maps by W. H. Bromage. Praeger.*

Browne, Lewis. *This Believing World; A Simple Account of the Great Religions of Mankind.* Macmillan.*

Chubb, Thomas C. *Slavic Peoples.* World Pub., 1962.

Churchill, Sir Winston. *A History of the English Speaking Peoples.* 4 vols. Bantam.*

Clough, Shepard B. and Cole, Charles. *Economic History of Europe.* 3d ed. Heath, 1952.

The Columbia-Lippincott Gazetteer of the World. 2nd Printing with Supplement, ed. by L. E. Seltzer. Columbia, 1962.

Contemporary Civilization 2, ed. by Henry Steele Commager. Scott, Foresman.*

Ellis, Harry B. *The Arabs.* World Pub., 1958.

Fairservis, Walter A., Jr. *Horsemen of the Steppes.* World Pub., 1962.

Fenichell, Stephen S. *The United Nations, Design for Peace.* Holt, 1960.

Goode's World Atlas, ed. by E. B. Espenshade, Jr. 11th ed. Rand McNally, 1960.

Hayes, Carlton J. H. *Contemporary Europe Since 1870.* Rev. ed. Macmillan, 1958.

Herring, Hubert. *A History of Latin America from the Beginnings to the Present.* Knopf, 1961.

Kenworthy, Leonard. *Leaders of New Nations.* Doubleday, 1959.

Ketchum, Richard M., ed. *What is Communism? A Picture Survey of World Communism,* rev. by Abraham Brumberg. Dutton, 1962.

Lansing, Marion F. *Liberators and Heroes of the West Indian Islands.* Farrar, Straus, 1953.

Life (Periodical). *The World's Great Religions,* by the Editors of Life. Golden Press, 1958. (Young Reader's Edition)

Müller, Herbert J. *Uses of the Past; Profiles of Former Societies.* Mentor.*

Palmer, R. R., ed. *Historical Atlas of the World.* Rand McNally.*

Rand McNally Cosmopolitan World Atlas. New ed. Rand McNally, 1962.

Shepherd, W. R. *Historical Atlas.* 8th rev. ed. Barnes and Noble, 1956.

The South American Handbook, 1962; A Year Book and Guide to the Countries and Resources of South and Central America, Mexico and Cuba, ed. by Howell Davies. Rand McNally, 1962.

Swearingen, Rodger. *The World of Communism,* ed. by Howard R. Anderson. Houghton.*

Van Loon, Hendrik. *Story of Mankind.* Washington Square.*

———

Paperback volumes are indicated by an asterisk.*

Webster's Biographical Dictionary. Merriam, 1961.

Webster's Geographical Dictionary. Rev. ed. Merriam, 1960.

Wells, H. G. *The Outline of History,* rev. by Raymond Postgate. Doubleday, 1961.

The World Almanac and Book of Facts, ed. by Harry Hansen. World-Telegram and Sun.

NATIONAL HISTORIES

Borden, Charles A. *Hawaii . . . Fiftieth State.* Macrae Smith, 1960.

Crow, John A. *Mexico Today.* Harper, 1957.

Dilts, Marion M. *The Pageant of Japanese History.* 3d ed. McKay, 1961.

Fairservis, Walter A., Jr. *India.* World Pub., 1961.

Life World Library Series. Time, Inc.

Lin Yutang. *The Chinese Way of Life.* World Pub., 1959.

Payne, Robert. *The Splendor of Persia.* Knopf, 1957.

Portraits of the Nations Series. Lippincott.

Rabling, Harold and Hamilton, Patrick. *Under the Southern Cross.* St. Martin's, 1962.

Schurz, William L. *Brazil: The Infinite Country.* Dutton, 1961.

Seeger, Elizabeth. *The Pageant of Chinese History.* 4th rev. ed. McKay, 1962.

Weston, Christine. *Ceylon.* Scribner, 1960.

ILLUSTRATED HISTORIES

American Heritage. *Discoverers of the New World,* by the Editors of American Heritage; narrative by Josef Berger. American Heritage, 1960.

American Heritage. *Pirates of the Spanish Main,* narrative by Hamilton Cochran. American Heritage, 1961.

Brosse, Jacques and others. *100,000 Years of Daily Life: A Visual History,* tr. by Anne Carter. Golden Press, 1961.

Bullock, Alan and others, eds. *World History; Civilization from Its Beginnings.* Doubleday, 1962. (Doubleday Pictorial Library)

Horizon Magazine. *The Horizon Book of Lost Worlds,* by the Editors; narrative by Leonard Cottrell. American Heritage, dist. by Doubleday, 1962.

Horizon Magazine. *The Horizon Book of the Renaissance,* by the Editors and J. H. Plumb. American Heritage, dist. by Doubleday, 1961.

Life (Periodical). *Life's Picture History of Western Man.* Simon and Schuster, 1951.

Paton, Alan. *South Africa in Transition.* Scribner, 1956.

Quennell, Peter and Hodge, Alan, eds. *The Past We Share; An Illustrated History of the British and American Peoples.* Prometheus, 1960.

Rubin, Jacob A. *A Pictorial History of the United Nations.* Yoseloff, 1962.

SCIENCE, TECHNOLOGY, AND THE ARTS

Allen, Agnes. *The Story of Sculpture.* Roy, 1958.

American Heritage. *Men of Science and Invention,* by the editors of American Heritage; narrative by Michael Blow. American Heritage, 1960.

Asimov, Isaac. *Breakthroughs in Science.* Scholastic Book Services.*

Asimov, Isaac. *Inside the Atom.* 2d rev. ed. Abelard, 1961.

Borek, Ernest. *The Atoms Within Us.* Columbia.*

Britten, Benjamin and Holst, Imogen. *The Wonderful World of Music.* Garden City Books, 1958.

Caidin, Martin and Caidin, Grace. *Aviation and Space Medicine.* Dutton, 1962.

Ceram, C. W., pseud. *The March of Archaeology*; tr. from the German by Richard and Clara Winston. Knopf, 1958.

Daugherty, Charles M. *The Great Archaeologists.* Crowell, 1962.

Del Ray, Lester. *The Mysterious Earth.* Chilton, 1960.

Deuel, Leo, ed. *The Treasures of Time.* Avon.*

Ewen, David, ed. *The World of Great Composers.* Prentice-Hall, 1962.

Fermi, Laura. *The Story of Atomic Energy.* Random House, 1961. (World Landmark Books)

Gardner, Helen. *Art Through the Ages,* ed. by Sumner Crosby. 4th rev. ed. Harcourt, 1959.

Gorsline, Douglas. *What People Wore; A Visual History of Dress from Ancient Times to Twentieth-Century America.* Viking, 1952.

Hogben, Lancelot. *Mathematics in the Making.* Doubleday, 1960.

Irwin, Keith Gordon. *The Romance of Weights and Measures.* Viking, 1960.

Jaffe, Bernard. *Michelson and the Speed of Light.* Anchor.*

Janson, Horst W. and Janson, Dora Jane. *The Story of Painting for Young People, from Cave Painting to Modern Times.* Abrams, 1962.

Kline, Morris. *Mathematics and the Physical World.* Anchor.*

Laird, Helene and Laird, Charlton. *The Tree of Language.* World Pub., 1957.

Lester, Katherine M. *Historic Costume; A Resume of the Characteristic Types of Costume from the Most Remote Times to the Present Day.* 4th enl. ed. Bennett, 1956.

Life (Periodical). *The Universe,* by the Editors of Life and David Bergamini. Time, Inc., 1962. (Life Nature Library)

Life (Periodical). *The Wonders of Life on Earth,* by the Editors of Life and Lincoln Barnett. Time, Inc., dist. by Prentice-Hall, 1960.

McKown, Robin. *The Fabulous Isotopes: What They Are and What They Do.* Holiday, 1962.

Mann, Martin. *Peacetime Uses of Atomic Energy.* Rev. ed. Viking, 1961.

Mead, Margaret. *People and Places.* Bantam.*

Moore, Ruth. *Man, Time, and Fossils; The Story of Evolution.* 2nd ed., rev. Knopf, 1961.

Poole, Lynn and Poole, Gray. *Scientists Who Changed the World.* Dodd, 1960.

Priestly, J. B. *The Wonderful World of the Theatre.* Doubleday, 1959.

Rogers, Frances. *Painted Rock to Printed Page.* Lippincott, 1960.

Samachson, Dorothy and Samachson, Joseph. *The Fabulous World of Opera.* Rand McNally, 1962.

Samachson, Dorothy and Samachson, Joseph. *Good Digging; The Story of Archaeology.* Rand McNally, 1960.

Silverberg, Robert. *Lost Cities and Vanished Civilizations.* Bantam.*

Space, the New Frontier. Supt. of Documents, Government Printing Office, 1962. (Catalog No. NAS 1.: SP 1/4/962)

Suggs, Robert C. *Modern Discoveries in Archaeology.* Crowell, 1962.

Taylor, Francis H. *Fifty Centuries of Art.* Rev. ed. Harper, 1960.

We Seven, by the Astronauts Themselves. Simon and Schuster, 1962.

Williams, Greer. *Virus Hunters.* Knopf, 1959.

Wright, Helen and Rapport, Samuel, eds. *The Amazing World of Medicine.* Harper, 1961.

Yost, Edna. *Modern Americans in Science and Technology.* Dodd, 1962.

UNIT 1 • THE DAWN OF CIVILIZATION

Baumann, Hans. *The World of the Pharaohs,* tr. by Richard and Clara Winston. Pantheon, 1960.

Chiera, Edward. *They Wrote on Clay.* Phoenix.*

Chubb, Mary A. *Nefertiti Lived Here.* Crowell, 1955.

Contenau, Georges. *Everyday Life in Babylon and Assyria*; tr. by K. R. and A. R. Maxwell-Hyslop. St. Martin's, 1954.

Coon, Carleton S. *The Story of Man; From the First Human to Primitive Culture and Beyond.* 2d ed. rev. Knopf, 1962.

Cottrell, Leonard. *Land of the Pharaohs.* World Pub., 1960.

Cottrell, Leonard. *Land of the Two Rivers.* World Pub., 1962.

Cottrell, Leonard. *Life Under the Pharaohs.* Holt, 1960.

Falls, C. B. *The First 3000 Years: Ancient Civilizations of the Tigris, Euphrates, and Nile River Valleys, and the Mediterranean Sea.* Viking, 1960.

Montagu, Ashley. *Man: His First Million Years.* Signet.*

Quennell, Marjorie and Quennell, C. H. B. *Everyday Life in Prehistoric Times.* Putnam, 1959.

Sellman, R. R. *Ancient Egypt.* Roy, 1962.

UNIT 2 • THE CLASSICAL WORLD

Bulfinch, Thomas. *Bulfinch's Mythology,* abr. by Edmund Fuller. Dell.*

Bulwer-Lytton, Edward. *The Last Days of Pompeii.* Dolphin.*

Burn, Andrew R. *Alexander the Great and the Hellenistic Empire*. Rev. ed. Collier.*

Coolidge, Olivia. *Men of Athens*. Houghton, 1962.

Coolidge, Olivia. *Roman People*. Houghton, 1959.

Coolidge, Olivia. *The Trojan War*. Houghton, 1952.

Cottrell, Leonard. *The Bull of Minos*. Universal.*

Cottrell, Leonard. *The Great Invasion*. Coward-McCann, 1962.

Dolan, Mary. *Hannibal of Carthage*. Abr. Avon.*

Duggan, Alfred. *Julius Caesar*. Knopf, 1955.

Graves, Robert. *Greek Gods and Heroes*. Doubleday, 1960.

Gunther, John. *Julius Caesar*. Random House, 1959. (World Landmark Books)

Hamilton, Edith. *Mythology*. Mentor.*

Johnston, Mary. *Roman Life*. Scott, Foresman, 1957.

Lamb, Harold. *Hannibal: One Man Against Rome*. Bantam.*

Plutarch. *Life Stories of Men Who Shaped History*, abr. by E. C. Lindeman. Mentor.*

Quennell, Marjorie and Quennell, Charles. *Everyday Things in Ancient Greece*. 2d ed. Putnam, 1954.

Wallace, Lew. *Ben-Hur*. Dolphin.*

UNIT 3 • THE MIDDLE AGES

Boardman, Fon W. *Castles*. Oxford (dist. by Walck), 1957.

Buehr, Walter. *Knights and Castles and Feudal Life*. Putnam, 1957.

Chubb, Thomas C. *The Byzantines*. World Pub., 1959.

Horizon Magazine. *Knights of the Crusades*, by the Editors and Jay Williams. American Heritage, 1962.

Kielty, Bernadine. *The Fall of Constantinople*. Random, 1957. (World Landmark Books)

Lamb, Harold. *The Crusades*. Bantam.*

Lamb, Harold. *Genghis Khan*. Bantam.*

Lamb, Harold. *Genghis Khan and the Mongol Horde*. Random, 1954. (World Landmark Books)

Painter, Sidney. *A History of the Middle Ages*. Knopf, 1953.

Quennell, Marjorie and Quennell, C. H. B. *Everyday Life in Roman and Anglo-Saxon Times; Including Viking and Norman Times*. Rev. ed. Putnam, 1959.

Sutcliff, Rosemary. *Beowulf*, retold. Dutton, 1962.

Sutcliff, Rosemary. *Dawn Wind*. Walck, 1962.

Trease, Geoffrey. *Escape to King Alfred*. Vanguard, 1958.

Twain, Mark, pseud. *A Connecticut Yankee in King Arthur's Court*. Washington Square.*

UNIT 4 • EARLY CIVILIZATIONS IN ASIA, AFRICA, AND AMERICA

Bakeless, Katherine and John. *They Saw America First; Our First Explorers and What They Saw*. Lippincott, 1957.

Byrne, Donn. *Messer Marco Polo*. Washington Square.*

Nevins, Albert J. *The Young Conquistador*. Dodd, 1960.

Schiffers, Heinrich. *The Quest for Africa; 2,000 Years of Exploration*, tr. from the German by Diana Pyke. Putnam, 1958.

Von Hagen, Victor W. *The Incas; People of the Sun*. World Pub., 1961.

Von Hagen, Victor W. *Maya, Land of the Turkey and the Deer*. World Pub., 1960.

UNIT 5 • MEDIEVAL EUROPE IN TRANSITION

Allen, Agnes. *The Story of Michelangelo*. Roy, 1957.

Armitage, Angus. *The World of Copernicus*. Mentor.*

Bainton, Roland H. *Here I Stand; A Life of Martin Luther*. Mentor.*

Bradford, Ernle. *The Great Siege*. Harcourt, 1962.

Brooks, Polly S. and Walworth, Nancy Z. *The World Awakes; The Renaissance in Europe*. Lippincott, 1962.

Burton, Elizabeth. *Pageant of Elizabethan England*. Scribner, 1958.

Busoni, Rafaello. *The Man Who Was Don Quixote; The Story of Miguel Cervantes*. Prentice-Hall, 1958.

Chute, Marchette. *Geoffrey Chaucer of England*. Everyman.*

Chute, Marchette. *Shakespeare of London*. Everyman.*

Daugherty, James. *The Magna Charta*. Random House, 1956. (World Landmark Books)

Dumas, Alexandre. *The Three Musketeers*. Pyramid;* Washington Square.*

Fermi, Laura and Bernardini, Gilberto. *Galileo and the Scientific Revolution*. Basic Books, 1961.

Irwin, Margaret. *Elizabeth, Captive Princess*. Harcourt, 1948. (Sequel to *Young Bess*.)

Irwin, Margaret. *Young Bess*. Harcourt, 1945.

Johnson, William. *Captain Cortés Conquers Mexico*. Random, 1960. (World Landmark Books)

Kendall, Paul Murray. *The Yorkist Age; Daily Life During the Wars of the Roses*. Norton, 1962.

Morison, Samuel Eliot. *Christopher Columbus, Mariner*. Mentor.*

Pearson, Lu Emily. *Elizabethans at Home*. Stanford, 1957.

Ripley, Elizabeth. *Leonardo da Vinci; A Biography*. Walck, 1952.

Schmitt, Gladys. *Rembrandt*. Dell.*

Scott, Sir Walter. *Quentin Durward*. Dolphin.*

Smith, Bradley. *Columbus in the New World*. Doubleday, 1962.

Vance, Marguerite. *Scotland's Queen; The Story of Mary Stuart*. Dutton, 1962.

Vance, Marguerite. *Song for a Lute*. Dutton, 1958.

Walsh, Ronald, pseud. *Ferdinand Magellan*. Criterion, 1956.

UNIT 6 • EARLY MODERN TIMES

Alden, John R. *The American Revolution, 1775-1783.* Torchbooks.*

American Heritage. *Thomas Jefferson and His World,* by the Editors of American Heritage; narrative by Henry Moscow. Dist. by Golden Press, 1960.

Bradford, William. *Of Plymouth Plantation,* ed. by Harvey Wish. Abr. Capricorn.*

Bristow, Gwen. *Celia Garth.* Pocket Books.*

Burton, Elizabeth. *The Pageant of Stuart England.* Scribner, 1962.

Butterfield, Herbert. *Napoleon.* Collier.*

Cunliffe, Marcus. *George Washington, Man and Monument.* Mentor.*

Dickens, Charles. *A Tale of Two Cities.* Dolphin;* Signet Classics;* *Washington Square.**

Edmonds, Walter D. *Drums Along the Mohawk.* Bantam.*

Forester, C. F. *Hornblower and the Hotspur.* Bantam.*

Ludwig, Emil. *Napoleon.* Pocket Books.*

Padover, Saul K. *Jefferson.* Rev. and abr. Mentor.*

Tannenbaum, Beulah, and Stillman, Myra. *Isaac Newton, Pioneer of Space Mathematics.* McGraw-Hill, 1959.

Tolstoy, Leo. *War and Peace;* tr. by Louise and Aylmer Maude. Modern Library.

Vance, Marguerite. *Marie Antoinette, Daughter of an Empress.* Dutton, 1950.

UNIT 7 • NINETEENTH-CENTURY EUROPE

Cecil, Lord David. *Melbourne.* Charter.*

Curie, Eve. *Madame Curie;* tr. by Vincent Sheean. Pocket Books.*

Davenport, Marcia. *Garibaldi: Father of Modern Italy.* Random, 1957. (World Landmark Books)

Dumas, Alexandre. *The Count of Monte Cristo.* Abr. Bantam.*

Haycraft, Molly. *Queen Victoria.* Messner, 1956.

Moore, Ruth. *Charles Darwin.* Knopf, 1955.

Spencer, Cornelia, pseud. *More Hands for Man: The Story of the Industrial Revolution (1760-1850).* Day, 1960.

Streatfield, Noel. *Queen Victoria.* Random House, 1958. (World Landmark Books)

Woodham-Smith, Cecil. *Lonely Crusader: The Life of Florence Nightingale.* Avon.*

Woodham-Smith, Cecil. *The Reason Why.* Everyman.*

UNIT 8 • GROWTH AND EXPANSION
OUTSIDE EUROPE

Bailey, Bernadine. *Famous Latin-American Liberators.* Dodd, 1960.

Benét, Laura. *Stanley, Invincible Explorer.* Dodd, 1954.

Catton, Bruce. *A Stillness at Appomattox.* Pocket Books.*

Gavin, Catherine. *The Cactus and the Crown.* Doubleday, 1962.

Horgan, Paul. *Citizen of New Salem.* Crest.*

Kruger, Rayne. *Good-Bye Dolly Gray; The Story of the Boer War.* Lippincott, 1960.

Landon, Margaret. *Anna and the King of Siam.* Pocket Books.*

Miers, Earl Schenck. *Robert E. Lee.* Vintage.*

Mitchell, Margaret. *Gone With the Wind.* Pocket Books.*

Sandburg, Carl. *Abraham Lincoln: The Prairie Years and the War Years.* 3 vols. Dell.*

Tully, Andrew. *When They Burned the White House.* Popular.*

UNIT 9 • NATIONAL RIVALRIES AND
WORLD WAR I

Baldwin, Hanson W. *World War I: An Outline History.* Black Cat.*

Fenner, Phyllis, comp. *Over There! Stories of World War I.* Morrow, 1961.

Lord, Walter. *The Good Years.* Bantam.*

Remarque, Erich. *All Quiet on the Western Front.* Crest.*

Sellman, R. R. *The First World War.* Criterion, 1962.

UNIT 10 • CHALLENGES TO DEMOCRACY
AND WORLD WAR II

Allen, Frederick Lewis. *Only Yesterday: An Informal History of the Nineteen Twenties.* Bantam.*

Chamberlain, William. *Combat Stories of World War II and Korea.* Day, 1962.

Churchill, Sir Winston. *Memoirs of the Second World War,* abridged by Denis Kelly. Houghton, 1959.

Churchill, Sir Winston. *The Second World War,* by Winston S. Churchill and the Editors of Life. Golden Press, 1960.

Eisenhower, Dwight D. *Crusade in Europe.* Dolphin.*

Ellsberg, Edward. *The Far Shore.* Popular.*

Fenner, Phyllis, comp. *No Time for Glory; Stories of World War II.* Morrow, 1962.

Forester, C. S. *Sink the Bismarck!* Bantam.*

Frank, Anne. *The Diary of A Young Girl,* tr. from the Dutch by B. M. Mooyaart. Pocket Books.*

Hersey, John. *A Bell for Adano.* Avon.*

Howarth, D. A. *D-Day: The Sixth of June, 1944.* Pyramid.*

Lengyel, Emil. *They Called Him Ataturk.* Day, 1962.

Lord, Walter. *Day of Infamy.* Bantam.*

Ogburn, Charlton, Jr. *The Marauders.* Crest.*

Shirer, William L. *Berlin Diary.* Popular.*

Shirer, William L. *The Rise and Fall of Adolf Hitler.* Random, 1961. (World Landmark Books) A simplified edition of *The Rise and Fall of the Third Reich; A History of Nazi Germany.* Crest.*

Tregaskis, Richard. *Guadalcanal Diary.* Popular.*

Wouk, Herman. *The Caine Mutiny.* Doubleday;* Dell.*

AFRICA

Ames, Sophia Ripley. *Nkrumah of Ghana.* Rand McNally, 1961.

Cousins, Norman. *Dr. Schweitzer of Lambaréne.* Harper, 1960.

Dughi, Nancy. *Strait Passage.* Coward, 1962.

Gunther, John. *Meet North Africa.* Harper, 1957.

Gunther, John and others. *Meet South Africa.* Harper, 1958.

Gunther, John. *Meet the Congo and Its Neighbors.* Harper, 1959.

Hughes, John. *The New Face of Africa South of the Sahara.* Longmans, 1961.

Italiaander, Rolf. *The New Leaders of Africa,* tr. by James McCovern. Prentice-Hall, 1961.

Kittler, Glenn D. *Equatorial Africa; The New World of Tomorrow.* Nelson, 1959.

Luthuli, Albert John. *Let My People Go.* McGraw-Hill, 1962.

Moorehead, Alan. *No Room in the Ark.* Harper, 1959.

Ostergaard-Christensen, L. *At Work With Albert Schweitzer;* tr. by F. H. Lyon. Beacon, 1962.

Paton, Alan. *Cry, the Beloved Country.* Scribner.*

Pond, Seymour. *African Explorer; The Adventures of Carl Akeley.* Dodd, 1957.

St. John, Robert. *The Boss; The Story of Gamal Abdel Nasser.* McGraw-Hill, 1960.

Wallbank, T. Walter. *Contemporary Africa: Continent in Transition.* Anvil.*

ARCTIC AND ANTARCTIC

Bixby, William. *The Impossible Journey of Sir Ernest Shackleton.* Little, 1960.

Bixby, William. *McMurdo, Antarctica.* McKay, 1962.

Dufek, George John. *Through the Frozen Frontier.* Harcourt, 1959.

Horizon Magazine. *Heroes of Polar Exploration,* by the Editors and Ralph K. Andrist. American Heritage, 1962.

Les Tina, Dorothy. *Icicles on the Roof.* Abelard, 1961.

Siple, Paul. *90° South: The Story of the American South Pole Conquest.* Putnam, 1959.

Steele, George P. *Seadragon: Northwest Under the Ice.* Dutton, 1962.

AUSTRALIA

Glaskin, G. M. *The Land that Sleeps.* Doubleday, 1961.

Polishuk, Nancy. *Four Against the River.* Dutton, 1962.

Rabling, Harold and Hamilton, Patrick. *Under the Southern Cross; the Story of Australia.* St. Martin's, 1961.

CHINA

Buck, Pearl. *My Several Worlds.* Pocket Books.*

Chow, Chung-cheng. *The Lotus Pool.* Appleton, 1961.

Greene, Felix. *China; The Country Americans Don't Know.* Ballantine.*

Hersey, John. *A Single Pebble.* Bantam.*

Scovel, Myra. *The Chinese Ginger Jars.* Harper, 1962.

Wong, Jade Snow. *Fifth Chinese Daughter.* Scholastic Book Services.*

EUROPE

Gunther, John. *Inside Europe Today.* Rev. ed. Pocket Books.*

McClellan, Grant S., ed. *The Two Germanies.* Wilson, 1959. (Reference Shelf V. 31, No. 1)

Sulzberger, C. L. *The Test: DeGaulle and Algeria.* Harcourt, 1962.

GREAT BRITAIN

Cathcart, Helen. *Her Majesty the Queen; The Story of Elizabeth II.* Dodd, 1962.

Harrity, Richard and Martin, Ralph G. *Man of the Century: Churchill.* Duell, 1962.

Rowland, John. *The Penicillin Man: The Story of Sir Alexander Fleming.* Roy, 1957.

INDIA, BURMA, AND TIBET

Bartholomew, Carol. *My Heart Has Seventeen Rooms.* Macmillan, 1959.

Bowles, Cynthia. *At Home in India.* Pyramid.*

The Dalai Lama of Tibet. *My Land and My People: The Memoirs of His Holiness, the Dalai Lama of Tibet.* McGraw-Hill, 1962.

Douglas, William O. *Exploring the Himalaya.* Random House, 1958. (World Landmark Books)

Eaton, Jeannette, *Gandhi: Fighter Without a Sword.* Morrow, 1950.

Guthrie, Anne. *Madame Ambassador: The Life of Vijaya Lakshmi Pandit.* Harcourt, 1962.

Moraes, Frank. *India Today.* Macmillan, 1960.

Moraes, Frank. *Jawaharlal Nehru; A Biography.* Macmillan, 1956.

Rama Rau, Santha. *Gifts of Passage.* Harper, 1961.

Sheean, Vincent. *Nehru: The Years of Power.* Random, 1960.

Thubten, Jigme Norbu. *Tibet is My Country.* Dutton, 1961.

INDO-CHINA

Dooley, Thomas A. *Deliver Us from Evil.* Signet.*

Dooley, Thomas A. *The Edge of Tomorrow.* Signet.*

Dooley, Thomas A. *The Night They Burned the Mountain.* Signet.*

Meeker, Oden. *The Little World of Laos.* Scribner, 1959.

INDONESIA

Mintz, Jeanne S. *Indonesia.* Van Nostrand.*

JAPAN

Bosworth, Allan R. *The Lovely World of Richi-San.* Harper, 1960.

Simon, Charlie May. *The Sun and the Birch: The Story of Crown Prince Akihito and Crown Princess Michiko.* Dutton, 1960.

Velen, Elizabeth and Velen, Victor, eds. *The New Japan.* Wilson, 1958. (Reference Shelf, Vol. 30, No. 2)

Vining, Elizabeth Gray. *Return to Japan.* Lippincott, 1960.

Vining, Elizabeth Gray. *Windows for the Crown Prince.* Lippincott, 1962.

KOREA AND OKINAWA

Engle, Eloise. *Dawn Mission: A Flight Nurse in Korea.* Day, 1962.

Leckie, Robert. *Conflict: The History of the Korean War.* Putnam, 1962.

Pak, Chong-Yong. *Korean Boy.* Lothrop, 1955.

Tibbets, Albert B., comp. *Courage in Korea, Stories of the Korean War.* Little, 1962.

LATIN AMERICA

Benton, William. *The Voice of Latin America.* Colophon.*

Crow, John A. *Mexico Today.* Harper, 1957.

Rivero, Nicolás. *Castro's Cuba: An American Dilemma.* Luce, dist. by McKay, 1962.

MIDDLE EAST

Dickson, Mora. *Baghdad and Beyond.* Rand McNally, 1961.

Douglas, William O. *West of the Indus.* Doubleday, 1958.

Edelman, Lily. *Israel: New People in an Old Land.* Nelson, 1958.

Hussein, King of Jordan. *Uneasy Lies the Head.* Geis, 1962.

Lengyel, Emil. *The Changing Middle East.* Day, 1960.

St. John, Robert. *Ben-Gurion: The Biography of an Extraordinary Man.* Doubleday, 1959.

PACIFIC ISLANDS

Attenborough, David. *People of Paradise.* Harper, 1961.

Borden, Charles A. *South Sea Islands.* Macrae Smith, 1961.

Heyerdahl, Thor. *Kon-Tiki.* Special edition for young people. Rand McNally, 1960.

Pole, James T. *Hawaii's First King.* Bobbs, 1959.

Romulo, Carlos. *I Walked With Heroes.* Avon.*

Sperry, Armstrong. *Pacific Islands Speaking.* Macmillan, 1955.

Suggs, Robert C. *Lords of the Blue Pacific.* New York Graphic Society, 1962.

Webb, Nancy and Webb, Jean Francis. *Kaiulani: Crown Princess of Hawaii.* Viking, 1962.

UNITED STATES OF AMERICA

Allen, Frederick Lewis. *The Big Change: America Transforms Herself, 1900-1950.* Bantam.*

Beach, Edward L. *Around the World Submerged: The Voyage of the 'Tritan.'* Holt, 1962.

Berding, Andrew. *Foreign Affairs and You! How American Foreign Policy is Made and What It Means to You.* Doubleday, 1962.

Caidin, Martin. *Rendezvous in Space: The Story of Projects Mercury, Gemini, Dyna-Soar, and Apollo.* Dutton, 1962.

Fermi, Laura. *Atoms in the Family.* Phoenix.*

Forsee, Aylesa. *Frank Lloyd Wright: Rebel in Concrete.* Macrae Smith, 1959.

Michelmore, Peter. *Einstein: Profile of the Man.* Dodd, 1962.

New York Times. *America's Race for the Moon.* Vintage.*

The Rockefeller Panel Reports. *Prospect for America.* Doubleday, 1961.

Solomon, Louis. *Telstar: Communication Breakthrough by Satellite.* McGraw-Hill, 1962.

Steinbeck, John. *Travels with Charley.* Bantam.*

White, Theodore H. *The Making of the President, 1960.* Pocket Books.*

Wolff, Perry. *A Tour of the White House with Mrs. John F. Kennedy.* Dell.*

U.S.S.R. AND SATELLITES

Armonas, Barbara and Nasvytis, A. L. *Leave Your Tears in Moscow.* Lippincott, 1961.

Gunther, John. *Inside Russia Today.* Rev. ed. Pyramid.*

Gunther, John. *Meet Soviet Russia.* 2 vols. Harper, 1962.

Jacquet, Eliane. *High Heels in Red Square;* tr. by Jerry Bothmer. Holt, 1961.

Kennan, George F. *Russia and the West Under Lenin and Stalin.* Mentor.*

Michener, James A. *The Bridge at Andau.* Bantam.*

Miller, Wright. *Russians as People.* Everyman.*

Rama Rau, Santha. *My Russian Journey.* Harper, 1959.

Rieber, Alfred J. and Nelson, Robert A. *A Study of the U.S.S.R. and Communism: An Historical Approach.* Scott, Foresman.*

Acknowledgments

QUOTED MATERIAL

Page

18 Allen Johnson, *The Historian and Historical Evidence* (New York: Charles Scribner's Sons, 1926), p. 21.

19 Bernard Norling, *Towards a Better Understanding of History* (South Bend, Ind.: Univ. of Notre Dame Press, 1960), p. 42.

19 Sherman Kent, *Writing History* (New York: Appleton-Century-Crofts, 1941), p. 1.

39 C. H. Johns, ed., *Babylonian and Assyrian Laws, Contracts and Letters,* "Library of Ancient Inscriptions" (New York: Charles Scribner's Sons, 1904), pp. 44-67 *passim.*

48 From *The Book of The Dead,* Oliver J. Thatcher, ed., *The Ideas That Have Influenced Civilization,* Milwaukee, 1901.

59 *Herodotus,* trans., H. G. Rawlinson, rev. and annoted, A. W. Lawrence (London: Nonesuch Press, Ltd., 1935, p. 735.

67 *Thucydides: The Peloponnesian War,* trans., Rex Warner (Middlesex: Penguin Books, Ltd., 1954), pp. 117, 118, 119.

78 *Herodotus, History of the Persian Wars,* trans., George Rawlinson, in *The Greek Historians,* Vol. I, ed., Francis R. B. Godolphin, p. 378. Copyright 1942 by Random House, Inc., and reprinted with their permission.

87 *Thucydides Translated into English,* Benjamin Jowett, ed. and trans., Vol. I (Oxford: The Clarendon Press, 1900), p. 16.

113 Leon Bernard and Theodore B. Hodges, *Readings in European History* (New York: The Macmillan Company, 1958), p. 44. Cited from *Century Readings in Ancient Classical and Modern European Literature,* ed. John W. Cunliffe (New York: Century Co., 1925), pp. 577-578.

135 Quoted in G. G. Coulton, *Medieval Panorama* (N. Y.: Cambridge Univ. Press and The Macmillan Co., 1938), p. 242.

147 Sir Walter Scott, *Ivanhoe* (Chicago: Scott, Foresman & Co., 1919), pp. 188-189.

155 *The Portable Chaucer,* trans., Theodore Morrison (New York: The Viking Press, Inc., 1949), pp. 68-69.

158 Quoted in J. W. Thompson, *Economic and Social History of the Middle Ages* (New York: Century Co., 1928), p. 772. Reprinted by permission of Appleton-Century-Crofts.

159 Quoted in G. G. Coulton, *Medieval Panorama* (N. Y.: Cambridge Univ. Press and The Macmillan Co., 1938), p. 303.

166 Quoted in H. O. Taylor, *The Medieval Mind,* Vol. II (London: The Macmillan Company, Ltd., 1938), p. 524.

178 Geoffrey de Villehardouin, *Villehardouin's Chronicle of the Fourth Crusade and the Conquest of Constantinople.* Quoted in F. Marzials, *Memoirs of the Crusades,* Everyman's Library (London: J. M. Dent & Sons, Ltd., 1908), pp. 25-26.

179 (top) Charles Diehl, *Byzantium: Greatness and Decline* (New Brunswick, N. J.: Rutgers University Press, 1957), p. 197.

179 (bottom) Quoted in J. F. C. Fuller, *A Military History of the Western World,* Vol. I (N. Y.: Funk & Wagnalls, 1954), p. 522.

182 *Procopius,* Vol. I, trans., Henry B. Dewing, Loeb Classical Library (Cambridge: Harvard Univ. Press, 1914), pp. 231-233.

185 (col. 1) From *The Koran,* as quoted in James Harvey Robinson, *Readings in European History,* Vol. I (Boston: Ginn and Company, 1904), pp. 118-119.

185 (col. 2) From *The Koran,* as quoted in J. W. Thompson and E. N. Johnson, *An Introduction to Medieval Europe* (N. Y.: W. W. Norton & Co., Inc., 1937), p. 160.

192 *The Rubáiyát of Omar Khayyám,* trans., Edward Fitzgerald. Quoted in R. C. Pooley *et al., England in Literature* (Chicago: Scott, Foresman & Co., 1963), p. 470.

197 Bernard Pares, *A History of Russia* (New York: Alfred A. Knopf, 1956), p. 56.

201 *Asian Relations,* "Report of Proceedings of First Asian Conference, 1947" (New Delhi: Asian Relations Organization, 1948), p. 21.

205 Quoted in Michael Edwardes, *A History of India From the Earliest Times to the Present Day* (New York: Farrar, Straus & Cudahy, Inc., 1961), p. 43.

214 J. Legge, trans. and ed., "The Travels of Fa-Hsien," in *Chinese Literature* (London: Cooperative Publishing Co., 1900), p. 230.

217 Jawaharlal Nehru, *The Discovery of India* (N.Y.: John Day Co., 1946), p. 221.

218 Father Pierre du Jarric, *History of the most memorable things that took place in the East Indies and the countries discovered by the Portuguese.* Book IV, Chap. 8. Quoted in Michael Edwardes, *A History of India From the Earliest Times to the Present Day* (New York: Farrar, Straus & Cudahy, Inc., 1961), pp. 160, 161.

229 Quoted in Lin Yu-tang, *The Wisdom of China and India,* Modern Library ed. (N.Y.: Random House, Inc., 1942), p. 883.

233 Quoted in Robert Payne, *The White Pony* (New York: The John Day Company, 1949), pp. 198-199, 240.

243 Quoted in Marion May Dilts, *The Pageant of Japanese History* (New York, London, and Toronto: Longmans, Green and Company, 1938, 1947), p. 256. Copyright 1938, 1947, Marion May Dilts.

249 Reprinted by permission of the publishers, The Arthur H. Clark Company, from Francis Augustus MacNutt, trans. and ed., *Hernando Cortes, His Five Letters of Relation to the Emperor Charles V*, Vol. I.

269 Quoted in J. L. LaMonte, *The World of the Middle Ages* (New York: Appleton-Century-Crofts, 1949), p. 462. From J. F. Scott *et al.*, *Readings in Medieval History* (New York: Appleton-Century-Crofts, 1933), pp. 464-465.

354 John Locke, "Of Civil Government," from *The Second Treatise of Civil Government* (N. Y.: Hafner Pub. Co., 1947), p. 233.

357 Voltaire, *The Age of Louis XIV*, trans., Martyn P. Pollack, Everyman's Library (London: J. M. Dent & Sons, Ltd.: N. Y.: E. P. Dutton & Co., Inc., 1935), p. 314.

393 Arthur Young, *Travels in France and Italy*, Everyman's Library (London: J. M. Dent & Sons, Ltd., 1915; New York: E. P. Dutton & Co., Inc., 1915, 1927, 1934), p. 80.

406 *The Statutes of the Realm, Printed by Command of His Majesty, King George the Third* (London, 1819-1820), VI, 143-144; VII, 636-638.

406 U. S. Office of Education, *The Declaration of Independence and Its Story* (Washington, D. C., 1955), pp. 1-8.

407 Thomas Paine, *Rights of Man*, ed., Moncure Daniel Conway (New York: G. P. Putnam's Sons, 1894), pp. 351-353.

496 Karl Marx and Friedrich Engels, *Manifesto of the Communist Party*, Authorized English Translation, ed., Friedrich Engels (New York: New York Labor News Company, 1888), pp. 7-15, 28.

511 Quoted in Emil Ludwig, *Bolívar* (New York: Alliance Book Corp., 1942), p. 46.

555 Leon Wolff, *In Flanders Fields* (N. Y.: Ballantine Books, Inc., 1958), pp. 21, 22, 23.

570 Heinrich G. von Treitschke, *Politics*, Vol. I, trans. B. Dugdale and T. DeBille (London: Constable and Co., Ltd., 1916), pp. 66-67.

573 Viscount Grey of Fallodon, *Twenty-Five Years*, Vol. II (New York: Frederick A. Stokes Company, 1925), p. 20.

577 Quoted in W. M. Knight-Patterson, *Germany from Defeat to Conquest, 1913-1933* (London: George Allen and Unwin, Ltd., 1945), p. 43.

582 Woodrow Wilson, *Appeal for Neutrality*, Senate Document 566, 63rd Congress, 2nd Session (Washington, D. C., 1914), pp. 3-4.

585 *Treaty of Peace with Germany*, Senate Document 49, 66th Session, 1st Session (Washington, D. C., 1919).

595 (top) Alan Moorehead, *Winston Churchill in Trial and Triumph* (Boston: Houghton Mifflin Company, 1954, 1955), p. 57.

595 (bottom) Reprinted with the permission of Charles Scribner's Sons from *The World Crisis* by Winston Churchill. Copyright 1923, 1927, Charles Scribner's Sons; renewal copyright 1951, 1955, Winston S. Churchill.

600 League of Nations Official Journal, Special Supplement No. 44: Records of the 7th Ordinary Session of the Assembly.

606 Frederick Lewis Allen, *Only Yesterday* (New York: Harper & Brothers, 1931, 1957), pp. 297-298.

617 Quoted in N. N. Sukhanov, *The Russian Revolution, 1917: A Personal Record*, Joel Carmichael, ed. (New York: Oxford University Press, 1955), p. 273.

657 "General Eisenhower's Order of the Day to the Allied Troops Invading France," June 6, 1944. Copyright by the *New York Times*. Reprinted by permission.

677 U.S. Strategic Bombing Survey, *The Effects of Atomic Bombs on Health and Medical Services in Hiroshima and Nagasaki* (Washington, D. C., 1948). Courtesy of the Department of the Air Force.

695 Oswald Spengler, *The Decline of the West* (New York: Alfred A. Knopf, 1928), pp. 39-44 passim.

698 Robin Boyd, "The Counter-revolution in Architecture," *Harper's*, September 1959. Vol. 219, pp. 40-48.

GRAPHIC MATERIAL

This list shows the sources from which illustrations were obtained. Positions are shown in abbreviated form as follows: (t) top, (c) center, (b) bottom, (l) left, (r) right. If no abbreviations are used, order proceeds from left to right, starting at the top of each page.

Key:

ARB	Art Reference Bureau
BM	British Museum
F	R. B. Fleming & Co., Ltd., London
G	Giraudon, Paris
UPI	United Press International
WW	Wide World Photos

Front cover: Raymond V. Schoder, S.J. Back cover: (India) Metropolitan Museum of Art, Rogers Fund, 1930; (China) Alastair M. Taylor; (North America) National Museum of Anthropology, Mexico; (Africa) BM. **2**: Raymond V. Schoder, S.J.; De Wolf Perry, *American Heritage*. **4**: Georg Gerster. **7**: Bernadine Bailey. **9**: Arnold Newman. **13**: U. S. Navy.

UNIT 1

20: courtesy Oriental Institute, University of Chicago. **21**: Henri Lhote. **24**: (l, r) Chicago Natural History Museum; (c) Danish National Museum, Lennart Larsen. **27**: A. Petruccelli, courtesy *Life* magazine, copyright 1961 Time Inc. **30**: by permission of University Museum of Archaeology and Ethnology, Cambridge (Chinnery Collection,

1928); Ohio Historical Society. **31**: Henri Lhote; French Government Tourist Office. **33**: Wolfe Worldwide Films, Los Angeles; reproduced by permission of World Publishing Co. from Kaj Birket-Smith's *Primitive Man and His Ways,* copyright Kaj Birket-Smith, 1957, English translation; (c) Odhams Press, Ltd., 1960; Chicago Natural History Museum. **38**: (l, c) courtesy Oriental Institute, University of Chicago; (r) Metropolitan Museum of Art, anonymous gift, 1931. **44**: Daniel J. Czubak; courtesy Metropolitan Museum of Art (Museum Excavations and Rogers Fund, 1930). **46**: Nelson Gallery-Atkins Museum, Kansas City, Mo. (Nelson Fund); courtesy Oriental Institute, University of Chicago. **47**: courtesy Oriental Institute, University of Chicago. **52**: BM; courtesy Musée du Louvre; Yale University Art Gallery, after a copy by Herbert Gute. **53**: Raymond V. Schoder, S.J. **58**: (t) BM, F; (c, b) courtesy Oriental Institute, Univ. of Chicago.

UNIT 2
62: Ara Guler. **63**: BM. **66**: ARB. **69**: Herakleion (Greece) Museum, Editions d'Art Albert Skira; Marburg, ARB. **74**: Rijksmuseum Van Oudheden Te Leiden, Netherlands, Editions d'Art Albert Skira; National Museum, Athens. **75**: (tl) Bibliothèque Nationale, Paris; (bl) Museum Antiker Kleinkunst, Munich; (tr, br) Alinari, ARB. **84, 85**: Raymond V. Schoder, S.J. **90**: ARB; Alinari, ARB. **94**: Alinari, ARB. **99**: (t) Musée de Saint-Germain, G: (bl, br) Alinari, ARB. **105**: (1, 3, 4) Alinari, ARB; (2) Mansell. **106**: ARB, French Government Tourist Office; Raymond V. Schoder, S.J. **107**: Aramco; Raymond V. Schoder, S.J.

UNIT 3
112: courtesy K. Wilkinson Riddle, F. **116**: BM, F; Bibliothèque Nationale, Paris. **120**: (tl, tr) Alinari, ARB; (b) G. **121**: Detroit Institute of Arts. **123**: Alinari, ARB. **128**: "Saint Anthony Distributing His Wealth to the Poor," Sassetta, National Gallery of Art, Washington, D.C., Samuel H. Kress Collection. **129**: Marburg, ARB; Archives Photographiques, Paris; courtesy Art Institute of Chicago. **134**: Marburg, ARB; ARB. **140**: Pierpont Morgan Library; Raymond V. Schoder, S.J. **141**: (t, c) BM. **144**: Pierpont Morgan Library; Musée de Versailles, G. **145**: G; Pierpont Morgan Library. **146**: (tl) J. Allan Cash. **154**: Bibliothèque Nationale, Paris, *Horizon.* **160**: (t) Oxford University Press; (c, bl, br) BM. **161**: G; BM. **168**: Victoria and Albert Museum, F. **169**: Seattle Art Museum; Musée de Cluny, G; Ewing Galloway, New York; Pierpont Morgan Library. **174**: ARB; Bibliothèque Nationale, Paris. **181**: Turkish Press Broadcasting and Tourist Department; G; Biblioteca Nacional, Madrid. **184**: Library of the University of Edinburgh. **188**: Wolfe Worldwide Films, Los Angeles; BM; Metropolitan Museum of Art, Rogers Fund, 1913. **189**: Trans World Airlines. **194**: Sovfoto, V. Koshevoi.

UNIT 4
200: Metropolitan Museum of Art, ex coll. A. W. Bahr, Fletcher Fund, 1947. **201**: from *Symbols, Signs & Signets* by Ernst Lehner, World Publishing Co. **204**: National Museum, Pakistan, Abdul Hakim Khan; Nelson Gallery-Atkins Museum, Kansas City, Mo. (Nelson Fund); reproduced by courtesy of the Secretary of State for Commonwealth Relations, F. **208**: Wolfe Worldwide Films, Los Angeles; "The Offering of the Four Bowls," Gandharan stone relief, Baltimore Museum of Art, museum purchase, Julius Levy Memorial Fund; Chicago Natural History Museum. **219**: (t) Musée Guimet, Paris, J. A. Lavaud. **222**: Osaka Municipal Museum of Natural Science, Harumi Konishi; Seattle Art Museum. **226**: (tl, b) Boston Museum of Fine Arts; (tr) Seattle Art Museum. **230**: Brown Brothers. **234**: Boston Museum of Fine Arts; Seattle Art Museum. **235**: courtesy Art Institute of Chicago; Seattle Art Museum, Eugene Fuller Memorial Collection; University Museum of the University of Pennsylvania. **244**: Musée Guimet, Paris, J. A. Lavaud; Nelson Gallery-Atkins Museum, Kansas City, Mo. (Nelson Fund); courtesy Art Institute of Chicago, Clarence Buckingham Collection. **245**: courtesy Art Institute of Chicago, Clarence Buckingham Collection. **248**: BM, F; Museum of the American Indian, New York Graphic Society; courtesy Art Institute of Chicago. **251**: University Museum of the University of Pennsylvania; Authenticated News; Department of Antiquities, Nigeria. **254**: Museum of the American Indian, New York Graphic Society; National Park Service. **255**: collection of Amelia E. White, Santa Fe, N.M., Laura Gilpin; Stovall Museum, University of Oklahoma. **262**: Library of Congress. **263**: (tl) Max J. Putzel; (bl, br) courtesy Art Institute of Chicago.

UNIT 5
268: Munich Staatsbibliothek, ARB. **272**: BM, F. **276**: (t) BM; (bl) Oxford University Press. **277**: Editions du Pont Royal, Paris. **278**: BM, F. **286**: Rijksmuseum, Amsterdam, ARB; BM, F, ARB; Bibliothèque Nationale, Paris. **290**: (l) Louvre, G. **294**: John and Mable Ringling Museum of Art, Sarasota, Fla. **295**: (r) Bibliothèque Nationale, Paris, courtesy J. D. Aylward. **298**: Ashmolean Museum, Oxford; Civic Museum of Padua. **299**: Isabella Stewart Gardner Museum, Boston; BM; F. **302**: John and Mable Ringling Museum of Art, Sarasota, Fla.; Alinari, ARB. **303**: Alinari, ARB; Gérondal; "Lorenzo de' Medici," Verrocchio, National Gallery of Art, Washington, D.C., Samuel H. Kress Collection. **306**: Kunsthistorisches Museum, Vienna, Meyer Erwin; BM, F; Alte Pinakothek, Munich, ARB. **307**: reproduced by courtesy of the Trustees, The National Gallery, London, F. **310**: Johnson Collection, Philadelphia; Kress Collection, 1937. **314**: Campion Hall, Oxford, F. **315**: G; ARB. **322**: National Maritime Museum, Greenwich, England, F; Graphische Sammlung,

Munich, ARB. **323**: ARB; Brown Brothers. **325**: courtesy Colonial Williamsburg, Inc. **328**: Direzione Belle Arti del Comune, Genoa, Mario Agosto; Louvre, G. **332**: (tl, br) National Maritime Museum, Greenwich, England; (bl) Victoria and Albert Museum, F. **333**: (b) Rijksmuseum, Amsterdam. **340**: (t) Hispanic Society of America, New York. **346**: Boymans-van Beuningen Museum, Rotterdam.

UNIT 6

352: Leo Gundermann, Wurzburg, Germany. **360**: reproduced by courtesy of the Trustees, The National Gallery, London, F. **361**: *Horizon*, Jerry Cooke; G; photo Deutscher Kunstverlag München in *Das Grosse Buch der Kunst* by Westermann-Verlag, Braunschweig, printed in the U.S.A. by Frederick A. Praeger, Inc. **368**: (t) reproduced by courtesy of the Secretary of State for Commonwealth Relations. **369**: Peter Wenkworth Collection, F. **374**: Derby Corporation Museum and Art Gallery, England; Nelson Gallery-Atkins Museum, Kansas City, Mo. (Nelson Fund). **380**: (t, br) Bettmann Archive. **384**: (t) Mozart Museum, Salzburg, Austria; (bl) National Portrait Gallery. **386**: (t) Trustees of the Wallace Collection, F. **387**: (t) BM, F. **392**: (l) from the collections of the Historical Society of Pennsylvania. **399**: (bl, br) BM, F. **402**: National Maritime Museum, Greenwich, England, F. **403**: Archives Photographiques, Paris; Anne S. K. Brown Military Collection. **410**: Bettmann Archive; G. **415**: (t) Culver; (b) Brown Brothers. **418**: (tl) Louvre, G; (tr) Bettmann Archive.

UNIT 7

422: Aerofilms and Aero Pictorial, Ltd. **426**: Musée Carnavalet, Paris, G. **434**: (t) BM, F. **435**: Editions du Pont Royal, Paris. **439**: (bl) Austrian Information Service. **452**: (r) Culver. **453**: (tr) The National Trust, Hughenden Manor, Buckinghamshire, England, F; (cr) Brown Brothers; (br) Radio Times Hulton Picture Library. **456**: (b) Mannheim Municipal Art Museum, Germany. **457**: (b) Culver. **464**: Rijksmuseum Kröller-Müller, Otterlo, Netherlands, ARB; Merrimack Valley Textile Museum. **470**: by permission of the Walker Art Gallery, Liverpool; Mansell; courtesy Chicago Historical Society. **471**: Metropolitan Museum of Art, gift of Joseph Bucklin Bishop, 1924; Charles Phelps Cushing. **477**: (cr) Culver; (bl) by permission of Sigmund Freud Copyrights, Ltd.; (br) copyright 1933 by Sigmund Freud and 1961 by W. J. H. Sprott. **480**: Metropolitan Museum of Art, bequest of Mrs. H. O. Havemeyer, 1929, the H. O. Havemeyer Collection; Louvre, G. **481**: Columbus Gallery of Fine Arts, Ferdinand Howald Collection. **488**: A. von der Becke and Son, Berlin. **492**: George Eastman House. **497**: (tr) Brown Brothers.

UNIT 8

506: Museum of the City of New York. **507**: Museum of Science and Industry, Chicago. **510**: Pan American Union. **514**: Detroit Institute of Arts; Ira Glackens. **519**: (t) Public Archives of Canada; (br) Australian News and Information Bureau. **525**: "Candombe," oil, 14" x 24", Pedro Figari (1861-1928), Uruguay, San Francisco Museum of Art; from *Mexican Graphic Art*, © Arthur Niggli, Ltd., Teufen, Switzerland. **530**: reproduced by courtesy of the Secretary of State for Commonwealth Relations. **535**: (t) courtesy Peabody Museum, Salem. **538-539**: courtesy Art Institute of Chicago, Emily Crane Chadbourne Collection. **542**: (t) BM, F; (c) Julius E. Lips, *The Savage Hits Back* (Lovat Dickson & Thompson, 1937); (b) Chicago Natural History Museum. **547**: (br) University Museum, University of Pennsylvania.

UNIT 9

554: Musée d'Art Moderne, Paris, G. **555**: Smithsonian Institution. **558**: BM, F. **568**: (b) © *Punch*, London. **569**: (tr) © *Punch*, London. **572**: Smithsonian Institution. **578**: Bettmann Archive; WW; National Archives. **579**: UPI. **581**: European Picture Service; UPI; WW. **587**: Imperial War Museum, London, F.

UNIT 10

590: Mr. and Mrs. Dalton Trumbo, A. G. Lutjeans. **591**: Elderman in *The Washington Post*. **603**: UPI. **610**: Allen & Unwin; Brown Brothers; UPI. **616**: Sovfoto. **627**: UPI. **634**: courtesy Art Institute of Chicago, William McCallin McKee Memorial Collection; Radio Times Hulton Picture Library. **638, 639**: UPI. **646**: (t, br) UPI; (bl) Fitzpatrick in *The St. Louis Post-Dispatch*. **647**: Three Lions; reprinted by permission of David Low, copyright Low all countries. **656**: Zygmunt Menkes; Educational Television Films, Ltd. **662**: UPI. **663**: (t) WW; (cl) U.S. Navy; (cr, b) UPI; **664**: U.S. Coast Guard. **665**: U.S. Navy; UPI. **671**: U.S. Marine Corps; Three Lions; WW.

UNIT 11

676: "Electronics Industry," one of a series of six paintings created by Siegfried Reinhardt interpreting important industries and professions served by Mallinckrodt Chemical Works, St. Louis. **677**: Westinghouse Electric Corporation. **680**: UPI. **686**: (l, tr) National Aeronautics and Space Administration; (br) *Medical World News*. **687**: General Precision, Inc.; Westinghouse Electric Corporation. **692**: Pablo Picasso, "The Three Musicians," Philadelphia Museum of Art, A. E. Gallatin Collection; **693**: Mr. and Mrs. Joseph R. Shapiro; Ruth Culberg. **698**: Hedrich-Blessing, Bill Engdahl; courtesy The Museum of Modern Art, New York; courtesy Brazilian Consulate. **702**: UN headquarters. **707**: Peace Corps, Paul Conklin; UPI; Black Star. **714**: WW; (bl) UPI. **717**: WW.

Index

Illustrations are indicated in italics, thus; *illus*. Suggested pronunciations for difficult or unusual words are re-spelled according to the table below. The mark ' is placed after a syllable with primary or strong accent; the mark ' shows a secondary or light accent, as in civilization (siv'ə lə zā'shən). The local pronunciations of many foreign words are too unusual for persons untrained in linguistics, and pronunciations given here are those commonly acceptable in unaffected, educated American speech. Where important to the text of LIVING WORLD HISTORY, the life span of a ruler or other personage is shown in brackets: [1867-1925]. The pronunciation key is taken from the *Thorndike-Barnhart High School Dictionary*, published by Scott, Foresman and Company.

a	hat, cap	j	jam, enjoy	u	cup, butter	**FOREIGN SOUNDS**
ā	age, face	k	kind, seek	ů	full, put	
ã	care, air	l	land, coal	ü	rule, move	Y as in French du. Pronounce ē with the lips rounded as for English ü in **rule**.
ä	father, far	m	me, am	ū	use, music	
		n	no, in			
b	bad, rob	ng	long, bring	v	very, save	
ch	child, much			w	will, woman	
d	did, red	o	hot, rock	y	young, yet	œ as in French peu. Pronounce ā with the lips rounded as for ō.
		ō	open, go	z	zero, breeze	
e	let, best	ô	order, all	zh	measure, seizure	
ē	equal, see	oi	oil, voice			
ėr	term, learn	ou	house, out	ə represents:		N as in French bon. The N is not pronounced, but shows that the vowel before it is nasal.
				a	in about	
f	fat, if	p	paper, cup	e	in taken	
g	go, bag	r	run, try	i	in pencil	
h	he, how	s	say, yes	o	in lemon	
		sh	she, rush	u	in circus	H as in German ach. Pronounce k without closing the breath passage.
i	it, pin	t	tell, it			
ī	ice, five	th	thin, both			
		₮H	then, smooth			

A

Abacus, 237

Abbasside dynasty, 187

Abdul Hamid II [1876-1909], sultan of Turkey, 461

Abelard (ab'ə lärd), Pierre [1079-1142], 165

Abraham (ā'brə ham), 53

Absolutism: in Egypt, 43; in England, 278-279, 393-397; in France, 357-363; in Portugal, 459; in Prussia, 365-367; in Russia, 363-365, 617-623; in Spain, 521. See also Communism; Dictatorship.

Abyssinia, 508, 546, 560. See also Ethiopia.

Acre, 150, 151, 157

Acropolis, 73, 76, 78, 87; *illus*. 84

Actium, battle of, 82, 97, 100

Act on the Emancipation of the Peasants from Serfdom, 618

Act of the Settlement, 400

Adenauer (ad' ə nou ər), Konrad [1876-], 711

Adler, Alfred [1870-1937], 684

Adrianople, battle of, 124

Aegean (i jē'ən) civilization, 63, 68, 70, *illus*. 69

Aeneid, 108

Aeschylus (es'kə ləs) [525-456 B.C.], 87

Afghanistan, 213, 217, 543

Africa: art, 253; early cultures in, 249-250, *illus*. 251; European rivalry in, 531; exports, 346-347; imperialism in, 544, 546, 559, 560; Moslem culture in, 250; nationalism in, 607, 720; Nok culture, 249-250; partition of, 546, 549, 565; Portuguese in, 339; slaves from, 522; after World War I, 586, 607-608; in World War II, 667, 670; Zimbabwe culture, 250. See also North Africa.

Afro-Moslem kingdoms, 250

Age of Discovery, 329-343

Age of Reason, 385

Agincourt, battle of, 284

Agriculture: American Indian, 256, 265, 266; atomic energy, use of, in, 690; Australian, 518; Brazilian, 526; Chinese, 224, *illus*. 234; collectivization of (Russia), 617, 619, 628; early Egyptian, 40, 45, 46, *illus*. 47; European, 162; early Greek, 71, 73; improvements in, 190, 468, 690; irrigation, 40, 42, 45, 534; Japanese, 241, 242; in Middle Ages, 135, 139, 162; Moslem, 190; in New Stone Age, 32; revolution in, 468; early Roman, 92; rotation of crops, 468; Sumerian, 50; in the United States, 606, 650

Aguinaldo (ä'gē näl'dô), Emilio [1870?-1964], 560

Pan-African Congress, 607
Panama: independence, 523; republic, recognized, 551; United States in, 550-551
Pan American Union, 565
Pankhurst, Emmeline [1857-1928], 500
Pan-Slavism, 573, 574
Papacy: decrees of, 331; Donation of Pepin, 130; Eastern Church, split with, 177-178; Great Schism, 312; vs. lay rulers, 131, 149, 312, 317-318, *illus.* 418; rights of, challenged, 313; at Rome, established, 122
Papal States: created, 131; seized by Cavour, 449; captured by Napoleon, 416; pope reinstated in, 428
Paper, 191, 223, 233, 257-258, 265, 301
Papyrus, 48
Paracelsus (par' ə sel'səs) [1493?-1541], 382
Pares, Sir Bernard [1867-1949], 197
Paris: Commune, 455; in French Revolution, 408-409, 412; *illus.* 392, 410-411; in Middle Ages, 163; modernized by Napoleon, 447; revolt of 1848, 427, 437-438, 496, *illus.* 426; revolt of 1870, 451; revolt of 1871, 455, *illus.* 457; treaties of, 370, 427, 430, 520; university of, 164, 165; in World War I, 577; in World War II, 661, 673
Paris Peace Conference, 446, 448, 585, 598, 601, 607, 608
Park, Mungo [1771-1806?], 545
Parliament: in England, 280, 282, 394-395, 396, 397-398, 400, 436-437, 602; in France, 408, 409, 438, 454-455, 602; in Germany, 455; Model, 280; in Poland, 371; in Turkey, 461. *See also* Chamber of Deputies; National Assembly; Reichstag.
Parnell, Charles Stewart [1846-1891], 454
Parthenon, 78, 87, *illus.* 84
Pasternak (pas'tər nak), Boris [1890-1960], 694
Pasteur, Louis [1822-1895], 476, *illus.* 477
Pataliputra, 212
Paul III, [1468-1549], pope, 318
Paul I [1754-1801], czar of Russia, 618
Paulistas, 526
Pavlov, Ivan [1849-1936], 478-479
Pax Romana, 91, 101
Peace movements, 565-567
Peace Corps, *illus.* 707
Peace of God, 148
Peace, Palace of (the Hague), 565
Pearl Harbor, attack on, 669
Pechenegs, 196
Pedro II [1825-1891], emperor of Brazil, 526
Peel, Robert [1788-1850], 493
Peking, 236, 237, 239, 240, 536, 612; Dutch merchants in, *illus.* 341
Peking Man, 26, 223, *illus.* 27
Peloponnesus, 76
Peloponnesian League, 77, 78
Peloponnesian War, 80
Peninsulares, 523
Penn, William [1644-1718], 566
People's Republic of China, 709, 716

Pepin the Short [?-768 A.D.], king of the Franks, 130
Pericles (per'ə klēz) [490?-429 B.C.], 67, 78, 80
Period of Militant Communism, 625
Permanent Court of Arbitration, 567
Permanent Court of International Justice (World Court), 597
Permanent Mandates Commission, 597
Perón (pə rōn'), Juan [1902-], president of Argentina, 713
Perry, Matthew C. [1794-1858], 538
Persepolis (pər sep'ə lis), 57, 81
Pershing, John J. [1860-1948], 584
Persia: conquests of, 43, 57, 77; division of, 543; empire of, 57, 59; vs. the Greeks, 77-78; under Mongol control, 237; Moslems in, 186, 190; Persepolis, *illus.* 58; religion, 59; after World War I, 609. *See also* Iran.
Peru, 257, 523; Viceroyalty of, 521
Pétain (pā taN'), Henri [1856-1951], 580, 661
Peter I (the Great) [1672-1725], czar of Russia, 364, 365, *illus.* 361
Peter III [1728-1762], czar of Russia, 364, 365
Petition of Right, 395
Petrarch (pē'trärk) [1304-1374], 294, 295
Petrine (pē'trīn) Theory, 122
Pharaoh (definition), 42
Phidias (fid'i əs) [500?-432? B.C.], 87
Philip II (Augustus) [1165-1223], king of France, 150
Philip IV (the Fair) [1268-1314], king of France, 312
Philip II [382-336 B.C.], king of Macedonia, 80, 81
Philip II [1527-1598], king of Spain, 321
Philip V [1683-1746], king of Spain, 357, 363
Philippi, battle of, 100
Philippine Islands: independence granted, 720; Magellan in, 335; acquired by United States, 544, 550, 560; in World War II, 670, 673
Phoenicians: alphabet of, 53; trade, 53, 68; writing, 53
Physicists, 191, 378, 475, 681, 682-683
Physics, discoveries in, 191, 376-377, 375, 682-683
Picasso (pi kä'sō), Pablo [1881-], 696, *illus.* 692
Piedmont, 431
Pillnitz, Declaration of, 412
Pilsudski (pil sùt'ski), Józef [1867-1935], 604
Pisistratus (pī sis'trə təs) [605?-527 B.C.], 76
Pitt, William [1708-1778], 370
Pius VII [1740-1823], pope, *illus.* 418
Pius IX [1792-1878], pope, 438, 440
Pizarro, Francisco [1471?-1541], 264, 338
Plain of Shinar, 50, 51, 53
Planck (plängk), Max [1858-1947], 682
Plantagenet (plan taj'ə nit) dynasty, 278, 280
Plassey, battle of, 370, *illus.* 368-369
Platea, battle of, 78
Plato [427?-347? B.C.], 82, 83
Plebeians, 92, 93, 94, 98
Plow: development of, 472; invention of, 40
Plutarch [46?-120 A.D.], 109
Poe, Edgar Allan [1809-1849], 482

Religion *(continued)*:

liberty, 118, 388, 494, 512; religious persecution, 118; in Roman Empire, 117; sun worshipers, 48, 264. *See also* individual sects.

Rembrandt (rem'brant) [1606-1669], 305

Renaissance: Carolingian, 131; Italian, 291-301,
illus. 302-303; Northern, 301, 304-305, 308,
illus. 306, 307

Renoir (rən war'), Auguste [1841-1919], 483

Reparations Commission, 598

Restoration, the, 397

Rhazes (Al-Razi) [860?-925?], 191

Rhine River, 101, 122, 130, 135-136, 362, 366

Rhodes, Cecil [1853-1902], 546

Richard I (the Lion-Hearted) [1157-1199], king
of England, 150, 279

Richard II [1367-1400], king of England, 282

Richard III [1452-1485], king of England, 282

Richardson, Samuel [1689-1761], 388

Richelieu (rĭsh'ə lü) [1585-1642], Cardinal, 324,
358, *illus.* 360

*Rights of Man and of the Citizen, Declaration
of,* 407

Rig-Veda (rig vā'də), 210

Rimski-Korsakov, Nikolay [1844-1908], 485

Risorgimento (resurgence), 448

Rivera (rē vā'rä), Diego [1886-1957], 697

Riza Shah Pahlavi (ri zä' shä' pa'lə vē) [1877-
1944], 608, *illus.* 610

Roads and highways: Assyrian, 55; Byzantine,
176; Chinese, 240; improvements in, 473;
Inca, 261; in Middle Ages, 274-275; Persian,
57; Roman, 105, *illus.* 94

Robespierre (rōbz'pēr), Maximilien de [1758-
1794], 413

Rockets, 688, 690

Roentgen (rent'gən), Wilhelm K. [1845-1923],
475

Rollo, [860?-932 A.D.], 136

Roman Catholic Church: in Canada, 516; civilization, aid to, 126-127; Counter Reformation,
318-319; and feudalism, 138, 149; in Germany, 313-316, 455, 458; High Church party
(England), 394; *Index* book list, 318; in Latin
America, 338, 522; in Mexico, 523; in Middle
Ages, 126-127, 131, 138, 147-152, 311; organization (early), 122; and Reformation, 311-
317, 319; split with Eastern Church, 177-178;
Thirty Years' War, 324

Roman Empire: achievements, 104-105, 108-109;
Augustus, 64, 100-102, 105; city planning,
108; decline of, 103-104, 113, 122, 126, 277;
established, 100, German tribes in, 124, 125;
government, 64, 100, 101-104; Greek influence,
108, 109; Justinian code, 105, 176; law of, 64,
104-105; literature of, 108, 109; military conquest, 91; *Pax Romana,* 64, 101; religion, 101,
117, 118, 122; roads, 64, 105; trade, 101, 104,
306.

Roman Republic: agriculture, *illus.* 99; Caesar,
Julius, 98, 100; Carthage, war with, 96; civil
war in, 97; conquests of, 64, 93; established,

92; family life in, 93; First Triumvirate, 98;
government, 91-92, 93, 95, 97; land reform,
97, 98; laws of, 95, 104; literature of, 108;
military conquests, 92, 93, 95-97, *illus.* 94;
patricians, 92, 95; plebeians, 92, 93, 95; Punic
Wars, 95-97; tribunes, 93, 98

Romanov dynasty, 364, 618-623, 624, 625

Romanov (rō'mə nôf), Mikhail [1596-1645], 364

Romanticism, 479, 481, 482; reaction against,
482-483

Rome-Berlin Axis, 648, 667

Rome, city of, 91-92, 108, 118

Rommel, Erwin [1891-1944], 667, 670

Roosevelt, Franklin D. [1882-1945], President of
the United States, 635, 650, 651, 666, 669, 672,
673

Roosevelt, Theodore [1858-1919], President of
the United States, 550-551, 565, 570

Rouault (rö ō'), Georges [1871-1958], 696

Roundheads, 395, *illus.* 399

Rousseau (rü sō'), Jean Jacques [1712-1778],
385, 566, *illus.* 384

Rubáiyát, 192

Rubens (rü'bənz), Peter Paul [1577-1640], 305

Ruhr Valley, 472, 599, 604

Rumania, 446, 461, 561, 562, 573, 667, 706

Rurik [9th century], 193

Russia: absolutism in, 363-365, 617-623; agriculture, 617, 619, 628; alliances, 370, 371,
415, 416, 430, 432, 563, 564, 630; Allied intervention in, after World War I, 625, 630;
atheism (Communist doctrine), 628; and Balkans, 556-557, 560-562, 563, 573-574, 576;
Bloody Sunday, 619, 623; Bolshevik party,
founded, 502; Bolshevik revolution (1917),
624; Byzantine culture in, 193, 287; in China,
543, 619, 708; Church in, 177, 193, 197, 364;
Cominform, 706; Comintern, 630, 631, 706;
Communist regime, established, 624-625; Communist regime recognized, 630; in Congress of
Vienna, 428-430; in Crimean War, 445-447,
618; cultural isolation, 193; Decembrist Revolt, 618; democracy, suppression of, 618;
economic growth, 715; Five Year Plan, 626,
628, 706; government (after 1917), 625-631;
Holy Alliance, 430, 432; imperialism in, 536-
537, 543; industrialization of, 626; industry,
state control of, 624; in Korea, 709; kulaks,
619; labor, 619; land distribution, 624, 625;
admitted to League of Nations, 631; development of nation, 193, 196-197, 285, 287, 363-
365; New Economic Policy, 625, 626; nobility,
617; pogroms, 619; Poland, partition of, 371-
372, 429; revolution (1905), 619, 623; rocket
research in, 688; Russo-Japanese War, 540,
565, 574, 619; Russo-Turkish War (1877-1878),
560-561; satellite nations of, 715; serfs, emancipation of, 618-619; social gains, 628; soviets
(councils), 623; in space race, 689; support,
in Spanish Civil War, 631; in Summit Conference, 710; Tartars in, 196-197, *illus.* 194;
Treaty of San Stefano, 561; in United Nations,

Silver: Byzantine, 183, 191; mining, *illus.* 340; in South America, 264; from Spain, 101; in trade, 68
Simpson, Sir James, 476
Sino-Japanese War, 536, 540
Sioux Indians, 256
Six Acts, 432
Slavery: in Africa, 520; debt, 39, 76; in Egypt, 45; in Rome, 108; among Indo-Aryans, 209; in Moslem Empire, 190; in ancient Near East, *illus.* 52
Slave trade: in Africa, 253, 346-347, 545; in Latin America, 522, 526
Slavs, 136, 193, 287, 573, 574
Smith, Adam [1723-1790], 491, 492
Social contract theory, 383, 385, 400
Social Democratic party (Germany), 458, 502
Social Democratic party (Russia), 502, 617
Socialism: Louis Blanc, 438; Fabian, 502; Marxist, 424, 425, 496, 498, 499, 500; moderate, 502; political parties of, 502; revisionists, 502; Utopian, 424, 495-496
Socialist party (Italy), 636
Social reform: attempts at, 438; by Bismarck, 458; in England, 493-494, 495; Hatt-i Humayun, 461; in Russia, 628
Social security legislation, 650
Socrates (sok'rə tēz) [469-399 B.C.], 82-83
Solferino, battle of, 559
Solomon [10th century B.C.], king of Israel, 54, 250
Solon (sō'lən) [638?-558? B.C.], 76
Somaliland: British, 549, 667; French, 545, 549; Italian, 549, 644-645
Son of Heaven, 227
Sophocles (sof'ə klēz) [495?-406? B.C.], 87
Southeast Asia Treaty Organization (SEATO), 709
South Africa, Union of, 520, 601, 608
South America, 253, 256, 331, 335, 342, 343, 526, 713. *See also* Latin America.
Soviet Union. *See* Russia.
Space: competition in, 688, 689; exploration of, 688-689; manned space flight, 688-689; satellites, 688-689; women, in space flight, 689
Spain: Byzantines in, 176; Civil War (1936), 648, 649; colonies, 342, 521-523; vs. England (1588), 321; vs. England (1779), 402; exploration, 331, 335, 338; fascism in, 648; vs. France (1793), 412; Hapsburg family, 320, 321, 324, 363; Napoleon in, 416; Moslems in, 164, 170, 186, 284; *Reconquista*, 164, 285; Renaissance literature of, 307-308; republic, established, 648; revolution (1868), 459; Spanish Armada, 321, *illus.* 322; Thirty Years' War, 324; Treaty of Utrecht, 363; War of Austrian Succession, 370; War of Spanish Netherlands, 362; War of Spanish Succession, 363
Spanish-American War, 459, 544, 560
Sparta, 63, 76-77, 80
Speke, John, 545
Spengler, Oswald [1880-1936], 695
Spenser (spen'sər), Edmund [1552?-1599], 305
Stalin (stä'lin), Joseph [1879-1953], Communist party leader, 626, 628-629, 631, 706, 715; *illus.* 616, 627; in World War II, 658, 660, 672. *See also* Russia.
Stalin Constitution, 628
Stamp Act, 401
Stanley, Sir Henry M. [1841-1904], 546
Statute of Westminster, 601
Steam engine, development of, 465, 473
Steel, development of, 472
Steinbeck, John [1902-], 694
Stephenson, George [1781-1848], 473
Stoicism and stoics, 83, 86, 117
Stone Ages: 21, 27-29, 32, 34, *illus.* 24
Stonehenge, prehistoric monument, *illus.* 4
Strauss (strous), Richard [1864-1949], 699
Stravinsky (strə vin'ski), Igor [1882-], 699
Stresa Conference, 648
Strikes. *See* Labor.
Stuart dynasty, 394, 398
Sturm und Drang (Storm and Stress), 479, 481
Submarine warfare, 555, 580, 667, 673, *illus.* 579
Sudan (region), 250
Sudan, 545, 546
Sudetenland, 652
Suez Canal, 447, 545, 561, 608, 719
Suffrage: in Belgium, 458; in Denmark, 458; in England, 494, *illus.* 444; in Germany, 455; in Great Britain, 454; in Italy, 459, 637; manhood, universal, 455, 458, 499, 500, 564; in Mexico, 607; in New Zealand, 520; in Norway, 458; in Sweden, 458; in Switzerland, 500; in United States, 403, 513, 606; women, granted to, 458, 500, 520, 606
Suleiman (the Magnificent) [1495?-1566], sultan of Ottoman Empire, 320
Sulla (sul'ə), Lucius C. [138-78 B.C.], 98
Sullivan, Louis H. [1856-1924], 485
Sumeria, 51, *illus.* 52
Summa Theologica, 165-166
Summit Conference, 710
Sung dynasty, 236-237
Sun Yat-sen [1867-1925], Chinese leader, 611, 612, *illus.* 610
Surrealism, 697
Susa (su'sə), Iran, 39, 57, *illus.* 52
Suttee, 534
Sweden: democracy, advancement in, 604; in war with France, 412; Great Northern War, 364; Lutheranism in, 316; suffrage in, 458
Swift, Jonathan [1667-1745], 388, *illus.* 384
Switzerland: Calvinism in, 316; democracy in, 604; League of Nations, headquarters in, 595; Red Cross, organization established, 559; theocracy in, 316; suffrage, 500
Syllogism, 83
Synthetics, development of, 690
Syria: early history, 43, 50, 51, 82, 177, 178, 186, 212; independence of, 718; after World War I, 586, 609

T

Tacitus (tas′ə təs) [55?-120? A.D.], 91, 109, 123
T'ai tsung (tī′ dzüng′), 232
Taj Mahal, 220
Talleyrand-Perigord, Charles Maurice de [1754-1838], 428
Tamerlane. *See* Timur the Lame.
Tamils, 213-214
Tanganyika, 608
Tang dynasty, 231-233; *illus.* 235
Tang Empire, 231-233, 241
Tank warfare, 580, *illus.* 578
Tannenburg, battle of, 580
Taoism (tou′iz əm), 228
Tarquin the Proud, Etruscan king of Latin tribes, 92
Tartars, 196, 197, 236, 285, 287, *illus.* 195
Tasman, Abel [1602?-1659], 518
Tasmania, 517
Taxation: of American colonies, 401; in cities (19th century), 490; in England, 280, 395; under feudal law, 138, 142; in France, 361, 405, 408, 414, 419; in Great Britain, 454, 490; of merchants (Middle Ages), 158, 275; in Persia, 57, 59; Roman, 97, 103, 117, *illus.* 99; in towns (Middle Ages), 158; in towns (19th century), 490
Technology: advances in, 378, 684, 690, *illus.* 686, 687; in Africa, 253; development of, 469-474; effect of, 489, 682-691; Sung (China) 236; in World War I, 580
Telegraph: first electric, 475; in India, 534
Telephone, invention of, 475
Telescope, invention of, 377, 378
Television: development of, 685; use of, 685
Telford, Thomas [1757-1834], 473
Ten Commandments, 54
Ten Hours Act (1847), 494
Tennessee Valley Authority (TVA), 650
Tennis Court Oath, 408
Tennyson, Alfred, Lord [1809-1892], 482
Tenochtitlan (tā noch′ti tlän′), 260, 264
Tertullian (tèr tul′i ən) [150?-222?], 118
Teutoburg Forest, battle of, 101, 123
Textile making: American Indian, 256; in China, 224; in ancient Greece, 73; 18th century, 469, 472, *illus.* 464; in England, 469, 472, 491; in France, 404; in India, 206, 216, 534; in Italy, 291; in Industrial Revolution, 469, *illus.* 464; in Middle Ages, 143; Moslem, 192; prehistoric, 32; silk, 223; synthetics in, 690
Thackeray, William Makepeace [1811-1863], 483
Thebes (thēbz): Egypt, 42, 49; Greece, 80, 81
Theocracies, 43, 185, 257, 261, 316
Theodora [?-548 A.D.], Byzantine empress, 180, 182, *illus.* 174
Theodoric (thi od′ə rik) [454?-526 A.D.], 125
Theodosius I (thē′ə dō′shĭ əs) [346?-395 A.D.], emperor of Roman Empire, 104, 118, 175
Thermopylae (thər mop′lē), 78
Third Coalition, 415
Third Communist International, 630

Third Estate (France), 404, 405
Third Reform Bill, 454
Third Reich, 641, 643, 652, 653
Third World, 718, 721
Thirty Years' War, 324, 358, *illus.* 323
Three Emperors' League, 563
Thucydides (thü sid′ə dēz) [460?-400? B. C.], 86-87
Thutmose III [?-1447 B.C.], Egyptian pharaoh, 42-43
Tiahuanaco, 260-261, 265
Tiberius (tī bēr′i əs) [42 B.C.-37 A.D.], 97, 98, 102
Tigris River, 49, 50, 55, 187
Timbuktu, 250, 253
Timur the Lame [1333?-1405], 197, 217
Tin, 35, 101, 224, 250
Titian (tish′ən) [1477?-1576], 292
Tito (tē′tō) (Josip Broz) [1891-], president of Yugoslavia, 715
Togoland, 549, 608
Tojo (tō′jō), Hideki [1885-1948], 705
Tokugawa (tō kü′gä wä) family, 242, 537, 538, 539
Toleration Act, 398
Tolstoy, Leo [1828-1910], 483; *illus.* 484
Toltecs (tol′teks), 257
Tools: Bronze Age, 34-35, *illus.* 24; Egyptian, 40; Hittite, 51; Middle Stone Age, 29; Minoan, 68; New Stone Age, 32; Old Stone Age, 27-28, 29, *illus.* 24, 27
Tories, 397, 398, 432, 436, 493-494, 452
Torricelli (tôr ə chel′i), Evangelista [1608-1647], 378
Tours, battle of, 130
Toussiant L'Ouverture, 523
Towns. *See* Cities and towns.
Townshend, Charles (Turnip), Viscount [1674-1738], 468
Toynbee, Arnold J. [1889-], 695
Trade: in Africa, 250, 253; in Age of Discovery, effect of, 349; in the Americas, 342-343; Athenian, 79; in Brazil, 526: British, 416, 601; Byzantine, 179-180; Chinese, 225, 231, 536, 537, *illus.* 535; crusades, effect of, on, 152, 291; depression, effect of, on, 635, 640, 648; early, 45, 68; in East Indies, 329, 339, 343; Egyptian, 41, 43, 45, 50, 157; embargoes on, 669; European (Middle Ages), 155-157; expansion of, 156-157, 273-274, 329; fairs (Middle Ages), 157; in France, 404; fur traders, 342; in Ghana, 250; Greek, 70, 71, 155; guilds, 159; Hawaiian, 544; Inca, 261; Indian, 214, 215, 331; Japanese, 537-538, 540, *illus.* 539-540; mercantilism, 348-349; merchants, 156, 157, 158, 250, 291, 292, 347; Middle Ages, 156-157, 273-274; Minoan, 68, 70; Moslem, 191, 250; Netherlands, 343, 346, *illus.* 333, 341; opium, 536; Pan-American Union, 565; Phoenician, 53, 68; Portuguese, 239, 339; in Roman Empire, 101, 103; routes, 68, 156, 157, 215, 291, 330-331, 622; slave (*see* Slave trade); effect of tariff rates on, 606; in

Verrocchio (ver rōk'kyō), Andrea de [1435-1488], 301; *illus.* 303

Versailles (vărsĭ'): court of, 359-360; Estates-General at, 408; German Empire proclaimed at, 451; palace at, 359-360, *illus.* 359; Treaty of, 585-586, 588, 630, 645, *illus.* 587

Vesalius (və sa'lē ŭs), Andreas [1516-1564], 382

Vespucci (ves pü'chi), Amerigo [1451-1512], 335

Victor Emmanuel II [1820-1878], king of Italy, 449; *illus.* 453

Victor Emmanuel III [1869-1947], king of Italy, 636

Victoria [1819-1901], queen of Great Britain and Ireland and empress of India, 452

Vienna: Congress of, 427-430, 458

Vikings, 136, 157, 193

Vinci, Leonardo da. *See* da Vinci, Leonardo.

Vishnu, 210

Visigoths, 122, 125, 127, 186

Vision of Piers Plowman, The, 170

Volstead Act (1920), 605

Volta (vôl'tä), Alessandro [1745-1827], 475

Voltaire (vol tär'), Francois Marie Arouet de [1694-1778], 287, 383, 385

Voortrekkers, 520

Vote and voting. *See* Suffrage.

W

Wagner (väg'nər), Richard [1813-1883], 485, *illus.* 484

Wallenstein (wol'ən stīn'), Albrecht von [1583-1634], 324

Walpole, Sir Robert [1676-1745], 398, 400, *illus.* 399

War Between the States, 513

War crimes court (after World War II), 705

War of the Austrian Succession, 367, 370, 532

War of Devolution, 362

War of Liberation, 416

War of the Spanish Netherlands, 362

War of the Spanish Succession, 363

Wars of the Roses, 282

Washington, George [1732-1799]: in American Revolution, 403; in French and Indian War, 370; inaugurated as President, 512

Washington Conference, 605

Waterloo, battle of, 430

Watt, James [1736-1819], 465, 473

Weights and measures, 229, 241, 419; international agreements on, 565

Weimar republic, 602, 640, 641

Welfare legislation, 454, 494, 500-501, 618, 650

Wellington, Arthur Wellesley, Duke of [1769-1852], 416

Wells, H. G. [1866-1946], 502

Wessex, kingdom of, 277

West Indies, 342, 343

Westphalia, Peace of, 324

Wheel: early use of, 51; invention of, 35; potter's wheel, 35

Whigs, 397, 398, 436, 452, 494, 517

White Russians, 625

Whitney, Eli [1765-1825], 472

William I (the Conqueror) [1027?-1087], king of England, 278

William III [1650-1702], king of England and Ireland, 398, *illus.* 398

William I [1797-1888], king of Prussia and emperor of Germany, 445, 449, 451

William II [1859-1941], emperor of Germany, 458, 563, 564, 572, 577

Wilson, Woodrow [1856-1924], President of the United States, 582, 583, 584, 585, 596, *illus.* 587

Windischgrätz, Alfred [1787-1862], 440

Wolfe, James [1727-1759], 370

Wordsworth, William [1770-1850], 481

World Court, 576, 597

World War I, 555-556, 557, 575-584; events leading to 556, 559-564, 567-570, 573-574

World War II, 657-674; aggressions leading to, 640-648, 652-653

Wotan, 122

Wright, Frank Lloyd [1869-1959], 697, *illus.* 698

Wright, Orville and Wilbur, 684

Writing: African, 253; Chinese, 223, 224, 228; cuneiform, 51; in ancient Egypt, 40; hieroglyphic, 48; Mayan, 257-258; Minoan, 68; picture writing, 48, 224, 228, 258; Phoenician, 53; Sumerian, 50, 51

Wu Ti, 231

Wycliffe (wik'lif), John [1320?-1384], 312

X-Y-Z

Xerxes (zėrk'sēz) [519?-465 B.C.], 78, 86, *illus.* 58

X rays, discovery of, 475

Yalta Conference, 673, 706

Yangtze (yang'tsē) River, 225

Yaroslav (the Wise) [11th century], Kievan ruler, 193, 196

Yellow River (Hwang Ho), 224

Young, Arthur [1741-1820], 393

Young, Owen D. [1874-], 599

Young Turks, 461

Ypres, 157, 577

Yü, first Hsia prince, 224

Yüan Shih-k'ai [1859-1916], president of China, 611-612, 640

Yugoslavia: boundary claims of, 597; Communism in, 715; republic of, 586, 715; rivalries in, 604; in World War II, 667

Zama, 96

Zanzibar, 339

Zeno of Cyprus [336?-264? B.C.], 86

Zero symbol, 166, 192, 216, 258

Zeus (züs), 71

Zimbabwe, 250, *illus.* 251

Zimmerman telegram, 582

Zinjanthropus, 26

Zola, Emile [1840-1902], 483

Zoroaster (zô'rō as'ter), 59

Zoroastrianism, 59

Zwingli (zwing'gli), Huldreich [1484-1531], 316

Index of Maps

The Index of Maps includes place-names which the student will be asked to locate in the end-of-chapter activities, and gives the page numbers of the maps on which those places may be found. This index is not intended as a complete index of place-names. It has been planned to assist the student in map study and should be used as a check list together with the List of Maps, pages 14 and 15.

Marathon, 79
Marne River, 583
Marston Moor, 396
Masurian Lakes, 583
Midway Islands, 658
Naseby, 396
Newbury, 396
Orléans, 283
Pearl Harbor, 658
Philippi, 102
Plassey, 541
Plataea, 79
Poitiers, 283
Prince of Wales, 658
Repulse, 658
St. Mihiel, 583
Salamis, 79
Sevastopol, 446
Somme River, 583
Stalingrad, 659
Tannenburg, 583
Taranto, 659
Teutoburg Forest, 102
Thermopylae, 79
Tours, 186
Trafalgar, 417
Tyre, 81
Verdun, 583
Waterloo, 417
World War II, 658, 668, 672
Ypres, 583

ISLANDS
Aleutian, 658, 728
Bahama, 344, 728
Balearic, 137, 362, 599, 725
Bermuda, 344, 728
Canary, 548, 730
Cape Verde, 344
Caroline, 608, 645
Corfu, 599
Dodecanese, 599, 653, 704
East Indies, 345
Falkland, 729
Fiji, 672
Galapagos, 729
Gilbert, 672
Hawaiian, 645, 728
Hebrides, 137
Madeira, 548, 730
Mariana, 645
Marshall, 608, 645
Midway, 645
Moluccas, 345
Philippines, 345, 645, 727
Samoa, 608, 731
Solomon, 645
West Indies, 344, 728

LAKES
Athabaska, 728
Chad, 548
Great Bear, 728
Huron, 728
Ladoga, 725
Maracaibo, 729
Michigan, 728
Mweru, 548
Nyasa, 548, 730
Peipus, 196
Rudolf, 548, 730
Superior, 728
Tana, 726, 730
Tanganyika, 548, 730
Titicaca, 729
Victoria, 548, 730
Winnipeg, 728

MOUNTAINS
Alaska Range, 728
Alps, 725
Andes, 729
Apennines, 725
Appalachian, 728
Atlas, 102, 730
Carpathian, 196, 725
Cascade Range, 728
Caucasus, 102, 196, 725, 727
Himalaya, 206
Hindu Kush, 206
Mount Athos, 79
Mount Olympus, 79
Pyrenees, 285, 725
Rockies, 728
Sierra Madre, 728
Sierra Nevada, 728
Taurus, 726
Transylvanian Alps, 725, 726
Urals, 196, 725

RIVERS
Amazon, 729
Blue Nile, 548
Brahmaputra, 206, 727
Bug, 196, 366, 371
Colorado (Argentina), 729
Congo, 548, 730
Danube, 102, 196, 366, 725
Dnieper, 196, 371, 446, 725
Dniester, 196, 371, 446, 725
Don, 196, 725
Dvina, 371
Elbe, 366, 668, 725
Euphrates, 49, 726, 727
Ganges, 206, 212, 218, 727
Hwang Ho (Yellow), 224, 228, 229, 236

Indus, 81, 206, 212, 218, 726
Irrawaddy, 206
Lena, 629
Limpopo, 548
Loire, 725
Mackenzie, 728
Madeira, 729
Magdalena, 729
Main, 366
Marne, 583
Mississippi, 728
Napo, 729
Narbada, 206
Negro, 729
Nieman, 366, 371
Niger, 548, 730
Nile, 49, 548, 726, 730. *See also* Blue Nile; Upper Nile; White Nile.
Ob, 629, 727
Oder, 196, 366, 371
Orange, 548
Orinoco, 729
Oxus, 81
Paraguay, 729
Paraná, 729
Plata, 336, 729
Po, 102, 725
Pripet, 371
Prut, 371
Rhine, 102, 366, 725
Rhone, 725
Rio Grande, 728
St. Lawrence, 728
São Francisco, 729
Seine, 725
Sénégal, 548
Somme, 583
Spree, 366
Tagus, 725
Thames, 725
Tiber, 102
Tigris, 49, 726, 727
Ubangi, 548
Ucayali, 729
Upper Nile, 548
Ural, 196, 725, 727
Vistula, 196, 366, 371
Volga, 196, 725
Wesser, 366
West Dvina, 196
White Nile, 730
Yangtze, 224, 228, 229, 236, 727
Yellow (Hwang Ho), 224, 228, 229, 236
Yenisei (Yenisey), 629, 727
Zambezi, 548